COMMENTS ABOUT ERICH A. HELFERT AND THIS BOOK

"Erich Helfert's book is a bona fide treasury for executives, managers, and entrepreneurs who need to understand financial management. I have used and recommended this great work in both corporate and university programs for more than ten years. Erich Helfert possesses unique abilities to make clear the arcane that frequently enshrouds topics of financial management."

Allen B. Barnes
Past Provost
IBM Advanced Business Institute
(formerly Director of Executive Education, UCLA)

"Erich Helfert's book is a candidate for every consultant-to-management's bookshelf. The underlying agenda is financial management as it pertains to effective resource allocation decisions. Framed in a dynamic model of the Business System, the beauty of Helfert's presentation lies in its treatment of subsystems that differentiate between investment, operations and financing decisions, but which are also integrated into the overall managerial fabric."

Stanley Press CMC
Book review September 2000
C2M Consulting to Management Journal

"Erich Helfert possesses a rare ability to make financial concepts understandable to individuals who lack a financial background. As a result we had Dr. Helfert conduct shareholder value creation classes for all senior managers and create a shareholder value course for all other salaried and hourly employees. The results of these efforts exceeded our high expectations."

L. Pendleton Siegel
Chairman and Chief Executive Officer
Potlatch Corporation

"Erich Helfert has played an instrumental role in teaching HP managers of both financial and non-financial backgrounds in our long-standing Functional Management Program. His excellent financial overviews and simplified models effectively broaden our managers' understanding and ownership of their fiscal responsibility to HP and our shareholders."

Robert P. Wayman
Executive Vice President and
Chief Financial Officer
Hewlett-Packard Company

"Dr. Helfert's book and his teachings go a long way toward removing the mystery from the financial workings of an enterprise. His approach allows managers from all areas of the business to understand how their decisions impact shareholder value."

Stephen E. Frank
President and Chief Operating Officer
Southern California Edison

"Erich Helfert has contributed to the development of financial skills of TRW managers through his case study preparation and presentations, his book Techniques of Financial Analysis, and his instruction. He continues to be included as a highly rated faculty member in TRW's management development programs."

Peter S. Hellman
Past President and Chief Operating Officer
TRW Inc.

FINANCIAL ANALYSIS: TOOLS AND TECHNIQUES

A Guide for Managers

ERICH A. HELFERT, D.B.A.

McGraw-Hill

New York   Chicago   San Francisco
Lisbon   London   Madrid   Mexico City   Milan
New Delhi   San Juan   Seoul   Singapore   Sydney   Toronto

Library of Congress Cataloging–in–Publication Data

Helfert, Erich A.
   Financial analysis tools and techniques : a guide for managers / by Erich A. Helfert.
     p. cm.
   ISBN 0-07-137834-0
    1. Corporations—Finance. 2. Cash flow. 3. Financial statements. 4. Ratio analysis. I.
Title.

HG4026.H436 2001
658.15'1—dc21   2001301716

McGraw-Hill

A Division of The **McGraw·Hill** *Companies*

1 2 3 4 5 6 7 8 9 0   DOC/DOC   0 9 8 7 6 5 4 3 2 1

ISBN 0-07-137834-0

Printed and bound by RR Donnelley/Crawfordsville.

McGraw-Hill books are available at special quantity discounts to use as premiums and sales promotions, or for use in corporate training programs. For more information, please write to the Director of Special Sales, Professional Publishing, McGraw-Hill, Two Penn Plaza, New York, NY 10121-2298. Or contact your local bookstore.

This book is printed on recycled, acid-free paper containing a minimum of 50% recycled, de-inked fiber.

To Anne

ABOUT THE AUTHOR

Erich A. Helfert is an internationally recognized management consultant in corporate finance, strategic planning, and executive education in financial/economic decision making and shareholder value creation. He gained his professional experience from a combination of distinguished business and academic careers. Dr. Helfert was vice president, corporate planning, at Crown Zellerbach Corporation, a major integrated paper and forest products company. Prior to his 20-year corporate career, he served on the faculty of the Harvard Graduate School of Business for eight years, teaching finance and managerial economics in the MBA program, and consulting in management development and strategy with major companies.

A native of the Sudetenland, formerly Austria, he received his BS from the University of Nevada and earned both an MBA (with high distinction) and a DBA (as a Ford Foundation Fellow) at the Harvard Business School. Dr. Helfert writes and lectures extensively in his field, and his books and articles have been published in the United States and abroad. His first literary work, *Valley of the Shadow,* a factual historical novel about his experiences in central Europe at the end of World War II, was published recently.

Dr. Helfert is cofounder, chairman and CEO of Modernsoft, Inc., San Mateo, California, developers of *Financial Genome,* an advanced knowledge-based financial analysis and business modeling software, which is complementary to *Financial Analysis: Tools and Techniques.*

CONTENTS

Chapter 3

Managing Operating Funds   59

Chapter 4

Assessment of Business Performance   95

Chapter 5

Projection of Financial Requirements   161

Chapter 6

Dynamics and Growth of the Business System   191

Chapter 7

Cash Flows and the Time Value of Money   223

Chapter 8

Analysis of Investment Decisions   255

Chapter 9

Cost of Capital and Business Decisions   297

Chapter 10

Analysis of Financing Choices   325

Chapter 11

Valuation and Business Performance   357

Chapter 12

Managing for Shareholder Value   391

APPENDIX I

Financial Analysis Using *Financial Genome*   425

APPENDIX II

Glossary of Key Terms and Concepts   433

APPENDIX III

Financial Information and On-Line Sources   449

APPENDIX IV

Basic Inflation Concepts   463

APPENDIX V

Some Issues in Multinational Financial Analysis   469

INDEX   477

PREFACE

This volume is an adaptation for the professional market of the most recent 10th ("millennium") edition of Dr. Helfert's best-selling *Techniques of Financial Analysis,* which, with more than half a million copies in print over the past 38 years, has given the student, analyst, and business executive a concise, practical, usable, and up-to-date overview of key financial/economic analysis tools. The presentation format has always been carefully designed to help the reader understand the linkage between management decisions and their impact on the financial performance and the economic value of a business. This book helps the reader to interpret financial reports, develop basic financial projections, evaluate business investment decisions, assess the implications of financing choices, derive the value of a business or a security, and understand the role of analysis in achieving the goal of shareholder value creation. Every technique and measure is described and demonstrated in the context of important underlying financial and economic concepts, but without delving into theoretical abstraction.

A Unique Systems Approach to Financial Management

The concept that any business is essentially an integrated system of cash flows driven by management decisions provides the book's foundation. All analytical tools and related financial/economic concepts are discussed within this systems context, which reflects the three basic types of decisions made continuously by the management of any ongoing business: investment, operating, and financing. The materials are also structured around the viewpoints of the major parties interested in the analysis and performance of a business: managers, owners, and creditors. The book begins by providing a perspective on the recent speculative excesses in the new economy's "dotcom" revolution, with the argument that basic economics and financial analysis have never changed, but only were ignored at times. Next, the key concept of the business system and all of its relationships to financial analysis and statements is presented in detail, from which the discussion proceeds to explain the various techniques and concepts in a logical flow. Closure is provided by returning to the systems concept in the final chapters on valuation and managing for shareholder value. Within this structure, however, practicality always remains paramount. Any issues and concepts going beyond what is essential are left to the more specialized textbooks and articles identified in the references. The systems approach is also reflected in the commercially available *Financial Genome* business analysis and planning software and its accompanying interactive templates.

The Audience

Ever since the first edition appeared in 1963, the book has consistently maintained a unique appeal both for students (graduate and undergraduate) and practitioners because of its clarity and commonsense presentation. Straddling the educational and professional markets, the book requires little if any background in finance and accounting and provides an accessible, self-contained overview of the essential financial management concepts and tools. Countless students have found the book an understandable and useful guide for their studies and kept the book for ready reference in their careers, while large numbers of professionals—whether financial practitioners or nonfinancial managers—recognized the practicality and applicability of the book's approach to their needs and decision-making.

Originally an outgrowth of the compact technical briefing materials used in the MBA program at the Harvard Business School, which supplement practical case study discussion with essential background, the book has been regularly updated and modified approximately every four years. The tenth "millennium" edition reflects not only the latest practice in the use of the various financial techniques, but also the experience gained over nine editions from the widespread use the book has enjoyed in university finance courses, both graduate and undergraduate, and from hundreds of executive development seminars and in-company programs in the United States, Canada, Latin America, and overseas, including those conducted by the author in numerous Fortune 100 client companies. Frequently translated into nine foreign languages over the years, the book has transcended the confines of American business practice on which it is built, because the way in which the analytical methods are described makes them almost universally applicable.

What's New in this Book

The 10th edition of *Techniques of Financial Analysis,* on which this volume is based, has been refined and updated while preserving the logical, integrated flow of the materials. After setting the stage in Chapter 1, the coverage begins with an overview of the "business system" and the key financial analysis tools, all the way to the development of business valuation and the newly developed materials on managing for shareholder value. The discussion of the analysis of business investments and business valuation have been expanded into two chapters each, to provide additional insights, practical examples, and greater linkage to shareholder value creation. The various graphics supporting the text, several of them new additions, were tested for their effectiveness in numerous executive development programs over the past 12 years. Also, where appropriate, specific references to spreadsheet analysis have been included and examples are presented in this readily accessible format to ease the mechanical aspects of analysis.

An entirely new feature is the optional availability of the advanced, knowledge-based financial analysis software package, *Financial Genome,* created by

Modernsoft, Inc. This professional application enables the user to develop financial statements, the whole range of key financial measures, and integrated financial projections and plans, as well as ad hoc financial analyses. The patented knowledge-based technology enables the user to readily perform these tasks from spreadsheet data or data bases with assured internal consistency, without having to worry about cell locations and formulas. Knowledge of financial terms, relationships, and statement structures is built in, but can be accessed and displayed at will for enhanced understanding. The software is also accompanied by a series of interactive templates and displays relating to many of the key exhibits of this book, especially the core diagram of the business system. The templates are designed to enhance the learning experience by graphically illustrating the impact of changes in assumptions and conditions. Many templates are also designed for general use, such as break-even and present value analysis. *Financial Genome* is described in detail in Appendix I. Interested readers can download the software for trial, as well as the "TFA Templates," from Modernsoft, Inc's web site: www.modernsoft.com.

As before, chapters 2 through 6 of the book form an integrated set, built around the conceptual overview of the business system, its decisional context, and its relationship to financial statements and analytical tools as presented in Chapter 2. The coverage of analytical methods begins in Chapter 3 with funds flow analysis, moves on to financial performance analysis, covers financial projections, and culminates in a discussion of the financial dynamics useful in modeling financial conditions and growth capabilities.

Chapters 7 through 11 deal with more specialized topics such as business investment analysis, the cost of capital, financing choices, and valuation of securities and businesses, while the final Chapter 12 returns to the systems context in an expanded discussion of the conceptual and analytical aspects of managing for shareholder value. The informational Appendix III was updated to include key on-line references.

The process of revision and current adaptation has not, however, affected the book's primary focus on the doable and practical—in effect an "executive briefing" concept—and on building the reader's basic ability to grasp financial relationships and issues. As before, the book presupposes only that the user has some familiarity with basic accounting concepts.

Acknowledgments

I would again like to express my appreciation to my former colleagues at the Harvard Business School for the opportunity to develop the original concept of the book. My thanks also go to my business associates and to my colleagues at universities and in executive development programs here and abroad, too numerous to mention individually, for their continued extensive use of the book and for the many expressions of interest and constructive suggestions that have supported the book's evolution.

My special thanks go to my colleagues at Modernsoft, Inc., Edgar P. Canty, Dr. William J. Clancey, John W. Wu, and Lee Hecht for their enthusiasm and expertise in adapting the major concepts of the book and its approach in our development of the *Financial Genome* software and its accompanying educational templates. Their insights and suggestions were most valuable during the recent revision of this book, and their unwavering dedication to creating this unique professional financial analysis and planning software has been exemplary.

I would also like to state my sincere appreciation to the McGraw-Hill publishing team who made this edition a reality; Jeffrey Krames, Publisher, and Stephen Isaacs, sponsoring editor, have both consistently and generously guided the book through its various stages.

Finally, I continue to be most gratified by the positive responses from so many individual users, past and current, who have found the book helpful in their studies and an ongoing supportive resource in their professions.

Erich A. Helfert

INTRODUCTION

When an analyst, business executive, or student is dealing with a financial issue, or wishes to understand the financial implications and economic trade-offs involved in decisions about business investment, operations, or financing, a wide variety of analytical techniques—and sometimes rules of thumb—is available to generate quantitative answers. Selecting the appropriate tools from these choices is clearly an important part of the analytical task. Yet, experience has shown again and again that first developing a proper perspective for the problem or issue is just as important as the choice of the tools themselves.

Therefore, this book not only presents the key financial tools generally used, but also explains the broader context of how and where they're applied to obtain meaningful answers. To this end, the second chapter provides an integrated conceptual backdrop both for the financial/economic dimensions of systematic business management and for understanding the nature of financial statements, data, and processes underlying financial analysis techniques. All subjects are viewed in the context of creating shareholder value—a fundamental concept that is revisited in the final chapter on managing for shareholder value.

While the tools and techniques covered in this book are discussed and demonstrated in detail, the user must not be tempted to view them as ends in themselves. It's simply not enough to master the techniques alone! Financial/economic analysis is both an analytical and a judgmental process which helps answer questions that have been carefully framed in a managerial context. The process is at its best when the analyst's efforts are focused primarily on structuring the issue and its context, and only secondarily on data manipulation. We can't stress enough that the basic purpose of financial analysis is to help those responsible for results to make sound business decisions within a relevant cash flow framework.

Apart from providing specific numerical answers, "solutions" to financial problems and issues depend significantly on the points of view of the various parties involved, on the relative importance of the issue, and on the nature and reliability of the information available. In each situation, the objective of the analysis must be clearly understood before pencil is put to paper or computer keys are touched—otherwise, the process becomes wasteful "number crunching," even if the workload itself is eased by analytical software.

Management has been defined as "the art of asking significant questions." The same applies to financial analysis, which should be targeted toward finding meaningful answers to these significant questions—whether or not the results are fully quantifiable. In fact, the qualitative judgments involved in finding answers to financial/economic issues can often count just as heavily as the quantitative results, and no analytical task is complete until these aspects have been carefully spelled out and weighed.

The degree of precision and refinement to which any financial analysis is carried also depends on the specific situation. Given the uncertain nature of many of the estimates used in calculations, it's often preferable to develop ranges of potential outcomes rather than precise answers. At the same time, a lot of effort can be wasted in further refining answers that clearly suggest the choice of particular alternatives—there's no need to belabor the obvious! Moreover, common sense dictates that most of the analytical effort should be directed at areas where the likely payoff from additional analysis is largest—to match the amount of energy expended with the significance of the results.

The following points are a suggested checklist for review and consideration before any financial analysis task is begun. This list should be helpful to the person actually doing the work as well as to the manager who may have assigned the question or project to an associate:

1. What's the exact nature and scope of the issue to be analyzed? Is the issue and its relative importance in the overall business context truly understood, and have its attributes been clearly spelled out, including all the relevant alternatives that should be considered?
2. Which specific variables, relationships, and trends are likely to be helpful in analyzing the issue? What's the order of their importance, and in what sequence should they be addressed?
3. Are there possible ways to obtain a quick "ballpark" estimate of the likely result to help decide (a) what the critical data and steps might be, and (b) how much effort should be spent on refining these?
4. How precise an answer is necessary in relation to the importance of the issue itself? Would additional refinement be worth the effort?
5. How reliable are the available data, and how is this uncertainty likely to affect the range of results? What confirmation might be possible, and at what degree and cost of effort?
6. Are the input data to be used expressed in cash flow terms—essential for economic analysis—or are they to be applied within an accounting framework to test only the financial implications of a decision?
7. What limitations are inherent in the tools to be applied, and how will these likely affect the range of results obtained? Are the tools chosen truly appropriate to solving the issue?
8. How important are qualitative judgments in the context of the issue, and what's the ranking of their significance? Which analytical steps might in fact be made unnecessary by such considerations?

Only after having thought through these questions should specific analytical work on any issue proceed. The amount of care and effort expended on taking this critical first step at the beginning of the task will pay off in much more focused and meaningful work and results. In effect, we're talking about using a rational approach to problem solving in financial/economic analysis. In the end, this is what effective support of decision making involving a company's investments, operations, and financing is all about, because shareholder value creation is the logical result of sound business decisions carefully analyzed and successfully implemented.

CHAPTER 1

THE CHALLENGE OF FINANCIAL/ECONOMIC DECISION-MAKING

At the time the tenth edition of this book appeared in August 1999, the business world was caught up in a still-growing state of euphoria over the high technology sector and especially the "dot.com" phenomenon, which promised to revolutionize the way business was done, whether business-to-business or business-to-consumer. There was also the impression, actively promoted by many commentators, pundits and financial professionals, that a different era of analytical practice had arrived. It was argued that many of the "old" ways of judging performance and business prospects would no longer be valid, as market valuations of scores of new or emerging businesses skyrocketed. However, when the market bubble contracted sharply, beginning in the Spring of 2000 and into the first year of the new millennium, 2001, there was a great deal of soul searching among financial professionals and investors alike, all trying to explain the sharp reversal and to speculate on how it was possible that so many judgments and expectations were not founded in reality.

As a way of introducing the range of analytical concepts and tools contained in this book, we'll attempt to characterize some of the key attributes of the "new economy" phenomenon and draw conclusions about the implications for financial analysis. In fact, we'll argue that the "basics" of financial/economic analysis and thinking have never changed. Many of the excesses of the period might have been prevented if even the most elementary economic principles had been followed.

We'll put into perspective the constructive role of what we call the economic manager, a quintessential requirement for sustainable success in businesses large and small. This will also be an opportunity to comment briefly on the practice of financial/economic analysis in operating and assessing a business. Finally, we'll characterize the key attributes of the value-creating company, the successful enterprise with a robust business model and a sustainable strategic advantage, which fulfills and even exceeds expectations of the investing community.

For many years the purpose and contribution of this book have been to help make financial/economic analysis a practical, understandable and usable process for managers and analysts, and we argue with conviction that applying these concepts to both established and emerging businesses has rarely been more important than now. As we enter the new millennium, continuation of our strong economic performance in the fast-moving business environment will depend on how well internal decision-making processes support and extend the new technologies and productivity improvements—which, after all, have helped create a decade of record economic expansion. We believe that the decision criteria for these processes should be, and will remain, based on sound economic principles, on the use of cash flow reasoning, and on well-defined trade-offs involved in decisions large and small. In other words, we are talking about applying solid economic management.

Lessons for the Millennium

As we enter the new millennium, two sets of issues about financial/economic analysis principles and practice offer themselves for discussion as an introduction to this book. The first is the concept of the so-called new economy, and the second is the applicability and relevance of time-tested methodologies and tools in the years ahead.

The New Economy

Much has been written and said about the impact of new technologies, of the information revolution, and of the Internet on our economy, not only in the United States, but worldwide. There is no question that the changes in information technology and communications capability have drastically altered both actual and potential ways of doing business. For example, instant access to inventory status at both the customer and manufacturer/supplier levels, and creative linkages through order processing and outsourcing have not only reduced funds tied up in inventories, but have also aligned these companies much more closely with actual demand patterns. The ability to customize products and services has been greatly enhanced, while lead times have shrunk in the supply chain to unheard of low levels. Information technology has been the key to achieving much more effective processes throughout the business world, and once they are properly selected and managed, the processes of data access, storage, application and exchange become much easier. The Internet has become the facilitator for instant sharing of information, and for linking entities with common interests and needs. Beyond that, the Internet promises to become a preferred processing medium for countless services, including accounting, data storage, analytical software, investment analysis, and others, offering instant access from any point in the world. Not only can high technology companies take advantage of these capabilities, but the potential for productivity enhancement extends to even the most basic of industries and services.

The examples cited above, as well as new applications not yet developed, can have a significant impact on both operational and strategic conditions in most industries and services. The business models of existing companies have to be adjusted to reflect the capabilities of these developments, to the extent that they apply. Likewise, companies directly engaged in pursuing such emerging and fast-paced opportunities must develop business models that are likely to succeed, even though they find themselves on the leading edge of new developments that are not yet fully understood. Thus the new economy represents both an opportunity and a challenge to business management.

What are the implications of these trends for business financial analysis and economic decision-making? Clearly, the pace of business activity and the speed with which opportunities emerge has accelerated greatly, resulting in the need for quicker analysis and decision-making. This means, among other things, designing information gathering and interpretation processes to ensure that appropriate decision-making data are available when needed. It also means that internal decision practices need to be rationally attuned to these shorter time frames. All these issues can be addressed in methodical ways.

Some Key Questions

However, several business concepts have emerged in the recent past that give ample reason to pause and consider whether they represent a dose of wishful thinking. These concepts largely apply to the new and emerging businesses of the new economy, but also have cast a shadow over more established companies. We'll look at the most important ones briefly:

- Successive advances in innovation guarantee success.
- High volume position is the key to competitive advantage.
- Profitability is an old-fashioned concept.

Innovation. The idea that successive waves of innovation are the main driver of long-term performance in a new or emerging business—or an existing one, of course—appears to be sound when viewed in the abstract. Clearly, innovations in technology, processes, and methodology have occurred, sometimes dramatically, in the U.S. and world economies. Whole new businesses emerged over the past two centuries as advances in manufacturing, transportation, services and communication came in sometimes rapid, successive cycles, speeding up exponentially in the past several decades. But the important lesson from economic history is that innovation alone does not guarantee success to the individual enterprise, whether pioneering or merely riding along with the changing opportunities.

It is here that the interpretation of the new economy and its innovative aspects began to conflict with basic economic reality in the past several years. As high-technology and "dot.com" enterprises attempted to seize the potential of innovative advances, basic notions of achieving positive cash flow and profits were cast aside. Instead, the argument was: "As long as we keep innovating and are doing it faster than others, we'll have positioned ourselves to warrant the confidence of our investors." It was this argument that contributed to the phenomenon of initial public offering prices soaring to unprecedented heights, giving new and untried enterprises market valuations that rivaled those of long-established, successful Fortune 100 corporations. The magic lure of innovation became a substitute for economic performance, and rampant speculation rather than thoughtful analysis drove venture capitalists, investment bankers, analysts, and individual investors to participate in the ride to quick riches.

Forgotten was the fact that where a great many innovators try, only a very few succeed, and they succeed only because they achieve acceptable financial results within a time span over which investors are willing to commit themselves. Ignored was the fact that results depend on the ability to deliver products and services which customers are actually willing to buy at adequate prices. One only has to think of the number of automobile companies that were started at the beginning of the automotive age, and how many survived, despite technical innovations made by many firms that no longer exist. The reason the innovating company succeeds is because it is built on sound, sustainable strategies, effective management, and economic decision-making, enabling it to seize and exploit innovative opportunities better than its rivals. If successive innovations come along, the successful company will repeat these principles. Thus it is not innovation alone, but the consistent and difficult application of sound strategic and economic management that brings about eventual success. And the underpinnings of such successful strategic and economic management are sound financial/economic analysis and its interpretation—the very principles and tools we'll discuss in this book.

Volume position. The second concept we wish to highlight also appears sound when viewed in principle, namely, that obtaining a commanding volume position in the market as early as possible is a critical ingredient of successful strategies. This can lead to lower costs, more effective marketing, logistics, synergies and lasting competitive advantage. General Electric, one of the most successful long-run value builders for decades, preached and practiced Jack Welch's mantra of being No. 1 or No. 2 in any of the businesses in which it chose to engage and continue. When it came to the new economy, however, the same principle was often applied without much thought being given to one critical economic requirement: the trade-off between the outlays required to establish position, and the economic benefits to be derived over time from this investment. In the "dot.com" sector of the economy, the principle of large scale and volume was interpreted as, for example, getting the most "eyeballs" to view one's web site, or building up the largest customer base possible, using give-away prices for products and services.

As "clicks competed with bricks," little attention was paid to the size of the requisite outlays on advertising, promotion, and particularly the often massive investment in fulfillment infra-structure, with its related operating costs. In extreme cases, the spending of hundreds of millions of dollars of shareholder capital or borrowed funds was shrugged off as "necessary" to build scale, to get ahead of several other competitors and reach the dominant position. There are many examples of such new business models, established in the hope of reaching commanding volume positions, such as amazon.com, webvan.com, Etoys.com, and others; some of these have by now expired, especially those startups trying to serve consumer markets in new ways.

Expectations about positive operating results kept being postponed year after year in many of these situations—with investment soaring and operational contributions to the bottom line remaining negative. Cash flows consistently remained a one-way street. At some point of reckoning such companies faced bitter choices: trying to raise additional funds under prohibitive conditions, selling out, or folding up altogether. The expected positive trade-off between investment and expectations had not materialized, and shareholders were penalized by collapsing share prices.

We believe that one of the main reasons the trade-off failed was the lack of importance, or even outright disregard, with which management viewed the use of hardheaded financial/economic analysis. Successful companies generally subject their new initiatives to various forms of "no nonsense" testing, carefully weighing ranges of potential investment against ranges of potential outcomes. Even elementary analysis of this kind, when applied to a number of the new "dot.com" business models, suggests that economically recovering the kinds of investments necessary requires growth rates, market positions and operating results that far exceed any set of reasonable estimates an objective observer might make about the potential scale and profitability of the business sector in question.

The counter arguments made by some suggested that because these market opportunities and business models were so new, estimates were essentially blue-sky guesses, and one could not afford to lose time in becoming Number One. As we'll discuss in the later portions of this book, however, uncertainty about the future is a common theme in just about all business propositions, and the issue is one of carefully scoping the likely dimensions, and assessing the risks involved as the analysis proceeds. In the case of the new economy business models, the rush to gain position and to be the first to benefit from it, did overshadow economic principle in the eyes of analysts, venture capitalists, and investors. The hurry to position oneself for a huge run-up in share prices became a speculative race where caution was thrown to the wind.

Profit is old-fashioned   Related to the first two issues we discussed is the notion that in the new economy, the old fashioned principle of achieving sustained profitability is obsolete. Concepts such as "top line growth," a metaphor for rapid sales increases, and other physical measures having to do mainly with positioning are becoming increasingly popular. There is no denying that these measures have a place in the arsenal of analytical tools, as they help to interpret the trends affecting business performance. But they are by no means a substitute for the ultimate test of success over time: the economic performance of the business in terms of the cash flow returns generated through sustained profitability, as measured against the investment base.

As we'll show throughout this book, and especially in the last six chapters, when interpreting the performance of a business one must make a clear distinction between accounting results and economic results. The former are based on generally accepted accounting principles (GAAP), under which all publicly held businesses in the United States are required to record their transactions, and report their financial position and operating results. The latter represent a translation of these accounting data and results into a basic cash-in, cash-out framework, which is used to establish the ultimate test of economic performance and value creation. Both types of results, of course, depend on sound management of every aspect of the company, except that cash-flow based principles and tools give much more direct decision support and economic meaning to performance evaluation and value creation. Both sets of measures and tools have their place in business analysis, depending on the circumstances of their use. Over the past two decades there has been a growing shift in the direction of cash-flow based principles and measures, inflation-adjusted and applied across time and geographic boundaries. We believe this to be a sound development for better decision-making and investment analysis.

Returning to the new economy argument that profitability is old-fashioned, we can only say that such a mind set is a denial of the obvious. In the last several years it was often argued that an ascending company showing profits was somehow in the wrong, that huge deficits and negative cash flows were signs of progress in the competitive game, and many market valuations were based in a perverse way on such criteria. Yet, for over a century it has been established that the viability of any business depends on earnings, over time, at levels above the cost of capital of the investment committed. This is nothing more than rudimentary economics, which is ignored by the argument about profitability not being relevant.

There are, of course, many ways to interpret profitability, as we'll see, be it in accounting or economic terms. But one must interpret it—whether one is a financial analyst, a corporate manager or staff person, a banker, a venture capitalist, a business adviser, or an individual investor. And it is here that the new economy thinking has attempted to sweep away a fundamental principle, to the regret of countless shareholders whose stake in the ballooning valuations was brought back to earth by the inexorable gravity of unsupported profit and cash flow expectations.

The Basics Never Change

At the time of this writing, a very important and encouraging process is taking place, namely, a rediscovery of basic management principles and of the matching set of analytical tools and concepts. The stock market has deflated a significant part of the speculative bubble of the last three years (with the NASDAQ declining below 50 percent of its peak level), a slowing economy requires the stimulus of sizeable interest rate cuts and tax reductions, and a significant downsizing of corporate earnings expectations is taking place. All of these forces have contributed to a climate in which investors, analysts and managers alike are again turning to the time-tested ways of thinking about performance and valuation, and acting in accordance with them. The notion that valuations of newer companies can be established through earnings multiples that defy gravity has receded; similarly, financial commentaries have begun again to stress the importance of earnings and cash flows. This trend is accompanied by renewed attention being given to the economic trade-offs involved in analyzing business decisions, whether strategic, operational or financial.

One is reminded of an often used simile, the wheel of fashion, which turns slowly, and where any spot on its rim eventually returns to the original position in cycle after cycle; whether it be skirt lengths or the width of men's ties, or dressing down or dressing up, the fashion cycle rotates. We can find a parallel in business practices and analytical concepts. In recent memory, the hectic "anything goes" conglomeration and merger period of the late 1960s into the '80s was followed by a sobering decade of restructuring and divestiture, supported to a considerable extent by the rapidly emerging new shareholder value analysis concepts and tools. Economic cash flow methodologies and trade-offs were at the heart of this reversal, and while they were expressed in new and advanced computer-aided forms, their guiding principles harked back to the economic axioms of a century or more.

The waning years of the last decade of the twentieth century, to which Federal Reserve Bank Chairman Alan Greenspan's earlier characterization of investor behavior as "irrational exuberance" could certainly be applied, are being followed again by the nth rediscovery of time-tested principles. These are simple but critical maxims such as earning returns above the cost of capital, recovering investments within a foreseeable time frame, making prudent decision trade-offs, and developing careful risk assessments in business situations both new and old. Financial/economic analysis never loses its basic importance—only the degree of attention paid varies over time, with the performance of the economy, changes in investor psychology, investment advisor hype, management ambition, and entrepreneurial verve.

The Economic Manager

Given our emphasis on basic economic principles and the time-tested approach to financial/economic analysis, we prefer to think of successful managers at all levels as economic managers. This appellation certainly doesn't imply requiring a degree in economics, or a stint in an economic consulting firm. Instead, we define the economic manager as a person operating from a mind set of deliberate economic trade-offs, applied to every decision made. This mind set always leads to

the question: "What are the ultimate cash flow benefits to be derived from this action, and what are the cash flow commitments involved—is this trade-off appropriate, given the risks involved?" There is a degree of basic common sense about
this point of view, because whether knowingly, instinctively, or even subcon-
sciously, just about all individuals make such trade-offs in their daily lives. We all
have a sense of weighing value received for value given in our purchases or investments, or in reverse, of value given for value received when we sell assets, or
our own services. It's only the degree of understanding, quantification, and analytical discipline applied in practice that distinguishes the economic manager from
the average individual, and we'll discuss the key attributes in a little more detail.

Understanding Business Economics

The economic manager has a very clear understanding of the business economics
of the company and its parts, and especially of the segment he or she manages.
This understanding begins with the dimensions and implications of the business
model used, including customer needs and attributes, the supply chain, competitive positioning, and the company's operational design and effectiveness, all
within the larger societal setting. It extends to insights about the specific contributions and requirements of the various stakeholders, and the obligations the organization owes them.

With such solid background knowledge the economic manager is in a position to identify and prioritize key value drivers that are essential to the long-
term success of the business. A value driver can be as basic as a sustainable
cost and/or quality advantage due to a patented process, a protected resource,
or a unique set of operational skills. It can be as intangible as the technical expertise of a product development team or a group of service providers, or it can
be an attribute of the business model that is hard for others to emulate. Positioning on the preference spectrum of the customers, such as brand name, or
enjoying the advantage from an installed base of products or services can be
value drivers. The point is, most businesses can identify one or more of these,
and if properly addressed, managed, and measured they can lead to a tangible
advantage or at least acceptable results. In the end every value driver is a lever
for improved cash flow performance, and the economic manager will be very
familiar not only with the nature of the value drivers impacted by decisions,
but also the trade-offs to be made in using the drivers well. Thus the economic
manager views the business not only as a complete system, but also as a finely
tuned assembly of interrelated parts. The economic manager knows where the
priority areas of attention are and how to enhance them, and understands the
business model and its parts sufficiently to have a positive impact through
carefully analyzed and executed decisions.

Parallel to this understanding is the economic manager's comfort with the
decision-making process itself. The mind set is oriented toward clearly defining the issue at hand, establishing the appropriate alternatives, identifying which

information and data are relevant for the purpose, and judging the analytical results from a long-term viewpoint of value creation. The economic manager is
sufficiently familiar with information sources within the company, and works in
close collaboration with financial and other staff persons to make sure that relevant data are at hand for sound analysis and judgments. There's sufficient understanding of such data to know what to ask for, to judge whether data or
analyses provided by others are truly relevant, and to hold one's own in discussions with specialized personnel whose job it is to delve into the details of analytical data, constructs, and tools. We're talking about a level of practical insight
that stops well short of the intricate specialization implicit in accounting, economic analysis, and planning expertise, but which is pronounced enough to insist on and achieve justifiable approaches and answers. The economic manager
thus actively and successfully merges practical line experience with effective
use of available staff capabilities.

Appropriate Economic Tools

Specifically, the economic manager knows the major tools for economic analysis
well enough to be comfortable with their application and the interpretation of the
results achieved. This is part of a deliberate effort to take responsibility for the
process, and to draw in assistance from specialized staffs as needed. It's a natural
aspect of managerial leadership to be cognizant of the need to apply the best techniques whenever necessary, and to base the choice on the cost benefit trade-off involved in such an effort.

Once appropriate analytical tools to prepare the groundwork for a decision
have been identified, the role of the economic manager becomes that of decision-
maker—one who guides the process, probes for the appropriate information, and
challenges the preliminary results and insights presented by staff, until a level of
comfort is reached with the output of the analysis. Practicality is paramount at all
times, as is realism stemming from the collective experience of the players involved. In line with this principle, for example, we'll discuss in Chapters 7 and 8
not only the technical aspects of the investment analysis tools presented there, but
also frame their meaning and use in the larger context of the decision process involved. Economic tools must be an extension of management practice, not an exercise in number crunching.

The economic manager embracing such an approach will be in a better position to interpret and argue the case for a significant initiative with the ultimate
decision-makers, whether senior executives or even the board of directors. The
manager's involvement in the framing of the issue, the choice of tools, and guidance of analytical effort leads to greater effectiveness not only in the manager's
ability to handle decisions large and small, but also, by virtue of the manager's
leadership, in the organization's ability to operate the business by appropriate economic criteria and by making the necessary trade-offs. This is, of course, a pre-
requisite for the value-creating company we address next.

The Practice of Financial/Economic Analysis

The financial/economic analysis sponsored and used by the economic manager can be viewed within a broad hierarchy of decision-making needs. The diagram in Figure 1–1 shows four key areas in the typical business where financial/economic analysis is a necessary ingredient. This conceptual pyramid rests on the broadest area: day-to-day decisions and operational planning. It successively rises via strategy development, investment analysis and capital structure planning, on to performance assessment and incentives, and finally to valuation and investor communication. Each of these areas contains challenges and issues in the practice of analysis and decision-making that the economic manager must address.

Day-to-Day Decisions and Operational Planning

One of the most important areas of applying basic financial/economic analysis is the support of day-to-day decisions made by managers and employees. We're talking about the operational part of the enterprise, in which strategic direction and operational plans are translated into action. Despite its importance, analytical practice in this area often tends to be the least developed, because the pressure of daily activities foreshortens the time for reflective thinking about operational issues and trade-offs. Too busy to ponder the impact of a decision on the bottom line, the harried manager or employee acts on the spur of the moment. Such seat-

FIGURE 1–1 —————————————————————————————————

Areas for Financial/Economic Analysis

of-the-pants decision-making can become the ingrained way of doing things, unless the company has instilled a basic sense of decisional discipline and provided guidance through simple but useful decision rules and processes. The successful company will have an integrated set of metrics and criteria, and provide information that clearly supports intelligent decision-making.

Without such guidance, non-economic and damaging choices such as spending funds because there's room in the budget or in the allowable head count become decision criteria. Operational effectiveness should be a function of sound trade-offs, with careful cost management and close attention paid to the quality and efficiency of production or services rendered, and with constant vigilance in serving customers through sustainable pricing, credit, and support actions.

While this book contains a large number of the key tools and measures to assist in making such trade-offs, the issue we're addressing here is larger than availability of tools. We're talking about a mind set, an organizational climate in which managers and all employees are encouraged, indeed challenged, to approach their jobs and the daily decisions they make with a rational trade-off mentality. Before making a decision, answers to questions such as "Is this really a necessary outlay and will it bring in more cash than I will spend?" or "Should I in fact spend more because I expect an opportunity to improve service will pay off in higher profit contribution?" should be second nature, as would the deliberation: "Should I engage in this activity, or is it more economical to have it performed by an outside service?" Such thinking might run counter to a corporate culture which does not encourage employee initiative and "thinking outside the box," but will be a natural consequence of the leadership of the economic manager we discussed earlier. It's reinforced by a combination of training and specific decision support, and clearly communicated expectations at all levels.

Supporting Strategy Development

The practice of financial/economic analysis is generally more developed in this area, as it is subject to more senior management scrutiny and authority because of the size and implications of the decisions made. Also, support by qualified internal staff or outside advice is often available. Yet, as we discussed earlier, there are significant exceptions to this in new economy companies; but even old economy businesses are certainly not uniform in the quality of analytical processes they employ in these areas.

The analysis of strategic alternatives and the commitment of resources to investments involves a complex set of economic trade-offs, viewed within a competitive framework. The ultimate goal is to find areas of activity that can be performed with a sustainable competitive advantage. The major challenge lies in establishing the key variables involved, making estimates of the risks surrounding them, and ultimately expressing the likely alternatives in the form of expected cash flow patterns. This is a difficult undertaking, where the problem is not so much the eventual application of the economic tools, but the development of a coherent structure of the proposal, its relevant alternatives, and all of its key variables and the risks expected. It is here where judgment and interpretation are critical, that is, clearly defining the opportunities and choices to be made, and thinking through all the implications of a potential decision on the existing organization, on the customer base, on the competitive situation.

It is also here where experience shows that profit expectations can be overblown, that the difficulties of implementation can be underestimated, and that market acceptance of an initiative might not materialize. This is not only true when introducing a new business model, as we mentioned, but is especially prevalent in mergers and acquisitions, which more often than not fail to create value because economic analysis becomes secondary to bidding contests and resultant overpricing. Economic managers will insist on creating and assessing a range of risk-adjusted summary cash flow estimates for any strategic change, perhaps based on different scenarios, as the basis for weighing the strategy's ultimate economic impact and value contribution.

The analysis of the current and prospective financing structure similarly involves many economic trade-offs, integrating the degrees of risk connected with various financing options with their costs and the long-run viability of the capital structure. Key influences are the rate of growth envisioned in the business, the trade-off between internal growth versus acquisitions and partnering, domestic versus global operations, and the nature of the main business activities themselves and their attendant risks. None of the choices of funding sources are obvious, and the economic impact on the business as well as on share values must be judged carefully. The role of informed judgment in gauging risks versus rewards, while not fully quantifiable in itself, is a critical requirement in, for example, avoiding credit problems, or financing constraints that can interfere with strategy.

In the end, the role of financial/economic analysis in strategy development and financing should be seen as an integrative force. Applied properly, it leads to testing as closely as possible the planned strategic structure of investment and necessary financing against the goal of earning above the cost of capital, and creating shareholder value.

Performance Assessment and Incentives

The main issue in this area is the relevance of the measures to the goals set, and the need to establish not only indicators of deviation from desired norms, but also to interpret these indicators so they can be used to reinforce value creation. It's an area where the quality of the concepts and tools employed varies widely in both established and new companies. If the relevance of measures employed has not been clearly established in an organization, performance data can be meaningless, or subject to manipulation. "Gaming" the budget or the business plan is an ever-present temptation. The tools for analysis, and the judgments required for interpreting performance vary widely, whether one measures performance from outside the business, which is the task of investors, creditors, and suppliers, or internally, which is a necessary function of managing the various levels and segments of a company.

One of the critical challenges in evaluating the performance of a business from the outside is to interpret the results as expressed in financial statements. These are the most readily available data for publicly held companies. But the various ratios and measures that can be applied to this information are subject to limitations inherent in the financial accounting process and to a number of choices management has in applying its rules and thus "managing" the reported results. The outside analyst endeavors to measure operational effectiveness, the success with which capital has been employed, and the risks represented by the capital structure and its parts. Measures and their meaning vary by industry segment and type of organization, and the challenge is always to derive insights from relevant comparisons to other companies or groupings, a difficult task in most instances. The ratios and relationships used as measures are easy to derive, but their effective use depends on the skill of the analyst in interpreting trends and recognizing exceptions and changes due to management actions or accounting policies. The sophisticated analyst is able to look beyond accounting results to make an evaluation of cash flow patterns underlying the data made available, as we'll observe frequently throughout the book.

Performance evaluation within the organization benefits from access to more detailed and current information, which usually goes far beyond publicly released data. But here the challenge is to develop measures that represent the cause and effect between decisions made and results achieved, a challenge not fully addressed in many situations. A vast range of statistical data can be used to measure effectiveness of operations, many of which are physical in nature, such as output data, failure rates, yields, customer contact frequencies, timeliness information, and project completions. Intangible data such as customer satisfaction, employee attitudes, and community feedback are important supplements. The point we're making is that financial performance begins with the roots of operational activity, and evaluating financial ratios and measures must rest on an understanding of these activity-based indicators. In well-managed companies there is a close connection between physical and financial indicators, and performance evaluation is made with this total view of the operation. This recognizes that accounting transactions and their compilation provide at best a partial view, and that financial measures have to be supplemented with judgments about organizational activity.

When it comes to internally assessing the effectiveness with which capital has been employed by various parts of the organization, accounting measures tend to loom larger. Rate-of-return measures and other criteria that we'll discuss represent a summarized, periodic view of net benefits, usually after-tax profit, versus the recorded resources employed. Here the potential deviation from economic results is larger, and many companies are attempting to move closer to the cash flow measures we'll discuss in the latter portion of the book. There has been a steady evolution in these processes, in parallel with a better understanding of the economic dynamics of the securities markets.

Incentives to enhance short- and long-term performance are the opposite side of the performance evaluation challenge we just discussed. We won't deal directly with the complex issues of designing incentive programs, as this is a subject deserving full treatment by itself. However, the principles of decision-driven management we support, the focus on cause and effect in making appropriate trade-offs, and the need for long-term cash flow generation will echo through a well-designed incentive system. Operational, largely activity-based incentives for employees are less difficult to design, because of their direct, statistical underpinnings.

More challenging are higher level finance-based incentives, which due to their more encompassing nature and usual reliance on accounting data, can introduce problems of interpretation and opportunities for "gaming." How periodic revenues are recorded, and expenses are recognized can affect the outcome of such measures and the resulting payout to the manager. There is also the issue of the time horizon over which incentives are established. The higher the level of management, the more emphasis should be given to long-term cash flow generation, to avoid the temptation for making short-term trade-offs that damage long-run value creation. Finally, there is the always present issue of how high to set the standard to ensure some degree of excellence and significant effort, without making the incentive unachievable. In short, incentives represent a form of using financial/economic analysis heavily overlaid not only with challenges of interpretation but of human motivation and proper rewards.

Valuation and Investor Communication

The most integrative aspect of financial/economic analysis is the area of valuation and investor communication. It is here that some of the most complex tools and methodologies are commonly employed, and it's also the area where much of the theoretical and empirical research of the past two decades has been focused. As we'll discuss in the final chapters, valuation is a function of the expectations held by the company's existing and potential investors, and by the securities markets in general. There is a two-fold challenge involved in this analytical area. First, outside analysts and managers alike must understand and properly apply the principles of valuation we'll discuss. Second, the story of the company's performance and future expectations has to be made available and explained—obviously within the legal and regulatory constraints to which such communication is subject—in a way that reasonable assumptions can be derived from this information.

Because valuation by necessity is a future-oriented process, existing performance must be projected over a time horizon befitting the nature of the business and its industry segment. This is best done in a cash flow framework to which various tools are applied to derive ranges of valuation, although short-cut methods can of course be used for "ballpark" estimates. Thus the challenge is quite daunting: It begins with understanding the business model and its key attributes, an appreciation of the strategies in place and any changes expected, an assessment of key performance criteria, a feel for the competitive realities and the future environment of the industry, and a judgment about the position and likely success of the company within this environment. We again are faced with a systems view of financial/economic analysis at the highest level, which integrates the insights about all aspects of the business under review. The external communication challenge similarly requires a systems view of the company's performance and prospects. In both the analytical and communications areas a fully integrated approach is still lacking in the majority of corporate situations, and we began this chapter by saying that there was an obvious hiatus during the excesses of the dot.com era. The rediscovery of basic economics is coming none too soon for this important area of analysis.

The Value Creating Company

While we've already brought up most of the requirements for creating economic value through economic management, let's reflect briefly on what the key attributes of a successful company are. In our view, the value creating company can be defined as an organization in which management has achieved integration of the interests and actions of its key stakeholders, that is, shareholders, managers, employees, customers, suppliers, creditors, and the community. This integration is based on managing, through sound decision-making, the business system we'll describe in Chapter 2, and the many economic trade-offs implicit in this system. Such a company achieves, as nearly as possible, an optimization of the system's performance over time, driven by a sound business model, strategies with a sustainable competitive advantage, and superb operational execution, supported by an appropriate, balanced capital structure. This should result in achieving positive cash flows as well as expectations of future cash flow patterns that exceed the cost of capital. In turn, this will provide superior returns to shareholders, superior rewards for managers and employees, excellence in customer satisfaction, first rate performance and loyalty from suppliers, and superior credit relations. Financial/economic analysis properly applied plays a key role in all of these aspects, and we'll discuss some of the underlying requirements.

Relevant Decision Information

No sound decisions are possible in a business setting without relevant information being available to the decision-maker. This axiom applies to all types of decision situations, whether large or small. The value creating company has established information sources and access to this information to enable persons at all levels to make rational trade-offs, whenever faced with an issue to be decided. This requires several supportive management practices:

- Sharing of relevant information.
- Decision support by financial staff.
- Distinction between accounting and economic data.

Sharing. The first practice is a deliberate management attitude of sharing. Too often old economy companies have fostered a climate in which information and knowledge is limited to those "in the know," while new economy companies often have been too busy to even develop appropriate information flows. The principle here is one of delegation, of entrusting people at all levels with relevant data that will help them make sound decisions in the interest of value creation. This fits well with the modern management concepts of flat organizations and empowered employees. Empowerment begins with knowledge and is expanded by targeted training, which includes understanding the nature and relevance of financial/economic data, and is reinforced by a climate of trust.

Decision support. The second practice defines the support role of financial staffs in the organization. If sharing of information and its appropriate use is to succeed, the financial staffs must be proactive, because they are the basic supervisors of transactions and data collection, sponsors of internal information and accounting systems, and guardians of financial information. Again we're describing a mind set, a shifting away from the primary attitude of control and stewardship—which historically has been the orientation of accounting professionals—to an attitude of business advisor and facilitator of decision support. The significance of this shift cannot be overemphasized. The value creating company looks upon its qualified financial staffs as business consultants, working closely with the line managers—our economic managers—and bringing to bear their insights and access to information in order to empower the decision-makers up and down the line to make appropriate trade-offs. This is an educational function as well as a support role, because even when information is shared, it's necessary to explain the meaning and relevance of the financial/economic data, and to assist the non-financial personnel in the appropriate use of decision criteria and tools. At the same time, as we observed earlier, non-financial managers must not simply delegate the analytical aspects of their economic decisions to the experts, because understanding the principles involved as well as being clear about the nature of the trade-offs is part of the overall effectiveness of the enlightened modern manager.

Accounting versus cash. The third practice is related to the first two, and also echoes an important theme mentioned earlier and carried throughout this book. The value creating company has managed to draw a clear distinction between the two points of view with which financial information is gathered and interpreted, namely, the accounting viewpoint and the economic decision viewpoint. The blurring between these two, which is too often found in financial analysts' commentary and security analysts' reports, can lead senior management to pursue results in accounting terms, such as managing quarterly earnings results and expectations, when in fact cash flows are increasingly being recognized as the real key to building value. The value creating company encourages internal decision-making on the basis of managerial economics and cash flow data, tasking the financial staffs to develop decision rules and decision information, and provide support that clarifies the economic trade-offs to be made.

In this process, such a company certainly doesn't ignore the requirements of financial accounting and reporting, which are still the mainstay of published financial information. But the company actively promotes, in parallel fashion, the view of its performance in cash flow terms, and embraces appropriate shareholder value techniques of the kind described in the final chapters of this book. As it sends clear signals to its personnel that decision-making must be economic and cash trade-off oriented, it also requires that the accounting implications are to be recognized as a separate view. At times, divergent near-term accounting impacts might have to be explained in external communications, if a strategic move is at stake which could depress near-term reported earnings but promises strong cash flow results over time. The value creating company does this as a matter of course, confident in the integrity of its decision-making processes, and communicating clearly why financial accounting cannot express the true economic results, given its different orientation.

In short, the value creating company has established a corporate climate in which all decisions and all actions are viewed as economic trade-offs, and which fosters access to and sharing of carefully developed, relevant information, decision rules, and tools in a collaborative fashion. Because the common objective is value creation for the long term, such a supportive climate for decision-making is the vital underpinning of success.

Economic Incentives

One of the critical attributes of the value creating company is the degree of attention paid to providing appropriate near-term and long-term incentives to its managers and employees. As we mentioned earlier, there should be a true cause-and-effect phenomenon surrounding incentives and results. If a company's incentives are based on some of the common, broad accounting measures such as return on equity, or return on assets, or even earnings per share, there is a real risk that decisions, large and small, will suffer from the economic disconnect and time lag inherent to these measures, as we'll discuss in the final chapters of this book. While the complex subject of management incentives is not one of the areas we'll cover, we believe the principles involved are the same basic economic choices that affect financial analysis and planning.

Therefore, both near-term and long-term incentive programs should reflect a careful set of measures designed to reinforce shareholder value creation. Since value creation depends on consistent cash flow generation in excess of the cost of capital, incentives chosen will tend to reward results from consistent cash-flow-based decision-making. Targets are set and measured with yardsticks as close as possible to cash. As we said earlier, this approach is directly applicable in the operational area, where the cause-and-effect relationship between incentives and results can be found in fairly basic targets, such as volume goals in sales or production, carefully calibrated against quality standards and relative contribution from products and services, or cost effectiveness standards that encourage enhanced performance within required service and quality levels. We're not talking merely about managing budgetary variances, but about setting specific sub-goals within a broader set of systematic expectations, accompanied by open communication about the fit of these sub-goals into the overall strategic context. The process in effect focuses on identifiable and measurable value drivers, which we mentioned earlier.

In the strategic area, long-term incentives should primarily be based on the cash flow expectations from specific plans, whether for a product or service sector in the business, or for the company as a whole. In essence, incentives are founded on the ability to bring about the cash flow streams committed to in strategic plans, and rewards fluctuate in response to such performance. The value creating company structures true incentives, that is, underperformance means a tangible penalty, while excellence is well rewarded. In addition, there is great emphasis on long-term performance to avoid the temptation to make decisions that enhance short-term results to the detriment of shareholder value creation.

Total Systems Management

As we've mentioned before, and as we'll illustrate in much more detail, the most important attribute of a successful, value creating company is its deliberate emphasis on managing the company and its parts as a total system. In simple terms, this means that there is coherence and positive, economic reinforcement reaching across all operational, investment and financing activities. The pattern of strategies and policies chosen is well-matched with the purpose and core capabilities of the company and its stakeholders. Senior management constantly monitors and reinforces this systems view through its feedback and actions, and stands ready to remedy any conflicting actions that could detract from the aim to optimize the overall system. Every major decision, whether affecting operational execution, investments, acquisitions or disinvestments, or financing choices and funding sources, is made within the systems context to ensure that all implications and linkages are considered and the appropriate trade-offs established. Decision rules and practices for day-to-day decisions are calibrated to reflect the systems view as well.

To achieve such integration of corporate purpose, strategies, policies, activities and decision-making is not an easy task. Only a few companies experience it fully and consistently, but it is here where the attributes of the economic manager we discussed can be applied most effectively. It requires constant vigilance and communication, as well as very consistent management behavior with responses that match this image. The rewards to shareholders, managers and other stakeholders are obvious, when value creation at the levels of, say, General Electric is considered. Every management team must ask itself from time to time whether it is managing the system entrusted to it by the shareholders in a coherent systems manner, and financial/economic analysis as we'll discuss it in this book is a critical component supporting this integrated approach.

Summary

In this chapter we've attempted to provide a broad, introductory perspective for the role and the challenges of financial/economic analysis in the modern business setting. We started by characterizing the attributes and issues of the new economy, and the recent welcome return to the unchanging basics of analyzing and understanding business performance and prospects. Then we stressed the need for all managers to become economic managers to best fulfill their and their companies' potential, and discussed some of the key issues in using financial/ economic analysis within the general hierarchy of business management. In each of these cases we referred to the challenges posed by current or emerging practice. We ended with an overview of the critical attributes of the successful, value creating company. This was a reemphasis of the critical need for a systems approach to economic management, the theme that is being carried throughout this book.

CHAPTER 2

A SYSTEMS CONTEXT FOR FINANCIAL MANAGEMENT

Any business, large or small, is a system of financial relationships and cash flows, which are activated by management decisions—a key principle we established in Chapter 1. This concept gained importance in the 1990s, when creation of shareholder value emerged as a critical performance challenge and became one of the primary goals of modern management. Creating shareholder value depends on bringing about a positive pattern of cash flows in excess of investor expectations. A business that is successfully managed in all parts as an integrated system will generate such cash flows over time and well into the future—thus becoming a value creating company.

Given that the basic purpose and value of business activity depend on long-term cash flow generation, it's necessary for us to understand more specifically how the dynamics of the integrated business system work. Moreover, we must directly relate the various analytical concepts and tools we'll discuss in this book to the business system. As we observed, they should assist decisionmakers at all levels in specific ways to support cash flow generation and shareholder value creation. Finally, we must provide an appropriate context for the use of commonly available financial information with which such analytical activity is supported.

In this chapter we'll expand the picture we've developed in the previous chapter, by presenting three conceptual overviews for the context and meaning of financial/economic analysis and the key economic trade-offs it supports. The purpose is to provide the reader with a realistic structure that goes beyond mere coverage of technical tools and methods:

- A graphic representation of the generalized, integrated business system, showing the relationships and dynamics of the three basic management decision areas which are common to all organizations which have an economic purpose:
  Investment decisions.

Operating decisions.

Financing decisions.

- A broad perspective of the nature, meaning, and limits of the major published financial statements, which are the primary source of financial data, and their relationship to the business system:

    Balance sheets.

    Income (operating) statements.

    Cash flow statements.

    Statements of changes in shareholders' (owners') equity.

- A generalized overview of the key analytical processes used in interpreting the performance and value of the business system, grouped by three major viewpoints:

    Financial accounting.

    Investor analysis.

    Managerial economics.

In our discussions we'll continue to differentiate between purely financial analysis on one hand, and economic analysis and trade-offs on the other. As we mentioned, the first is largely based on financial statements and accounting data, while the second focuses on cash flows. We make this important distinction because the tasks of analyzing, judging, and guiding a firm's activities are far broader and more complex than the mere manipulation of reported financial data. Ultimately, the performance and value of any business must be judged in economic terms; that is, expressed in cash flows achieved and future cash flows expected.

Yet, we must remind ourselves that much of the available data and many of the analytical techniques generally used are based on financial accounting and its special conventions, which by their nature don't necessarily reflect current and future economic performance and value. Therefore, the manager or analyst must at all times carefully interpret and even translate the available data to properly match the context and purpose of the analysis. It's the both the manager's and the analyst's duty to make sure that the process selected and the results obtained in any analysis clearly fit the desired objectives, whether they express a financial viewpoint or an economic insight when judging performance, expectations, or valuation.

A Dynamic Perspective of Business

Decision Context

As we've established, successful operation, performance, and long-term viability of any business, depend on a continuous sequence of sound decisions made individually or collectively by the management team. Every one of these decisions ultimately causes, for better or worse, an economic impact on the business. In essence, the process of managing any enterprise requires ongoing economic choices; each time trading off costs and benefits. These choices in turn activate specific, identifiable shifts in the physical and financial resources supporting the business. Ultimately these shifts cause movements of cash, which is the final economic result.

For Example

> Hiring an employee means incurring a future series of salary or wage payments in exchange for useful services. Selling merchandise on credit releases goods from inventory to the customer and creates a documented obligation by the customer to remit payment within 30 or 60 days. Investing in a new physical facility causes, among other effects, a potentially complex set of future financial obligations to be fulfilled. Developing a new software application involves a significant period of cash commitments for salaries, technical support, and testing before marketing efforts result in a revenue stream. Successful negotiation with a lender for a line of credit brings an inflow of cash into the business, to be repaid in future periods.

Some decisions are major, such as investing in a new manufacturing plant, raising large amounts of debt, or adding a new line of products or services. Most other decisions are part of the day-to-day processes through which every functional area of a business is managed. We earlier established the common theme that all decisions are economic trade-offs; that is, before a decision is made the decision maker must weigh the cash benefits expected against the cash costs incurred.

In normal day-to-day decisions, these underlying trade-offs can be quite apparent and identifiable. In complex situations, however, managers must carefully evaluate whether the net pattern of resources committed directly or indirectly by the decision is likely to be profitably recovered over time through the changes in revenues and expenses caused by this commitment. Managers also must identify the relevant information needed to support this analysis. The collective effect of the series of trade-off analyses and decisions ultimately impacts both the performance and value of the business. Results are then judged periodically, either by means of financial statements or with the help of special economic analyses.

Fundamentally, managers make decisions on behalf of the owners of the business, while addressing the interests of the various stakeholders involved, that is employees, suppliers, creditors and the community. In this process, managers are responsible for effectively deploying available internal and external resources in ways that create an economic gain for the owners—a gain reflected over time in the combination of dividends and share price appreciation received by the owner/shareholders. This concept, called *total shareholder return (TSR),* is one of the key criteria for measuring the success of the company relative to its peers and the market as a whole, as we'll discuss in Chapters 4 and 12.

Despite the great variety of issues faced every day by managers of different businesses, and within the hierarchy of business activities we discussed in the first chapter, management tasks are so similar in principle that we can effectively group all business decisions into three basic areas:

- The investment of resources.
- The operation of the business using these resources.
- The proper mix of financing that funds these resources.

Figure 2–1 reflects the continuous interrelationship of these three areas.

Today's business world has infinite variety. Enterprises of all sizes engage in activities such as trade, manufacturing, finance, and myriad services, using a variety of business models, and legal and organizational structures. They frequently involve international operations, far-flung investments and internet support. Common to all businesses, however, is the following definition of the basic economic purpose of sound management:

Strategic deployment of selected resources in order to create, over time, economic value sufficient to recover all of the resources employed while earning an acceptable economic return on these resources under conditions that match the owners' expectations of risk.

Over time, therefore, successful resource deployments should result in a net improvement in the economic position of the owners of the business. Only when such an improvement is achieved has additional shareholder value been created, as we'll discuss later. The primary effect of value creation normally will be a higher valuation of the business. If the company's stock is traded publicly, its value is judged by the securities markets. If the company is privately held, its value will be reflected in the price offered by potential buyers of the business. If no value increment is achieved over time, or if there is a declining trend, the firm's economic viability might be in question.

FIGURE 2–1

The Three Basic Business Decisions

Therefore, creating shareholder value ultimately depends on properly managing the three basic decision areas common to all organizations

- Selecting, implementing, and monitoring all *investments* based on sound, sustainable strategies, economic analysis and effective management.
- Guiding the *operations* of the business profitably through proper trade-off decisions and cost-effective use of all resources employed.
- Prudently *financing* the business by consciously trading off the rewards expected against the risks encountered in balancing internal and external financing in the capital structure.

Making successful economic trade-offs in all of these decisions is fundamental to driving the value creation process. These trade-offs must also be explicitly chosen and managed in a consistent way to achieve long-run success, instead of focusing on occasional short-term improvements that cannot be sustained or might detract from longer-term results. Figure 2–2 depicts the definition and purpose of the three interrelated decision areas.

As we observed earlier, the basic task—and the fundamental challenge—of financial/ economic analysis lies in constructing and sharing a reasonably consistent and meaningful set of data and relationships that will support the decision-making process for the purpose of value creation. If this is done well, the chosen frameworks and tools should enable the analyst and the manager to judge the economic trade-offs involved in investment choices, financing options, and operational effectiveness, and help define and judge the company's economic performance, future expectations, and value.

Figure 2–3 illustrates, in the form of background layers, the analytical framework and tools, data sources, and the general backdrop of competitive and economic conditions to the three decision areas. This picture presents an integrated set of concepts for the ideal interplay of management decisions and the interpretation of results.

FIGURE 2-2

The Process of Value Creation

FIGURE 2–3

The Broad Context of Financial/Economic Analysis

The Business System

As we know, there's a dynamic interrelationship among decisions made by managers. Decisions cause resource movements in various forms that ultimately change the cash flow pattern of the business as a whole. The process might involve some intermediate steps before cash movements occur, as we'll discuss in Chapter 3, but increases or decreases in cash will invariably follow any decision made. We observed that in a successful business, the balancing of cash uses and sources over time generates positive cash flow patterns that lead to the desired buildup of economic value and long-term viability. In fact, creation of shareholder value and cash flow patterns—achieved and expected—are inseparable concepts.

As we take up the analytical concepts and tools in the book, we'll relate them, as appropriate, to the simple principle that "cash in" versus "cash out" is the key to any economic analysis. In Chapter 3, we'll discuss the formal ways of tracking and analyzing overall resource flow patterns and their cash impact. In Chapters 7, 8, 11, and 12 we'll show how the specific cash flows associated with an investment project or a business as a whole can be established, analyzed, and valued.

Let's now develop a practical, simplified view of how a typical business operates. With the help of an intuitive systems diagram we'll demonstrate the basic cash flow patterns, the key relationships, and the key decisions involved in an integrated fashion. Then we'll show how the major financial/economic analysis measures and key business strategies relate to this business system. Every one of the measures and concepts will, of course, be discussed in greater depth in the appropriate chapters of this book, but this overview provides a structure for keeping the individual elements in proper perspective.

Figure 2–4 presents the basic flow chart of the business system, which contains all major elements necessary to understand the broad cash flow patterns of any business. The arrangement of boxes, lines, and arrows is designed to show that we're dealing with a system in which all parts are interrelated to each other— and which therefore has to be managed as a whole. The solid lines with arrows represent cash flows, while the dashed lines symbolize trade-off relationships. The system is organized into three segments that match the three major decision areas we've defined: investment, operations, and financing.

- The top segment represents the three components of business investment: the *investment base* already in place, the addition of *new investments,* and any *disinvestment* (divestment) of resources no longer deemed effective or strategically necessary. In addition, it shows the *depreciation effect* caused by accounting write-offs of portions of depreciable assets against the investment base and against profits. This box, which effectively enhances the funding potential shown in the bottom segment, represents available cash that was masked when the accounting-based operating profit after taxes was calculated, as we'll discuss in Chapter 3.

- The center segment represents the operational interplay of three basic elements: *price, volume,* and *costs* of products and/or services. It also recognizes that usually costs are partly fixed and partly variable relative to volume changes. The ultimate result of the complex set of continuously made trade-offs in the operations area is the periodic operating profit or loss, after applicable income taxes. Operating profit is shown as part of the bottom segment in the diagram, because profit represents one of the key elements of financing the business.

- The bottom segment represents, in two parts, the basic financing choices open to a business:

  1. The normal disposition of the *operating profit after taxes* (or loss after taxes) that has been achieved for a period:

     This is a three-way split among *dividends* paid to owners, *interest* paid to lenders (adjusted for taxes because of its tax deductibility), and *earnings* retained for reinvestment in the business. As the arrows indicate, the cash used for paying dividends and interest leaves the system.

  2. The available choices for using long-term capital sources:

     This reflects *shareholders' equity* (ownership), augmented by retained earnings, and *long-term debt* held by outsiders. Trade-offs

The Business System: An Overview*

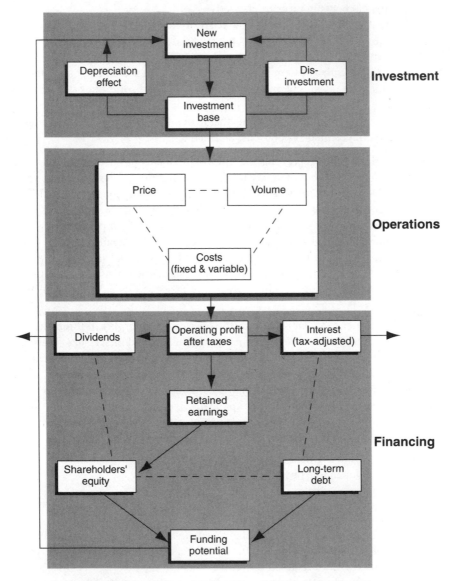

*This diagram is available in an interactive format (TFA Template) – see "Analytical Support" on p. 57.

and decisions that affect the levels of shareholders' equity, retained profits, or long-term capital sources impact the company's *funding potential,* which, as the arrow moving from the left to the top indicates, affects the amount of new investment that can be added to the investment base. As was already mentioned, the depreciation effect shown in the top segment enhances the funding potential, because it reflects cash that was masked in the accounting profit calculation. Alternatively, of course, some of the enhanced funding potential can be used to reduce long-term debt, or to repurchase outstanding ownership shares in the market. These actions will, of course, change the capital structure proportions and cause cash to leave the system.

Now we'll examine each part of the business system in further detail to highlight the three types of decisions and the various interrelationships among them.

Investment Decisions

Investment is the basic driving force of any business activity. It's the source of growth, supports management's explicit competitive strategies, and it is normally based on careful plans (capital budgets) for committing existing or new funds to three main areas:

- Working capital (cash balances, receivables due from customers, and inventories, less trade credit from suppliers and other normal current obligations).
- Physical assets (land, buildings, machinery and equipment, office furnishings, computer systems, laboratory equipment, etc.).
- Major spending programs (research and development, product or service development, promotional programs, etc.) and acquisitions.

Note that investment is broadly defined here in terms of resource commitments to be recovered over time, not by the more narrow accounting classification which would, for example, categorize most spending programs as ongoing expenses, despite their longer-range impact. Figure 2–5 shows the investment portion of the systems diagram, accompanied by major yardsticks and key strategies that can be identified in this area.

During the periodic planning process, when capital budgets are formulated, management normally chooses from a variety of options those new investments that are expected to exceed or at least meet targeted economic returns. The level of these returns generally is related to shareholder expectations via the cost of capital calculation, as described in Chapter 9. Making sound investment choices and implementing them successfully—so that the actual results in fact exceed the cost of capital standard—is a key management responsibility that leads to value creation. New investment is the key driver of growth strategies that cause enhanced shareholder value, but only if carefully established investment standards are met or exceeded.

FIGURE 2–5

The Business System: Investment Segment

Key yardsticks
- Economic measures
  - Net present value
  - Internal rate of return
  - Discounted payback

- Accounting measures
  - Return on investment
  - Return on net assets
  - Return on assets
    employed

- Value-based measures
  - Economic profit
  - Cash flow return
  - Cash value added

New
investment

Depreciation
effect

Dis-
investment

Investment
base

Key strategies
- Portfolio assessment
- Strategic alternatives
- Capital budgeting
- Priorities and deployment
- Acquisitions
- Disinvestment

At the same time, successful companies periodically make critical assessments of how their existing investment base (portfolio) is deployed, to see if the actual performance and outlook for the individual products, services, and business segments warrant continued commitment within the context of the company's strategic posture. If careful analysis demonstrates below-standard economic results and expectations about a particular market or activity, then the opposite of investment, *disinvestment,* becomes a compelling option. As we'll see, such poor performing activities destroy shareholder value. Disposing of the assets involved or selling the operating unit as a going concern will allow the funds received to be redeployed more advantageously elsewhere. Also, the sale of any equipment being replaced by newer facilities will provide funds for other purposes. Shareholder value creation thus depends on a combination of ongoing successful performance of existing investments, and the addition of successful new investments—a continued reassessment of the company's total portfolio of activities.

The yardsticks helpful in selecting *new investments* and *disinvestments* are generally economic criteria. They are based on cash flows, measuring the tradeoff between investment funds committed now and the expected stream of future operational cash flow benefits, and residual values. The cash flow tools listed here, net present value, internal rate of return, and discounted payback, are discussed in detail in Chapter 7. In contrast, common yardsticks that measure the effectiveness of the existing investment base generally are based on accounting data and relationships, as we'll describe in Chapter 4. These measures—return on investment, return on assets, and return on assets employed—relate balance sheet and income statement data as basic ratios. We'll show that there's a real disconnect between the economic measures commonly used for new investments, and the accounting-based measures for existing investments. This gap in comparability must be bridged in order to achieve a consistent approach to shareholder value creation. In fact, this bridging process has been underway since the '90s with the significant shift of corporate America toward *value-based management.* Measures such as economic profit, cash flow return on investment, and cash value added have become widely used in judging the performance and value of existing operations. As we'll discuss in Chapter 12, these measures are cash-flow oriented and thus are comparable to the economic yardsticks used for new investment, which are described in Chapter 7.

Operating Decisions

Here key strategies and decisions should focus on effective utilization of the funds invested to ensure that their implementation and continued operation meet the criteria and expectations on which the commitment was originally based. The basic set of trade-offs in operations, as was already mentioned, lies in the price, volume, and cost relationship, but surrounding this simple concept is an extensive array of complex choices and decisions.

To begin with, the company must develop its product and service offerings to achieve excellence relative to market expectations. This must be accompanied by positioning its operations competitively to make use of its core competencies and to differentiate itself from its competitors. Here we're talking not only about a strategic concept, but about a very practical operational application of such advantages as cost-effective facilities, superior skills and systems in delivery and customer service, highly effective information systems linked with customer networks, and unique technology or research capabilities. Deploying its resources in carefully selected target markets, the company must use appropriate pricing and service policies that are competitive in filling customers' needs. Management must anticipate and deal with the impact of changing prices and competitors' actions on sales volume and on the profitability of individual products or services. At the same time, all operations of the business, whether carried on inside the company or outsourced with others must not only be made cost effective, but maintained as such to achieve competitive success. Figure 2–6 highlights key elements of the operations segment of the financial system.

Successful operating results also depend on a realistic understanding of the business processes employed, the economic costs and benefits of each part of the organization, and the relative contribution of products and services to overall results. This requires the use of appropriate information systems, data collection, and reporting. Part of the insight is the effect on the company's profitability of the level and proportion of fixed (period) costs committed to the operations, versus the amount and nature of variable (direct) costs incurred in manufacturing, service, or trading operations. These concepts will be discussed in detail in Chapter 6.

Sound operational planning is an essential support process. Goals and incentives are established to reinforce the need for making economic decisions. Budgeting and analysis processes are designed to give relevant feedback, and provide

FIGURE 2–6

The Business System: Operations Segment

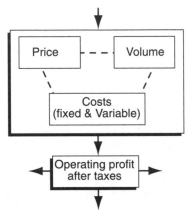

Key yardsticks
- Operating ratios
- Contribution analysis
- Activity analysis
- Effectiveness criteria
- Benchmarking

Price — — Volume

Costs (fixed & Variable)

Operating profit after taxes

Key strategies
- Product/service excellence
- Competitive positioning
- Core capabilities
- Resource deployment
- Market selection
- Pricing strategy
- Cost effectiveness
- Operating leverage
- Outsourcing; partnering

action signals for corrective measures should targets not be met. Enterprise modeling and activity-based accounting represent modern information structures made possible by ever more powerful computer systems and networks. We'll discuss basic budgeting and projection of operating activity in Chapter 5, and take up the subject of modeling in Chapter 6.

The key yardsticks in the operations segment include a variety of operating ratios that measure the effectiveness with which revenues and costs are managed. Among these are financial expressions such as operating profit percentages and various ratios of cost elements to sales revenue. There are overall expressions such as sales and assets per employee, and a host of operating statistics such as output per hour, yield percentages in production, or indicators of customer satisfaction with services rendered. Operating ratios vary greatly by type of business, as they have to be tailored to the specific variables that drive performance. In fact, operating ratios are ideally derived from those variables that represent key drivers for the business, whether they be physical conditions, human skills and attitudes, resource utilization, or technology application. From an economic standpoint, the relative profit and cash flow contribution margins of different products and services are important measures, not only for tracking current performance but as an input to strategic decisions about the portfolio of products and services.

The distinction between accounting ratios and economic analysis is again important in the operations segment, because the answers provided by each can vary significantly. This problem has led to the wide use of a relatively recent methodology that directly addresses the need for economic answers, namely, *activity-based analysis*, which was mentioned earlier. This process is essentially a step-by-step identification of the physical activities involved in a specific function of the company, or the activities required to support a particular product line, followed by a careful economic analysis of the costs and benefits incurred in each step and in total. Because it amounts to an economic assessment, activity-based analysis has become an important technique for supporting the current emphasis on corporate reengineering and value-based management. In addition, benchmarking activities against best practices in the specific industry or in general business usage represents yet another popular way of refining the measures and standards to be applied. We'll discuss a variety of key financial and economic operational criteria in Chapters 4, 5, and 6.

Financing Decisions

Here we must deal with the various choices available to management for funding the investments and operations of the business over the long term. Note that the financing section begins with profit after taxes, which normally is a major source of funding for a company. Two key areas of strategy and trade-off decisions are identified:

- The disposition of profits.
- Shaping the company's capital structure.

Normally this set of trade-offs and decisions is made at the highest levels of management and endorsed by the board of directors of a corporation because the choices are crucial to the firm's long-term viability. Figure 2–7 displays the relationships, yardsticks, and strategies in the financing segment. The first area, the disposition of profits, amounts to a basic three-way split of after-tax profit among:

- Owners.
- Lenders.
- Reinvestment in the business.

Every one of these choices is affected by current or past management policies, trade-offs, and decisions. For example, payment of dividends to owners is made at the discretion of the board of directors. Here, the critical trade-off choice is the relative amount of dividends to be paid out to shareholders as part of their overall return versus the alternative of retaining these funds to invest in the company's growth, with the goal of creating additional value which will be reflected in greater share price appreciation for the shareholders.

Payment of interest to lenders is a matter of contractual obligation. The level of tax-adjusted interest payments incurred (the cost to the company is the net amount after applying the corporate tax rate) relative to operating profit, however, is a direct function of management policies and actions regarding the use of debt, symbolized by the dashed line. The higher the proportion of debt in the capital structure, the greater the demand will be for profit dollars to be used as interest expense, and the greater the firm's risk exposure will be; that is, its potential inability to meet interest obligations and/or repayment during a business downturn.

FIGURE 2–7

The Business System: Financing Segment

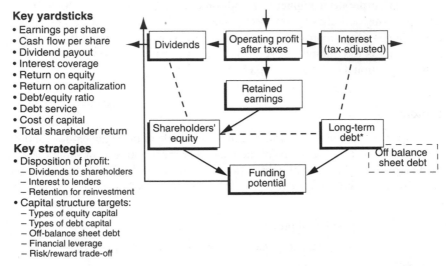

Key yardsticks
- Earnings per share
- Cash flow per share
- Dividend payout
- Interest coverage
- Return on equity
- Return on capitalization
- Debt/equity ratio
- Debt service
- Cost of capital
- Total shareholder return

Key strategies
- Disposition of profit:
  - Dividends to shareholders
  - Interest to lenders
  - Retention for reinvestment
- Capital structure targets:
  - Types of equity capital
  - Types of debt capital
  - Off-balance sheet debt
  - Financial leverage
  - Risk/reward trade-off

*Assumes a continuous rollover of debt (refinancing), that is, there is no reduction in existing debt levels from repayments, as new funds are raised to cover these, unless a policy change in debt proportions is specified. No specific provision is made here for use of off-balance sheet debt, such as operating leases.

Retained earnings represent the residual profit after taxes for the period, a net amount which remains in the company after payment of interest and dividends. This normally forms a significant part of the funding potential for additional investment and growth as shown on the bottom of the chart. We recall that the depreciation effect was added to this funding potential and reflected in the investment section, to correct for the amount of cash masked by the depreciation deduction made in arriving at operating profit after taxes, as will be discussed in Chapter 3. Additional funding potential can be found in new funds provided by lenders and investors, depending on the company's policies governing the use of such long-term sources.

Key measures in the area of earnings disposition are earnings and cash flow (after-tax profit plus the depreciation effect), calculated on a per-share basis, which are viewed as broad indicators of the company's ability to compensate both lenders and owners. In addition, specific ratios are used that measure the proportion of dividends paid out, the degree to which earnings cover the current interest on debt, and how well total debt service requirements are covered. These measures are discussed in Chapter 4.

The second area, the planning of capital structure targets, involves selecting and balancing the relative proportions of funding obtained over time from ownership sources and long-term debt obligations. The chosen combination, after taking into account business risk and debt service requirements, is intended to support an acceptable level of overall profitability while matching the degree of risk exposure deemed appropriate by management and the board of directors. A key consideration in choosing funding methods is the impact of financial leverage (see Chapter 6). It can be defined as the prudent use of funds obtained from fixed-cost debt obligations for financing opportunities that promise potential earnings higher than the interest cost on the borrowed funds—the difference benefiting the owners of the company.

Again, this process requires a series of economic trade-offs, which include weighing the rewards obtained versus the risks involved in the different alternatives open to management. As we'll discuss in Chapter 10, numerous types of equity, ranging from straight common equity to convertible shares and preferred stocks, can be used for new ownership funding. On the other hand, existing ownership funds also can be returned through repurchase of the company's shares in the open market, using some of the current funding potential. The latter choice has become an important aspect of capital structure management, because repurchasing stock with corporate cash flow reduces the number of shares outstanding, making each remaining share proportionately more valuable. At the same time, no dividends need be paid on the purchased shares, which can be used at a later time for purposes such as acquisitions. The trade-off is between adding value through new investment and adding share value through a reduced number of shares.

The choices among debt instruments are even more varied, as we'll discuss in Chapter 10. These include operating leases and similar long-term obligations, which are called *off-balance sheet debt* because they are not listed on the balance sheet and only impact the income statement as annual expenses. Major measures in the area of capital structure strategy include ratios that measure the return on equity and the return on capitalization (equity and long-term debt combined), various debt service coverage ratios (Chapter 4), ratios for relative levels of debt and equity (Chapter 6), measures of the cost of various forms of capital as well as the combined cost of capital for the company as a whole (Chapters 9 and 10), and finally, shareholder value creation concepts, such as total shareholder return, economic value added, and so forth (Chapters 11 and 12). As we'll see, one of the fundamental principles of running a successful business system is that the returns from the investments supported by the capital structure must exceed the combined cost of the equity and debt capital employed, in order to create shareholder value and a satisfactory total shareholder return. Returns just matching the cost of capital will leave value unchanged, while returns below the cost of capital will destroy value. As we'll discuss in Chapter 12, the analyst again must distinguish carefully between accounting-based and cash flow–based measures in this area.

The footnote to Figure 2–7 refers to an assumption about continuous rollover of debt. This is necessary because the business system as described here is a simple growth model with stable capital structure policies, also called target proportions. Normally, as the amount of shareholders' equity grows with incremental retained earnings, management will likely wish to match this increase, in the proper proportion, with an incremental amount of new debt—unless management decides that a change in debt policy is appropriate for a variety of reasons. In that case, specific assumptions will have to be made about the pattern of repayments planned, which, of course, will change the relative proportions of debt and equity outstanding, and also change the cash flow patterns in the model.

Interrelationship of Strategy and Value Creation

It should be obvious by now that our concept of the basic business system (Figure 2–4) forces us to recognize and deal with the many dynamic interrelationships of key management strategies, policies, and decisions, and the major cash flows they cause. In effect, the system amounts to a basic financial growth model which illustrates the interplay of key variables in support of the ultimate goal—value creation through positive cash flows in excess of the cost of capital over time. Achieving consistency in the choices and decisions regarding these variables is critical to managing a firm's long-term success and shareholder expectations, because only a well-tuned business system will perform in a superior fashion.

For Example

> It would be ineffective for a company to set aggressive growth strategies for its operations, while at the same time restricting itself to a set of rigid and conservative financial policies—especially when operating margins are narrow and funding needs sizable. Similarly, paying out a high proportion of current operating profit in the form of dividends, or repurchasing significant amounts of the company's shares, while at the same time maintaining a restrictive debt policy would clash with an objective to hold market share in a rapidly expanding business that requires substantial funding. Under such circumstances, adequate funds for new investment simply wouldn't be available, unless new equity was raised in the market. The company's strategic position could be at risk, and the stock market would adversely assess future cash flow expectations, thereby lowering the valuation of the company.

The basis for successful management, therefore, is to develop and maintain a consistent set of business strategies, investment objectives, operating goals, and financial policies that reinforce each other rather than conflict. They must be chosen through conscious and careful analysis of the various economic trade-offs involved, both individually and in combination. Proper measures and incentives must be employed, all reinforcing a long-term pattern of performance that will establish and reinforce positive shareholder expectations about current and future cash flows from successful existing investments and sound new investments—or from divestments of underperforming parts of the company. As we'll demonstrate in later chapters, understanding the dynamics of business strategies and financial policies is essential, whether they involve operational cash flow management, key drivers of financial performance, investment and divestment analysis, or capital structure planning. Our simplified systems diagram has provided a way to recognize the main interrelationships in a broad context of management decisions and cash flows.

The Nature of Financial Statements

To apply the insights gained from the conceptual overview of the business system, we must now look for available information that will:

- Allow the manager or analyst to track the financial condition and operating results of the business.
- Assist in understanding the cash flow patterns in more specific terms.

In the process of financial/economic analysis, a variety of formal or informal data are normally reviewed and tested for their relevance to the specific purpose of the analysis. The most common form in which basic financial information is available publicly, unless a company is privately held, is the set of financial statements issued under guidelines of the Financial Accounting Standards Board (FASB) of the public accounting profession and governed by the U.S. Securities and Exchange Commission (SEC). Such a set of statements, prepared according to generally accepted accounting principles (GAAP), usually contains balance sheets as of given dates, income statements for given periods, and cash flow statements for the same periods. A special statement highlighting changes in owners' equity on the balance sheet is commonly provided as well.

Since financial statements are the source for a good portion of analytical efforts, we must first understand their nature, coverage, and limitations before we can use the data and observations derived from these statements for our analytical judgments. Financial statements reflect the cumulative effects of all of management's past decisions. However, they involve considerable ambiguity. Financial statements are governed by rules that attempt to consistently and fairly account for every business transaction using the following conservative principles:

- Transactions are recorded at values prevailing at the time.
- Adjustments to recorded values are made only if values decline.
- Revenues and costs are recognized when committed to, not when cash actually changes hands.
- Periodic matching of revenues and costs is achieved via accruals, deferrals, and accounting allocations.
- Allowances for negative contingencies are required in the form of estimates that reduce both profits and recorded value, usually affecting shareholders' equity or special set-asides.

These rules leave reported financial accounting results open to considerable interpretation, especially if the analyst seeks to understand a company's economic performance and to establish the basis for shareholder value results. It's common practice among professional analysts to adjust the data reflected on financial statements for known accounting transactions which do not affect cash flows, and to make assumptions about the economic values underlying recorded asset values. We'll discuss the most important of these adjustments in Chapters 4 and 12.

The Balance Sheet

The balance sheet, prepared as of *a specific date,* records the categories and amounts of assets employed by the business (i.e., the resources committed) and the offsetting liabilities incurred to lenders and owners (i.e., the funds obtained). Also called the *statement of financial condition* or *statement of financial position,* it must always balance. By definition, the recorded value of the total assets invested in the business at any point in time must be matched precisely by the recorded liabilities and owners' equity supporting these assets. Liabilities are specific obligations that represent claims against the assets of the business, ranking ahead of the owners in repayment priority. In contrast, the recorded shareholders' equity in effect represents a residual claim of the owners on the remaining assets after all liabilities have been subtracted.

The major categories of assets, or resources committed, are:

- Current assets (items that turn over in the normal course of business within a relatively short period of time, such as cash, marketable securities, accounts receivable, and inventories).

- Fixed assets (such as land, mineral resources, buildings, equipment, machinery, and vehicles), all of which are used over a longer time frame.

- Other assets, such as deposits, patents, and various intangibles, including goodwill that arose from an acquisition.

Major sources of the funds obtained are:

- Current liabilities, which are obligations to vendors, tax authorities, employees, and lenders due within one year or less.

- Long-term liabilities, which are a variety of debt instruments repayable beyond one year, such as bonds, loans, and mortgages.

- Owners' (shareholders') equity, which represents the recorded net amount of funds contributed by various classes of owners of the business as well as the accumulated earnings retained in the business after payment of dividends.

Balance sheets are *static* in that, like snapshots, they reflect conditions on the date of their preparation. They're also cumulative because they represent the effects of all decisions and transactions that have taken place since the inception of the business and have been accounted for up to the date of preparation.

As we indicated earlier, financial accounting rules require that all transactions be recorded at costs and values as incurred at the time, and retroactive adjustments to recorded values are made only under very limited circumstances. As a consequence, balance sheets (being cumulative) display assets and liabilities acquired or incurred at different times. Because the current economic value of assets can change, particularly in the case of longer-lived items (such as buildings and machinery) or basic resources (such as land and minerals), the costs stated on the balance sheet are not likely to reflect true economic values. Moreover, changes in the value of the currency in which the transactions are recorded can, over time, distort the balance sheet.

Ultimately, the recorded book value of owners' equity is affected by all of these value differentials. There generally is quite a divergence between this residual accounting value and the current economic value of the business as reflected in share prices or in valuations for acquisition. In fact, the shares of successful companies are usually traded at price levels far above their recorded book value (see Chapter 12).

Finally, a number of relatively recent accounting rules require the estimation and recording of contingent liabilities arising from a variety of future obligations, such as pension and health-care costs, further introducing a series of value judgments. These are frequently shown as "other liabilities," listed just ahead of shareholders' equity, and, in effect, amount to a reclassification from being part of the owners' residual claims, to a special form of long-term liability.

The accounting profession's FASB is expending a great deal of effort to resolve these and other issues affecting the meaning of the balance sheet, but only with partial success. Accounting standards continue to evolve, and a manager or analyst must be aware of the underlying issues and processes when reviewing and analyzing this statement. We'll discuss the most important of these more specifically as we examine analytical techniques in later chapters.

In our decisional context of investment, operations, and financing, the balance sheet is a cumulative listing of the impact of past investment and financing decisions, and of the net operational results from using these resources. It's a historical record of all transactions that affected the current business over time. The net effect of operations in the form of periodic profit or loss is reflected in the changing shareholders' equity account. Figure 2–8 is a simple conceptual picture of the balance sheet as it relates to the three areas of management decisions.

Only the major categories normally found on the balance sheet are listed in Figure 2–8, which is an oversimplification. In actual practice, the analyst encounters a large variety of detailed asset, liability, and net worth accounts because balance sheets reflect the unique nature of a given company and the business sector to which it belongs. But the actual accounts always can be grouped into the basic categories listed.

To provide an example of the balance sheet of a major corporation, Figure 2–9 shows the consolidated balance sheets for December 31, 1997, and December 31, 1996, of TRW Inc., as published in its 1997 annual report, but presented here

FIGURE 2-8

Balance Sheet in Decisional Context

Management Decision Area

| Investment | Operations | Financing |

| Assets | **Balance Sheet**
(on a given date) | Liabilities and
net worth |

Current
assets

plus

Fixed
assets

plus

Other
assets

equals

**Total
assets**

Net profit or loss

Current
liabilities

plus

Long-term
liabilities

plus

Shareholders'
equity

equals

**Total
liabilities and
net worth**

without accompanying notes. (These are reproduced in Chapter 4, Figure 4–6). TRW Inc. is a global manufacturing and service company headquartered in Cleveland, Ohio. It's strategically focused on providing products and services with a high technology or engineering content to the automotive, space and defense, and information systems markets. TRW holds leading positions in most of its market segments. Founded in 1901, the company employs about 72,500 people in 24 countries, and is ranked 146th in sales in the Fortune 500 listing for 1997. We'll use TRW's published financial statements as examples in Chapters 3 and 4 and demonstrate the use of analytical techniques on their data.

The Income Statement

The income statement reflects the effect of management's operating decisions on business performance and the resulting accounting profit or loss for the owners of the business *over a specified period of time.* The profit or loss calculated in the statement increases or decreases owners' equity on the balance sheet. Thus, the income statement is a necessary adjunct to the balance sheet in explaining this major component of change in owners' equity, and it provides a variety of performance assessment information. The income statement, also referred to as the *operating statement, earnings statement,* or *profit and loss statement,* displays the

---

FIGURE 2–9

TRW INC. AND SUBSIDIARIES
Consolidated Balance Sheets
December 31, 1997 and 1996 ($ millions)

	1997	1996
Assets		
Current assets:		
Cash and cash equivalents	$ 70	$ 386
Accounts receivable	1,617	1,378
Inventories	573	524
Prepaid expenses	79	69
Deferred income taxes	96	424
Total current assets	2,435	2,781
Property, plant, and equipment at cost	6,074	5,880
Less: Allowances for depreciation and amortization	3,453	3,400
Total property, plant, and equipment—net	2,621	2,480
Intangible assets:		
Intangibles arising from acquisitions	673	258
Other	232	31
Total intangible assets	905	289
Less: Accumulated amortization	94	78
Total intangible assets—net	811	211
Investments in affiliated companies	139	51
Other assets	404	376
Total assets	$6,410	$5,899
Liabilities and Shareholders' Investment		
Current liabilities:		
Short-term debt	$ 411	$ 52
Accrued compensation	338	386
Trade accounts payable	859	781
Other accruals	846	775
Dividends payable	38	39
Income taxes	99	52
Current portion of long-term debt	128	72
Total current liabilities	2,719	2,157
Long-term liabilities	788	767
Long-term debt	1,117	458
Deferred income taxes	57	272
Minority interests in subsidiaries	105	56
Shareholders' investment:		
Serial preference stock II	1	1
Common stock	78	80
Other capital	462	437
Retained earnings	1,776	1,978
Cumulative translation adjustments	(130)	47
Treasury shares—cost in excess of par value	(563)	(354)
Total shareholders' investment	1,624	2,189
Total liabilities and shareholders' investment	$6,410	$5,899

Source: Adapted from 1997 TRW Inc. annual report.

revenues recognized for a specific period, and the costs and expenses charged against these revenues, including write-offs (e.g., depreciation and amortization of various assets) and taxes. Revenues and costs involve elements such as:

- Sales for cash or credit.
- Purchases of goods for resale or manufacture, or cost of services provided.
- General and administrative expenses.
- Sales and marketing expenses.
- Research and development costs.

The income statement represents the best effort of the firm's accountants to match the relevant items of revenue with the relevant items of cost and expense for the period, a process which involves accrual accounting and extensive use of allocation of prior and future revenues and costs.

Among the judgmental areas involving costs are:

- Recognizing the incidence of revenues received in advance or delayed in time.
- Depreciation of assets being used over more periods than the current reporting period.
- Cost of goods purchased or manufactured in previous periods.
- Proper allocation of general expenses to a specific period.

We'll take up the more critical of these elements and choices as we apply the analysis techniques in later chapters.

When viewed in our decisional context, the income statement in the center column of Figure 2–10 expands the details of the transactions and allocations that make up one of the key performance elements, profit or loss.

Again, we are providing an actual example of an income statement in Figure 2–11, the consolidated statement of earnings for TRW Inc. for the years ending December 31, 1997, and December 31, 1996.

The Cash Flow Statement

Because we are interested in the combined effects of investment, operating, and financing decisions, analyzing both the income statement for the period and the balance sheets at the beginning and the end of the period together provides more basic insights than either statement alone. Management decisions not only affect the profit for the period, but cause accompanying changes in most assets and liabilities, particularly in the accounts making up working capital, such as cash, receivables, inventories, and current payables. The statement that captures both the current operating results and the accompanying changes in the balance sheet is the *cash flow statement, statement of cash flows,* or *funds flow statement.* It gives us

Income Statement in Decisional Context

Management Decision Area

Investment	*Operations*	*Financing*

Assets	**Balance Sheet** (on a given date)	Liabilities and net worth
Current assets	**Income statement**	Current liabilities
plus	Revenues	plus
Fixed assets	less — Cost of sales	Long-term liabilities
plus	equals — Gross margin	plus
Other assets	less — Operating expenses	Shareholders' equity
equals	equals — Operating earnings/loss	equals
Total assets	less — Income taxes	**Total liabilities and net worth**
	equals — Net profit or loss	

a dynamic picture of the ultimate changes in cash resulting from the combined de-cisions made during a given period.

The statement is prepared by comparing beginning and ending balance sheets and using key items of the income statement for the period, all interpreted in terms of uses and sources of cash:

- Cash generated by profitable operations or drained by unprofitable results.
- Cash impact of changes in working capital requirements.
- Commitments of cash to invest in assets or to repay liabilities.
- Raising of cash through additional borrowing or by reducing asset investments.
- Cash impact of issuance of new shares or repurchase of shares.
- Cash impact of dividends paid.
- Adjustments for accounting allocations, write-offs, and other noncash elements in the income statement and the balance sheets.
- Net impact of the period's cash movements on the company's cash balance.

The cash flow statement thus offers a ready overview of the combined cash impact of all management decisions during the period. The user can judge both

FIGURE 2–11

TRW INC. AND SUBSIDIARIES
Statements of Earnings
For the Years Ended December 31, 1997 and 1996 ($ millions)

	1997	1996
Sales	$10,831	$ 9,857
Cost of sales	8,826	8,376
Gross profit	2,005	1,481
Administrative and selling expenses	684	613
Research and development expenses	461	412
Purchased in-process research and development	548	—
Interest expense	75	84
Other expenses (income) net	(3)	70
Total expenses	1,765	1,179
Earnings (loss) from continuing operations before taxes		
Excluding purchased R&D; special charges ('96)	788	687
Reported earnings (loss) before income taxes	240	302
Income taxes	289	120
Earnings (loss) from continuing operations		
Excluding purchased R&D; special charges ('96)	499	434
Reported earnings (loss) after income taxes	(49)	182
Discontinued operations, gain on disposition, after taxes	—	298
Net earnings (loss)	$ (49)	$ 480
Preference dividends	—	1
Earnings (loss) applicable to common stock	$ (49)	$ 479
Per share of common stock:		
Average number of shares outstanding (millions)		
Diluted	123.7	132.8
Basic	123.7	128.7
Diluted net earnings (loss) per share		
From continuing operations		
Excluding purchased R&D; special charges	$ 4.03	$ 3.27
Reported	(0.40)	1.37
From discontinued operations	—	2.25
Diluted net earnings (loss) per share	$ (0.40)	$ 3.62
Basic net earnings (loss) per share		
From continuing operations		
Excluding purchased R&D; special charges	$ 4.03	$ 3.29
Reported	(0.40)	1.41
From discontinued operations	—	2.31
Basic net earnings (loss) per share	$ (0.40)	$ 3.72
Book value per share (year-end)	13.19	17.29
Tangible book value per share (year-end)	6.58	15.62
Other data ($ millions):		
Depreciation of property, plant, and equipment	$ 480	$ 442
Amortization of intangibles, other assets	10	10
Capital expenditures	549	500
Dividends paid	154	148

Source: Adapted from 1997 TRW Inc. annual report.

the magnitude and the relationships of these cash movements, such as the company's ability to fund investment needs from operational results, the magnitude and appropriateness of financing changes, and disproportional movements in working capital needs. Observing the cash flow patterns can stimulate questions about the effectiveness of management strategies as well as the quality of operational decisions. The amount of detail can vary widely, depending on the nature of the business and the different types of movements emphasized.

In the past, basic formats for these statements differed widely as well. In more recent times, the FASB and SEC required that all published cash flow statements follow a common format, listing uses and sources by the familiar three decision areas: investments, operations, and financing. This rule recognized the usefulness of this arrangement in understanding the dynamics of the business system, as described earlier. Figure 2–12 shows how the cash flow statement fits into our management decision context.

One aspect of the cash flow statement that requires some explanation is the treatment of accounting write-offs. From a cash flow standpoint, write-offs such as depreciation and amortization merely represent bookkeeping entries that have *no* effect on cash. The reason is simply that the assets being amortized by these entries represent cash that was committed in *past* periods. Consequently, the write-off categories, insofar as they had reduced net profit, must be added back here as a positive cash flow, thus restoring the cash generated by operations to the original level before the write-off was made. The reader will recall that we recognized the cash flow implications of the depreciation effect in the earlier discussion of the business system. Handling of this adjustment will be illustrated more specifically in Chapter 3.

The cash flow statement has the same inherent limitations as the balance sheet and the income statement, because it's derived from the accounting data

---

FIGURE 2–12

Cash Flow Statement in Decisional Context

Management Decision Area		
Investment	*Operations*	*Financing*
Cash flow statement		
Investments	**Operations**	**Financing**
Investment (increases) in all types of assets are uses of cash; disinvestment (reductions) in all types of assets are sources of cash.	Profitable operations are a source of cash; losses drain cash from the system. Accounting write-offs or write-ups do not affect cash; their profit impact must be adjusted for.	Trade credit and new financing (increasing in liabiliites and equity) are sources of cash; repayments of liabilities, dividends, and returns of capital are uses of cash.

contained in these statements. However, because it focuses on the *changes* incurred during the period, the limitations due to historical valuation are usually not significant. However, we must remember that by displaying the net change from the beginning to the end of the chosen period in each asset, liability, and ownership account reported, the statement might "bury" major individual transactions that occurred during the period and perhaps offset each other. Normally, however, material transactions of this kind (such as major investments, acquisitions, or divestitures) are noted specifically in the company's cash flow statement. The statement therefore affords the user the most detailed picture of the impact of major events of the period.

TRW's consolidated cash flow statement for the years ended December 31, 1997, and December 31, 1996, in Figure 2–13 shows how the various elements are listed in practice. A number of adjustments based on information only internally available have been made by TRW to show more clearly the nature of cash movements during the periods covered, especially in view of the sale of some businesses in 1996, and two major acquisitions in 1997, as we'll discuss in Chapter 3.

The Statement of Changes in Shareholders' (Owners') Equity

The fourth financial statement commonly provided by a business is an analysis of the main changes, during a specific period, in the shareholders' capital accounts, or net worth. We know from the earlier discussion that one of these changes is the net income or loss for the period, as displayed in the income statement. But other management decisions could have affected shareholders' equity.

For example, most corporations, including TRW, pay dividends on a quarterly basis. Such dividends are normally paid in cash, reducing both the cash balance and retained earnings, the latter being part of shareholders' equity. Another decision might be to provide additional capital through sale of new shares of common stock, or conversely, the repurchase of shares in the open market using excess cash balances—some of which may be resold to employees under stock purchase or option plans. A third area might involve write-offs or adjustments of asset values connected with disposition of assets or with business combinations. A fourth area concerns the complex adjustments related to the exchange of foreign currencies by companies doing business internationally.

The net change in owners' equity can thus be selectively split into its major components to highlight the impact of these decisions. Figure 2–14 provides a conceptual view of this special analytical statement. Its limitations largely depend on how much the issuing company chooses to disclose beyond what's legally required.

Again TRW's consolidated statement of changes in shareholders' (owners') equity for the years ended December 31, 1997, and December 31, 1996, is given as an actual example in Figure 2–15. The format used by the company displays the changes in each of the key areas involved, by type of stock, other capital, retained earnings, currency translation effects, and treasury stock (repurchased shares).

FIGURE 2–13

TRW INC. AND SUBSIDIARIES
Statements of Cash Flows
For the Years Ended December 31, 1997 and 1996 ($ millions)

	1997	1996
Operating Activities:		
Net earnings (loss)	$ (49)	$ 480
Adjustments to reconcile net earnings (loss) to		
net cash provided by continuing operations:		
Purchased in-process research and development	548	—
Depreciation and amortization	490	452
Deferred income taxes	116	(182)
Discontinued operations	—	(298)
Other—net	10	23
Changes in assets and liabilities, net of effects of		
businesses acquired or sold:		
Accounts receivable	32	(46)
Inventories and prepaid expenses	(26)	8
Accounts payable and other accruals	(166)	298
Other—net	(1)	(24)
Net cash provided by operating activities	954	711
Investing Activities:		
Capital expenditures	(549)	(500)
Acquisitions, net of cash acquired	(1,270)	(76)
Net proceeds from divestitures	—	789
Other—net	2	34
Net cash provided by (used in) investing activities	(1,817)	247
Financing Activities:		
Increase (decrease) in short-term debt	912	(127)
Proceeds from debt in excess of 90 days	113	51
Principal repayments in excess of 90 days	(89)	(91)
Dividends paid	(154)	(148)
Acquisition of common stock	(247)	(361)
Other—net	41	51
Net cash provided by (used in) financing activities	576	(625)
Effect of exchange rate changes on cash	(29)	(6)
Increase (decrease) in cash and cash equivalents	(316)	327
Cash and cash equivalents at beginning of year	386	59
Cash and cash equivalents at end of year	$ 70	$ 386
Supplemental Cash Flow Information:		
Interest paid (net of amount capitalized)	$ 76	$ 89
Income taxes paid (net of refunds)	78	615

Source: Adapted from 1997 TRW Inc. annual report.

In this portion of the chapter, we have provided an overview of the nature and relationships of the four major financial statements as the background for analysis of the results of management decisions and their impact on funds movements. Within our decisional framework, these four statements can be combined

Statements of Changes in Owners' Equity in Decisional Context

Management Decision Area

Investment	*Operations*	*Financing*

Assets	**Balance Sheet** (on a given date)	Liabilities and net worth
Current assets		Current liabilities
plus		plus
Fixed assets		Long-term liabilities
plus	Net profit or loss	plus
Other assets		**Statement of changes in shareholders' equity** Owners' equity (plus/minus) New equity (plus) Profit/loss (plus/minus) Return of capital (minus) Dividends (minus) Adjustments (plus/minus)
equals		equals
Total assets		**Total liabilities and net worth**

to help us visualize their coverage and relationship as an integrated whole. Note that the generalized overview in Figure 2–16 displays not only what the four statements cover in terms of key information, but also how they are related, being derived from the same basic information. The dotted lines indicate the impact of any accounting write-offs.

To summarize, the balance sheet describes the financial condition of a business at a point in time. It shows the cumulative effect of previous decisions and includes the profits or losses for preceding periods. The income statement matches revenues and expenses for a specific period, including write-offs and allocations. It provides more detail about the elements making up the after-tax net profit and loss that was recorded in the owners' equity on the balance sheet.

In contrast to the two previous statements, the cash flow statement is a dynamic representation in that it highlights the net changes in assets, liabilities, and ownership accounts over a specific period. It reflects the pattern of cash uses and sources that resulted from management's decisions concerning investments, operations, and financing. The statement corrects for the fact that write-offs and amortization of assets acquired in the past are bookkeeping entries and not cash movements.

Finally, the statement of changes in owners' equity gives more details concerning the change in ownership accounts as recorded on the beginning and ending balance sheets. Within the limitations of GAAP rules and the accountants'

TRW INC. AND SUBSIDIARIES
Statement of Changes in Shareholders' Investment
For the Years Ended December 31, 1997 and 1996

	1997	1996
Serial Preference Stock II:		
Series 1:		
Balance at January 1 and December 31	$ —	$ —
Series 3:		
Balance at January 1 and December 31	$ 1	$ 1
Common Stock:		
Balance at January 1	80	40
Stock dividend	—	42
Purchase of shares and other	(2)	(2)
Balance at December 31	78	80
Other Capital:		
Balance at January 1	437	398
Sale of stock and other	25	39
Balance at December 31	462	437
Retained Earnings:		
Balance at January 1	1,978	1,688
Net earnings (loss)	(49)	480
Stock dividend and other	—	(39)
Dividends declared:		
Preference stock	(1)	(1)
Common stock ($1.84 and $1.80 per share)	(152)	(150)
Balance at December 31	1,776	1,978
Cumulative Translation Adjustments:		
Balance at January 1	47	76
Translation adjustments	(177)	(29)
Balance at December 31	(130)	47
Treasury Shares—Cost in Excess of Par Value:		
Balance at January 1	(354)	(31)
ESOP funding	2	17
Purchase of shares	(262)	(372)
Sold under stock options	51	32
Balance at December 31	(563)	(354)
Total shareholders' investment:	$1,624	$2,189

Source: Adapted from 1997 TRW Inc. annual report.

judgments, financial statements are an effort to reflect, with reasonable consistency, all business transactions that, over time, result in a net improvement or worsening of the recorded value of owners' equity. But as we'll discuss in the ensuing chapters, the manager or analyst must carefully interpret their meaning, due to the implications of recorded values and their conservative bias. This requires using standard techniques as well as explicit judgments and adjustments

FIGURE 2–16

Generalized Overview of Financial Statements

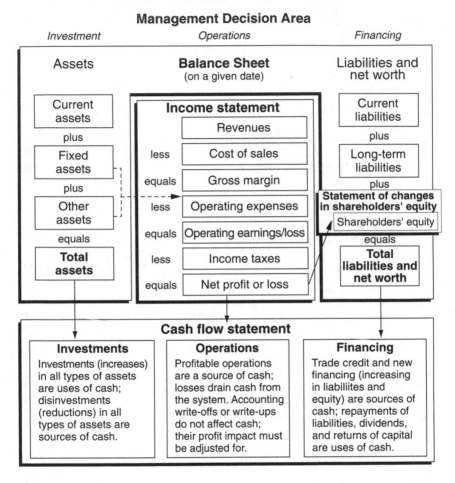

in evaluating the financial, and more importantly, the economic, performance of the business under review.

The Context of Financial Analysis

Now that we've explored the broad background of business system dynamics and the nature of commonly available financial statements that describe performance and values from a specific, limited viewpoint, it's useful to provide one more context that allows us to put the materials of the book into proper perspective. It will reinforce a number of the references we have made earlier to the judgmental aspects involved in financial analysis, and to the distinction between financial and economic analysis.

The Different Objectives of Financial/Economic Analysis Processes

Financial Accounting	Investor Analysis	Managerial Economics
Profit Determination	**Financial Information**	**Activity Economics**
• Revenue recognition	• Adjustment process	• Task analysis
• Expense recognition	• Trend analysis	• Economic allocation
• Cost allocation	• Profit projection	• Contribution analysis
• Profit definition	• Cash flow projection	• Trade-off determination
Value Determination	**Comparative Data**	**Resource Effectiveness**
• Historical costs	• Industry analysis	• Investment base
• Conservatism	• Competitor analysis	• Capital investments
• Equity as residual value	• Economic conditions	• Capital divestments
• Contingency recognition	• Adjustment areas	• Human resources
Tax Determination	**Market Analysis**	**Shareholder Value Creation**
• Legal data requirements	• Share price patterns	• Cash flow patterns
• Income/expense timing	• Market trends	• Cost of capital
• Tax management issues	• Value drivers	• Investor expectations
• Statement adjustments	• Market models	• Ongoing business value

Managers or analysts performing various kinds of financial/economic analysis normally do so with a specific purpose in mind. During the process of analysis, financial statements, special analyses, databases, and other information sources are used to derive reasonable judgments about past, current, and prospective conditions of a business and the effectiveness of its management.

We must recognize that not only does the person performing the analysis and interpretation have a purpose and viewpoint, but so do the preparers and providers of the various types of data and information on which the analysis is based. For example, during our discussion of financial statements, we referred to the accounting rules and principles governing the compilation of these documents, and to the need to allow for the specific biases introduced by them. This isn't to say that financial statements are right or wrong in an absolute sense, but rather that the information might have to be adjusted in some cases, or discarded in others, in order to suit the purpose of the analysis.

Figure 2–17's descriptive overview presents the key objectives of three major financial/economic processes as a context for understanding the differences in data generation and analytical orientation involved in each:

- Financial accounting.
- Investor analysis.
- Managerial economics.

The table identifies these three as processes whose objectives differ, although they frequently have to draw on each other for information and data. We must consider the orientation and focus of these processes when information is shared between them, or exchanged for use by any one of them. Our ultimate aim is to analyze and judge business problems, company performance, and shareholder value in *economic* terms, which requires careful adjustment of data and analyses that often were prepared with different objectives in mind.

When we speak of basic financial analysis in this book, we put more emphasis on the objectives of the left column (financial accounting) and to some extent on the middle column (investor analysis). When we refer to economic analysis, however, the focus is on the right column (managerial economics) and also on a number of the areas in the center column. Despite the obvious differences among the three areas, the majority of the available data are originated on the left, by financial accounting, while some are obtained from the right, from analytical efforts or internal databases on which managerial economics depends. In addition, databases covering the stock market and economic activity come into play in the center column.

Financial accounting has three major objectives as governed by professional standards and SEC regulations:

- Profit determination.
- Value determination.
- Tax determination.

Profit determination focuses on recognizing when revenue is earned during a period, and how to determine the matching costs and expenses. A clear distinction must be drawn between the recording of a revenue or expense transaction, and the actual receipt or disbursement of cash, which might lag by days or months. Similarly, costs incurred in the past are allocated to current or future periods with the objective of determining a profit figure that matches only "recognized" revenue and expense elements. A similar allocation process might apply to anticipated future costs that are apportioned to current periods. These allocations have significant implications for cash flow analysis, as we'll see in Chapter 4.

Value determination rests firmly on the principle of historical costs, a conservative concept that uses only actual transaction evidence as the value criterion. When economic values of assets acquired in the past change, adjustments to values generally are made only if they decline. This is commonly done for accounts receivable that have become uncollectible, or inventories where market value has declined below cost. Increases are recognized (realized) only when assets are sold, not while they're being held. The residual value of the business, that is, its recorded shareholders' equity (book value), therefore might over time bear only limited resemblance to the equity's market value (economic value). In addition, the growing emphasis on recording contingencies of all kinds in the liability section of the balance sheet introduces a negative bias in value, because only potential liabilities are established, not potential gains. Examples are long-term pension and benefit obligations, and potential liabilities arising from all types of operational, legal, and contractual issues. Generally such contingent liabilities are set-asides of shareholders' equity, further diminishing the recorded book value of equity.

Meanwhile, appreciation of assets like land, buildings, natural resources, technologies, and patents is left unrecognized until they're disposed of. As the wave of corporate takeovers in the past fifteen years demonstrated, careful analysis of the target companies' balance sheets often uncovered massive amounts of unrecorded potential gains, which could be turned into cash from the eventual breakup of the acquired companies, and used in part to pay for the acquisition.

Tax determination is governed by the legal requirements of the current income tax code, which often requires modified principles of income and expense recognition, including disallowance of certain costs and expense—in effect amounting to a different set of books. Tax rules tend to speed up the timing of revenue recognition compared with financial accounting rules, and at the same time, delay expense recognition. These rules are clearly designed to enhance current tax receipts for the government. Differences between financial accounting for reporting purposes and for tax accounting give rise to tax management issues (legally minimizing taxes) in companies and industries where the amounts involved could be significant enough to affect actual decisions on investments, operations, and financing.

From the standpoint of financial analysis, the important question is what effect tax accounting has on the financial statements used for analysis. As we'll see, the amount of taxes actually paid versus the amount shown on the income statement can differ materially, and adjustments made on the balance sheet to compensate for this situation might involve significant funds movements. From an analytical standpoint, we'll show the importance of recognizing the tax implications of various types of decisions in Chapters 7 through 12.

Investor analysis in this context has three objectives:

- Interpretation of financial information.
- Use of comparative data.
- Analysis of financial markets.

Interpretation of financial information essentially amounts to analyzing financial statements and other financial data about a company in order to assess and project its performance and value. The key judgments focus on the adjustment process through which reported accounting data are modified or converted into information that permits economic and cash flow assessments to be made. Only rarely can financial data, as generally provided, be used in their exact form to derive analytical judgments. Applying the various ratios and relationships discussed in Chapter 4, for example, often leads to significant questions and actual adjustments during the analysis.

Trend analysis uses various series of adjusted past data to look for and analyze significant changes in magnitudes and ratio relationships over time, and it becomes one of the bases of profit projection. Finally, the ultimate adjustment leads to understanding the pattern of net cash flows generated by the business, and the projection of these cash flows as an indicator of expected economic performance and value.

Comparative data are an essential part of financial analysis, as they help put judgments about a particular company or business in perspective. By implication, all judgments made about performance and value are relative to the standards and perceptions of the analyst; comparable data assist in confirming these judgments. Industry analysis involves the selection of relevant groupings of companies and compiling appropriate data and ratios (generally available in on-line databases) against which to measure the attributes of the company being studied. The important issue here again is the need to interpret and adjust the financial data so that they match the data used for the original company.

Competitor analysis applies the same process to individual companies or divisions of those companies that compete directly with the business. Economic conditions and the competitive dynamics of the markets served are brought into the analysis as a backdrop for explaining past variations, and as a guide to projecting future performance and value.

Market analysis involves the study and projection of the pattern of share prices of the company and its competitors relative to trends in the stock market, in relation to general economic and political conditions, and with reference to industry and company-specific forces. It is here that financial analysis becomes a bridge between published financial statements and stock market trends that reflect the economic value of a company. The analyst focuses on the value drivers behind the market value of the shares, which are basic economic variables like cash flow generated and the relative cost effectiveness of the business, along with judgments about the expected impact of known strategies in the competitive setting. Market models range from simple relationships of key variables and share price to complex computer simulations, in an effort to determine the current and potential shareholder value created by the expected cash flows of the business.

Managerial economics encompasses three basic objectives:

- Determining activity economics.
- Determining resource effectiveness.
- Creating shareholder value.

All three areas deal with economic insights management can use to make decisions that will enhance shareholder value. In that sense, the orientation of managerial economics is closely allied to the basic purpose of economic analysis as we define it here. In fact, the third objective directly supports the ultimate question: Is the business creating value for its owners? In later chapters, we'll address the most important aspects of these areas.

Activity economics is a summary term for various types of processes and analyses that define and establish economically relevant data to describe and judge the relative attractiveness of any operational aspect of a business and its subdivisions. Among these, task analysis amounts to determining the true economic cost of a task, whether it be a functional area like purchasing, or legal services, or a line area like selling. This is done by identifying and measuring the series of steps required to provide a service, or the phases of a manufacturing process, and to establish the resources used directly or indirectly in each case. This kind of analytical process, referred to previously as activity-based accounting, goes far beyond cost accounting principles. These principles often fall short of a proper economic allocation of jointly used resources or often they can't recognize all aspects of a task or an activity.

Contribution analysis refers to measuring the difference between revenues created and the economic costs involved in a given line of business or a particular product or service. Such information on economic contribution helps management plan which combination of activities will create the most economic value over time. The choices always require economic trade-offs based on economic data, not accounting information. By using activity-based accounting information, management can make both operational and strategic choices in monitoring and adjusting its portfolio of products and services.

Resource effectiveness addresses the important question of how well, from an economic standpoint, the resources employed by a business are currently being utilized or will be utilized in the future. The process includes measuring the returns from the existing investment base, gauging the economic justification of new capital investments or capital divestments, and measuring the returns from human resources. These questions will be discussed in more detail in Chapters 3, 7, and 8 where again we'll highlight the need to develop an economic basis for these judgments.

Shareholder value creation, management's ultimate goal, is measured by means of a combination of past and projected cash flow patterns, the cost of capital of the particular company, and the overall return expectations of investors for this type of business. In essence, shareholder value creation becomes a tangible expression of the risk/reward trade-off the investor has to judge when investing in the equity of a company. Management has to assess at all times whether cash flow expectations from the strategies, policies, and decisions employed are likely to serve the investors' interest by creating additional shareholder value. The approach will be discussed in detail in Chapters 8, 11, and 12.

Key Issues

The following is a recap of the key issues raised directly or indirectly in this chapter. They are enumerated here to help the reader keep the materials discussed within the perspective of financial theory and business practice.

1. Managing a business successfully requires an understanding of the systematic relationships among the key elements in the areas of investment, operations, and financing, and the impact of decisions on these relationships. Total systems thinking is a critical requirement both in setting strategies and in their execution.

2. Cash flow is the ultimate driver of business performance and value, but its use in internal and external analysis generally requires considerable care in selecting data, constructing proper analytical frameworks, and interpreting the results.

3. Expectations by shareholders about future cash flows are the basis for deriving shareholder value. The value of a business relative to its peers and the stock market as a whole will change with these expectations. This requires a future orientation in analyzing business performance.

4. Creating shareholder value is a key responsibility of business management, the success of which depends on consistent use of sound economic trade-offs in all decisions made by the management team. This requires an understanding of the cash flow implications of decisions, and an organizational climate and incentives that will foster such consistency in strategies, policies, and in making and implementing management decisions.

5. While published financial statements are the most widely available source for financial analysis, the limitations inherent in their preparation (based on generally accepted accounting principles) require a basic understanding on the part of the user of how analytical results in the areas of performance and valuation can be distorted and what adjustments might be necessary.

6. The context of any analytical effort is critical to successfully addressing the issue or problem to be resolved by the analysis. Much of the thought process underlying an analysis should be directed to ensuring consistency between the objectives and the data sources and processes employed.

Summary

First, we provided a conceptual overview of the business system to show the dynamic interrelationship of cash flows activated by management decisions. Three basic decision areas were recognized—investment, operations, and financing—that underlie all business activity. The cash impact of decisions in any or all of these areas on the system was shown. The systems view also demonstrated how decisions in each area were affected by key strategies and policies, and how consistency was essential in optimizing the system to achieve the ultimate goal—enhanced shareholder value. The overview also provided a first look at major areas of financial and economic analysis, and how these were related to management strategies and decisions.

Second, we gave an overview of the major financial statements commonly prepared by companies, and their relationship both to each other and to the three decisional areas defined earlier. We also indicated how the origin, rationale, and limitations of financial statements affect the potential for analyzing performance and value, and how important the cash flow statement is as a useful dynamic view of the changing cash flow patterns in the system.

Third, we established the context within which most financial analysis takes place, and provided an overview of the various objectives of analysis and data preparation. This was done to highlight the need for building a bridge between accounting-oriented data and the ultimate objective of financial/economic analysis, that is, judging business performance and shareholder value creation in economic terms. Adjustment areas were suggested as prerequisites for developing useful information, and the analyst's judgmental role was emphasized.

The chapter served as a contextual preview of the various analytical concepts explored in the remainder of the book. Its intent was to reinforce the point that financial/economic analysis is not a freestanding activity or an end in itself, but rather an effort to understand and judge the characteristics and economic performance of a highly interrelated system of financial relationships.

Analytical Support

Financial Genome, the commercially available financial analysis and planning software described in Appendix I, is accompanied by an interactive template (TFA Template under "extras"), representing the business system diagram in Figure 2–4 on page 28. The template allows the user to vary the key assumptions about the investments, operations, and financing conditions of a sample company, and to observe the changes resulting from these modifications on the graphic representation of the business system. The template also contains a set of abbreviated financial statements linked to the systems diagram, displaying the results of the changes made. Moreover, the major positive and negative cash flow movements are highlighted on an active bar graph. The template helps the user explore and understand in depth the linkages within the system and its accompanying financial statements, and to simulate and test the impact of any one, or a combination of, modifications in financial policies, investment commitments, and price/volume/cost conditions. (see "Downloads Available" on p. 431)

Selected References

Copeland, Tom; Tim Koller; and Jack Murrin. *Valuation: Measuring and Managing the Value of Companies.* New York: John Wiley & Sons, 1990.

Johnson, H. Thomas, and Robert S. Kaplan. *Relevance Lost: The Rise and Fall of Management Accounting.* Boston: Harvard Business School Press, 1987.

Kaplan, Robert S., and David P. Norton. *The Balanced Scorecard.* Boston: Harvard Business School Press, 1996.

Knight, James A. *Value Based Management: Developing a Systematic Approach to Creating Shareholder Value.* Burr Ridge, IL: Irwin/McGraw-Hill, 1998.

Martin, John D., and J. William Petty, *Value Based Management.* New York: The Financial Management Association Survey and Synthesis Series, 2000.

McTaggart, James M.; Peter W. Kontes; and Michael C. Mankins. *The Value Imperative: Managing for Superior Shareholder Returns.* New York: Free Press, 1994.

Porter, Michael E. *Competitive Advantage: Creating and Sustaining Superior Performance.* New York: Free Press, 1985.

Rappaport, Alfred. *Creating Shareholder Value.* New York: Free Press, 1997.

Stewart, B. Bennett. *The Quest for Value.* New York: Harper Business, 1991.

CHAPTER 3

MANAGING OPERATING FUNDS

We now turn to the key issues surrounding the flow of funds through a business, that is, how to properly manage, on an ongoing basis, cash inflows and funding requirements for day-to-day operations. Managers must understand the specific cash movements within the business system, which are caused by their daily decisions on investment, operations, financing, and the many external circumstances affecting the business. These decisions and events, in one form or another, affect the company's ability to pay its bills, obtain credit from suppliers and lenders, extend credit to its customers, and maintain a level of operations that matches the demand for the company's products or services, supported by appropriate investments. In the end, the combined effect of these decisions is the creation of shareholder value—but, as we've stated before, only if the net cash flows achieved by the business exceed the market's expectations over time.

It should be obvious by now that every decision has a monetary impact on the ongoing pattern of uses and sources of cash. Management's job is to maintain at all times an appropriate balance between cash inflows and outflows, and to plan for the cash impact of any changes in operations—whether caused by management's decisions or by outside influences—that might affect these flows. Properly managing operating cash flows is, therefore, fundamental to successful business performance.

The principle is quite simple: Obtain the most performance over time with the least commitment of resources. In practice, however, leads and lags in receipts and payments, unexpected deviations from planned conditions, delays in receiving cash from funding sources, and myriad other factors can make cash flow management a complex challenge. New businesses often find that balancing operating funds needs and sources is a continuous struggle for survival. Yet, even well-established companies need to devote considerable management time and effort to balance the ongoing funding of their operations as they strive for optimal economic results.

In addition to managing working capital, balancing operating funds flows requires dealing with the changing cash flow patterns of periodic profits and losses, and with the ultimate cash impact of current decisions on both new investment and new financing choices.

As we'll demonstrate, managing operating funds requires a thorough understanding of the combined systems effect of investment, operating, and financing decisions. This includes recognizing the impact on funds uses and sources caused by various basic operating conditions, such as seasonal peaks and valleys, cyclical variations, rapid growth, or gradual decline. In every circumstance the resulting cash flow patterns will behave in very different ways, and will put stresses on the financial system at different points and in different time frames.

For Example

Managing working capital soundly is a major operating cash flow challenge. The key components of working capital, accounts receivable, inventories, and accounts payable often represent significant funds commitments and sources for a business. In fact, the basic level of working capital (commonly defined as the difference between current assets and current liabilities) with which a business operates represents a long-term investment supported by long-term capital sources. Each component, however, must be carefully managed to match the changing requirements of operations—with the objective of minimizing the resources committed at any point in time while meeting all operational needs, such as ensuring smooth production and customer service goals.

Current assets	Current liabilities
Working capital	Long-term debt
Fixed assets	Share-holders' equity
Other assets	

Management should plan for fluctuations in working capital as a result of changing conditions, rather than be surprised by soaring inventories or overextended supplier credit. As in all business decisions, economic trade-offs apply here: Is the cost of carrying extra inventory outweighed by better service to customers? Is the cost of granting higher discounts for early payment offset by the reduction in receivables likely to be outstanding? What is the real cost of not meeting the credit terms extended by the company's vendors?

In Chapter 4, we'll examine a variety of performance measures drawn from financial statements, which we know to be periodic summaries of financial condition and operating results. As we'll see, these summaries often mask peaks and valleys of funds movements—for example, a seasonal buildup causing critical near-term financing needs—because these points mights lie within the period spanned by the statements. Obviously, managing a business is an ongoing day-to-day process, which must deal with peaks and valleys of cash flows as they occur.

   In this chapter, we'll describe how operating funds cycle through a business, what the implications of these movements are, and how to identify the critical financial variables that must be weighed in making daily operating decisions. We'll demonstrate how significantly different types of operations impact a company's cash flow pattern, and also highlight key accounting issues, such as inventory costing and methods of depreciation. Then we'll return to the interpretation of cash flow statements, using our sample of TRW's 1997 and 1996 financial data, and demonstrate how to use cash flow statements in a meaningful way. Finally, we'll discuss the key levers available to managers with which to minimize funds needs, moderate the impact of fluctuations, and generally optimize the management of operating funds as part of shareholder value creation.

Funds Flow Cycles

Businesses vary widely in orientation, size, structure, and products or services, but they all experience operating funds cycles that eventually affect cash needs and availability. To illustrate the simplest of circumstances, let's observe a solitary ice cream vendor who sells cones from his cart for cash. To carry on this business, he has to provide an inventory on wheels, which he slowly converts into cash as the day progresses. Let's also assume that he has invested his own cash at the beginning of the day to purchase the ice cream from his supplier. He obviously hopes to recoup these funds as well as pocket a profit by the end of the day.

   Our vendor's decision to commit his own cash to inventory can be visualized in Figure 3–1, which traces the funds movements in a simple diagram. Note that the layout reflects the three decision areas we discussed in Chapter 2.

FIGURE 3–1

Ice Cream Vendor
Initial Cash Investment to Start the Day

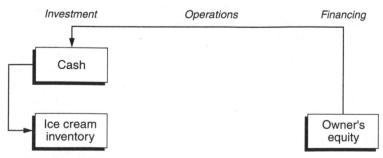

Management Decision Context

The initial cash investment is financed from the owners' equity, and in turn, the cash is used to invest in the first day's inventory. If our vendor was short of cash, he could sign an IOU for the supplier, promising to pay for the inventory the next morning, using the day's cash receipts as funding. This assumption modifies the diagram, as shown in Figure 3–2. Here, the creditor's funds effectively supplant the owner's funds, if only for a single day.

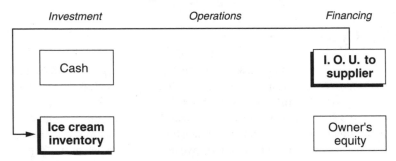

F I G U R E 3–2

Ice Cream Vendor
Initial Use of Credit to Start the Day

Management Decision Context

Investment   *Operations*   *Financing*

| Cash | | **I. O. U. to supplier** |

| **Ice cream inventory** | | Owner's equity |

In any event, our vendor's funds cycle is very short. The initial investment in inventory, funded either with his own cash or with credit from his supplier, is followed by numerous individual cash sales during the day. These receipts build up his cash balance for the following day's operations.

Next, we've represented the first day of operations—assuming the vendor financed the inventory himself—in Figure 3–3, where cash on hand is built up by sales receipts, inventory is drawn down during the day, and the difference between sales revenue and the cost of the ice cream sold represents the profit earned. This profit increases ownership equity, reflecting the value created during the day.

The following morning, our vendor uses the accumulated cash either to replenish his inventory, or to pay off the supplier so that he'll be extended credit for another day's cycle. Any profit he has earned above the cost of the goods sold will, of course, be his to keep, or to invest in more inventory for the next day.

Figure 3–4 shows the alternative funds movements that would arise had our vendor used supplier credit for the first day. He would find that the amount of cash left after repayment of the initial supplier credit—the amount of his profit for the first day—would purchase only a portion of the next day's inventory. To continue operating on the second day he would have to decide whether to

- Ask for renewed credit from his supplier, or
- Provide the additional funds from any resources of his own that aren't yet committed to the business.

Ice Cream Vendor
Profitable Operations during the First Day

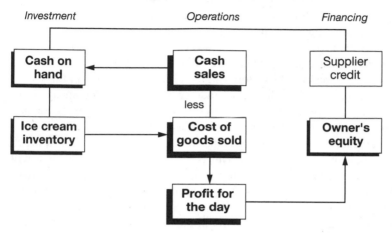

Management Decision Context

Ice Cream Vendor
Repayment of Credit after Profitable First Day

Management Decision Context

Funds cycles of larger and more structured businesses differ from this simple situation only in complexity, not in concept. Even for the most complex international conglomerate, the ultimate form of settlement of any transaction is cash. However, such a company's operational funds cycle usually involves a variety of partially offsetting credit extensions, changes in inventories, transformations of assets, etc., that precede the cash collections or payments.

In essence, any funds cycle arises because of a series of lags in the timing of business transactions. Our ice cream vendor has a lag of only a few hours between the purchase of his inventory and its conversion into cash through many small transactions. In contrast, a large manufacturer might have a lag of months between the time a product is made in the factory and the ultimate collection of the selling price from customers who purchased on trade credit. A service company might have a lag of weeks between the time salaried or contract professionals are paid for their work and the ultimate collection of service fees.

Management must plan for and find the financing for company funds which are tied up because of these timing lags. This is important because these funds will remain committed for the foreseeable future, unless there are significant changes in the company's operations. As with any type of investment, management should attempt to minimize this resource commitment while maintaining operational effectiveness. Ways to reduce the funding required include methods such as "just-in-time" delivery of materials or parts in manufacturing, or purchasing merchandise on consignment in retailing.

To illustrate the nature of the concept further, we'll further explore the following three processes:

- The funds cycle of a simplified manufacturing operation.
- The funds cycle for selling the manufactured products.
- The funds cycle for a service organization.

We've separated these processes for purposes of illustration and discussion, even though the first two cycles are always intertwined in any ongoing business that both produces and sells products. The sales cycle alone, of course, applies to any retail, wholesale, or trading operation that purchases goods for resale, while the service cycle amounts to a modification of the sales cycle.

The Funds Cycle for Manufacturing

To keep the illustration simple, let's assume that the Widget Manufacturing Company has just begun operations and is going to produce widgets for eventual sale. Figure 3–5 shows the company's funds flow cycle in the form of an overview, using minimal detail. We've again arranged the diagram to reflect the three management decision areas.

As is readily apparent, the company was initially financed through a combination of owners' equity, long-term debt, and three kinds of short-term debt:

FIGURE 3–5

Funds Flow Cycle for Manufacturing

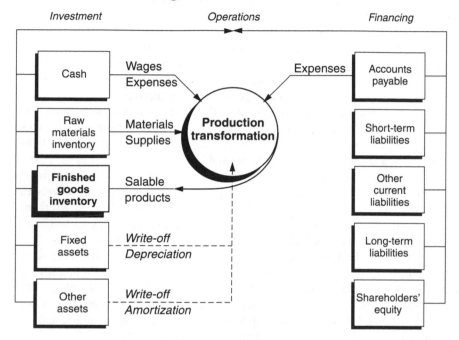

Management Decision Context

Investment   *Operations*   *Financing*

- Accounts payable due vendors of materials and supplies.
- Some short-term loans from banks.
- Other current liabilities, such as accrued wages and taxes.

The initial investments involve fixed assets (such as plant facilities), other assets (such as patents and licenses), and three kinds of current assets:

- Cash.
- Raw materials inventory.
- Finished goods inventory.

Of course, the last of these won't appear until the plant actually starts producing widgets. We can assume that long-term debt and owners' equity are the logical sources of funds for investing in plant and equipment, because they match the long-term funding commitment involved. In contrast, the short-term loans most likely provided the ready cash needed to start operations. Materials and supplies were bought with short-term trade credit extended by the company's vendors.

As production begins, a basic transformation process takes place. Some of the available cash is used to pay weekly wages and various ongoing expenses. Materials and supplies are withdrawn from inventory and are used in manufacturing widgets. Inventories are replenished with additional credit. Some operating inputs, like power and fuel oil, are obtained on credit, and are temporarily financed through accounts payable.

Use of the plant and equipment is reflected in the form of a depreciation charge, which becomes part of the cost of the transformation process. Any patents and licenses are similarly amortized and charged to the production cost. As widgets are finished on the factory floor, they're moved into the warehouse and their cost is added to the growing finished goods inventory account.

In the absence of any widget sales, the production process continuously transforms cash, raw materials, expense accruals, and trade credit into a growing buildup of finished goods inventory. A fraction of the original cost of the building, machinery, and other depreciable assets used has now become part of the cost of finished goods via the depreciation charge—even though no cash is actually moved by this allocation process. This accounting write-off merely affects the company's books by transferring a portion of the recorded cost of the assets into the cost of the inventory. Remember, the only time cash actually changed hands was when the assets were originally acquired.

What are the funds implications of this transformation? The operational funds flows, which occurred after the business was established, so far had affected only working capital components. The major sources of funding for the production process largely came from drawing down cash and raw materials, which were among the initial funds committed. An additional source was found in increased trade credit and in expenses accrued but not yet paid.

The major use of these funds was in the buildup of finished goods inventory. Unless the company can eventually turn finished goods into cash through successful sales to its customers, the continued inventory buildup will eventually drain both the cash reserves and the stores of raw material. These will have to be replenished by new infusions of credit or owners' equity, or both. Adding to the cash drain is the obligation to begin the repayment— on normal terms such as 30 or 45 days from the invoice date—of accounts payable for trade credit incurred.

From a funds flow standpoint, several timing lags are significant in our example:

- A supply of raw materials sufficient for several days of operation has to be kept on hand to ensure uninterrupted manufacturing, assuming that just-in-time delivery arrangements are not possible.

- The physical lag in the number of days required to produce a widget causes a buildup of an inventory of work in process, that is, widgets in various stages of completion.

- A sufficient number of widgets must be produced and kept at all times in finished goods inventory to support an ongoing sales and service effort.

The combined funds commitment caused by these lags has to be financed on a *continuous* basis through resources provided by owners and creditors, as long as the pattern of lags remains unchanged.

Offsetting this funding requirement, but only in part, is the length of time over which credit is extended by the company's suppliers. This is a favorable lag because purchases of raw material and supplies, as well as certain other expenses, will be financed by vendors as accounts payable for 30 or 45 days, or for whatever length of time is common usage in the industry. New credit will continue to be extended as repayments are made of the accounts coming due.

Another significant favorable lag is the temporary funding provided by the employees of the company whose wages are paid periodically. In effect, employees are extending credit to their employer for a week, two weeks, or even a month, depending on the company's payroll pattern. Such funding is recognized among current liabilities as accrued wages. Other expense accruals, such as income taxes currently owed, will provide temporary funds as well.

As we observed before, however, the buildup of finished goods in the warehouse cannot go on indefinitely, and at some point, revenues from the sale of the widgets become essential to replenishing cash in order to meet the company's obligations as accounts become due. To complete the picture, we must examine the funds implications of the selling process.

The Funds Cycle for Sales

The funds flows caused by selling the widgets can be examined within our decisional framework, as shown in Figure 3–6. The operations segment in the center of the diagram now includes the main elements of an income statement:

- Sales revenue.
- Cost of goods sold.
- Selling expenses.
- General and administrative expenses.
- Net income.

The selling cycle is based on a major timing lag, which arises from the extension of credit to the company's customers. If the widgets were sold for cash, collection would, of course, be instantaneous. If the company provides normal trade credit, however, the collection of accounts receivable will be delayed by the terms extended to customers, such as 30 or 45 days, depending on prevailing practice in the business sector.

This sales lag, like the lags incurred during the production cycle, has to be financed *continuously*, because for any given volume of sales, the equivalent of 30, 40, or 50 days' worth of sales will always be outstanding. As accounts becoming due are collected, new credit will be extended to customers on current sales—as was the case with the vendors supplying materials and other items to the company itself.

FIGURE 3–6

Funds Flow Cycle for Sales

Cost of goods sold represents the value of the widgets withdrawn from finished goods inventory, each of which contains a share of the labor, raw material, and overhead. Other costs expended in its manufacture include apportioned depreciation for the use of the facilities and a share of the amortization of any patents or licenses involved.

Selling expenses, which consist of the salaries of the sales force, the marketing support staff, and advertising and promotional costs, will be paid partly in cash and partly with funds obtained from creditors. General and administrative expenses will be paid in a similar fashion. Once all these costs and expenses have been subtracted from sales revenue, the resulting net income (or loss), after allowing for state and federal income taxes, causes an increase (or decrease) in owners' equity.

What are the funds flow implications of this picture? First of all, assuming that the company is maintaining a level volume of sales and manufacturing operations, management must plan for a continuous long-term commitment of funds to support the necessary amount of working capital. This means that sufficient funds must be provided to carry inventories of raw materials and work in process in support of production. In addition, funds are needed to maintain a proper level of finished goods to support smooth sales and deliveries, and to allow for sufficient accounts receivable balances outstanding to permit normal credit extension to customers. Also, a minimum cash balance must be maintained for punctual payment of currently due obligations.

Beyond these working capital requirements, additional funds are likely to be needed for any investment outlays on fixed and other assets that support growing operations. Finally, arrangements have to be made for payment of declared dividends, any scheduled repayment of debt, or for refinancing long-term obligations.

The sources of this financing will be derived only in relatively small part from outstanding accounts payable, which can usually support a portion of raw materials, supplies, and ongoing operating expenses in line with the normal number of days' credit extended by the suppliers. The difference between the amount of funds continually tied up in inventories and receivables, and the funds provided by current accounts payable, must come from sources that are relatively permanent, such as long-term debt and owners' equity—the latter augmented by after-tax profits or diminished by net losses.

The dynamics of the system are such that once desired conditions and relationships have been reached, the requirement for operating funds will be constant as long as the business operates on a sustained level. As we shall see in the section on the variability of funds flows, however, the level of funding requirements will change significantly when operational conditions themselves change.

The Funds Cycle for Services

The funds flows characterizing a service organization are similar to the sales cycle we just discussed. Service businesses for the most part do not produce any physical goods, but instead make available a wide range of activities to their customers. These include providing information and advisory services, electronic communication, equipment servicing, physical or electronic delivery, retailing or wholesaling functions, transportation services, temporary staffing, data processing, and so on. Services, whether based on contractual arrangements, trade credit, or cash remittances, will produce periodic cash inflows to the provider, with normal lags in collection matching the service pattern. While certain service businesses require extensive physical infrastructure resources, such as stores and warehouse facilities, delivery fleets, diagnostic and repair equipment, or data processing networks, the funds flow cycle tends to be centered more on working capital elements and their leads and lags. Infrastructure resources are frequently obtained through leasing arrangements, which effectively transform their funding into periodic cash payments. Human resources are a significant portion of the funds flow mix, again representing near-term cash requirements.

Thus the funds flow implications are largely the interplay of payment for current expenses, current infrastructure support, and collection of services billed. Inventories have a significant role in manufacturing but are minor elements in many service businesses. There they are limited to supplies or parts used in carrying out service activities—except in the case of retailing and wholesaling operations, where they are a critical part of the funds picture. The funds flow cycle pattern of Figure 3–6 applies to service businesses with minor modifications, the main differences being the relative importance of working capital elements and the relative impact of infrastructure elements represented by fixed assets. As in the case of the sales cycle, basic working capital needs will require permanent funding, and the interplay of sales, cost of services (or goods) sold, and attendant support expenses will result in operational cash inflows. Increased infrastructure needs will have to be funded over time through leasing or ownership. Major marketing or new service initiatives also will require funding from the normal mix of profit, the depreciation effect, and long-term sources. Under stable conditions, operational cash flow patterns for service businesses will level out, given an integrated set of operational and financial policies. But stable conditions are the exception rather than the rule, and we now turn to the implications of changing conditions.

Variability of Funds Flows

Unless there are significant changes in a company's internal conditions or in its markets, the level of ongoing financing needed to support operations will mainly depend on effective inventory management, sound management of customer credit, and prudent use of supplier credit, as well as reliable relations with other lenders, such as banks. Also, cost-effective and profitable operations will generate cash that can be used as part of the funding pattern. The company's continuous funding needs will, of course, be increased if collections from customers worsen, credit terms extended by suppliers or lenders tighten, or profits decline.

Rarely does a company enjoy the steady-state conditions that made financing so predictable in our simple illustrations. In reality, several internal and external factors can affect any business. Major internal forces include management's ability to seize growth opportunities, its effectiveness in managing all activities, or its inability to stem a decline in the company's volume of operations. Major external forces include the competitive interplay in the industry, as well as seasonal variations and cyclical movements in the economy, which go beyond the impact of specific actions taken by the company's competitors. Each of these conditions has its own particular cash flow implications, and we'll illustrate the most important of these now.

Growth/Decline Variations

Growth A pattern of steady growth in a business brings with it the need to fund the underlying expansion of all financial requirements. Successful growth can't be achieved without providing for appropriate increases in working capital, long-term investments, and other expenditures. These growing funds commitments will be permanently tied up as long as growth continues or as long as operations remain at a given level. Normal profits earned from successful operations usually supply only a portion of these funding needs.

Consider the following rules of thumb:

- If the business sells on 30-day credit, the value of each incremental layer of sales will be added to accounts receivable for 30 days and must be funded continually, because as prior sales are collected, new and larger current sales are added.

- Similarly, if the business turns over its inventory nine times per year, the value of the incremental cost of the goods sold will have to be added to inventories in the form of 40 days' worth of inventory ($360 \div 9$), which must also be funded continually.

- Offsetting this additional use of funds, but only in part, will be the incremental growth in accounts payable and other minor accruals. The credit from the company's vendors will amount to an equivalent value of the additional purchases for, say, 30 days, if that is the usual credit pattern.

For Example

Let's take the simple example of a wholesaling company, which sells on terms of 45 days, buys on terms of 40 days, and turns over its inventory every 30 days (twelve times per year). Cost of goods sold is 72 percent of sales, and profit after taxes 6 percent. As the company grows, funding needs for every *incremental* $100 in annual sales will be:

- Accounts receivable increase by $12.50 ($100 × 45/360).
- Inventories of goods purchased increase by $6.00 ($72 × 30/360).
- Accounts payable to vendors increase by $8.00 ($72 × 40/360).

The net effect is a funding requirement of $10.50 in additional working capital ($12.50 + $6.00 − $8.00), assuming no other changes take place in the company's financial system. At the normal level of after-tax profits of 6 percent, the company could provide only $6.00 of the funding needed— that is, if no other uses of these profits existed, such as paying dividends to shareholders, or expanding the warehouse and associated equipment to support the growth trend. Thus, a minimum of $4.50 would have to be continuously financed for every $100 in additional sales generated.

Since the required investment in accounts receivable and inventories is normally much more than twice the credit obtained from current payables and accruals, it should be clear that successful growth requires extensive funding of additional working capital. Add to this the funds required for any expansion of physical facilities or for contractual arrangements to support the growth in sales.

The pattern of sales, operating assets (working capital plus fixed and other assets supporting operations), and profits of the typical growing company will look something like the graph shown in Figure 3–7, where growth requires additional working capital every single year as receivables and inventories expand. This growth is only partially offset by increasing accounts payable. Periodically, new investments must be made in expanded facilities, as is indicated by the jump in the operating assets in 2003 and again in 2006. The asset column continues to grow as long as volume growth persists, and constant funding of this increase will be necessary through a combination of profit and other sources.

The dotted funding line indicates the total need for funds required to finance growing operating assets, reduced by total after-tax profits in every year. It is assumed that an amount equal to annual depreciation is spent every year on maintaining the facilities. No dividend payments have been allowed for in this line, and as a result the actual funding need is understated. Note that growing profits in the later years are able to gradually reduce the total funding requirements.

FIGURE 3–7

Typical Growth Pattern

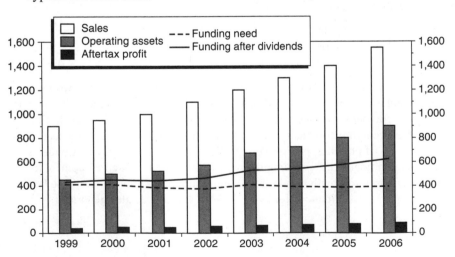

FIGURE 3–8

Managed Decline Pattern

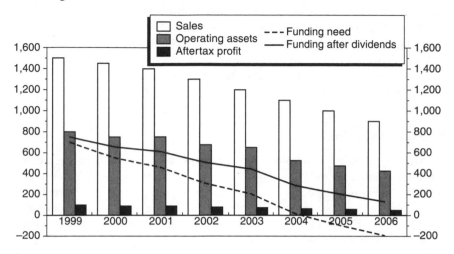

When dividend payments are provided for, however—in this case rising gradually from $20 in 1997 to $40 in 2004—what was essentially a level funding need becomes a steadily growing requirement for permanent funding, as shown in the solid line. By now it should be clear that successful growth typically requires an ongoing and growing funding commitment, which must be financed over the long term through the use of additional owners' equity and long-term debt. Frequently, reinvestment of profits alone is not a sufficient source, because in a high-growth business, the contribution from the profit margin might be far outweighed by the cumulative funding demands (as Chapter 5 details).

Decline In the opposite case, when a business declines in volume and is deliberately managed to achieve such shrinkage efficiently—a difficult assumption not always realized—the company will in fact turn into a strong generator of cash. Here the reverse of the growth situation prevails. As sales decline, management must carefully seek to reduce operations, working capital, and other operating assets to match the decline in volume, thus releasing the funds that had been tied up over time.

This idealized situation is demonstrated in Figure 3–8. Note the dramatic decline in the basic funding needs, which turned into positive funds generation during the last two years. When dividend payments of as much as 50 percent of after-tax profits are assumed in every year, the funding requirements decline more slowly, but still represent only a fraction of the level at the beginning of the period.

Basically, the ability of the business system to release cash depends on the careful removal of all layers of activity that no longer need to be supported. A proportional shrinkage of receivables and inventories, partially offset by declining payables, becomes the major potential cash source, apart from the disposal of other assets no longer needed. If the decline pattern becomes precipitous or cannot be managed properly, however, the specter of inventory markdowns, operating inefficiencies, and emergency actions will seriously impede the release of funds. Under these conditions, real difficulties can arise and the expected cash flow might not materialize.

Seasonal Variations

A fairly large number of industries experience distinct seasonal operating patterns (specific months or weeks of high sales, followed by a dramatic decline in demand). These ups and downs repeat themselves quite predictably. Examples are most common in retailing operations, many of which are geared to special holiday periods or specific customer segments with seasonal style or gift requirements. Producers of seasonal items, like snowmobiles or bathing suits, will experience high fluctuations in demand, unless they can sell into global markets that have offsetting climates, or diversify their offerings. Similar patterns impact businesses such as canneries that process specific crops or other seasonal foods, or service firms that prepare income tax returns.

Common to all seasonal businesses is a funds cycle with large short-term swings during the period of a year or less. The financial implications of such a pattern are quite obvious. During the low point of demand, ongoing operations have to be supported with cash from internal or external sources, unless the business can be shut down, as some seasonal resorts are. In many seasonal manufacturing businesses, inventories are gradually built up, either through production or through purchases from suppliers.

As was the case in our earlier example, funding for this buildup must come from credit, loans, and owners' equity. Once the selling activity begins, growing amounts of receivables due from customers buying on normal credit terms have to be funded by the company. It is not until the first receivables are actually collected that cash starts flowing back into thebusiness. The financial lags are usually such that collection of the receivables from peak sales will occur well after the peak of funding requirements has occurred.

Figure 3–9 demonstrates a typical seasonal pattern on a month-by-month basis which reflects the dramatic rise and fall in funding needs over the year, before any dividends are even considered. In this case, management must make several critical decisions. Among them are the size of the buildup of inventories needed to support anticipated demand, the level of operating and other expenditures to be made during the different phases of the operating cycle, and the nature of the funding to finance the bulge in requirements. Contingencies—such as lower-than-expected demand or prices, or both, delays in collections from customers, or the

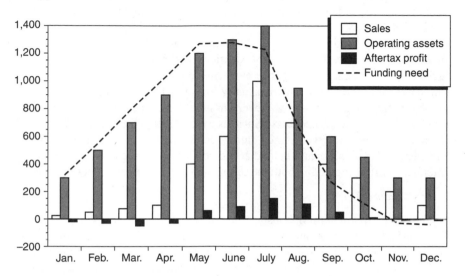

FIGURE 3–9

Typical Seasonal Pattern

time involved in arranging for short-term financing with banks and other lenders—must be allowed for. Otherwise, the business could find itself strapped because its own financial obligations must be met well before collections are made.

We'll discuss applying turnover relationships and the aging of receivables as a means of judging the effectiveness of asset use by management in Chapter 4. Under highly seasonal conditions such relationships become unstable, because lags and surges in the accounts within the period spanned by financial statements make most ratio comparisons difficult.

As we'll see in Chapter 5, a more direct evaluation of a seasonal business is possible. Rather than comparing quarterly or year-end financial statements, a month-to-month (or week-to-week) analysis of funds movements and a careful assessment of changes in the funds cycle of the company from peak to peak, or trough to trough can be done.

Cyclical Variations

A variant of the seasonal picture is the cyclical pattern of funds movements. It mainly reflects external economic changes that impact the company over a period of several years. Economic variations and specific industry cycles are generally long term and not as regular and predictable as seasonal variations. Economic swings that affect a business or industry tend to bring many more variables into play, such as changes in raw materials, prices and availability, competitive conditions in the market, and capital investment needs. Nevertheless, the cash flow principles we observed in dealing with the seasonal pattern apply here as well.

Funds lags during a cyclical upturn or downturn tend to be magnified by a mostly unavoidable lag in decision making. As conditions begin to change, it can be very difficult for management to gauge, from daily experience, whether the economy or the market is undergoing a long-term shift and what the specific timing is likely to be.

Thus a cyclical downturn results in significant challenges: First, management must recognize, with reasonable confidence, that a turning point has indeed arrived. Next, management must prevent inventories from rising by curtailing purchases and production. This is usually followed by reducing staffing levels, and by cutting ongoing costs wherever possible. Careful management of credit, both extended and used, becomes critical as well. Meeting these challenges is easier said than done, because data on current economic trends available at any one time tend to lag significantly behind actual conditions, while economic forecasts often fall short of predicting both the timing and the degree of economic change.

For Example

A gradual downturn in housing construction will leave many producers and wholesalers of building materials with inventories in excess of declining demand. As the sales slump accelerates, and prices of lumber, plywood, and other commodities fall, management faces a funding crisis. Continuing normal production will transform raw material into products that cannot be sold; thus, production must be curtailed. Lower volume and prices also decrease the eventual cash flow generated from current sales, while the stream of collections from past higher sales begins to run out.

Figure 3–10 demonstrates a typical cyclical pattern, where sales volume and prices swing with economic conditions, but, due to the factors just mentioned, operating asset levels and their accompanying funding needs lag behind the volume changes. Note the steady increase in funding required during the decline phase is brought about by a combination of rising investment (mostly a buildup of working capital) and plummeting profits. If dividends are maintained at the level of $30, and if we assume that these are paid every year, the funding line rises to a new high, indicating that the company isn't able to make up for the funds drain of the cyclical decline.

In the cyclical upswing, lags in decision making can cause inventory and production levels to be insufficient as sales volume begins to surge. To compensate, extra shifts or outside purchases might be used, even though the costs incurred with these alternatives are typically higher than normal and will depress profitability. Growing sales will also raise the amount of receivables credit extended to customers.

Thus, a cyclical boom will likely require the infusion of additional funds to provide the increased working capital needed and to finance increased physical operations. The latter might involve additional investment in plant and facilities. Overall, it can be said that a cyclical upswing will usually require an increase in medium- to long-term financing to support added levels of working capital and

F I G U R E   3–10

Typical Cyclical Pattern

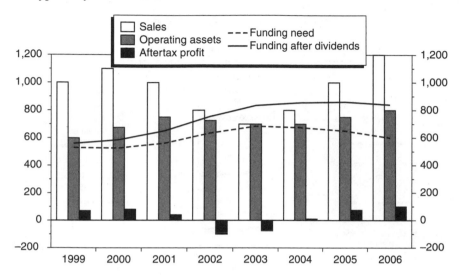

other financial requirements. A downswing, however, will first result in rising inventories—until management can adjust its operations—and then will begin to release cash, which can be used to repay credit obligations. The latter condition, however, will hold true only if both working capital and production levels are carefully managed downward.

In summary, variability in funds flows is caused by management actions, by external conditions, or by both. We know that a business operating in a steady state must maintain a permanent stock of working capital, as well as properties, facilities, equipment, and other assets. As a general rule of thumb, the amount of funds tied up in current assets far exceeds trade credit sources and normal short-term borrowings. Therefore, when significant variability in the level of operations is introduced, major shifts in the company's financial condition might be caused by changes in working capital alone. Funding for other needs, such as investments in facilities or infrastructure and major spending programs, must be superimposed on this pattern. In Chapter 4, we'll discuss these issues in the context of the techniques of forecasting funds requirements.

Generalized Funds Flow Relationships

At this point, it's useful once again to examine the overall relationships of funds movements in a generalized framework, as shown in Figure 3–11. The diagram is applicable to any type of business, large or small. We have added flow lines, which show the potential funds movements and linkages between the main accounts of the balance sheet and the income statement. A summary, in terms of our

FIGURE 3–11

Generalized Funds Flow Model

Management Decision Context

familiar management decision context, of the sources and uses of the ultimate cash flows is given at the bottom of the diagram.

This representation will be a useful reference when we discuss the interpretation of cash flow statements in the next section, as we follow the convention of the three decisional areas, and the general rules governing cash inflows and outflows.

Interpreting Funds Flow Data

We're now ready to examine in more detail the use and implications of a company's funds flow information, as normally represented in its cash flow statements. As we discussed in Chapter 2, companies that are publicly held and publish regular financial statements are required by the SEC to provide a statement of cash flows along with balance sheets and income statements. Where such statements aren't readily available, however, or in situations where the analyst wishes to project future funds movements, it's relatively straightforward to develop meaningful cash flow statements from standard balance sheets and income statements. With the help of the cash flow statement, we can develop many insights about the actual funds changes that took place, and also obtain clues for further analysis of the nature and quality of management decisions in operations, investments, and financing.

In this section, we'll illustrate how to quickly draw up a basic cash flow statement from available balance sheets and income statements, and discuss the major principles involved in transforming this accounting information into the funds flow pattern in which we are interested. For this purpose, we'll again use the 1997 and 1996 TRW Inc. financial statements originally shown in Chapter 2 as Figures 2–9 and 2–11.

We'll work back from these to develop a derived cash flow statement, which we can then compare to the more detailed one published by TRW. Not having access to the detailed records of the company, we'll find that our own version of the cash flow statement will approximate, but not be identical to, the key funds movements shown in TRW's statement. This is because some informational details required are not directly represented on the published statements.

We'll begin with a look at the differences in the key balance sheet items between the two dates, and sort these into a listing of funds sources and uses as a convenient way of identifying positive and negative cash flows. This format is called a *sources and uses statement*, mainly distinguished from the formal cash flow statement by the arrangement of the information, which in the latter case follows our three familiar decisional areas. Then we'll turn to the income statement to obtain additional details necessary to expand our insights in the operational area of funds movements. The objective is not accounting refinement, but simply an understanding of the principles involved in transforming data about key changes into cash flow patterns.

TRW's consolidated balance sheets are reproduced as Figure 3–12, which also shows changes in the accounts between the two balance sheet dates. To develop a cash flow statement, these changes must be classified as either funds uses or sources. We've done this in Figure 3–13, where increases and decreases in assets and liabilities are assigned to the appropriate categories, following the rules we displayed earlier in Figure 3–11. However, some of the balance sheet categories are too broad for our purpose. As a result, several of the funds flows cannot be specifically delineated:

- Net profit (or loss) from operations is not recognized as such, but is part of the net change in retained earnings.
- Cash dividends are also immersed in the net change in retained earnings.

FIGURE 3–12

TRW INC. AND SUBSIDIARIES
Consolidated Balance Sheets at December 31
($ millions)

	1997	1996	Change
Assets			
Current assets:			
Cash and cash equivalents	$ 70	$ 386	$ − 316
Accounts receivable	1,617	1,378	+ 239
Inventories	573	524	+ 49
Prepaid expenses	79	69	+ 10
Deferred income taxes	96	424	− 328
Total current assets	2,435	2,781	− 346
Property, plant, and equipment at cost	6,074	5,880	+ 194
Less: Allowances for depreciation			
and amortization	3,453	3,400	+ 53
Total property, plant, and equipment			
—net	2,621	2,480	+ 141
Intangible assets:			
Intangibles arising from acquisitions	673	258	+ 415
Other	232	31	+ 201
	905	289	+ 616
Less: Accumulated amortization	94	78	+ 16
Total intangible assets—net	811	211	+ 600
Investments in affiliated companies	139	51	+ 88
Other assets	404	376	+ 28
Total assets	$6,410	$5,899	+ 511
Liabilities and Shareholders' Investment			
Current liabilities:			
Short-term debt	$ 411	$ 52	$ + 359
Accrued compensation	338	386	− 48
Trade accounts payable	859	781	+ 78
Other accruals	846	775	+ 71
Dividends payable	38	39	− 1
Income taxes	99	52	+ 47
Current portion of long-term debt	128	72	+ 56
Total current liabilities	2,719	2,157	+ 562
Long-term liabilities	788	767	+ 21
Long-term debt	1,117	458	+ 659
Deferred income taxes	57	272	− 215
Minority interests in subsidiaries	105	56	+ 49
Shareholders' investment:			
Serial Preference Stock II	1	1	0
Common stock	78	80	− 2
Other capital	462	437	+ 25
Retained earnings	1,776	1,978	− 202
Cumulative translation adjustments	(130)	47	− 177
Treasury shares—cost in excess of par	(563)	(354)	− 209
Total shareholders' investment	1,624	2,189	− 565
Total liabilities and shareholders' investment ..	$6,410	$5,899	+ 511

Source: Adapted from 1997 TRW Inc. annual report.

F I G U R E 3–13

TRW INC. AND SUBSIDIARIES
Statement of Balance Sheet Changes
For the Year Ended December 31, 1997
($ millions)

Sources:

Decrease in cash and cash equivalents	$ 316
Decrease in deferred income taxes	328
Increase in allowances for depreciation	53
Increase in accumulated amortization	16
Increase in short-term debt	359
Increase in trade accounts payable	78
Increase in other accruals	71
Increase in income taxes payable	47
Increase in current portion of long-term debt	56
Increase in long-term liabilities	21
Increase in long-term debt	659
Increase in minority interests in subsidiaries	49
Increase in other capital	25
	$2,078

Uses:

Increase in accounts receivable	239
Increase in inventories	49
Increase in prepaid expenses	10
Increase in property, plant, and equipment	194
Increase in intangibles arising from acquisitions	415
Increase in other intangibles	201
Increase in investments in affiliated companies	88
Increase in other assets	28
Decrease in accrued compensation	48
Decrease in dividends payable	1
Decrease in deferred income taxes	215
Decrease in common stock	2
Decrease in retained earnings	202
Decrease in cumulative translation adjustments	177
Increase in treasury shares	209
	$2,078

- Depreciation and amortization write-offs are buried in the changes in the respective accounts for accumulated depreciation and amortization.

- Special items, such as write-offs and adjustments incurred with acquisitions or restructuring activities, are combined in the net amounts of affected accounts.

- New investments in facilities, as well as acquisitions, disposals, and divestments, are similarly netted out in the balance sheet accounts.

TRW's statement of earnings, or income statement, reproduced in Figure 3–14, provides us with helpful information on the first four elements, while we have to rely on additional information from the company about the amount of new investments, acquisitions, disposals, and divestments. We've provided some of these data in summarized form at the bottom of the income statement.

The simple sources and uses statement in Figure 3–13 is an indication of the broad financial implications of growth to record sales volume and earnings from continuing operations, the remaining impact of restructuring activities in 1996, and the significant effects of two major acquisitions in 1997.

The key net funds sources were:

- A net increase in long-term debt of $659 million, accompanied by an increase of $59 million in the current portion of long-term debt. This change occurred in connection with the $1.0 billion acquisition of BDM International, an information technology company, and the acquisition of an 80 percent interest in Magna International, an automotive component company, for approximately $0.5 billion.

- A net increase in short-term debt of $359 million, also part of the funding of TRW's growth and of temporary financing needs related to the acquisitions.

- A significant reduction of cash and cash equivalents of $316 million, reflecting part of the financing changes put in place during 1997 and the cash transactions involved in the two acquisitions.

- A reduction in the company's deferred income tax assets, which represents a timing shift in actual tax payments, effectively using accumulated credit and thereby conserving cash. This was, to a large extent, offset by a reduction in deferred income tax liabilities, and a reverse shift in the timing of tax payments, effectively requiring the use of cash to reduce tax obligations. The two opposing cash flows netted out to a $113 million source.

- Other sources reflect a variety of working capital changes and minor increases in minority interests and other capital.

- The period's depreciation and amortization, which we would expect to be major sources, are so far hidden in the overall changes of the accumulated allowances shown on the balance sheet.

The major net funds uses during 1997 were:

- Large increases in intangible assets caused by the acquisition ($415 million) and by other investments ($201 million).

- An increase of $239 million in accounts receivable, reflecting volume growth and the impact of the acquisitions.

- A net increase of $194 million in property, plant, and equipment, reflecting new capital spending as well as disposals, and the impact of the

FIGURE 3-14

TRW INC. AND SUBSIDIARIES
Statements of Earnings
For the Years Ended December 31, 1997 and 1996
($ millions)

	1997	1996
Sales	$10,831	$ 9,857
Cost of sales	8,826	8,376
Gross profit	2,005	1,481
Administrative and selling expenses	684	613
Research and development expenses	461	412
Purchased in-process research and development	548	—
Interest expense	75	84
Other expenses (income) net	(3)	70
Total expenses	1,765	1,179
Earnings (loss) from continuing operations before taxes		
Excluding purchased R&D; special charges ('96)	788	687
Reported earnings (loss) before income taxes	(240)	302
Income taxes	289	120
Earnings (loss) from continuing operations		
Excluding purchased R&D; special charges ('96)	$ 499	$ 434
Reported earnings (loss) after income taxes	(49)	182
Discontinued operations, gain on disposition, after tax . . .	—	298
Net earnings (loss)	$ (49)	$ 480
Preference dividends	—	1
Earnings (loss) applicable to common stock	$ (49)	$ 479
Per share of common stock:		
Average number of shares outstanding (millions)		
Diluted	123.7	132.8
Basic	123.7	128.7
Diluted net earnings (loss) per share		
From continuing operations		
Excluding purchased R&D; special charges	$ 4.03	$ 3.27
Reported	$ (0.40)	$ 1.37
From discontinued operations	—	$ 2.25
Diluted net earnings (loss) per share	$ (0.40)	$ 3.62
Basic net earnings (loss) per share		
From continuing operations		
Excluding purchased R&D; special charges	$ 4.03	$ 3.29
Reported	$ (0.40)	$ 1.41
From discontinued operations	—	$ 2.31
Basic net earnings (loss) per share	$ (0.40)	$ 3.72
Book value per share (year-end)	$ 13.19	$ 17.29
Tangible book value per share (year-end)	$ 6.58	$ 15.62
Other data ($ millions):		
Depreciation of property, plant, and equipment	$ 480	$ 442
Amortization of intangibles, other assets	10	10
Capital expenditures	549	500
Dividends paid	154	148

Source: Adapted from 1997 TRW Inc. annual report.

acquisitions, accompanied by an increase of $88 million in investments in affiliated companies.

- A retained earnings decrease of $202 million, despite record earnings from ongoing operations, due to a major write-off of purchased research and development of $544 million and dividend payments of $154 million.

- Repurchases of shares in the open market that amounted to $209 million, a continuation of the share repurchase policy TRW has carried out over several years.

- Unfavorable currency translation that caused a drain of $177 million.

Although we do, at this point, have a broad picture of TRW's sources and uses of funds, we should make a few modifications to our statement using what information is readily available to us:

1. The net change in retained earnings can be separated into profit or loss from operations and cash dividends paid. In the case of TRW, we know from the income statement that there was net income (earnings) for 1997 of $499 million from ongoing operations before a write-off of $548 million of purchased research and development after the acquisition of BMD International. The net amount, a loss of $49 million, must have been subtracted from retained earnings. The income statement further indicated that cash dividends paid were $154 million, which was also subtracted from retained earnings. The total of these two amounts is $203 million, very close to the change in retained earnings of $202. The $1.0 million is due to the difference between dividends declared and dividends actually paid, and to other small adjustments.

2. The amount of depreciation and amortization charged against income during the period should be shown as a positive funds movement, in order to reverse the impact of these noncash charges. Normally the largest is depreciation of plant and equipment, followed by amortization of patents, licenses, and other intangibles. In some cases, depletion of mineral deposits and standing timber is charged. We remember that such write-offs reflect the apportionment of past expenditures and do not involve current cash flows, serving to mask the total cash generation implicit in net income. Therefore, they must be added back to income to arrive at cash flow. This proper practice, however, results in a common misconception—to view depreciation and amortization as actual sources of cash. Remember that depreciation and amortization as such do not create any cash—they are only accounting entries that reduce reported income and thus understate the actual cash flow obtained. They do, of course, directly affect the amount of income taxes paid, but this positive funds impact has already been recognized in the income tax charge which was deducted before

arriving at net income. In TRW's case, depreciation and amortization were shown at the bottom of the income statement as $480 million and $10 million, respectively. These amounts should be listed as sources because their addition in effect restores net income to its pre–write-off level.

3. Capital expenditures for new investment are often provided as a line item in published statements and in a company's annual report. If we did not have direct information about new investments, acquisitions, disposals, and divestments made during the period, we would have to approximate the amount of funds used by arguing that the net change of the property, plant, and equipment account was affected by two main elements:

   • The amount of depreciation charged during the year.
   • All the other transactions combined.

Because we know that the net change in TRW's property, plant, and equipment was an increase of $141 million (increase in gross property of $194 million less increase in allowances for depreciation of $53 million), we can derive the net effect of all the other movements by adding back the amount of depreciation of $480 million, for a net change in investments of $621 million. This result suggests, at the very least, that the actual new investments of $549 million shown below the income statement in Figure 3–14 must have been accompanied by some additional amounts, both positive, due to the acquisitions, and perhaps negative, due to disposals of equipment. We can use the same approach to approximate the net change in intangible investments by adding back the amortization charge of $10 million to the net balance sheet change of $600 million, for a total of $610 million. Note that the company separated intangibles into two categories: those arising from acquisitions (essentially the difference between the purchase price and the recorded value of the assets), and other intangibles, such as intellectual property. As we'll see, the published cash flow information provided by the company shows the details of the positive and negative movements in this area.

Now we can assemble a modified sources and uses statement in Figure 3–15, using the basic information displayed earlier in Figure 3–13. The statement will be improved somewhat by the adjustments we've discussed in owners' equity, net income, and plant and equipment, but will be somewhat lacking in terms of understanding the specific impact of TRW's two major acquisitions in 1997. We've rearranged the derived TRW data in our three familiar areas of management decisions: operations, investment, and financing, as well as by sources and uses to highlight the specific impact of each element. This provides a preliminary picture of the effect of TRW management decisions in 1997.

We observe that operational decisions resulted in a net funds source of $951 million, which represents the 1997 net loss of $49 million—adjusted for the write-off of $548 million of purchased research and development related to the acquisition of BDM International, depreciation of $480 million, amortization of

FIGURE 3–15

TRW INC. AND SUBSIDIARIES
Derived Funds Sources and Uses Statement
For the Year Ended December 31, 1997
($ millions)

	Sources	Uses
Funds from Operations:		
Net loss		$ 49
Write-off of purchased research and development	$ 548	
Depreciation (noncash item)	480	
Amortization (noncash item)	10	
Change in deferred income taxes (net)	113	
Change in current liabilities		
(payables, accruals, taxes, dividends, etc.)	147	
Change in current assets other than cash		
(receivables, inventories, prepaid expenses)	—	298
Total operational funds flows	1,298	347
Net funds from operations	951	
Funds for Investment:		
Capital investments (adjusted for depreciation of $480) . .		621
Investment in intangible assets		
(adjusted for amortization of $10)		610
Purchased research and development		548
Investment in affiliated companies		88
Increase in other assets		28
Total investment funds flows		1,895
Funds from Financing:		
Increase in short-term debt	359	
Increase in long-term debt (including current portion)	715	
Increase in long-term liabilities	21	
Increase in minority interests	49	
Decrease in common stock		2
Increase in other capital	25	
Increase in treasury shares		209
Currency translation adjustments		177
Dividends paid		154
Adjustments to retained earnings	1	
Financing funds flows	1,170	542
Net funds provided by financing	628	
Change in Cash:	316	
Totals	$1,895	$1,895

$10 million, and reduction in deferred taxes of $113 million. The final two items represent changes in working capital elements, with net changes in current liabilities providing a source of $147 million, and net changes in current assets (other than cash; see bottom of statement) amounting to a use of $298 million.

Funds required for investment amounted to $1,895 million, which included our derived capital investment figure of $621 million, plus a similarly derived investment of $610 million in intangible assets. We must also reflect here the known purchase of research and development of $548 million during the acquisition of BDM International in 1997, which was written off against earnings in the same year, as shown above. Smaller uses are the investment in affiliated companies of $88 million, and the increase in other assets of $28 million.

Funds from financing decisions, a net amount of $628 million, are characterized by significant increases in TRW's debt, with short-term debt raised by $359 million and long-term debt growth of $715 million, largely related to the major acquisitions. Other capital grew by $25 million, while repurchases of stock for cash raised treasury shares by $209 million. Currency translations affected cash negatively by $177 million, and dividends paid amounted to $154 million. Minor elements account for the remainder.

A check of the company's annual report reveals that, as we know, actual 1997 capital investment for new property, plant, and equipment was $549 million, as compared to our derived total of $621. We also learn that the total cost of the acquisitions, net of cash acquired, was $1,270 million. This figure could not be directly derived from the balance sheet changes because the acquired assets were in part written off ($548 million of purchased research and development was charged against earnings), and the various assets and liabilities were merged with the balance sheet totals. However, we can regard the combined increase in intangible assets of $1,150 million ($610 million largely due to the acquisitions, and purchased research and development of $540 million) as a reasonable proxy for the cost of the acquisitions, even though this total falls short by $120 million. These differences can only be reconciled by inside information not available in the published data.

When we compare TRW's actual cash flow statement, reproduced in Figure 3–16, to our derived statement in Figure 3–15, we find that, apart from differences in presentation, the figures we have developed are directionally representative. The various items on which the statements disagree—and some of them are significant—require more detailed knowledge. This is particularly true of details in the financing section, which reflects a lot of information not available to us, and in the investment section, where the major aspect is the acquisition of BDM International and Magna International. The impact of these acquisitions, which were made for cash, is reflected there as the original total amount of $1,270, financed temporarily by a large increase in short-term debt. As the three companies were combined, assets and liabilities were consolidated and the difference between the price and the recorded values brought about the sizable increase in intangibles (goodwill). For purposes of the TRW cash flow statement, the intangibles increases we had recognized separately are part of acquisition cost shown, and the changes specified in the financing section are designed to highlight the acquisition transaction. From an overall standpoint, however, the totals in the three major funds flow categories are reasonable approximations of the TRW presentation, varying by no more than $78 million in the largest category—the funds used for investment—and by far less in the other two, $3 million and $52 million respectively.

FIGURE 3–16

TRW INC. AND SUBSIDIARIES
Statements of Cash Flows
For the Years Ended December 31, 1997 and 1996
($ millions)

	1997	1996
Operating Activities:		
Net earnings (loss)	$ (49)	$ 480
Adjustments to reconcile net earnings (loss) to		
net cash provided by continuing operations:		
Purchased in-process research and development	548	—
Depreciation and amortization	490	452
Deferred income taxes	116	(182)
Discontinued operations	—	(298)
Other—net	10	23
Changes in assets and liabilities, net of effects of		
businesses acquired or sold:		
Accounts receivable	32	(46)
Inventories and prepaid expenses	(26)	8
Accounts payable and other accruals	(166)	298
Other—net	(1)	(24)
Net cash provided by operating activities	954	711
Investing Activities:		
Capital expenditures	(549)	(500)
Acquisitions, net of cash acquired	(1,270)	(76)
Net proceeds from divestitures	—	789
Other—net	2	34
Net cash provided by (used in) investing activities	(1,817)	247
Financing Activities:		
Increase (decrease) in short-term debt	912	(127)
Proceeds from debt in excess of 90 days	113	51
Principal repayments in excess of 90 days	(89)	(91)
Dividends paid	(154)	(148)
Acquisition of common stock	(247)	(361)
Other—net	41	51
Net cash provided by (used in) financing activities	576	(625)
Effect of exchange rate changes on cash	(29)	(6)
Increase (decrease) in cash and cash equivalents	(316)	327
Cash and cash equivalents at beginning of year	386	59
Cash and cash equivalents at end of year	$ 70	$ 386
Supplemental Cash Flow Information:		
Interest paid (net of amount capitalized)	$ 76	$ 89
Income taxes paid (net of refunds)	78	615

Source: Adapted from 1997 TRW Inc. annual report.

To summarize, in this section we constructed a cash flow statement that goes beyond simply listing the changes readily observed in a comparison of beginning and ending balance sheet accounts. We achieved this by making some broad adjustments in several of the accounts. The purpose of the refinements was to highlight significant results that reflect management decisions involving investments, operations, and financing. If a company's cash flow statement is not made available as a matter of course, the analyst can usually approximate the main elements of the statement, which an insider could prepare by going through the basic adjustment process we've demonstrated.

Funds Management and Shareholder Value

It will be useful to reflect once more on the nature of funds movements in the context of shareholder value creation. We've demonstrated the complex interrelationship of funds movements, driven by management decisions, external forces, and the intrinsic nature of a company's business. We've further shown how to determine and illustrate the impact of funds movements on cash flows.

The overriding principle for successful management of operating funds is constant attention to the economical use of the resources these funds represent. The best-managed companies tailor their information systems and management incentives to minimize funds use relative to the level of each activity. If the foundation of shareholder value creation is to earn returns on the resources employed at levels above shareholder expectations, taking a "scarcity" approach to resource deployment should be natural for managers at all levels. Such thinking must not be limited to funding new capital outlays alone, as we'll discuss in Chapters 7 and 8, but must reach into all aspects of the business, including working capital management, employment practices, funding of research, product and service development, marketing and promotional programs, and so on. We'll now briefly discuss some of the key elements involved in managing operational funds.

Cash Management

As we've stated before, all management decisions and the funds movements caused by them eventually materialize in the form of a cash impact. But we also must realize that a company's cash balance at any one time represents a resource commitment, even though its movements are more frequent and extensive than those of other investments. The principle that applies to this resource is the same as with any other resource:

> Minimize its size relative to the needs it supports, and obtain the greatest possible return by investing cash balances in ways that reflect its unique characteristics.

Therefore, the economics of sound cash management requires that any time there is a lag in cash receipts it should be minimized, and disbursements should be made no sooner than required by commercial and legal terms. Ways to achieve time compression range from the use of lockboxes, to which remittances from customers are mailed for speedier processing, to the growing use of electronic funds transfers, which allows immediate collection of amounts due without the delays of paperwork. Effective banking relationships are a great asset in this process, and companies with widespread locations will attempt to concentrate cash management into regional processing arrangements.

Minimization of cash balances can be achieved by transferring any excess cash into marketable securities of short maturities, including U.S. treasury bills, commercial paper issued by corporations, and certificates of deposit issued by banks. While returns from these temporary investments will not approach the returns from a company's normal business activities, the trade-off between leaving cash idle versus earning a modest return until the cash can be used for longer-term investments, dividends, or repurchase of shares, will be positive and therefore in the shareholders' interest.

Working Capital Management

Investments in customer credit in the form of accounts receivable, and in inventories of goods or materials, are long-term resource commitments as part of the stock of working capital, as we discussed earlier. Minimization of these investments relative to the level and pattern of a company's operations is a crucial element in the total management of operating funds. The key to successful management of customer credit and inventories is a clear understanding of the economic trade-offs involved.

Credit terms are a function of the competitive environment as well as of a careful assessment of the nature and creditworthiness of customers. For example, the issue might be whether extended credit terms, and the resulting rise in receivables outstanding, are compensated for by the contribution from any incremental sales gained. Similarly, extending normal credit to marginal customers has to be judged in terms of the risk of late payment or default versus the contribution from the sales gained. Techniques in the customer credit area include constant updating of credit performance, aging of accounts receivable into time categories, and developing sound criteria for credit extension.

Inventory management in successful companies has evolved into a rigorous process of asset minimization. Information technology has permitted a general reduction in inventory levels, whether in manufacturing, wholesaling, or retailing. In an effort to push inventories as low as possible, techniques such as just-in-time deliveries by suppliers to their customers' manufacturing or trading locations, and carefully scheduled restocking triggered by instantaneous purchase data from major wholesalers and retailers, have become widespread. In effect, these techniques have created a very close relationship between major suppliers and major customers, often with electronic linkages of inventories, order processing, and production scheduling. Such ties allow for timely coordination of schedules and minimization of inventories on both sides.

Normal trade credit from suppliers in the form of accounts payable helps to offset receivables and inventories. Here the appropriate principle is to make use of the credit terms extended, but to watch for potential favorable trade-offs such as discounts for early payment. Accounts payable is one form of financing working capital, and therefore, maximum use of trade terms is appropriate. If discounts offered for early payment are attractive—for example, 2 percent for payment in 10 days rather than 30 days amounts to a sizable interest rate of 36 percent per year (2 percent gained for a 20-day speedup in remittance)—there is an obvious advantage in using less-expensive bank credit in order to remit to the vendor in 10 days. Deliberately exceeding the normal credit terms might make the interest trade-off more favorable, but there is the risk of affecting the company's credit standing if delays beyond the terms granted become habitual. Sound management of supplier credit, as was true with customer credit, relies on current up-to-date information on accounts and aging of payables to ensure proper payment.

As we discussed earlier, funding of working capital must be considered a long-term commitment, unless the business is characterized by significant seasonal or cyclical fluctuations. Given that even tightly managed receivables and inventories require long-term financial support, successful management of operational funding requires the use of a combination of reinvested earnings and long-term debt, augmented as needed by temporary short-term funding.

Investment Management

Funding of operations also involves periodic investments in facilities, programs, and other long-term resource commitments beyond working capital needs. As we'll discuss in Chapters 7 and 8, the principles of sound investment management are no different in terms of shareholder value creation—the minimization of funds needs relative to the expected benefits is paramount. The main complications arise because of the longer time frame and greater degree of uncertainty surrounding the expectations about the cash flows to be generated. The techniques of analysis are somewhat more involved, but still are based on the basic notion of cash flow trade-offs. The funding for such commitments will naturally tend to have a longer time horizon as well.

Key Issues

The following is a recap of the key issues raised directly or indirectly in this chapter. They are enumerated here to help the reader keep the materials discussed within the perspective of financial theory and business practice.

1. Operational funding needs and sources are woven into the larger systems context of managing the company for shareholder value, and must also be viewed from both a short-term and a long-term perspective. It is not appropriate to attempt to separate specific operational funding issues from this larger context.

2. Operational funding is affected by both internal and external conditions and causes, which must be understood in terms of the business environment, economic conditions, and specific company processes and policies. Identifying the key drivers of operational funds patterns and tracing their impact over appropriate periods of time is a valuable effort for minimizing unexpected shortfalls or ineffective use of resources.

3. Operational funding requirements and the trade-offs surrounding them are special applications of the broader economic principles that govern all resource commitments and sources. The main difference lies in the timing of the flow patterns, which are generally more short-term oriented, but still belong within the larger framework of resource management.

4. Several key questions arise as funds movements are analyzed. Most relate to the types of funds commitments (uses) made compared to the sources of funds available. Are enough long-term funds provided to fund ongoing growth in working capital and fixed asset expansion given a strategic context? Are most sources of funds temporary loans and credit extensions? Is the business counting on profits to fund peak needs that might exceed such expectations?

5. As modern management embraces greater degrees of cash flow thinking, the interpretation and use of cash flow statements increases, as does the amount of detail presented in them. Analysis of published financial statements materially benefits from these displays of cash flow patterns, and familiarity with the development and limitations of the statements is a necessary skill for the financial analyst and manager.

6. Funds flow patterns represent the essential nature of business decisions, and are the key ingredient in shareholder value creation. The challenge to the analyst and manager is to understand the difference between economic cash flows and noncash accounting transactions, and to interpret the pattern of funds movements accordingly. Judging the performance and value of a business largely depends on such discriminating insights.

Summary

In this chapter, we've demonstrated the funds flow cycle involved in any business, large or small, and its implications for management. We began with a simple illustration of basic funds movements, and then discussed operating funds cycles from the standpoints of manufacturing, sales, and service. We observed the nature and behavior of working capital, highlighted the impact of different types of variability in operations, and demonstrated the effect of funds lags on the nature and duration of financing required to support a business. Major insights gained included the need to consider the permanence of basic working capital requirements, the financial drain encountered even with successful growth, and the potential funds release from decline in volume.

We then turned to a demonstration of how public financial statement information can be used to develop a meaningful cash flow statement, which summarizes the total cash flow picture of a business. It became clear that much of the insight to be gained about the cash impact of a company's decision pattern could be expressed by analyzing balance sheet changes and supplementary income statement information. At the same time, the need for specific detail not normally published was apparent, in order to refine the cash flow information. Fortunately, publicly held companies publish detailed cash flow statements arranged in a standard format, allowing direct access to the major cash effects of significant decisions.

In essence, funds flow analysis is a broad-brush dynamic view of the management of the business. It relates changes in major conditions to their key financial implications by reconstructing the cash implications of major transactions during the period. The techniques are relatively simple, requiring only basic accounting knowledge to provide this extra dimension in assessing balance sheets and income statements. The transformation into cash flow thinking achieved by funds flow analysis matches the dynamics of the systems concept we discussed in Chapter 2. It is also a precursor to the topics covered in later chapters, where cash flow patterns and expectations are a significant aspect of financial analysis techniques and practices.

Analytical Support

Financial Genome, the commercially available financial analysis and planning software described in Appendix I, has the capability to develop cash flow statements from databases, spreadsheets, and direct inputs. (see "Downloads Available" on p. 431)

Selected References

Anthony, Robert N. *Essentials of Accounting*. 5th ed. Reading, MA: Addison Wesley, 1993.
Brealey, Richard, and Stewart Myers. *Principles of Corporate Finance*. 5th ed. Burr Ridge, IL: Irwin/McGraw-Hill, 1996.
Ross, Stephen; Randolph Westerfield; and Bradford Jordan. *Fundamentals of Corporate Finance*. 4th ed. Burr Ridge, IL: Irwin/McGraw-Hill, 1998.
Weston, J. Fred, and Thomas E. Copeland. *Managerial Finance*. 10th ed. Hinsdale, IL: Dryden Press, 1992.

CHAPTER 4

ASSESSMENT OF BUSINESS PERFORMANCE

When we wish to assess the performance of a business, we're looking for ways to measure the financial and economic consequences of past management decisions that shaped investments, operations, and financing over time. The important questions to be answered are whether all resources were used effectively, whether the profitability of the business met or even exceeded expectations, and whether financing choices were made prudently. Shareholder value creation ultimately requires positive results in all these areas—which will bring about favorable cash flow patterns exceeding the company's cost of capital.

As we'll see, there is a wide range of choices among many individual ratios and measures, some purely financial and some economic. No one ratio or measure can be considered predominant. In this chapter, we'll demonstrate primarily the analysis of business performance based on published financial statements. These represent the most common data source available for the purpose, even though they are not designed to reflect economic results and conditions. We'll also discuss the more important measures that help assess economic performance aspects. Our focus will be on key relationships and indicators that allow the analyst to assess past performance and also to project assumed future results (as discussed in Chapter 5). We'll point out their meaning as well as the limitations inherent in them. In the final chapters we'll discuss the larger context of valuing a company or its parts in economic terms, a process that is based on an intense assessment of performance drivers and strategic positioning, and that requires developing expected cash flow results for which past performance is only a starting point.

Ratio Analysis and Performance

Because there are so many tools for doing performance assessment, we must remember that different techniques address measurement in very specific and often narrowly defined ways. One can be tempted to "run all the numbers," particularly given the speed and ease of computer spreadsheets. Yet normally, only a few selected relationships will yield information the analyst really needs for useful insights and decision support. By definition, a ratio can relate any magnitude to any other—the choices are limited only by the imagination. To be useful, both the meaning and the limitations of the ratio chosen have to be understood. Before beginning any task, therefore, the analyst must define the following elements:

- The viewpoint taken.
- The objectives of the analysis.
- The potential standards of comparison.

Any particular ratio or measure is useful only in relation to the viewpoint taken and the specific objectives of the analysis. When there is such a match, the measure can become a standard for comparison. Moreover, ratios are not absolute criteria: They serve best when used in selected combinations to point out changes in financial conditions or operating performance over several periods and as compared to similar businesses. Ratios help illustrate the trends and patterns of such changes, which, in turn, might indicate to the analyst the risks and opportunities for the business under review.

A further caution: Performance assessment via financial statement analysis is based on past data and conditions from which it might be difficult to extrapolate future expectations. Yet, any decisions to be made as a result of such performance assessment can affect only the future—the past is gone, or sunk, as an economist would call it.

No attempt to assess business performance can provide firm answers. Any insights gained will be relative, because business and operating conditions vary so much from company to company and industry to industry. Comparisons and standards based on past performance are especially difficult to interpret in large, multibusiness companies and conglomerates, where specific information by individual lines of business is normally limited. Accounting adjustments of various types present further complications. To deal with all these aspects in detail is far beyond the scope of this book, although we'll point out the key items. The reader should strive to become aware of these issues and always be cautious in using financial data.

To provide a coherent structure for the many ratios and measures involved, the discussion will be built around three major viewpoints of financial performance analysis. While there are many different individuals and groups interested in the success or failure of a given business, the most important are:

- Managers.
- Owners (investors).
- Lenders and creditors.

Closest to the business on a day-to-day basis, but also responsible for its long-range performance, is the management of the organization, whether its members are professional managers or owner/managers. Managers are responsible and accountable for operating efficiency, the effective deployment of capital, useful human effort, appropriate use of other resources, and current and long-term results—all within the context of sound business strategies.

Next are the various owners of the business, who are especially interested in the current and long-term returns on their equity investment. They usually expect growing earnings, cash flows, and dividends, which in combination will bring about growth in the economic value of their "stake." They are affected by the way a company's earnings are used and distributed, and by the relative value of their shares within the general movement of the security markets.

Finally, there are the providers of "other people's money," lenders and creditors who extend funds to the business for various lengths of time. They are mainly concerned about the company's liquidity and cash flows that affect its ability to make the interest payments due them and eventually to repay the principal. They'll also be concerned about the degree of financial leverage employed, and the availability of specific residual asset values that will give them a margin of protection against their risk.

Other groups such as employees, government, and society have, of course, specific objectives of their own—the business' ability to pay wages, the stability of employment, the reliability of tax payments, and the financial wherewithal to meet various social and environmental obligations. Financial performance indicators are useful to these groups in combination with a variety of other data.

The principal financial performance areas of interest to management, owners, and lenders are shown in Figure 4–1, along with the most common ratios and measures relevant to these areas. We'll follow the sequence shown in the figure and discuss each subgrouping within the three broad viewpoints. Later, we'll relate the key measures to each other in a systems context.

Management's Point of View

Management has a dual interest in the analysis of financial performance:

- To assess the efficiency and profitability of operations.
- To judge how effectively the resources of the business are being used.

Judging a company's operations is largely done with an analysis of the income statement, while resource effectiveness is usually measured by reviewing both the balance sheet and the income statement. In order to make economic judgments, however, it's often necessary to modify the available financial data to reflect current economic values and conditions.

For purposes of illustration, we'll again use information from the sample statements of TRW Inc. for 1997 and 1996, which were reproduced in Chapter 2. The same statements are shown here in Figures 4–2 and 4–3. We'll use this information for the remainder of this chapter. For added convenience, we've also expressed the various items on the income statement as a percent of sales, a common

FIGURE 4–1

Performance Measures by Area and Viewpoint

Management	Owners	Lenders
Operational Analysis	**Investment Return**	**Liquidity**
Gross margin	Return on total net worth	Current ratio
Profit margin	Return on common equity	Acid test
EBIT; EBITDA	Earnings per share	Quick sale value
NOPAT	Cash flow per share	
Operating expense analysis	Share price appreciation	
Contribution analysis	Total shareholder return	
Operating leverage		
Comparative analysis		
Resource Management	**Disposition of Earnings**	**Financial Leverage**
Asset turnover	Dividends per share	Debt to assets
Working capital management	Dividend yield	Debt to capitalization
• Inventory turnover	Payout/retention of earnings	Debt to equity
• Accounts receivable patterns	Dividend coverage	
• Accounts payable patterns	Dividends to assets	
Human resource effectiveness		
Profitability	**Market Performance**	**Debt Service**
Return on assets (after taxes)	Price/earnings ratio	Interest coverage
Return before interest and taxes	Cash flow multiples	Burden coverage
Return on current value basis	Market to book value	Fixed changes coverage
EVA and economic profit	Relative price movements	Cash flow analysis
Cash flow return on investment	Value drivers	
Free cash flow	Value of the firm	

way of highlighting the relative magnitude of the various categories in relation to the base of sales.

In addition, Addendum 4–1 at the end of this chapter contains major selections from the "Notes to Financial Statements," as published in TRW's 1997 annual report. They are provided as explanatory background for the company's key accounting policies, recent restructuring and acquisitions, income tax provisions, deferred income taxes, post-retirement benefits accounting change, debt, and industry segments. Because these items affect the development of many of the ratios in this chapter, the notes will help in understanding some of the choices an analyst must make in using financial statement information.

Operational Analysis

An initial assessment of the operational effectiveness for the business as a whole or any of its subdivisions is generally performed through a "common numbers" or percentage analysis of the income statement. Individual costs and expense items

FIGURE 4-2

TRW INC. AND SUBSIDIARIES
Consolidated Balance Sheets at December 31
($ millions)

	1997	1996
Assets		
Current assets:		
Cash and cash equivalents	$ 70	$ 386
Accounts receivable	1,617	1,378
Inventories	573	524
Prepaid expenses	79	69
Deferred income taxes	96	424
Total current assets	2,435	2,781
Property, plant, and equipment at cost	6,074	5,880
Less: Allowances for depreciation and amortization	3,453	3,400
Total property, plant & equipment—net	2,621	2,480
Intangible assets		
Intangibles arising from acquisitions	673	258
Other	232	31
Total intangible assets	905	289
Less: Accumulated amortization	94	78
Total intangible assets—net	811	211
Investments in affiliated companies	139	51
Other assets	404	376
Total assets	$6,410	$5,899
Liabilities and Shareholders' Investment		
Current liabilities:		
Short-term debt	$ 411	$ 52
Accrued compensation	338	386
Trade accounts payable	859	781
Other accruals	846	775
Dividends payable	38	39
Income taxes	99	52
Current portion of long-term debt	128	72
Total current liabilities	2,719	2,157
Long-term liabilities	788	767
Long-term debt	1,117	458
Deferred income taxes	57	272
Minority interests in subsidiaries	105	56
Shareholders' investment:		
Serial preference stock II	1	1
Common stock	78	80
Other capital	462	437
Retained earnings	1,776	1,978
Cumulative translation adjustments	(130)	47
Treasury shares − cost in excess of par value	(563)	(354)
Total shareholders' investment	1,624	2,189
Total liabilities and shareholders' investment	$6,410	$5,899

Source: Adapted from 1997 TRW Inc. annual report.

FIGURE 4-3

TRW INC. AND SUBSIDIARIES
Statements of Earnings
For the Years Ended December 31, 1997 and 1996
($ millions)

	1997	Percent of Sales	1996	Percent of Sales
Sales	$10,831	100.0%	$9,857	100.0%
Cost of sales.........................	8,826	81.5	8,376	85.0
Gross profit..........................	2,005	18.5%	1,481	15.0%
Administrative and selling expenses	684	6.3	613	6.2
Research and development expenses.......	461	4.2	412	4.2
Purchased in-process research and development	548	5.1	—	—
Interest expense........................	75	0.7	84	0.9
Other expenses (income) net..............	(3)	—	70	0.7
Total expenses	1,765	16.3%	1,179	12.0%
Earnings (loss) from continuing operations before taxes				
Excluding purchased R&D; special charges ('96)	788	7.3	687	7.0
Reported earnings (loss) before income taxes	240	2.2	302	3.1
Income taxes	289	2.7	120	1.2
Earnings (loss) from continuing operations				
Excluding purchased R&D; special charges ('96)	499	4.6	434	4.4
Reported earnings (loss) after income taxes	(49)	(0.5)	182	1.8
Discontinued operations, gain on disposition, after tax	—	—	298	3.0
Net earnings (loss).....................	$ (49)	(0.5)%	$ 480	4.8%
Preference dividends	—	—	1	—
Earnings (loss) applicable to common stock ..	$ (49)	(0.5)%	$ 479	4.8%
Per share of common stock:				
Average number of shares outstanding (millions)				
Diluted	123.7		132.8	
Basic.............................	123.7		128.7	
Diluted net earnings (loss) per share				
From continuing operations				
Excluding purchased R&D; special charges	$4.03		$ 3.27	
Reported........................	(0.40)		1.37	
From discontinued operations	—		2.25	
Diluted net earnings (loss) per share	$ (0.40)		$ 3.62	
Basic net earnings (loss) per share				
From continuing operations				
Excluding purchased R&D; special charges	$4.03		$ 3.29	
Reported........................	(0.40)		1.41	
From discontinued operations	—		2.31	
Basic net earnings (loss) per share	$ (0.40)		$ 3.72	
Cash dividends paid.....................	1.24		1.135	
Book value per share (year-end)	13.19		17.29	
Tangible book value per share (year-end)	6.58		15.62	
Other data ($ millions):				
Depreciation of property, plant, and equipment	$ 480		$ 442	
Amortization of intangibles, other assets	10		10	
Capital expenditures.....................	549		500	
Dividends paid	154		148	

Source: Adapted from 1997 TRW Inc. annual report.

are normally related to sales, that is, gross sales revenues adjusted for any returns and allowances. The common base of sales permits a ready comparison of the key costs and expenses from period to period, over longer stretches of time, and against competitor and industry databases.

Expense-to-sales ratios are used both to judge the relative magnitude of selected key elements and to determine any trends toward improving or declining performance. However, we must keep in mind the type of industry involved and its particular characteristics, as well as the individual trends and special conditions of the company being studied. For example, the gross margin of a jewelry store with slow turnover of merchandise and high markups will be far greater (50 percent is not uncommon) than that of a supermarket, which depends on low margins and high volume for its success (gross margins of 10 to 15 percent are typical). In fact, comparing a particular company's ratios to those of similar companies in its industry over a number of time periods will usually provide the best clues as to whether the company's performance is improving or declining.

Many published annual overviews of company and industry performance use ranking approaches, such as the annual Fortune 500 listings. Individual companies usually develop their own comparisons with the performance of comparable units within the organization or with relevant competitors on the outside. It's also often useful to graphically depict a series of performance data over time, a process now easily achieved with the ubiquitous availability of computer spreadsheets and online financial databases and services.

Gross-Margin and Cost-of-Goods-Sold Analysis

One of the most common ratios in operational analysis is the calculation of cost of goods sold (cost of sales) as a percentage of sales. This ratio indicates the magnitude of the cost of goods purchased or manufactured, or the cost of services provided, in relation to the gross margin (gross profit) left over for operating expenses and profit.

The ratios calculated from our TRW sample statements appear as follows:

$$\text{Cost of goods sold} = \frac{\$8,826}{\$10,831} = 81.5\% \ (1996{:}\ 85.0\%)$$

$$\text{Gross margin} = \frac{\$2,005}{\$10,831} = 18.5\% \ (1994{:}\ 15.0\%)$$

The cost of goods sold (81.5 percent) and the gross margin (18.5 percent) indicate the margin of "raw profit" from operations. Remember that gross margin reflects the relationship of prices, volume, and costs. A change in gross margin can result from a combination of changes in:

- The selling price of the product.
- The level of manufacturing costs for the product.
- Any variations in the product mix of the business.

In a trading or service organization, gross margin can be affected by a combination of changes in:

- The price charged for the products or services provided.
- The price paid for merchandise purchased on the outside.
- The cost of services from internal or external sources.
- Any variation in the product/service mix of the business.

The volume of operations also can have a significant effect if, for example, a manufacturing company has high fixed costs (see Chapter 6 for a discussion of operating leverage), or a small trading company has less buying power and economies of scale than a large competitor.

In the case of TRW, the cost of goods sold and the gross margin shown in the annual report represented a consolidation of the two major business segments. In other words, the income statement combined the automotive business and space, defense, and information systems. We note a gross margin improvement of three and one-half percentage points from the prior year, which was in part affected by the restructuring and acquisition activities during the two years. For a more detailed insight, we should calculate the gross margins for the individual business areas, if this information was publicly available.

In its annual report, TRW provided a selective breakdown, by major product line, of sales, operating profit, identifiable assets, depreciation and amortization, and capital expenditures, which would allow the analyst to make some overall comparisons (see p. 157, "Industry Segments"). These data would have to be supplemented by additional internal information, however, to be able to perform a detailed ratio analysis—something routinely done within the company.

There are particular complications in the analysis of manufacturing companies. The nature of manufacturing cost accounting systems governs the specific costing of products for inventory and for current sale. Significant differences can exist in the apparent cost performance of companies when using standard full cost systems (all costs, fixed and variable, are allocated to each unit of production based on an estimate of normal cost levels) as compared to using direct costing (fixed manufacturing costs are not allocated to individual products but charged as a block against operations). The charges against a particular period of operations can be affected to some degree by the choice of accounting methods. Increasingly, however, companies are turning to various forms of activity-based accounting for internal purposes, which provides a more precise basis for judging the real economic costs of products and services. Inflation, which affects the prices of both cost inputs and goods or services sold, or currency fluctuations, in the case of international businesses, further distort the picture. We'll take up some of these issues later in this chapter.

Any major change in a company's cost of goods sold or gross margin over a relevant period of time would call for further analysis to identify the cause. The length of the time period chosen for such trend analysis depends on the nature of the business. For example, as we demonstrated in Chapter 3, many businesses have normal seasonal fluctuations, while others are affected by longer-term business cycles. Thus, this ratio serves as a signal rather than an absolute measure, as is the case with most of the measures discussed.

Profit Margin

The relationship of reported net profit after taxes (net income) to sales indicates management's ability to operate the business with sufficient success. Success in this case means not only recovering the cost of the merchandise or services, the expenses of operating the business (including depreciation), and the cost of borrowed funds, but also leaving a margin of reasonable compensation to the owners for putting their capital at risk. The ratio of net profit (income) to sales (total revenue) essentially expresses the overall cost/price effectiveness of the operation. As we'll demonstrate later, however, a more significant ratio for this purpose is the relationship of profit to the amount of capital employed in generating it.

At this point, we should note that earnings can be affected significantly by mandated changes in accounting methods issued from time to time by FASB. There might be sizable adjustments, as occurred in the early 90s, when future employee medical benefits had to be recognized as a liability with an offsetting charge to earnings. For purposes of ratio analysis and for period-to-period comparisons, extraordinary adjustments should be excluded, along with any other extraordinary gains or losses a company might encounter in a particular period. In most cases, significant items of this kind are highlighted in the company's financial statements, allowing the analyst to choose whether to include them in the analysis. The calculation of the net profit (net earnings) ratio is simple, as the figures from our TRW example show. We have chosen to use net profit before special charges and discontinued operations in these calculations, to permit a clearer comparison of the results of TRW's continuing operations for the two years:

$$\text{Profit margin} = \frac{\$499}{\$10,831} = 4.6\% \ (1996: 4.4\%)$$

Note the increase of two-tenths of a percentage point from 1996, which is the result of both record volume and aggressive cost containment.

A variation of this ratio uses net profit *before* interest and taxes. This figure represents the operating profit before any compensation is paid to debt holders. It's also the profit before the calculation of federal and state income taxes, which are often based on modified sets of deductible expenses and accounting write-offs. The ratio represents a purer view of operating effectiveness, undistorted by financing patterns and tax calculations. Referred to as earnings before interest and taxes (EBIT), this pretax, pre-interest income ratio for TRW appears as follows, again using the results from ongoing operations only:

$$\text{EBIT} = \frac{\$788 + \$75}{\$10,831} = 8.0\% \ (1996: 7.8\%)$$

In its published data TRW reported that the pretax operating margin for its two major businesses, a measure which corresponds to EBIT, was 9.0 percent (9.4 percent for 1996) for the automotive segment (65 percent of 1997 sales), and 8.4 percent (7.3 percent for 1996) for space, defense, and information systems (35 percent of 1997 sales), providing some additional insight into their comparative performance.

A modification frequently used by security analysts is EBIT, adjusted for depreciation and amortization, in an attempt to show the pretax earnings unaffected by taxes and the allocation of past expenditures in the form of depreciation and amortization. Called EBITDA, this income measure affects the ratio as follows, using TRW's figures from continuing operations:

$$\text{EBITDA} = \frac{\$788 + \$75 + \$480 + \$10}{\$10,831} = 12.5\% \ (1996: 12.4\%)$$

A sound argument can be made, however, for considering income taxes an ongoing expense of being in business. The EBIT formula can therefore be modified by using profit *before* interest but *after* taxes, which requires a tax adjustment for the interest amount. Again, the intent is to focus on operating efficiency by leaving out any compensation to the various holders of capital.

Using the TRW figures, this modified result appears as follows:

$$\text{EBIAT} = \frac{\$499 + (1 - .37) \ 75}{\$10,831} = 5.0\% \ (1996: 4.9\%)$$

For convenience in removing the effect of interest from aftertax profit, we usually assume that the interest paid during the period was fully tax deductible. Thus, we simply add back to the stated profit figure the after-tax cost of interest. We obtain the latter by multiplying pretax interest by a factor of "one minus the tax rate," employing either the effective (average) tax rate paid on earnings (37.0 percent in TRW's case) or, ideally, the marginal (highest bracket) corporate tax rate for the firm in question.

The choice of tax rates depends on the complexity of the company's taxation pattern. TRW operates worldwide, and therefore is subject to a variety of taxes, which are combined in the provision for income taxes on the income statement. It's most straightforward to rely on the effective overall rate paid, which for TRW approximated the marginal U.S. corporate tax rate prevailing in 1997. Chapter 9 contains a specific discussion of the cost of debt and the nature of the necessary tax adjustments to be made to interest cost.

The EBIAT concept can be further refined in the form of NOPAT, the net operating profit after taxes, which excludes interest expense and income as well as any nonoperating income and expense items. The NOPAT measure has gained in importance with the shift toward shareholder value measures, which we'll discuss in more detail in Chapter 12. As an expression of the after-tax earnings power of the operations of the business, NOPAT becomes an input to such measures as economic value added. In TRW's case, the calculation from published data requires only the elimination of other income and expenses on the same basis as interest, that is, tax-adjusting them before subtracting or adding them:

$$\text{NOPAT} = \frac{\$499 + (1 - .37)(\$75 - \$3)}{\$10,831} = 5.1\% \ (1996: 5.4\%)$$

It should be mentioned that the result for 1996 was improved by about one-third of a percentage point because other expenses of $70 were added back after tax adjustment.

As a general rule, when there are unusual or nonrecurring income and expense elements not directly related to ongoing operations, the analyst should adjust the ratios by excluding these items when measuring operating effectiveness. The adjustment should be done on the same basis as we demonstrated for interest—that is, the tax effect of revenue or expense items must be calculated if after-tax comparisons are desired.

Operating Expense Analysis

Various expense categories are routinely related to sales. These comparisons include such items as administrative expense, selling and promotional expenses, and many others typical of particular businesses and industries.

The general formula used to calculate this expense ratio is:

$$\text{Expense ratio} = \frac{\text{Various expense items}}{\text{Sales}} = \text{Percent}$$

There are relatively few expense categories shown in the abbreviated income statement of TRW, but the ratio to sales was calculated for each item in Figure 4–3. In practice, a much finer breakdown would be desirable, something that is internally available as a matter of course. Most trade associations collect extensive financial data—many of them company confidential—from their members and compile published summary statistics on expense ratios, as well as on most of the other ratios discussed in this chapter. These publications help provide broad standards of comparison and can serve as a basis for trend analysis. As in any statistical references, however, care must be taken to select reasonably comparable groupings of companies and businesses to obtain meaningful insights.

In such statistics, businesses should be carefully categorized within an industry by size and other characteristics to reduce the degree of error introduced by large-scale averaging. Moreover, companies with complex product or service offerings, or companies with many international operations, might be hard to categorize. Yet, even without specific comparative data available, a skilled analyst will scan the revenue and expense categories on an income statement as a matter of course over a number of time periods to see if any of them seem out of line or are trending adversely within the particular company's experience.

Contribution Analysis

This type of analysis has been used mainly for internal management, although it is increasingly applied in broader financial analysis. It involves relating sales to the contribution margin of individual product groups or of the total business. Such calculations require a very selective analysis or estimate of the fixed and variable costs and expenses of the business, and take into account the effect of operating leverage (see Chapter 6). Usually only directly variable costs are subtracted from sales to show the contribution of operations toward fixed costs and profits for the period.

The contribution margin is calculated as follows:

$$\text{Contribution margin} = \frac{\text{Sales} - \text{Direct costs (variable costs)}}{\text{Sales}}$$

$$= \text{Percent}$$

Significant differences can exist in the contribution margins of different industries, due to varying needs for capital investment and the resultant cost-volume conditions. Even within a particular company, various lines of products or services might contribute quite differently to fixed costs and profits. Note that the measure is sensitive to three key drivers—volume, price and direct costs—which are traded off in the process of managing the operations of the business. Understanding changes in contribution therefore depends on understanding the changes in the drivers underlying this result, as we pointed out in our discussion of the business system in Chapter 2.

Contribution margins as derived from financial statements are useful as a broad, if limited, tool in judging the risk characteristics of a business. The measure suggests the amount of leeway management enjoys in pricing its products and services, and the scope of its ability to control costs and expenses under different economic conditions. Analysis of *operating leverage* and pricing strategies as related to volume becomes important in this context. Chapter 6 contains a more extensive discussion of these points.

As mentioned before, a great deal of effort has been expended in recent years on so-called activity-based accounting analysis. This approach can be used for an assessment of the relative economic contribution of various parts of a company, thereby going beyond the limitations of existing cost accounting systems. During this process, all phases of an activity are first carefully defined in terms of physical relationships and process steps. Then a specific financial/economic allocation is made of all resources and cost elements, direct or indirect, internal or external, which support the activity, product line, operation, or line of business. The result serves as the basis for periodic strategic assessment of the current and prospective relative economic contribution of the area under study. The insights gained often differ from a straight accounting analysis, because the activity-based process is much more precise in defining and allocating relative effort, cost, and support capital required. The techniques involved go beyond the scope of this book; for more information see the references at the end of the chapter.

Resource Management

Here we are interested in judging the effectiveness with which management has employed the assets entrusted to it by the owners of the business. When examining a balance sheet, an analyst can draw company-specific conclusions about the size, nature, and value of the assets listed, look at relative proportions, and judge whether the company has a viable asset base. Clues such as high accumulated depreciation relative to recorded property, plant, and equipment may suggest that aging facilities are in need of upgrading. Similarly, a significant jump in cash balances might suggest lagging new investments and an accumulation of excess funds. Surges in working capital items like inventories and receivables might signal problems with inventory management or customer credit policies.

In a more overall sense, a few ratios are used to judge broad trends in resource utilization. Such ratios essentially involve turnover relationships and express, in various forms, the relative amount of capital used to support the volume of business transacted.

Asset Turnover

The most commonly used ratios relate sales to gross assets, or sales to net assets. The measure indicates the size of the recorded asset commitment required to support a particular level of sales or, conversely, the sales dollars generated by each dollar of assets.

While simple to calculate, overall asset turnover is a crude measure at best, because the balance sheets of most well-established companies list a whole variety of assets recorded at widely differing cost levels of past periods. These stated values often have little relation to current economic values, and the distortions grow with time, with any significant change in the level of inflation, or with the appreciation of assets such as real estate. Such discrepancies in values can attract corporate raiders intent on realizing true economic values through the breakup and selective disposal of the company, as we'll discuss in Chapter 12.

Another distortion is caused by a company's mix of product or service lines. Most manufacturing activities tend to be asset-intensive, while others, like services or wholesaling, need relatively fewer assets to support the volume of revenues generated. Again, wherever possible, a breakdown of total financial data into major product or service lines should be attempted when a company has widely different businesses.

Basically, the turnover ratio serves as one of several clues that, in combination, can indicate favorable or unfavorable performance. If total assets are used for the purpose of averaging the beginning and ending amounts for the year, the calculation for TRW's turnover ratios appears as follows:

$$\text{Sales to assets: } \frac{\text{Sales}}{\text{Average total assets}} = \frac{\$10,831}{.5(\$5,899 + \$6,410)}$$

or
$$= 1.76 \text{ times (1996: 1.70)}$$

$$\text{Assets to sales: } \frac{\text{Average total assets}}{\text{Sales}} = \frac{\$6,154}{\$10,831} = 57\% \text{ (1996: 59\%)}$$

If net assets (total assets less current liabilities, representing the capitalization of the business) are used, the calculations are either:

$$\text{Sales to net assets: } \frac{\text{Sales}}{\text{Average net assets}} = \frac{\$10,831}{.5(\$3,742 + \$3,691)}$$

$$= 2.91 \text{ times (1996: 2.61)}$$

or

$$\text{Net assets to sales: } \frac{\text{Average net assets}}{\text{Sales}} = \frac{\$3,716}{\$10,831} = 34\% \text{ (1996: 38\%)}$$

The difference between the two sets of calculations lies in the choice of the asset figure, that is, whether to use total assets or net assets. Using net assets eliminates current liabilities from the ratio. Here the assumption is that current liabilities, which are mostly operational in nature (accounts payable, current taxes due, current repayments of short-term debt, and accrued wages and other obligations), are available to the business as a matter of course. Therefore, the amount of assets employed in the business is effectively reduced by these ongoing operational credit relationships. This concept is especially important for trading firms, where the size of accounts payable owed suppliers is quite significant in the total balance sheet.

Again TRW provided some additional information in its published data, indicating the turnover of identifiable assets in its two major businesses. The automotive segment had a turnover of 1.6 times (1.8 in 1996), while the space, defense, and information systems segment had results of 2.5 times and 2.8 times, respectively.

Working Capital Management

Among the assets of a company, the key working capital accounts, inventories and accounts receivable, are usually given special attention. The ratios used to analyze them attempt to express the relative effectiveness with which inventories and receivables are managed. They aid the analyst in detecting signs of deterioration in value, or excessive accumulation of inventories and receivables. The amounts as stated on the balance sheet are generally related to the single best indicator of activity levels, such as sales or cost of sales (cost of goods sold), on the assumption that a reasonably close relationship exists between assets and the indicator.

Inventory levels cannot be judged precisely, short of an actual count, verification, and appraisal of current value. Since an outside analyst can rarely do this, the next best step is to relate the recorded inventory value to sales or to cost of goods sold, to see whether there is a shift in this relationship over time. Normally, *average* inventories are used to make this calculation (the average of beginning and ending inventories). At times, it might be desirable to use only ending inventories, especially in the case of rapidly growing firms where inventories are being built up to support steeply rising sales.

Furthermore, it's necessary to closely observe the method of inventory costing employed by the company—such as last-in, first-out (LIFO), first-in, first-out (FIFO), average costing—and any changes made during the time span covered by the analysis, as these can significantly affect the amounts recorded on the balance sheet. (We'll discuss inventory costing and other key accounting issues later.)

While the simple relationship of sales and inventories will often suffice as a broad measure of performance, it's usually more precise to relate inventories to the cost of sales. Only then will both elements of the ratio be stated on a comparable cost basis. Using sales causes a distortion, because recorded sales include a profit markup that is not included in the stated cost of the inventories on the balance sheet.

The difference in the two methods of calculating the size of inventory relative to sales or cost of sales is reflected in the equations below:

$$\text{Inventory to sales: } \frac{\text{Average inventory}}{\text{Sales}} = \frac{.5(\$573 + \$524)}{\$10,831} = 5.1\% \ (1996\text{: } 5.3\%)$$

or

$$\text{Inventory to cost of sales: } \frac{\text{Average inventory}}{\text{Cost of sales}} = \frac{\$548}{\$8,826} = 6.2\% \ (1996\text{: } 6.3\%)$$

In the sample calculations, we've used total TRW sales and total cost of goods and services. The fact that TRW has two rather different major businesses and numerous product lines within each again suggests that a more refined analysis is desirable. TRW's inventories essentially relate to materials and manufactured products of the automotive and the space, defense, and information systems segments. Given the different nature of the two businesses, it would be useful to develop separate ratios for each, if detailed inventory information were available to the outsider.

When dealing with any manufacturing company, we also must be particularly aware of the problem of accounting measurements—so often encountered when using other analytical methods—because the stated value of inventories can be seriously affected by the specific cost accounting system employed.

In assessing the effectiveness of a company's inventory management, it's more common to use the number of times inventory has turned over during the period of analysis, again using average amounts.

The TRW inventory turnover figures appear as follows:

$$\text{Inventory turnover} \over \text{(Sales)} \cdot \frac{\text{Sales}}{\text{Average inventory}} = \frac{\$10,831}{\$548}$$

$$= 19.8 \text{ times (1996: 18.7 times)}$$

or

$$\text{Inventory turnover} \over \text{(Cost of sales)} \cdot \frac{\text{Cost of sales}}{\text{Average inventory}} = \frac{\$8,826}{\$548}$$

$$= 16.1 \text{ times (1996: 15.9 times)}$$

These calculations reflect the frequency with which the inventory was turned over during the operating period. In TRW's case, turnover remained relatively high due to a combination of inventory management and a change in the mix of products. Generally speaking, the higher the turnover number the better, because low inventories often suggest a minimal risk of non-salable goods and indicate efficient use of capital. Electronic linkages have materially improved turnover in recent years.

However, inventory turnover figures that are well above prevailing industry practice might signal the potential for inventory shortages, resultant poor customer service, and thus the risk of suffering a competitive disadvantage. The final judgment about what a desirable turnover goal should be depends on the specific circumstances and on a much finer breakdown of inventory data into separate businesses and product lines.

The analysis of *accounts receivable* again is based on sales. Here, the question is whether accounts receivable outstanding at the end of the period closely approximate the amount of credit sales we would expect to remain uncollected under prevailing credit terms. For example, a business selling under terms of net/30 would normally expect an accounts receivable balance approximating the recorded sales of the prior month. If 40 or 50 days' sales were reflected on its balance sheet, this could mean that some customers had difficulty paying or were abusing their credit privileges, or that some sales had to be made on extended terms.

An exact analysis of accounts receivable can only be made by examining the *aging* of the individual accounts recorded on the company's books. Aging involves classifying accounts receivable into brackets of days outstanding, 10 days, 20 days, 30 days, 40 days, and so on, and relating this pattern to the credit terms applicable in the business. Since this type of analysis requires access to detailed inside information about individual customer accounts, financial analysts assessing the business from the outside must be satisfied with the relatively crude overall approach of restating accounts receivable outstanding in terms of the number of days' sales they represent.

This is done in the following two steps, using TRW's figures:

$$(1) \text{ Sales per day: } \frac{\text{Sales}}{\text{Days in the year}} = \frac{\$10,831}{360} = \$30.09/\text{day (1996: } \$27.38/\text{day)}$$

and

$$(2) \text{ Days outstanding: } \frac{\text{Accounts receivable}}{\text{Sales per day}} = \frac{\$1,617}{\$30.09}$$

$$= 53.7 \text{ days (1996: 50.3 days)}$$

TRW is showing a slowdown in the turnover of its total receivables from the prior year, which was in part affected by the impact of the recent acquisition.

A complication arises when a company's sales are normally made to different types of customers under varying terms, or when sales are made partly for cash and partly on account. If at all possible, cash and credit sales should be separated. If no detailed information is available on this aspect and on the terms of sale used, the rough average calculated above must suffice to provide a broad indication of trends.

A similar process can be used to judge a company's performance regarding the management of *accounts payable*. The analysis is a little more complicated, because accounts payable should be related specifically to the purchases made during the operating period. Normally purchase information is not readily available to the outside analyst, except in the case of trading companies, where the amount of purchases can be readily deduced by adding the change from beginning to ending inventories to the cost of goods sold for the period. In a manufacturing company, purchases of goods and services are buried in the cost-of-goods-sold account and in the inventories at the end of the operating period. We can make a crude approximation in such cases by relating accounts payable to the average daily use of raw materials, if this expense element can be identified from the available information.

In most cases, we can follow the approach used for analyzing accounts receivable, if it's possible to approximate the average daily purchases for the period. The number of days of accounts payable is then directly related to the normal credit terms under which the company makes purchases, and serious deviations from that norm can be spotted.

Optimal management of accounts payable involves remitting payment within the stated terms, but no sooner—yet taking discounts whenever offered for early payment, such as 2 percent if paid in 10 days versus remitting the full amount due in 30 days. Credit rating agencies can be a source of information to the analyst because they will express an opinion on the timeliness with which a company is meeting its credit obligations, including accounts payable.

The ultimate issue in interpreting working capital conditions is the flow of cash through the business, as we discussed in detail in Chapter 2. Over time, all working capital elements are converted into cash, and the analyst must assess the nature and quality of the company's cash conversion cycle. Excessive lags in receivables and payables, and a steady buildup in inventories, for example, can significantly affect the normal cash conversion patterns and lead to distortions in the company's financial system performance.

Human resource effectiveness has been gaining increased attention in recent years. Ratios used in measuring this complex area often go beyond purely financial relationships, and are based on carefully developed statistics on output data, such as various productivity indicators, call volume for sales personnel, deliveries completed, etc. They also extend to managing human resources, such as costs of employment, training, and development, and the complex issue of compensation and benefits administration. Examples of broad measures, per employee, are units of output, dollars of investment, costs of hiring and training, benefits costs, and so on. In TRW's case, the company published overall employee-related data, based on employee totals of 79,726 at the end of 1997 (65,218 in 1996); sales per average employee were $159,528 ($154,274 in 1996); earnings from continuing operations per average employee were $7,350 ($6,793); and year-end assets per year-end employee were $80,400 ($90,450).

Profitability

Here the issue is the effectiveness with which management has employed both the total assets and the net assets as recorded on the balance sheet. This is judged by relating net profit, defined in a variety of ways, to the resources utilized in generating the profit, for the company as a whole or for any of its parts. The relationship is used quite commonly, although the nature and timing of the stated values on the balance sheet and the accounting aspects of recorded profit will again tend to distort the results. As we'll see later, the approach can be refined to reflect the cash flow concepts underlying shareholder value creation.

Return on Assets (ROA or RONA)

The easiest form of profitability analysis is to relate reported net profit (net income) to the total assets on the balance sheet. Net assets (total assets less current liabilities) might also be used, with the argument (already mentioned earlier) that current operating liabilities are available essentially without cost to support a portion of the current assets. Net assets are also called the *capitalization* of the company, or *invested capital*, representing the portion of the total assets supported by equity and long-term debt. Whether total or net assets are employed, it's also appropriate to use *average* assets for the period, instead of ending balances. Using average assets allows for changes due to growth, decline, or other significant influences on the business.

The calculations for both forms of return on assets for TRW, in this case using ending balances, appear as follows:

$$\text{Return on total assets: } \frac{\text{Net profit}}{\text{Assets}} = \frac{\$499}{\$6,410}$$

$$= 7.8\% \ (1996: 7.4\%)$$

or

$$\text{Return on net assets: } \frac{\text{Net profit}}{\text{Net assets}} = \frac{\$499}{\$6,410 - \$2,719} = 13.5\% \text{ (1996: 11.6\%)}$$
(capitalization)

While either ratio is an indicator of overall profitability, the results can be seriously distorted by nonrecurring gains and losses during the period, changes in the company's capital structure (the relative proportions of interest-bearing long-term debt and owners' equity), significant restructuring and acquisitions, and changes in the federal income tax regulations applicable for the period analyzed. It's usually desirable to make further adjustments if some of these conditions prevail, and in this case we again have used the earnings from ongoing operations before the adjustments for purchased research and development and discontinued operations. Note that the use of reported earnings would cause a negative return for 1997, and a lower figure for 1996.

Return on Assets before Interest and Taxes

As we stated before, net profit (net income or net earnings) is the final operating result after interest and taxes have been deducted. It's therefore affected by the proportion of debt contained in the capital structure through the resultant interest charges that were deducted from profit before taxes. A more meaningful result can be obtained when we eliminate both interest and taxes from the profit figure and use EBIT (earnings before interest and taxes), which was demonstrated earlier. Moreover, it will again be useful to eliminate any significant unusual or nonrecurring income and expense items. The revised return ratio expresses the gross earnings power of the capital employed in the business, independent of the pattern of financing that provided the capital, and independent of changes in the tax laws.

The calculation of return on assets before interest and taxes, based on average assets, is as follows for TRW:

Return on average total assets before interest and taxes:

$$\frac{\text{Net profit before interest and taxes (EBIT)}}{\text{Average assets}} = \frac{\$863}{\$6,154} = 14.0\% \text{ (1996: 13.3\%)}$$

or

Return on average net assets before interest and taxes:

$$\frac{\text{Net profit before interest and taxes (EBIT)}}{\text{Average net assets (capitalization)}} = \frac{\$863}{\$3,716} = 23.2\% \text{ (1996: 20.5\%)}$$

If we accept the argument that income taxes are a normal part of doing business, this result can be modified by using net profit before interest but after taxes. We can again employ the simple adjustment shown earlier to add back to net profit the after-tax cost of interest and the after-tax effect of any nonrecurring income and expense items.

When there is reason to believe that income taxes paid were modified for any reason and the effective tax rate does not reflect normal conditions, the marginal income tax rate should be used to calculate the net effect of interest and other items added back by determining the earnings before interest, after taxes (EBIAT).

The calculations for TRW are as follows:

Return on average total assets before interest, after taxes:

$$\frac{\text{Net profit after taxes, before interest}}{\text{Average assets}} = \frac{\$546}{\$6,154} = 8.9\% \ (1996: 8.4\%)$$

or

Return on average net assets before interest, after taxes:

$$\frac{\text{Net profit after taxes, before interest}}{\text{Average net assets (capitalization)}} = \frac{\$546}{\$3,716} = 14.7\% \ (1996: 12.9\%)$$

Note that the results of the last two sets of more refined calculations show a moderate change in TRW's overall effectiveness of asset utilization, as did the first calculation, which was based on net profit alone. Again, it would be useful to break down these results into major product lines, but in most cases there's not enough information to make all the adjustments from published data.

Another refinement used at times is the relationship of profit, defined in the various ways we have described, to the net assets of the business restated on a *current value* basis. This requires a series of very specific assumptions about the true economic value of various assets or business segments of a company, and it is employed particularly by analysts developing a case for the takeover of a company that might be underperforming on this basis. The Financial Accounting Standards Board (FASB) is engaged in developing new rules that are designed to take some changes in value into account, which are already being applied to certain financial investments held by banks and other financial institutions.

A relatively recent measure of profitability that is finding wide use is the concept of *economic profit,* or *economic value added* (EVA). It is based on the premise that to create shareholder value, the profits earned on the resources employed must exceed the cost of the capital that supports these resources. In its simplest form, economic profit is derived by subtracting from after-tax operating profits a capital charge which represents this cost of capital. To arrive at the capital charge, it's necessary first to define the asset base involved, which usually is net assets (with some adjustments to arrive at net operating assets), and second, to derive the weighted cost of capital of the company's capital structure (discussed in detail in Chapter 9). Then the asset base is multiplied by the cost of capital percentage, and the result is subtracted from after-tax operating profits. If the net amount is positive, value has been created; if it's negative, value has been destroyed. We'll explore this concept in more detail in Chapter 12.

As we'll discuss in Chapters 7 and 8, profitability also depends on the economic analysis and successful implementation of new investment projects. Here it's critical to define and develop the relevant cash flow changes brought about by the investment decision, and to judge the results through an economic appraisal process based on discounted cash flow techniques. In recent years, this methodology has been expanded to measure the *cash flow return on investment* on both existing and new investments, in effect treating the company as a whole or its major parts as if they were a series of investment projects. This calls for a number of specialized techniques, and we will return to this subject when we discuss valuation concepts in Chapters 11 and 12.

The concept of *free cash flow* also will be discussed in Chapter 12. It's the basis for cash flow valuation techniques that help establish the value of a company or its parts. In its simplest form, free cash flow is the net amount of (1) reported profit, adjusted for depreciation, depletion, and other noncash accounting elements, less (2) net new investment in facilities and net acquisitions, and plus or minus (3) changes in working capital. Free cash flow comes closest to a cash-in, cash-out concept of performance, and is used in valuing current and prospective cash flow as the driver of a company's value.

In summary, the various ratios available for judging a business from management's point of view deal with the effectiveness of operations, the effectiveness of capital deployment, and the profitability achieved on the assets deployed. These measures are all affected to some degree by uncertainties involving accounting and valuation methods, but together they can provide reasonable clues to a firm's performance, and suggest areas for further analysis.

Owners' Point of View

We now turn to the second of the three viewpoints relevant in analyzing performance, that of the owners of a business. These are the investors to whom management is responsible and accountable. It should be quite clear that the management of a business must be fully cognizant of, and responsive to, the owners' viewpoint and their expectations in the timing, execution, and appraisal of the results of operations. This is the basis for shareholder value creation, as we've said before. Similarly, as we'll learn, management must be alert to the lender's viewpoint and criteria.

The key interest of the owners of a business—the shareholders in the case of a corporation—is investment return. In this context, we are talking about the returns achieved, through the efforts of management, on the funds invested by the owners. The owners are also interested in the disposition of earnings that belong to them; that is, how much is reinvested in the business compared to how much is paid out to them as dividends, or, in some cases, through repurchase of outstanding shares. Finally, they are concerned about the effect of business results achieved—and future expectations about results—on the market value of their investment, especially in the case of publicly traded stock. The key concepts related to this last aspect are discussed in detail in Chapters 10 and 11; therefore we'll make only brief reference to them here.

Investment Return

The relationship of profits earned to the shareholders' stated investment in a company is watched closely by the financial community. Analysts track several key measures that express the company's performance in relation to the owners' stake. Two of these, return on shareholders' investment and return on common equity, address the profitability of the total ownership investment, while the third, earnings per share, measures the proportional participation of each unit of investment in corporate earnings for the period.

Return on Equity (Shareholders' Investment)
The most common ratio used for measuring the return on the owners' investment is the relationship of net profit to equity, or total shareholders' investment. In performing this calculation, we don't have to make any adjustment for interest, because the net profit available for shareholders already has been properly reduced by interest charges, if any, paid to creditors and lenders. However, we do have to consider the impact of nonrecurring and unusual events, such as restructuring and major accounting changes and adjustments.

Net profit for purposes of this calculation is the residual result of operations and belongs totally to the holders of common and preferred equity shares. Within the shareholder group, only those holding common shares have a claim on the residual profit after obligatory preferred dividends have been paid.

The ratio is calculated for TRW's shareholders' investment as follows, again using only earnings from continuing operations:

$$\text{Return on equity: } \frac{\text{Net profit}}{\text{Shareholders' investment}} = \frac{\$499}{\$1,624} = 30.7\% \text{ (1996: 19.8\%)}$$

Here we have used TRW's ending shareholders' investment. It's quite common, however, to use the average equity for this calculation, on the assumption that profitable operations build up equity during the year, and that therefore the annual profit should be related to the midpoint of this buildup. Moreover, in TRW's case, significant changes in shareholder investment were brought about by the two acquisitions, stock repurchases, and currency effects in 1997, lowering the balance by about $500 million.

The ratio for TRW is calculated as follows:

Return on average equity:

$$\frac{\text{Net profit}}{\text{Average shareholders' investment}} = \frac{\$499}{.5(\$1,624 + \$2,189)}$$
$$= 26.2\% \text{ (1996: 19.9\%)}$$

A possible accounting distortion must be mentioned here. Frequently, questions arise about the way a particular liability account on the balance sheet, "deferred taxes," should be handled in this analysis. Less frequently, there is even a deferred taxes account on the asset side of the balance sheet. As we mentioned before, deferred taxes represent the accumulated difference between the accounting treatment and the tax treatment of a variety of revenue and expense elements. Essentially, they are tax payments deferred (or advanced) due to a timing difference in recognizing tax deductions allowable under prevailing Internal Revenue Service (IRS) rules.

In addition, a larger similar issue involves so-called long-term liabilities, which are generally shown before interest-bearing long-term debt on the liability side of the balance sheet. These growing amounts ($788 million and $767 million in the case of TRW) mostly represent the results of changes in accounting rules designed to establish estimated liabilities—and corresponding reductions in equity—for such obligations as postretirement benefits, previously paid as incurred. Such liabilities are noninterest-bearing estimates, and in effect, represent permanent set-asides of portions of the shareholder's investment.

Some analysts argue that such liabilities should be treated as equity, while others argue that they represent a form of long-term debt. Since there is no consensus on the analytical treatment, deferred income taxes and long-term liabilities often are not included in any of the ratio calculations. However, because their combined accumulation on the liability side of the balance sheet might be quite large, material differences can result depending on how they are considered in the calculations.

Return on Common Equity (ROE)

A somewhat more refined version of the calculation of return on the shareholders' investment is necessary if there are several types of stock outstanding, such as preferred stock in different forms. The goal is to develop a return based on earnings accruing to the holders of common shares only. The net profit figure is first reduced by dividends paid to holders of preferred shares and by other obligatory payments, such as distributions to holders of minority interests. The total equity is likewise reduced by the stated amount of preferred equity and any minority elements, to arrive at the common equity figure. TRW in effect has only common stock outstanding, since its Serial Preference Stock II is reflected at the very nominal value of just $1.0 million. Thus, we'll show only the formula for the calculation, because the results will be the same:

$$\text{Return on common equity: } \frac{\text{Net profit to common}}{\text{Average common equity}} = \text{Percent}$$

Return on common equity is a widely published statistic. Rankings of companies and industry sectors are compiled by major business magazines and rating agencies. The ratio is closely watched by stock market analysts and, in turn, by management and the board of directors. Since the ratio focuses only on the ownership portion of the capital structure, however, the ROE of companies with widely different proportions of long-term debt in their capital structure is not directly comparable. As we observed before, successful use of leverage will boost the owners' return and make it higher than that of an otherwise identical company that uses no debt. Moreover, the accuracy of recorded balance sheet values and earnings calculations is an issue in this ratio as well, and adjustments might be necessary if the analyst is aware of major inconsistencies. Such inconsistencies could include assets with sizable economic values that are not reflected on the balance sheet and thereby leave owners' equity understated.

Finally, there is the basic issue of using book value versus market value. Since recorded common equity is the residual value of all accounting transactions and adjustments, the value shown on the balance sheet is generally quite different from the market value of the shares representing it. In publicly traded companies with successful operations and outlook, the market value of common shares will be much higher than the book value of these shares, often two to three times or even more. When return on common equity is calculated on a market value basis, the result will therefore tend to be proportionately lower. Therefore, despite the widespread use of return on equity on a book value basis, the measure is certainly not a reflection of the economic return to the shareholder. We'll discuss these issues in more detail when we return to valuation and value-based management in Chapter 12.

Earnings per Share

The analysis of earnings from the owners' point of view usually centers on earnings per share in the case of a corporation. This ratio simply involves dividing the net profit to common stock by the average number of shares of common stock outstanding:

Earnings per share:

$$\frac{\text{Net profit to common}}{\text{Average number of shares outstanding}} = \text{Dollars per share}$$

Earnings per share is a measure to which both management and shareholders pay a great deal of attention. It is widely used in the valuation of common stock, and often is the basis for setting specific corporate objectives and goals as part of strategic planning. Yet, the rise of shareholder value concepts during the past decade has been causing a reassessment of the importance of earnings per share which, as a pure accounting measure, does not adequately reflect cash flow performance and expectations that drive shareholder value creation. Chapters 10, 11, and 12 contain more background on the uses and limitations of this measure. Normally, the analyst doesn't have to calculate earnings per share because the result is readily announced by corporations large and small.

In TRW's 1997 annual report, earnings per share from continuing operations before special charges and write-offs were reported as $4.03 for 1997, and

$3.27 for 1996 (see Figure 4–3). Earnings per share are available on both an annual and a quarterly basis, and are a matter of record whenever a company's shares are publicly traded.

A recent requirement by the Financial Accounting Standards Board and the Securities and Exchange Commission calls for the calculation of earnings per share on two bases: The first is the so-called *basic* earnings per share, which uses average shares actually outstanding during the period. The second basis makes the assumption that all shares potentially outstanding be counted in addition to actual shares outstanding. These would include shares resulting from the conversion of preferred and debt securities that are convertible into common shares under various provisions, as well as rights, warrants, and stock options outstanding.

The second result is referred to as *diluted* earnings per share, and reflects the reduced earnings per share that would result from any overhang of such potential shares—putting the investment community on notice that such a dilutive effect is possible. In TRW's case, there is no significant potential dilution, and diluted earnings per share before special charges and write-offs are practically identical to basic earnings in both years, as can be seen in Figure 4–3.

Even though the earnings per share figure is one of the most readily available statistics reported by publicly held corporations, there are some complications in its calculation. Apart from possible unusual elements in the quarterly and annual net profit pattern, the number of shares outstanding varies during the year in many companies, either because of newly issued shares (new stock offerings, stock dividends paid, options exercised, and so on), or because outstanding existing shares are repurchased (acquired as treasury stock). Therefore, the *average* number of shares outstanding during the year is commonly used in this calculation. Moreover, any significant change in the number of shares outstanding (such as would be caused by a stock split) requires retroactive adjustments in past data to ensure comparability.

A great deal of interest among analysts is focused on past earnings per share, both quarterly and annual. Future projections are frequently made on the basis of past earnings levels. Fluctuations and trends in actual performance are compared to the projections and watched closely for indications of strength or weakness. Again, great caution is advised in interpreting these data. Allowances must be made for unusual elements both in the earnings figure and in the number of common shares outstanding. As we pointed out earlier, however, the importance of earnings per share is waning relative to the use of cash-flow-based performance and valuation measures, which will be discussed in more detail in Chapter 12.

Cash Flow per Share

Representing a calculation to approximate the cash flow per share from operating results this figure is frequently used as a very rough indicator of the company's ability to pay cash dividends. It's developed from the net profit figure to which accounting write-offs such as depreciation, amortization, and depletion have been added back. We recall from our earlier discussion of the cash flow statement that such write-offs do not represent cash movements. Adding back these bookkeeping entries restates the net profit in a form that partially reflects the cash generated by operations, but leaves out many other significant funds movements, such as changes in working capital, investments in new assets, and so on.

The calculation parallels the earnings per share ratio:

Cash flow per share:

$$\frac{\text{Net profit to common plus write-offs}}{\text{Average number of shares outstanding}} = \text{Dollars per share}$$

In the case of TRW, we know that depreciation and amortization amounted to $480 million and $10 million, respectively. The average number of shares outstanding was given in the annual report as 123.7 million for purposes of calculating basic earnings per share. Write-offs thus amounted to $3.96 per share, which when added to basic earnings per share of $4.03, results in a cash flow per share from continuing operations of $7.99 in 1997, and $6.80 in 1996.

Since the use of all funds in a business is largely at the discretion of management, this limited cash flow per share concept is at best only a crude indication of the potential to pay dividends. A more extensive analysis of overall cash flows is required to judge the total pattern of sources and uses, including dividend payments, as demonstrated in Chapter 3.

Share Price Appreciation

Apart from current earnings generated for the shareholders, some of which will be received as dividends, investors expect an appreciation in the value of their common shares in the stock market over time. The main driver for this appreciation is the creation of additional economic value by management, that is, the generation of more positive cash flows than outlays in the long run through the combined effect of sound investment, operating, and financing decisions. We'll discuss shareholder value creation more fully in Chapter 12, but suffice it to say that the analyst will look for movement in the share prices that at least matches and hopefully outperforms the trend in the stock market as a whole. Similarly, the performance trend of particular business segments in a large company will be related to the share price trends of relevant composites of comparable companies.

Total Shareholder Return (TSR)

The return achieved by investors holding shares in a company is a combination of share price appreciation (or decline) and cash dividends received over appropriate time periods selected for analysis. Since usually only part of the earnings belonging to shareholders is paid out in the form of dividends, the relevant positive inflow to the shareholder is the stream of dividends received, not the announced earnings per share. The full economic benefit received by the shareholder is the sum of this stream of dividends plus any change in the price of the stock. The calculation simply involves taking the market price of stock at the beginning of the period, summing the quarterly dividends for the period, determining the change in price at the end of the period, and calculating the annualized return this pattern represents on the initial market price (the present value techniques of Chapter 7 are helpful in this process).

The results of this process are published annually in the spring by *Fortune* magazine for publicly held companies in the Fortune 500 listings. The previous year's TSR and the annual rate of TSR for the prior ten-year period is provided for companies in each major segment. TRW was listed among 37 companies in the motor vehicles and parts segment, even though a large portion of its operations involve space and defense and information services. Its TSR for 1997 was 10 percent (31 percent for 1996), while the more meaningful long-term return from 1987 to 1997 was 12 percent (13 percent for 1986 to 1996). Comparable figures for the median of the segment were 37 percent for 1997 (16 percent for 1996), and 14 percent for the decade (11 percent for 1986 to 1996). Median figures for 13 aerospace companies were 20 percent for 1997 (32 percent for 1996), and 21 percent for the decade (16 percent for 1986 to 1996).

The TSR concept is critical to assessing the relative performance of a company within the market as a whole, compared with its peers, and within broad industry groupings. We'll again discuss TSR in relation to shareholder value analysis in Chapter 12.

Disposition of Earnings

The periodic split of earnings (net profit) into dividends paid and earnings retained for reinvestment is watched closely by shareholders and the financial community, because of the trade-off between cash leaving the financial system and the retained residual, which builds up the owners' equity and is a source of funds for management's use. The trade-off amounts to giving value directly to the shareholders as part of TSR, versus reinvesting the funds for future value creation. This is not an either/or proposition, however, because dividend policy is hardly ever changed abruptly. Instead, the board of directors usually considers whether dividends should be increased incrementally as earnings grow, focusing on the stability of the dividend record which shareholders can expect from the company. Only in dire circumstances will the dividend be reduced or omitted.

Cash dividends are the most common form of payment, although stock dividends are also frequently used. In the latter case, no cash is involved. Instead, additional shares are issued to the holder in proportion to the shares owned. If a regular cash dividend is paid as well, stock dividends will, in the end, result in fractionally higher cash dividends.

Dividends per Share

Dividends are generally declared on a per share basis every quarter by a corporation's board of directors, the elected representatives of the shareholders. Therefore no calculation is necessary. Dividend policy is the prerogative of the board, which has legal authority to set payments at any level it deems appropriate. Since the market value of common stock is partially influenced by both dividends paid and dividends anticipated, the board generally deals with this periodic decision carefully. Dividends are declared each quarter and paid subsequently on a specified date, which can lead to slight differences between the dividends declared and those actually paid in a given year. TRW Inc. paid common dividends of $1.24 per share in 1997 and $1.135 in 1996 (versus declared dividends of $1.24 and $1.17, respectively).

Dividend Yield

Annual dividends paid per share can be related to current or average share prices to derive the dividend yield:

$$\text{Dividend yield:} \frac{\text{Annual dividend per share}}{\text{Average market price per share}} = \text{Percent}$$

This is a measure of the return on the owners' investment from cash dividends alone. In the case of TRW, the 52-week range of stock prices from January 1997 to December 1997 was 61.19 to 47.38, with an average of approximately 54.25. The dividend yield at $1.24 per share thus amounts to 2.3 percent on the average price. This ratio falls short as a basis for comparison with other companies, however, because dividend policies differ widely. As we stated earlier, the more important measure is TSR, a combination of dividends and market appreciation (or decline) of the stock.

Payout/Retention

A ratio commonly used in connection with dividend policy is the so-called payout ratio, which represents the proportion of earnings paid out to the shareholders in the form of cash during any given year:

$$\text{Payout ratio:} \frac{\text{Cash dividend per share}}{\text{Earnings per share}} = \frac{\$1.24}{\$4.03} = 30.8\% \ (1996: 34.5\%)$$

Because most boards of directors tend to favor paying a fairly stable dividend per share, adjusted only gradually, the payout ratio of a company might fluctuate widely in the short run in response to swings in earnings performance. Over a period of several years, however, the payout ratio can often be used to indicate the tendency of directors to reinvest funds in the business versus paying out earnings to the shareholders.

There are no firm standards for this ratio, but the relationship is significant in characterizing the style of the corporation. High-growth companies tend to pay out relatively low proportions of earnings because they prefer to reinvest earnings to support profitable growth. Stable or moderate-growth companies tend to pay out larger proportions. Some companies pay no cash dividends at all, or provide stock dividends only. Many more factors must, of course, be considered in making judgments in this area. The reader is directed to the references at the end of this chapter for further insight into both concepts and practices.

Dividend Coverage

Owners are also interested in the degree to which their dividends are covered by earnings and cash flow. Furthermore, they are concerned about the degree to which the proportion of debt in the capital structure and its associated interest and repayment requirements will affect management's ability to achieve reasonably stable and growing earnings, and to pay dividends commensurate with the owners' expectations. A variety of coverage ratios can be calculated, but they hardly differ from the ones we'll take up in the discussion of the lender's point of view.

Dividends to Assets

Finally, it is sometimes useful to relate the annual dividends paid by a company to the total assets or net assets involved in generating them. The rationale is similar to the dividend yield discussed earlier, except that in this case, it's not the market value of the shares, but the book value of the assets they represent, which is used as the denominator. It can be argued that market valuation is a more current indicator for the yield relationship than the historical basis of the asset values as recorded on the balance sheet. Nevertheless, dividends to assets is at times found as part of an analytical set of performance data.

Market Indicators

We'll briefly mention two ratios which are commonly used as indicators of stock market values: the price/earnings ratio and the market-to-book ratio. The subject of market valuation will be covered in more detail in Chapters 11 and 12.

Price/Earnings Ratio

The simple relationship between current or expected earnings per share and the current market price of the stock is often quoted by both management and owners. The ratio also is called the earnings multiple, and it is used as a broad indicator of how the stock market is judging the company's earnings performance and prospects. The calculation is quite straightforward, and relates current market prices of common shares to the most recent available earnings per share on an annual basis:

$$\text{Earnings multiple (Price/earnings ratio):} \frac{\text{Market price per share}}{\text{Earnings per share}} = \text{Factor}$$

The result is a simple factor. If diluted earnings differ significantly from basic earnings per share, the calculation can be done on both bases. The earnings multiple is used quite commonly as a rough rule of thumb in valuing companies for purposes of acquisition to arrive at a first approximation of value.

Earnings multiples vary widely by industry and by company, and are, in effect, a simple overall approximation of the market's current judgment of industry and company risk versus past and prospective earnings performance. They are tracked by various investor services and related to total market averages, as well as to average price earnings multiples for selected industry groups, to assess the relative performance of a particular company. Earnings multiples will tend to be higher in emerging industries, such as high technology companies or Internet-based firms, than in more established industries, such as public utilities or basic manufacturing. The reason for this divergence lies in the collective expectations of the market about the ability of an industry to achieve superior growth, technological breakthroughs with above average earnings, cash flow potential, and other ways of achieving shareholder returns well above average through sustainable differentiation. The same is true for individual companies in their respective industry classifications—standouts like innovative Wal-Mart within the mature retailing field come to mind.

The reverse of the earnings per share formula is the so-called earnings yield, which relates earnings per share to the market price. Although it is sometimes used to express the current yield the owner enjoys, the measure can be misleading, because earnings are not normally paid out in full as dividends. Thus, the earnings yield cannot be compared to, for example, the yield on a bond where interest payments are contractual cash remittances. As we already know, the real economic return to the shareholder is a combination of the dividends received and the appreciation (decline) of the stock.

Cash Flow Multiples

A variant of relating current earnings performance to current market value is the use of cash flow per share, as discussed earlier, where we learned that TRW's cash flow per share in 1997 was $7.99. Usually the definition of cash flow for this purpose is after-tax profit plus depreciation and amortization, divided by the average number of shares outstanding. We know from the discussion in Chapter 3 that this represents only a limited view of the actual cash generation of the business, but the measure is widely used and quoted as a rule of thumb that relates this definition of operating cash flow to share values.

Market-to-Book Ratio

This indicator relates current market value on a per share basis to the stated book value of owners' equity on the balance sheet, also on a per share basis. TRW's December 31, 1997, book value per share was $13.19, while the average market value for 1997 at $54.25 was more than four times this figure. The market-to-book ratio leaves much to be desired as a measure of performance for many of the reasons mentioned in earlier discussions of other ratios. It's not an economic measure of performance, because it relates market values to stated historical accounting values, which are further affected by equity set-asides and similar accounting effects. In addition, while in a given company the relationship between stated balance sheet values and market values might be favorable, the ratio doesn't truly help the analyst judge what the comparable expectations for other firms should be. Thus, the measure is only a beginning step in the appraisal of long-term performance and outlook.

Relative Price Movements

While the typical investor is interested in the absolute change in the value of the shares held, the insights from the relative performance of the stock to the market as a whole and to appropriate averages for specific industries can be useful in assessing the trend of a particular company. As we'll discuss in Chapter 12, targeting for shareholder value creation is often based on relative price performance as one of the measures used. Price movements can be expressed in absolute dollar terms, or in several of the ratios mentioned above. In view of the growing importance of cash flow thinking, fueled by the acquisition and leveraged buyout boom of the past decade, services like Value Line provide trends in cash flow multiples as an additional indicator of relative price movements.

Value Drivers

An approach that has gained increased recognition in recent years is the identification of key elements that stand out as significant in the creation of shareholder value of a specific company. From the owners' standpoint, key value drivers might be the growth potential of key products or services of the company, key technology capabilities that provide a competitive advantage, superior cost-effectiveness in its processes, or differentiated strategic positioning. All of these affect the market's expectations about the future success and cash flow generation potential of the company. Clearly, these and many more narrowly defined value drivers, which may be specific operational ratios, have to be developed and managed by the organization, and are part of an integrated value-based management process, as we'll discuss in Chapter 12.

Value of the Firm

This is a common concept which recognizes that the two main components of a company's capital structure, equity and debt, are valued separately in the marketplace. At any time, the market value of the firm is the sum of the market values of its shares and its debt:

$$VF = VS + VD$$

where VS is the market price per share times the number of shares outstanding, and VD is the market value of the various classes of long-term debt the company has outstanding. The formula can, of course, be restated to show that the value of the company's shares is a function of the total value of the firm less the value of its debt:

$$VS = VF - VD$$

We'll return to a more detailed discussion of valuation principles and shareholder value creation in Chapters 11 and 12.

In summary, the ratios pertinent to the *owners' view* of a company's performance are measures of the return owners have earned on their stake and the cash rewards they have received in the form of dividends, as well as their expectations about future returns. These results depend on the earning power of the company and on management policies and decisions regarding the use of financial leverage and reinvestment, and the exploitation of the company's value drivers. Ultimately, all management actions affect the economic value of the owners' capital commitment, as reflected in stock market prices. This will be discussed in more detail in Chapter 12.

Lenders' Point of View

While the main orientation of management and owners is toward the business as a going concern, the lender—of necessity—has to be of two minds. Lenders are interested in funding the needs of a successful business that will perform as expected. At the same time, they must consider the possible negative consequences of default and liquidation. Sharing none of the rewards of success other than receiving regular payments of interest and principal, the lender must carefully assess the risk involved in recovering the original funds extended—particularly if they have been provided for a long period of time. Part of this assessment must be the ultimate value of the lender's claim in case of serious difficulty.

The claims of a general creditor rank behind federal tax obligations, accrued wages, and the claims of secured creditors, who lend against a specific asset, such as a building or equipment. Thus, caution often dictates that lenders look for a margin of safety in the assets held by the company, a cushion against default.

Several ratios are used to assess this protection by testing the liquidity of the business. Another set of ratios tests the relative debt exposure, or leverage of the business, in order to weigh the position of lenders versus owners. Finally, there are so-called coverage ratios relating to the company's ability to provide debt service from funds generated by ongoing operations.

Liquidity

One way to test the degree of protection afforded lenders focuses on the short-term credit extended to a business for funding its operations. It involves the liquid assets of a business, that is, those current assets that can readily be converted into cash, on the assumption that they form a cushion against default.

Current Ratio

The ratio most commonly used to appraise the debt exposure represented on the balance sheet is the current ratio. This relationship of current assets to current liabilities is an attempt to show the safety of current debt holders' claims in case of default. The calculation is shown using TRW's relevant totals from Figure 4–2:

$$\text{Current ratio: } \frac{\text{Current assets}}{\text{Current liabilities}} = \frac{\$2,435}{\$2,719} = 0.90 : 1 \ (1996: 1.29 : 1)$$

Presumably, the larger this ratio, the better the position of the debt holders. From the lender's point of view, a higher ratio would certainly appear to provide a cushion against drastic losses of value in case of business failure. A large excess of current assets over current liabilities seems to help protect claims, should inventories have to be liquidated at a forced sale and should accounts receivable involve sizable collection problems.

Seen from another angle, however, an excessively high current ratio might signal slack management practices. It could indicate idle cash balances, inventory levels that have become excessive when compared to current needs, and poor credit management that results in overextended accounts receivable. At the same time, the business might not be making full use of its current borrowing power.

A very common rule of thumb suggests that a current ratio of 2 : 1 is about right for most businesses, because this proportion appears to permit a shrinkage of up to 50 percent in the value of current assets, while still providing enough cushion to cover all current liabilities. The problem with this concept is that the current ratio measures an essentially static condition and assesses a business as if it were on the brink of liquidation. The ratio does not reflect the dynamics of a going concern, which should be the top priority of management. A lender or creditor looking for future business with a successful client should bear this in mind, and will likely turn to the type of cash flow analysis described in Chapter 3 to judge the viability of the business as a client. In TRW's case, the short-term portion of financing related to the two major acquisitions in 1997 caused a temporary decline in the ratio below 1 : 1, with no implication about any liquidity issues.

Acid Test

An even more stringent test, although again on a static basis, is the acid test or quick ratio, which is calculated using only a portion of current assets—cash, marketable securities, and accounts receivable—which are then related to current liabilities as follows:

Acid test:

$$\frac{\text{Cash} + \text{marketable securities} + \text{receivables}}{\text{Current liabilities}} = \frac{\$70 + \$1,617}{\$2,719}$$
$$= 0.62 : 1 \ (1996: 0.82 : 1)$$

The key concept here is to test the collectibility of current liabilities in the case of a real crisis, on the assumption that inventories would have no value at all. As drastic tests of the ability to pay in the face of disaster, both the current ratio and acid test are helpful.

From an operational standpoint, however, it is better to analyze a business in terms of the expected total future cash flow pattern, which projects inflows and outflows over the period for which credit is extended. The proportion of current assets to current liabilities normally covers only a small part of this picture.

Quick Sale Value

Another stringent test that can be applied to the business as a whole is to determine, through a series of assumptions, what cash value the various assets of the company would bring in a hurried sale, and relating this total to the liabilities of the business. Again, this is a liquidation point of view that does not allow for recognizing the ongoing cash flow patterns.

Financial Leverage

As we'll discuss in greater detail in Chapters 6 and 10, successful use of debt enhances earnings for the owners of the business, because the returns earned on these funds—over and above the interest paid—belong to the owners, and thus will increase the return on owners' equity. From the lender's viewpoint, however, when earnings do not exceed or even fall short of the interest cost, fixed interest and principal commitments must still be met. The owners must fulfill these claims, which might severely affect the value of owners' equity. The positive and negative effects of leverage increase with the proportion of debt in a business. With higher leverage, the risk exposure of the providers of debt grows, as does the risk exposure of the owners.

From the lender's point of view, a variety of ratios that deal with total debt, or long-term debt only, in relation to various parts of the balance sheet, are more inclusive measures of risk than leverage alone. These ratios measure the risk exposure of the lenders in relation to the available asset values against which all claims are held.

Debt to Assets

The first and broadest test is the proportion of total debt, both current and long-term, to total assets, which is calculated as follows:

$$\text{Debt to assets: } \frac{\text{Total debt}}{\text{Total assets}} = \frac{\$4,681^*}{\$6,410} = 73.0\% \ (1996:\ 61.9\%)$$

This ratio describes the proportion of "other people's money" to the total claims against the assets of the business. The higher the ratio, the greater the risk for the lender. This is not necessarily a true test of the ability of the business to

---

*Includes long-term liabilities and deferred income taxes.

cover its debts, however. As we've already observed, the asset amounts recorded on the balance sheet are generally not indicative of current economic values, or even liquidation values. Nor does the ratio give any clues as to likely earnings and cash flow fluctuations that might affect current interest and principal payments.

Debt to Capitalization

A more refined version of the debt proportion analysis involves the ratio of long-term debt to capitalization (total invested capital). The latter is again defined as the sum of the long-term claims against the business, both debt and owners' equity, but doesn't include short-term (current) liabilities. This total also corresponds to net assets, unless some adjustments were made, such as ignoring deferred taxes.

The calculation appears as follows, when the current portion of long-term debt, long-term liabilities, and deferred taxes are included in the debt total:

Debt to capitalization:

$$\frac{\text{Long-term debt}}{\text{Capitalization (net assets)}} = \frac{\$2,090}{\$3,691} = 56.6\% \ (1996: 41.9\%)$$

If deferred taxes are excluded from debt, the ratio changes to 55.1 percent and 34.7 percent, respectively.

The ratio is one of the elements that rating companies such as Moody's take into account when classifying the relative safety of debt. Another definition of debt is sometimes used, which includes (1) short-term debt (other than trade credit), (2) the current portion of long-term debt, and (3) all long-term debt in the form of contractual obligations. In this case, long-term liabilities like set-asides representing potential employee benefit claims and deferred taxes are not counted as part of the capitalization of the company, which is (1) the sum of debt as defined above, plus (2) minority interests, and (3) shareholders' investment (equity). In TRW's case, the debt total thus becomes \$1,656 (\$411 + \$128 + \$1,117), and the capitalization becomes \$3,385 (\$1,656 + \$105 + \$1,624), resulting in a ratio of 48.9 percent for 1997 and 20.6 percent for 1996. As is apparent, the greater the uncounted portions of the capital structure, the less this version of the debt ratio represents the full balance of the various elements of the capital base of a company.

A great deal of emphasis is placed on the ratio of debt to capitalization, carefully defined for any particular company, because many lending agreements of both publicly held and private corporations contain covenants regulating maximum debt exposure expressed in terms of debt to capitalization proportions. There remains an issue of how to classify different liabilities, and how to deal with accounting changes, as most companies, including TRW, experienced establishing long-term liabilities for future employee benefits. As we'll see later, however, there is growing emphasis on a more relevant aspect of debt exposure, namely, the ability to service the debt from ongoing funds flows, a much more dynamic view of lender relationships.

Debt to Equity

A third version of the analysis of debt proportions involves the ratio of total debt, frequently defined as the sum of current liabilities and all types of long-term debt, to total owners' equity, or shareholders' investment. The debt to equity ratio is an attempt to show, in another format, the relative proportions of all lender's claims to ownership claims, and it is used as a measure of debt exposure. The measure is expressed as either a percentage or as a proportion, and in the example shown below, the figures again were taken from TRW's balance sheet in Figure 4–2:

Debt to equity:

$$\frac{\text{Total debt}}{\text{Shareholders' investment (equity)*}} = \frac{\$4,681}{\$1,729} = 271\% \ (1996: 163\%)$$

In preparing this ratio, as in some earlier instances, the question of deferred income taxes and other estimated long-term liabilities is often sidestepped by leaving these potential long-term claims out of the debt and capitalization figures altogether. We have included all of these elements here. One specific refinement of this formula uses only long-term debt, as related to shareholders' investment, ignoring long-term obligations and deferred taxes.

Debt to equity (alternate):

$$\frac{\text{Long-term debt}^{\dagger}}{\text{Shareholders' investment (equity)}^{\ddagger}} = \frac{\$1,245}{\$1,729} = 72.0\% \ (1996: 23.6\%)$$

The various formats of these relationships imply the care with which the ground rules must be defined for any particular analysis, and for the covenants governing specific lending agreements. They only hint at the risk/reward trade-off implicit in the use of debt, which we'll discuss in more detail in Chapters 9 and 11.

Debt Service

Regardless of the specific choice from among the several ratios just discussed, debt proportion analysis is in essence static, and does not take into account the operating dynamics and economic values of the business. The analysis is totally derived from the balance sheet, which in itself is a static snapshot of the financial condition of the business at a single point in time.

Nonetheless, the relative ease with which these ratios are calculated probably accounts for their popularity. Such ratios are useful as indicators of trends when they are applied over a period of time. However, they still don't get at the heart of an analysis of creditworthiness, which involves a company's ability to pay both interest and principal on schedule as contractually agreed upon, that is, to service its debt over time.

---

*Includes minority interests.
†Includes current portion of long-term debt.
‡Includes minority interests.

Interest Coverage

One very frequently encountered ratio reflecting a company's debt service uses the relationship of net profit (earnings) before interest and taxes (EBIT) to the amount of the interest payments for the period. This ratio is developed with the expectation that annual operating earnings can be considered the basic source of funds for debt service, and that any significant change in this relationship might signal difficulties. Major earnings fluctuations are one type of risk considered.

No hard and fast standards for the ratio itself exist; rather, the prospective debt holders often require covenants in the loan agreement spelling out the number of times the business is expected to cover its debt service obligations. The ratio is simple to calculate, and we can employ the EBIT figure developed for TRW earlier in the management section:

Interest coverage:

$$\frac{\text{Net profit before interest and taxes (EBIT)}}{\text{Interest}} = \frac{\$863}{\$75}$$

$$= 11.5 \text{ times (1996: 9.2 times)}$$

The specifics are based on judgment, often involving a detailed analysis of a company's past, current, and prospective conditions.

Burden Coverage

A somewhat more refined analysis of debt coverage relates the net profit of the business, before interest and taxes, to the sum of current interest and principal repayments, in an attempt to indicate the company's ability to service the burden of its debt in all aspects. A problem arises with this particular analysis, because interest payments are tax deductible, while principal repayments are not. Thus, we must be on guard to think about these figures on a comparable basis.

One correction often used involves converting the principal repayments into an equivalent pretax amount. This is done by dividing the principal repayment by the factor "one minus the effective tax rate." The resulting calculation appears as follows, using the $89 million in principal repayments (due in over 90 days) TRW paid in 1997, as shown in the cash flow statement in its 1997 annual report (see Chapter 3):

Burden coverage:

$$\frac{\text{Net profit before interest and taxes (EBIT)}}{\text{Interest} + \dfrac{\text{Principal repayments}}{(1 - \text{tax rate})}} = \frac{\$863}{\$75 + \dfrac{\$89}{(1 - .37)}} = \frac{\$863}{\$75 + \$141}$$

$$= 3.99 \text{ times}$$

An alternate format uses operating cash flow (net profit after taxes plus write-offs), developed from Figure 4–3, to which after-tax interest has been added back. This is then compared to the sum of after-tax interest and principal repayment, and the calculation for 1997 appears as follows:

Burden coverage:

$$\frac{\text{Operating cash flow} + \text{Interest } (1 - \text{tax rate})}{\text{Interest } (1 - \text{tax rate}) + \text{Principal repayments}} = \frac{\$989* + \$75\,(.63)}{\$75\,(.63) + \$89}$$

$$= \frac{\$1,036}{\$136} = 7.62 \text{ times}$$

Fixed Charges Coverage

A more inclusive concept is the combination of interest and rental expenses into a fixed charges amount, which is then compared to pretax earnings to which these fixed charges are added back. In the case of TRW, its published statistics included a calculation of fixed charges coverage which combined one-third of rental expenses and interest paid, which was then related to pretax earnings plus this total. In 1997, the fixed charges coverage was 2.9 times, and in 1996 it was 3.4 times.

Cash Flow Analysis

Determining a company's ability to meet its debt obligations is most meaningful when a review of past profit and cash flow patterns is made over a long enough period of time to indicate the major operational and cyclical fluctuations that are normal for the company and its industry. This might involve financial statements covering several years or several seasonal swings, as appropriate, in an attempt to identify characteristic high and low points in earnings and funds needs. The pattern of past conditions must then be projected into the future to see what margin of safety remains to cover interest, principal repayments, and other fixed payments, such as major lease obligations. These techniques will be discussed in Chapter 5.

   If a business is subject to sizable fluctuations in after-tax cash flow, lenders might be reluctant to extend credit when the debt service cannot be covered several times at the low point in the operational pattern. In contrast, a very stable business would encounter less-stringent coverage demands. The type of dynamic analysis involved is a form of financial modeling that can be greatly enhanced both in scope and in the number of possible alternative conditions explored by using spreadsheets or full-fledged corporate planning models.

Ratios as a System

The ratios discussed in this chapter have many elements in common, as they are derived from key components of the same financial statements. In fact, they're often interrelated and can be viewed as a system. The analyst can turn a series of ratios into a dynamic display highlighting the elements that are the most important levers used by management to affect operating performance.

   In internal analysis, many companies employ a variety of systems of ratios and standards that segregate into their components the impact of decisions affecting operating performance, overall returns, and shareholder expectations. Du Pont was one of the first to do so early in the last century. The company published a chart showing the effects and interrelationships of decisions in these areas, which focused on the linkages to return on equity as the key result and represented a first "model" of its business. The Du Pont system was built on accounting relationships only, as cash flow concepts and measures were not in vogue at that time. Companies that engage in value-based management, as we'll discuss in Chapter 12, develop relationships in their planning models and operational systems that focus on value drivers and shareholder value creation, using a mix of cash flow measures and appropriate physical and accounting ratios.

For purposes of illustrating the basic principles here we'll demonstrate the relationships between major accounting ratios discussed earlier, using two key parameters segregated into their elements: *return on assets*, which is of major importance for judging management performance, and *return on equity*, which serves as the key measure from the owners' viewpoint. We'll leave aside the refinements applicable to each to concentrate on the linkages. As we'll show, it's possible to model the performance of a given company by expanding and relating these ratios. Needless to say, careful attention must be paid to the exact definition of the elements entering into the ratios for a particular company to achieve internal consistency. Also, it's important to ensure that the ratios are interpreted in ways that foster economic trade-offs and decisions in support of shareholder value creation.

Elements of Return on Assets

We established earlier that the basic formula for return on assets (ROA) was a simple ratio, into which different versions of the elements can be inserted:

$$\text{Return on assets} = \frac{\text{Net profit}}{\text{Assets}}$$

We also know that net profit was related both to asset turnover and to sales. Thus, it is possible to restate the formula as follows:

$$\text{Return on assets} = \frac{\text{Net profit}}{\text{Sales}} \times \frac{\text{Sales}}{\text{Assets}}$$

Note that the element of sales cancels out in the second formula, resulting in the original expression. But we can expand the relationship even further by substituting several more basic elements for the terms in the equation:

$$\text{ROA} = \frac{(\text{Gross margin} - \text{expenses})(1 - \text{tax rate})}{\text{Price} \times \text{Volume}}$$
$$\times \frac{\text{Price} \times \text{Volume}}{\text{Fixed} + \text{Current} + \text{Other assets}}$$

The relationships expressed here serve as a simple model of the key drivers on which management can focus to improve return on assets. For example, improvement in gross margin is important, as is control of expenses. Price/volume relationships are canceled out, but we know they are essential factors in arriving at a satisfactory gross margin, as is control of cost of goods sold. (We could have substituted "price/volume less cost of goods sold" for gross margin in the first bracket.)

All along we've said that asset management is very important. The model shows that the return on assets will rise if fewer assets are employed and if all the measures of effective management of working capital are applied. Minimizing taxes within the legal options available also will improve the return.

Elements of Return on Equity

A similar approach can be taken with the basic formula for return on owners' equity (ROE), which relates profit and the amounts of recorded equity:

$$\text{Return on equity} = \frac{\text{Net profit}}{\text{Equity}}$$

If we use some of the basic profit and turnover relationships to expand the expression, the following formula emerges:

$$\text{Return on equity} = \frac{\text{Net profit}}{\text{Assets}} \times \frac{\text{Assets}}{\text{Equity}}$$

Note that, in effect, the formula states that return on equity (ROE) consists of two elements:

- The net profit achieved on the asset base.
- The degree of leverage or debt capital used in the business.

"Assets to equity" is a way of describing the leverage proportion. We can expand the formula even more to include the key components of return on assets:

$$\text{ROE} = \frac{\text{Net profit}}{\text{Sales}} \times \frac{\text{Sales}}{\text{Assets}} \times \frac{\text{Assets}}{\text{Assets} - \text{Liabilities}}$$

Once again we can look for the key drivers management should use to raise the return on owners' equity. It's not a surprise that improving profitability of sales (operations) comes first, combined with effective use of the assets that generate sales. An added factor is the boosting effect from successful use of debt in the capital structure. The greater the liabilities, the greater the improvement in return on equity—assuming, of course, that the business is profitable to begin with and at a minimum continues to earn more on its investments than the cost of debt. As we know, of course, value creation depends on overall returns above the cost of capital, which is not expressed in this particular formula.

Using other people's money can be quite helpful—until the risk of default on debt service in a down cycle becomes significant. The analyst can use this simple framework to test the impact on the return on equity from one or more changed conditions, and to test how sensitive the result is to the magnitude of any change introduced.

A more inclusive format of the relationship of key ratios to each other and to the three major decision areas is displayed in Figure 4–4. We've added the major drivers behind the ratios on the left, as an indication of the levers management can use in managing the company. Note that in this diagram, we've included the cost of interest on debt as part of the "net contribution from leverage" in the financing area, while properly defining operating earnings as excluding the cost of interest.

This representation can be viewed as a simple model of a business in an accounting ratio format. It can be useful in tracing through the ultimate effects from changes in any of the basic drivers that are brought about by management decisions. For example, note that an increased level of inventories will reduce working capital turnover, which lowers the return on investment, and in the end, the return on equity. Or take an increase in debt (leverage), where the funds obtained are successfully invested with a rate of return higher than the interest cost—this will make a positive contribution to the return on equity. The latter example also illustrates that different degrees of leverage employed by companies being compared can affect the comparability of the return on equity measure.

A word of caution is in order, however. The neat precision implied in this arrangement must not blind us to the fact that while accounting ratios are commonly used indicators, the ultimate driver of TSR and shareholder value is the pattern of cash flows achieved and, more importantly, expected by the stock market. This represents an economic viewpoint which transcends the shortcomings of accounting statements and relationships, and expresses market valuation as a cash flow mechanism—a concept which has been confirmed by many empirical studies. The roots of the system on the left of the diagram are the basic conditions which drive success or failure as expressed in these accounting ratios. These drivers are common to accounting and cash flow reasoning; The difference is in the way the results are expressed. As we'll discuss in Chapter 12, value creation depends on effective management of all the basic drivers, but the ultimate result must be viewed in cash flow terms.

Does this mean that we cannot really use the various tools and relationships we've discussed in this chapter? Not at all. The challenge to analysts and managers is to constantly be aware of the cash flow implications of their decisions in addition to any accounting-based analysis. Accounting ratios and data at times will conflict with economic choices, especially in the near term, and some of them will not be useful for a particular decision. Over the long run, measures such as return on equity and return on net assets will tend to converge with cash flow results. The rule to observe at all times is that true economic trade-offs must be

FIGURE 4–4

A Systems View of Key Ratios and Their Elements*

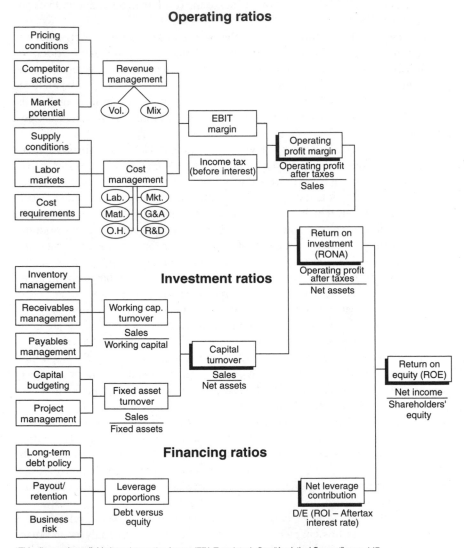

*This diagram is available in an interactive format (TFA Templates). See "Analytical Support" on p. 147.

based on cash flows, and if decisions are consistently analyzed and executed in this manner, positive accounting results will follow in due course.

We'll return to the subject of business modeling again in Chapters 5 and 6, and highlight economic cash flow trade-offs in Chapters 7 through 12.

Integration of Financial Performance Analysis

We've discussed the great variety of financial ratios and measures available to anyone wishing to analyze the performance of a company and its various units, or of an individual business. We've also grouped the measures by points of view and shown their many interrelationships as well as the key management drivers that impact them. At this point, it'll be helpful to provide a few practical guidelines for structuring the process of using the measures. We'll briefly address the following key points:

- Careful definition of the issue being analyzed and the viewpoint to be taken.
- Identifying a combination of primary and secondary measures and tools.
- Identifying key value drivers that affect performance.
- Trending performance data over time, both historical and prospective.
- Finding comparative indicators and supplementary information.
- Using past performance as a clue to future expectations.
- Recognizing systems issues and obstacles to optimal performance.

First, there is nothing more important in any kind of financial/economic analysis than a clear *definition of the issue* to be addressed, and the *viewpoint to be taken*. For example, when a banker ponders whether to extend a short-term loan to a business for working capital needs, the key issue is the company's ability to repay within a relatively short time period. Immediately, the analysis focuses on past and prospective cash flow patterns, supplemented by measures on working capital management and profitability. When a security analyst wishes to assess the quality of a company's management, the focus will be on past and prospective strategic direction, competitive position, and investment effectiveness. Measures of profitability benchmarked against comparative industry data will be important, as will be indicators of shareholder return and value creation. The point is that every type of analysis—complex or simple—should be preceded by a careful issue definition and choice of viewpoint that will naturally lead to a focused selection of measures to be applied.

Second, it should be obvious that most financial/economic analysis has to use a *combination of primary and secondary measures* to be effective. Rarely will a situation require only a single measure or indicator, since all ratios are limited to some extent both by the nature of the data and by the relationships underlying them. Looking only at the return on equity as a measure of profitability, for example, falls far short of the insights gained when it is combined with key measures of operating earnings, asset turnover, and contribution from leverage, as we saw earlier. It's good practice to decide which key indicators best fit the specific issue, and which subsidiary ratios or other measures can provide additional insight or verification. The analytical results should then be expressed in these terms.

Third, sound analytical practice includes *identifying the key value drivers* underlying the performance of any business. Whether production-oriented, such as the yield in producing electronic chips, or service-based, such as call volume by sales personnel, performance ratios and measures are usually directly affected by variations in these key drivers. While one can find many kinds of value drivers—internal or external—varying greatly between types of business, there are generally just a few in each situation that really make a difference. The effective analyst makes it a practice to understand what these drivers are, how they affect the broader financial/economic measures used, and how trends in the drivers themselves impact both past and prospective performance. It's good practice to test the sensitivity of key measures chosen to various value driver conditions, and to include critical value drivers as part of the combination of measures chosen to address the performance issue under review.

Fourth, the results of performance analysis are much more meaningful when placed in the *context of comparable data* about the industry, key competitors, or intracompany comparisons of organizational units. It's here that both the level of performance and key trends can be judged in relative terms. While it's often hard to find truly comparative data, particularly for multidivisional businesses, the notion of benchmarking business results whenever possible has grown in the past decade as U.S. management has begun to focus on improving competitive effectiveness. The references at the end of this chapter and in Appendix III contain published sources of industry data and ratios, which companies often supplement with special efforts to develop even more specific data through detailed benchmarking activities, that is, by sharing experiences with noncompeting companies. Depending on the importance of the issue being analyzed, the industry/competitive context for viewing performance results can be critical.

Fifth, it's an axiom of good analysis that *trends in financial/economic performance* be judged in a time frame befitting the nature of the business and its industry, including the aspects of cyclicality, seasonality, growth, and decline discussed in Chapter 3. This calls for developing data series that cover at least several years, in order to judge the trends affecting various aspects of the company's performance. Sound analysis uses the perspective gained from positive or adverse trends in the primary and secondary performance indicators, and carefully weighs their relative importance to the issue being addressed. Remember also that performance analysis is not just an exercise in historical assessment—rather, it's the basis from which future expectations are developed. Trend analysis becomes especially important in this context, for the analyst often needs to project future conditions and must decide whether the trends observed are likely to continue, or change, because of foreseeable events.

Sixth, viewing past performance as a *clue to potential future expectations* is a common practice in financial/economic analysis. We've already touched on this aspect in our discussion of trend analysis. A word of caution is necessary, however. While it's proper to identify past trends in both value drivers and the broader ratios and measures, and to extrapolate them into the future, this is only a first step. As we'll see in Chapter 5 and later chapters, historical conditions are merely an indication that might not be relevant for the company's prospective results. Past performance trends have to be carefully tested against expectations about future conditions, both internal to the company and external in the broader context of business, competitive, and economic conditions. It might very well be true that recent actions taken by management, or discernible changes in the environment, require a different set of assumptions about the future.

Finally, performance analysis in the broadest sense has to be viewed in the *context of the business system,* as described in Chapter 2. When the issue selected is an overall assessment of a company or a major business unit, it's good practice to test the results and trends of the various measures not only in the form of absolute and relative performance against proper benchmarks, but also in relation to each other. As we pointed out in Chapter 2, sound economic/financial performance requires optimizing the systems results over time. This simply means that policies and strategies in the areas of investment, operations, and financing should reinforce each other. The skilled analyst will put performance analysis into this broader context, and view the historical results as well as the projected expectations as indicators of systems balance. Are growth policies matched by appropriate financing plans? Are operating results in cash flow terms sufficient to support dividend policies and investment plans? Do the results reflect sound trade-offs over time? Many of these points will be discussed in more detail in later chapters.

Some Special Issues

The impact of accounting practices and decisions on the management of funds was briefly mentioned in Chapter 2, where accounting write-offs and deferred taxes were identified as aspects to be considered. At this point, it'll be useful to refine our understanding of these issues a little further because possible alternative treatments of these matters at times significantly affect the assessment of operations as well as understanding the patterns of cash flows. Addendum 4–1 at the end of this chapter reproduces the notes to TRW's financial statements to illustrate the many accounting and tax considerations underlying the reported financial data of any large U.S. corporation. Appendix V contains some of the more specialized issues of interpreting performance statements in an *international setting,* especially the problem of judging the profitability of parts of a multibusiness company operating in different countries.

We'll limit ourselves to a review of the key choices available to management in the areas of *inventory costing and depreciation methods* to help the reader in forming individual judgments when faced with interpreting financial statements and cash flows. We'll also briefly mention the effects of *inflation,* although no satisfactory methods of dealing with that issue have been established so far.

Inventory Costing

One accounting challenge present at all times is the proper allocation of a portion of the costs that are accumulated in the inventory account to the actual goods being sold. We can visualize *layers of cost* built up over time in the inventory account, which correspond to the physical movement of raw materials, work in process, and finished goods into storage. The accountant wants to *match revenues and expenses* in keeping track of the inventory account, yet from a physical standpoint, it is just as possible to ship the oldest unit on hand as it is to ship the most recent arrival. The warehouse supervisor can even pick the goods at random.

If unit costs never changed, matching costs to revenues would not be a problem, because the accountant would simply track the number of units shipped and multiply them by the unchanged unit cost, regardless of the actual physical choices made by the warehouse supervisor. In real life, however, several problems arise. A manufacturing company might experience fluctuations that affect the recorded unit cost of the products inventoried. This effectively results in different layers of cost in the finished goods inventory account. Further, the prices of raw materials and other inputs might be positively or negatively influenced by supply and demand. The materials inventory account will therefore reflect different layers of cost. A merchandising company will similarly encounter variations in the cost of inventory items, as supplier prices change. Most cost accounting systems allow for variances to the extent they are predictable, but larger swings do affect costs that are charged to periodic income statements.

Finally, there is the impact of general inflation, or, more rarely, deflation. The impact of inflation on inventories generally is a steady rise in the cost of the more recent additions, resulting in successive layers of escalating costs.

The accountant is therefore faced with a real problem in the effort to match costs and revenues. If unit costs are growing significantly from period to period, deciding which costs to charge against the revenues for a period can have significant effects on the financial statements. If the more "logical" method of removing the oldest units first is used, the oldest, and presumably lowest, unit costs will be charged against current revenues. Depending on how quickly the inventory turns over, such costs might lag current conditions by months and even longer. Therefore, under rising price levels, first-in, first-out (FIFO) inventory costing causes the profit on the income statement to be higher than it would be if current unit costs had been charged. At the same time, the balance sheet will reflect inventory values that are reasonably current, because the oldest, lowest cost units are being removed.

If the opposite method is employed, that is, last-in, first-out (LIFO) costing, the income statement will be charged with current costs and thus reflect lower but more realistic profits. The balance sheet, however, will show inventory values that in time, might be highly *understated,* because only the oldest and lowest layers of cost remain.

We could argue that the choice of methods does not really matter, because one of the two financial statements will be distorted in *either* case. The question then simply becomes whether more realistic balance sheet values or more realistic reported profits are preferred. There is a significant *cash flow* aspect involved, however. The choice of methods affects the amount of income taxes paid for the period. The higher earnings under FIFO are taxed as income from operations, even though they contain a profit made from old inventories. Therefore, one criterion in making the choice is the difference in tax payments, which *does* affect the company's funds. LIFO is preferable from this standpoint, even though with continued inflation, inventory values stated on the balance sheet will become more and more obsolete. Yet surprisingly, FIFO has remained a very common form of inventory costing, despite the fact that it can lead to a funds drain from higher tax payments. Apparently, the higher reported profit under FIFO costing is attractive enough to many managers to outweigh the actual tax disadvantage—a trade-off between reporting and economics.

In contrast to other permissible choices of accounting methods for tax purposes, current federal tax laws do not allow the use of one inventory costing method for tax calculation and another for bookkeeping and reporting. Thus, the ideal combination of LIFO for tax purposes and FIFO for reporting earnings is not possible. In fact, many firms employ an averaging method for inventory costing, or a combination of methods.

Trading firms, retailers, and companies experiencing significant fluctuations in the current values of inventories often adjust inventory values, usually at year-end, using the conservative method of restating inventories at cost or market value, whichever is lower, and writing off the difference against current profits. Such periodic adjustments tend to reduce stated values, not raise them, and allow the company to reflect the negative effects of changed conditions so as not to overstate inventory values. Under inflationary conditions, this practice does not, of course, assist in resolving the inventory costing issues we have just discussed.

Depreciation Methods

Depreciation is based on the accountant's objective to reflect as a charge against current operations some appropriate fraction of the cost of assets employed in producing revenues. Since physical assets other than land deteriorate with use and eventually wear out, the accounting challenge is to establish an appropriate period of time over which portions of the cost of the asset are charged against revenues. Moreover, the accountant has to decide on the pattern of the depreciation write-off, that is, level, declining, or variable depreciation. Another issue involves estimating any salvage value that might be realized at the end of an asset's useful life. Only the difference between asset cost and such salvage value is normally depreciated.

A similar rationale is applied to intangible assets such as patents and licenses, which are amortized and charged against operations over an appropriate period of years, and to specialized assets such as mineral deposits and timber, on which depletion allowances are calculated.

In the case of physical assets, the depreciation write-off is shown as a charge in the income statement, and is accumulated on the balance sheet as an offset to the fixed assets involved, in an account called accumulated depreciation or reserve for depreciation. Thus, over time, the original asset value stated on the balance sheet is reduced, as periodic charges are made against operations. For performance assessment, the significance of depreciation write-offs is in the appropriateness of the charges in light of the nature of the assets and industry conditions, and thus, depreciation's impact on profits and balance sheet values. The significance for purposes of cash flow management is the tax impact of depreciation. Under normal circumstances, depreciation is a tax-deductible expense, even though it is only an accounting allocation of past expenditures. The highest depreciation write-off legally possible will normally be taken by management to minimize the cash outlay for taxes, unless operating profits are insufficient during the taxable period (including tax adjustments like operating-loss carryback and carryforward, which permit using losses to reduce the taxes of profitable periods) to take full advantage of the deductions.

The choice of depreciation methods is made easier by the provision in the current tax laws allowing the use of one method for bookkeeping and reporting purposes and another for income tax calculation. Recall that this was not possible for inventory valuation. Thus, a company can enjoy the best aspects of both depreciation concepts: slower depreciation for reporting higher profits, and faster depreciation for paying lower taxes.

The difference between the taxes actually paid versus what would be due, had the book profit been taxed, is accumulated on the balance sheet as a liability called deferred taxes, which we encountered earlier in our discussion. This liability will keep growing if a company continually adds to its depreciable assets and consistently uses faster write-offs for tax purposes. If the company stops growing or changes its depreciation policies, actual tax payments in future periods will increase and the differences will begin to reduce the deferred taxes account. There is no current consensus on how to treat this often significant amount in the calculation of performance assessment measures.

What are the most common choices for depreciation write-offs? Historically, accounting practice has favored *straight-line depreciation*. This is determined by dividing the cost of the asset (less the estimated salvage value) by its expected life. For example, an asset costing $10,000, with a salvage value of $400 and a 6-year life, would be depreciated at the annual rate of $1,600 (one-sixth, or $16\frac{2}{3}$ percent of $9,600). A variant of this method is *unit depreciation*, in which the allocation is based on the total number of units estimated to be produced over the life of the asset and the annual depreciation is based on the number of units produced in that year.

Since many types of assets, such as automobiles, lose more of their value in early years, and since allowing faster write-offs provides an incentive to reduce current income taxes, several methods of *accelerated depreciation* were developed over time. The two most common methods are described here.

Double-declining balance depreciation is calculated by using twice the annual rate of straight-line depreciation (33⅓ percent for a 6-year life), multiplying the full original cost of the asset for the first year with this factor, and the declining balance for each successive year. In other words, in our example, one-third of the remaining balance would be depreciated in each year (see Figure 4–5). The last year's depreciation is the remaining balance, and any salvage value is recognized by reducing the amount charged in the *final* year.

Sum-of-years-digits depreciation is calculated by adding the digits for all the years of the asset's life (1 + 2 + 3, and so on). The total is the denominator in a fraction (for a 6-year life, this sum would be 21: 1 + 2 + 3 + 4 + 5 + 6). The numerators represent each year of useful life, in reverse order. (In our example, the fractions are $6/21$, $5/21$, $4/21$, $3/21$, $2/21$, and $1/21$.) In a given year, the depreciation write-off is the asset's original cost (less salvage value) multiplied by the fraction for that year.

The different patterns of depreciation resulting from the use of the various methods for accounting purposes are shown in Figure 4–5, using our simple example for illustrating the differences in the annual amounts.

The depreciation methods permitted under prevailing IRS codes have changed frequently, especially during the 1980s. Under the 1986 revision of the tax code, the IRS lengthened the lives over which various classes of depreciable assets could be written off. Six asset classes were established for personal property, with lives of 3, 5, 7, 10, 15, and 20 years. For real property (e.g., buildings), two classes of 27.5 and 31.5 years were defined, which must be depreciated straight-line. All classes have in common the assumption that new assets are in service for only 6 months in the first year, which lowers the first-year write-off across the board. The IRS stipulated the double-declining balance method for as-

---

F I G U R E   4–5

Comparative Annual Depreciation Patterns
($10,000 Asset with Six-Year Life and $400 Salvage Value)

	Straight-Line Method	Double-Declining Balance Method*	150 Percent Declining Balance Method†	Sum-of-Years Digits Method
Year 1	$1,600	$3,333	$2,500	$2,743
Year 2	1,600	2,222	1,875	2,286
Year 3	1,600	1,482	1,407	1,829
Year 4	1,600	988	1,406	1,371
Year 5	1,600	658	1,406	914
Year 6	1,600	917	1,006	457
Total:	$9,600	$9,600	$9,600	$9,600

*Year 6 is shown net of salvage value of $400.

†Switch to straight-line in Year 4; required for 15- and 20-year IRS asset classes.

sets with up to 10 years of life, and a variation of this method, the 150 percent de-clining balance method, for assets with a 15- and 20-year life.

Figure 4–6 shows the tax write-off patterns for the six different asset classes established by the IRS under the so-called accelerated cost recovery system (ACRS), using the percentage of the depreciable investment allowed as a deduction in each year.

The IRS permits a switch to straight-line depreciation in the latter years, when this becomes advantageous. These methods must be used if a company chooses to use accelerated depreciation for *tax* purposes, while *any* other method can be employed for bookkeeping and reporting. The specifics of the tax regulations applicable at the time of the analysis are best examined in the detailed materials provided by the Internal Revenue Service.

The Impact of Inflation

The extreme inflationary conditions in the United States beginning in the early 1970s resulted in significant distortions in many of the calculations we discussed. In recent years, inflationary trends have improved greatly in the major countries, to the extent that inflation is now considered relatively benign. Many other countries have, of course, had to deal with far more insidious levels of inflation for much longer periods of time, and some still do.

In the United States, the accounting profession and the Securities and Exchange Commission have expended much effort in developing new ways to ac-

FIGURE 4–6

Tax Depreciation Percentages by ACRS Asset Class

Year(s)	3-Year	5-Year	7-Year	10-Year	15-Year	20-Year
1	33.33	20.00	14.29	10.00	5.00	3.75
2	44.45	32.00	24.49	18.00	9.50	7.22
3	14.81	19.20	17.49	14.40	8.55	6.68
4	7.41	11.52	12.49	11.52	7.70	6.18
5		11.52	8.93	9.22	6.93	5.71
6		5.76	8.93	7.37	6.23	5.28
7			8.93	6.55	5.90	4.89
8			4.45	6.55	5.90	4.52
9				6.55	5.90	4.46
10				6.55	5.90	4.46
11				3.29	5.90	4.46
12					5.90	4.46
13					5.90	4.46
14					5.90	4.46
15					5.90	4.46
16					2.99	4.46
17–20						4.46
21						2.25

count for and disclose the impact of changes in prices of goods and services and of fluctuating exchange rates due in part to inflation. However, the intricacies and arguments abundant in this difficult area are beyond the scope of this book. We are mentioning only a few of the basic mechanisms commonly employed to deal with price level changes where this is necessary to understand the impact on financial analysis. Thus, Chapters 3, 5, and 11 contain a brief discussion of essential price level adjustments pertaining to the subjects of operating funds management, projections, and valuation. Appendix IV contains a discussion of the basic concepts underlying the inflation phenomenon.

In performance analysis, the main problem associated with inflation is the use of *historical costing* as a generally accepted accounting principle. The original cost of assets utilized in and charged to operations is reflected on the balance sheet. Depreciation and amortization reflect past values, which are often lower than current values. Financial statements of particularly heavily capitalized industries with long-lived depreciable assets and physical resources tend to reflect overstated profits and taxes, and understated asset values. This raises the issue of comparability of companies of different ages, and certainly of comparability of whole industries. Even short-term fluctuations in values will affect companies with high inventory turnover, such as wholesalers.

Another area of distortion affects the *viewpoint of the lender.* In inflationary times, the declining value of currency will affect borrowing/lending relationships, because eventual repayment will be made in less valuable dollars. Thus, the lender would be at a disadvantage unless the interest rate contracted for is high enough to offset this risk. The dramatic rise in the 1970s and subsequent fall in the 1980s and early 1990s of short- and long-term interest rates in response to growing and waning inflationary pressures will remain in the memories of long-term lenders in particular.

Among the many methods used to deal with price level changes are replacement cost accounting, new forms of inventory valuation, and partial or full periodic restatement of financial reports. In fact, inflation has turned the deceptively simple accounting principle of matching costs and revenues into an economic and intellectual challenge. As yet, there are no consistent ways of appraising the difference between this type of recast statement and the original accounting statements. A current proposal by the Financial Accounting Standards Board goes part way toward recasting financial statements for banks and financial institutions, asking that loans and investments be valued at current values. This raises a variety of issues that are far from resolved at the time of this writing.

Key Issues

The following is a recap of the key issues raised directly or indirectly in this chapter. They are enumerated here to help the reader keep the materials discussed within the perspective of financial theory and business practice.

1. Analysis of business performance is a complex process, which requires a clearly defined viewpoint, careful selection of appropriate measures, and an understanding of the interrelationships of the measures chosen.

2. The context of any analytical effort is critical to successfully addressing the issue or problem to be resolved by the analysis. Much of the thought process underlying an analysis should be directed to ensuring consistency between the objectives and the data sources and processes employed.

3. While published financial statements are the most widely available source for financial analysis, the limitations inherent in their preparation (based on generally accepted accounting principles) require a basic understanding on the part of the user of how analytical results in the areas of performance and valuation can be distorted and what adjustments may be necessary.

4. There is no one measure or set of measures that fits every situation in which business performance is assessed. The choice is always dependent on the viewpoint and circumstances involved.

5. Performance analysis of a company or business unit is ultimately related to shareholder value creation. Therefore, past performance and future expectations have to be viewed at some point in terms of cash flow generation, investment returns, and operational effectiveness.

6. Many performance measures are related to each other in various ways, and sound analysis requires a thorough understanding of these linkages.

7. Comparative analysis of companies and business units is challenged by the frequent lack of truly comparable data, because of differences in product/service mix, accounting choices, size and age of the businesses, differences in the portfolio, and geographic scope. Industry statistics available from various sources often suffer from comparability issues as well.

8. Performance analysis is best performed as a dynamic process, using financial models where possible, to assess combinations of data and measures over time.

Summary

In this chapter, we discussed essential aspects of the main financial statements as a basis for appraising business performance, although we again established that true value creation is based on cash flow reasoning and criteria. With this background, we then demonstrated that the assessment of performance is made meaningful when seen from the points of view of the key groups interested in the company's success.

We chose to concentrate on the particular viewpoints of three groups—management, owners, and lenders—which are essential to the functioning of the business. The insights of these groups are used and expanded by others for their own particular needs. All three groups are concerned about the success of the business, each from its own standpoint.

It is management's prime duty to bring about stability, growth, and reliable earnings performance with the investment entrusted to it by the owners. We found that within the wide range of ratios displayed, the crucial test is the return on the capital employed in the business and its attendant effect on the value of the ownership stake, which will be discussed in more detail in Chapters 11 and 12. We also found that the ratios are linked by their common information base, and many are directly connected through the common use of certain elements. They are best interpreted when the business is viewed as a system of interdependent conditions responding to the decisions of management, and the specific impact of carefully defined value drivers. To this end, modeling and computer simulation are meaningful processes, because many individual ratios are, by their nature, only static tests that cannot do justice to the dynamics of a business.

Shortcomings in the analysis relate to the limitations of the accounting principles commonly used, and we strongly suggested that managers and analysts take an economic (cash flow) viewpoint for decision making, which will in the long run result in good accounting performance. Further distortions are introduced through price level changes stemming from inflation, currency fluctuations, and economic value changes. No definitive ways of compensating for these measurement problems have as yet been found to make financial analyses readily comparable and economically meaningful. As a result, the manager and analyst must use care and judgment at all times when dealing with performance assessment.

Analytical Support

Financial Genome, the commercially available financial analysis and planning software described in Appendix I has the capability to develop and display all common financial ratios, grouped by decision area, from databases, spreadsheets, and direct inputs. The software is accompanied by an interactive template (TFA Template under "extras"), representing the main features of Figure 4–4 on p. 136, ratios as a system, which allows the user to vary key assumptions and to study their impact on the various interrelated ratios. (See "Downloads Available" on p. 431.)

Selected References

Anthony, Robert N. *Essentials of Accounting.* 5th ed. Reading, MA: Addison Wesley, 1993.
Bandler, James P. *How to Use Financial Statements.* Burr Ridge, IL: Irwin Professional Publishing, 1994.
Brealey, Richard, and Stewart Myers. *Principles of Corporate Finance.* 5th ed. Burr Ridge, IL: Irwin/McGraw-Hill, 1996.
Dun & Bradstreet. *Industry Norms and Key Business Ratios* (annual). New York.
Merrill Lynch. *How to Read a Financial Report.* 7th ed. New York: Merrill Lynch, 1993.

Robert Morris Associates. *Annual Statement Studies*. Philadelphia.

Palepu, Krishna G.; Victor L. Bernard; and Paul M. Healy. *Business Analysis and Valuation: Using Financial Statements*. Cincinnati: Southwestern College Publishing, 1996.

Ross, Stephen; Randolph Westerfield; and Jeffrey Jaffe. *Corporate Finance*. 5th ed. Burr Ridge, IL: Irwin/McGraw-Hill, 1999.

Standard & Poor's. *Analysts Handbook* (annual issues with monthly supplements). New York.

Troy, Leo. *Almanac of Business and Financial Ratios* (annual issues). Englewood Cliffs, NJ: Prentice Hall.

Weston, J. Fred; Scott Besley; and Eugene F. Brigham. *Essentials of Managerial Finance*. 11th ed. Hinsdale, IL: Dryden Press, 1997.

TRW INC. AND SUBSIDIARIES
Notes to Financial Statements

Summary of Significant Accounting Policies

Principles of consolidation–The financial statements include the accounts of the company and its subsidiaries except for two insurance subsidiaries. The wholly owned insurance subsidiaries and the majority of investments in affiliated companies, which are not significant individually, are accounted for by the equity method.

Use of estimates–The preparation of financial statements in conformity with generally accepted accounting principles requires management to make estimates and assumptions that affect the reported amounts of assets and liabilities and disclosures of contingent assets and liabilities as of December 31, 1997 and 1996, respectively, and reported amounts of sales and expenses for the years ended December 31, 1997, 1996, and 1995, respectively. Actual results could differ from those estimates.

Long-term contracts–The percentage-of-completion (cost-to-cost) method is used to estimate sales under fixed-price and fixed-price incentive contracts. Sales under cost-reimbursement contracts are recorded as costs are incurred. Fees based on cost, award fees, and incentive fees are included in sales at the time such amounts are reasonably estimable. Losses on contracts are recognized when determinable.

Accounts receivable–Accounts receivable at December 31, 1997 and 1996, included $698 million and $547 million, respectively, related to long-term contracts, of which $209 million and $257 million, respectively, were unbilled. Unbilled costs, fees, and claims represent revenues earned and billable in the following month as well as revenues earned but not billable under terms of the contracts. A substantial portion of such amounts is expected to be billed during the following year. Retainage receivables and receivables subject to negotiation are not significant.

Inventories–Inventories are stated at the lower of cost, principally the first-in, first-out (FIFO) method, or market. Inventories applicable to long-term contracts are not significant.

Depreciation–Depreciation is computed over the assets' estimated useful lives using the straight-line method for the majority of the company's depreciable assets. The remaining assets are depreciated using accelerated methods.

Asset impairment–The company records impairment losses on long-lived assets used in operations when events and circumstances indicate that the assets may be impaired and the undiscounted net cash flows estimated to be generated by those assets are less than their carrying amounts.

Intangible assets–Intangible assets are stated on the basis of cost. Intangibles arising from acquisitions prior to 1971 ($49 million) are not being amortized because there is no indication of diminished value. Intangibles arising from acquisitions after 1970 are being amortized by the straight-line method principally over 40 years. The carrying value of intangible assets is assessed for impairment on a quarterly basis.

Forward exchange contracts–The company enters into forward exchange contracts, the majority of which hedge firm foreign currency commitments and certain intercompany transactions. At December 31, 1997, the company had contracts outstanding amounting to approximately $186 million denominated principally in the Canadian dollar, the U.S. dollar, the German mark, the British pound, and the European currency unit, maturing at various dates through December 1998. Changes in market value of the contracts are generally included in the basis of the transactions. Foreign exchange contracts are placed with a number of major financial institutions to minimize credit risk. No collateral is held in relation to the contracts, and the company anticipates that these financial institutions will satisfy their obligations under the contracts.

Fair values of financial instruments

In millions	1997 Carrying Value	1997 Fair Value	1996 Carrying Value	1996 Fair Value
Cash and cash equivalents	$ 70	$ 70	$386	$386
Short-term debt	411	411	52	52
Floating rate long-term debt	736	736	31	31
Fixed rate long-term debt	509	584	499	553
Interest rate hedges—(liability)	—	(5)	—	(1)
Forward currency exchange contracts—(liability)	—	(2)	—	(4)

149

The fair value of long-term debt was estimated using a discounted cash flow analysis, based on the company's current borrowing rates for similar types of borrowing arrangements. The fair value of interest rate hedges and forward currency exchange contracts is estimated based on quoted market prices of offsetting contracts.

Environmental costs–TRW participates in environmental assessments and remedial efforts at operating facilities, previously owned or operated facilities, and Superfund or other waste sites. Costs related to these locations are accrued when it is probable that a liability has been incurred and the amount of that liability can be reasonably estimated. Estimated costs are recorded at undiscounted amounts based on experience and assessments and are regularly evaluated as efforts proceed. Insurance recoveries are recorded as a reduction of environmental costs when fixed and determinable.

Earnings per share–In 1997, TRW adopted SFAS No. 128, "Earnings per Share." Statement 128 replaced the calculation of primary and fully diluted earnings per share with basic and diluted earnings per share. Unlike primary earnings per share, basic earnings per share excludes any dilutive effects of options and convertible securities. Diluted earnings per share is similar to the previously reported fully diluted earnings per share. All earnings per share amounts for all periods presented have been restated to conform to Statement 128 requirements. The effects of preferred stock dividends, convertible preferred stock, and employee stock options were excluded from the calculation of 1997 diluted earnings per share as they would have been antidilutive.

In millions except per share data	1997	1996	1995
Numerator			
Earnings (loss) from continuing operations	$(48.5)	$182.4	$395.4
Preferred stock dividends	(.7)	(.7)	(.8)
Numerator for basic earnings per share— earnings (loss) available to common shareholders	(49.2)	181.7	394.6
Effect of dilutive securities Preferred stock dividends	—	.7	.8
Numerator for diluted earnings per share— earnings (loss) available to common shareholders after assumed conversions	$(49.2)	$182.4	$395.4

Denominator

Denominator for basic earnings per share— weighted-average common shares	123.7	128.7	130.6
Effect of dilutive securities			
Convertible preferred stock	—	1.1	1.2
Employee stock options	—	3.0	2.6
Dilutive potential common shares	—	4.1	3.8
Denominator for diluted earnings per share— adjusted weighted-average shares and assumed conversions	123.7	132.8	134.4
Basic earnings (loss) per share from continuing operations	$(0.40)	$1.41	$3.02
Diluted earnings (loss) per share from continuing operations	$(0.40)	$1.37	$2.94

Research and Development

In millions	1997	1996	1995
Customer-funded	$1,501	$1,425	$1,360
Company-funded Research and development	461	412	392
Product development	174	160	139
	635	572	531
	$2,136	$1,997	$1,891

Company-funded research and development programs include research and development for commercial products and independent research and development and bid and proposal work related to government products and services. A portion of the cost incurred for independent research and development and bid and proposal work is recoverable through overhead charged to government contracts. Product development costs include engineering and field support for new customer requirements.

The 1997 amounts exclude the $548 million charge for purchased in-process research and development.

Acquisitions

On February 5, 1997, the company acquired an 80 percent equity interest in the air bag and steering wheel businesses of Magna International for cash of $415 million plus assumed net debt of $50 million. These businesses supply air bag modules, inflators, propellants, steering wheels, and other related automotive components. The results of operations have been included in the financial statements from the date of acquisition. The acquisition was accounted for by the purchase method; accordingly, the purchase price has been allocated to the net assets acquired based on their estimated fair values and to costs for certain restructuring actions to be completed in 1998. The purchase price in excess of the net assets is $276 million and is being amortized over 40 years.

On December 24, 1997, the company acquired the shares of BDM International, Inc. (BDM), for cash of $880 million plus assumed net debt of $85 million. BDM is an information technology company operating in the systems and software integration, computer and technical services, and enterprise management and operations markets. The acquisition was accounted for by the purchase method, with the purchase price tentatively allocated to the net assets acquired based on their fair values. An independent valuation was performed primarily using the income approach for valuing the intangible assets. As a result of the valuation, $548 million was allocated to in-process research and development projects that had not reached technological feasibility and have no alternative future use. This amount was recognized as an expense with no tax benefit at the date of acquisition. The intangible assets of $306 million will be amortized over an average period of 15 years.

The following unaudited pro forma financial information reflects the consolidated results of operations of the company as if the acquisitions had taken place at the beginning of the respective periods. The pro forma information includes adjustments for interest expense that would have been incurred to finance the acquisitions, additional depreciation based on the fair market value of the property, plant and equipment acquired, write-off of purchased in-process research and development, and the amortization of intangible assets arising from the transactions. The pro forma financial information is not necessarily indicative of the results of operations as they would have been had the transactions been affected on the assumed dates.

In millions, ext per share amounts

Year ended (unaudited)	1997	1996
Sales	$11,758	$11,231
Loss from continuing operations	(85)	(392)
Loss per share	(.69)	(3.05)

Divestiture and Special Charges

During 1996, the company sold substantially all of the businesses in its Information Systems & Services segment. The financial statements reflect as discontinued operations for all periods presented that segment's net assets and operating results, as well as the related transaction gain.

Net proceeds of $1.1 billion in cash resulted in a gain of $484 million ($260 million after tax, or $1.96 per share). Sales of the discontinued operations were $453 million and $604 million in 1996 and 1995, respectively.

During 1996, the company recorded before-tax charges of $385 million ($252 million after tax, or $1.90 per share) primarily for actions taken in the automotive and space, defense and information systems businesses. The components of the charge include severance costs of $40 million, contract reserves of $99 million, litigation and warranty expenses of $127 million, asset writedowns of $96 million, and other items of $23 million. Cash expenditures related to the severance costs were substantially completed during 1997.

The charges are included in the Statements of Earnings for 1996 as follows: $321 million included in cost of sales; $18 million included in interest expense; $65 million included in other expense (income)—net; and a reduction of $19 million included in other captions. For balance sheet purposes, other accruals in 1997 and 1996 include $96 million and $225 million, respectively, relating to these charges.

Other Expense (Income)—Net

In millions	1997	1996	1995
Other income	$(66)	$(67)	$(37)
Other expense	48	119	25
Minority interests	20	12	11
Earnings of affiliates	(12)	(1)	(2)
Foreign currency translation	7	7	10
	$(3)	$70	$7

Other income in 1997 includes a $15 million gain on the sale of a property. Other expense in 1996 includes $65 million of special charges.

Income Taxes

Earnings from continuing operations before income taxes

In millions	1997	1996	1995
U.S.	$95	$133	$428
Non-U.S.	145	169	197
	$240	$302	$625

Provision for income taxes

In millions	1997	1996	1995
Current			
U.S. federal	$136	$176	$90
Non-U.S.	84	73	57
U.S. state and local	23	20	17
	243	269	164
Deferred			
U.S. federal	46	(130)	31
Non-U.S.	(4)	(6)	14
U.S. state and local	4	(13)	21
	46	(149)	66
	$289	$120	$230

Effective income tax rate

	1997	1996	1995
U.S. statutory income tax rate	35.0%	35.0%	35.0%
Nondeductible expenses	2.7	2.4	1.3
U.S. state and local income taxes net of U.S. federal tax benefit	7.6	3.0	3.8
Non-U.S. tax rate variances net of foreign tax credits	(2.2)	3.4	(.1)
Prior years adjustments	(3.5)	(1.9)	(3.0)
Purchased in-process research and development	80.0	—	—
Other	.7	(2.3)	(.2)
	120.3%	39.6%	36.8%

subsidiaries and thereby indefinitely postpone their remittance. Accordingly, deferred income taxes have not been provided for accumulated undistributed earnings of $451 million at December 31, 1997.

In millions	Deferred Tax Assets		Deferred Tax Liabilities	
	1997	1996	1997	1996
Pensions and postretirement benefits other than pensions	$260	$269	$6	$23
Completed contract method of accounting for long-term contracts	49	53	457	421
State and local taxes	23	33	—	8
Reserves and accruals	85	186	—	—
Depreciation and amortization	10	11	91	86
Insurance accruals	22	32	—	—
Non-U.S. net operating loss carryforwards	30	23	—	—
Other	180	143	41	40
	659	750	595	578
Valuation allowance for deferred tax assets	(25)	(20)	—	—
	$634	$730	$595	$578

The effective tax rate in 1997 was 120.3 percent compared to 39.6 percent in 1996. Excluding the write-off of purchased in-process research and development, the effective tax rate would have been 36.6 percent.

Deferred income taxes reflect the net tax effects of temporary differences between the carrying amounts of assets and liabilities for financial reporting purposes and the amounts used for income tax purposes. At December 31, 1997 and 1996, the company had unused tax benefits of $30 million and $23 million, respectively, related to non-U.S. net operating loss carryforwards for income tax purposes, of which $13 million and $18 million can be carried forward indefinitely and the balance expires at various dates through 2004. A valuation allowance at December 31, 1997 and 1996, of $25 million and $20 million, respectively, has been recognized to offset the related deferred tax assets due to the uncertainty of realizing the benefit of the loss carryforwards.

It is the company's intention to reinvest undistributed earnings of certain of its non-U.S.

Pension Plans

The company has defined benefit pension plans (generally noncontributory except for those in the United Kingdom) for substantially all employees. Plans for most salaried employees provide pay-related benefits based on years of service. Plans for hourly employees generally provide benefits based on flat-dollar amounts and years of service.

Under the company's funding policy, annual contributions are made to fund the plans during the participants' working lifetimes, except for unfunded plans in Germany and certain non-qualified plans in the United States which are funded as benefits are paid to participants. Annual contributions to funded plans have met or exceeded ERISA's minimum funding requirements or amounts required by local law or custom.

The company sponsors a contributory stock ownership and savings plan for which a majority of its U.S. employees are eligible. The company matches employee contributions up to 3 percent of the participant's qualified compensation. The

In millions	1997 U.S.	1997 Non-U.S.	1996 U.S.	1996 Non-U.S.	1995 U.S.	1995 Non-U.S.
Defined benefit plans						
Service-cost benefits earned during the year	$ 72	$ 16	$ 73	$ 14	$ 52	$ 15
Interest cost on projected benefit obligation	179	29	165	28	153	27
Actual return on plan assets	(441)	(30)	(344)	(23)	(508)	(38)
Net amortization and deferral	207	6	137	8	306	19
Defined benefit plans	17	21	31	27	3	23
Defined contribution plans	1	5	1	5	1	5
Employee stock ownership and savings plan	44	—	40	—	36	—
Total pension cost	$ 62	$ 26	$ 72	$ 32	$ 40	$ 28

In millions	1997 U.S.	1997 Non-U.S.	1996 U.S.	1996 Non-U.S.
Actuarial present value of benefit obligations				
Vested benefit obligation	$2,343	$ 382	$1,947	$ 368
Overfunded plans	$2,291	$ 260	$2,050	$ 253
Underfunded plans	167	138	55	129
Total accumulated benefit obligation	$2,458	$ 398	$2,105	$ 382
Projected benefit obligation	$2,869	$ 429	$2,381	$ 412
Overfunded plans	$3,031	$ 301	$2,782	$ 300
Underfunded plans	105	21	5	14
Total plan assets at fair value (primarily listed stocks and bonds)	3,136	322	2,787	314
Plan assets in excess of (less than) projected benefit obligation	267	(107)	406	(98)
Unrecognized net gain	(162)	(39)	(253)	(47)
Unrecognized net assets from January 1, 1986 (January 1, 1989 for non-U.S. plans)	(23)	(11)	(41)	(11)
Unrecognized prior service cost	33	11	22	9
Additional minimum liability	(16)	(7)	(16)	(7)
Net pension asset (liability) recognized in the balance sheet	$ 99	$(153)	$ 118	$(154)

Actuarial assumptions:

	1997 U.S.	1997 Non-U.S.	1996 U.S.	1996 Non-U.S.
Discount rate	7.0%	6.0–7.0%	7.5%	6.5–7.75%
Rate of increase in compensation levels	4.4%	3.5–4.0%	4.4%	4.0–5.0%

company contributions are held in an unleveraged employee stock ownership plan. The company also sponsors other defined contribution pension plans covering employees at some of its operations.

The expected long-term rate of return on plan assets for U.S. plans was 9 percent for 1997, 1996, and 1995. For non-U.S. plans, the expected long-term rate of return ranged from 7 percent to 9 ½ percent in 1997, 7 percent to 9 ¾ percent in 1996, and 7 percent to 9 ½ percent in 1995.

Postretirement Benefits Other Than Pensions

The company provides health care and life insurance benefits for a majority of its retired employees in the United States and Canada. The health care plans provide for cost sharing, in the form of employee contributions, deductibles and coinsur-

ance, between the company and its retirees. The postretirement health care plan covering a majority of employees who retired since August 1, 1988, limits the annual increase in the company's contribution toward the plan's cost to a maximum of the lesser of 50 percent of medical inflation or 4 percent. Life insurance benefits are generally noncontributory. The company's policy is to fund the cost of postretirement health care and life insurance benefits in amounts determined at the discretion of management. Retirees in certain other countries are provided similar benefits by plans sponsored by their governments.

In millions	1997	1996
Accumulated postretirement benefit obligation		
Retirees	$511	$512
Fully eligible active participants	43	35
Other active participants	240	213
	794	760
Plan assets at fair value (primarily listed stocks and bonds)	129	83
Accumulated postretirement benefit obligation in excess of plan assets	(665)	(677)
Unrecognized prior service cost	(6)	(6)
Unrecognized net gain	(30)	(35)
Net liability recognized in the balance sheet	$(701)	$(718)

In millions	1997	1996	1995
Service cost	$13	$13	$10
Interest cost	54	54	54
Actual return on plan assets	(13)	(7)	(9)
Net amortization and deferral	4	2	5
Net periodic postretirement benefit cost	$58	$62	$60

The discount rate used in determining the accumulated postretirement benefit obligation as of December 31, 1997 and 1996, was 7 percent and 7 ½ percent, respectively. At December 31, 1997, the 1998 annual rate of increase in the per capita cost of covered health care benefits was assumed to be 8 percent for all participants. The rate was assumed to decrease gradually to 5 percent in the year 2009 and remain at that level thereafter. At December 31, 1996, the 1997 annual rate of increase in the per capita cost of health care benefits was assumed to be 9 percent for participants under age 65 and 8 percent for participants age 65 or older. The rates were assumed to decrease gradually to 6 percent and 5 percent, respectively, in the year 2009 and remain at that level thereafter. A one percent annual increase in these assumed cost trend rates would increase the accumulated postretirement benefit obligation at December 31, 1997, by approximately 14 percent and the aggregate of the service and interest cost components of net periodic postretirement benefit cost for 1997 by approximately 14 percent. The weighted average expected long-term rate of return on plan assets was 8 percent for 1997, 1996, and 1995. The trust holding the majority of the plan assets is not subject to federal income taxes.

Debt and Credit Agreements

Short-term debt

In millions	1997	1996
U.S. borrowings	$ 318	$ 9
Non-U.S. borrowings	93	43
	$411	$ 52

Long-term debt

In millions	1997	1996
U.S. borrowings	$ 691	$ —
Non-U.S. borrowings	54	44
7.3% ESOP obligations due 1997	—	20
Medium-term notes		
9.35% Notes due 2020 (due 2000 at option of note holder)	100	100
9 ⅜% Notes due 2021	100	100
Other medium-term notes	278	234
Other	22	32
Total long-term debt	1,245	530
Less current portion	128	72
	$1,117	$458

TRW maintains two committed U.S. revolving credit agreements. The first agreement allows the company to borrow up to $750 million with 17 banks and extends through June 2002. The second agreement allows the company to borrow up to $750 million with 15 banks and extends to December 8, 1998. The interest rate under the agreements is either a negotiated rate, the banks' prime rates, a rate based on the banks' costs of funds in the secondary certificate of deposit market, or a rate based on an Interbank Offered Rate. TRW's commercial paper borrowings are supported by these agreements. At December 31, 1997, there were $60 million and $65 million in outstanding borrowings under the U.S. revolving credit agreements, respectively. At December 31, 1997, $600 million of short-term U.S. borrowings were reclassified as long-term debt as the company intended to refinance these borrowings on a long-term basis and has the ability to do so under its U.S. revolving credit agreements. In January 1998, the company issued $500 million of notes and debentures which mature at various dates through 2028.

The company also maintains a committed multicurrency revolving credit agreement with 17 banks. The agreement allows the company to borrow up to $250 million and extends through June 2002. The interest rate under the agreement is based on various interest rate indices. At December 31, 1997, there were no outstanding borrowings under the multicurrency credit agreement.

On December 24, 1997, the company acquired the shares of BDM International. BDM maintained a committed multicurrency revolving credit agreement with six banks. At December 31, 1997, there were $91 million in outstanding borrowings under the BDM committed multicurrency revolving credit agreement. The borrowings were paid and the credit agreement was terminated in January 1998.

As of December 31, 1997, the company has interest rate swap agreements for notional borrowings of $28 million in which the company pays a fixed rate and receives a floating rate. The weighted average pay rate and receive rate under these agreements is 6.2 percent and 3.4 percent, respectively. These agreements mature at various dates through 1998. The floating rates under the interest rate swap agreements are based on LIBOR rates and have been calculated using these rates at December 31, 1997. Net payments or receipts under the agreements are recognized as an adjustment to interest expense. The agreements were entered into with a major financial institution, and the company anticipates that the financial institution will satisfy its obligations under the agreements. No collateral is held in relation to the agreements.

The weighted average interest rate on short-term borrowings outstanding, including amounts reclassified to long-term debt, at December 31, 1997 and 1996, is 6.4 percent and 9.9 percent, respectively.

The other medium-term notes bear interest at rates ranging from 5.98 percent to 9.25 percent and mature at various dates through 2020.

Long-term non-U.S. borrowings bear interest, stated in terms of the local currency borrowing, at rates ranging from 3.6 percent to 9.48 percent at December 31, 1997, and mature at various dates through 2005.

The maturities of long-term debt are, in millions: 1998—$128; 1999—$37; 2000—$12; 2001—$33; 2002—$602; and $433 thereafter.

The indentures and other debt agreements impose, among other covenants, restrictions on funded debt and maintenance of minimum net worth. Under the most restrictive interpretation of these covenants, the payment of dividends was limited to approximately $729 million at December 31, 1997.

Compensating balance arrangements and commitment fees were not material.

Lease Commitments

TRW leases certain offices, manufacturing and research buildings, machinery, automobiles, and data processing and other equipment. Such leases, some of which are noncancelable and in many cases include renewals, expire at various dates. The company pays most maintenance, insurance, and tax expenses relating to leased assets. Rental expense for operating leases was $146 million for 1997, $130 million for 1996, and $124 million for 1995.

At December 31, 1997, the future minimum lease payments for noncancelable operating leases totaled $372 million and are payable as follows: 1998—$103; 1999—$79; 2000—$53; 2001—$34; 2002—$26; and $77 thereafter.

Capital Stock

Serial Preference Stock II–Cumulative—stated at $2.75 a share; 5 million shares authorized.

Series 1–Each share convertible into 8.8 shares of common; redeemable at $104 per share; invol-

untary liquidation price of $104 per share; dividend rate of $4.40 per annum.

Series 3–Each share convertible into 7.448 shares of common; redeemable at $100 per share; involuntary liquidation price of $40 per share; dividend rate of $4.50 per annum.

Series 4–Not convertible into common shares; redemption price and involuntary liquidation price of $125 per one one-hundredth of a share; annual dividend rate per one one-hundredth of a share of the lesser of $4.00 or the current dividend on common stock; no shares outstanding at December 31, 1997.

Common stock–$0.625 par value; authorized 500 million shares; shares outstanding were reduced by treasury shares of 10.9 million in 1997 and 7.2 million in 1996.

TRW has a shareholder purchase rights plan under which each shareholder of record as of May 17, 1996, received one-half of one right for each TRW common share held. Each right entitles the holder, upon the occurrence of certain events, to buy one one-hundredth of a share of Cumulative Redeemable Serial Preference Stock II, Series 4, at a price of $300. In other events, each right entitles the holder, other than the acquiring party, to purchase $600 of TRW common stock or common stock of another person at a 50 percent discount. The company may redeem these rights at its option at one cent per right under certain circumstances.

At December 31, 1997, 15.8 million shares of common stock were reserved for the exercise and issuance of stock options and conversion of the Serial Preference Stock II, Series 1 and 3. There were 1.2 million shares of Cumulative Redeemable Serial Preference Stock II, Series 4, reserved for the shareholder purchase rights plan.

Stock Options

TRW has granted nonqualified stock options to certain employees to purchase the company's common stock at the market price on the date of grant. Stock options granted become exercisable to the extent of one-third of the optioned shares for each full year of employment following the date of grant and expire 10 years after the date of grant. The company applies the provisions of Accounting Principles Board Opinion No. 25 in accounting for its employee stock options and, as such, no compensation expense is recognized as the exercise price equals the market price of the stock on the date of grant.

	1997		1996		1995	
	Millions of shares	Weighted-average exercise price	Millions of shares	Weighted-average exercise price	Millions of shares	Weighted-average exercise price
Outstanding at beginning of year	8.5	$29.72	9.2	$26.45	9.4	$25.09
Granted	2.0	50.19	1.7	43.98	1.4	32.32
Exercised	1.6	25.96	1.9	25.28	1.4	23.33
Canceled, expired or terminated	.4	38.63	.5	35.51	.2	28.23
Outstanding at end of year	8.5	34.94	8.5	29.72	9.2	26.45
Exercisable	5.3	27.81	5.6	25.18	6.6	24.07
Weighted-average fair value of options granted		11.92		9.45		8.24

At December 31, 1997, approximately 1,100 employees were participants in the plan. As of that date, the per share exercise prices of options outstanding ranged from $19.88 to $58.88. The weighted-average remaining contractual life of those options is approximately six years.

Had the compensation cost for the stock options granted in 1997, 1996 and 1995 been determined based on the fair value at the grant date consistent with the fair value method of SFAS No. 123, the company's net earnings and earnings per share would have been reduced by $9 million ($.08 per share) in 1997, $5 million ($.04 per share) in 1996, and $2 million ($.02 per share) in 1995. The effect on 1996 and 1995 net earnings may not be representative of the effect on future years' net earnings amounts as the compensation cost reflects expense for only two years' vesting in 1996 and one year's vesting in 1995.

Fair value was estimated at the date of grant using the Black-Scholes option pricing model and the following weighted-average assumptions for 1997, 1996, and 1995, respectively: risk-free interest rate of 5.83%, 5.43%, and 7.44%; dividend yield of 2.54%, 2.84%, and 2.80%; expected volatility of 20%, 20%, and 19%; and an expected option life of six years for 1997, 1996, and 1995.

TRW grants performance share rights to certain employees under which the employees are entitled to receive shares of the company's common stock based on the achievement of a certain return on assets employed. The rights specify a target number of shares which the employee would receive for each year that goals for returns on assets employed are met. If the goals are exceeded, the employee could receive up to 200 percent of the target shares, with the excess over 100 percent payable in cash, unless the Compensation and Stock Option Committee of TRW's Directors determines to pay the excess in shares. If the goals are not met, the employee would receive fewer than the target shares or no shares. The target number of performance share rights granted to employees and still outstanding were .2 million and .4 million at December 31, 1997 and 1996, respectively.

Contingencies
The company is subject to various investigations, claims, and legal proceedings covering a wide range of matters that arise in the ordinary course of its business activities. In addition, the company is conducting a number of environmental investigations and remedial actions at current and former company locations and, along with other companies, has been named a potentially responsible party for certain waste management sites. Each of these matters is subject to various uncertainties, and some of these matters may be resolved unfavorably to the company. A reserve estimate for each matter is established using standard engineering cost estimating techniques. In the determination of such costs, consideration is given to professional judgment of company environmental engineers in consultation with outside environmental specialists when necessary. At multiparty sites, the reserve estimate also reflects the expected allocation of total project costs among the various potentially responsible parties. At December 31, 1997, the company had reserves for environmental matters of $71 million, including $6 million of additional accruals recorded during the year. The company aggressively pursues reimbursement for environmental costs from its insurance

carriers. However, insurance recoveries are not recorded as a reduction of environmental costs until they are fixed and determinable. At December 31, 1997, the "Other assets" caption on the balance sheet includes $30 million of insurance recoveries related to environmental matters. The company believes that any liability that may result from the resolution of environmental matters for which sufficient information is available to support these cost estimates will not have a material adverse effect on the company's financial position. However, the company cannot predict the effect on the company's financial position of expenditures for aspects of certain matters for which there is insufficient information. In addition, the company cannot predict the effect of compliance with environmental laws and regulations with respect to unknown environmental matters on the company's financial position or the possible effect of compliance with environmental requirements imposed in the future.

Further, product liability claims may be asserted in the future for events not currently known by management. Although the ultimate liability from these potential claims cannot be ascertained at December 31, 1997, management does not anticipate that any related liability, after consideration of insurance recovery, would have a material adverse effect on the company's financial position.

During 1997, TRW Vehicle Safety Systems Inc., a wholly owned subsidiary of the company, reported to the Arizona Department of Environmental Quality (ADEQ) potential violations of the Arizona hazardous waste law at its Queen Creek, Arizona, facility for the possible failure to properly label and dispose of waste water that might be classified as hazardous waste. ADEQ is conducting an investigation into these potential violations, and the company is cooperating with the investigation. If ADEQ initiates proceedings against the company with respect to such matters, the company could be liable for penalties and fines and other relief. The company has been apprised by state and federal officials that there are ongoing civil and criminal investigations with respect to these potential violations. Management is currently evaluating this matter and is unable to make a meaningful estimate of the amount or range of possible liability, if any, at this time.

During 1996, the company was advised by the Department of Justice (DOJ) that it had been named as a defendant in two lawsuits brought by a former employee and filed under seal in 1994 and 1995, respectively, in the United States District Court for the Central District of California under the QUITAM provisions of the civil False Claims Act. The Act permits an individual to bring suit in the name of the United States and share in any recovery. The allegations in the lawsuits relate to the classification of costs incurred by the company that were charged to certain of its federal contracts. Under the law, the government must investigate the allegations and determine whether it wishes to intervene and take responsibility for the lawsuits. On February 19, 1998, the DOJ intervened in the litigation with respect to a limited number of the allegations. The company cannot presently predict the outcome of these matters, although management believes that the company has meritorious defenses.

Industry Segments

TRW Inc. is a United States–based company providing advanced technology products and services for the automotive and space, defense, and information systems markets. The principal markets for the company's automotive products are North American, European, and Asian original equipment manufacturers and independent distributors. Space, Defense & Information Systems primarily provides products and services to the United States Government, agencies of the United States Government, and commercial customers.

Automotive–Occupant restraint systems, including sensors, steering wheels, air bag, and seat belt systems. Steering systems, including power and manual rack and pinion steering for light vehicles, hydraulic steering systems for commercial truck and off-highway vehicles, and suspension components. Electrical and electronic controls, engineered fasteners, and stud welding and control systems. Engine valves, valve train parts, and pistons.

Space, Defense & Information Systems– Spacecraft, including the design and manufacture of military and civilian spacecraft equipment, propulsion subsystems, electro-optical and instrument systems, spacecraft payloads, high-energy lasers and laser technology, and other high-reliability components. Systems integration, systems engineering services, and software in the fields of military command and control, intelligence collection, public safety, modeling and simulation, training, telecommunications, image processing, earth observation, nuclear waste management, air traffic control, security and counterterrorism, and other high-technology space, defense, and civil government support systems. Electronic systems, equipment, components and services, including the design and manufacture of space communication systems, airborne reconnaissance systems, unmanned aerial vehicles, avionics systems, commercial telecommunications and other electronic technologies for tactical and strategic space, defense, and selected commercial applications. Information technology systems, products and services for government and commercial markets focused on defense, health, and human safety, integrated supply chain, warehousing, logistics, criminal justice, tax systems modernization, and financial reporting applications.

In millions	Year ended December 31	Automotive	Space, Defense & Information Systems	Company Staff & Other	Total
Sales	1997	$7,032	$3,799	$ —	$10,831
	1996	6,493	3,364	—	9,857
	1995	6,468	3,100	—	9,568
Operating profit (loss)	1997	$ 631	$ (228)(A)	$(163)	$ 240(A)
	1996	319	157	(174)	302
	1995	607	192	(174)	625
Identifiable assets	1997	$4,307	$1,546	$ 557	$ 6,410
	1996	3,683	1,278	938	5,899
	1995	3,706	1,113	851	5,670
Depreciation and amortization of property, plant and equipment	1997	$ 352	$ 115	$ 9	$ 476
	1996	321	112	10	443
	1995	304	102	9	415
Capital expenditures	1997	$ 390	$ 156	$ 3	$ 549
	1996	342	157	1	500
	1995	314	114	38	466

(A) Excluding the write-off of purchased in-process research and development, Space, Defense & Information Systems and Total operating profit would have been $320 million and $788 million, respectively.

Company Staff assets consist principally of cash and cash equivalents, current deferred income taxes, and administrative facilities. Intersegment sales were not significant. Sales to agencies of the U.S. Government, primarily by the Space, Defense & Information Systems segment, were $3,523 million in 1997, $3,121 million in 1996, and $2,890 million in 1995. Sales to Ford Motor Company by the Automotive segment were $1,469 million in 1997, $1,470 million in 1996, and $1,474 million in 1995.

Geographic Segments

In millions	Year ended December 31	United States	Europe	Other Areas	Company Staff & Other	Total
Sales	1997	$6,919	$3,002	$910	$ —	$10,831
	1996	6,469	2,522	866	—	9,857
	1995	6,212	2,525	831	—	9,568
Operating profit (loss)	1997	$ 94	$ 245	$ 64	$(163)	$ 240
	1996	212	224	40	(174)	302
	1995	514	220	65	(174)	625
Identifiable assets	1997	$3,415	$1,980	$554	$ 461	$ 6,410
	1996	3,056	1,411	590	842	5,899
	1995	2,871	1,464	537	798	5,670

Interarea sales are not significant to the total revenue of any geographic area.

Quarterly Financial Information (Unaudited)

In millions except per share data

	First 1997	First 1996	Second 1997	Second 1996	Third 1997	Third 1996	Fourth 1997	Fourth 1996
		(C)				*(D)*	*(A)(B)*	*(E)*
Sales	$2,660	$2,514	$2,852	$2,572	$2,521	$2,320	$2,798	$2,451
Gross profit	482	463	534	479	466	133	523	406
Earnings (loss) from continuing operations before income taxes	195	165	219	188	166	(218)	(340)	167
Net earnings (loss)	119	117	135	130	108	106	(411)	127
Net earnings (loss) per share *(F)*								
Diluted	.92	.86	1.05	.97	.85	.82	(3.34)	.98
Basic	.95	.89	1.09	1.00	.88	.82	(3.34)	1.01

(A) Earnings (loss) from continuing operations before income taxes includes a $548 million ($4.46 per share) one-time noncash charge related to in-process research and development with no income tax benefit.

(B) Earnings (loss) from continuing operations before income taxes includes a $15 million gain ($10 million aftertax, 8 cents per share) related to the sale of property.

(C) Earnings (loss) from continuing operations before income taxes included an $18 million benefit ($12 million after taxes, 9 cents per share) related to an insurance claim settlement and a $15 million noncash charge ($13 million aftertax, 10 cents per share) related to SFAS No. 121.

(D) Net earnings (loss) included a $243 million gain ($1.90 per share) related to the sale of the information services business and a $233 million charge ($1.83 per share) for actions taken in the automotive and space, defense, and information systems businesses.

(E) Net earnings (loss) included a $17 million gain (13 cents per share) related to the sale of the remaining interest in the information services business, a $10 million benefit (8 cents per share) related to the recovery of certain tax costs, and a $28 million charge (22 cents per share) related primarily to product warranties.

(F) Amounts have been restated to comply with SFAS No. 128, "Earnings per Share." Under the provisions of SFAS No. 128, the sum of net earnings (loss) per share for the four quarters may not equal the total year amount.

Stock Prices and Dividends (Unaudited)

The book value per common share at December 31, 1997, was $13.19 compared to $17.29 at the end of 1996. TRW's directors declared the 238th consecutive quarterly dividend during December 1997. Dividends declared per share in 1997 were $1.24, up 6 percent from $1.17 in 1996. The following table highlights the market prices of TRW's common and preference stocks and dividends paid for the quarters of 1997 and 1996.

	Quarter	Price of Traded Shares 1997 High	Price of Traded Shares 1997 Low	Price of Traded Shares 1996 High	Price of Traded Shares 1996 Low	Dividends Paid per Share 1997	Dividends Paid per Share 1996
Common stock	1	$55 ⅞	$48 ⅛	$46 ⅛	$37 ⁷⁄₁₆	$.31	$.275
Par value $0.625 per share	2	58 ⅜	47 ⅜	48 ½	43 ½	.31	.275
	3	61 ⁵⁄₁₆	51 ¼	50 ¾	41 ¹⁄₁₆	.31	.275
	4	61 ⁹⁄₁₆	50 ½	52	43 ¾	.31	.31
Cumulative Serial	1	500	300	379	379	1.10	1.10
Preference Stock II	2	457 ½	442	418	414	1.10	1.10
$4.40 Convertible	3	600	300	500	300	1.10	1.10
Series 1	4	495	495	427	427	1.10	1.10
Cumulative Serial	1	400	364	332 ½	288	1.125	1.125
Preference Stock II	2	402	396	352	350	1.125	1.125
$4.50 Convertible	3	423 ¼	423 ¼	425	250	1.125	1.125
Series 3	4	420	400	329	329	1.125	1.125

The $4.40 Convertible Series 1 was not actively traded during the first quarter of 1997 and the third quarters of 1997 and 1996. The $4.50 Convertible Series 3 was not actively traded during the third quarter of 1996. The prices shown for these quarters represent the range of asked (high) and bid (low) quotations.

CHAPTER 5

PROJECTION OF
FINANCIAL REQUIREMENTS

Up to this point, we've discussed appraisal of performance and management of operating funds in the context of *past* decisions involving investments, operations, and financing. This chapter shifts the emphasis to a *forward* look, that is, forecasting likely future conditions, a critically important task in managing any business. We'll discuss the key concepts and techniques of projecting operating performance and expected financial requirements with which to support future operations. Such projections normally involve alternative plans developed for different sets of conditions, and testing of the sensitivity of the results to changes in key assumptions.

Projection of financial requirements is only part of the business planning process with which management positions the company's future activities relative to the expected economic, competitive, technical, and social environment. When business plans are developed, they are usually structured around specific goals and objectives cooperatively set by the organization and its subgroups. The plans normally spell out strategies and actions for achieving desired short-term, intermediate, and long-term results, with special attention to the need for creating shareholder value by exceeding the cost of capital in ongoing operations as well as sound new growth investments.

Eventually, such plans are quantified in financial terms, in the form of projected financial statements (pro forma statements) and a variety of operational budgets. Detailed cash budgets and cash flow statements are used to provide greater insight into the funding implications of the projected activities. Also, key ratios are usually calculated and presented. The concepts and techniques discussed in Chapters 3 and 4 are necessary for this quantification.

The scope of this book allows us to focus only on the major methods and formats of financial projection. We cannot explicitly take into account the broader strategic planning framework through which the future direction of the company should be explored before any financial quantification can become fully mean-ingful. Nor can we go into the details of various statistical methods which are at times used to support the judgments involved in estimating future conditions.

Nevertheless, financial projection techniques by themselves can be useful simulations of the likely results of broad assumptions made by management about a variety of future conditions. The ease with which pro forma financial statements and cash flow projections can be developed makes them attractive as convenient approximations—which can then be refined with additional information and in-sights—especially as the number of alternatives for action is narrowed down.

Computer spreadsheets and planning models have become ubiquitous, and a growing selection of software packages offers financial simulation and projec-tion capabilities. Many of these applications have helped reduce the drudgery of tracing investment, operational, and financing assumptions through the financial framework of a business. While commercial software offerings differ in their specific orientation and degree of sophistication, they are all built around the basic concepts we'll be discussing in this chapter, as is the commercially available advanced *Financial Genome* software described in Appendix I.

The most important requirement for making successful use of projection methods, however, is a solid understanding of basic financial techniques and rela-tionships, because spreadsheets and analytical packages cannot remove the over-riding need for judgment and consistency. Only with such understanding can the analyst take full advantage of their capabilities. Therefore, this book doesn't focus on the technicalities of how to use spreadsheets, but rather on explaining the fi-nancial concepts and techniques themselves, structured around our decisional context.

The main techniques of financial projection fall into three categories:

- Pro forma financial statements.
- Cash budgets.
- Operating budgets.

Pro forma statements, as the name implies, are projected financial state-ments embodying a set of assumptions about a company's future performance and funding requirements. Cash budgets are detailed projections of the specific inci-dence of cash moving in and out of the business. Operating budgets are detailed projections of company-wide or departmental revenue and/or expense patterns, and they are subsidiary to both pro forma statements and cash flow statements.

All three projection categories involve organized arrays of financial and economic data for the purpose of assessing future performance and funds require-ments. As we'll see, the three methodologies are also closely interrelated—a link-age that can be exploited to achieve consistent financial forecasts.

After discussing each category in detail, we'll examine basic financial mod-eling concepts and the use of sensitivity analysis for testing the impact of changes in critical assumptions underlying the financial projections, subjects we'll revisit in a broader context in Chapter 6.

Pro Forma Financial Statements

The most comprehensive look at the future financial performance of a company can be obtained by developing a set of pro forma statements. These are merely an income statement and a related balance sheet extended into the future by a variety of assumptions. The pro forma income statement represents a broad operational plan for the business, while the pro forma balance sheet reflects the anticipated cumulative impact of assumed future decisions on its financial condition. Both statements are prepared by taking the most readily available estimates of future activity and projecting, account by account, the assumed results and conditions. As we'll see, the approach is not based on detailed accounting transactions, but rather on a creative use of the financial statement framework as a structure on which to arrange future expectations.

Most of the time a third statement, the pro forma cash flow statement, is prepared to add further insight by displaying the funds movements expected during the forecast period, arranged into our familiar categories of operations, investments, and financing. Cash flow statements provide the most dynamic view of the expected changes in the company's funding picture, as we saw in Chapter 3.

Pro forma projections can be done for any time frame and at any level of detail desired. In summarized form, these statements are one of the most widely used ways of quickly making estimates of funding needs. They are particularly favored by bank loan officers, who must assess the creditworthiness of the client company from a total financial standpoint. Detailed plans aren't needed to construct complete pro forma statements, even though using the results of a formal planning process would increase the degree of precision. Instead, selected ratios can be employed to produce statements that are entirely satisfactory, particularly as a first look. As we'll demonstrate, an important aspect of pro forma analysis is the ability to establish the company's net cash requirements as of the future date for which the pro forma balance sheet is prepared.

To show how pro forma statements are developed, we'll use the example of a fictitious manufacturing company called XYZ Corporation. We've chosen a manufacturing company here because such statements tend to be more complex than those of service organizations, especially in the operations area, and thus provide an opportunity to show more interrelationships. XYZ company makes and sells three different products, has a seasonal pattern with the low point occurring in December, and is currently profitable. The most recent actual results available are for the third quarter of 1999. This initial set of data allows us to project ahead, but we can also ask management for additional information as needed. The pro forma projection is to be made for the last quarter of 1999, and the objective is to determine both the level of profit for the quarter and the amount of additional funds that will be needed as of the end of the year. A quarterly pattern was chosen for this illustration because it permits us to consider seasonal changes in addition to simple period-to-period changes. We've also included an annual view, showing the estimated results for all of 1999, and a pro forma projection for the year 2000. There is no difference in the basic principles for projecting either annual or quarterly periods—only the length of the time interval itself.

Pro Forma Income Statement

We begin the process with the pro forma income statement for XYZ Corporation. The income statement is normally prepared first, because the amount of after-tax profit developed there also must be reflected in the pro forma balance sheet as a change in retained earnings, in order to ensure consistency between the two statements.

The starting point for the income statement, as shown on the first line in Figure 5–1, is a projection of the unit and dollar volume of *sales*. This can be estimated in a variety of ways, ranging from trend-line projection to detailed departmental sales forecasts by individual product, often built up from field estimates. In the absence of any other information we can, of course, make our own "guesstimates" based on past overall results. In the case of XYZ Corporation, we know that a seasonal pattern exists, and that sales can be expected to decline in the last quarter. On an annual basis, we are showing the estimated results for all of 1999, which include the projected last quarter, and a pro forma projection for 2000.

In the first column of Figure 5–1, we've reproduced the actual income statement for the third quarter of 1999. Dollar amounts are given for key revenue and cost elements, as well as a breakdown into percent of sales, or common numbers. In making the necessary series of assumptions for the fourth quarter, we'll use the third quarter experience as a guide, because we've been assured that the quarterly pattern over the years has been reasonably stable. Company statistics from past years suggest that a drop of 18 to 20 percent in sales volume is normal during the fourth quarter. We'll take the midpoint of this range as a beginning assumption. After calculating a 19 percent drop in unit volume, we'll further assume that both prices and product mix will remain unchanged. It's possible, of course, to make different assumptions about volume, prices, and the mix of the three individual products in order to reflect specific insights or to test the sensitivity of operating profit to the impact of "what if " questions. In our case, an inquiry to sales management will confirm that this set of assumptions about sales matches their own forecast.

In establishing the volume for the estimated full year 1999, we are told that units sold through 9/30/99 were 399,000, to which we can add the fourth quarter estimate of 111,000 units. With no change in price and mix, 1999 sales revenue will be $47,100,000. In the pro forma year 2000, sales management expects a 40,000 unit increase over 1999, with product mix and prices still unchanged, for total sales of $52,250,000.

Next we turn to *cost of goods sold*. The actual third quarter income statement provides details on the main components—labor, materials, overhead, and

FIGURE 5–1

XYZ CORPORATION
Pro Forma Income Statements
For the Quarter Ended December 31, 1999,
and for the Years Ended December 31, 1999 and 2000
($ thousands)

	Actual Quarter Ended 9-30-99		Pro Forma Quarter Ended 12-31-99		Estimated Full Year Ended 12-31-99		Pro Forma Year Ended 12-31-00		
Units sold	137,000		111,000		510,000		550,000		Last quarter is seasonal low; past data show 18 to 20 percent decline from third quarter.
Sales	$12,650	100.0%	$10,250	100.0%	$47,100	100.0%	$52,250	100.0%	Projection for the quarter has 19 percent lower volume, same price and mix; pro forma year assumes 7.3 percent growth
Cost of goods sold:									
Labor	2,210		1,810		8,250		9,050		Continued at 21.5 percent of total cost of goods sold
Materials	2,045		1,680		7,675		8,400		Continued at 20 percent of total cost of goods sold
Overhead	5,685		4,660		21,315		23,350		Continued at 55.5 percent of total cost of good sold
Delivery	305		250		1,150		1,250		Continued at 3.0 percent of total cost of goods sold
Total cost of goods sold	10,245	81.0	8,400	82.0	38,390	81.5	42,050	80.5	
Gross margin	2,405	19.0	1,850	18.0	8,710	19.5	10,200	19.5	Margin reduced for the quarter by 1 percentage point due to inefficiencies; improvement for pro forma year
Expenses:									
Selling expense	875	6.9	825	8.0	3,340	7.1	3,550	6.8	Lower activity in last quarter; increase in pro forma year
General and administrative	585	4.6	600	5.9	2,215	4.7	2,350	4.5	Slight increase for quarter; improvement in pro forma year
Total expenses	1,460	11.5	1,425	13.9	5,555	11.8	5,900	11.3	
Operating profit (EBIT)	945	7.5	425	4.1	3,160	6.7	4,300	8.2	Quarter shows impact of slowdown; improvement for pro forma year
Interest	190	1.5	175	1.7	785	1.7	850	1.6	Based on outstanding debt and temporary borrowing
Profit before taxes	755	6.0	250	2.4	2,375	5.0	3,450	6.6	
Income taxes	272	2.2	90	0.9	855	1.8	1,250	2.4	Projected at 36 percent
Net income	483	3.8	160	1.5	1,520	3.2	2,200	4.2	
Dividends	100	0.8	0	0.0	300	0.6	400	0.8	No payment in last quarter; higher in pro forma year
Retained earnings	383	3.0%	160	1.5%	1,220	2.6%	1,800	3.4%	Carried to balance sheet
Depreciation effect added back	575		600		2,330		2,450		From fixed asset records (tax and book depreciation the same)
Net cash flow after dividends	958		760		3,550		4,250		
Add back tax-adjusted interest	122		112		502		544		
Add back dividends	100		0		300		400		
Cash flow from operations	$ 1,180		$ 872		$ 4,352		$ 5,194		

delivery—contained in cost of goods sold. The simplest approach to projection is to calculate the proportion of cost that each of these elements represents in the total cost of goods sold, and assume that the same proportions will hold during the fourth quarter.

We must also remember that the last quarter is the company's seasonal low point, and we can assume that overall production costs are likely to rise, because as operations slow down, some inefficiencies will likely occur. Without more data, we can probably assume a rise of something like one percentage point in the ratio of cost of goods sold to sales as a quick way to allow for the seasonal distortion. The dollar penalty of this assumption is a reduction in the gross margin by 1 percent of sales, or $102,500. We could, of course, test the impact of other levels of the cost of goods sold ratio, using the detailed cost breakdown (labor, materials, etc.) given in the third-quarter income statement. If more precision were desired, specific assumptions could be made about each of these components. This is a basic form of sensitivity analysis—testing the impact on the outcome from changes in one or more key assumptions.

As was done in the case of sales, to estimate the full year 1999 our cost of goods sold projection for the fourth quarter was added to the year-to-date amounts provided to us by management. Note that the gross margin percentage for the full year is above both the third and fourth quarters, because of better performance in the first two quarters. The projection for the year 2000 assumes unchanged annual performance at 19.5 percent.

The main expense categories can be estimated by examining again the actual statement for the third quarter. The figures provided there might simply be accepted and used as the base for our projection, or more detailed assumptions could be tested. For a quick first look, such an overall approach is usually acceptable. *Selling expense* is shown as $875,000. Given that the fourth quarter has lower sales activity, we can probably assume a small decrease, such as $50,000. A reduction fully proportional to the 19 percent drop in volume would not be realistic, however, given that many of the costs, such as base salaries of sales and marketing personnel, are essentially fixed in the near term. This assumption, when added to the results to date given to us by the finance staff, leads to a full year 1999 estimate of $3,340,000, and a projection for 2000 of $3,550,000, assuming higher sales efforts to support the increased volume.

Administrative expenses should be rounded off a little higher for purposes of our quarterly projection because of expected nonrecurring year-end outlays. Note that both expense elements now represent a higher proportion of sales than was true for the actual prior quarter. If there's reason to believe that this result seems out of line, it can, of course, be modified. But we must remember that even if historical patterns were available in great detail, our projection has to deal with the future, and the purpose of the exercise is to make the most realistic assumptions possible. These will, of course, remain assumptions until actual experience supersedes them. Including the fourth quarter figure, the estimate for all of 1999 becomes $2,215,000, again based on year-to-date information given us, and $2,350,000 for pro forma 2000.

As a result of all our assumptions, the fourth quarter *operating profit* falls by half a million dollars, and the profit ratio drops to almost one-half its former level. This is due mostly to the 19 percent drop in sales volume and the associated loss in profit contribution. This volume reduction represents $2.4 million of lost sales which, with a normal cost of goods sold ratio of 81 percent, would have contributed $456,000 to profit. Moreover, we assumed certain inefficiencies in operations and expected only a partial ability to reduce what are mostly fixed expenses. As stated before, this result can and should be examined against the best available experience to judge its appropriateness. For the year as a whole, operating profit is expected to amount to $3,160,000, while the year 2000 results are boosted to $4,300,000. This is due in part to the assumed volume increase of 40,000 units, and also because of the improvements in operating expenses as reflected in their lower percentages of sales compared with expected 1999 results.

Interest expense is charged according to the provisions of the company's outstanding debt, information which is provided to us by the financial organization for all the pro forma periods. The income statement will be complete once we calculate *income taxes* (assumed here at an effective rate of 36 percent) to arrive at *net income*. We note that net income for the quarter has dropped significantly in response to the slowdown in operations, while results for 2000 versus estimated 1999 are up by almost $700,000.

A further assumption needs to be made about *dividends* to arrive at *retained earnings* for the period, which will be reflected in the pro forma balance sheet. In XYZ's case, no dividends have been declared for the quarter, although payments already made during 1999 amount to $300,000. Dividends are expected to rise to $400,000 for the year 2000. As a last step, we've added back the depreciation effect for each of the periods, as well as tax-adjusted interest and dividends to calculate the *cash flow from operations*. As we recall from Chapter 4, this total is a quick approximation which we'll review later in the context of all other expected funds movements.

Pro Forma Balance Sheet

Armed with the data about expected operations, we can now develop the pro forma balance sheets at the end of 1999 and 2000, as illustrated in Figure 5–2. Again, we must make specific assumptions about each account, using the actual balance sheet data at the beginning of the forecast period and applying any additional information we can obtain from management. Fortunately, we have relative freedom to make and vary our estimates in this statement—except that there must always be complete consistency between any assumptions affecting *both* the income statement and the balance sheet. The objective is not accounting precision, of course, but rather to develop an indication of approximate funds needs three months hence and a look at the overall financial condition of the company at that time, as well as one year later.

FIGURE 5-2

XYZ CORPORATION
Pro Forma Balance Sheets
As of December 31, 1999, and December 31, 2000
($ thousands)

	Actual 9/30/99	Change	Pro Forma 12/31/99	Change	Pro Forma 12/31/00	
Assets						
Current assets:						
Cash	$ 1,450	$ −200	$ 1,250	$　　0	$ 1,250	Cash set at estimated minimum balance.
Accounts receivable	4,250	−1,200	3,050	450	3,500	Represents 30 days' sales (projected December sales)
Raw materials	1,500	0	1,500	100	1,600	Safety level; requirements purchased as needed
Finished goods	4,050	−750	3,300	500	3,800	Reduced production by 19 percent for quarter; up for 2,000
Total current assets	11,250	−2,150	9,100	1,050	10,150	Drop from September to December reflects seasonal pattern
Fixed assets:						
Land	2,500	0	2,500	0	2,500	No change assumed
Plant and equipment	20,800	−1,500	19,300	1,750	21,050	Machine sold; cost $1,500, accum. depreciation $950; new equipment bought in 2000
Less: Accumulated depreciation .	8,350	−350	8,000	2,450	10,450	Depreciation for quarter $600; less $950 reduction from sale; normal depreciation for 2000
Net plant and equipment	12,450	−1,150	11,300	−700	10,600	
Total fixed assets	14,950	−1,150	13,800	−700	13,100	
Other assets	1,250	0	1,250	200	1,450	No change in quarter; purchased patents in 2000
Total assets	27,450	−3,300	24,150	550	24,700	
Liabilities and Net Worth						
Current liabilities						
Accounts payable	1,120	−410	710	600	1,310	45 days' purchases from estimated pattern in Figure 5–4; increase for 2000
Notes payable	3,000	−1,500	1,500	−1,500	0	Scheduled repayments
Due contractor	3,400	−2,900	500	−500	0	Scheduled payments on building contract
Accrued taxes	1,250	−310	940	400	1,340	Payment for quarter $400; plus accrual of $90; net increase for 2000
Total current liabilities	8,770	−5,120	3,650	−1,000	2,650	
Long-term liabilities	8,500	0	8,500	0	8,500	No change assumed
Common stock	4,250	250	4,500	0	4,500	Sale of stock under option during quarter; none in 2000
Retained earnings	5,930	160	6,090	1,800	7,890	Retained earnings as calculated on income statement; net of dividends in 2000
Total liabilities and net worth	$27,450	$ −4,710	$22,740	$　800	$23,540	
Funds required		1,410	1,410	-250	1,160	"Plug" figure representing financing needs as of December 31; same amount as in Figures 5-3 and 5-4

We'll start the process with the first account, *cash,* and assume that three months hence, the company would need to keep only the minimum working balance in its bank accounts, and that this will also apply to 12/31/00. The information source for this figure ($1,250,000) is again the finance staff. In the absence of such specific data, we could assume a level of cash that is common among companies of this size. As we'll see later, the desired amount of cash on hand directly affects the amount of funds the company may have to borrow. Also, we must not forget that any cash balance maintained as an ongoing requirement on he balance sheet represents an investment like any other commitment of resources.

Next we turn to *accounts receivable.* If the company sells its products on terms of net 30, it can expect to have at least 30 days' sales outstanding; more, if some of its customers are late in paying. Given no abnormal delays in collections, the accounts receivable balance on the December 31 balance sheet should represent the sales for the whole month of December. However, we do not have exact December sales estimates, because our pro forma income statement for the quarter shows the last three months' sales combined, and we have only an annual sales estimate for 2000. As a simple shortcut, we could assume that one-third of the projected quarterly sales would be outstanding at the end of the fourth quarter, and one-twelfth of the annual sales outstanding on 12/31/00.

For XYZ Corporation, the figure for 12/31/99 would be one-third of the sales of $10,250,000 in Figure 5–1, or $3,417,000. But we learn after some discussion with sales management that in view of the seasonal low in December, the company's sales force projects the month's sales at only $3,050,000. This amount thus represents the 30 days of sales we can assume to be outstanding in the form of accounts receivable at the end of 1999, given normal collection experience. Similarly, the estimate for December sales in 2000 is given to us as $3,500,000.

Raw material inventory could be projected by using monthly withdrawal and purchase patterns, information that the company would be able to provide. However, manufacturing management informs us that for reasons of continuity, they like to keep $1,500,000 worth of raw materials on hand at all times, and frequent purchases are made as needed to maintain that level, which is assumed both for 1999 and 2000.

Finished goods inventory is likely to decline in concert with lower sales and production activity, and we have allowed for a 19 percent reduction. If we considered this an optimistic assumption, because of likely inefficiencies in adjusting production exactly to the seasonal low, a higher amount can, of course, be specified. This would necessarily mean, however, that a lesser amount of funds would be released from declining inventories. A somewhat higher figure is assumed for the end of 2000, reflecting the higher volume of sales in that year net of the seasonal slowdown.

When we add up all our changes in the *current asset accounts,* we find that this total at the end of the fourth quarter is projected to decline by over $2 million, in effect releasing these funds for other uses in the company. Note that this pattern reflects the normal funds flow characteristics of seasonal operations, as discussed in Chapter 3. By the end of 2000, however, the higher sales volume will have caused an increase of about $1.0 million, requiring funding instead.

Fixed assets are affected by several events. While *land* remains unchanged, we are told that some machines will be sold during the last quarter. Their original cost was $1.5 million, against which $950,000 of depreciation has been accumulated. They are to be sold for their book value of $550,000, involving no taxable gain or loss. To reflect this transaction, the *plant and equipment* account on our pro forma balance sheet must be reduced by the original cost, while *accumulated depreciation* must be reduced by the $950,000 of past write-offs recorded there. This effectively removes all traces of the machinery from the company's books, while cash in the amount of $550,000 will have been received.

We also know from the pro forma income statement that the company's normal depreciation charges for the quarter will be $600,000. This amount has to be added to the accumulated depreciation account. As a net result of the two changes, accumulated depreciation will decline by $350,000. Overall, the combined effect of these fixed asset transactions will decrease the net plant and equipment account by $1,150,000.

During the year 2000, new equipment is expected to be purchased for $1,750,000, which must be added to the plant and equipment account. Depreciation charges for the year as calculated by the finance staff and shown on the pro forma income statement will amount to $2,400,000, and this figure must be added to the accumulated depreciation account. *Other assets* are assumed to be unchanged during the last quarter of 1999, but during 2000 some patents are expected to be purchased for $200,000.

On the liability side, *accounts payable* are expected to decline in response to lower activity in the final quarter. We're told that payables are mostly related to purchases of raw material. We could approximate accounts payable, which have payment terms of net 45, by assuming that because the pro forma income statement reflects 90 days of raw materials use, about one-half of this amount would be outstanding ($840,000). But we have additional inside information on the actual level of purchases scheduled (Figure 5-4 on p.176), and are able to refine our assumption to show all of December's purchases ($460,000) and one-half of November's ($250,000) as total accounts payable outstanding at year end 1999 ($710,000). At the end of 2000, about $1.3 million are expected to be outstanding.

Other current liabilities must be analyzed in terms of specific payment schedules. We're informed that *notes payable* carry a provision for repayment of $1.5 million during the quarter, and for payment of the balance in the year 2000. Moreover, the account *due contractor* requires XYZ Corporation to make a payment of $2.9 million owed on construction in progress, which will become due in the final quarter, with the balance of $0.5 million due in 2000. *Accruals* largely involve income tax obligations. We already know from the pro forma income statement that tax accruals projected for the quarter will be $90,000. We're also told that the company must make an estimated tax payment of $400,000 during the quarter. The two items cause a net reduction in accrued taxes of $310,000. During the year 2000, tax accruals are assumed to increase because of overall higher tax obligations and payments. Note that with all these changes, total current liabilities are estimated to be reduced by about $5.1 million by 12/31/99, a significant drain of funds during the quarter, with another $1.0 million net reduction occurring by 12/31/00.

Long-term liabilities are assumed to remain unchanged both during the quarter and during 2000, while the recorded value of *common stock* is expected to increase by $250,000, because stock options are about to be exercised in late 1999. Finally, *retained earnings* should increase by the amount of net profit (income) of $160,000 as calculated on the pro forma income statement for the quarter, and by the net amount after dividends of $1.8 million for the year 2000.

When all these results are added up, we find that neither of the pro forma balance sheets balances! However, this shouldn't be surprising because we didn't use double-entry bookkeeping to balance our calculations. Instead, we made a variety of independent assumptions about many of the accounts, taking care only to be consistent with related projections in the respective pro forma income statements. Having maintained this consistency, and given that we're reasonably satisfied with our assumptions, the balancing figure required to equalize assets and liabilities at the end of both periods will represent either the company's net *funds need* or *excess funds* as of the pro forma balance sheet date.

This *plug* figure, as it's often called, serves as a quick estimate of what additional indebtedness the company will face on the date of the statement, or what uncommitted funds it will have at its disposal. But the plug won't indicate what peaks and valleys in funds requirements might have occurred during each of the three months. These fluctuations could, of course, be found by generating intermediate balance sheets more frequently than every 90 days.

In other words, we could find any major variations in funding conditions by taking financial "snapshots" in more closely spaced intervals, such as months or even weeks. As we'll see shortly, however, preparing a detailed cash budget is a much more direct way of tracing the ups and downs of funding requirements within the forecast period. But before illustrating the detailed cash budget for XYZ Corporation, we need to discuss the further interpretation of balance sheet changes by means of a cash flow analysis, using the third financial statement commonly prepared in pro forma projections. This approach allows us to see the cash uses and sources individually, and to reconcile them with the cash balances on hand.

Pro Forma Cash Flow Statement

As we observed in Figure 5–2, some very significant changes took place between the beginning and ending balance sheets of the two forecast periods. A pro forma cash flow statement will help us highlight the cash movements caused by these changes and their impact on the company's financial condition. Using the techniques discussed in Chapter 2, we can take the changes in the respective balance sheets and selected information from the related income statements to construct the pro forma cash flow analysis shown in Figure 5–3.

Reflecting prevailing practice, we've separated the various cash flow items into cash flow from operations, cash flow from investment, and cash flow from financing. It becomes quite obvious that the reduced operations of the last quarter of 1999 are expected to release a significant net amount of working capital ($1,230,000) of which $1.2 million comes from reduced accounts receivable

FIGURE 5–3

XYZ CORPORATION
Pro Forma Cash Flow Statements
For the Quarter Ended December 31, 1999, and the Year Ended December 31, 2000
($ thousands)

	Quarter Ended 12/31/99	Year Ended 12/31/00
Cash flow from operations:		
Net income.............................	$ 160	$ 2,200
Depreciation effect........................	600	2,450
Changes in working capital:		
Decrease (increase) in receivables	1,200	−450
Decrease (increase) in raw materials	0	−100
Decrease (increase) in finished goods	750	−500
Increase (decrease) in payables	−410	600
Increase (decrease) in accruals..............	−310	400
Total changes in working capital	1,230	−50
Net cash flow from operations	1,990	4,600
Cash flow from investments:		
Purchase of new equipment	0	−1,750
Purchase of patent (other asset)	0	−200
Proceeds from sale of machines	550	0
Net cash flow from investments..............	550	−1,950
Cash flow from financing:		
Repayment of notes........................	−1,500	−1,500
Repayment of construction loan	−2,900	−500
Proceeds from stock options	250	0
Dividends paid............................	0	−400
Net cash flow from financing	−4,150	−2,400
Net cash flow..............................	−1,610	250
Beginning cash balance.......................	1,450	−160
Ending cash balance	−160	90
Minimum cash balance	$ 1,250	$ 1,250
Funding requirement as of December 31	1,410	1,160

alone. These working capital funds sources almost triple the basic operating cash flow (net income of $0.16 million plus depreciation of $0.6 million) into a total cash inflow from operations of about $2.0 million.

In contrast, the growth assumed during all of 2000, affected by a similar seasonal pattern late in the year, will cause essentially unchanged working capital requirements. The higher net income, plus somewhat higher depreciation charges, will almost totally be available for funding other needs, as we'll see.

During the quarter, operating funds sources are far outweighed by significant funding needs for financing, however. To meet various financial obligations currently due, $4.4 million are scheduled for repayment. Of this total, the notes payable of $1.5 million represent repayment of seasonal funding, made possible by the significant release of working capital as the seasonal low approaches, while a sizable payment of $2.9 million is due the building contractor. Cash received from the sale of machinery and the exercise of stock options assists somewhat in this. But in the end there is a cash outflow of $1.61 million for the quarter, only slightly offset by the planned reduction in the minimum cash balance. The remainder to be financed is $1.41 million, as we already observed from the pro forma balance sheet of 12/31/99.

The conditions for the year 2000 are also affected by the repayment of notes ($1.5 million), and the balance due the contractor ($0.5 million). In addition, there are significant investment outlays for machinery ($1.75 million) and patents ($0.2 million). Dividend payments of $0.4 million require funding as well. In contrast to the fourth quarter pattern, there is a net cash inflow of $0.24 million for the year, but in order to maintain a minimum cash balance of $1.25 million, funding of $1.16 million must be obtained. Again, this is the same figure we observed as the "plug" in the pro forma balance sheet of 12/31/00. It appears that for the foreseeable future XYZ Corporation will have to rely on financing of between $1.0 million and $1.5 million to carry out the intentions reflected in the operational, investment, and financing areas of its business system.

It should be clear by now that any changes in the various assumptions for the pro forma cash flow projections will directly affect the size of the funding gap. In fact, it's often very helpful to test the sensitivity of the projected conditions to variations in key assumptions, such as sales volume, collection patterns, and major cost deviations.

However, because we've looked at the fourth quarter as a whole, the likely funding stresses falling within the three individual months of the last quarter of 1999 still haven't been dealt with. These occur because the gradual release of operating funds caused by the seasonal slowdown during the quarter will likely lag the decline in operating volume. As a consequence, the exact scheduling of repayments within the three-month period could cause significant temporary shortfalls. For example, if all repayments came due in October, the funding gap would be much higher during that month than the pro forma statements suggest at the end of December. As we'll see shortly, only a detailed cash budget can reveal such hidden fluctuations.

To summarize, pro forma statements are a convenient and relatively simple way of projecting expectations about a company's performance. To create these statements requires maintaining consistent assumptions between the income statement and the balance sheet, but otherwise, a great degree of subjective judgment is allowed. The balancing element in the pro forma balance sheet is the funds need or funds excess resulting from the conditions assumed. The "plug" figure will of course vary as assumptions are changed.

Pro forma cash flow statements help highlight the funds movements implied by changes in the balance sheet. Pro forma analysis is limited by the static nature of the balance sheet, which shows funds needs only at a specific point in time, and not their ebb and flow. A more dynamic intraperiod analysis requires either generating several short-term pro forma statements at key decision points, or making the detailed budgetary forecast embodied in the cash budget.

Cash Budgets

Cash budgets, or detailed cash flow projections, are very specific month-by-month or even week-by-week planning vehicles normally prepared by a company's financial staff. These budgets focus exclusively on the specific incidence of cash receipts and payments—as distinguished from the leads and lags embodied in the accrual accounting approach used by most enterprises. A financial analyst who develops a cash budget is very interested in observing the ongoing changes in the cash account as assumptions are made, with the objective of maintaining a level sufficient to allow timely payments of all obligations as they become due. Consequently, the analyst must plan cash activity in very specific detail, reflecting the exact timing of the inflows and outflows of cash in response to planned operational, investment, and financing decisions.

As we'll see, cash budgets again indicate the level of any funds needs or excesses. In fact, the amount at the end of the planning period will match exactly the funding need or excess shown on the pro forma balance sheet—if the cash budget was prepared with the same basic assumptions as those underlying the pro forma statements.

Cash budgeting is quite simple in principle. It's very similar to personal budgeting, where bills due are matched with receipts from paychecks, dividend checks, bank interest payments, and so on. This matching is necessary, period by period, to align funds requirements on the one hand, and cash available for payment on the other. Normally, the cash balance will fluctuate from day to day, week to week, month to month, whether a personal or company budget is involved. If a company's collections from credit sales tend to lag for weeks while wages and purchases must be paid currently, serious cash shortages can occur. (The concept of lags in relation to cash flow patterns was extensively demonstrated in Chapter 3.) Similarly, cash payments for nonrecurring items, such as outlays for capital equipment, might cause temporary funding problems that must be met. Given its focus and detail, the cash budget is the ultimate expression of cash flow analysis, because in the end, all funds movements wind up as changes in the cash balance.

When preparing a cash budget, a time schedule of estimated receipts and payments of cash must be laid out carefully. This schedule shows, period by period, the net effect of projected activity on the cash balance, leaving out accounting allocations such as depreciation, which do not represent cash flows. The selection of the time intervals covered by the cash budget depends on the nature of the business and the trade terms under which it operates. If daily fluctuations are likely to be large, as in the banking business, day-by-day projections are necessary. In other cases, weekly, monthly, or even quarterly projections will suffice.

Let's now return to the data of XYZ Corporation and prepare a monthly cash budget for the last quarter of 1999. This will increase our understanding of the company's cash flow patterns beyond what was provided by the pro forma analysis alone. Figure 5–4 presents some of the basic data of the company's operations regarding sales, production, and purchases. We show two months of actual activities *prior* to the last quarter, because (due to the nature of the credit terms for sales and purchases) the cash lag from these past months will influence the three months being projected. Also, we're again showing matching totals for the year ended 12/31/00, even though we've omitted the details behind these figures. Accordingly, we'll focus on the quarter in this discussion, knowing the totals for the year 2000 were similarly derived.

The lag effect can be demonstrated clearly in the first item of the *cash receipts,* collection of *receivables.* On the assumption that the company's customers will continue to remit within the 30-day terms, cash receipts for any month should be the sales made in the prior month. In contrast, if there was a 60-day collection period, collections would represent the sales made two months earlier. Thus, any expected change in customer behavior or in credit terms themselves must be reflected in a different receipts pattern.

It's often helpful to draw a scale of time periods on which the days, weeks, or months of dollar sales are recorded when they first occur. Using this scale, any assumed collection experience can be simulated by "staggering" (that is, delaying) the dollar receipts according to the appropriate number of days. For example, a schedule of sales and collections on 30-day credit would appear as follows:

	January	February	March	April	May	June
Credit sales	$25,000	$30,000	$40,000	$42,000	$35,000	$30,000
Collections	(Dec. sales)	25,000	30,000	40,000	42,000	35,000

In XYZ Corporation, proceeds from the exercise of *stock options* and from the sale of used *machinery* have been budgeted in their respective months of incidence. The total cash receipts for each month show a diminishing pattern which lags the declining sales by a month. This reduction in collections is moderated somewhat by the nonoperating proceeds from options and sale of used machinery.

As we turn to *cash disbursements,* we encounter another lag in payments for *purchases* made on credit. Under the normal credit terms of 45 days extended to XYZ Corporation, we can assume that the company's payments will trail by 45 days. Consequently, purchases made in the second half of August and the first half of September will be paid for in October, with a similar pattern repeating itself in November and December. In other words, one month's worth of purchases staggered by 45 days will be paid in a given month. Under these conditions, a time scale with 15-day intervals will help illustrate the payment pattern.

Inasmuch as the last quarter of 1999 is projected with a declining monthly pattern, assuming a December seasonal low in sales and manufacturing activities, the staggered timing shifts earlier, somewhat higher cash receipts into a period of lower operating activity, with reduced purchase and payroll payments being experienced as well. Net funds are released in the process, but these are not sufficient to overcome the heavy debt repayments scheduled in October and

FIGURE 5–4

XYZ CORPORATION
Sample Cash Budget for the Quarter Ended December 31, 1999
and for the Year ended December 31, 2000
($ thousands)

	Aug.	Sept.	Oct.	Nov.	Dec.	Total for Quarter	Total for Year Ended 12/31/00
Basic data:							
Unit sales..............	48,000	46,000	42,000	36,000	33,000	111,000	550,000
Unit production	50,000	50,000	35,000	34,000	31,000	100,000	560,000
Change in units in inventory ..	2,000	4,000	−7,000	−2,000	−2,000	−11,000	10,000
Sales volume (on credit)	$4,450	$4,250	$3,850	$3,350	$3,050	$10,250	$52,250
Purchases (on credit)	$ 760	$ 740	$ 520	$ 500	$ 460	$ 1,480	$ 8,400
Cash receipts:							
Collection of receivables (prior month's sales)		$4,250	$3,850	$3,350		$11,450	$52,100
Proceeds from exercise of stock options...........................		0	250	0		250	0
Proceeds from sale of machines at book value		0	0	550		550	0
Total cash receipts		4,250	4,100	3,900		12,250	52,100
Cash disbursements:							
Payment for purchases*...........................		750	630	510		1,890	8,300
Production payroll (from operating budget)........................		560	545	500		1,605	9,050
Manufacturing expenses (from operating budget)........................		1,265	1,260	1,235		3,760	21,700
Selling and delivery expenses (from sales budget)		350	345	335		1,030	4,800
General overhead (from administrative budget)		200	200	200		600	2,350
Interest payment on debt......................		0	0	175		175	850
Principal payment on note payable................................		1,500	0	0		1,500	1,500
Federal tax payment		400	0	0		400	850
Payment on construction of new plant		0	2,000	900		2,900	500
Purchase of new equipment.....................		0	0	0		0	1,750
Purchase of patent (other assets)...........................		0	0	0		0	200
Dividends paid.............................		0	0	0		0	400
Total cash disbursements..................		5,025	4,980	3,855		13,860	51,850
Net cash receipts (disbursements)		−775	−880	45		−1,610	250
Cumulative net cash flow......................		$−775	$−1,655	$−1,610			
Analysis of cash requirements:							
Beginning cash balance		1,450	675	−205		1,450	−160
Net cash receipts...........................		−775	−880	45		−1,610	250
Ending cash balance		675	−205	−160		−160	90
Minimum cash balance		1,250	1,250	1,250		1,250	1,250
Cash requirements		$ 575	$1,455	$1,410		$1,410	$1,160

*For the quarter, normal terms of 45 days are assumed. Payments represent one month's purchases prior to last 1.5 months (e.g., one-half of August and one-half of September's payables are disbursed during October).

November, and only December just about breaks even in terms of net cash receipts and disbursements.

Had there instead been a rising volume of operations, more cash would have become tied up in working capital, requiring additional funding. In fact, we observed that effect in the results for 2000, where working capital was assumed to grow enough to offset the seasonal decline in the last quarter. Had the last quarter of 1999 been a growth period, the cash budget would have reflected the lag effect of the lower activities of the earlier months, with staggered collections rising, and growing manufacturing outlays. It should be apparent by now that there is a critical need for careful cash budgeting in any business where operating levels, receipts, and payments tend to vary significantly.

Other cash disbursements (*payroll, manufacturing expenses, selling and delivery,* and *general overhead*) are shown here without lags, on the assumption that payments for these expenses and obligations will be made within the month they are incurred. This assumption could be slightly incorrect in the case of payroll disbursements and certain manufacturing expenses. Such items could indeed lag by one or two weeks. How precisely these lags are dealt with is a function of the relative size and importance of the cash flow issues they represent.

Production-related payments, such as payroll and raw materials purchases, are based on the declining pattern of production shown in the basic data section of Figure 5–4, which also reflects a gradual inventory reduction. Yet, in the pro forma income statement for the period, cost of goods sold assumptions were based on the pattern of *selling* activities, to make the projection a little easier. Thus, the pro forma statement and the more detailed cash budget might differ because the assumptions concerning sales and production are different. To ensure complete consistency, it's therefore necessary to determine carefully whether the pattern of production is projected on a different basis than the pattern of sales.

As an example of such a potential difference, it's entirely possible that the seasonal low could be used by management to build up inventories in advance of the expected resurgence of sales. If that were so, the inventory assumption for the pro forma balance sheet would have to be adjusted upward to show the buildup of inventories and the resultant additional funds need. The cash budget, in turn, would have to reflect the higher expenditures involved in producing for inventory. Recognizing such differences in production and selling patterns is a key to refining the projection of company performance, and to making cash budgeting results consistent with the pro forma statements.

The final result of our cash budget exercise is a picture of the monthly cash effect of the operating plans on which it is based, and the net cash needs or excesses incurred each month. Note that the cash needs at the end of December 31, 1999 ($1.41 million), and December 31, 2000 ($1.16 million), exactly match the indications we received from the pro forma statements—not surprising, because the same assumptions were used throughout.

While we've focused on a manufacturing setting for our example, the same principles apply to the somewhat less complex conditions in a service business or a retailing or wholesaling operation. Payrolls and leasing costs, for example, will loom much larger in a service business, while purchases, inventories, and credit terms take on greater importance in a retailing or wholesaling company. In a financial institution, short- and long-term investment changes will be significant, as will shifts in deposits and other liabilities, with operations focused on personnel and infrastructure costs. However, the process of developing assumptions for pro forma statements and cash budgets is very similar to whatwe have shown here. In all cases they must be based on the physical as well as financial levers particular to each situation. The reader might recall our discussion in Chapter 3 about retailing and wholesaling examples.

To summarize, cash budgets lay out in specific detail the exact timing incidence of cash receipts and disbursements. Like household budgets, they allow us to watch for peaks and valleys in cash availability and to schedule additional financing or repayments as needed. Unlike pro forma statements (which are generally limited to the beginning and end of a specific period or to its total net effects), cash budgets can be drawn up for as many intervals as desired within the period to simulate the fluctuations in cash flow. Given the same assumptions in terms of the volume of production and sales, and the handling of receipts, payments, and credit, the cash budget and pro forma statements will agree in signaling the amount of funds need or excess at the end of the period covered.

Operating Budgets

The pro forma statements and cash budget we prepared for XYZ Corporation provide an overall view of the company's future performance. But in any sizable company, a whole hierarchy of more specific operating budgets is normally prepared. Operating budgets are essentially internal documents. As expressions of the details of ongoing operations, such budgets are linked closely to the organizational structure and to the type of performance measurement used by the particular company. They're part of the planning process we mentioned earlier, and are very useful as background for pro forma and cash flow projections when a higher degree of detail and accuracy is desired.

Most companies structure their operations into manageable parts, and for each of them an executive or manager is held responsible. The structure might be organized by *functions,* that is, sales, production, purchasing, and so on. In other cases, the organization might be composed of a set of smaller *profit centers,* each of which is expected to make a profit contribution to total company performance. Some activities might be grouped into *cost centers,* focusing the managers' attention on cost-effectiveness. More recently, cross-functional teams have been used for certain activities, with budget arrangements to match. Growing activity-based costing and analysis efforts, which we've mentioned before, have refined budgetary processes even as they caused rethinking and restructuring—and outsourcing—of certain activities in many companies. Even though there are countless variations of organizational structures, the principles of budgeting and financial projection are straightforward and commonly applicable.

Any projection of operating results must be done in a form that reflects the scope of the business unit involved. It must be related to the elements controllable by the responsible manager, and should be done on the same basis as the one with which the manager's performance is measured. These criteria obviously require that operating budgets be carefully designed to fit the particular unit's conditions and the management style of the company as a whole. This means that there'll be a great deal of difference in the approach taken by various companies, even in the same industry. There might even be differences within the same company in the operating budgets used for different organizational units and processes. A growing body of literature has recognized the positive contribution of so-called responsibility accounting for tracking managers' results, more recently expanded to include team management and process management concepts.

For purposes of our discussion, a few illustrations of basic operational budgeting will suffice. Among the various internal operating budgets routinely prepared by XYZ Corporation are the *annual sales budget by quarters* and a *quarterly factory budget*. The sales budget is designed to show the sales unit's projected contribution to total corporate profits, while the factory budget reflects expected output and the total costs incurred in producing the forecast volume. There are many other types of profit and expense budgets, but we'll limit our discussion to these two, showing how they're used to provide background information for the financial analyst preparing and analyzing pro forma statements and cash budgets. The principles employed in our examples are the same for any other kind of budgeting arrangement.

Sales Budget

As is shown in Figure 5–5, the sales manager must first project the level of *unit sales* expected in the market territories served by the business. The projection is made by major product lines. Most likely, this forecast will be built up from the individual judgments of the persons closest to current and potential customers. Economic conditions will likely be factored in, as will the impact of marketing strategies XYZ Corporation and its competitors are likely to employ.

Next the *price levels* for each product must be estimated. Prices commonly are a function of three factors:

- Industry pricing practices.
- The competitive environment.
- The cost-effectiveness of the company's manufacturing operations.

Once the price has been established, the *sales revenue* can be calculated. Then the *cost of goods sold* for the products transferred internally or possibly purchased on the outside must be determined. The difference between the revenue and cost is the *margin before delivery* achieved by the sales unit. Next are the projected *delivery costs* to the customers, if these are borne by the company. Controllable *selling expenses* include *compensation* of sales personnel, *travel and entertainment,* and *sales support costs.*

FIGURE 5-5

XYZ CORPORATION
Sample Quarterly Sales Budget
For the Year Ended December 31, 1999

		Quarter			
	First	Second	Third	Fourth	Total
Basic data:					
Unit sales (number of units):					
Product A	2,700	2,900	3,000	2,800	11,400
Product B	8,000	8,500	10,000	8,000	34,500
Product C	17,500	18,500	21,000	16,000	73,000
Price level (per unit):					
Product A	$ 145	$ 145	$ 150	$ 150	—
Product B	92	92	95	95	—
Product C	74	74	74	74	—
Number of salespersons	25	25	25	26	—
Operating budget ($000):					
Sales revenue	$2,423	$2,572	$2,954	$2,364	$10,313
Less: returns, allowances	25	26	28	24	103
Net sales	2,398	2,546	2,926	2,340	10,210
Cost of goods sold	1,916	2,051	2,322	1,868	8,157
Margin before delivery	482	495	604	472	2,053
Delivery expense	56	60	68	54	238
Gross margin	426	435	536	418	1,815
Selling expense (controllable):					
Salespersons' compensation	94	94	94	98	380
Travel and entertainment	32	32	32	33	129
Sales support costs	23	23	26	24	96
Total selling expenses	149	149	152	155	605
Gross contribution	277	286	384	263	1,210
Departmental period costs	18	18	18	18	72
Net contribution	259	268	366	245	1,138
Corporate support (transferred):					
Staff support	23	25	25	27	100
Advertising	50	50	75	50	225
General overhead	63	63	63	63	252
Total corporate support	136	138	163	140	577
Profit contribution (before taxes)	$ 123	$ 130	$ 203	$ 105	$ 561

The result is the *gross contribution* from selling activities, which must be reduced by estimated *departmental period costs* (like rent, managers' salary, and other items that do not vary with short-term fluctuations in volume) to arrive at the *net contribution* provided by the department. After deducting allocated *corporate support costs,* which are staff support, advertising, and general overhead, the *profit contribution* for the period is established. In making all of these estimates, the sales manager can use past relationships and selected ratios, tempered by his or her judgment concerning changes in future conditions.

In our example, both basic data and dollar elements have been estimated and set out by the four quarters and the full year of 1999. There's nothing unique about the format we have selected here, because many different arrangements of such information are possible to suit any specific organization. Generally, a company prescribes the format for its managers to follow in preparing projected activity budgets, both to maintain a degree of uniformity and to lessen the accounting problem of consolidating the projections when preparing overall financial forecasts. From the standpoint of financial projection, the sales and contribution data in our example are the raw material which goes into the company's total operating plan.

Production Budget

The sales budget we just discussed is basically a projection of profit contribution. However, companies also must forecast for operations or activities that involve only costs or expenses. An example of this type of projection, a cost budget for a factory, is shown in Figure 5–6. This time the data are given for each month. We've included three months and the total for the quarter. The period shown is the second quarter, during which sales and production are expected to increase.

Again, the amount of detail included and the presentation format are chosen to suit the particular needs and preferences of the organization. This time we've arranged the headings and data to show that certain cost items (both direct and period costs) are under the control of the local manager. (Other costs, like allocated general overhead, are transferred in from corporate headquarters and thus are beyond the local manager's control.) This arrangement of data will also be useful if the operating plan serves as a control device with which to measure the unit's performance.

Both sales and cost budgets commonly include additional columns in which *actual* as opposed to *projected* figures are recorded. In addition, *variance* columns are frequently used to measure deviations from plan. We'll not go into such refinements here, because our examples were only meant to show the type of internal budgeting and projection used formally or informally in most organizations preparatory to developing an overall financial forecast.

Interrelationship of Financial Projections

It should be obvious by now that the various types of projection presented in this chapter are closely related. If all three forecasts—pro forma statements, cash budgets, and operating budgets—are based on the same set of assumptions about

FIGURE 5-6

XYZ CORPORATION
Sample Production Budget
For the Quarter Ended June 30, 1999

	April	May	June	Total
Basic data:				
Number of shifts (5-day week)	3	3	3	3
Days worked.	20	21	22	63
Hourly employees per shift	33	33	33	33
Number of machines.	35	35	34	—
Unit production:				
Product A	1,000	1,050	1,100	3,150
Product B	2,400	2,510	2,640	7,550
Capacity utilization	94%	94%	96%	95%
Downtime for repairs (hours)	0	36	0	36
Operating budget:				
Direct costs (controllable):*				
Manufacturing labor	$57,600	$60,500	$63,400	$181,500
Raw materials.	53,800	56,400	59,200	169,400
Operating supplies	6,500	6,900	7,300	20,700
Repair labor and parts	7,300	12,400	6,500	26,200
Power, heat, light	4,200	4,500	4,800	13,500
Total direct costs.	129,400	140,700	141,200	411,300
Period costs (controllable):				
Supervision.	5,500	5,500	5,500	16,500
Support labor	28,500	28,500	28,500	85,500
Insurance, taxes	8,700	8,700	8,700	26,100
Depreciation	20,500	20,500	20,500	61,500
Total period costs	63,200	63,200	63,200	189,600
Total controllable costs	192,600	203,900	204,400	600,900
General overhead (allocated)	72,000	72,000	72,000	216,000
Total cost.	$264,600	$275,900	$276,400	$816,900

*Where appropriate, unit costs can be shown.

receipts and collections, repayment schedules, operating rates, inventory levels, and so on, they will all precisely fit together as illustrated in Figure 5–7.

The financial plans and the projected funds need or excess will differ only if different assumptions concerning the various drivers affecting cash flows are used, particularly between the pro forma statements and the cash budget. It is easy to reconcile pro forma statements and cash budgets, however, by carefully thinking through the key assumptions to be made, one by one, and by laying out formats that contain sufficient detail and properly timed background data.

The diagram shows how the various operational budgets flow into a consolidated cash budget, which in turn is reinforced by specific data from the investment and financing plans. The combined information supports the pro forma statements at the top of the diagram. Thus, pro forma statements are the all-encompassing expression of the expected conditions for the projected period. If

FIGURE 5–7

Interrelationship of Financial Projections

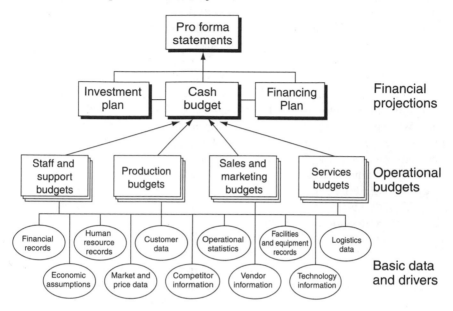

we choose for planning purposes to develop a broad overall financial projection using pro forma statements directly (rather than building them up from the company's detailed plans and budgets), the results will in effect *imply* specific assumptions about all the other elements in the diagram.

We haven't yet discussed some of the other elements shown in Figure 5–7. *Investment plans (capital budgets)* are projections of new outlays for land, buildings, machinery and equipment, and related incremental working capital, as well as major outlays for new products and services, expanding markets, new technology, etc. They also contain plans to divest any of the company's assets. Acquisitions and divestitures of whole companies, lines of business, or activities are usually part of these projections.

We recall that XYZ Corporation made a minor reduction in its fixed assets by selling some used machines in 1999, and planned to purchase new equipment items in 2000. Also, a recently constructed plant was in the final stages of completion, as evidenced by the amount that had become due and payable to the contractor. This facility investment was already reflected on the actual balance sheet of September 30, 1999, largely supported by long-term debt raised earlier. Only the current payment due the contractor was properly scheduled as a pro forma cash disbursement. Given the size of the plant investment, the company might consider raising some additional long-term debt to fund the new facility, because our projections of ongoing operations show insufficient cash flow to pay off the contractor liabilities.

Financing plans are schedules of proposed future additions to or reductions in indebtedness or ownership funds during the forecast period. They might involve significant expansion or restructuring of a company's capital structure, depending on the projected capital requirements. XYZ Corporation planned no specific future financing, but provisions will have to be made for financing the sizable near-term funds need revealed with the help of our pro forma analysis, and to avoid straining current funds as the plant is paid off.

Staff budgets, as the name implies, are spending plans based on the expected cost of operating various support functions of a company, such as the finance organization, human resources, legal and governmental affairs, and so on. These budgets are prepared and used in the same fashion as other expense budgets, with personnel expenses usually being the largest element. *Services budgets* are spending plans representing such service activities as customer or technical support, delivery and communication, online services of various kinds, and so on. Budgetary categories will differ depending on the nature of the activity, of course.

Underlying the operating budgets and financial projections, Figure 5–7 shows a selection of key data sources, formal or informal, from which the relevant drivers of physical and financial activities can be derived. Whether they are made apparent or not, the structure of projections is supported by explicit or implicit assumptions about such basic data and conditions. In our example of XYZ Corporation we touched on a limited number of these areas, relying in all cases on information given to us by management—who would have to base their expectations on their understanding of all the conditions affecting their company.

A word about projection methodology should be added here. Any form of financial projection involves both an examination of past trends and specific assumptions about future behavior of revenues, costs, expenses, and other receipts and payments. Past trend analysis can range from simple "eyeballing" of obvious patterns to applying a variety of statistical methods to the available data in order to establish a trend line or curve as the basis for judging future conditions. The projection of key variables might start with such a trend, but hard, informed judgments about likely changes must override the temptation merely to extrapolate past conditions. The mathematical elegance of statistical methods should not be allowed to supplant the effort of making realistic future assumptions about specific company and market conditions, industry performance, and the national and world economic outlook affecting the likely financial performance of the business. The end-of-chapter references and Appendix V are sources of information on forecasting techniques and other processes that will assist the analyst in technical and judgmental aspects of financial projection.

Financial Modeling

In recent years, software developed for financial modeling has vastly expanded the financial analyst's ability to explore the consequences of different assumptions, conditions, and plans. In principle, such software packages are mathematical representations and templates of key financial accounting relationships, ratios, and formats, supported by automatic subroutines that calculate, update, and display data and results in whatever form is desired. While the degree of sophistication varies widely in these approaches, the process is based on the very same steps and reasoning we discussed in this chapter.

The simplest form of financial modeling is found in the common use of spreadsheets to represent a particular set of relationships for analysis and manipulation. Here the analyst specifies the basic formulas and connections underlying the data and formats under review, but must take special care to maintain internal consistency. At the other extreme is a full-fledged financial model, usually developed by a company's staff in collaboration with software vendors, which encompasses many elements such as the company's accounting procedures, depreciation schedules, tax calculations, debt service schedules, debt covenants and restrictions, inventory policies, and so on. In most cases, the terms used, key assumptions, and output formats are "custom tailored" so that the model reflects the specific characteristics of a given company. This allows the analyst to calculate the projected results of the conditions expected by the company, examine several sets of assumptions, and assess alternative outcomes.

The major difference between the projection techniques we discussed earlier in this chapter and the use of computer models is only the degree of automation in the process. A cash budget, even if done by hand, is essentially a model of the cash flow patterns of the company. In constructing such a budget, the analyst must take into account corporate policies regarding accounting methods, tax reporting, and other detailed operating rules. These constraints also can be incorporated into a basic financial planning software package, or even a powerful modeling program. The main difference is that the computer can run different options, while simultaneously tracking all important interrelationships much more easily and quickly than is possible when doing an analysis on a simple spreadsheet.

The financial modeling software available on the market is constantly evolving, and the reader should become familiar with the available offerings. In relative scope, the modeling packages range all the way from simple spreadsheet templates with which to calculate condensed pro forma statements to highly sophisticated representations of a company's financial accounting system, and to so-called enterprise models. In the last case, a generalized model is extensively refined by experts to reflect the company's specific situation. Some companies have developed models that not only will calculate the results of specific sets of assumptions, but also will contain optimizing routines that select the most desirable alternative investment and financing patterns according to criteria stipulated by management. Other models include statistical projection programs that can be used for initial trending of key variables from past experience. It's clearly beyond the scope of this book to detail the vast number of concepts and specialized techniques involved in the building and use of computerized financial models. However, the reader can refer to Appendix I, which describes Modernsoft, Inc.'s *Financial Genome,* an advanced financial analysis application commercially available for use in connection with this book and for general professional usage.

Figure 5–8 depicts a broad overview of the major relationships represented in a full-fledged financial model, with linkages to internal and external databases.

FIGURE 5–8

Financial Modeling: An Overview of Key Interrelationships

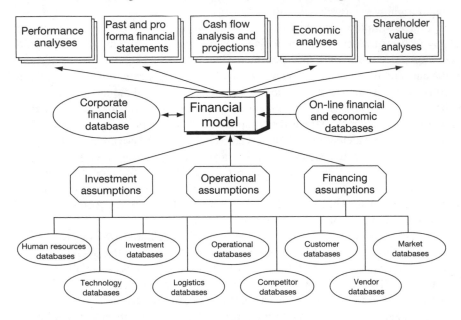

The central element is the software program that governs the calculations and displays, with the inputs coming from various sources and databases as needed, and the outputs grouped into our familiar categories of analysis, including special economic analyses and shareholder value calculations. Such analytical capability permits the use of clearly defined assumptions about corporate strategy and operational plans, backed by trend analysis of relevant historical internal data and external information, to develop meaningful, consistent statements and analyses. Once key drivers of performance and financial conditions are specified, the task of projecting financial statements, cash flow patterns, and valuation aspects is relatively straightforward, as is the use of extensive sensitivity analysis and scenario planning. Strategic plans for several years ahead, the impact of potential acquisitions or restructuring, or more near-term operational conditions can all be expressed in financial terms.

Sensitivity Analysis

As we mentioned, one of the advantages of financial modeling is the ability to perform sensitivity analysis with considerable ease. This approach involves selecting a few key performance drivers and altering them to determine the sensitivity of the result to such changes. For example, one of the key assumptions in our pro forma analysis of XYZ Corporation was the usual seasonal pattern of an

18 to 20 percent decline in sales volume in the last quarter. If there were reason to believe that a more serious drop might occur, the analyst could estimate the dollar decline in contribution from each additional 1 percent decrease in volume. Assuming all other conditions remain the same, that dollar decline would be the lost contribution from the units left unsold.

The impact on cash needs would be traced by adjusting after-tax profits, and by recognizing that there would be a change in working capital because sales levels are lower, except in inventory where the unsold units might remain. If prices were considered unstable, the impact of a series of assumptions about the effect of lower prices for one or all of the product lines could be tested. In every case, the critical issue would be the sensitivity of the cash needs to the changes in each of the three months. Clearly, many other tests could be applied and related to the altered result brought about by the change in any given assumption.

The key to this type of reasoning is the analyst's judgment as to which elements in the operating and financial patterns being projected are most subject to variability. Then the task is to simulate how sensitive the desired result is to each change. Care must be taken to observe any interrelationships among the chosen variables. These interrelationships include the inverse impact of price changes on volume, and nonlinear conditions such as varying changes in some costs and certain activities in response to volume assumptions and load factors. Given such a range of results, the decision maker using the analysis can judge the risk of the proposed course and adjust operating and financial policies accordingly. A full-fledged financial model is not critical to applying such sensitivity tests. Even our simple pro forma statements and cash budgets can be modified easily on a spreadsheet to answer basic questions of this sort.

Nonetheless, with appropriate software, the analyst can examine many more possibilities and determine the impact of a far greater number of assumptions. Sensitivity tests can be performed on more than one variable simultaneously, and whole scenarios can be developed with the financial impact reflected in the output. We'll return to the topic of sensitivity analysis again in the chapters that follow.

Key Issues

The following is a recap of the key issues raised directly or indirectly in this chapter. They are enumerated here to help the reader keep the materials discussed within the perspective of financial theory and business practice.

1. Projecting the financial requirements of a business is a logical extension of financial statement preparation and cash flow thinking. It's the culmination of a set of planning assumptions that must be applied consistently in the process to ensure consistency among the different representations of the business provided by financial statements and cash budgets. Given such consistency, the common link among the displays will be the financing requirement identified.

2. The process of financial projections rests on explicit and implicit assumptions about the expected behavior of key drivers in the future periods under review. These can be derived from a detailed planning process including strategic direction, operational budgeting, and other key conditions affecting future performance, or they can be specified in broad terms for a quick assessment. The main issue is to think through the financial systems effects in all areas of the business.

3. Extrapolation of past trends, such as margin percentages, expense ratios, credit conditions, and asset turnover should be considered only as a starting point, from which refinements must be made to allow for likely changes in future conditions. Such key forecast drivers should be identified and tracked to ensure reasonableness.

4. Sensitivity analysis is a key requirement for thoughtful planning of financial requirements as well as of other projections involving future events. The impact on the final result from varying assumptions about individual variables considered key drivers must be tested to assist in judging the range of possible outcomes. Focusing on drivers with the most impact will tend to sharpen the analytical and decision-making process.

5. Whenever projections and plans are subject to uncertainty, especially if forecast periods are extensive, it's useful to develop alternate scenarios based on consistent assumptions about sets of key drivers under different potential conditions.

6. Financial modeling is an important activity which provides varying degrees of automatic linkage among key variables and output formats. It is not a substitute for judgment, however, because the underlying assumptions necessary for an analysis require thoughtful choices and insights, whether the model is highly evolved or merely a simple spreadsheet.

Summary

The principles of financial projection discussed in this chapter revolve around the use of *pro forma statements* and various types of *budgets*. We observed that financial projection is only part of the broader process of *business planning*. Financial projection can be expressed in the familiar form of financial statements and in many specifically tailored budget formats. The process is simple in that it represents an orderly way of sorting out the financial impact of investment, operating, and financing decisions. The process is difficult in that judgments about future conditions are fraught with uncertainty—as planning of any sort must be.

Here, the use of *sensitivity analysis,* the calculation of the impact of alternative assumptions, can narrow the range of uncertainty. Financial projection basically is a form of modeling the future within the context of operational and policy constraints. To the extent that more detail and more options for future plans are desired, *financial modeling* can yield the significant benefits of speed and accuracy of calculation. Greater insights can be derived from such modeling, but the judgmental requirements for proper inputs and assumptions remain the same.

Analytical Support

Financial Genome, the commercially available financial analysis and planning software described in Appendix I, has the capability to develop and display pro forma financial statements in its forecasting mode, using forecast drivers and assumptions specified by the user. The statements are fully integrated to provide the net impact on cash needs or surpluses (the "plug" figure) resulting from any set of assumptions made. The software is also accompanied by an interactive template (TFA Template under "extras"), which provides a detailed cash budgeting problem. The templates allow the user to vary key assumptions and to study their impact on the various results and statements (see "Downloads Available" on p. 431).

Selected References

Anthony, Robert N. *Essentials of Accounting.* 5th ed. Reading, MA: Addison Wesley, 1993.
Brealy, Richard, and Stewart Myers. *Principles of Corporate Finance.* 5th ed. New York: McGraw-Hill, 1996.
Ross, Stephen; Randolph Westerfield; and Jeffrey Jaffe. *Corporate Finance.* 5th ed. Burr Ridge, IL: Irwin/McGraw-Hill, 1999.
Weston, J. Fred; Scott Besley; and Eugene Brigham. *Essentials of Managerial Finance.* 11th ed. Hinsdale, IL: Dryden Press, 1997.

CHAPTER 6

DYNAMICS AND GROWTH
OF THE BUSINESS SYSTEM

$\mathbf{I}$n Chapter 2 we characterized the business system as a dynamic growth model and described in broad terms the interrelationship of decisions, financial yardsticks, and management policies used in the pursuit of shareholder value creation. In the previous three chapters, we dealt with several specific aspects of financial management: the movement of cash through the system, the evaluation of the financial results of the system, and the projection of future financial requirements. We ended Chapter 5 with a broad description of financial modeling as a valuable assist in developing financial projections, after demonstrating basic pro forma and cash budgeting processes as common tools for financial planning. Now we need to return to our systems concept and become more specific about how some of the system's internal characteristics and dimensions affect changes in the cash flow patterns that lead to shareholder value creation.

There are two important subjects that so far we've touched on only briefly, but that are an integral part of understanding and modeling the business system, namely leverage and the potential for growth. The reader will recall that financial leverage and the funding potential with which to support growth were represented in the financing sector of the business system diagram. We also recognized the interplay of fixed and variable costs in the operational sector. At the time we briefly indicated the trade-offs and choices that could be made by management in dealing with these areas. Now it's time to integrate these concepts into a more thorough financial planning discussion that deals with the operational and policy drivers underlying the pro forma statements and cash budgets covered in the previous chapter.

We'll focus first on the concept of *leverage*—the impact of fixed elements on overall results—in two critical areas:

- Operating leverage.
- Financial leverage.

Here we'll explore in detail the impact of volume changes on profitability under a variety of assumptions about the nature and level of fixed elements in the company's cost pattern, and deal with their implications for structuring and managing the operational part of the system. Then we'll illustrate the impact of financial leverage on a company's profitability, and how the introduction of fixed interest charges into the financial system can both benefit a company's return and magnify the variability of these returns, based on a trade-off of risk versus return.

Last, we'll turn to an integrated modeling approach that'll demonstrate the drivers of growth in the system and their financial implications. Our focus will be on testing the financial impact of top-level policy changes in investment, operations, and financing. The vehicle for this process will be a basic financial growth plan format, which in a highly summarized way allows us to visualize the interrelationship of the key financial dimensions and drivers affecting the performance and growth of the total business system. We'll cover the following concepts in detail:

- The basic financial growth model.
- Determining sustainable and affordable growth.
- The integrated financial plan.

The reader is encouraged to revisit the first section of Chapter 2, which describes the business system and its key linkages, many of which we'll test in this discussion. The broader concept of shareholder value creation will be dealt with extensively in Chapter 12.

Leverage

Leverage, as previously mentioned, refers to the often favorable, but at times problematic, condition of having within the overall cost pattern of the business system a stable element which supports a wide range of activity. *Operating leverage* simply means that part of the ongoing costs of a business are fixed over a broad range of operating volume. As a result, profits are boosted or depressed more than proportionally for given changes in sales volume. The phenomenon is positive as long as volume is increasing; when volume turns down due to unfavorable market conditions, there can be a large negative impact on operating profit. Similarly, *financial leverage* occurs when a company's capital structure contains obligations with fixed interest rates. Earnings after interest and return on equity are boosted or depressed more than proportionally as volume and profitability fluctuate. However, there are differences in the specific elements involved and in the methods of calculation of each type of leverage. Both operating and financial leverage can be present in any business, depending on the choices made by management in structuring operations and the financing requirements, and the respective impact on net profit will tend to be mutually reinforcing. We need to understand the specific impact of leverage whenever it's encountered in a business, as it is an important element in the financial planning process.

Operating Leverage

Distinguishing between fixed and variable costs (those costs that vary with time and those that vary with the level of activity) is an old idea. This separation of costs by behavior is the basis for *break-even analysis*. The idea of "breaking even" is based on the simple question of how many units of product or service a business must sell in order to cover its fixed costs before beginning to make a profit. Presumably, unit prices are set at a level high enough to recoup all direct (that is, variable) unit costs and leave a margin of contribution toward fixed (period) costs and profit. Once sufficient units have been sold to accumulate the total contribution needed to offset all fixed costs, the margin from any additional units sold will become profit—unless a new layer of fixed costs has to be added at some future point to support the higher volume.

Understanding this principle will improve our insight into how the operational aspects of a business relate to financial planning and projections. This knowledge is also helpful in setting operational policies, which, especially in a volatile business setting might, for example, focus on minimizing fixed costs through outsourcing certain activities. But in a broader sense, it'll allow us to appreciate the distorting effect which significant operating leverage might exert on the measures and comparisons used in financial analysis.

A word of caution must be added here. There's nothing absolute about the concept of fixed costs, because in the long run, every cost element becomes variable. All costs rise or fall as a consequence of management policies and decisions, and can therefore be altered. As a result, the break-even concept must be handled with flexibility and judgment.

As we mentioned, introducing fixed costs to the operations of a business tends to magnify profits at higher levels of operation up to the point when another layer of fixed costs might be needed to support greater volume. This is due to the buildup of incremental contribution which each additional unit provides over and above the strictly variable costs incurred in producing it. Depending on the proportion of fixed versus variable costs in the company's cost structure, the total incremental contribution from additional units can result in a sizable overall jump in profit.

Analyzing a leveraged operating situation is quite straightforward. Once all fixed costs have been recovered through the cumulative individual contributions from a sufficient number of units, profits begin to appear as additional units are sold. Profits will grow proportionally faster than the growth in unit volume. Unfortunately, the same effect holds for declining volumes of operations, which result in a profit decline and accelerating losses that are disproportional to the rate of volume reduction. Operating leverage is definitely a double-edged sword!

We can establish the basic definitions as follows:

$$\text{Profit} = \text{Total Revenue} - \text{Total Cost}$$
$$\text{Total Revenue} = \text{Volume (Quantity)} \times \text{Price}$$
$$\text{Total Cost} = \text{Fixed Cost} + \text{Variable Cost}$$

The formal way of describing leverage conditions is quite simple. We're interested in the effect on profit (I) of changes in volume (V). The elements that bear on this are the unit price (P), unit variable costs (C), and fixed costs (F). The relationship is:

$$I = VP - (VC + F)$$

This formula can be rewritten as:

$$I = V(P - C) - F$$

which illustrates that profit depends on the number of goods or services sold times the difference between unit price and unit variable cost—which is the contribution to the constant element, namely fixed costs.

As unit volume changes, the unit contribution ($P - C$) multiplied by the change in volume will equal the total change in profit. Under normal conditions, the constant, fixed costs (F) will remain just that. The relative changes in profit for a given change in volume will be magnified because of this fixed element.

Another way of stating the leverage relationships is to use profit as a percent of sales (s), one of the ratios developed in Chapter 4. Using the previous notation,

$$s = \frac{I}{VP}$$

and defining I in terms of the components, the formula becomes:

$$s = \frac{V(P - C) - F}{VP}$$

and slightly rewritten:

$$s = \left[1 - \frac{C}{P}\right] - \frac{F}{VP}$$

The relationship indicates that the profit/sales ratio depends on the contribution per unit of sales, less fixed costs as a percent of sales revenue. We observe that, to the extent fixed costs are present, they cause a reduction in the profit ratio. The larger F is, the larger the reduction. Any change in volume, price, or unit cost, however, will tend to have a disproportional impact on s because F is constant.

Now let's examine how the process works, using some concrete examples. We'll use the cost/profit conditions of a simple business with relatively high fixed costs of $200,000 in relation to its volume of output and variable costs per unit. The fixed costs are largely overhead and costs related to owning and operating the production facilities, including the depreciation effect. Our company has a maximum level of production of 1,000 units, and for simplicity, we assume there's no lag between production and sales. Units sell for $750 each, and variable costs of materials, labor, and supplies amount to $250 per unit. Every unit therefore provides a contribution of $500 toward fixed costs and profit.

Figure 6–1's *break-even chart* is a simple representation of the conditions just outlined. At zero volume, fixed costs amount to $200,000, and they remain level as volume is increased until full capacity has been reached. Variable costs, on the other hand, accumulate by $250 per unit as volume is increased until a level of $250,000 has been reached at capacity, for a total cost of $450,000. Revenue rises from zero, in increments of $750, until total revenue has reached $750,000 at capacity.

Where the revenue and variable cost lines cross (at 400 units of output), a break-even condition—no profit and no loss—has been reached. This means that

---

FIGURE 6–1

ABC CORPORATION
Simple Operating Break-Even Chart*

Break-even volume 400 units

Profits and Losses as a Function of Volume Changes of 25 Percent

Volume	Increase	Profits	Increase
400	—	-0-	—
500	25%	$ 50,000	Infinite**
625	25	112,500	125%
781	25	190,500	69
976	25	288,000	51
Volume	Decrease	Losses	Increase
400	—	-0-	—
300	25%	$ 50,000	Infinite**
225	25	87,500	75%
169	25	115,500	32
127	25	136,000	18

*This diagram is available in an interactive format (TFA Template)—see "Analytical Support" on page 222.

**Infinite because the base is zero.

the total cumulative revenue of $300,000 at that point is just sufficient to offset the fixed costs of $200,000, plus the total variable costs of $100,000 (400 units at $250 each). If operations increase beyond this point, profits are generated; at volumes of less than 400 units, losses are incurred. The break-even point can be found numerically, of course, by simply dividing the total fixed costs of $200,000 by the unit contribution of $500, which results in 400 units, as we expected:

$$\text{Break-even point } (I = \text{zero}): \frac{F}{P - C} = V$$

$$\text{Zero profit} = \frac{\$200,000}{\$500} = 400 \text{ units}$$

The most interesting aspect of the break-even chart, however, is the clear demonstration that increases and decreases in profit are not proportional. A series of 25 percent increases in volume above the break-even point will result in much larger percentage jumps in profit growth.

The relevant change data are displayed in the table under the chart. They show a gradual decline in the growth rate of profit from infinite to 51 percent. Similarly, as volume decreases below the break-even point in 25 percent decrements, the growth rate of losses goes from infinite to a modest 18 percent, as volume approaches zero. Thus, changes in operations *close* to the break-even point, whether up or down, are likely to produce *sizable* swings in earnings. Changes in operations well above or below the break-even point will cause lesser fluctuations.

We must be careful in interpreting these changes, however. As in any percentage analysis, the specific results depend on the starting point and on the relative proportions of the components. In fact, managers will generally be much more concerned about the total dollar amount of change in profit than about percentage fluctuations. Moreover, it's easy to exaggerate the meaning of profit fluctuations unless they are viewed carefully in the context of a company's total cost structure and its normal level of operations.

Nevertheless, the concept should be clear: The closer to its break-even point a firm operates, the more dramatic will be the profit impact of volume changes. The analyst assessing a company's performance or making financial projections must attempt to understand where the level of its current operations is relative to normal volume and the break-even point, and then interpret the analytical results accordingly.

Clearly, the greater the relative level of fixed costs, the more powerful the effect of operating leverage becomes. Therefore, we need to understand this aspect of the company's cost structure. In capital-intensive industries, such as steel, mining, forest products, and heavy manufacturing, most of the costs of production are indeed fixed for a wide range of volumes. This tends to accentuate profit swings as companies move away from break-even operations.

Another example is the airline industry, which from time to time substantially increases the capacity of its flight equipment. The fixed costs associated with leasing and operating these expensive aircraft initially cause sharp drops in profit for many airlines. As business and private travel rise to approach the new levels of capacity, well-managed airlines experience dramatic improvements in profits, while marginal performers continue to suffer losses. In contrast, service industries, such as consulting firms, can directly influence their major cost—salaries and wages—by adjusting the number of employees as demand changes. Thus, they're much less subject to the effects of the operating leverage phenomenon. In many businesses, the use of temporary or contract employees has risen dramatically in recent years, reflecting the desire to reduce in part the more long-term obligations associated with regular employees.

As we mentioned before, in most situations management should assess whether there would be value in reducing the level of fixed costs through creative solutions such as outsourcing, partnering, and contract work arrangements that move the responsibility for fixed expense obligations elsewhere. Such assessments became a growing phenomenon in the 90s during the widespread efforts at corporate restructuring and reengineering. Naturally, there are trade-offs involved in such choices, such as giving up control over what might be important elements of value-creating activities.

There are three main elements management can influence in the operating leverage relationship:

- Fixed costs.
- Variable costs.
- Price.

All three are in one way or another related to *volume*. We'll demonstrate the effect of changes in all three by varying the basic conditions in our example.

Effect of Lower Fixed Costs

If management can lower *fixed costs* through energetic reductions in overhead by using facilities more intensively, by contracting out part of its production, or through other restructuring of the company's activities, the break-even point might be lowered significantly. As a consequence, the boosting effect on profits will start at a lower level of operations. Figure 6–2 shows this change.

Note that reducing fixed costs by one-eighth has led to a corresponding reduction in break-even volume. It will now take one-eighth fewer units contributing $500 each to recover the lower fixed costs. From the table we can observe that successive 25 percent volume changes from the reduced break-even point lead to increases or decreases in profit that are quite similar to our first example in Figure 6–1. Reducing fixed costs, therefore, is a very direct and effective way of lowering the break-even point to improve the firm's profit performance.

Effect of Lower Variable Costs

If management is able to reduce the variable costs of production (direct costs), thereby increasing the contribution per unit, the action can similarly affect profits

FIGURE 6–2

ABC CORPORATION

Simple Operating Break-Even Chart: Effect of Reducing Fixed Costs
(reduction of $25,000)

Contribution per unit	
Revenue	$750
Variable costs	250
Contribution	$500

Break-even volume 350 units

Profits and Losses as a Function of Volume Changes of 25 Percent

Volume	Increase	Profits	Increase
350	—	-0-	—
438	25%	$ 44,000	Infinite*
547	25	98,500	125%
684	25	167,500	69
855	25	252,000	51
Volume	Decrease	Losses	Increase
350	—	-0-	—
262	25%	$ 44,000	Infinite*
196	25	77,000	75%
147	25	101,500	32
110	25	120,000	18

*Infinite because the base is zero.

at current levels and influence the movement of the break-even point itself. In Figure 6–3, we've shown the resulting change in the slope of the variable cost line, which in effect widens the area of profits. At the same time, loss conditions are reduced.

However, the change in break-even volume resulting from a 10 percent change in variable costs is not as dramatic as the change experienced when fixed costs were lowered by one-eighth. The reason is that the reduction applies only to a small portion of the total production cost, as variable costs are relatively low in this example. (This illustrates the point we made earlier about having to consider the relative cost proportions in this type of analysis.)

FIGURE 6–3

ABC CORPORATION
Simple Operating Break-Even Chart: Effect of Reducing Variable Costs
(reduction of $25 per unit)

Break-even volume 381 units

Profits and Losses as a Function of Volume Changes of 25 Percent

Volume	Increase	Profits	Increase
381	—	-0-	—
476	25%	$ 49,900*	Infinite†
595	25	98,500	125%
744	25	167,500	69
930	25	252,000	51
Volume	*Decrease*	*Losses*	*Increase*
381	—	-0-	—
286	25%	$ 50,150	Infinite†
215	25	87,125	75%
161	25	115,475	32
121	25	136,475	18

*First 25 percent change not exactly equal due to rounding.
†Infinite because the base is zero.

Only at the full capacity (1,000 units) does the profit impact of $25,000 correspond to the effect of the reduction of $25,000 in fixed costs in the earlier example. At lower levels of operations, lower unit volumes and the lesser impact of variable costs combine to minimize the effect. Nevertheless, the result is a clear improvement in the break-even condition, and a profit boost is achieved earlier on the volume scale. Again, 25 percent incremental changes are tabulated to show the specific results.

Effect of Lower Prices

Up to this point, we've concentrated on *cost* effects which are largely under management's control. In contrast, price changes are for the most part dependent on the firm's competitive environment. As a result, price changes normally affect the competitive equilibrium and will directly influence the unit volume a business is able to sell. Thus, it's not enough to trace the effect of raised or lowered prices on the break-even chart, but we also must anticipate the likely impact on volume resulting from the price change. In other words, raising the price could more than proportionally affect the unit volume the company will be able to sell competitively, and the price action could actually result in lower total profits. Conversely, lowering the price could more than compensate for the lost contribution per unit by significantly boosting the total unit volume that can be sold against competition.

Figure 6–4 demonstrates the effect of lowering the price by $50 per unit, a 6.7 percent reduction. Note that this change raises the required break-even volume by about 11 percent, to 444 units. In other words, the company needs to sell an additional 44 units just to recoup the loss in contribution of $50 from the sale of every unit.

For example, if the current volume was 800 units, with a contribution of $400,000 and a profit of $200,000, the price drop of $50 per unit would require the sale of enough additional units to recover 800 times $50, or $40,000. The new units required will, of course, provide the lower per-unit contribution of $45

Under these conditions, as many as 89 additional units ($40,000 ÷ $450) have to be sold at the lower price to maintain the $200,000 profit level, which represents a volume increase of 11 percent. Note that this results in a more than proportional change in unit volume (11 percent) versus the drop in price (6.7 percent). Price changes affect internal operating results, but they could have an even more pronounced and lasting impact on the competitive environment. If a more than proportional volume advantage—and therefore improved profits—can be obtained over a significant period of time after the price has been reduced, this could change the competitive situation to the company's advantage. Otherwise, if price reductions can be expected to be quickly matched by other competitors, the final effect could simply be a drop in profit for everyone, because little if any shift in relative market shares would result. The airline price wars mentioned earlier are a prime example of this phenomenon.

This isn't the place to discuss the many strategic issues involved in pricing policy; the intent is merely to show the effect of this important factor on the operating area of the business system and to provide a way of analyzing likely conditions.

Multiple Effects on Break-Even Conditions

Up to now, we've analyzed cost, volume, and price implications and their impact on profit separately. In practice, the many conditions and pressures encountered

FIGURE 6–4

ABC CORPORATION

Simple Operating Break-Even Chart: Effect of Reducing Price
(reduction of $50 per unit)

Break-even volume 444 units

Profits and Losses as a Function of Volume Changes of 25 Percent

Volume	Increase	Profits	Increase
444	—	-0-	—
555	25%	$ 49,750*	Infinite†
694	25	112,300	125%
867	25	190,150	69
1084	25	287,800	51

Volume	Decrease	Losses	Increase
444	—	-0-	—
333	25%	$ 50,150*	Infinite†
249	25	87,950	75%
187	25	115,850	32
140	25	136,000	18

*First 25 percent change not exactly equal due to rounding.
†Infinite because the base is zero.

by a business often affect these variables *simultaneously*. Cost, volume, and price for a single product might all be changing at the same time in subtle and often non-measurable ways. The analysis is further complicated when several products or services are involved, as is true of most major companies. In such cases, changes in the sales mix can introduce many additional complexities.

Moreover, our simplifying assumption to make production and sales simultaneous doesn't necessarily hold true in practice; the normal lag between production and sales has a significant effect. In a manufacturing company, sales and production can be widely out of phase. Some of the implications of this condition were discussed in Chapter 3, when we dealt with funds flow patterns caused by varying levels of operations, and in Chapter 5 when we examined the relationship of cash budgets and pro forma income statements.

So far we've also assumed that operating conditions were essentially *linear*. This allowed us to simplify our analysis of leverage and break-even conditions. A more realistic framework is suggested in Figure 6–5. The chart shows potential changes in both fixed and variable costs over the full range of operations. Possible price–revenue developments are also indicated. In other words, changes in all three factors affecting operating leverage are reflected at the same time.

Figure 6–5 further shows that the simple straight-line relationships used in Figures 6–1 through 6–4 are normally only approximations of the "step functions" and the gradual shifts in cost and price often encountered under realistic circumstances. Inflationary distortions arising over time also must be considered. A few examples of the possible changes and likely reasons are described below.

Target Profit Analysis

One application of operational leverage calculations is the use of target profit analysis as part of the planning process of a company. It takes into account the

FIGURE 6–5

ABC CORPORATION
Generalized Break-Even Chart:
Allowing for Changing Cost and Revenue Conditions

A. A new layer of fixed costs is triggered by growing volume.
B. A new shift is added, with additional requirements for overhead costs.
C. A final small increment of overhead is incurred as some operations require overtime.
D. Efficiencies in operations reduce variable unit costs.
E. The new shift causes inefficiencies and lower output, with more spoilage.
F. The last increments of output must be sold on contract at lower prices.

relative proportions of fixed and variable costs expected to occur in the company's system. Given projections of total fixed costs (F), estimates of variable costs (C), and expected price (P), the unit volume required to achieve any desired pretax target profit (TP) can be determined with the basic break-even formula:

$$\text{Volume for target profit: } V = \frac{F + TP}{P - C}$$

Similarly, if management wishes to test the level of variable costs (C) allowable for any desired pretax target profit (TP), with an estimated unit volume (V) and price (P) based on expected market conditions and projected fixed costs (F), the formula can be rewritten as:

$$\text{Variable unit cost for target profit: } C = P - \frac{(F + TP)}{V}$$

The reader is invited to rewrite the formula for the required price to achieve a desired pretax profit, and also to determine the change required to put the formula on an after-tax basis. Calculations of this kind serve well to scope the dimensions of the planning process, but cannot be substituted for detailed analysis and projections as discussed in Chapter 5. The approach is helpful for analysts and managers to recognize in broad terms the implications of the company's operating leverage.

Financial Leverage

The concept of introducing an element of fixed cost into the financial system also applies to financial leverage. In the case of operating leverage, we saw that advantage can be gained from a fixed level of cost that serves a wide variety of volume conditions. With financial leverage, advantage is gained from the expectation that funds borrowed at a fixed interest rate can be used for investment opportunities earning rates of return higher than the interest paid on the funds. The difference, of course, accrues as profit to the owners of the business and boosts the return on equity, as seen in Chapter 4. Viewed superficially, the implication would be that as long as a company's investments consistently provide returns above this rate of interest, the augmented rate of return on equity would benefit the shareholders. The opposite would, of course, apply if the company earned returns on its investments below the rate of interest paid.

We remember, however, that the basic principle of value creation requires that the return on all investments already in place as well as on any future investments must exceed not only the interest paid on debt but also the expectations of the holders of the company's shares. Shareholder value can be created only if the combined cost of capital, representing all long-term funding sources, is consistently exceeded. We established this principle early on and will revisit it in detail in Chapters 9 and 12. This return requirement doesn't affect or alter the principles of leverage itself, but it forces us to think carefully about the minimum level of return with which resources have to be employed. Instead of considering the rate of interest as the threshold return, it's the overall cost of capital that must be met and exceeded.

Given that higher standard, however, the effect of financial leverage is still derived from the fixed nature of the interest charges relative to the overall return created, with the difference, positive or negative, accruing to the shareholders. The principle is simple: Using return on shareholders' equity as the criterion, the higher the proportion of debt—and its fixed interest charges—in the capital structure, the greater will be the leverage contribution to the return on shareholders' equity, for a given positive return achieved on the investments. Conversely, as achieved returns drop below the rate of interest (tax-adjusted), the fixed nature of the interest charges will begin to magnify the reduction in return on equity. The reader will recall the diagram in Chapter 4, p. 136, which shows the connection of financial leverage to return on equity.

To illustrate the relationships further, Figure 6–6 shows the leverage effect on the return on equity measure under three different levels of return on net assets. All three curves are drawn with the assumption that funds can be borrowed at 4 percent per year after taxes. If the normal return before interest, after taxes on the company's capitalization is 20 percent (curve *A*), growing proportions of debt cause a dramatic rise in return on equity. This return jumps to infinity as debt nears 100 percent—obviously a dangerous extreme in capital structure

F I G U R E   6–6

ABC CORPORATION
Return on Equity as Affected by Financial Leverage
(after-tax interest on debt is 4 percent)

A: Return on net assets = 20%
B: Return on net assets = 12%
C: Return on net assets = 5%

proportions. Curves B and C show the leverage effect under more modest invest-ment return conditions. While somewhat lessened, the return on equity still shows sharp increases as the proportion of debt rises. We haven't drawn the downward sloping curves that would reflect a sharp plunge in negative return on equity when the return drops below 4 percent, the after-tax cost of interest. This effect is also suggested by the increase in the distances between curves A, B, and C at higher debt levels.

To express financial leverage relationships formally, we begin by defining the components, as we did in the case of operating leverage. Profit after taxes (I) now has to be related to shareholders' equity (E) and long-term debt (D). We also single out the return on shareholders' equity (R), and the return on capitalization (net assets) (r) before interest and after taxes, and the after-tax rate of interest (i).

First we define the return on shareholders' equity as:

$$R = \frac{I}{E}$$

and the return on capitalization (the sum of equity and debt) as:

$$r = \frac{I + Di}{E + D}$$

We now restate profit (I) in terms of its components:

$$I = r (E + D) - Di$$

which represents the difference between the return on the total capitalization $(E + D)$ and the after-tax cost of interest on outstanding debt (Di). We substitute this restated profit for R in our initial return on equity formula, which now reads:

$$R = r \frac{(E + D) - Di}{E}$$

and which can be further rewritten as:

$$R = r + \frac{D}{E}(r - i)$$

This formulation highlights the leverage effect, represented by the positive expression after r (that is, the proportion of debt to equity), multiplied by the dif-ference between the earnings power of net assets and the after-tax cost of interest. Thus, to the extent that debt is introduced into the capital structure, the return on equity is boosted as long as after-tax interest cost doesn't exceed earnings power. This is the *net leverage contribution,* which we displayed in our systems view of key ratios in Chapter 4 on p. 136. Companies with different degrees of leverage will, even if their earnings power is the same, achieve different returns on equity due to the specific net leverage contribution (or detraction) caused by their capi-tal structures. Analysts must therefore be careful in making direct comparisons of ROE results.

When we apply the formula to one set of conditions that pertained to Figure 6–6, the results can be calculated as follows. Given $i = 4$ percent, and $r = 12$ percent, if

(1) $D = \quad 0$ and $E = \$100$, then R equals 12.0%

(2) $D = \$25$ and $E = \quad \$75$, then R equals 14.7%

(3) $D = \$50$ and $E = \quad \$50$, then R equals 20.0%

(4) $D = \$75$ and $E = \quad \$25$, then R equals 36.0%

In this illustration, we have four different debt/equity ratios, ranging from no debt in the first case to a 3:1 debt/equity relationship in the fourth case. Given an after-tax cost of interest of 4 percent, and the normal opportunity to earn 12 percent after taxes on net assets invested, the return on equity in the first case is also 12 percent after taxes—because no debt exists, and the total capitalization is represented by equity.

As increasing amounts of debt are introduced to the capital structure, however, the return on equity is boosted considerably, because in each case, the return on investment far exceeds the cost of interest paid to the debt holders. This was, of course, demonstrated in the graph of Figure 6–6. The reader is invited to work through the opposite effect, that is, interest charges in excess of the ability to earn a return on the investments made with the funds.

We're also interested in the impact of leverage on the return on net assets, or capitalization (r), which we obtain first by reworking the formula

$$R = r + \frac{D}{E}(r - i)$$

into

$$r = \frac{RE + Di}{E + D}$$

Given $i = 4$ percent, and $R = 12$ percent, we can determine the minimum return on capitalization necessary to obtain a return on equity of 12 percent, for

(1) $D = \quad 0$ and $E = \$100$, then R equals 12%

(2) $D = \$25$ and $E = \quad \$75$, then R equals 10%

(3) $D = \$50$ and $E = \quad \$50$, then R equals 8%

(4) $D = \$75$ and $E = \quad \$25$, then R equals 6%

This is a useful way of testing the expected return from new investments. The approach simply turns the calculation around by fixing the return on equity and letting the expected return on investment vary. The process is straightforward. Note that the required amount of earnings on net assets, or capitalization, drops sharply as leverage is introduced, until it begins to approach the 4 percent after-tax interest cost. It'll never quite reach this figure, however, because normally some amount of equity must be maintained in the capital structure to keep the company viable.

While it's simple to work out the mathematical relationships, the translation of these conditions into the appropriate financial strategies is much more complex. No management is completely free to vary the capital structure at will, and there are practical, as well as legal and contractual constraints, on any company to maintain some normalcy on the liability side of the balance sheet. While no absolute rules exist, the various tests of creditworthiness run the gamut of the ratios discussed in Chapter 4, particularly the measures oriented to the lenders' point of view.

With enlightened self-interest in mind, lenders will impose upper limits on the amount of debt capital to be utilized by any potential borrower. For manufacturing companies, the amount of long-term debt will normally range between 0 and 50 percent of their capitalization, while public utilities will range between 30 and 60 percent. Trading companies with highly liquid assets might have even higher debt proportions. At the same time, restructuring and corporate reengineering are shifting both capital requirements and debt levels in many instances. For example, outsourcing as part of corporate strategy might serve to reduce the need for capital, including debt, because part of the asset base is effectively transferred to suppliers. The vast increase in leveraged buyouts during the 1980s introduced far higher than normal levels of debt into the capital structures of many companies. In those cases, financial leverage is used to the ultimate extent, which also vastly increases the companies' exposure to the adverse effects of cash flow falling below expectations.

The most important issue around the use of financial leverage, however, relates to its impact on a company's overall market value. Financial theory has firmly established that introduction of financial leverage into an unleveraged capital structure will raise the market value of the company because of the change in total return to debt and equity holders—but only up to a point. The lift in market value is in fact a function of the corporate tax deductibility of the interest cost of debt, as demonstrated in Figure 6–7. As debt levels increase, the value of this favorable tax shield impact increases. Here we've assumed a total capital of $2.0 million, on which pretax operating earnings are 30 percent, or $600,000. With no debt, there are no interest charges and net income after taxes of 40 percent is $360,000. If instead we assume a 50 percent debt level, interest at 8 percent on $1.0 million amounts to $80,000, lowering taxable income and income taxes paid, thus dropping net income to $312,000. At 75 percent debt we've assumed a higher interest rate of 10 percent, due to the greater financial exposure, and net income drops to $270,000.

Note, however, that XYZ Corporation's investors can claim potential distribution of after-tax income in the form of dividends to the shareholders, plus actual payment of interest to the debt holders, a total which rises from $360,000 to $420,000 under the three conditions. As it turns out, the increase of $32,000 in potential distribution from zero to 50 percent debt is exactly the amount of taxes saved through the deductibility of interest (40 percent of $80,000). The increase

FIGURE 6–7

XYZ CORPORATION
Impact of Leverage on Earnings and Distribution
($ thousands)

	Debt Proportion		
	0	50	75
Total capital	$2,000	$2,000	$2,000
EBIT @ 30% of capital.	600	600	600
Interest expense @ 8% and 10%	0	80	150
Income before taxes.	600	520	450
Income taxes @ 40%.	240	208	180
Net income.	360	312	270
Distribution of after-tax income:			
Dividends	360	312	270
Interest	0	80	150
Total income to investors*	360	392	420
Distribution of income assuming no taxes:			
Dividends	600	520	450
Interest	0	80	150
Total income to investors	$ 600	$ 600	$ 600

*Before personal income taxes.

in distribution of $60,000 from zero to 75 percent debt likewise represents the tax savings of 40 percent on $150,000 of interest. Shown in the next set of figures is the result if income taxes didn't exist—and, as we might expect, there's no change in the distribution potential, regardless of the amount of leverage introduced, because the tax shield has disappeared. Naturally, in a no-tax environment the total available for distribution would be much higher; in fact it would remain at the level of EBIT, with the pattern of distribution again shifting gradually toward the holders of debt as leverage and risk increased.

We've demonstrated here in very basic terms that successful employment of financial leverage does in fact create higher overall returns, if all potential distributions are taken into account, because there is a true economic savings from employing fixed, tax-deductible interest in the capital structure. As we'll see in Chapter 12, the stock market ascribes a higher market value to a company that is able to bring about an improved result from a cash flow standpoint.

There is a risk-reward trade-off, however. As the proportion of debt with its fixed requirements rises to levels at which the risk of nonperformance and even bankruptcy looms ever higher, the expectations of shareholders and creditors will increasingly factor in the potential for difficulties, and the market value of the company will level off and even decline. The trade-off here is simply between the economic cash flow implications from the obtainable tax savings and the cash flow implications from financial stress and even failure. The "right" level of leverage will differ greatly among companies, industries, and management styles.

Finding the optimal degree of leverage for a business requires a careful assessment of potential financial risks, which are a function of the variability of performance of the company's business system, the outlook for the markets served, competitive conditions, strategic positioning, and so on. In short, successful application of financial leverage is much more than a numerical exercise, and we'll return to it when discussing capital structure planning in Chapter 10. The reader is also referred to the various sources listed at the end of this chapter for more insights.

Our main interest for the rest of the chapter is in the demonstrable effect of financial leverage on the broader area of financial planning for a company. As such, it's only one of several aspects affecting overall performance. In the next section, we'll integrate the numerical aspects of financial leverage as well as other key factors into a broader financial plan.

Financial Growth Plans

Most managers aspire to building ever larger businesses, whenever the opportunities in the marketplace permit this. Typically, common shareholders also expect growing economic benefits to accrue from share ownership. As a consequence, profitable and sustainable growth within the competitive environment is one of the key underpinnings of shareholder value creation, as we'll discuss in detail in Chapter 12. Thus, it's not surprising that one important dimension of financial planning is continual assessment of the effects of growth on investment, operations, and financing. The choices of financial policy open to management have different impacts on the expected results, and therefore must be tested along with the operational aspects of the plans.

Management can set a variety of financial objectives and financial policies to direct and constrain the company's planning effort and the specific financial projections based on these plans. One of the most commonly used financial objectives is return on shareholders' equity, even though this measure is accounting based and not necessarily an indicator of value creation. We'll use it here to demonstrate the planning process. The objective of a specific return on shareholders' equity in turn is derived from underlying objectives about:

- Growth in earnings per share.
- Growth in dividends per share.
- Growth in total profits.
- Growth in shareholders' equity.
- Growth in market value.

None of these objectives can be used singly as an overall standard, of course. In fact, the strong emphasis in recent years on shareholder value creation and total shareholder return achieved has put many of the accounting-based measures into a secondary role. As we'll discuss and demonstrate in more detail in

Chapters 11 and 12, shareholder value creation ultimately is based on cash flows and market expectations, while total shareholder return takes into account the combined return to the investor from dividends and changes in the market price of the stock. The accounting measures remain important, however, because they're conveniently derived from published financial statements, and can be visibly linked to financial policies. Foremost among these financial policies is the amount of financial leverage the company considers prudent, while subsidiary to it are the various measures of creditworthiness that management will wish to observe as constraints.

To demonstrate the buildup of an integrated financial plan that enables us to observe the effect of growth and its relationship to financial objectives and policies, we will begin by selecting just one of the objectives named above to work through a simple conceptual model of a hypothetical company. The format of this model is the basic framework that we'll use later to build a more detailed integrated financial plan. It'll also serve to demonstrate the concept of sustainable growth.

Basic Financial Growth Model

A simple way of demonstrating the interrelated elements that affect growth in the business system is to use the objective of growth in shareholders' equity, as recorded on the balance sheet. Not only is this particular element easy to calculate, but it also encompasses the effects of profit growth and dividend payout—apart from any changes caused by issuing new shares or repurchasing existing shares in the market.

Figure 6–8 represents this simplified financial model that allows us to trace the aspects affecting equity growth in a company, namely, leverage, profitability, earnings disposition, and financing. With its help, we can demonstrate the effect that different financial policies have on this objective. In fact, the model is a broad representation of our business system as discussed in Chapter 2.

Three cases have been worked out. The first represents an unleveraged company with $500,000 in equity, which pays no dividends and reinvests all of its profits in operations similar to its present activities. The second case shows the same company, but in a leveraged condition with debt at 50 percent of capitalization. In the third case, we take the conditions of the second case, but assume a dividend payout of 50 percent of earnings. All other financial conditions are assumed to remain constant.

Let's trace through the data for Case I. Given a gross return on net assets (capitalization) of 10 percent after taxes, the amount of net profit generated for the year is $50,000, all of which is the basic funding potential that can be reinvested in the company's activities in the form of new investment for expansion, profit improvements, and so on.

FIGURE 6-8

Financial Growth Model: Three Different Policies* ($ thousands)

	Case I	Case II	Case III
Capital structure:			
Debt as percent of capitalization.........	0	50%	50%
Debt	0	$250	$250
Equity	$500	$250	$250
Net assets (capitalization)............	$500	$500	$500
Profitability (after taxes):			
Gross return on net assets**............	10%	10%	10%
Amount of profit.....................	$ 50	$ 50	$ 50
Interest rate........................	0	4%	4%
Amount of interest....................	0	10	10
Profit after interest..................	$ 50	$ 40	$ 40
Disposition of profit:			
Dividend payout	0%	0%	50%
Dividends paid	0	0	20
Reinvestment of profit...............	$ 50	$ 40	$ 20
Financing:			
Additional debt	0	40	20
Funding potential	$ 50	$ 80	$ 40
Cash flow implications:			
Amount of after-tax profit	$ 50	$ 40	$ 40
Depreciation effect	25	25	25
Cash flow from operations	75	65	65
Dividends paid	0	0	20
Cash flow available for reinvestment	75	65	45
Additional debt	0	40	20
Total investment potential	$ 75	$105	$ 65
Results:			
Net return on net assets†	10%	8%	8%
Return on equity	10%	16%	16%
Growth in equity‡	10%	16%	8%

*This exhibit is available in an interactive format (TFA Template)—see "Analytical Support" on p. 222.

**Profits before interest, after taxes related to net assets (capitalization).

†Profits after interest and taxes related to net assets.

‡Growth in recorded equity based on earnings reinvested after payment of dividends.

The results of Case I are a net return on net assets (capitalization) after interest, which is zero in this example, of 10 percent, and a return on equity of 10 percent. The latter also represents a growth in equity of 10 percent during the period. This condition holds because all profits are retained in the business for reinvestment.

In Figure 6–9, we've calculated three additional periods of operations for the Case I company, without changing any of the assumptions. We can quickly observe that given stable policies and conditions, equity growth will indeed continue at 10 percent per year for periods 2 and 3, matched by growth in profit after interest.

Returning to Figure 6–8, we next examine the cash flow implications for Case I, which show that when the depreciation effect of $25,000 is added in, the total cash available for investment in fact is $75,000, without raising any additional debt. For purposes of this model we'll assume that this amount of depreciation is also reinvested, but in the form of equipment replacement necessary to maintain the profitability of the existing facilities. By this choice, therefore, the return on net assets of 10 percent is maintained. We've applied this approach to the additional periods of Figure 6–9 in every case.

Case II differs only with regard to the use of debt financing. Because $250,000 has been borrowed at 4 percent after taxes, $10,000 of after-tax interest must be deducted from the amount of profit earned on net assets, which reduces the amount available for reinvestment to $40,000. If management wishes to maintain its policy of a 50 percent debt level, an additional $40,000 can be borrowed, matching the increase in equity. This raises the funding potential for reinvestment to $80,000. From a cash flow standpoint, however, the total investment potential now is $105,000, because the depreciation effect must be added, as done in Case I.

Compared to Case I, the results have changed in several ways. Net return on net assets (capitalization) has dropped to 8 percent because interest charges were introduced. As we expected, however, the return on equity was boosted to 16 percent because of the financial leverage effect. Figure 6–9 again demonstrates that under these conditions, growth in equity can be similarly maintained at a level of 16 percent for periods 2 and 3, as long as all of the internally generated funds are reinvested in opportunities returning 10 percent, and matching amounts of debt funds are obtained and similarly invested.

The cash flow implications of Case II once more show that the total investment potential is higher by the amount of depreciation, and we'll again assume that this amount will be reinvested to maintain the return on net assets, which was done in Figure 6–9. There we observe the faster growth in net assets in periods 2 and 3, due to the higher reinvestment, which is also supported by increasing amounts of new debt raised in each subsequent period to maintain the 50 percent debt proportion desired by management.

In Case III, the only change is the introduction of dividends. The assumed 50 percent payout reduces the internal funds available for reinvestment to only $20,000, and also reduces the available additional debt to $20,000, under the stated 50 percent debt policy. The funding potential from reinvestment has thus been reduced to $40,000. This dividend action seriously affects our objective of growth in equity, which is now only half the level in Case II. From a cash flow standpoint, the total investment potential including the depreciation effect is now

FIGURE 6-9

Financial Growth Model Results of Three Different Policies Held Constant over Three Periods* ($ thousands)

	Case I			Case II			Case III		
	Period 1	Period 2	Period 3	Period 1	Period 2	Period 3	Period 1	Period 2	Period 3
Capital structure:									
Debt as percent of capitalization	0%	0%	0%	50%	50%	50%	50%	50%	50%
Debt	0	0	0	250.0	290.0	336.4	250.0	270.0	291.6
Equity	$500.0	$550.0	$605.0	250.0	290.0	336.4	250.0	270.0	291.6
Net assets (capitalization)	$500.0	$550.0	$605.0	$ 500.0	$ 580.0	$ 672.8	$500.0	$540.0	$583.2
Profitability (after taxes):									
Gross return on net assets**	10%	10%	10%	10%	10%	10%	10%	10%	10%
Amount of profit	$50.00	$55.00	$60.50	$ 50.00	$ 58.00	$ 67.28	$50.00	$54.00	$58.32
Interest rate	0	0	0	4%	4%	4%	4%	4%	4%
Amount of interest	0	0	0	10.00	11.60	13.46	10.00	10.80	11.66
Profit after interest	$50.00	$55.00	$60.50	$ 40.00	$ 46.40	$ 53.82	$40.00	$43.20	$46.66
Disposition of profit:									
Dividend payout	0%	0%	0%	0%	0%	0%	50%	50%	50%
Dividends paid	0	0	0	0	0	0	$20.00	$21.60	$23.33
Reinvestment of profit	$50.00	$55.00	$60.50	$ 40.00	$ 46.40	$53.82	$20.00	$21.60	$23.33
Financing:									
Additional debt (next year)	0	0	0	40.00	46.40	53.82	20.00	21.60	23.33
Funding potential (next year)	$50.00	$55.00	$60.50	$ 80.00	$ 92.80	$107.64	$40.00	$43.20	$46.66
Cash flow implications:									
Amount of after-tax profit	$50.00	$55.00	$60.50	$ 40.00	$ 46.40	$ 53.82	$40.00	$43.20	$46.66
Depreciation effect	25.00	28.00	31.00	25.00	30.00	36.00	25.00	27.00	29.00
Cash flow from operations	75.00	83.00	91.50	65.00	76.40	89.82	65.00	70.20	75.66
Dividends paid	0.00	0.00	0.00	0.00	0.00	0.00	20.00	21.60	23.33
Cash flow available for reinvestment	75.00	83.00	91.50	65.00	76.40	89.82	45.00	48.60	52.33
Additional debt	0.00	0.00	0.00	40.00	46.40	53.82	20.00	21.60	23.33
Total investment potential	$75.00	$83.00	$91.50	$105.00	$122.80	$143.64	$65.00	$70.20	$75.66
Results:									
Net return on net assets†	10%	10%	10%	8%	8%	8%	8%	8%	8%
Return on equity‡	10	10	10	16	16	16	16	16	16
Growth in equity‡	10	10	10	16	16	16	8	8	8
Growth in profit after interest	—	10	10	—	16	16	—	8	8

*This exhibit is available in an interactive format (TFA Template)—see "Analytical Support" on p. 222.

**Profits before interest, after taxes related to net assets (capitalization) as a measure of operational return on assets.

†Profits after interest and taxes related to net assets, as often shown in financial reports.

‡Growth in recorded equity based on earnings reinvested after payment of dividends.

only $65,000. This figure is lower than in the other two cases, because of the combined impact of a high dividend payout and the more limited incremental debt. Periods 2 and 3 reflect the continued lower growth induced by the new dividend policy.

The simple framework in Figures 6–8 and 6–9 illustrates the effects of a combination of decisions about investment, operations, earnings disposition, and financing strategy. It permits easy analysis of changes, and testing of the sensitivity of results in response to changed assumptions. Clearly we've oversimplified the conditions for purposes of demonstration, but refinements in the assumptions about such items as return on net assets, dividend payout ratios, and increments of additional borrowing, will only be variations on the basic theme expressed here.

Sustainable Growth and the Sustainable Growth Equation

One of the key issues in planning the future successful growth of a company is to grapple with the inherent limitations and constraints of the business system. Limitations are such inherent aspects as the amount of assets required to support a given level of sales, which will depend greatly on the nature of the activity and vary widely between service companies, trading companies, and manufacturing or natural resource companies, or the basic profitability of the activities. Constraints are the policies under which management operates, such as the degree of leverage to be employed, the readiness to issue new equity, or the dividend policy followed.

When it comes to establishing the potential for normal growth, we must make specific assumptions about the key limitations and policies, as we previously did in our simple financial growth model. There we observed that growth in shareholders' equity in fact is a good surrogate for expressing growth potential under the stipulated assumptions. If we visualize a growing company under stable policies, increasing sales volume will require proportional increases in working capital, as well as proportional investments in fixed assets and other assets supporting the operations. The funding of these requirements has to come from two sources, ownership funds and debt. To the extent that profits are retained in the business, they build up recorded shareholder equity and this buildup, together with incremental debt, represents the funding potential for growth, as we saw. Given stable policies and performance, the rate of increase in shareholders' equity will therefore represent the rate of expansion of the balance sheet necessary to support the growth. If the company wished to grow faster than the growth in equity implied by stable policies, additional funds would have to be raised from new debt or new equity, thus changing one or more financial policy constraints. If the company wished to grow at a lower rate, some of the funding potential could be used to pay increased dividends, buy back outstanding shares, or retire debt instead of providing an expanded asset base, again changing some of the policy constraints. The concept of sustainable growth, therefore, is simply defined as the growth in the business that can be sustained by stable policies over a period of time, and it is reflected by growth in shareholder equity.

Let's now turn to a formal way of describing the drivers of growth and their relationships. Revisiting our simple growth model in Figures 6–8 and 6–9, we noted that in Case I, when no debt was employed and no dividends were paid, the following relationship held:

$$g = r$$

where g is growth in equity and r is the after-tax rate of return on capitalization. This equation simply expresses the fact that under these basic conditions, return on capitalization is *equal* to return on equity, and growth in equity is *equal* to return on equity.

In Case II, debt was introduced to the capital structure, and we therefore have to add the leverage effect to the formula to arrive at this expression of growth:

$$g = r + \frac{D}{E}(r - i)$$

where D is debt, E is equity, and i is the after-tax interest rate. Leverage, as we discussed earlier, is a direct function of these two elements:

- Proportion of debt in the total capital structure.
- Difference between the return on capitalization and the interest cost of debt funds, both after taxes.

Because in Case II all earnings are assumed to be reinvested, the rate of growth in equity must again be equal to the *return* on equity—which in this case is a combination of the return on net assets and the net contribution from leverage.

In Case III, the introduction of dividend payments slowed the growth in equity, because only the earnings retained could be reinvested. We now have to adjust each of the two components of the expression to reflect this change. The factor p stands for the proportion of earnings retained as a percentage of total earnings. The resulting equation is:

$$g = rp + \frac{D}{E}(r - i)\, p$$

We now have a generalized formula for the rate of growth in equity that can be sustained by a business if stable conditions and policies hold. It's called the *sustainable growth equation.** If the business, over the long run, is managed within the following parameters, the growth in equity achieved will stabilize at the rate determined by the equation:

---

*This equation is available in an interactive format (TFA Template)—see "Analytical Support" on p. 000

- Continually able to invest funds at the return indicated.

- Maintain the debt/equity proportion stable.

- Interest rates and the dividend payout ratio do not change.

As changes in policies or conditions are introduced, however, the fluctuations in year-to-year performance can be severe. In fact, most companies are unlikely to operate for extended periods at a particular sustainable growth rate.

We can examine in more detail the drivers of growth that are implicit in this equation. Foremost is the return on capitalization (r), which is the key indicator of the effectiveness with which working capital, fixed assets, and other assets funded by the capitalization are employed. Not surprisingly, the greater the return, the higher the growth potential. The numerator r, operating profit after taxes, is clearly a function of the profitability of sales, while the denominator, debt plus shareholders' equity, expresses the relative size of the asset base it supports. Thus both operating profits and effective use of assets are key drivers of growth. Next is the policy of earnings retention versus dividend payout. As we saw in Case III, sustainable growth can be significantly reduced if a high payout policy is pursued. Finally, the degree of financial leverage directly influences growth potential. The higher the successful use of leverage, the greater the growth potential—within the constraints of prudent financing, of course.

Another way of looking at sustainable growth is to multiply the profit margin on sales (profit after taxes P divided by sales S) (in percent), asset turnover (number of times), financial leverage (assets A divided by the beginning balance of shareholders' equity E_b) (number of times), and the retention rate (p) of earnings (in percent). These elements, of course, also underlie our earlier formulation, only the form of expressing them here has changed.

Our modified formula appears as follows:

$$g = \frac{P}{S}\,(\%) \times \frac{S}{A} \times \frac{A}{E_b} \times p\,(\%)$$

Now the drivers of growth reflect the focus on sales profitability, asset effectiveness in terms of turnover, the degree of leverage, and the retention of earnings. Again sustainable growth boils down to managing profitability, managing resource utilization, using leverage prudently, and choosing a sustainable dividend policy.

What are the implications of sustainable growth analysis? Clearly, a company in a fast-growing industry that is characterized by thin operating margins and high asset requirements isn't likely to be able to sustain its desired growth from internal sources alone, even if it pays out very little in dividends. The financial policies that management must consider will include expanding the equity base beyond retained earnings by issuing new shares, and using increasing leverage, especially if rapid growth in the early stages of the product/service life cycle is essential to attaining a strategic advantage. There are likely to be repeated, significant cash shortfalls during the growth period. In contrast, a company in a mature business setting might have a sustainable growth rate that exceeds its internal strategic growth needs, resulting in a buildup of excess cash. Management may have to reexamine its financial policies, consider higher dividends, share repurchases, and reduction of debt, unless other strategic opportunities can be found to employ the resources being created by its older products and services.

When doing trend analysis of past performance, it's useful to calculate the sustainable growth rate for the years examined and to compare the results to the actual year-to-year growth achieved. The differences will indicate whether the company has exceeded or lagged relative to its growth potential, and a further check of the financial policies in place at the time will indicate whether significant changes were made in them or could perhaps be in the offing.

As we've stated before, however, growth in equity is only one of several different types of financial objectives. Figure 6–9 indicated that our basic model is applicable to testing other objectives, such as growth in earnings. As the last line of the "Results" section indicates, under our stable sets of policies, growth in total earnings (profit after taxes) stabilizes at the same rate as growth in equity. In fact, the formula used for growth in equity applies to this objective as well, because profit growth depends on the same variables.

Similar models can be developed for the variables affecting earnings per share, dividends per share, debt service, or any other financial area of the business. We won't attempt to go into detail about these, but rather let growth in equity and growth in earnings serve as examples. Creative use of spreadsheets is a natural assistance in these types of analysis.

Integrated Financial Plan

We can now turn to an illustration of an integrated financial plan, which in concept and format is based on the models in Figures 6–8 and 6–9. This time, however, our focus is on taking a set of changing operating and financial assumptions and working them through the format, in a more realistic representation of the impact of the economic and competitive environment. As part of its strategy development, the XYZ Company is considering a number of modifications in its financial policies, and management wishes to study the impact of the combination of operating projections and policy modifications on its rate of growth and profitability over the next five years. The resulting integrated financial plan in Figure 6–10 encompasses changes in debt proportions, return on net assets, interest cost (changing as debt proportions rise), and dividend payout.

One key benefit of displaying the interrelationships in this form is that any obviously inconsistent conditions will show up in the results. As undesirable effects occur, the analyst can explore them with more tenable assumptions and calculate the impact of such changes. Basic planning frameworks of this kind are fairly easy to construct on spreadsheets, while more inclusive financial models can be programmed to provide output of this kind.

FIGURE 6–10

XYZ CORPORATION
Integrated Financial Plan:*
Sample Five-Year Projection of Effect of Policy Changes ($ thousands)

	Year 1	Year 2	Year 3	Year 4	Year 5
Capital structure:					
Debt as percent of capitalization.......	33.3%	43.0%	43.0%	50.0%	50.0%
Debt...........................	$300.0	$ 470.7	$ 492.5	$ 688.9	$ 728.5
Equity..........................	600.0	624.0	652.9	688.9	728.5
Net assets (capitalization).........	$900.0	$1,094.7	$1,145.4	$1,377.8	$1,457.0
Profitability (after taxes):					
Gross return on net assets**..........	8%	7%	8%	8%	9%
Amount of profit....................	$ 72.0	$ 76.6	$ 91.6	$ 110.2	$ 131.1
Interest rate......................	4%	4%	4%	4.5%	4.5%
Amount of interest.................	$ 12.0	$ 18.8	$ 19.7	$ 31.0	$ 32.8
Profit after interest................	$ 60.0	$ 57.8	$ 71.9	$ 79.2	$ 98.3
Disposition of profit:					
Dividend payout....................	60%	50%	50%	50%	40%
Dividends paid.....................	$ 36.0	$ 28.9	$ 35.9	$ 39.6	$ 39.3
Reinvestment of profit.............	$ 24.0	$ 28.9	$ 36.0	$ 39.6	$ 59.0
Financing (next year):					
New debt, old ratio	$ 12.0	$ 21.8	$ 27.2	$ 39.6	$ 59.0
New debt, revised ratio..............	158.7	0	169.2	0	0
Funding potential.................	$194.7	$ 50.7	$ 232.4	$ 79.2	$ 118.0
Cash flow implications:					
Amount of after-tax profit............	$ 60.0	$ 57.8	$ 71.9	$ 79.2	$ 98.3
Depreciation effect	40.0	46.0	50.0	65.0	72.0
Cash flow from operations	100.0	103.8	121.9	144.2	170.3
Dividends paid.....................	36.0	28.9	35.9	39.6	39.3
Cash flow available for reinvestment ...	64.0	74.9	86.0	104.6	131.0
Additional debt.....................	170.7	21.8	196.4	39.6	59.0
Total investment potential.........	$234.7	$ 96.7	$ 282.4	$ 144.2	$ 190.0
Results:					
Net return on net assets†	6.7%	5.3%	6.3%	5.8%	6.8%
Return on equity	10.0%	9.3%	11.0%	11.5%	13.5%
Growth in equity‡	4.0%	4.6%	5.5%	5.8%	8.1%
Earnings per share (100,000 shares)...	0.60	0.58	0.72	0.79	0.96
Dividends per share	0.36	0.29	0.36	0.40	0.39

*This exhibit is available in an interactive format (TFA Template)—see "Analytical Support" on p. 000.
**Profits before interest, after taxes related to net assets (capitalization).
†Profits after interest and taxes related to net assets.
‡Growth in recorded equity based on earnings reinvested after payment of dividends.

XYZ Corporation has a total capitalization of $900,000 and starts with a debt proportion of 33.3 percent (every dollar of equity is matched by 50 cents of long-term debt). The current return on net assets after taxes but before interest is 8 percent, which provides a profit of $72,000. Interest after taxes requires $12,000, which leaves a net profit of $60,000.

With an assumed dividend payout of 60 percent, cash dividends of $36,000 are required, which leaves a balance of retained earnings of $24,000 for reinvestment in new assets. This is in addition to the amount of depreciation we assume to be spent automatically to keep facilities in good repair. If the debt proportion of 33.3 percent in Year 1 were to be maintained, new debt of $12,000 supported by the increased equity could be incurred and used for new investment in Year 2.

In anticipation of major expansion plans, XYZ management has considered raising its debt proportion for Year 2 to 43 percent. This change would allow additional borrowing of $158,700 beyond the increase of $12,000 that would be possible under the old debt proportion. (The total amount of new debt is found by simply letting the increased equity of $624,000 represent 57 percent of net assets for Year 2.) For simplicity, we've assumed that all changes take place at year-end.

The results for the first year show a net return on capitalization of 6.7 percent, a return on equity of 10 percent, and growth in equity of 4 percent. Earnings per share are $0.60 and dividends per share are $0.36. The influx of new funds at the beginning of Year 2 raises the company's capitalization to almost $1.1 million.

For Year 2, the assumption about returns is lowered to reflect some normal inefficiencies as the new funds are invested; the overall return on net assets is expected to be 7 percent. After making proper allowance for interest payments, profits after taxes are $57,800. The assumed reduction in dividend payout to 50 percent requires only $28,900—which leaves $28,900 for reinvestment. Under the existing debt proportion of 43 percent, this amount permits raising of $21,800 of new debt (28,900 represents 57 percent of the increase in capital). These combined funds are added to the investment base for Year 3.

The process is repetitive as changes in policies are anticipated at the end of each year's operations. For example, we find a sizable new influx of capital in Year 4, as the debt proportion is again raised, this time to 50 percent. A small increase in the after-tax interest rate to 4.5 percent is assumed, because lenders will require higher interest as the capital structure becomes more leveraged and thus more risky. At the same time, however, the effectiveness of employing capital (after-tax return on net assets) has been left at 8 percent in Years 3 and 4, but was raised to 9 percent in Year 5, to allow some time for the new investments to become effective.

The results at the bottom of the table show some fluctuations in the net return on capitalization over the years, as either profitability or interest cost is changed. The return on equity, however, after dropping in Year 2, rises steadily to a sizable 13.5 percent in Year 5. Growth in equity jumps, after some intermediate boosts, to about double the original 4 percent rate in Year 5, that is, to 8.1 percent. Changes in total profit after interest are quite significant, as policy changes from year to year take effect. Similarly, growth in earnings per share fluctuates while dividends per share are somewhat diminished—showing little or no growth for most years as funds are reserved for investment.

The results from such a model raise some realistic questions. For example, it might not be prudent to change the dividend payout ratio in sizable steps as was done here. We observe a drop in dividends per share of almost 20 percent in the second year. In the absence of general economic problems, the corporation's directors might be very reluctant to make this change because a consistent dividend pattern is generally considered desirable. The main reason is that dividends represent part of the total shareholder return the investors have come to expect. Therefore, the dividend payout ratio for Year 2 might be maintained near the original level with the purpose of avoiding a drop in dividends per share. The dividend payout ratio would be lowered only as total earnings rise sufficiently to permit paying a level, or even growing, dividend.

At the same time, it might be useful to refine the assumptions about return on net assets. We've used an overall percentage in this example. It would be more realistic if, specifically taking into account the lag in expected returns on the new investments made, we split the analysis into

- Return on existing assets.
- Return on incremental assets.

Such a refinement might be particularly useful if a company were diversifying its operations and would expect a significantly different return from some of these new activities. More attention might also be paid to our current assumption that depreciation will be reinvested without generating additional profits. A company with short life cycles of products or services, or one that's consolidating some of its ongoing operations to free funds for redeployment in more diversified lines of business, might not be willing to reinvest the equivalent of depreciation in old product lines. Dealing with capital expenditures as a separate input would help clarify some of these questions.

The main purpose of this illustration is to show the usefulness of financial planning in the context of the overall business system. By observing how the key results respond to a variety of different inputs, the analyst can arrive at a set of assumptions and recommendations that fairly reflect management's desires and capabilities. Many more refined formats are, of course, possible.

Key Issues

The following is a recap of the key issues raised directly or indirectly in this chapter. They are enumerated here to help the reader keep the materials discussed within the perspective of financial theory and business practice.

1. The business system is a dynamic linkage of decisions, policies, and constraints, which must be considered as a whole when dealing with any subset of elements. Leverage in operations and financing has significant effects extending throughout the system, and these should be understood in specific terms as conditions are analyzed and changes are considered.

2. Operating leverage has both financial and strategic implications, because it cannot be separated from the trade-offs involved in pricing, cost effectiveness including outsourcing, and insights from activity-based analysis. It is intimately tied to all operational aspects of the business system, but also has implications for investment choices and financing considerations.

3. Use of financial leverage is a complex policy issue which not only relates to the specific impact of tax-deductible fixed interest charges on the return characteristic of the business, but requires fundamental understanding of the risk/reward trade-offs implicit in exposing a particular company to the risk of financial distress. Financial leverage thus is part of the policy mix that both enables successful performance and matches the management style of the company involved.

4. The ultimate purpose of using financial leverage is to enhance the overall market value of the firm, and as such the risk/reward trade-offs in the operational and competitive setting of the company have to be made explicit to find the optimum level.

5. Sustainable growth is a concept based on stable policies in investment, operations, and financing. Given the assumption of such stability, sustainability is subject to significant change as key conditions and constraints are altered. The sustainable growth concept can serve, however, as a yardstick against which the actual performance of a company can be held over time.

6. Financial modeling is useful in displaying the key drivers and results of assumed sets of conditions affecting growth. The degree of sophistication can vary widely; usually adequate ballpark estimates can be achieved with fairly basic sets of relationships. Integrated financial models will give more precise and interrelated results, but these also will be dominated by a limited set of key variables.

Summary

In this chapter we've attempted to integrate some key concepts discussed in the earlier parts of the book into the dynamic system framework established in Chapter 2. We added an expanded treatment of operating and financial leverage to demonstrate the important impact of fixed cost elements on changing operating conditions, and the risk/reward trade-off implicit in using debt financing. Through the use of a simplified financial growth model, we illustrated the need for consistency in setting operating and financial objectives and policies. We highlighted the various implications of growth, and developed the policy rationale for sustainable growth over time, given a stable set of conditions and choices. Finally, we applied the modeling approach to the needs and policies of a sample company and developed an integrated financial plan with which we tested the impact of planned changes in various key policies on the company's growth and performance.

In the end, the key test of financial analysis is the viability of the methods and results as predictors of future activity, which was a major point made in the earlier chapters. Often the optimal approach requires use of quite detailed and sensitive financial models of the business. Yet the outside analyst, and even insiders, often will be well served with simplified yardsticks and models which can sufficiently approximate solutions to planning alternatives. In this sense, the chapter draws together many of the points of earlier materials to give the reader an overall, albeit simplified, framework for analysis.

Analytical Support

Financial Genome, the commercially available financial analysis and planning software described in Appendix I, is accompanied by several interactive templates (TFA Template under "extras") for analyzing and displaying different assumptions for operating and financial leverage (Fig. 6-1 on p. 195), exploring the sustainable growth equation (p. 215) and testing the implications of future growth under different conditions. A graphic display permits break-even analysis with varying assumptions, while sustainable growth relationships are displayed in graphic form. The growth model format of Figure 6–8 on p. 211 and Figure 6–9 on p. 213 is available for testing the whole range of policy options. Finally, there is an interactive integrated financial plan template based on Figure 6–10 on p. 218. All of these templates allow the user to vary key assumptions and to study their impact on the various ratios and relationships. (see "Downloads Available" on p. 431)

Selected References

Brealey, Richard, and Stewart Myers. *Principles of Corporate Finance.* 5th ed. Burr Ridge, IL: Irwin/McGraw-Hill, 1996.

Donaldson, Gordon. *Strategy of Financial Mobility.* Boston: Division of Research, Graduate School of Business Administration, Harvard University, 1969. (A classic.)

Donaldson, Gordon. *Corporate Restructuring: Managing the Change Process from Within.* Boston: Harvard Business School Press, 1994.

Donaldson, Gordon. *Managing Corporate Wealth: The Operation of a Comprehensive Financial Goals System.* New York: Praeger, 1984.

Drucker, Peter F. "The Information Executives Truly Need." *Harvard Business Review,* January/February 1995.

Ross, Stephen; Randolph Westerfield; and Jeffrey Jaffe. *Corporate Finance.* 5th ed. Burr Ridge, IL: Irwin/McGraw-Hill, 1999.

CHAPTER 7

CASH FLOWS AND THE TIME VALUE OF MONEY

Throughout this book we've referred to the primary business objective of creating shareholder value through successful economic decisions made by the company's managers. We've defined value creation in terms of a positive trade-off of cash generated versus cash given up when making investment, operating, and financing decisions. We've also made the point that the cash flows involved in most decisions have a future dimension. To properly analyze the implications of a decision, therefore, we need to understand how to measure, at a given point in time, future cash flows and their value to the decision maker. The techniques and indicators required for this purpose are relatively straightforward due to their basic mathematical nature—involving discounting and compounding methodologies—although their application and especially the interpretation of results require a deeper understanding of the context of the decision and the many judgments involved in developing the estimates and implications of the underlying data and the cash flows expected. The various techniques we'll discuss are fundamental to financial/economic decisions, whether these are made in a corporate context, in the financial markets, or by individuals dealing with investments or financial instruments of various kinds.

In this chapter we'll concentrate first on defining the basic concepts underlying the time value of money. Then we'll provide a review of the common components involved in structuring the pattern of investment analyses in the business setting, followed by a discussion of the major techniques and indicators employed in the economic analysis of cash flows. We'll illustrate the techniques by using simple examples. In Chapter 8 we'll focus on the broader context of business investment decisions, identify the issues and complexities encountered, and provide numerous illustrations of more complex cases. We'll discuss in some detail the derivation of the underlying data, and the interpretation of the results of the analysis. Finally, we'll take up the issue of risk and how to factor uncertainty into the analytical process.

The Time Value of Money

Given the future orientation of most decisions, the proper application of economic reasoning requires us to recognize the intimate connection between two elements:

- The specific timing of every cash inflow and outflow relevant to the decision.
- The combined value of all relevant cash flows at the point of decision.

It's a simple axiom that a dollar received today is worth more than a dollar received one year hence, because we forgo the opportunity of profitably investing today the future dollar for which we must wait. Similarly, spending a dollar a year later is preferable to spending it now, because it can earn a return in the meantime. Thus, in principle the time value of money is related both to the timing of any receipt or expenditure and to the individual's or company's opportunity to earn a return on funds invested.

Discounting, Compounding, and Equivalence

Common sense tells us that we won't be indifferent between two investment propositions that are exactly alike in all aspects except for a difference in timing of the future benefits. An investor will obviously prefer the one providing more immediate benefits. The reason, of course, is that funds available earlier give an individual or a company the opportunity to invest these funds and earn a return, be it in a savings account, a government bond, a loan, a new piece of equipment, a promotional campaign, or any one of a great variety of other economic possibilities. Having to wait for a period of time until funds become available entails an opportunity cost in the form of lost earnings potential.

Conversely, common sense also dictates that given the choice between making an expenditure now versus making the same expenditure some time in the future, it's advantageous to defer the outlay. Again, the reason is the opportunity to earn a return on the funds in the meantime. As we stated earlier, the time value of an amount of money, or a series of cash flows, is affected directly by the specific timing of the receipt or disbursement, and the level of return the investor or the business can normally achieve on invested funds.

A simple example will help illustrate this point. If a person normally uses a savings account to earn interest of 5 percent per year on invested funds, a deposit of $1,000 made today will grow to $1,050 in one year. (For simplicity, we ignore the practice of daily or monthly compounding commonly used by banks and savings institutions.) If for some reason the person had to wait one year to deposit the $1,000, the opportunity to earn $50 in interest would be lost. Without question, a sum of $1,000 offered to the person one year hence has to be worth less today than the same amount offered immediately. Specifically, today's value of the delayed $1,000 must be related to the person's normally chosen opportunity to earn a

5 percent return. Given this earnings goal, we can calculate the *present value* of the $1,000 to be received in one year's time as follows:

$$\text{Present value} = \frac{\$1,000}{1 + 0.05} = \$952.38$$

The equation shows that with an assumed rate of return of 5 percent, $1,000 received one year from now is the *equivalent* of having $952.38 today. This is so because $952.38 invested at 5 percent today will grow into $1,000 by the end of one year. The calculation clearly reflects the economic trade-off between dollars received today versus a future date, based on the length of time involved and the available opportunity to earn a return. If we ignore the issue of risk for the moment, it also follows that our investor should be willing to pay $952.38 today for a financial contract that will pay $1,000 one year hence. Under these assumed conditions, our investor should in fact be indifferent between $952.38 today and $1,000 one year from now.

The longer the waiting period, the lower becomes the present value of a sum of money to be received, because for each additional period of delay, the opportunity to earn a return during the interval is forgone. Principal and interest left in place would have compounded by earning an annual return on the growing balance. As we already pointed out, the concept applies to outlays as well. It'll be advantageous to defer an expenditure as long as possible, because this allows the individual to earn a return during every period on the amount not spent plus any earnings left in place.

Calculating this change in the value of receipts or expenditures is quite simple when we know the time period and the opportunity rate of return. For example, a sum of $1,000 to be received at the end of five years will be worth only $783.53 today to someone normally earning a rate of return of 5 percent, because that amount invested today at 5 percent compounded annually would grow to $1,000 five years hence, if the earnings are left to accumulate and interest is earned on the growing balance each year.

The formula for this calculation appears as follows:

$$\text{Present value} = \frac{\$1,000}{(1 + 0.05)^5} = \frac{\$1,000}{1.27628} = \$783.53$$

The result of $783.53 was obtained by relating the *future value* of $1,000 to the *compound earnings factor* at 5 percent over five years, shown in the denominator as 1.27628—which is simply 1.05 raised to the fifth power. When we divide the future value by the compound factor, we have in effect *discounted* the future value into a lower *equivalent* present value.

Note that the mathematics are straightforward in achieving what we described in concept earlier: The value of a future sum is lowered in precise relationship to both the opportunity rate of return and the timing incidence. The opportunity rate of return in this example is our assumed 5 percent compound interest, while the timing incidence of five years is reflected in the number of times the interest is compounded to express the number of years during which earnings were forgone.

Naturally it's possible to calculate *future* values for today's values by multiplying the present value by the compound interest factor. If we take the conditions of the example just cited, we can derive the future value of $1,000 to be received in Year 5 from the present value of $783.53 as follows:

$$\text{Future value} = \$783.53 \times (1 + 0.05)^5 = \$783.53 \times 1.27628 = \$1,000$$

We refer to the calculation of present values as discounting, while the reverse process, the calculation of future values, is called compounding. These basic mathematical relationships allow us to derive the equivalent value of any sum to be received or paid at any point in time, either at the present moment, or at any specified future date.

The process of discounting and compounding is as old as money lending and has been used by financial institutions from time immemorial. Even though the application of this methodology to business investments is of relatively more recent vintage, techniques employing discounting and compounding have now become commonplace. Electronic calculators and ubiquitous computer spreadsheets with built-in discounting and compounding capability have made deriving time values and time-based investment measures a matter of routine.

Even though we recommend the use of calculator and spreadsheet programs to quickly arrive at time-adjusted cash flow results, we'll display in our examples the actual discount factors that are embedded in those routines, in order to highlight their impact. These factors are taken from present value tables, which analysts used before electronic means were available. While these tables are no longer needed for making the actual calculations, they do provide a visual demonstration of the effect of discounting, which becomes ever more powerful the higher the rate and the longer the time period. Two of the tables are provided at the end of this chapter as a reference.

We can clarify a few points with the help of these tables. Table 7–I (p. 252) contains the factors that translate into equivalent present values a single sum of money received or disbursed at the end of any period, under different assumptions about the rate of earnings. They are based on this general formula:

$$\text{Present value of sum} = \frac{1}{(1 + i)^n}$$

where i is the applicable opportunity rate of return (also referred to as discount rate) and n is the number of periods over which discounting takes place. In effect, the table factors are compound interest factors divided into 1. The table covers a range from 1 to 60 *periods,* and discount rates from 1 to 50 percent. The rates are related to these periods, however defined. For example, if the periods represent years, the rates are annual, while if months are used, the rates are monthly. The present value of a sum of money therefore can be found by simply multiplying the amount involved by the appropriate factor:

$$\text{Present value} = \text{Factor} \times \text{Sum}$$

while the future value of any sum can be found by dividing the present value by the appropriate factor from the table:

$$\text{Future value} = \frac{\text{Present Value}}{\text{Factor}}$$

Note that the present value results from our savings account example on pages 224–225 can be found in Table 7–I (p. 252) in the 5 percent column, lines 1 and 5, for the 1-year and 5-year illustrations, respectively. The same result for the first case can be obtained from a spreadsheet, by using the *npv* (net present value) function, entering 5 percent, and placing $1,000 in the first time period. The second result can be obtained again by using the *npv* function, entering 5 percent, zero values in periods 1 through 4, and $1,000 in period 5. Similarly, future values can be derived from a spreadsheet, by using the *fv* (future value) function, and entering the percentage rate, the number of time periods, and the present value into the appropriate openings.

The factors in Table 7–II (p. 253), a variation of Table 7–I, allow the direct calculation of the present value of a *series* of equal receipts or payments occurring over a number of periods. Such even series of cash flows are called *annuities,* and occur mostly in connection with financial instruments, such as mortgages. The same result could, of course, be obtained by using Table 7–I and repeatedly multiplying the periodic amount with the appropriate series of successive factors and adding all of the results. Table 7–II directly provides a set of such additive factors, which allow obtaining the present value of an annuity in a single step, that is, multiplying the period receipt or payment by the appropriate factor:

$$\text{Present value} = \text{Factor} \times \text{Annuity}$$

For example, the present value of an annuity of $100 per year for seven years is 5.206 × $100, or $520.60. Using a spreadsheet, we can obtain this result by selecting the *pv* (present value) function, entering 8 percent, and seven periods @ $100 per period, taking care to properly interpret the sign of the value displayed. The mathematical relationships embedded in the table and in the spreadsheet routine are represented by the annuity formula:

$$\text{Present value of annuity} = \frac{1}{i} - \frac{1}{i(1 + i)^n}$$

In practice one can choose many possible variations and refinements in timing, such as more frequent discounting (monthly or weekly), or assuming that the annuity is received or disbursed in weekly or monthly increments rather than at the end of the period, a distinction which is important for financial institutions.

The use of the continuous flow option introduces a forward shift in timing that leads to slightly higher present values, both for single sums and annuities. Refinements such as daily discounting or compounding are commonly applied to financial instruments, such as mortgages, bonds, charge accounts, and so on, all of which involve specific contractual arrangements.

For the practical purpose of analyzing business investments, such refinements are not critical, because as we'll see, the inherent imprecision of many of the estimates involved easily outweighs any incremental numerical refinement that might be obtained. The normal settings of calculators and spreadsheet programs use the periodic discounting embodied in the formulas of the two tables at the end of the chapter. This is quite adequate for most analytical needs in a business environment, but if more precision is sought, the optional settings in calculators and spreadsheets easily accommodate such refinements.

We'll now turn to the discussion of the basic analytical framework for business investments, and identify the critical components involved. Then we'll take up one by one the commonly used measures for investment analysis, most of which employ these discounting principles. We'll cover the basic rationale on which the measures are based, and their applicability to business investment analysis, as well as their shortcomings. Our illustrations and discussion will be built around simple business investment projects, but their applicability to the broader variety of cash-flow-based investments and instruments will become obvious.

Since the economic analysis of business investments involves projecting a whole series and pattern of incremental cash flows, both positive and negative, and usually uneven, we need to apply time value adjustments to develop a consistent translation of these future flows into equivalent values at the point of decision. Figure 7–1 shows the pattern of cash flows connected with a typical

---

F I G U R E   7–1

Typical Cash Flow Pattern for a Business Investment

investment, consisting of an initial outlay, a series of positive benefits, an intermediate additional outlay, and ultimate recovery of part of the resources committed in the form of a terminal value.

All of these future cash flows have to be brought back in time to the present
point of decision by an appropriate methodology, in order to determine whether
the trade-off between the expected positive and negative cash flows is favorable.
As we've discussed, expressing future dollars in the form of *equivalent* present
dollars requires discounting. It's the basis for all the modern techniques of investment analysis and valuation discussed in this book. We'll return to describing the
key tools employing the time value of money after we've discussed the basic layout and elements of the cash flow analysis.

Components of Analysis

In essence, financial resources are invested for one basic reason: to obtain sufficient future economic returns to warrant the original outlay and any related future
outlays, that is, sufficient cash receipts over the life of the project to justify the
cash spent. This basic trade-off of current cash outflow against expected future
cash inflow must be recognized by any of the analytical methods used in one way
or another.

To judge the attractiveness of any investment, we must consider the following four elements involved in the decision:

- The amount expended—the *net investment.*
- The potential benefits—the *net operating cash inflows.*
- The time span of benefits—the *economic life.*
- Any final recovery of capital—the *terminal value.*

A proper economic analysis must take these four elements into account to
be able to determine whether or not the investment is worthwhile.

For Example

An outlay of $100,000 for equipment needed to manufacture a new
product is expected to provide an after-tax cash flow of $25,000 over a
period of six years, without significant annual fluctuations. Although the
equipment will not be fully worn out after six years, it's unlikely that
more than scrap value will be realized at that time, due to technical
obsolescence. The cost of removal is expected to offset this scrap value.
The effect of straight-line depreciation over the six years ($16,667 per
year) was correctly adjusted for in the annual cash flow figure of $25,000,
having been added back to the expected net after-tax improvement in
profits of $8,333.

Net Investment

The first element in the analysis, the net investment, normally consists of the gross capital requirements for new assets, reduced by any funds recovered from the trade or sale of any existing assets caused by the decision. Such recoveries must be adjusted for any change in income taxes arising from a recognized gain or loss on the disposal of existing assets.

The basic rule for finding the investment amount committed to the decision is to calculate the net amount of initial outlays and recoveries actually caused by the decision to invest. In our simple example, no funds are recovered at the decision point and therefore the net investment is the full outlay of $100,000.

When an investment is made to support a new product or service, or to provide an increased volume of existing products or services, any additions to working capital required by the increased level of sales also must be included in the analysis. Normally, any initial incremental working capital is added to the net investment, and future requirements or releases are shown as cash flows in the respective time periods. For our simple example this refinement is ignored, but in Chapter 8 we'll demonstrate how working capital increments are handled.

Further investment outlays might also become necessary during the life of the project, and might be foreseeable enough to be estimated at the time of analysis. If such future outlays are a potential consequence of the initial decision, they must be considered as part of the current decision process, and reflected as cash outflows in the time periods when they are expected to occur. We'll also demonstrate examples which involve sequential investments in Chapter 8.

Net Operating Cash Inflows

The operational basis for defining the economic benefits over the life of the investment is the expected period-by-period *net change* in revenues and expenses caused by the investment, after adjusting for applicable income taxes and the effect of accounting elements such as depreciation. These incremental changes include such elements as operating savings from a machine replacement, additional profits from a new product line or a new service, increased profits from a plant expansion, or profits created by developing land or other natural resources. Generally, these changes will be reflected in the form of increased profit as reported in periodic operating statements, once the investment is in place and functioning. Our main focus, however, has to be on finding the estimated net impact on periodic cash flow, adjusted for all applicable taxes and for accounting elements like depreciation. They must be carefully defined as only the changes actually caused by the decision to invest, that is, only relevant cash inflows and outflows. Later, we'll give examples of how such project cash flows are derived.

For our simplified illustration, we'll assume that the net annual operating after-tax cash inflow will be a level amount of $25,000 over the project's life. This figure represents the sum of estimated net after-tax profits of $8,333 to which is added the depreciation effect of $16,667. As we'll see later, introducing a variable pattern of periodic cash flows can significantly influence the analytical results. Level periodic flows are easiest to deal with, and are generally found in financial contracts of various kinds, but they are quite rare in the business setting. Uneven cash flows are more common and they make the analysis a little more complex—but such patterns can be handled readily for calculation purposes, as we'll demonstrate.

Economic Life

The third element, the time period selected for the analysis, is commonly referred to as the *economic life* of the investment project. For purposes of investment analysis, the only relevant time period is the economic life, as distinguished from the *physical* life of equipment, or the *technological* life of a particular process or service.

Even though a building or a piece of equipment might be perfectly usable from a physical standpoint, the economic life of the investment is finished if the market for the product or service has disappeared. Similarly, the economic life of any given technology or service is bound up with the economics of the marketplace—the best process is useless if the resulting product or service can no longer be sold. At that point, any resources still usable will have to be repositioned, which requires another investment decision, or they might be disposed of for their recovery value. When redeploying such resources into another project, the net investment for that decision would, of course, be the estimated recovery value after taxes.

In our simple example, we have assumed a six-year economic life, the period over which the product manufactured with the equipment will be sold. The *depreciation life* used for accounting or tax purposes doesn't normally reflect an investment's true life span, and in this case we've only made it equal to the economic life for simplicity. As we discussed earlier, such write-offs are based on standard accounting and tax guidelines, and don't necessarily represent the investment's expected economic usefulness.

Terminal (Residual) Value

At the end of the economic life an assessment has to be made whether any residual values remain to be recognized. Normally, if one expects a substantial recovery of capital from eventual disposal of assets at the end of the economic life, these estimated amounts have to be made part of the analysis. Such recoveries can be proceeds from the sale of facilities and equipment (beyond the minor scrap value assumed in our example), as well as the release of any *working capital* associated with the investment. Also, there are situations in which an ongoing value of a business, a facility, or a process is expected beyond this specific analysis period chosen. This condition is especially important in valuation analyses, which we'll discuss in Chapters 11 and 12. For our simple illustration no terminal value is assumed, but later we'll demonstrate the handling of this concept.

Methods of Analysis

We've now laid the groundwork for analyzing any normal business investment by describing the four essential *components* of the analysis. Our purpose was to focus on *what* must be analyzed. We'll now turn to the question of *how* this is done—the methods and criteria of analysis that will help us judge the economics of the decision.

How do we relate the four basic components—

- Net investment
- Operating cash inflow
- Economic life
- Terminal value

—to determine the project's attractiveness? First we'll dispose quickly of some simplistic methods of analysis, which are merely rules of thumb that intuitively (but incorrectly) grapple with the trade-off between investment and operating cash flows. They are the *payback* and the *simple rate of return,* both of which are still used in practice occasionally despite their demonstrable shortcomings.

Our major emphasis will be on the measures employing the time value of money as discussed earlier, which enable the analyst to assess the trade-offs between relevant cash flows in equivalent terms, that is, regardless of the timing of their incidence. Those key measures are *net present value,* the *present value payback,* the *profitability index,* and the *internal rate of return (yield),* and in addition, the *annualized net present value.* We'll focus on the meaning of these measures, the relationships between them, and illustrate their use on the basis of simple examples. In Chapter 8, we'll discuss the broader context of business investment analysis, within which these measures play a role as indicators of value creation, and discuss more complex analytical problems. As part of this broader context, we'll also deal with risk analysis, ranges of estimates, simulation, probabilistic reasoning, and risk-adjusted return standards.

Simple Measures

Payback
This crude rule of thumb directly relates assumed level annual cash inflows from a project to the net investment required. Using the data from our simplified example, the calculation is straightforward:

$$\text{Payback} = \frac{\text{Net investment}}{\text{Average annual operating cash flow}} = \frac{\$100,000}{\$25,000} = 4 \text{ years}$$

The result is the number of years required for the original outlay to be repaid, answering the question, How long will it be until I get my money back? It's a rough test of whether the amount of the investment will be recovered within its economic life span. Here, payback is achieved in only four years versus the estimated economic life of six years. Recovering the capital is not enough, of course, because from an economic standpoint, one would hope to earn a return on the funds while they are invested.

Visualize a savings account in which $100 is deposited, and from which $25 is withdrawn at the end of each year. After four years, the principal will have been repaid. If the bank statement showed that the account was now depleted, the saver would properly demand to be paid the 4 or 5 percent interest that should have been earned every year on the declining balance in the account.

We can illustrate these basics of investment economics in Figure 7–2, where we've shown how both principal repayment and earnings on the outstanding balance have to be achieved by the cash flow stream over the economic life. We're again using the simple $100,000 investment, with a level annual after-tax operating cash flow. If the company typically earned 10 percent after taxes on its investments, part of every year's cash flow would be considered as normal earnings return, with the remainder used to reduce the outstanding balance.

The first row shows the beginning balance of the investment in every year. In the second row, normal earnings of 10 percent are calculated on these balances. In the third row are operating cash flows which, when reduced by the normal earnings, are applied against the beginning balances of the investment to calculate every year's ending balance. The result is an amortization schedule for our simple investment that extends into the sixth year—requiring about two more years of

---

FIGURE 7–2

Amortization of $100,000 Investment at 10 Percent

	Year 1	Year 2	Year 3	Year 4	Year 5	Year 6
Beginning balance	$100,000	$85,000	$68,500	$50,350	$30,385	$ 8,424
Normal company earnings @ 10%	10,000	8,500	6,850	5,035	3,039	842
Operating cash inflows of project	25,000	25,000	25,000	25,000	25,000	25,000
Ending balance to be recovered	85,000	68,500	50,350	30,385	8,424	−15,734
Simple payback (4 × $25,000)				Year 4		

annual benefits than the simple payback measure would suggest. If the project ended in Year 4, an opportunity loss of about $30,400 would be incurred, and in Year 5, the loss would be about $8,400. Only in Year 6 will the remaining principal balance have been recovered and an economic gain of about $15,700 achieved. As we'll see shortly, all modern investment criteria are based on the basic rationale underlying this example, with some refinements in the precise calculations used.

We can now quickly dispose of the payback measure as an indicator of investment desirability: It's insensitive to the economic life span and thus not a meaningful criterion of earnings power. It'll give the same "four years plus something extra" reading on other projects that have similar cash flows but 8- or 10-year economic lives, even though those projects would be clearly superior to our example. It implicitly assumes level annual operating cash flows, and cannot properly evaluate projects with rising or declining cash flow patterns—although these are very common. It cannot accommodate any additional investments made during the period, or recognize capital recoveries at the end of the economic life.

The only situation where the measure has some applicability is in comparing a series of simple projects with quite similar cash flow patterns, but even then it is more appropriate to apply the economic techniques that are readily available on calculators and spreadsheets.

However, it's possible to make use of a refined concept of payback that is expressed in economic terms, but this measure requires the discounting process to arrive at the so-called present value payback. It's one of the indicators of investment desirability that build a return requirement into the analysis, and we'll discuss it in detail later.

Simple Rate of Return

Again, only passing comments are warranted about this simplistic rule of thumb, which in fact is the inverse of the basic payback formula. It states the desirability of an investment in terms of a percentage return on the original outlay. The method shares all of the shortcomings of the payback, because it again relates only two of the four critical aspects of any project, net investment and operating cash flows, and ignores the economic life and any terminal value:

$$\frac{\text{Return on}}{\text{investment}} = \frac{\text{Average annual operating cash flow}}{\text{Net investment}} = \frac{\$25,000}{\$100,000} = 25\%$$

What this result actually indicates is that $25,000 happens to be 25 percent of $100,000, because there's no reference to economic life and no recognition of the need to amortize the investment. The measure will give the *same* answer whether the economic life is 1 year, 10 years, or 100 years. The 25 percent return indicated here would be economically valid only if the investment provided $25,000 per year *in perpetuity*—not a very realistic condition!

Economic Investment Measures

Earlier, we described business investment analysis as the process of weighing the economic trade-off between current dollar outlays and future net cash flow benefits that are expected to be obtained over a relevant period of time. This economic valuation concept applies to all types of investments, whether made by individuals or businesses. The time value of money is employed as the underlying methodology in every case. We'll use the basic principles of discounting and compounding discussed earlier to explain and demonstrate the major measures of investment analysis. These measures utilize such principles to calculate the quantitative basis for making economic choices among investment propositions.

Net Present Value

The net present value (NPV) measure has become the most commonly used indicator in corporate economic and valuation analysis, and is accepted as the preferred measure in the widest range of analytical processes. It weighs the cash flow trade-off among investment outlays, future benefits, and terminal values in *equivalent* present value terms, and allows the analyst to determine whether the net balance of these values is favorable or unfavorable—in other words, the size of the economic trade-off involved relative to an economic return standard. From the standpoint of creating shareholder value, a positive net present value implies that the proposal, if implemented and performing as expected, will add value because of the favorable trade-off of time-adjusted cash inflows over outflows. In contrast, a negative net present value will destroy value due to an excess of time-adjusted cash outflows over inflows. As a basic rule one can say the higher the positive NPV, the better the value creation potential.

To use the tool, a rate of discount representing a normal expected rate of return first must be specified as the standard to be met. As we'll see, this rate is commonly based on a company's weighted average cost of capital, which embodies the return expectations of both equity and debt providers of the company's capital structure, as described in Chapter 9. Next, the inflows and outflows over the economic life of the investment proposal are specified and discounted at this return standard. Finally, the present values of all inflows (positive amounts) and outflows (negative amounts) are summed. The difference between these sums represents the net present value. NPV can be positive, zero, or negative, depending on whether there is a net inflow, a matching of cash flows, or a net outflow over the economic life of the project.

Used as a standard of comparison, the measure indicates whether an investment, over its economic life, will achieve the expected return standard applied in the calculation, given that the underlying estimates are in fact realized. Inasmuch as present value results depend on both timing of the cash flows and the level of the required rate of return standard, a positive net present value indicates that the cash flows expected to be generated by the investment over its economic life will:

- Recover the original outlay (as well as any future capital outlays or recoveries considered in the analysis).
- Earn the specified return standard on the outstanding balance.
- Provide a "cushion" of economic value over and above meeting the minimum standard.

Conversely, a negative net present value indicates that the project is not achieving the return standard and thus will cause an economic loss if implemented. A zero NPV is value neutral. Obviously, the result will be affected by the level of benefits assumed, the specific timing pattern of the various cash flows, and the relative magnitudes of the amounts involved.

Another word should be said at this point about the rate of discount. From an economic standpoint, it should be the rate of return an investor normally enjoys from investments of similar nature and risk, as we explained in our discussion of the time value of money. In effect, this standard represents an opportunity rate of return. In a corporate setting, the choice of a discount rate is complicated both by the variety of investment possibilities and by the types of financing provided by both owners and lenders. The corporate return standard normally used to discount business investment cash flows should reflect the minimum return requirement that will provide the normally expected level of return on the company's investments, under normal risk conditions.

The most commonly employed standard is based on the overall corporate *cost of capital,* which takes into account shareholder expectations, business risk, and leverage. As we've mentioned before, shareholder value can be created only by making investments whose returns exceed the cost of capital. Therefore, the actual standard established by a company will often be set above the cost of capital, reflecting a specific management objective to achieve returns higher than the cost of capital. Sometimes a corporate return standard is separated into a set of multiple discount rates for different lines of business within a company, in order to recognize specific risk differentials. We'll deal with these concepts in greater depth in Chapters 8 and 9. For purposes of this discussion, we'll assume that management has chosen an appropriate return standard with which to discount investment cash flows, and we'll focus on how present value measures are used to assess potential investments on an economic basis.

As a first step, it's generally helpful to lay out the pertinent information period by period to give us a proper time perspective. A horizontal time scale matching spreadsheet patterns should be used, on which the periods are marked off, as Figure 7–3 shows. Positive and negative cash flows are then inserted as arrows at the appropriate positions in time, scaled to the size of the dollar amounts. Note that the time scale begins at point 0, the present decision point, and extends out as far as the project's economic life requires. Any events that occurred prior to the decision point (shown as negative periods) are not relevant to the analysis, unless the decision specifically causes a recovery of past expenditures, such as the sale of old assets.

FIGURE 7–3

Generalized Time Scale for Investment Analysis

FIGURE 7–4

Net Present Value Analysis at 8 Percent*

	Year 0	Year 1	Year 2	Year 3	Year 4	Year 5	Year 6	Totals
Investment outlay								
(outflow)	$−100,000	0	0	0	0	0	0	$− 100,000
Benefits (inflows) ..	0	$25,000	$25,000	$25,000	$25,000	$25,000	$25,000	150,000
Present value								
factors @ 8%** ..	1.000	0.926	0.857	0.794	0.735	0.681	0.630	
Present values of								
cash flows	−100,000	23,150	21,425	19,850	18,375	17,025	15,750	15,575
Cumulative present								
values	−100,000	−76,850	−55,425	−35,575	−17,200	−175	15,575	
Net present value								
@ 8%								$ 15,575

*This exhibit is available in an interactive format (TFA Template)—see "Analytical Support" on p. 250.

**From Table 7–I (p. 252), which assumes benefits occur at year-end. Because the inflows are level, we could instead use an annuity factor of 4.623 from Table 7–II (p. 253) for an identical result.

    To illustrate the process, let's return to the simple investment example used earlier in the chapter. We'll show the numerical information as a table in Figure 7–4. Note the similarity in approach to the simple amortization process we used in Figure 7–2 (p. 233). Figure 7–4 demonstrates that the pattern in our sample net investment of $100,000, with six annual benefit inflows of $25,000 from Year 1 through Year 6, results in a net present value of almost $16,000. This assumes that our company considers the relatively low rate of 8 percent after taxes a normal earnings standard. The total initial outflow will have been recovered over the six-year period, while 8 percent after taxes will have been earned all along on the declining investment balance outstanding during the project life. The positive net present value shows that a value creation of about $15,600 in equivalent present value dollars can be expected if the cash flow estimates are correct and if the project does live out its full economic life.

In the simple payback concept we discussed earlier, we referred to the recovery of the original investment plus "something extra." The critical difference between simple payback and net present value, however, is the fact that net present value has a built-in return requirement in addition to full recovery of the investment. Thus, the value "cushion" implicit in a positive net present value is truly a calculated economic value gain that goes beyond satisfying the required return standard. In fact, we can see from the cumulative present value line that if the project performs as expected, the cash flows are sufficient to recover the principal and earn 8 percent by the end of period five, where the cumulative present value is very close to zero.

If a higher earnings standard had been required, say 12 percent, the results would be those shown in Figure 7–5. The net present value remains positive, but the size of the value creation has dramatically decreased to only $2,800. We would expect such a decrease, because at the higher discount rate, the present value of the future cash inflows must decline, with all other circumstances unchanged. Note that this time the present value payback requires almost the full six years.

At an assumed earnings standard of 14 percent, the net present value shrinks even further. In fact, it is transformed into a negative result ($25,000 \times 3.889 -$ $100,000 = -$2,775). These results reflect the great sensitivity of net present value to the choice of earnings standards, especially at higher rates.

The cumulative present value row in the two sets of calculations illustrates the importance of the length of the economic life of the investment. We can observe that the time required for the cumulative present value to turn positive (and thus achieve a present value payback) was lengthened as the earnings standard

FIGURE 7–5

Net Present Value Analysis at 12 Percent*

	Year 0	Year 1	Year 2	Year 3	Year 4	Year 5	Year 6	Totals
Investment outlay (outflow) ...	$−100,000	0	0	0	0	0	0	$−100,000
Benefits (inflows) ...	0	$ 25,000	$ 25,000	$ 25,000	$ 25,000	$ 25,000	$25,000	150,000
Present value factors @ 12%** ...	1.000	0.893	0.797	0.712	0.636	0.567	0.507	
Present values of cash flows	−100,000	22,325	19,925	17,800	15,900	14,175	12,675	2,800
Cumulative present values ...	$−100,000	$−77,675	$−57,750	$−39,950	$−24,050	$−9,875	$ 2,800	
Net present value @ 12%							$	2,800

*This exhibit is available in an interactive format (TFA Template)—see "Analytical Support" on p. 250.

**As in Figure 7–4, we could use 4.112 times $25,000 from Table 7–II, p. 253.

was raised. At 8 percent, the economic life had to last about five years for the switch to occur (the net present value after the benefits of Year 5 is almost zero), while at 12 percent, most of the sixth year of economic life was necessary for a positive turnaround (approximately $10,000 of negative present value remaining at the end of Year 5 has to be recovered from the benefits of Year 6). At 14 percent more time than the economic life was required to achieve a positive net present value, making the project uneconomic.

In our example we assumed a level operating cash inflow of $25,000. Uneven cash flow patterns have a notable impact on the results, although the method of calculation remains the same. The net present value approach can, of course, accommodate any combination of cash flow patterns without difficulty. The reader is invited to test this, using a cash inflow pattern that rises from, say, $15,000 to $40,000, and one that falls from $40,000 to $15,000, each totaling $150,000 over six years. When using a spreadsheet, the reader can select the *npv* function, specify the discount rate, enter the cash flows from Year 1 through 6, and subtract the net investment from the result to arrive at the net present value.

Net present value is a direct measure of value creation as well as a screening device that indicates whether a stipulated minimum return standard, such as the cost of capital, can be met over an investment proposal's economic life. We stated before that when net present value is positive, there is potential for a return in excess of the standard and therefore, economic value creation. When net present value is negative, the minimum return standard and capital recovery cannot be achieved with the projected cash flows. When net present value is close to or exactly *zero*, the return standard has just been met. In this case the investment will be value neutral. All of these conditions, of course, hold only on the assumption that the cash flow estimates and the projected life will in fact be achieved. The graphic representation of net present value in Figure 7–6 demonstrates the three outcomes.

While net present value is the most frequently used tool in evaluating investment alternatives, it doesn't answer all our questions about the economic

---

FIGURE 7–6

A Representation of Net Present Value

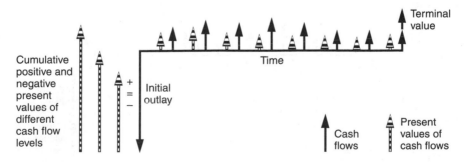

attractiveness of capital outlays. For example, when comparing different projects, how does one evaluate the respective size of the value creation calculated with a given return standard, particularly if the investment amount differs significantly? Also, to what extent is achieving the expected economic life a factor in such comparisons?

Furthermore, how does one quantify the potential errors and uncertainties inherent in the cash flow estimates, and how does the measure assist in investment choices if such deviations are significant? Finally, one can ask what specific return the project will yield if all estimates are in fact realized? Further measures and analytical methods are necessary to answer these questions, and we'll show later how a combination of techniques helps to narrow the choices to be made.

Present Value Payback

We've already referred to this measure during our discussion of net present value. As we saw, the concept establishes the *minimum life* necessary for an investment to operate as expected, and still meet the return standard of the present value analysis, a break-even condition in value creation. In other words, present value payback is achieved at the specific point in time when the cumulative positive present value of cash benefits equals the cumulative negative present value of all the cash outlays—in fact, a zero net present value condition. It's the point in the project's economic life when the original investment has been fully amortized and a return equal to the built-in return standard has been achieved on the declining balance—the point at which the project becomes economically attractive and can begin to create value. Figure 7–7 below provides a visual representation of this concept similar to the one for net present value.

Recall that in Figures 7–4 and 7–5, we included a row for the cumulative net present value of the project. It served as a visual check for determining the point at which net present value turned positive. The present value payback for our example, using a discount rate of 8 percent was about 5 years, while a 12 percent standard required almost 6 years, just about the full economic life of

---

FIGURE 7–7

A Representation of Present Value Payback

the investment. The minimum time needed to recover the investment and earn the return standard on the declining balance of the investment, when compared to the economic life, is also a way of expressing the potential risk of the project. The measure doesn't specifically address the nature of the risk, but merely identifies any remaining part of the economic life as an overall risk allowance. One can then judge whether the risk entailed in the combination of the key drivers of the project—or any one key variable in particular—is likely to outweigh the cushion of safety implied in the additional time the project might operate once it has passed the present value payback point. Remember, however, that the measure focuses only on the life span of the project, assuming implicitly that the estimated annual operating conditions will in fact continue to be achieved.

When uneven and more complicated cash flows patterns are projected, a condition we'll examine later, the minimum life test of the present value payback again requires a year-by-year accumulation of the negative and positive present values, as was done in simplified form in Figures 7–5 and 7–6.

If a project is a straightforward combination of a single outlay at point zero and expected level annual operating cash inflows, in effect representing an annuity, the analysis is especially simple and can, of course, be done readily on a calculator or spreadsheet. To illustrate the concept, however, we'll again make use of our present value tables, this time using the annuity factors in Table 7–II to quickly identify the present value payback. The following relationship is utilized:

$$\text{Present value} = \text{Factor} \times \text{Annuity}$$

We're looking for the condition under which the present value of the outflows is exactly equal to the present value of the inflows. Inasmuch as the net investment (outflow) must be recovered by the inflows, we can change the formula to:

$$\text{Net investment} = \text{Factor} \times \text{Annuity}$$

Because we know the level of the annuity, which is represented by the annual operating cash inflows, we can find the factor that satisfies the condition:

$$\text{Factor} = \frac{\text{Net investment}}{\text{Annuity}}$$

For our machine example, we can calculate the following results: $100,000 ÷ $25,000 = 4.0. We can look for the closest factor in the 8 percent column of Table 7–II. The answer lies almost exactly on the line for period 5 (3.993), which indicates that the project's minimum life under the assumed operating conditions must be 5 years to achieve the standard 8 percent return. If the standard is 12 percent, the minimum life has to be approximately 5⅔ years (an interpolation between 3.605 and 4.112).

The test for present value payback (minimum life) at any given return standard thus becomes one more factor in assessing the margin for error in the project estimates. It sharpens the analyst's understanding of the relationship of economic life and acceptable performance, and is a much improved version of the simple payback rule of thumb. The measure is a useful companion to the net present value criterion. It does not, however, address specific risk elements and in fact leaves weighing of any favorable difference between minimum and economic life to the decision maker's judgment.

Profitability Index (BCR)

After calculating the net present values of a series of projects, we might be faced with a choice that involves several alternative investments of different sizes. In such cases, we cannot ignore the fact that even though the net present values of the alternatives might be close or even equal, they involve initial funds commitments of widely varying amounts.

In other words, it does make a difference whether an investment proposal promises a net present value of $1,000 for an outlay of $10,000, or whether in another case, a net present value of $1,000 requires an investment of $25,000—even if we can assume equivalent economic lives and equivalent risk. Although both projects will create value if implemented successfully, the value creation in the first case is a much larger fraction of the net investment, which makes the first investment clearly more attractive, given that all other conditions are comparable.

The profitability index is a formal way of expressing this relationship of benefits to cost, a ratio which also is called the *benefit cost ratio (BCR):*

$$\text{Profitability index} = \frac{\text{Present value of operating inflows }(benefit)}{\text{Present value of net investment outlays }(cost)}$$

The present values in this formula are the same amounts we used earlier to derive the net present value, although then we subtracted inflows from outflows. In the case of the profitability index, the question is simply: How much in present value is being created for each dollar of net investment outlay?

The two cases we cited above would yield the following results:

$$1. \quad \text{Profitability index} = \frac{\$11,000}{\$10,000} = 1.10$$

$$2. \quad \text{Profitability index} = \frac{\$26,000}{\$25,000} = 1.04$$

The higher the index, the better the project. As we expected, the first project is much more favorable, given the assumption that all other aspects of the investment are reasonably comparable. If the index is 1.0 or less, the project is just meeting or even below the minimum return standard used to derive the present values. An index of exactly 1.0 corresponds to a zero net present value and no value creation. Our simple machine example has a profitability index of 1.16 at 8 percent in Figure 7–4 ($115,575 ÷ $100,000), and 1.03 at 12 percent in Figure 7–5 ($102,800 ÷ $100,000).

The profitability index provides results that directionally are consistent with the net present value measure. It's based on the same inputs but differs in format, focusing on the relative size of the trade-off. When used in conjunction with net present value, it provides additional insight for the analyst or manager. As already mentioned, it allows us to choose between investment alternatives of differing magnitudes. But it still leaves several points unanswered, and there are some theoretical issues involved that we'll point out later.

Internal Rate of Return (IRR, Yield)

The concept of a "true" return yielded by an investment over its economic life, also referred to as the *discounted cash flow return,* or *DCF,* was briefly mentioned in our earlier discussion of net present value. The internal rate of return is simply the unique discount rate that, when applied to both cash inflows and cash outflows over the investment's economic life, provides a zero net present value—that is, the present value of the inflows is exactly equal to the present value of the outflows. Stated another way, if cash flow estimates are achieved, the principal of an investment will be amortized over its specified economic life, while earning the exact return implied by the underlying discount rate. Figure 7–8 visually presents the dimensions of this measure.

The project's IRR might coincide with the return standard desired, might exceed it, or might fall short of the standard. These three conditions parallel those of net present value. One of the attractions of the internal rate of return for many practitioners is its ease of comparison with the return standard, and/or the cost of capital, being stated in percentage terms.

Naturally, the result of a given project will vary with changes in the economic life and the pattern of cash flows. In fact, the internal rate of return is found by letting it become a variable that is dependent on cash flows and economic life. In the case of net present value and profitability index, we had employed a specified return standard to discount the investment's cash flows. For the internal rate

---

FIGURE   7–8

A Representation of Internal Rate of Return (DCF)

of return, we switch the problem around to find the one discount rate that makes cash inflows and outflows exactly equal.

We can again employ our basic formula (Present value = Factor X Annuity) if the project is simple enough to involve a single investment outlay and only level annual cash inflows. The formula can then be expressed as follows:

$$\text{Factor} = \frac{\text{Present value (net investment)}}{\text{Annuity}}$$

The factor then can be located in the present value table for annuities (Table 7–II). Because the economic life is a given, we can find the rate of return by moving along the proper period row to the column containing a factor that approximates the formula result. Obviously, the result can be quickly obtained using a programmed calculator or a spreadsheet (using the *irr* function and specifying the cash flows by period), but again we're showing the details here to improve our understanding of the underlying mechanics.

To illustrate, our earlier investment example has a factor of 4.0 ($100,000 ÷ $25,000). On the line for period 6 in Table 7–II we find that 4.0 lies almost exactly between 12 percent (4.112) and 14 percent (3.889). Approximate interpolation suggests that the result is about 13 percent. (The precise result from a spreadsheet is 12.98%.)

When a project involves a more complex cash flow pattern, a trial-and-error approach is implied. Successive application of different discount rates to all cash flows over the investment's economic life can be made until a reasonably close approximation of a zero net present value has been found. We observed this effect in our earlier example, when the net present value declined as the discount rate was raised from 8 to 12 percent (see Figures 7–4 and 7–5). Again, programmed calculators and computer spreadsheets will arrive at the result directly, once the cash flows have been specified for all the periods involved.

As a ranking device for investments, the internal rate of return isn't without problems. First, there's the mathematical possibility that a complex project with many varied cash inflows and outflows over its economic life might in fact yield two different internal rates of return. Although a relatively rare occurrence, such an inconvenient outcome is caused by the specific pattern and timing of the various cash inflows and outflows.

More important, however, is the practical issue of choosing among alternative projects that involve widely differing net investments and that have internal rates of return inverse to the size of the project (the smaller investment has the higher return). A $10,000 investment with an internal rate of return of 50 percent cannot be directly compared to an outlay of $100,000 with a 30 percent internal rate of return, particularly if the risks are similar and the company normally requires a 15 percent earnings standard. While both projects exceed the desired return and thus create value, it might be better to employ the larger sum at 30 percent than the smaller sum at 50 percent, unless sufficient funds are available for both projects to be undertaken. If the economic life of alternative projects differs widely, it might similarly be advantageous to employ funds at a lower rate for a longer period of time than to opt for a brief period of higher return. This condition applies if a choice must be made between two investments, both of which exceed the return standard.

It should be apparent that the internal rate of return, like all other measures, must be used with some caution. Because it provides the analyst with a unique rate of return inherent to each project, the IRR of an investment permits a ranking of potential alternatives by a single number and by a direct comparison to the return standard. In contrast, the net present value method builds in a specified earnings standard reflecting the company's expectations from such investments, and the ranking is based on relative present value creation in dollar terms.

When the internal rates of return of different projects are compared, there's also the implied assumption that the cash flows thrown off during each project's economic life can in fact be reinvested at their unique rates. We know, however, that the company's earnings standard usually is an expression of the long-run earnings power of the company, even if only approximate. Thus, managers applying a 15 or even 20 percent return standard to investments must realize that a project with its own internal rate of return of, say, 30 percent, cannot be assumed to have its cash flows reinvested at this unique higher rate. Unless the general earnings standard is quite unrealistic, funds thrown off by capital investments can only be expected to be reemployed over time at this lower average rate.

This apparent dilemma does not, however, invalidate the internal rate of return measure, because any project will certainly yield its calculated internal rate of return if all conditions hold over its economic life, regardless of what is done with the cash generated by the project. Therefore, it's appropriate to rank projects by their respective IRRs.

In the last part of Chapter 8, we'll return to a comparative overview of all measures and develop basic rules for their application. The reader is invited to turn to the references listed at the ends of this chapter and of Chapter 8 for more extensive discussions of the many theoretical and practical arguments surrounding the use of present value techniques, particularly in the case of the internal rate of return.

Annualized Net Present Value

Another useful way of employing the annuity principle of discounting is to estimate how much of an annual shortfall in operating cash inflows would be permissible over the full economic life of a project, while still meeting the minimum return standard. We know that the net present value calculation normally results in either a cumulative excess or a cumulative deficiency of present value benefits vis-à-vis the net investment. We also know that if the net present value is positive, the amount can be viewed as value creation in excess of the cost of capital, if that is the standard employed. This figure also can be considered, at least in part, as a cushion against any estimating error contained in future cash inflows, especially when the discount rate has been set much higher than the cost of capital.

Unless a project has highly irregular annual flows, it's often useful to transform the positive net present value at the decision point into an *equivalent annuity* over the project's economic life. Such an annual equivalent, representing the allowable margin of error, can then be directly compared to the original estimates of annual operating cash inflow. This is possible because the net present value has in effect been "reconstituted" into a series of level cash flows on the same basis as the estimates themselves, that is, in the form of annual cash flows unadjusted for time value. To illustrate, we can transform the net present value shown in Figure 7–4, $15,575, into an annuity over the six-year life by simply using the familiar present value relationship:

$$\text{Present value} = \text{Factor} \times \text{Annuity}$$

or by using the annuity routines in calculators and spreadsheets, choosing the *pmt* (payment) function and specifying the discount rate, the number of periods and the present value to be recovered. Because we're interested in finding the annuity represented by the net present value, and wish to do so over a known economic life and at a specified discount rate—which is the earnings standard employed in the net present value calculation in the first place—we can transform the annuity formula as follows:

$$\text{Annuity} = \frac{\text{(Net) present value}}{\text{Factor}}$$

Our example has the following result:

$$\text{Annuity} = \frac{\$15,575}{4.623} = \$3,369$$

The annual operating cash inflows were originally estimated to be $25,000. Given the result above, the actual cash flow experienced could be lowered by about $3,400 per year, and the project would still meet the minimum standard of 8 percent, but obviously not create value. Note, however, that the investment would have to operate at that lower level of cash flows over its full economic life for this value-neutral condition to be true.

In this case, the shortfall allowance directly translates into a permissible downward adjustment of estimated operating cash inflows by 22 percent. We must remember from page 229, however, that the annual cash flow consists of an estimated after-tax operating profit of $8,333, to which depreciation of $16,667 has been added back. In view of this sizable depreciation allowance—which is not subject to uncertainty—the relevant permissible reduction applies to the after-tax profit alone. The adjustment reduces the after-tax profit to about $5,000 ($8,333 − $3,369 = $4,964), which amounts to a hefty 40 percent! As we can see, this type of analysis represents a more direct approach to judging the allowable variation in the key estimates than did the present value payback, which focused on the time period instead of the cash flow estimates.

Annualization can be more generally applied as a very practical and quick preliminary "scoping" of the attractiveness of a tentative investment proposal that has not yet been fleshed out in detail. This method turns the normal investment analysis around by finding the approximate annual operating cash flow required to justify an estimated capital outlay, at a time when specific operating benefits have yet to be determined. Given an estimate of the economic life and an earnings standard, we can employ the formula

$$\text{Operating cash flow} = \frac{\text{Net investment}}{\text{Factor}}$$

to find the annual cash flow equivalent that, on average, will be the minimum target benefit. We can, of course, readily use electronic means to make this transformation directly by again applying the *pmt* function and entering the discount rate, the number of periods, and the investment to be amortized.

We must be careful, however, to interpret this figure properly. Because by definition it's an after-tax cash flow, the result has to be correctly adjusted for the assumed annual depreciation in order to transform it into the minimum pretax operating improvement necessary to justify the outlay. The process simply involves working backward through the analysis, using the knowledge that cash flow consists of the sum of after-tax operating profit and annual depreciation. We can apply this to our example from Figure 7–4.

First, we find the target cash flow benefits over six years at 8 percent, using the appropriate factor from Table 7–II or obtaining them directly from a spreadsheet, using the *pmt* function and entering 8 percent, 6 periods, and the $100,000 present value:

$$\frac{\$100,000}{4.623} = \$21,631$$

Next we transform this required after-tax cash flow into its equivalent pretax operating improvement:

Aftertax cash flow	$21,631
Less: Depreciation	16,667
Aftertax profit	$ 4,964
Tax at 34% of *pretax* profit	$ 2,557
Pretax profit	$ 7,521
Add back depreciation	16,667
Minimum pretax operating improvement	$24,188

Thus, our investment has to provide a minimum of about $24,200 in direct operating improvements such as lower costs, incremental revenues, and so on. Clearly, this method provides a quick look at the amount of pretax profit benefits required and allows the decision maker to think about the likely potential of the investment to achieve them. In other words, annualization applied in this way is a useful tool for making a first assessment of the chances that an investment will be in the ballpark.

Applying Time-Adjusted Measures

As we stated earlier, the practice of discounting and compounding is inextricably connected with the services and instruments of the financial community world-wide. In our discussion we have concentrated on the use of discounting and compounding methodologies for the more specific purpose of analyzing business investments, defining the four key parameters of such investments and demonstrating the major tools used in the process. It should be clear to the reader, however, that minor rethinking of the key inputs as defined here will make the analysis process generally applicable to analyzing financial instruments, contracts, and any situation which involves cash flow trade-offs extending from the present into the future. In fact, we've used simple analogies to financial instruments in our discussion, and also indicated that the process would be present again in the valuation discussions in the final chapters of the book. The general applicability of discounting and compounding is also apparent from the general wording contained in calculator and spreadsheet routines, which are structured to handle any problem that involves present values, future values, payments, receipts, time periods, and rates for discounting and compounding.

As we also mentioned, applying the methodology is relatively easy once a degree of comfort has been acquired in understanding the basic mathematics and relationships. Manipulating data within the various frameworks can become quite routine. The real challenge in the application of time-adjusted methodologies relates to defining the problem, establishing the relevant data, defining the key risk factors, and interpreting the results. Chapter 8 illustrates many of these challenges. Business investments generally are more complex in these aspects than straightforward contracts and financial instruments, and the skills acquired from studying the materials in this chapter will provide a sound basis for handling the process in the many other areas to which it applies.

Key Issues

The following is a recap of the key issues raised directly or indirectly in this chapter. They are enumerated here to help the reader keep the analysis tools and methods within the perspective of financial theory and business practice.

1. Decisions involving trade-offs between present and future cash flows
    are a common occurrence in any business. They require a consistent
    framework for analyzing these cash flows at the point of decision
    in equivalent terms.

2. Discounting and compounding methodologies use basic mathematical relationships to integrate timing, monetary returns, and cash flow amounts into a value framework. They are not a substitute for judgment, however, only numerical assists.

3. Business investment analysis requires careful definition of the key inputs and variables underlying the cash flow pattern, which involves an understanding of the expected changes brought about by the decision, independent of accounting methodology, adjusted for tax implications, and fitted to the economic life span.

4. Economic analysis of investment decisions must be based on differential revenues and costs in the form of cash flows that are caused by the decision, and not on changes that are merely due to accounting conventions.

5. The major investment measures are designed to take into account the timing of inflows and outflows of an investment and relate to economic attractiveness to defined return expectations. Simple rules of thumb violate these criteria, and the ease of spreadsheet analysis has made the use of economic measures fully accessible to any interested person.

6. Creating shareholder value through economic returns above the cost of capital is the key criterion in business investment analysis, and the net present value and IRR measures can be used to test the analytical results for this outcome.

7. Testing for potential leeway in achieving lesser cash flow returns while still meeting or exceeding the standard used in the analysis is a useful application of economic payback and annualization, although care must be taken in the interpretation of such modifications.

8. While all economic measures discussed here directionally give the same reading of desirability, using only one measure in isolation can lead to misinterpretation of project desirability, depending on such elements as project size, interdependence, and funding limits.

9. Analytical techniques can provide ranges of results as well as quantitative insights of considerable sophistication, but they can't supplant qualitative business judgments that must deal with the broader context of strategy and risk assessment.

10. The use of discounting and compounding in the financial and economic environment is far broader than its specific application to business investments as described here; however, business investments represent the most complex set of conditions due to the uncertainty of estimates and the need to integrate projects into business strategy.

Summary

In this chapter, we've presented the basic analytical framework for business investment analysis within the context of the key parameters required for most business applications. Even though the material dealt largely with the time value of money and the specific techniques used to analyze the cash flow trade-offs in examples of simple business investments, we made the point repeatedly that the most critical aspect of the process was thoughtful attention to defining the parameters of net investment, net operating cash flows, economic life, and terminal value before any quantitative techniques are applied.

We discussed the importance of dealing with the net effect of the investment decision on future cash flows, that is, to focus on the relevant changes attributable to the decision. We pointed out the importance of deriving cash flows adjusted for accounting allocations, of recognizing the tax shield effect of write-offs such as depreciation, and generally dealing with the net after-tax cash impact of net investment, operating cash flows, and any terminal recoveries.

After introducing the basic mathematics of time adjustment through discounting and compounding, we presented a step-by-step approach to the various tools of analysis. We discarded as uneconomic the simple rules of thumb still being used at times, and demonstrated how the major economic tools, net present value, discounted payback, internal rate of return and annualization all gave indications of value creation in excess of the cost of capital, albeit in different form. We laid out a common format for analysis, and related this visual representation to the internal routines of calculators and spreadsheets. Working through a series of simple examples, we provided the reader with the ability to perform the key numerical aspects of investment analysis. But we cautioned that numerical results were only one input to the broader management task of selecting investment projects in a strategic context with defined corporate objectives and goals, and with the ultimate purpose of creating shareholder value, and indicated that the next chapter will be devoted to viewing business investment analysis in this broader, judgmentally more difficult, setting.

Analytical Support

Financial Genome, the commercially available financial analysis and planning software described in Appendix I, is accompanied by general purpose present value analysis templates and graphic displays (TFA Template under "extras"), which can be used to directly calculate the various discounted cash flow measures discussed in this chapter from any pattern of cash flows and discount rates, as well as different depreciation assumptions and tax rates. They match the format used in this chapter (Figs. 7–4 and 7–5 on pp. 237 and 238) and in Chapter 8. (see "Downloads Available" on page 431)

Selected References

Brealey, Richard, and Stewart Myers. *Principles of Corporate Finance*. 5th ed. Burr Ridge, IL: Irwin/McGraw-Hill, 1996.

Grant, Eugene L., et al. *Principles of Engineering Economy*. 8th ed. New York: John Wiley & Sons, 1990. (A classic.)

Ross, Stephen; Randolph Westerfield; and Bradford D. Jordan. *Fundamentals of Corporate Finance*. 4th ed. Burr Ridge, IL: Irwin/McGraw-Hill, 1998.

Thorndike, David. *The Thorndike Encyclopedia of Banking and Financial Tables, 1995 Yearbook*. Boston: Warren, Gorham & Lamont.

Weston, Fred; Scott Besley; and Eugene Brigham. *Essentials of Managerial Finance*. 11th ed. Hinsdale, IL: Dryden Press, 1997.

TABLE 7-1

Present Value of Single Sum of $1 Received or Paid at End of Period

Period of Receipt or Payment	1%	2%	4%	5%	6%	8%	10%	12%	14%	15%	16%	18%	20%	22%	24%	25%	26%	28%	30%	35%	40%	45%	50%
1	0.990	0.980	0.962	0.952	0.943	0.926	0.909	0.893	0.877	0.870	0.862	0.847	0.833	0.820	0.806	0.800	0.794	0.781	0.769	0.741	0.714	0.690	0.667
2	0.980	0.961	0.925	0.907	0.890	0.857	0.826	0.797	0.769	0.756	0.743	0.718	0.694	0.672	0.650	0.640	0.630	0.610	0.592	0.549	0.510	0.476	0.444
3	0.971	0.942	0.889	0.863	0.840	0.794	0.751	0.712	0.675	0.658	0.641	0.609	0.579	0.551	0.524	0.512	0.500	0.477	0.455	0.406	0.364	0.328	0.296
4	0.961	0.924	0.855	0.823	0.792	0.735	0.683	0.636	0.592	0.572	0.552	0.516	0.482	0.451	0.423	0.410	0.397	0.373	0.350	0.301	0.260	0.226	0.198
5	0.951	0.906	0.822	0.784	0.747	0.681	0.621	0.567	0.519	0.497	0.476	0.437	0.402	0.370	0.341	0.328	0.315	0.291	0.269	0.223	0.186	0.156	0.132
6	0.942	0.888	0.790	0.746	0.705	0.630	0.564	0.507	0.456	0.432	0.410	0.370	0.335	0.303	0.275	0.262	0.250	0.227	0.207	0.165	0.133	0.108	0.088
7	0.933	0.871	0.760	0.711	0.665	0.583	0.513	0.452	0.400	0.376	0.354	0.314	0.279	0.249	0.222	0.210	0.198	0.178	0.159	0.122	0.095	0.074	0.059
8	0.923	0.853	0.731	0.677	0.627	0.540	0.467	0.404	0.351	0.327	0.305	0.266	0.233	0.204	0.179	0.168	0.157	0.139	0.123	0.091	0.068	0.051	0.039
9	0.914	0.837	0.703	0.645	0.592	0.500	0.424	0.361	0.308	0.284	0.263	0.225	0.194	0.167	0.144	0.134	0.125	0.108	0.094	0.067	0.048	0.035	0.026
10	0.905	0.820	0.676	0.614	0.558	0.463	0.386	0.322	0.270	0.247	0.227	0.191	0.162	0.137	0.116	0.107	0.099	0.085	0.073	0.050	0.035	0.024	0.017
11	0.896	0.804	0.650	0.585	0.527	0.429	0.350	0.287	0.237	0.215	0.195	0.162	0.135	0.112	0.094	0.086	0.079	0.066	0.056	0.037	0.025	0.017	0.012
12	0.887	0.788	0.625	0.557	0.497	0.397	0.319	0.257	0.208	0.187	0.168	0.137	0.112	0.092	0.076	0.069	0.062	0.052	0.043	0.027	0.018	0.012	0.008
13	0.879	0.773	0.601	0.530	0.469	0.368	0.290	0.229	0.182	0.163	0.145	0.116	0.093	0.075	0.061	0.055	0.050	0.040	0.033	0.020	0.013	0.008	0.005
14	0.870	0.758	0.577	0.505	0.442	0.340	0.263	0.205	0.160	0.141	0.125	0.099	0.078	0.062	0.049	0.044	0.039	0.032	0.025	0.015	0.009	0.006	0.003
15	0.861	0.743	0.555	0.481	0.417	0.315	0.239	0.183	0.140	0.123	0.108	0.084	0.065	0.051	0.040	0.035	0.031	0.025	0.020	0.011	0.006	0.004	0.002
16	0.853	0.728	0.534	0.458	0.394	0.292	0.218	0.163	0.123	0.107	0.093	0.071	0.054	0.042	0.032	0.028	0.025	0.019	0.015	0.008	0.005	0.003	0.002
17	0.844	0.714	0.513	0.436	0.371	0.270	0.198	0.146	0.108	0.093	0.080	0.060	0.045	0.034	0.026	0.023	0.020	0.015	0.012	0.006	0.003	0.002	0.001
18	0.836	0.700	0.494	0.416	0.350	0.250	0.180	0.130	0.095	0.081	0.069	0.051	0.038	0.028	0.021	0.018	0.016	0.012	0.009	0.005	0.002	0.001	0.001
19	0.828	0.686	0.475	0.396	0.331	0.232	0.164	0.116	0.083	0.070	0.060	0.043	0.031	0.023	0.017	0.014	0.012	0.009	0.007	0.003	0.002	0.001	
20	0.820	0.673	0.456	0.377	0.312	0.215	0.149	0.104	0.073	0.061	0.051	0.037	0.026	0.019	0.014	0.012	0.010	0.007	0.005	0.002	0.001	0.001	
21	0.811	0.660	0.439	0.359	0.294	0.199	0.135	0.093	0.064	0.053	0.044	0.031	0.022	0.015	0.011	0.009	0.008	0.006	0.004	0.002	0.001		
22	0.803	0.647	0.422	0.342	0.278	0.184	0.123	0.083	0.056	0.046	0.038	0.026	0.018	0.013	0.009	0.007	0.006	0.004	0.003	0.001	0.001		
23	0.795	0.634	0.406	0.326	0.262	0.170	0.112	0.074	0.049	0.040	0.033	0.022	0.015	0.010	0.007	0.006	0.005	0.003	0.002	0.001			
24	0.788	0.622	0.390	0.310	0.247	0.158	0.102	0.066	0.043	0.035	0.028	0.019	0.013	0.008	0.006	0.005	0.004	0.003	0.002	0.001			
25	0.780	0.610	0.375	0.295	0.233	0.146	0.092	0.059	0.038	0.030	0.024	0.016	0.010	0.007	0.005	0.004	0.003	0.002	0.001	0.001			
26	0.772	0.598	0.361	0.281	0.220	0.135	0.084	0.053	0.033	0.026	0.021	0.014	0.009	0.006	0.004	0.003	0.002	0.002	0.001				
27	0.764	0.586	0.347	0.268	0.207	0.125	0.076	0.047	0.029	0.023	0.018	0.011	0.007	0.005	0.003	0.002	0.002	0.001	0.001				
28	0.757	0.574	0.333	0.255	0.196	0.116	0.069	0.042	0.026	0.020	0.016	0.010	0.006	0.004	0.002	0.002	0.002	0.001	0.001				
29	0.749	0.563	0.321	0.243	0.185	0.107	0.063	0.037	0.022	0.017	0.014	0.008	0.005	0.003	0.002	0.002	0.001	0.001					
30	0.742	0.552	0.308	0.231	0.174	0.099	0.057	0.033	0.020	0.015	0.012	0.007	0.004	0.003	0.002	0.001	0.001	0.001					
35	0.706	0.500	0.253	0.181	0.130	0.066	0.036	0.019	0.010	0.008	0.006	0.003	0.002	0.001									
40	0.672	0.453	0.208	0.142	0.097	0.046	0.022	0.011	0.005	0.004	0.003	0.001	0.001										
45	0.639	0.410	0.171	0.111	0.073	0.031	0.014	0.006	0.003	0.002	0.001	0.001											
50	0.608	0.372	0.141	0.087	0.054	0.021	0.009	0.003	0.001	0.001	0.001												
60	0.550	0.305	0.095	0.054	0.030	0.010	0.003	0.001															

1. To find present value (PV) of future amount: PV = Factor × Amount.
2. To find future amount representing given PV: Amount = PV/Factor.
3. To find period given future amount, PV and yield: Factor = PV/Amount; locate in column.
4. To find yield given future amount, PV and period: Factor = PV/Amount; locate in row.

TABLE 7-II

Present Value of $1 per Period Received or Paid at End of Period (Annuity)

Number of Periods	1%	2%	4%	5%	6%	8%	10%	12%	14%	15%	16%	18%	20%	22%	24%	25%	26%	28%	30%	35%	40%	45%	50%
1	0.990	0.980	0.962	0.952	0.943	0.926	0.909	0.893	0.877	0.870	0.862	0.847	0.833	0.820	0.806	0.800	0.794	0.781	0.769	0.741	0.714	0.690	0.667
2	1.970	1.942	1.886	1.859	1.833	1.783	1.736	1.690	1.647	1.626	1.605	1.566	1.528	1.492	1.457	1.440	1.424	1.392	1.361	1.289	1.224	1.165	1.111
3	2.941	2.884	2.775	2.722	2.673	2.577	2.487	2.402	2.322	2.283	2.246	2.174	2.106	2.042	1.981	1.952	1.923	1.868	1.816	1.696	1.589	1.493	1.407
4	3.902	3.808	3.630	3.545	3.465	3.312	3.170	3.037	2.914	2.855	2.798	2.690	2.589	2.494	2.404	2.362	2.320	2.241	2.166	1.997	1.849	1.720	1.605
5	4.853	4.713	4.452	4.329	4.212	3.993	3.791	3.605	3.433	3.352	3.274	3.127	2.991	2.864	2.745	2.689	2.635	2.532	2.436	2.220	2.035	1.876	1.737
6	5.795	5.601	5.242	5.075	4.917	4.623	4.355	4.112	3.889	3.784	3.685	3.498	3.326	3.167	3.020	2.951	2.885	2.759	2.643	2.385	2.168	1.983	1.824
7	6.728	6.472	6.002	5.786	5.582	5.206	4.868	4.564	4.288	4.160	4.039	3.812	3.605	3.416	3.242	3.161	3.083	2.937	2.802	2.508	2.263	2.057	1.883
8	7.652	7.325	6.733	6.463	6.210	5.747	5.335	4.968	4.639	4.487	4.344	4.078	3.837	3.619	3.421	3.329	3.241	3.076	2.925	2.598	2.331	2.108	1.922
9	8.566	8.162	7.435	7.108	6.802	6.247	5.759	5.328	4.946	4.772	4.607	4.303	4.031	3.786	3.566	3.463	3.366	3.184	3.019	2.665	2.379	2.144	1.948
10	9.471	8.983	8.111	7.722	7.360	6.710	6.145	5.650	5.216	5.019	4.833	4.494	4.192	3.923	3.682	3.571	3.465	3.269	3.092	2.715	2.414	2.168	1.965
11	10.368	9.787	8.760	8.307	7.887	7.139	6.495	5.937	5.453	5.234	5.029	4.656	4.327	4.035	3.776	3.656	3.544	3.335	3.147	2.752	2.438	2.185	1.977
12	11.255	10.575	9.385	8.863	8.384	7.536	6.814	6.194	5.660	5.421	5.197	4.793	4.439	4.127	3.851	3.725	3.606	3.387	3.190	2.779	2.456	2.196	1.985
13	12.134	11.343	9.986	9.393	8.853	7.904	7.103	6.424	5.842	5.583	5.342	4.910	4.533	4.203	3.912	3.780	3.656	3.427	3.223	2.799	2.468	2.204	1.990
14	13.004	12.106	10.563	9.898	9.295	8.244	7.367	6.628	6.002	5.724	5.468	5.008	4.611	4.265	3.962	3.824	3.695	3.459	3.249	2.814	2.477	2.210	1.993
15	13.865	12.849	11.118	10.379	9.712	8.559	7.606	6.811	6.142	5.847	5.575	5.092	4.675	4.315	4.001	3.859	3.726	3.483	3.268	2.825	2.484	2.214	1.995
16	14.718	13.578	11.652	10.838	10.106	8.851	7.824	6.974	6.265	5.954	5.669	5.162	4.730	4.357	4.033	3.887	3.751	3.503	3.283	2.834	2.489	2.216	1.997
17	15.562	14.292	12.166	11.274	10.477	9.122	8.022	7.120	6.373	6.047	5.749	5.222	4.775	4.391	4.059	3.910	3.771	3.518	3.295	2.840	2.492	2.218	1.998
18	16.398	14.992	12.659	11.690	10.828	9.372	8.201	7.250	6.467	6.128	5.818	5.273	4.812	4.419	4.080	3.928	3.786	3.529	3.304	2.844	2.494	2.219	1.998
19	17.226	15.678	13.134	12.086	11.158	9.604	8.365	7.366	6.550	6.198	5.877	5.316	4.844	4.442	4.097	3.942	3.799	3.539	3.311	2.848	2.496	2.220	1.999
20	18.046	16.351	13.590	12.462	11.470	9.818	8.514	7.469	6.623	6.259	5.929	5.353	4.870	4.460	4.110	3.954	3.808	3.546	3.316	2.850	2.497	2.221	1.999
21	18.857	17.011	14.029	12.821	11.764	10.017	8.649	7.562	6.687	6.312	5.973	5.384	4.891	4.476	4.121	3.963	3.816	3.551	3.320	2.852	2.498	2.221	2.000
22	19.660	17.658	14.451	13.163	12.042	10.201	8.772	7.645	6.743	6.359	6.011	5.410	4.909	4.488	4.130	3.970	3.822	3.556	3.323	2.853	2.498	2.222	2.000
23	20.456	18.292	14.857	13.489	12.303	10.371	8.883	7.718	6.792	6.399	6.044	5.432	4.925	4.499	4.137	3.976	3.827	3.559	3.325	2.854	2.499	2.222	2.000
24	21.243	18.914	15.247	13.799	12.550	10.529	8.985	7.784	6.835	6.434	6.073	5.451	4.937	4.507	4.143	3.981	3.831	3.562	3.327	2.855	2.499	2.222	2.000
25	22.023	19.523	15.622	14.094	12.783	10.675	9.077	7.843	6.873	6.464	6.097	5.467	4.948	4.514	4.147	3.985	3.834	3.564	3.329	2.856	2.499	2.222	2.000
26	22.795	20.121	15.983	14.375	13.003	10.810	9.161	7.896	6.906	6.491	6.118	5.480	4.956	4.520	4.151	3.988	3.837	3.566	3.330	2.856	2.500	2.222	2.000
27	23.560	20.707	16.330	14.643	13.211	10.935	9.237	7.943	6.935	6.514	6.136	5.492	4.964	4.524	4.154	3.990	3.839	3.567	3.331	2.856	2.500	2.222	2.000
28	24.316	21.281	16.663	14.898	13.406	11.051	9.307	7.984	6.961	6.534	6.152	5.502	4.970	4.528	4.157	3.992	3.840	3.568	3.331	2.857	2.500	2.222	2.000
29	25.066	21.844	16.984	15.141	13.591	11.158	9.370	8.022	6.983	6.551	6.166	5.510	4.975	4.531	4.159	3.994	3.841	3.569	3.332	2.857	2.500	2.222	2.000
30	25.808	22.396	17.292	15.372	13.765	11.258	9.427	8.055	7.003	6.566	6.177	5.517	4.979	4.534	4.160	3.995	3.842	3.569	3.332	2.857	2.500	2.222	2.000
35	29.408	24.999	18.665	16.374	14.498	11.654	9.664	8.176	7.070	6.617	6.215	5.539	4.992	4.541	4.164	3.998	3.845	3.571	3.333	2.857	2.500	2.222	2.000
40	32.835	27.355	19.793	17.159	15.046	11.925	9.779	8.244	7.105	6.642	6.234	5.548	4.997	4.544	4.166	3.999	3.846	3.571	3.333	2.857	2.500	2.222	2.000
45	36.094	29.490	20.720	17.774	15.456	12.108	9.863	8.282	7.123	6.654	6.242	5.552	4.998	4.545	4.166	4.000	3.846	3.571	3.333	2.857	2.500	2.222	2.000
50	39.196	31.424	21.482	18.256	15.762	12.234	9.915	8.304	7.133	6.661	6.246	5.554	4.999	4.545	4.167	4.000	3.846	3.571	3.333	2.857	2.500	2.222	2.000
60	44.955	34.761	22.623	18.929	16.161	12.376	9.967	8.324	7.140	6.665	6.249	5.555	5.000	4.545	4.167	4.000	3.846	3.571	3.333	2.857	2.500	2.222	2.000

1. To find present value (PV) of series of equal receipts or payments: PV = Factor × Annuity.
2. To find annuity representing given PV: Annuity = PV/Factor.
3. To find number of periods to recover investment: Factor = Investment/Annuity; locate in column.
4. To find yield of annuity given investment: Factor = Investment/Annuity; locate in row.

CHAPTER 8

ANALYSIS OF INVESTMENT DECISIONS

The decision to invest resources is one of the key drivers of the business financial system, as we established in Chapter 2. Sound investments that implement well-founded strategies are essential to creating shareholder value, and they must be analyzed both in a proper context and with sound analytical methods. Whether the decision involves committing resources to new facilities, a research and development project, a marketing program, additional working capital, an acquisition, or investing in a financial instrument, an economic trade-off must be made between the resources expended now and the expectation of future cash benefits to be obtained. Analyzing this trade-off is essentially a valuation process that makes an economic assessment of a combination of positive and negative cash flow patterns. The task is difficult by nature because it deals with future conditions subject to uncertainties and risks—yet this basic valuation principle is common to all investments, large and small.

In this chapter, we'll examine in some detail both the key conceptual and practical aspects of investment decisions, using the analytical techniques described in Chapter 7. In Chapters 9 and 10, we'll address the related issues of financing costs and the choice among financing alternatives. In Chapters 11 and 12, we'll expand on these concepts and demonstrate how the process applies to valuing a business and to the creation of shareholder value. From time to time, we'll introduce applicable portions of managerial economics and financial theory. In keeping with the scope of this book, however, we'll avoid the esoteric in favor of the practical and useful. At the end of each chapter, we'll summarize, as before, the key conceptual issues underlying the analytical approaches covered, both as a reminder and as a guide for the interested reader in exploring the references listed.

The analysis of decisions about new investments (as well as the opposite, disinvestments) involves a particularly complex set of issues and choices that must be defined and resolved by management. We'll discuss these in several categories:

- Strategic perspective.
- Decisional framework.
- Refinements of investment analysis.
- Application of economic measures.

Because business investments, in contrast to operational spending, are normally long-term commitments of resources, they should always be made within the context of a company's explicit strategy. In fact, investment in the absence of a sound strategy is an invitation to economic ruin. An effective approach to value creation cannot be built on retroactively trying to make sense out of sunk resource commitments. In addition, the financial analysis underlying the decisions and the trade-offs involved must be carried out within a consistent economic framework of accepted conceptual and practical guidelines.

As we discussed in Chapter 7, most business investment projects have several key components of analysis in common. These must be understood and made explicit, as well as comparable, in order to arrive at a proper choice among different investment alternatives, as we'll demonstrate on the basis of more complex examples. Finally, the economic nature of the process requires that the analytical methods supporting the decisions focus on the true cash flow impact of the investment or disinvestment and be properly interpreted.

We'll take up each area in turn, emphasizing in greater detail the analytical components and methodologies. Once we've demonstrated the fundamental concepts, we'll introduce certain specialized aspects of the analytical process, such as sensitivity analysis, simulation, and the broader issues of dealing with risk. Some comments about related topics will follow, and we'll close with a checklist of key issues affecting investment analysis.

Strategic Perspective

Investments in land, productive equipment, buildings, natural resources, research facilities, product development, employee development, marketing programs, working capital acquisitions, and other resource deployments made for future economic gain should represent physical expressions of a company's strategy—which management must carefully develop and periodically reevaluate. Investment choices should always fit into the desired strategic direction the company wishes to take, with due consideration of:

- Expected economic conditions.
- Outlook for the company's specific industry or business segment.
- Competitive position of the company.
- Core competencies of the organization.

An almost infinite variety of business investments is available to most firms. It doesn't matter how the resource commitment is reflected on the company's books, whether in the form of an asset or as an expense for the period—the critical point is that the outlay is being made with an expectation of future returns. A company might invest in new facilities for expansion, expecting that incremental profits from additional volume will make the investment economically desirable. Investments might also be made for upgrading worn or outmoded facilities to improve cost-effectiveness. Here, savings in operating costs are the justification.

Some strategies call for entering new markets, which could involve setting up entirely new facilities and associated working capital, or perhaps a major repositioning of existing facilities through rebuilding or through sale and reinvestment. In a service business, expansion strategies could involve significant employee training outlays and electronic infrastructure investments. Other strategic proposals might involve creating a new business model of Internet connectivity, or establishing a research program, justified on the basis of its potential for developing new products or processes. Business investment also could involve significant promotional outlays, targeted on raising the company's market share over the long term and, with it, the profit contribution from higher volumes of operation. At times, acquiring a company whose product or service lines fit into the company's strategy, or purchasing a supplier to integrate the technology base, might be appropriate. At other times, partnering or outsourcing part of the company's product or service offerings might create additional value.

These and other choices are conceived continuously by the organization. Typically, lists of proposals are examined during the company's strategic planning process within the context and constraints of corporate and divisional objectives and goals. Then the various alternatives are narrowed down to those options that should be given serious analysis, and periodic spending plans are prepared which contain those capital outlays that have been selected and approved.

The many steps involved in identifying, analyzing, and selecting capital investment opportunities—as well as opportunities for divestiture—are collectively known as capital budgeting. This process includes everything from a broad scoping of ideas to very refined economic analyses. In the end, the company's capital budget normally contains an acceptable group of projects that individually and collectively are expected to provide economic returns meeting long-term management goals in support of shareholder value creation.

In essence, capital budgeting is like managing a personal investment portfolio. In both cases, the basic challenge is to select, within the constraint of available funds, those investments that promise to yield the desired level of economic rewards in relation to the degree of acceptable risk. The process thus involves a series of conscious economic trade-offs between exposure to potential adverse conditions and the expected profitability of the investments. As a general rule, the higher the profitability, the higher the risk exposure. Moreover, the choice among alternatives in which to invest the usually limited funds available invariably involves opportunity costs, because committing to one investment can mean rejecting others, thereby giving up the opportunity to earn perhaps higher but riskier returns.

In an investment portfolio, cash commitments are made in order to receive future inflows of cash in the form of dividends, interest, and eventual recovery of the principal through sale of the investment instrument—which over time might have appreciated or declined in market value. In capital budgeting, the commitment of company funds is made in exchange for future cash inflows from incremental after-tax profits and from the potential recovery of a portion of the capital invested, or from the value of a going business at the end of the planning horizon.

However, the analogy carries only so far. In a typical company, managing business investments is complicated by the need not only to select a portfolio of sound projects, but also to implement them well and to operate the facilities, service functions, or other new resources deployed with quality and cost effectiveness. In addition, analyzing potential investments in a business context is far more complex than selecting among stocks and bonds because the outlays often involve multiple expenditures spread over a period of time and a wide variety of operational cash flows that are expected over the economic life. Examples are constructing and equipping a new factory, or the gradual building up of a service business and its infrastructure.

Determining the economic benefits to be derived from the outlay is even more complex. An individual investor generally receives specific contractual interest payments or regular dividend checks. In contrast, a business investment typically generates additional profit contributions from higher volume, new products and services, or cost reduction. The specific incremental cash flow from a business investment might be difficult to identify, because it's intermingled in the company's financial reports with other accounting information. As we'll see, the analysis of potential capital investments involves a fair degree of economic reasoning and projection of future conditions that goes beyond merely using normal financial statements.

If we follow the analogy between a capital budget and an investment portfolio to its logical conclusion, capital budgeting would ideally amount to arraying all business investment opportunities in the order of their expected economic returns, and choosing a combination that would meet the desired portfolio return within the constraints of risk and available funding. The theoretical concepts that have evolved around these issues rely heavily on portfolio theory, both in terms of risk evaluation and in the comparison between investment returns and the cost of capital incurred in funding the investments.

These concepts are highly structured and depend on a series of important underlying assumptions. Not easy to apply in practice, they continue to be the subject of much learned argument. In simple terms, the theory argues that business investments—arrayed in declining order of attractiveness—should be accepted up to the point at which incremental benefits equal incremental cost, given appropriate risk levels. The economic attractiveness is most frequently expressed via the amount of net present value created.

This theory encounters several problems when applied in a practical setting. First, at the time the capital budget is prepared, it's simply not possible to foresee all investment opportunities, because management faces a continuously revolving planning horizon over which new opportunities keep appearing, while known opportunities might fade as conditions change even more rapidly. In recent times the speed of change in the business environment has increased dramatically.

Second, capital budgets are generally prepared only once a year in most companies. As various timing lags are encountered, actual implementation can be delayed or even canceled, because circumstances often change.

Third, economic criteria, such as the cost of capital and return standards based thereon, are merely approximations. Moreover, they are not the sole basis for the investment decision. Instead, the broader context of strategy and its attendant risks, the competitive environment, the ability of management to implement the investment, organizational considerations, and other factors come into play as management weighs the risk of an investment against the potential economic gain. Thus, there is nothing automatic or simple in arriving at decisions about the stream of potential investments that are continuously surfaced within a business organization.

In this chapter, we'll explore the decisional framework and apply the analytical techniques discussed in Chapter 7 to the decision process for analyzing and choosing business investments. We won't delve into the broader conceptual issues of capital budgeting and portfolio theory, except to point out some of the key issues. Readers wanting more information on these topics should check the references at the end of the chapter. The important question of the cost of capital as related to capital budgeting will be taken up in the next chapter. Then, Chapter 10 will cover analytical reasoning behind the choice among types of potential funding sources for capital investments.

Decisional Framework

Effective analysis of business investments requires that both the analyst and the decision maker be very conscious of and specific about the many dimensions involved. We need to set a series of ground rules to ensure that our results are thorough, consistent, and meaningful. These ground rules cover:

- Problem definition.
- Nature of the investment.
- Estimates of future costs and benefits.
- Incremental cash flows.
- Relevant accounting data.
- Sunk costs.

A good rule of thumb to keep in mind is that of the total time and effort required to analyze a business investment, at least 85 percent should be spent on meeting the important requirements of framing and refining these elements of the decision, and only 15 percent on various forms of "running the numbers." Because of the ease with which our spreadsheets can calculate data, however, there is the strong temptation to develop numerical approaches before proper framing has been done. Thus, unfortunately, the proportions of effort are often reversed in practice, resulting in potentially costly omissions of insight and clarification.

Problem Definition

We should begin any evaluation by stating explicitly what the investment is supposed to accomplish. Carefully defining the problem to be solved (or the opportunity presented) by the investment and identifying any potential alternatives to the proposed action are critically important to proper analysis. This elementary point is often overlooked, at times deliberately, when the desire to proceed with a favorite investment project overrides sound judgment.

In most cases, at least two or three alternatives are available for achieving the purpose of an investment, and careful examination of the specific circumstances might reveal an even greater number. The simple diagram in Figure 8–1 can help us to visualize the key options for deciding on which alternatives to pursue in an investment proposal.

For example, the decision of whether to replace a machine nearing the end of its useful life at first appears to be a relatively straightforward "either/or" problem. The most obvious alternative, as in any case, is to do nothing, that is, to continue patching up the machine until it falls apart. The ongoing, rising costs likely to be incurred with that option are compared with the expected cost pattern of a

---

FIGURE 8–1

Alternatives for a Business Investment Decision

new machine when we decide whether or not to replace it. But the alternative of doing nothing always exists for any investment project, and sound analysis requires that its implications be tested before proceeding.

But there are some not-so-obvious alternatives. Perhaps the company should stop making the product or providing the service altogether! This "go out of business" option should at least be considered—painful as it might be to think about—before new resources are committed.

The reasoning behind this seemingly radical notion is quite straightforward. While the improved efficiency of a new machine or a whole new service infrastructure might raise this particular operation's economic performance from poor to average, there might indeed be alternatives elsewhere in the company that would yield greater returns from the overall funds committed. By going ahead with the investment, an opportunity cost from losing a higher return option might be incurred. In the interest of shareholder value creation, it might indeed be better to redeploy all existing resources now devoted to the product or service instead of prolonging its substandard performance through an incremental investment that viewed by itself might be quite acceptable.

Moreover, even if the decision to continue making a product is economically sound under prevailing conditions, there still are several additional alternatives open to management. Among these, for example, are replacement with the same machine, or with a larger, more automated model, or with equipment using an altogether different technology and manufacturing process—or outsourcing the manufacture and thereby avoiding the investment.

It's crucial to select the appropriate alternatives for analysis and to structure the problem in such a way that the analytical tools are applied to the real issue to be decided. For decisions of major strategic importance, formal processes are available which use the disciplines of decision theory to aid in structuring the problem and in establishing an array of creative alternatives (see end-of-chapter references). As a general rule, however, no investment should be undertaken unless the best analytical judgment allows it to clear the basic hurdles implied in the first two branches of the decision tree in Figure 8–1.

Nature of the Investment

Most business investments tend to be independent of each other, that is, the choice of any one of them doesn't preclude also choosing any other—unless there are insufficient funds available to do them all. In that sense, they can be viewed as a portfolio of choices. The analysis and reasoning behind every individual decision will be relatively unaffected by past and future choices.

There are, however, circumstances in which investments compete with each other in their purpose so that choosing one will preclude the other. Typically, this arises when two alternative ways of solving the same problem are being considered. Such investment projects are called mutually exclusive. The significance of this condition will become apparent when we discuss some of the specific examples later on. A similar condition can, of course, arise when management sets a strict limit on the amount of spending, often called capital rationing, which will preclude investing in some worthy projects once others have been accepted. This situation is quite common, because companies will more often than not find their funding potential limited, whether due to debt proportions that already are at target levels, fluctuations in profitability, or exercising caution in preserving cash flow for yet unspecified needs.

Another type of investment involves sequential outlays beyond the initial expenditure. For example, any major capital outlay for plant and equipment also might entail additional future outlays for major maintenance, upgrading, and partial replacement some years hence. These future outlays—to which the company is committing itself by the initial decision—must be formally considered when the initial analysis is made. Another example is the introduction of a new product or service with high growth potential, where additional working capital and perhaps future capacity expansions are a natural consequence of the decision to proceed.

The most logical evaluation of such investments comes from taking into account the whole pattern of major outlays recognizable at the time of analysis. If this isn't done, such a project might be viewed more favorably than a more straightforward one, because a number of future negative cash flows have been left out of the cash flow pattern. Moreover, if the project is chosen, management could become trapped into having to approve these unanticipated future outlays as they arise later—on the argument that these incremental funds are clearly justifiable because the project is "already in place." While that argument might be true given the earlier decision, the fact remains that the project originally was not judged on its full implications, and under those conditions might not have been justifiable to begin with. This type of incrementalism invariably causes undesirable economic results.

Future Costs and Benefits

As we stated earlier, one of the key principles in making investment decisions is that the economic calculations used to justify any business investment must be based on projections and forecasts of future revenues and costs. It's not enough to assume that the past conditions and experience, such as operating costs or product prices, will continue unchanged and be applicable to a new venture. While this might seem obvious, there's a practical human temptation to extrapolate past conditions instead of carefully forecasting likely developments. We must at all times remember that the past is at best a rough guide, and at worst irrelevant for analysis.

The success of an investment, whether the time horizon is two, five, ten, or even twenty-five years, rests entirely on future events and the uncertainty surrounding them. It therefore behooves the analyst to explore as much as possible the likely changes from present conditions in the key variables relevant to the analysis. If potential deviations in several areas are large, it might be useful to run the analysis under different sets of assumptions, thus testing the sensitivity of the quantitative result to changes in particular variables, such as product volumes, prices, key raw material costs, and so on. (Recall our references to this type of analysis in earlier chapters.) This task has been eased with the availability of software packages specifically designed for comprehensive sensitivity analysis, yet even basic spreadsheets make the effort of testing a variety of assumptions about key variables quite manageable.

The uncertainty of future conditions affecting an investment is the cause of the risk of not meeting expectations and being left with an insufficient economic return or even an economic loss—the degree of risk being a function of the relative uncertainty about the key variables of the project. Careful estimates and research are often warranted to narrow the margin of error in the predicted conditions on which the analysis is based, although removing all risk is clearly a futile endeavor. Since the basic rationale of making investments relies on a conscious economic trade-off of risk versus reward, as we established earlier, the importance of explicitly addressing key areas of uncertainty should be obvious. Identifying key variables also will be helpful in judging the actual performance of the project after implementation. This is because tracking of these elements is usually much easier than trying to reconstruct the full scope of the incremental project from the overall accounting data flow into which it has been merged.

Incremental Cash Flows

The economic reasoning behind any capital outlay is based strictly on the incremental changes which result directly from the decision to make the investment. In other words, the test question must always be "what is different between the current state of affairs and the new situation introduced by the decision," and the differences will be reflected in the form of

- Incremental investment.
- Incremental revenues.
- Incremental costs and expenses.

Moreover, proper economic analysis recognizes only cash flows, that is, the after-tax cash effect of positive or negative funds movements caused by the investment. Any accounting transactions related to the decision but not affecting cash flows are irrelevant for the purpose.

The first basic question to be asked is: What additional investment funds will be required to carry out the chosen alternative? For example, the investment proposal can, in addition to the outlay for new equipment, entail the sale or other disposal of assets that will no longer be used. Therefore, the decision might actually free some previously committed funds. In such a case, it's the net outlay that counts, after any applicable incremental tax effects have been factored in.

Similarly, the next question is: What additional revenues will be created over and above any existing ones? If an investment results in new revenues, but at the same time causes the loss of some existing revenues, only the net impact, after applicable taxes, is relevant for economic analysis.

The third question concerns the costs and expenses that will be added or removed as a result of the investment. The only relevant items here are those costs, including applicable taxes, that will go up or down as a consequence of the investment decision. Any cost or expense that is expected to remain the same before and after the investment has been made is not relevant for the analysis.

These three basic questions illustrate why we refer to the economic analysis of investments as an incremental process. The approach is relative rather than absolute, and is tied closely to carefully defined alternatives and the differences between them. The only data relevant and applicable in any investment analysis are the differential investment funds commitments as well as differential revenues and costs caused by the decision, all viewed in terms of after-tax cash flows.

Relevant Accounting Data

Investment analysis in large part involves the use of data derived from accounting records, not all of which are relevant for the purpose. Accounting conventions that don't involve cash flows must be viewed with extreme caution. This is true particularly with investments that cause changes in operating costs. Therefore we must distinguish clearly between those cost elements that in fact vary with the operation of the new investment and those which only appear to vary. The latter are often accounting allocations which might change in magnitude but do not necessarily represent a true change in costs incurred.

For example, for accounting purposes, general overhead costs (administrative costs, insurance, etc.) might be allocated on the basis of a chosen fixed level of operating volume expressed in units produced. At other times, direct labor hours are the basis for allocation. In the former case, the accounting system will charge a new machine, which has a higher output, with a higher share of overhead than it charged the machine it replaces.

Yet it is likely that there was no actual change in overhead costs that could be attributed to the decision to substitute one machine for the other. Therefore, the reported change in the allocation is not relevant for purposes of economic analysis. The analyst must constantly judge whether there has been a change in the true cash outlays and revenues—not whether the accounting system is redistributing existing costs in a different way. A sound rule that helps prevent being trapped by allocations is to avoid unit costs whenever possible and to perform the analysis on the basis of annual changes in the various cost categories expected to be caused by the investment decision.

We should point out that the growing use of activity-based costing, which we mentioned earlier, is a very positive development insofar as determining relevant data for economic analysis is concerned. Essentially a system which expresses the economic costs and benefits of activities, product lines, and organizational units, activity-based analysis and accounting establishes a flow of information that directly relates to economic choices and trade-offs. Based on a careful assessment of the physical flow of activities, the data collected and stored in the system are in most cases representative of the type of information that must be stipulated when analyzing the changes in revenues and costs brought about by a business investment. The nature of cost assessments and economic allocations is much more transparent than in customary cost accounting systems, although the need for judgment in selecting appropriate data still remains.

Sunk Costs

There's a common temptation to include in the analysis of a new investment all or some portion of outlays that occurred in the past, expenditures that perhaps were incurred preparatory to making the new commitment being considered. No basis in economic analysis exists, however, that would justify such backtracking to expenditures that have already been made and that are not recoverable in part or as a whole. Past decisions simply do not count in the economic trade-off underlying a current investment decision. The basic reason for this is that such sunk costs, even if they are connected in some way to the decision at hand, simply cannot be altered by making the investment now.

If, for example, significant amounts had been spent on research and development of a new product in excess of original plans, the current decision about whether to invest in new facilities to make the product should in no way be affected by those sunk costs. Perhaps the earlier decision to do research and development in retrospect turned out to be less rewarding than expected because of such overspending, and shouldn't have been made at the prior decision point. But now the only relevant question is: If the new investment required to exploit the results of such past research appears economically justified on its own merits from future benefits, it should be undertaken at the present time. There's nothing that can be done about sunk costs, except to learn from any mistakes made.

Another, more specialized situation arises, however, when an incremental productive investment is added to a group of operating facilities, all of which are supported by a large past infrastructure investment, such as power generation, shipping docks, service networks, and so on, which is not fully utilized at this point. The infrastructure might have been sized to allow for the addition of several future operating investments before the infrastructure itself has to be expanded. In such a case, it'll be relevant to make an economic allocation of an appropriate share of the cost of the existing infrastructure as part of the investment, and to do the same with other similar alternative productive investments, if the strategy of the company calls for continued expansion in the foreseeable future. In contrast, if the current operating investment proposal were the only remaining planned addition, the infrastructure in place would be irrelevant and sunk in the true sense of the word, because no other use of the excess infrastructure was envisioned.

Somewhat differently, if the productive investment triggered another round of infrastructure expansion as part of a long-term growth strategy, a share of such infrastructure would have to be considered part of the productive investment requirements, with other portions allocated to other current or future expansion investments planned. Again, the effort here must be to judge the specific investment proposition on its full set of implications, and to view the specific proposition within the larger context of the company's strategy and future plans.

Economic decisions are always forward-looking and must involve only those things that can be changed by the action being decided. This is the essential test of relevance for any element to be included in the analysis.

Refinements of Investment Analysis

We'll now turn to some more realistic and complex examples in order to refine various aspects of both the components of analysis and the methodology itself. No new concepts or techniques will be introduced here; instead, some expanded practical examples will help us work through the implications of many of the points that so far we've only mentioned in passing. As we go through the projects step by step, the essentials of economic investment analysis should become firmly implanted in your mind.

At this point, we'll stress once more that it's always essential as the first step in any economic analysis to carefully define the problem in all of its aspects. From this flows the rationale for deriving the net investment, operating cash flows, the economic life, and any terminal values. Once these detailed aspects have been properly established and understood, the actual calculation of the appropriate yardsticks becomes almost automatic, as we'll see in the examples we're about to discuss.

A Machine Replacement

A company is analyzing whether to replace an existing 5-year-old machine with a more automatic and faster model. Acquiring a new machine of some sort is viewed as the only reasonable alternative under the circumstances, because the product fabricated on the equipment is expected to continue to be profitable for at least 10 years. Moreover, the markets served could absorb additional output beyond the current capacity, as much as one-third more than the present volume.

The old machine is estimated to have at most 5 years' life left before it becomes physically worn out, while the new machine will operate acceptably for 10 years before it has to be scrapped. The old machine originally cost $25,000 and has a current book value of $12,500, having been depreciated straight-line at $2,500 per year. It can be sold for $15,000 in cash to a ready buyer.

The new machine will cost $40,000 installed. Also to be depreciated straight-line over 10 years, it will likely be salable at book value if it is disposed of prior to the end of its physical life. It has an annual capacity of 125,000 units (compared to the present equipment's 100,000 unit ceiling), and it will produce at lower unit costs for both labor and materials. In fact, the new machine will involve slightly lower total labor costs because of fewer setups, releasing the required time of the skilled mechanic for other productive tasks in the plant. One operator will run the machine as before. Materials usage will be reduced due to a lower level of rejects. The company expects no difficulty in selling the additional volume at the current price of $1.50, and will incur only modest incremental selling and promotional expense in the process.

Such a set of conditions is both common and fairly realistic except for the stable long-term market conditions we've assumed—yet the same analytical principles do apply in a shorter time frame. As we analyze this project, we'll expand on several aspects of economic capital investment analysis and draw generalized conclusions where appropriate.

Net Investment Refined

Net investment has been defined as the net change in cash committed to a project as a result of the investment decision. Two specific changes in cash flow must be considered in this case: (1) the initial outlay of $40,000 for the new machine, which is a straightforward cash commitment, and (2) the recovery of cash from the sale of the old machine.

Since the sale of the old machine is a direct consequence of the decision to replace it, the release of these funds is relevant to the analysis. The amount received, however, will have to be adjusted below the $15,000 cash value because the capital gain realized on the sale is a taxable event. We recall that the book value was only $12,500; thus the company will be taxed on the difference of $2,500. For simplicity, we'll assume that the applicable tax rate is the full corporate income tax rate of 34 percent, resulting in an incremental tax outlay of $850.

We now have all the components of the initial net investment figure relevant for this example:

Cost of the new machine	$40,000
Cash from sale of old machine	(15,000)
Tax payable on capital gain	850
Net investment	$25,850

In this economic analysis, we don't recognize the remaining book value of the old machine, except for its brief role in the income tax calculation. As we've observed before, any funds expended in the past are irrelevant because they are sunk, and we're interested only in the changes caused by the current decision. Therefore, the proceeds from the equipment sale and the incremental tax due on the capital gain are the only relevant elements.

Had the old machine not been salable despite its stated book value of $12,500, the only item of relevance would be the tax savings on the capital loss incurred with this condition. While there might be a temptation to include the loss of sizable book values in such analyses, doing so would confuse accounting with cash flow economics.

The net investment shown represents the difference between current cash movements, both in and out, that are direct consequences of the investment decision. If we assume that the decision caused working capital (incremental receivables and inventories less incremental payables) to rise in support of the expected higher sales volume, any funds committed for this purpose would also become relevant for our analysis. Similarly, if the current decision were expected to directly cause further capital outlays in later years, such amounts would have to be recognized in the analysis. In our second example, we'll demonstrate how incremental working capital and sequential investments are handled.

Operating Cash Inflows Refined

As we established before, operating cash inflows are the net after-tax cash changes in revenue and cost elements resulting from the investment decision. In our replacement example, we must first carefully sort out the expected conditions to identify relevant differential revenues and costs. Each element should be carefully tested as to whether the decision to replace will make a cash difference in operating conditions. The decision to replace has three significant effects:

- The new machine will bring about greater efficiency that should result in operating savings vis-à-vis the old machine.
- The additional volume of product produced will provide an incremental profit contribution, if we assume the sales efforts will be successful.
- There'll be a tax impact from the change in the amount of depreciation charged against operations.

The calculations in Figure 8–2 illustrate how to deal with these elements in three clearly labeled successive stages.

Stage 1: Operating Savings. Operating savings for the existing level of output (100,000 units) are found by simply comparing the annual costs of operating the two machines at that volume. While each requires one operator, the new machine will incur $1,000 less in setup costs because the time of the skilled mechanic involved can be employed elsewhere in the plant. We were also told earlier that the new machine uses materials more efficiently, and this attribute will save about $2,000.

Overhead changes, in contrast, are not relevant for this comparison, because overhead costs are represented by allocations at the rate of 120 percent of direct labor. The fact that direct labor cost has declined does not automatically mean that spending on overhead has changed. The only change is in the basis of allocation, which in this case happens to be a lower labor cost against which an unvarying percentage rate is applied. Clearly, the plant manager and the office staff still receive the same salaries, and other overhead costs are not affected.

FIGURE 8–2

Differential Benefit and Cost Analysis

	Old Machine	New Machine	Relevant Annual Differences
1. Operating savings from current volume of 100,000 units:			
Labor (operator plus setup)	$ 31,000	$ 30,000	$ 1,000
Material	38,000	36,000	2,000
Overhead (120% of direct labor)	37,200	36,000	—*
	$106,200	$102,000	$ 3,000
2. Contribution from additional volume 25,000 units sold at $1.50 per unit		$ 37,500	
Less:			
Labor (no additional operators)		—	
Material cost at 36¢/unit		(9,000)	
Additional selling expense		(11,500)	
Additional promotional expense		(13,000)	$ 4,000
Total savings and additional contribution			$ 7,000
3. Differential depreciation (additional expense; for tax purposes only)	$ 2,500	$ 4,000	$(1,500)
Taxable operating improvements			5,500
Income tax at 34%			1,870
After-tax profit improvement			3,630
Add back depreciation			1,500
After-tax operating cash flow			$ 5,130

*Not relevant, because it represents an allocation only.

Only if the decision to replace directly caused an actual change in overhead spending, such as higher property taxes, insurance premiums, additional maintenance, and technical and other staff support, would a change have to be reflected in the calculation. Under those conditions, we'd estimate the annual overhead expenditures before and after the installation of the new machine, and calculate the differential cost to be included in the analysis, just as we did for the other differential operating cash inflows.

Whenever we're comparing operating costs, it's usually more appropriate to use annual totals rather than to rely on per-unit figures. The latter could cause the analyst to inadvertently apply accounting allocations, which as a rule are irrelevant for this type of economic analysis—even though they are necessary and appropriate for cost accounting (determining cost of goods sold, inventory values, price estimating, and so on) in line with generally accepted accounting principles.

Stage 2: Contribution from Additional Volume. Now we're ready to determine the incremental contribution from the increased output. This change must be counted as an additional benefit from the decision to replace, because the old machine had a ceiling of 100,000 units of production. The additional sales revenue of $37,500 from the extra 25,000 units available for sale at $1.50 each is relevant, as are any additional costs which can be attributed to the higher sales volume.

We know that the existing operator is able to produce the higher output, and thus there will be no additional labor cost. The higher volume will require additional materials, however, which are charged at the usage rate of the more efficient machine, that is, 36 cents per unit, or $9,000. We've also been told that additional selling and promotional expenses of $24,500 will be incurred to move the higher volume, and these are relevant as well. The combination of operating savings and incremental product profit totals $7,000.

Stage 3: Differential Depreciation. The only remaining relevant item is the tax impact of differential depreciation. As we discussed in Chapters 2 and 3, depreciation as such is not relevant to cash flows. For purposes of our analysis, it merits attention only because depreciation is tax deductible. Remember that because depreciation charges normally reduce income tax payments, they're called a tax shield. If an investment decision causes higher or lower depreciation charges than before, such a difference must be reflected as a change in the tax shield.

For our replacement example, the differential depreciation for the next 5 years will be $1,500, an increase due to the higher cost basis of the new machine. We're assuming that straight-line depreciation also is used for tax purposes, to keep the calculations simple.

As is shown in Figure 8–2, the analysis results in taxable operating improvements of $7,000, an incremental tax of $1,870, and a change in after-tax profit of $3,630. The applicable tax rate normally is the rate a company would be paying on any incremental profit. As the final step, the differential depreciation is added back to arrive at the after-tax operating cash flow of $5,130.

In following these steps, we have correctly reflected a tax reduction due to the differential depreciation, but then removed depreciation itself from the picture to leave us with the economic cash effect of the investment.

We could have obtained the same result by doing the analysis in two phases: (1) determining the tax on the operating improvement before depreciation, and (2) directly determining the tax shield effect of the differential depreciation. This would appear as shown below, and as we might expect, the result is exactly the same.

Operating improvement before depreciation	$7,000
Tax at 34%	2,380
After-tax operating improvement	$4,620
Tax shield at 34%* of depreciation of $1,500	510
After-tax operating cash flow	$5,130

*Each dollar of depreciation provides a tax shield of $1 times the applicable tax rate.

Unequal Economic Lives

In Chapter 7, we defined economic life as the length of time over which an investment yields economic benefits. Now we find that a complication has been introduced because of the expected difference in the physical lives of the two machines. Inasmuch as the old machine is assumed to wear out in 5 years while the new one will last for 10 years, with no change in the market for the product assumed, the two investments are comparable only over the next 5 years. After that, the original alternative no longer exists, and a new decision will have to be made at that point in any case. The situation is illustrated in Figure 8–3.

Differential revenues and costs can be defined only as long as both alternatives exist together. After 5 years, the old machine will be gone, which means that we can't analyze the situation beyond 5 years without making some assumptions about the remaining life of the new machine. While we have assumed that the product is likely to be salable for at least the total 10-year life of the new machine, the economic comparison for the current replacement decision can be made only over the 5 years the two alternatives have in common.

There are two ways of handling this problem. First, we can cut off the analysis at the end of Year 5 and assign an assumed recovery value to the new machine at that point, because it should be able to operate well for another 5 years. This terminal value estimate must be counted as a capital recovery in Year 5, that is, its present value should be recognized as a cash flow benefit. This approach is widely used in practice, and usually, as a simplifying assumption, the amount of terminal value is considered to be at least the amount of the remaining book value. But if the asset's value is quite predictable (as is the case with automobiles or trucks), the estimated sales value (adjusted for any tax consequences) is entered in the present value analysis as a cash flow benefit.

FIGURE 8–3

Overlapping Economic Life Spans

Comparison of lives

Only five years are comparable. If the new machine lasts longer, its life has to be cut off for purposes of comparison.

An alternative way of dealing with the problem is to assume that the old machine will be replaced by a new one in Year 5, and that a similar replacement will be made in Year 10 when the current new machine wears out. This approach involves a great deal of sequential guessing about possible replacement options 5 and 10 years hence. Moreover, in spite of such extra analytical effort, the economic lives of the two machines still will not be the same. Admittedly, the power of discounting will make the estimates of the later years almost immaterial. On balance, unless there are compelling reasons to develop such a series of replacement assumptions, the cutoff analysis described earlier is far more straightforward and less fraught with judgmental traps.

Capital Additions and Recoveries

The treatment of terminal values deserves a few more comments here. It's quite common for larger projects to require a series of additional capital outlays over time, and eventually provide likely recoveries of at least part of these funds. As a practical matter, any increments of capital committed or recovered must be entered in the present value framework as cash outflows or cash inflows at the point in time when they occur. This also applies to incremental working capital commitments, which must be shown as outflows when incurred, and which can be assumed to be recovered in part or in total at the end of the economic life of the project.

In our replacement example, we've made no provision for additional working capital in order to keep the problem focused on the other basic refinements. The assumed terminal value of the new machine after 5 years, however, is to be treated as a capital recovery and entered as a positive cash inflow at the end of Year 5. For simplicity, we'll assume that its economic value (realizable through sale or trade) will be equal to its book value. This would amount to $20,000 ($40,000 less five years' depreciation at $4,000 per year), with no taxable capital gain or loss expected.

We'd have to modify this amount, of course, if circumstances indicated a higher or lower value due to changes in technology or other conditions. Book value is frequently used because it's easy to do, causes no taxable gains or losses, and also because the need for precision in terminal values is diminished by the exponential impact of discounting in later years.

Analytical Framework

With all the basic data at hand, we now can lay out the framework for a present value analysis. We'll assume a 10 percent return standard and again set up the figures in a table. The results, as displayed in Figure 8–4, indicate a sizable net present value of $6,013—assuming, of course, that all of our assumptions are borne out in fact! It suggests that the replacement is desirable, at least on a numerical basis.

FIGURE 8-4

Present Value Analysis of Machine Replacement*

	Year 0	Year 1	Year 2	Year 3	Year 4	Year 5	Year-end 5	Totals
Net investment outlay and recovery	$-25,850	0	0	0	0	0	$20,000	$-5,850
Operating cash inflows	0	$ 5,130	$ 5,130	$ 5,130	$ 5,130	$ 5,130	0	25,650
Present value factors @ 10%	1.000	0.909	0.826	0.751	0.683	0.621	0.621	
Present values of investment cash flows	-25,850	0	0	0	0	0	12,420	-13,430
Present values of operating cash flows	0	4,663	4,237	3,853	3,504	3,186	0	19,443
Cumulative present values	$-25,850	$-21,187	$-16,949	$-13,097	$-9,593	$-6,407	$ 6,013	
Net present value @ 10%								$ 6,013
Profitability index (BCR) @ 10%								1.45/1.23

*This exhibit is available in an interactive format (TFA Template)—see "Analytical Support" on p. 295.

As in Chapter 7, we've laid out the cash flow analysis with the present value factors displayed. Using a spreadsheet will, of course, give the same result when the *npv* function is applied at 10 percent to the cash flows of Years 1 through 5 (including the year-end recovery), and the net investment of Year 0 is subtracted from the result.

Note that the analysis is affected significantly by the assumed recovery of the book value of $20,000 in Year 5, which amounts to a present value inflow of $12,420. In effect, this terminal inflow reduces the investment, when viewed over the 5-year span, to only $13,430 in present value terms as can be determined in row 4 of the analysis by netting the present values of the investment cash flows. Remember, economic analysis requires that the recovery value must be counted as a cash benefit at the end of Year 5, even though there might be no intention of actually selling the machine at that point.

This value inclusion is relevant because the company would have the option of selling the machine at the end of Year 5 and thereby realizing this economic value. After the 5 years are over, the alternative of selling could, of course, be compared with the alternative of recommitting the realizable value of $20,000 in order to preserve the profitable business at the level of 125,000 units. But these latter considerations deal with a future set of decisions and therefore are not relevant today.

The profitability index (BCR) of the project is positive, as we might expect from the sizable net present value of about $6,000. Dividing $13,430 (net investment less recovery) into the operating benefits of $19,443 results in an index of 1.45, which should give the project a favorable ranking against an implied average return of only 10 percent from the company's investment opportunities. Because of the uncertainty implicit in establishing a terminal value, many analysts prefer to express the profitability index by relating the original net investment to the total of all inflows, including capital recoveries. In our example, this alternative result would be $31,863 ÷ $25,850 = 1.23, again a very favorable showing even when this more stringent test is applied. While one could argue for and against either method, consistent application of one of them will be satisfactory.

The internal rate of return has to be found by trial and error when using the present value tables, both for the single sums and for the 5-year annuity, because the capital recovery at the end of Year 5 complicates an otherwise straightforward annuity. The analysis can be handled as shown in Figure 8–5. The trial at 15 percent indicates a positive net present value of $1,286, which at 16 percent is reduced to $466. Thus, the precise result lies somewhat above 16 percent. Again, we've used the present value tables of Chapter 7 to illustrate the process, and the reader can confirm the exact result of 16.6 percent by using the *irr* function on a spreadsheet and entering the total cash flow pattern over the 5-year period.

A simple risk analysis can be carried out by calculating the present value payback (minimum life) and the annualized net present value. For the former, we must cumulate the present values of operating cash inflows until they approximate the net investment of $25,850, as was made visible in the cumulative present values of Figure 8–4. A quick scanning of the sixth row shows that this will not happen until Year 5, when the terminal value of $20,000, discounted to $12,420, is required to turn the net present value positive. If we are reasonably certain that the machine will be salable as assumed here, we could argue that this terminal value should be subtracted from the net investment first. Under this assumption, the net present value payback would occur very early in Year 4. As a general rule, it is advisable not to count on terminal values in such a precise fashion, given that technological and competitive conditions are always subject to change even during a few years' time.

A minor technical question arises here as to whether we should bring the assumed recovery at the end of Year 5 forward in time nearer the payback point to obtain a more precise calculation of minimum life. This would involve a process of iteration, because not only would the present value of the recovery rise, but the sales value of the machine would also be higher in earlier years. Such a refinement normally is not called for even though it can be handled readily by altering the magnitudes on the spreadsheet or by a simulation routine.

FIGURE 8–5

Present Value Analysis to Find Internal Rate of Return*

	Year 0	Year 1	Year 2	Year 3	Year 4	Year 5	Year-end 5	Totals
Investment outlay and recovery	$-25,850	0	0	0	0	0	$20,000	$-5,850
Operating cash inflows	0	$5,130	$5,130	$ 5,130	$5,130	$5,130	0	25,650
Present value factors @ 15%	1.000	—	—	3.352	(annuity)	—	0.497	
Present values of cash flows	-25,850	—	—	17,196	—	—	9,940	
Net present value @ 15%								1,286
Present value factors @ 16%	1.000	—	—	3.274	(annuity)	—	0.476	
Present values of cash flows	$-25,850	—	—	$16,796	—	—	$ 9,520	
Net present value @ 15%								$ 466
Internal rate of return								16.6%

*This exhibit is available in an interactive format (TFA Template)—see "Analytical Support" on p. 295.

The annualized net present value can be found when we divide the net present value in Figure 8–4 by the 10 percent annuity factor in Year 5 from Table 7–II on page 253, or $6,013 ÷ 3.791, which amounts to $1,586 per year. On a spreadsheet, we would use the *pmt* function and specify the 10 percent discount rate, the five periods, and the net present value to obtain this amount. All other aspects being equal, the project would still meet the minimum standard of 10 percent if the annual operating cash inflows over the 5 years dropped from $5,130 to only $3,544, a possible shrinkage of over 30 percent. If we remove the depreciation tax shield of $510 from this test, the allowable drop in the pure after-tax operating improvement could be better than 34 percent ($1,586 against $4,620) to arrive at a value-neutral result. Remember, however, that under these conditions the project would just meet the return standard, but not create additional shareholder value, even if all the modified cash flows are in fact achieved.

Another way of interpreting the net present value amount from a risk standpoint is to ask how sensitive the result would be to a reduced expected capital recovery at the end of Year 5. The answer to a value-neutral condition can be found readily by reconstituting at the end of Year 5 a dollar amount that has the equivalent present value of the value creation of $6,013. To find this future dollar amount, we simply divide the net present value of $6,013 by the single sum factor given in Table 7–I on page 252 for 10 percent in period 5, which is 0.621, to obtain a required amount of $9,684. On a spreadsheet, we would use the *fv* function and specify the 10 percent discount rate, the 5 periods, and the net present value of $6,013 to obtain the same result. We can see that if the expected recovery of $20,000 were reduced by about $10,300, the project would still earn the 10 percent standard (at a zero net present value), given that all the other conditions hold.

While perhaps a little complex, the step-by-step process we've just completed has exposed most of the basic practical issues encountered in the methodology of investment analysis. Let's turn to another illustration which adds the handling of working capital as well as successive investments.

A Business Expansion

The cash flow patterns in Figure 8–6 reflect the kinds of commitments and recoveries normally associated with a major business expansion. In the early life of the project, we find not only an outlay for facilities, but also a buildup of working capital during the first and second years. Additional equipment outlays are required during Years 4 and 6, while recoveries of equipment and working capital are made as the economic life comes to an end in Year 8. All cash flows are assumed to represent the expected incremental revenues and expenses caused by the decision to invest, and they have been adjusted for tax consequences along the lines we discussed in our first example. The periodic operating cash flows show a growth stage, a peak in the middle years, and decline toward the end.

No new concepts are required for us to deal with this investment example. As we know from Chapter 3, new working capital additions (incremental inventories and receivables less new trade obligations) represent a commitment of

| FIGURE 8-6 |

Present Value Analysis of Complex Expansion Project* ($ thousands)

	Year 0	Year 1	Year 2	Year 3	Year 4	Year 5	Year 6	Year 7	Year 8	Totals
Equipment outlays and recovery**	$-130,000	0	0	0	$-15,000	0	$-10,000	0	$25,000	$-130,000
Working capital outlays and recovery†	0	$-25,000	$-20,000	0	0	0	0	0	35,000	-10,000
Operating cash inflows ...	0	20,000	40,000	$40,000	$40,000	$50,000	$50,000	$20,000	10,000	270,000
Total project cash flows ..	-130,000	-5,000	20,000	40,000	25,000	50,000	40,000	20,000	70,000	130,000
Present value factors @12%	1.000	0.893	0.797	0.712	0.636	0.567	0.507	0.452	0.404	
Present values of investment cash flows ..	-130,000	-22,325	-15,940	0	-9,540	0	-5,070	0	24,240	
Present values of operating cash flows	0	17,860	31,880	28,480	25,440	28,350	25,350	9,040	4,040	
Present values of total cash flows	-130,000	-4,465	15,940	28,480	15,900	28,350	20,280	9,040	28,280	
Cumulative present values	$-130,000	$-134,465	$-118,525	$-90,045	$-74,145	$-45,795	$-25,515	$-16,475	$11,805	
Net present value @ 12%...										11,805
Profitability index (BCR) @ 12%...										1.09
Internal rate of return										13.9%
Present value payback @12% (requires part of capital recovery)										Year 8

*This exhibit is available in an interactive format (TFA Template)—see "Analytical Support" on p. 295.

**Additional depreciation on investments in Years 4 and 6 has been reflected in the cash flows.

†Assume loss in liquidation of $10,000.

resources just as definite as an expenditure for buildings and equipment, except that no depreciation write-off is involved. If all inventories and receivables are expected to be successfully liquidated at the end of the economic life, these funds (net of payables) will become a cash inflow at that point, a capital recovery. If we assume some fraction of this investment to be not salable or uncollectible, the figure must be lowered accordingly.

Additional capital expenditures for equipment during the life of the project are simply recognized as cash outflows when incurred. We must take care, however, to reflect the additional depreciation pattern in each case as additional tax shields during future operating periods and we can assume that this was done in the cash flows shown. Of course, it's quite easy to lay out these patterns over time in successive series. The uneven cash flows of this project present no problems when we use spreadsheets or calculators to find the net present value of the overall cash flow pattern and derive directly the other measures listed. For the present value payback, the present values for each period must be calculated and accumulated period by period. But to demonstrate the background structure of the calculations, we've again employed the present value tables to show the factors involved.

As was shown in Figure 8–6, the expected result of the project is a positive net present value of almost $12 million. The profitability index is about 1.1, while the internal rate of return is approximately 14 percent, and present value payback is not achieved until Year 8, requiring about one-half of the terminal recovery. These results leave little margin for error. When we annualize the net present value, the result suggests that the annual operating cash inflows can be reduced by $11,815 ÷ 4.968, or at most, by about $2.4 million per year.

We've gone about as far as we can to carry out the quantitative financial aspects of the analysis with the data at hand. The various judgments leading to the final decision call for much more insight into the nature of the product, the technology, the requirements and outlook of the market place, the competitive setting, and so on. As we outlined in the first section of this chapter, we cannot overemphasize the importance of those areas for any well-informed business investment decision.

Mutually Exclusive Alternatives

So far we've dealt with individual investment projects without regard to the broader question of how these projects fit into the whole range of possibilities open to a company. We've assumed that our examples were independent investment projects that could be evaluated and ranked against other independent projects. At times, however, managers face the issue of evaluating projects that are not independent of each other. Such is the case with sets of different alternatives which might be available for achieving the same purpose. These are called mutually exclusive alternatives, because if one is chosen, the others are eliminated by that very decision.

Analyzing such a situation is merely a special case of economic analysis which uses the same underlying concepts as before but emphasizes incremental reasoning. To illustrate, let's first take the simple case of a choice between continuing a current process through relatively high maintenance outlays versus an up-front expenditure to replace the equipment, which entails low maintenance costs and a significant terminal value. Next, we'll take up the issue of choosing between a full-fledged, state-of-the-art solution to a facility upgrade versus an economy solution with lower capital costs and somewhat lower benefits, each of which can serve the purpose equally well. Finally, we'll discuss three individually feasible alternatives of investing in facilities and working capital to produce and sell a modified product and compare the economic implications of the choice.

Maintain versus Replace

This issue involves the often encountered trade-off of carrying on an operation by maintaining supporting equipment at significantly higher cost levels than would be required for new items, but forgoing the near-term outlay of funding new equipment. The decision must be seen within a larger context of market and technological change, and also withstand the question of whether maintenance of current equipment will in fact ensure an uninterrupted flow of quality products or services. Our example in Figure 8–7 assumes that over a 5-year horizon maintenance expenditures will rise from $40,000 in Year 1, until in Year 3 a partial

FIGURE 8–7

Comparison of Maintain versus Replace: 1. Maintain*

	Year 0	Year 1	Year 2	Year 3	Year 4	Year 5	Totals
Maintenance expenditures	0	$−40,000	$−60,000	$−180,000	$ −30,000	$ −40,000	$−350,000
Tax rate		36%	36%	36%	36%	36%	
After-tax cost	0	−25,600	−38,400	−115,200	−19,200	−25,600	−224,000
Depreciation tax shield	0	0	0	0	0	0	0
Total project cash outflows	0	−25,600	−38,400	−115,200	−19,200	−25,600	−224,000
Present value factors @ 12%	1.000	0.893	0.797	0.712	0.636	0.567	
Present values of cash outflows	0	−22,861	−30,605	−82,022	−12,211	−14,515	
Cumulative present values	0	$−22,861	$−53,466	$−135,488	$−147,699	$−162,214	
Net present value cost @ 12%							$ −162,214
Annualized net present value cost @ 12%							$ −45,000

*This exhibit is available in an interactive format (TFA Template)—see "Analytical Support" on p. 295.

FIGURE 8–8

Comparison of Maintain versus Replace: 2. Replace*

	Year 0	Year 1	Year 2	Year 3	Year 4	Year 5	Totals
Equipment outlay and recovery	$−400,000	0	0	0	0	$ 100,000	$−300,000
Maintenance expenditures	0	$ −8,000	$ −9,000	$ −10,000	$ −11,000	−12,000	−50,000
Tax rate		36%	36%	36%	36%	36%	
After-tax cost	0	−5,120	−5,760	−6,400	−7,040	−7,680	−32,000
Depreciation tax shield ($80,000 × .36)	0	28,800	28,800	28,800	28,800	28,800	144,000
Total project cash flows (incl. recovery)	−400,000	23,680	23,040	22,400	21,760	121,120	$−188,000
Present value factors @ 12%	1.000	0.893	0.797	0.712	0.636	0.567	
Present values of cash flows	−400,000	21,146	18,363	15,949	13,839	68,675	
Cumulative present values	$−400,000	$−378,854	$−360,491	$−344,542	$−330,703	$−262,028	
Net present value cost @ 12%							$ −262,028
Annualized net present value cost @ 12%							$ −72,689

*This exhibit is available in an interactive format (TFA Template)—see "Analytical Support" on p. 295.

overhaul of $100,000 becomes necessary in addition to $80,000 in regular maintenance, after which maintenance expenditures will settle back to earlier levels.

The replacement alternative shown in Figure 8–8 requires a current outlay for equipment of $400,000, which still will be worth $100,000 (tax-adjusted) at the end of Year 5, and which will be depreciated straight-line over 5 years. Maintenance costs rise slowly from $8,000 in Year 1 to $12,000 in Year 5.

It so happens that total cash outlays and recoveries are equal for both alternatives over the five years at $350,000 each, but with significant timing differences. A return standard of 14 percent has been stipulated, and the two alternatives are assumed to be the only feasible options of dealing with this situation.

Both analyses lay out the cash flow patterns in our now familiar format, focusing on the respective net present value cost, both in total and on an annualized basis. As they are two different ways of achieving the same objective, it's possible to use this cost focus. Note the significant impact of the tax shield effect of depreciation in the second alternative, which turns annual cash flows positive.

If we assume that either alternative will serve the product/service requirements equally well, the first alternative is far superior from an economic standpoint, representing about $100,000 less in present value cost. As we mentioned, the critical question, however, relates to whether in fact the first alternative will be able to perform to expectations, especially if heavy maintenance and the Year 3 overhaul were to cause business interruptions and lower volume and quality. The difference in net present value cost of the second alternative could be viewed as broad insurance against such potential disruptions, but it might be useful to try to quantify the cost of potential interruptions directly in analyzing the first alternative.

Full-Fledged versus Economy Solution

Another example of mutually exclusive alternatives is the often encountered situation where a full-fledged solution to a facility improvement or expansion, or for support equipment like computer systems, will create value by comfortably exceeding the return standard. On closer examination there might, however, be an economy solution which for significantly lower capital outlays and somewhat lower benefits creates even more value. Once these alternatives are stipulated and analyzed, the economic results clearly point to the economy version, and an incremental analysis demonstrates the value destruction caused by the additional capital outlay required in the full-fledged version. The practical issue in such a scenario is that because the full-fledged version easily meets the standard, the economy version might not even be analyzed and surfaced. The reason for this is simply that the full-fledged version also satisfies the less tangible but often encountered desire to have the latest in design, all possible "bells and whistles," and an extra margin of performance, most of which might not be relevant to the specific solution sought.

The analysis of the full-fledged version in Figure 8–9 shows a 7-year project with an outlay of $11.5 million, a recovery of $1.0 million in Year 7, and level

FIGURE 8–9

Comparing Alternatives: Full-Fledged Solution* ($ thousands)

	Year 0	Year 1	Year 2	Year 3	Year 4	Year 5	Year 6	Year 7	Totals
Equipment outlay and recovery	$−11,500	0	0	0	0	0	0	$1,000	$−10,500
Annual benefits	0	$ 4,000	$ 4,000	$ 4,000	$ 4,000	$4,000	$4,000	4,000	28,000
Tax rate		36%	36%	36%	36%	36%	36%	36%	
After-tax benefits	0	2,560	2,560	2,560	2,560	2,560	2,560	2,560	17,920
Depreciation tax shield ($1,500 × .36)	0	540	540	540	540	540	540	540	3,780
Total project cash flows (including recovery)	$−11,500	3,100	3,100	3,100	3,100	3,100	3,100	4,100	11,200
Present value factors @ 14%	1.000	0.877	0.769	0.675	0.592	0.519	0.456	0.400	
Present values of cash flows	−11,500	2,719	2,384	2,093	1,835	1,609	1,414	1,640	
Cumulative present values	$−11,500	$−8,781	$−6,397	$−4,305	$−2,470	$ −861	$ 553	$2,193	
Net present value @ 14%									$ 2,193
Profitability index (BCR) @ 14%									1.19
Internal rate of return									19.9%
Present value payback @ 14%									Year 6

*This exhibit is available in an interactive format (TFA Template)—see "Analytical Support" on p. 295.

annual benefits of $4.0 million before taxes. For simplicity we've assumed level cash flows and straight-line depreciation over 7 years, and the capital recovery in Year 7 is a net value after taxes. The company's return standard is 14 percent, and as the analysis shows, the project has a net present value of about $2.2 million, a profitability index of 1.2, and will be paid back in present value terms between Year 5 and Year 6, depending on the treatment of the recovery in Year 7. Thus, this project appears quite favorable.

When we analyze the economy alternative in Figure 8–10, however, an even more favorable result emerges. For an outlay of only $8.75 million, and a smaller recovery of $.75 million, benefits are expected to be 10 percent less at $3.6 million per year. But when the analysis is completed, the net present value is higher by about $1.0 million, the profitability index rises to 1.36, and the IRR jumps to 25 percent. Payback is achieved between Years 4 and 5. If thorough examination of the situation suggests that the objectives of the project can in fact be met by the economy alternative, this version is clearly superior.

To illustrate the value impact of choosing the full-fledged version over the economy alternative, we've prepared a differential analysis in Figure 8–11. The results clearly show that the incremental outlay of $2.75 million achieves only $.4 million per year incremental benefits, causing a negative net present value of about $1.0 million, with all other measures indicating a bad investment. The trade-off is clearly a poor one, and this simple example again illustrates the critical importance of defining all relevant alternatives for a project early on, to ensure that a company's resources are deployed with the highest possible value creation potential in net present value terms.

Comparing Different Scenarios

Carrying the analysis of the previous example a little further, we can take a more general case in which three potential ways of achieving the implementation of a

---

FIGURE 8–10

Comparing Alternatives: Economy Solution* ($ thousands)

	Year 0	Year 1	Year 2	Year 3	Year 4	Year 5	Year 6	Year 7	Totals
Equipment outlay and recovery	$−8,750	0	0	0	0	0	0	$ 750	$ −8,000
Annual benefits	0	$ 3,600	$ 3,600	$ 3,600	$ 3,600	$3,600	$3,600	3,600	25,200
Tax rate		36%	36%	36%	36%	36%	36%	36%	
After-tax benefits	0	2,304	2,304	2,304	2,304	2,304	2,304	2,304	16,128
Depreciation tax shield ($1,150 × .36)	0	414	414	414	414	414	414	414	2,898
Total project cash flows (including recovery) . .	−8,750	2,718	2,718	2,718	2,718	2,718	2,718	3,468	11,026
Present value factors @ 14%	1.000	0.877	0.769	0.675	0.592	0.519	0.456	0.400	
Present values of cash flows	−8,750	2,384	2,090	1,835	1,609	1,411	1,239	1,387	
Cumulative present values	$−8,750	$−6,366	$−4,276	$−2,442	$ −832	$ 578	$1,818	$3,205	
Net present value @ 14%									$ 3,205
Profitability index (BCR) @ 14%									1.36
Internal rate of return									25.0%
Present value payback @ 14%									Year 5

*This exhibit is available in an interactive format (TFA Template)—see "Analytical Support" on p. 295.

FIGURE 8–11

Comparing Alternatives: Differential Analysis* ($ thousands)

	Year 0	Year 1	Year 2	Year 3	Year 4	Year 5	Year 6	Year 7	Totals
Equipment outlay and recovery	$–2,750	0	0	0	0	0	0	$ 250	$ –2,500
Annual benefits.	0	$ 400	$ 400	$ 400	$ 400	$ 400	$ 400	400	2,800
Tax rate		36%	36%	36%	36%	36%	36%	36%	
After-tax benefits.	0	256	256	256	256	256	256	256	1,792
Depreciation tax shield ($350 × .36)	0	126	126	126	126	126	126	126	882
Total project cash flows (including recovery) . .	$–2,750	382	382	382	382	382	382	632	174
Present value factors @ 14%.	1.000	0.877	0.769	0.675	0.592	0.519	0.456	0.400	
Present values of cash flows	–2,750	335	294	258	226	198	174	253	
Cumulative present values.	$–2,750	$–2,415	$–2,121	$–1,863	$–1,637	$–1,439	$–1,265	$–1,012	
Net present value @ 14%									$ –1,012
Profitability index (BCR) @ 14%									0.63
Internal rate of return									1.46%
Present value payback @ 14%									none

*This exhibit is available in an interactive format (TFA Template)—see "Analytical Support" on p. 295.

new product investment have been identified, analyzed and quantified. Each alternative will achieve the purpose over the next 7 to 8 years, and the company's return standard is 14 percent. The first alternative represents existing technology, the second a more costly but advanced process, while the third provides higher capacity as well as the advanced process. Let's assume further that both the quality of the estimates and the uncertainty about the outcomes are the same in all three cases—which is not totally realistic but simplifies our example here.

The key dimensions of the three alternatives are presented as follows:

Alternative	Net Investment	Annual Inflows	Terminal Value
(1) Standard	$500,000	$112,000	$150,000
(2) Advanced	600,000	128,000	150,000
(3) Expanded	750,000	169,000	200,000

The three major investment measures were calculated and appear as follows:

Alternative	Net Present Value (NPV)	Internal Rate of Return (IRR)	Profitability Index (BCR)
(1) Standard	$40,256	16.3%	1.08
(2) Advanced	8,864	14.4	1.01
(3) Expanded	54,672	16.1	1.07

The first observation is that all three alternatives meet the company standard by every measure, although to different degrees. The issue is to select the best of the three alternatives, however, and we have to contend with somewhat different signals. From a net present value standpoint, Alternative 3 is clearly best, while the IRR and BCR results favor Alternative 1.

We must remember that the objective of successful investment is to create an economic trade-off that will increase shareholder value. Because only one alternative can be chosen, this would argue for Alternative 3 with the highest net present value. But Alternative 3 is also the most expensive one, and its creation of value per dollar invested (BCR) is somewhat less than Alternative 1.

A useful way of thinking through the purely economic aspects of mutually exclusive alternatives is again to examine the incremental benefits obtained as one moves from the least expensive to the most expensive, as we did in the prior example. In this situation, the incremental investment for Alternative 2 is $100,000, but it reduces net present value from $40,256 to $8,864. This clearly is not desirable, and the lower IRR and BCR measures for Alternative 2 confirm this. Going from Alternative 1 to Alternative 3, however, results in an incremental investment of $250,000, which improves net present value by $14,416. This incremental investment certainly exceeds the company standard of 14 percent, because its IRR can be calculated at 15.7 percent. This result is not quite as attractive as Alternative 1 with an IRR of 16.3 percent—but then the question becomes whether the company has any other projects that might give a return better than 15.7 percent. If not, Alternative 3 should be favored, assuming that all other judgmental aspects are comparable among the three alternatives—especially that the higher volume of business can in fact be counted on.

Many other factors, of course, will have to be considered for a final decision, such as the relative technological and operational risks of the alternatives, issues of implementation, and market aspects. What we've shown here is the interpretation of the economic results alone to illustrate their use in assessing value creation.

Dealing with Risk and Changing Circumstances

Throughout this discussion we have dealt with estimates of future costs and benefits largely as givens. In practice, estimates are more often than not proved wrong by actual experience—in either direction. When projects are performing better than expected, all is well. When actual results are disappointing, however, economic analysis becomes important if it is possible to terminate the project in midstream. Such an option is particularly important if a project contains another decision point for additional investment.

Figure 8–12 illustrates such a situation, where the first four years of the project's life have passed with disappointing results, and management is faced with whether or not to fund the second investment phase. The cardinal rule of economics to remember here is that past investments and cash flows are sunk, and that only present and future cash flows affect the decision to continue or quit. The economic trade-off, therefore, is between

- The net present value of the additional investment and the revised future cash flows on the one hand, and
- Any recovery value of the investment in place on the other.

If no additional investment is required, the trade-off is between the present value of expected future cash flows and the recovery value. In either case, the view taken must extend from the decision point onward into the future.

FIGURE 8–12

Actual Results Lower than Expected—New Decision

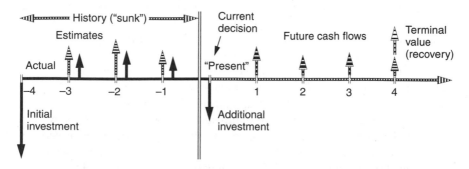

The same argument can be made when a company is faced with the decision to produce a product or service after having spent much more than planned on research and development. We touched on this issue earlier in our discussion of sunk costs. With hindsight, the past decision to invest in the total project was a poor one, because had this higher level of research spending been anticipated, the total project would not have met the return standard. But the current decision to proceed with funding the follow-on production stage might very well remain a sound economic choice, if the estimates about future price, volume, and cost continue to be favorable.

The weight of past mistakes cannot be allowed to suppress sound judgment, which must be based on only relevant factors, that is, present and future conditions which can be affected by a current decision. At the same time, it should be obvious that management must be careful not to create sunk costs through a series of such investments, each of which as a whole turns out to be unsatisfactory due to early overruns, despite the attractiveness of later stages. Remember, sunk costs were future costs at one time, and these should have been properly estimated and refined when they were relevant to the initial decision.

Specifying Risk

The estimates used to analyze business investments are inevitably uncertain because they are dealing with future conditions. As we stated before, business investments involve risk because of the uncertainties surrounding the key variables used. The analyst who prepares the investment calculations and managers who use these results for decision making must allow for a whole range of possible outcomes. Even the best estimates can go wrong as events unfold, yet decisions always have to be made in advance of the actual experience.

The analytical and judgmental challenge is to assess the risk inherent in the key variables of the investment proposal. Such risk analysis can take many forms. In earlier chapters, we mentioned sensitivity analysis as a formal means of testing the impact of changes in key assumptions. This process can be very informal, such as back-of-the-envelope reasoning, or it can involve systematically working through the impact of assumed changes in revenues, operating savings, costs, size of outlays, recovery of capital, and so on, either singly or in combination, and testing the impact on the results. We've also discussed using two of the present value measures, the present value payback and the annualized net present value, as simple risk assessment tools, which allow the user to test the impact of overall changes in periodic cash flows and terminal recoveries.

Earlier we briefly mentioned a more specific approach which involves using differing scenarios based on ranges of estimates, either for the total cash flows, or for individual key variables making up the cash flows. This method allows the decision maker to examine the most optimistic and pessimistic cases as well as the most likely figures, and it is far superior to single-point estimating, especially for significant investments. We'll first discuss the use of ranges of estimates, and their refined application in probabilistic simulation in more detail below. Finally, we'll touch on the subject of risk-adjusted rates.

Ranges of Estimates

Risk can be defined as the degree of variation in the actual versus estimated cash benefit levels of an investment. The wider the possible deviations, the greater the risk. Therefore, using a range of estimates is a more direct approach to investment risk analysis. It might not be necessary to do this for all types of investments, however, because degrees of risk vary widely among business and financial investments, as do the relative importance and magnitude of the investments themselves.

For example, the risk involved in holding a U.S. government bond is very small indeed, because default on the interest payments is extremely unlikely. Therefore, the range of possible benefits from the bond investment is narrowly focused on the contractual payments—in effect no range at all. In contrast, the risk of a business investment for a product or service is a function of the whole range of possible benefit levels that can go from very positive cash flows to negative loss conditions. The uncertainty surrounding these outcomes poses a challenge to the analyst and the decision maker.

The "single-point" estimates of annual cash flow projections we've used so far are the expected results based on the best judgment of the analyst and the type of information available. In effect, they amount to an average of the possible outcomes, implicitly weighed by their respective probabilities. By introducing a range of high, low, and expected levels of annual cash inflows and outflows, the analyst can employ a form of sensitivity analysis to indicate the consequences of expected fluctuations in the annual results—and thus the degree of risk. At times, past experience can provide clues to the range of future outcomes, but essentially, the projection of future conditions has to be judgmental and based on specific forward-looking estimates. The impact of changes in key variables on, say, net present value also can be shown in graphic form in diagrams which display the impact on the total result for each variable on a scale, which allows the decision maker to assess, for example, how important the relative impact of a change in price is compared to changes in key cost elements. A number of analytical computer programs have such built-in capabilities, and graph the results in bar charts that show the relative size of the change induced by modifying each variable.

The decision maker must assess the likelihood that the range of estimated outcomes fairly expresses the characteristics of the project, and decide whether the expected outcome is sufficiently attractive to compensate for the possibility that the actual results might vary as defined. Risk assessment in essence comes down to how comfortable the decision maker is with the possibility of experiencing adverse results—that is, a very personal risk preference or risk aversion. Stipulating a range helps the responsible person or group visualize the possible extremes in the expected results.

Business Investments as Options

When we discussed sequential investments earlier, our examples involved stages of commitments, such as research and development followed by implementation, or different stages of supporting a product or service expansion. We were looking at these stages in retrospect. At times, however, companies face strategic investment choices which offer sequential commitments and thus the option to abandon a project if at an early stage it becomes clear that the overall concept is a failure. Recognizing, during the initial analysis, the points in a complex project's pattern where the option to abandon exists and planning to act on the results after implementation can help reduce the impact of value destruction as expressed by changes in net present value.

For example, if a company wishes to invest in applying a new technology, recognizing that the chance of success is limited to say, 60 percent, it will be useful to develop a comparative analysis which includes the option to abandon early in the economic life, given that results are unacceptable. Two scenarios can be drawn up, one specifying the cash flow pattern given success, the other specifying the cash flow implications of failure. Weighting the cash flows by their respective probabilities, and discounting the expected cash flows at the return standard applicable to the type of business, the expected net present value can be determined, as shown in Figure 8–13. Without the option to abandon, as shown in the top portion of the analysis, the negative expected net present value is far larger than when the option to abandon is considered in the bottom portion. Note that there is a ramp-up of cash flow benefits if the project is successful, and a leveling out of negative cash flows in the unsuccessful situation. Viewed by itself, the success alternative provides a significant positive net present value of $103 million, as shown below the first alternative, but given the high chance of failure this is obviously not a realistic picture. The probability-weighted expected net present value reflects the risk/reward trade-off situation better.

Investing in New Technology ($ millions)

Stage 1 Investment Without Option to Abandon	Year 0	Year 1	Year 2	Year 3	Year 4	Year 5	Year 6	Year 7	Totals
After-tax cash flows if successful	$–250	$ 70	$ 80	$ 90	$ 100	$ 110	$ 120	$ 120	$ 440
After-tax cash flows if unsuccessful	–250	–110	–90	–90	–80	–80	–80	–80	–860
Weighted cash flows—success 60%	–250	42	48	54	60	66	72	72	164
Weighted cash flows—failure 40%	–250	–44	–36	–36	–32	–32	–32	–32	–494
Expected cash flows.....................	–250	–2	12	18	28	34	40	40	–80
Present value factors @ 18%..............	1.000	0.847	0.718	0.609	0.516	0.437	0.370	0.314	
Present values of cash flows	–250	–2	9	11	14	15	15	13	
Cumulative present values.................	$–250	$–252	$–243	$–232	$–218	$–203	$–188	$–175	
Expected net present value @ 18%									–175
Net present value—success @ 18%									103
With Option to Abandon									
After-tax cash flows if successful	$–250	$ 70	$ 80	$ 90	$ 100	$ 110	$ 120	$ 120	$ 440
After-tax cash flows if unsuccessful	–250	–110	–90	60	0	0	0	0	–390
Weighted cash flows—success 60%	–250	42	48	54	60	66	72	72	164
Weighted cash flows—failure 40%	–250	–44	–36	24	0	0	0	0	–306
Expected cash flows.....................	–250	–2	12	78	60	66	72	72	108
Present value factors @ 18%..............	1.000	0.847	0.718	0.609	0.516	0.437	0.370	0.314	
Present values of cash flows	–250	–2	9	48	31	29	27	23	
Cumulative present values.................	$–250	$–252	$–243	$–196	$–165	$–136	$–109	$ –87	
Expected net present value @ 18%									$ –87

Clearly, it's unlikely that the unsuccessful alternative would be maintained for its 7-year life, and accordingly, the option to abandon has been included in Year 3, with provision for a recovery of some of the initial investment built in. Note also that we have used a fairly high return standard of 18 percent, reflecting the risky nature of the business. Many managers would probably raise this hurdle even higher given the uncertainty, but this brings up the issue of doubly adjusting for risk in both the cash flows and the discount rate. We'll discuss multiple standards later.

The decision makers still face the question whether this uncertain investment fits their risk preferences, that is, whether a chance of 60 percent success is sufficient for the first, modest investment stage. But they might want to consider another option in the form of a potential large expansion stage in the second year, given that the technology has been proven workable in the first year. The chances of success at that point will have dramatically improved, and the larger follow-on investment could be viewed as a 90 percent success bet. Such a set of conditions is very typical in high technology companies, where initial investments in new advances can lead to significant exploitation of the full potential, once a smaller scale project has proved out. Note in Figure 8–14 the sizable investment in Year 2, followed by rising cash flow benefits.

The risk of failure was built into the analysis at 10 percent, and the expected cash flow and net present value results appear quite favorable, because the decision can be held off until success has been achieved in the first stage. Viewed by itself this analysis indicates an expected net present value of $313 million. But because the decision on the first stage has to be made in Year 0, we must adjust the

FIGURE 8–14

Exploiting New Technology ($ thousands)

Stage 2 Investment Given Success of Stage 1	Year 0	Year 1	Year 2	Year 3	Year 4	Year 5	Year 6	Year 7	Totals
After-tax cash flows if successful	0	0	$−1,000	$ 400	$ 500	$ 600	$ 600	$ 600	$ 1,700
After-tax cash flows if unsuccessful	0	0	−1,000	−450	−300	400	0	0	−1,350
Weighted cash flows—success 90%	0	0	−1,000	360	450	540	540	540	1,430
Weighted cash flows—failure 10%.	0	0	−1,000	−45	−30	40	0	0	−1,035
Expected cash flows.	0	0	−1,000	315	420	580	540	540	1,395
Present value factors @ 18%.	1.000	0.847	0.718	0.609	0.516	0.437	0.370	0.314	
Present values of cash flows	0	0	−718	192	217	253	200	170	
Cumulative present values.	0	0	$ −718	$−526	$−309	$ −56	$ 144	$ 313	
Expected net present value @ 18%									$ 313

net present value for the combined stages of the whole project by taking the expected net present value of the first stage of −$87 million (with the option to abandon built in), and add to it 60 percent of the expected net present value of the second stage (.6 × $313) or $188 million, for a tot al expectation of $101 million.

Using the option to abandon reduced the negative results of the first stage significantly, and adding the deferrable option to expand made the whole project attractive from a net present value standpoint, even though the individual outcomes of the two stages remain subject to the probabilities assigned to them. Thus this type of analysis has provided a clearer picture of the dimensions of the risk/reward trade-offs involved.

Probabilistic Simulation

A more refined approach to risk assessment consists of estimating ranges or probabilities not only for the total annual cash flows, but also for the individual key variables that make up these cash flows. Probability distributions are then assigned to the likelihood of the outcomes for each of the variables. A number of the variables are usually interdependent, such as changes in price causing changes in volume, and it is helpful to define such interdependencies and build them into the analysis. The possible outcomes of the project can then be simulated by running many iterations on the computer. The method is an extension of sensitivity analysis in that the potential changes in many variables are evaluated both simultaneously and relative to each other.

The result is a range of possible annual cash inflows in the form of a probability distribution, or even a range of net present values or internal rates of return arrayed by probability. Such a risk profile allows the decision maker to think about the relative attractiveness of a project in terms of statements such as: "chances are 9 out of 10 that the project will meet the minimum standard of 10 percent," or, "there is a probability of 60 percent that the net present value of the project will be at least $1.0 million or better." Cumulative probability distributions such as those shown in Figure 8–15 can be drawn up as an aid. The relative

FIGURE 8–15

Cumulative Probability Distribution for Two Projects

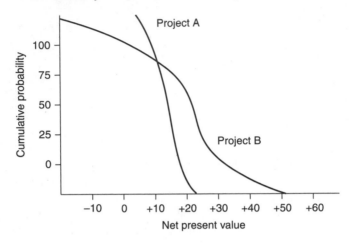

ease with which such simulations can be carried out does not eliminate the many practical issues involved in assigning specific probability distributions to the individual variables in the first place, or ease the problem of interpreting the final results. There are a number of commercial simulation models available to spreadsheet users, which permit doing this type of analysis to various degrees of complexity.

As we said before, judging both the likelihood of an event and one's own attitude toward the risk expressed in this fashion is a highly personal response that often defies precise quantification. The amount of risk a decision maker will accept is largely a matter of personal experience and preference. In addition, investment decisions in a business setting are as much a function of complex personal and group dynamics as they are dependent on the pure analytical results, the quality of presentation, and examination of specific economic data.

Risk-Adjusted Return Standards

Another way of adjusting for risk is to modify the return standard itself to include a risk premium where warranted. In a sense, the concept is quite simple—the greater the risk, the higher the return desired from the investment. Also, this reasoning is intuitively attractive to business decision makers, because the process parallels the way we think about personal investments. At the same time, however, letting the return standard be the main expression of riskiness deals only indirectly with the true source of risk, that is, the uncertainty about the investment cash flows themselves and the specific key variables they contain. It's usually preferable to expend considerable thought and analysis on understanding and evaluating the riskiness of the cash flows and the key drivers implicit in them, to avoid applying arbitrarily high return standards to specific projects or businesses.

Investments in businesses subject to wide profit swings and competitive pressures should command a significant premium above the return standard, while fairly predictable businesses might find a lesser return acceptable. This is no different from recognizing the basic risk/reward trade-off implicit in the premiums commanded by interest-bearing financial instruments, depending on the degree of risk involved, ranging from essentially risk-free government bonds to so-called junk bonds. Remember also that the corporate cost of capital, the basic minimum standard for value creation, has a built-in allowance for not only the market risk, but the specific risk implicit in a company's business. This is discussed in detail in Chapter 9.

When multiple return standards are employed, it's done on the assumption that a diversified company can use different standards which, in combination, will ensure an appropriate overall return to the shareholders and also fairly reflect the risk exposure of the individual lines of business. We'll return to the basis for earnings standards in Chapter 9, and discuss both the conceptual and practical issues involved.

When to Use Investment Measures

During our discussion of the measures in Chapter 7, and while using them with different examples in this chapter, we cautioned the reader about various shortcomings and issues of interpretation. We'll now review and expand some of these caveats. Basically, investment analysis measures exist to help analysts and managers determine whether a project meets the return standard established for the business and thereby satisfies the basic value creation criterion of exceeding the company's cost of capital. Also, they assist in ranking the relative desirability of a group of proposals during the capital budgeting process. If the projects being considered are independent of each other, the time-adjusted measures of net present value, profitability index, discounted payback, and internal rate of return will singly or in combination properly reflect the projects' relative economic attractiveness and result in an appropriate ranking sequence, although the net present value criterion is the most commonly used and accepted measure.

Shown in Figure 8–16 is a comparative view of the consistent readings of net present value, internal rate of return, and present value payback as applied to three types of independent projects. Project A exceeds the company standard, Project B falls short, and Project C just meets the standard. In every case, each measure gives an economic reading that indicates the proper ranking of the project.

As we demonstrated earlier, uneven lives of capital investments pose complications that are handled by adjusting the analysis to equalize the time spans for purposes of comparison. This can be done by truncating the life of a project with an assumed recovery of funds from disposal at an earlier point, as in our replacement example in Figure 8–3, or by extending the shorter alternative by assuming repeated investment. Mutually exclusive projects with different lives also can be compared by annualizing their net present values over their respective economic

FIGURE 8-16

Investment Measures Applied to Three Projects

lives to determine their respective annual equivalent benefits or cost. This process simply calls for dividing the net present value by the relevant annuity factor, or for using calculator or spreadsheet routines.

For mutually exclusive projects, the profitability index (BCR) will normally give a fair assessment, but the choice has to be considered in terms of the relative size and length of the commitment as well—the risk/reward trade-off. As we discussed earlier, a larger investment with a somewhat lower profitability index and yield might be preferable to a smaller investment, if both alternatives show benefits well above normal. If a company's identified projects exceed the limits of its funding potential, however—a fairly common condition—management has to apply what is called capital rationing. This involves spending the company's limited funds on the best selection of projects from the larger list of acceptable projects. Here the investment measure used must provide an economic ranking, that is, optimize the benefits obtained from the investment dollars spent. Essentially, the company should choose that group of projects within the budget limit that will generate the highest aggregate net present value.

To do this, projects can be ranked in declining order of their profitability index until the budgeted amount has been exhausted. This amounts to maximizing the present value benefits achieved per dollar of investment, because investment funds are the limiting factor. This concept ties closely to the principles of shareholder value creation, as will be discussed in more detail in Chapter 12. In practice, however, capital budgets are rarely so precise that truly attractive projects that were initially rejected for lack of funds or that appeared during the budget period could not at least be considered at another point in time.

Let's also remember that there should be nothing automatic about the use of any of the investment measures. The seemingly precise results achieved with present value calculations can tempt us to "let the numbers decide." Many more elements have to be weighed in even fairly straightforward projects, as we observed at the beginning of the chapter and hinted at in our examples. Besides the obvious constraints imposed by uncertainty in the economic estimates, management also must consider competitive, technical, human, societal, and other constraints within the company's strategic context, before significant investment or divestment decisions are made.

Some Further Considerations

Several specialized aspects of business investment analysis have been mentioned only briefly so far. A detailed treatment would go beyond the scope of this book. Yet, for completeness, we'll add some further comments on how the choice of leasing affects the economic analysis of an investment, on the impact of accelerated depreciation on present value analysis, and on the impact of inflation. Finally we'll once more put into perspective the degree of accuracy warranted in the calculations.

Leasing—A Financing Choice

Leasing is a popular means of obtaining a wide variety of capital assets for businesses as well as individuals, in exchange for making a pattern of periodic payments. For our purposes, however, the main point to consider is that leasing represents merely one form of financing, as we'll discuss in Chapter 10. Therefore, it's only after economic investment analysis has shown a project to be acceptable that alternative ways of financing should be considered. This principle is consistent with the business systems approach we've taken, where we clearly separated the decisions on investment, operations, and financing. While financing for business investments should come from appropriate sources—matching their long-term nature—the specific alternatives of financing, including leasing, must remain independent from the economic justification of the investment itself.

All along we've viewed investment analysis as a cash flow trade-off which is independent of the compensation paid for the funds that finance the asset. The cost of capital or a return standard related to it automatically takes into account the expectations of the various providers of capital for appropriate compensation. If such an economic analysis is favorable, a separate test can then be applied to determine whether the company is better off leasing or owning the assets involved. This involves comparing various funding methods, where the question clearly becomes "lease versus buy" not "invest versus not invest." A number of specialized software applications exist, which permit analysts and managers to make the necessary calculations and tests for comparing financing alternatives.

Because of the special complexities involved in these analytical methods, the reader is directed to the references at the end of the chapter for more information.

Accelerated Depreciation

For simplicity, we've used straight-line depreciation in our examples to derive the tax shield effect of depreciation charges as they affect economic analysis. However, we've also referred to the accelerated write-offs allowed under the Internal Revenue Code (see Chapter 4, p. 344), which are periodically modified by Congress. Rather than focus on any one of the several methods permitted, we'll make only a few generally applicable comments.

Remember, when doing investment analysis we're interested in depreciation, whatever pattern it might take, only insofar as it changes the tax expenditures of the company and provides a tax shield. From a present value standpoint, accelerated depreciation provides an advantage because it moves the favorable tax impact of the write-offs forward in time. In other words, in the early years of a project, the tax shield effect on cash flows will be greater than with straight-line write-offs.

Similarly, shorter lives permitted by the ever changing Internal Revenue Code will also place more tax benefits into the early stages of a project. Project benefits will be increased in the present value context, assuming, of course, that the company has sufficient taxable profits to take advantage of higher early write-offs. The calculations required to take account of accelerated depreciation in economic investment analysis can be handled easily with computer spreadsheets, just as any other uneven cash flow pattern can be accommodated.

The reader is encouraged to seek out the most current information published by the IRS to ascertain the proper depreciation class and write-off patterns for the assets being analyzed, and also to be aware of the particular tax management circumstances of the company that might affect its election of write-off patterns for tax purposes.

Inflation and Investment Analysis

The most important point to remember about the impact of inflation on investment analysis is the need for consistency between the measures used and data being analyzed. As we'll see in the next chapter, company return standards are commonly based on the weighted cost of capital. This cost specifically embodies inflation expectations both in the interest rate ascribed to debt, and the investors' return expectations on which the cost of shareholder equity is based.

The analysis of business investment projects should therefore be carried out with revenue and cost estimates that contain the same inflation expectations as the return standard employed. In other words, reasonable assumptions about price level changes affecting every part of the investment cash flow analysis should be built in, in order to make the discounting process meaningful. For example, using a return standard which contains an inflation allowance to discount constant dollar projections would give a result biased against the project. Similarly, using a constant dollar return standard to discount inflated cash flows would unduly improve the project's measures. The reader is referred to Appendix IV on inflation for a more detailed discussion of the underlying concepts.

Accuracy

At all times we must remember that the great precision implied by the mathematical basis of the investment analysis tools should be viewed with extreme caution. As we've pointed out before, the very nature of cash flow estimates—to which these tools are applied—is uncertain because the estimates are based on expectations, forecasts, projections, and sometimes plain guesses. Only rarely does the analyst deal with contractual sums, such as interest or lease payments, and even these are subject to a degree of uncertainty. Therefore it makes no sense to generate deceptively precise results or to allow highly specific numerical rankings to take on undue importance.

In our examples, we've been more precise than needed. Our intention was mainly to give the reader enough specific details to be able to follow the various methods step by step. In practice, liberal rounding of calculations (and certainly the final results) is highly advisable to keep the mathematical process from overwhelming the realistic business judgments required.

Keeping accuracy in proper perspective is even more important when we realize that the power of discounting is such that even widely different estimates for distant time periods can be so severely reduced in present value terms that they have relatively minor effects on the final result. A glance at the present value tables will confirm the rapid shrinkage of factors as discount rates rise and periods are more remote.

Key Issues

The following is a recap of the key issues raised directly or indirectly in this chapter. They are enumerated here to help the reader keep the analysis tools and methods within the perspective of financial theory and business practice.

1. Business investment decisions are made continuously within the larger context of business strategy. This context evolves over time, and the portfolio of potential investments never remains constant or visible in its entirety.

2. The trade-off between outlays and benefits must be made with the objective of increasing shareholder value, that is, the return standards employed in measuring this trade-off must reflect the earnings potential and risks expected from a given business.

3. Shareholder expectations are incorporated into relevant return yardsticks through the concept of weighted cost of capital, which reflects the expected level of future compensation to all providers of capital, but which must be exceeded for value creation.

4. To permit an economic judgment to be made, investment measures must take into account the timing of inflows and outflows of an investment and relate economic attractiveness to defined return expectations.

5. Economic analysis of investment decisions must be based on differential revenues and costs in the form of cash flows that are caused by the decision, and not on changes that are merely due to accounting conventions.

6. At times economic allocations of existing or potential infrastructure must be made to the investment analysis, if the proposal over the economic life requires such infrastructure that could be committed to other current or future alternatives.

7. Risk is inherent in all estimates of future conditions because of the uncertainty about most variables affecting an investment project. It must be expressed consistently in developing the expected cash flows, their potential range, and in applying the investment measures. Sensitivity analysis is a key aspect of business investment analysis of any significant size.

8. Inflation and specific price changes in revenues and costs can complicate both the estimating process and the level of the investment standards, and they must be handled consistently.

9. Capital budgets in practice are neither absolute ceilings on the amount of investments for a company, nor are they automatically affected by purely quantitative project ranking.

10. Financing patterns affect both the capability to make business investments and management's risk tolerance because of the impact of financial leverage and the need to cover fixed obligations.

11. Framing of investment decisions within the broader context of strategy, alternative solutions, capital constraints, and uncertainty—over an appropriate time horizon—is the critical prelude to economic analysis and to the use of analytical techniques, and this framework is also inextricably involved in the final decision process.

Summary

In this chapter, we've presented the basic analytical framework for investment analysis in the broad context of capital budgeting. The strategic backdrop of this activity was highlighted before we illustrated the use of the time-adjusted measures with a variety of realistic examples.

All along we've stressed, however, that the most critical aspect of the process was thoughtful structuring of the problem in all of its dimensions before any quantitative techniques are applied. We discussed the need to define the problem, including development of relevant alternatives, careful preparation of all relevant data about the investment and the changes in the operating conditions introduced by the decision, and any capital recoveries—all done in an economic cash flow context. We found conceptual problems in all of these aspects, particularly in the use and meaning of the investment measures themselves. Working through increasingly complex examples, we provided the reader with a basic ability to perform investment analysis. But we cautioned that numerical results were only inputs to the broader management task of strategic positioning of the business—the selection and matching of appropriate long-term capital commitments with appropriate funding sources, within the framework of defined corporate objectives and goals, and with the ultimate purpose of creating shareholder value.

Analytical Support

Financial Genome, the commercially available financial analysis and planning software described in Appendix I, is accompanied by general purpose present value analysis templates and graphic displays (TFA Template under "extras"), which can be used to directly calculate the various discounted cash flow measures discussed in this chapter and in Chapter 7, from any pattern of cash flows and discount rates, as well as different depreciation assumptions and tax rates. They match the format represented by Figures 8–4 through 8–11, and Figures 7–4 and 7–5 in Chapter 7. (see "Downloads Available" on p. 431)

Selected References

Aggarwal, R., ed. *Capital Budgeting under Uncertainty: Advances and New Perspectives.* Englewood Cliffs, NJ: Prentice Hall, 1991.

Bierman, Harold Jr., and Seymour Smidt. *The Capital Budgeting Decision.* 8th ed. New York: Macmillan, 1992. (A classic.)

Brealey, Richard, and Stewart Myers. *Principles of Corporate Finance.* 5th ed. Burr Ridge, IL: Irwin/McGraw-Hill, 1996.

Dixit, Avinash K., and Robert S. Pindyck. *The Options Approach to Capital Investment.* Harvard Business Review, May–June 1995.

Garrison, Raymond H., and Erick W. Noreen. *Managerial Accounting.* 8th ed. Burr Ridge, IL: Irwin/McGraw-Hill, 1997.

Grant, Eugene L., et al. *Principles of Engineering Economy*. 8th ed. New York: John Wiley & Sons, 1990. (A classic.)

Hertz, David B. *Risk Analysis in Capital Investment*. Harvard Business Review, September–December 1979. (A classic.)

McNamee, Peter, and John Celona. *Decision Analysis with Supertree*. 2d ed. South San Francisco, CA: The Scientific Press, 1990.

Perlman, Kalman I. *The Leasing Handbook*. Chicago and Cambridge, Eng.: Probus, 1992.

Weston, Fred; Scott Besley; and Eugene Brigham. *Essentials of Managerial Finance*. 11th ed. Hinsdale, IL: Dryden Press, 1997.

CHAPTER 9

COST OF CAPITAL
AND BUSINESS DECISIONS

$\mathbf{A}$ common theme of this book is to view business decisions as economic cost/ benefit trade-offs, designed ultimately to create value for the shareholders. Up to this point, however, we've focused mainly on the *economic benefits* obtained from investing in and operating a business. Now we'll deal in more specific terms with the *economic costs* associated with business decisions.

For example, during our discussion of financial leverage in Chapter 6, we encountered the special profit impact that is caused by the cost of long-term debt funds. We demonstrated how such fixed-cost obligations introduce magnified earnings fluctuations at different levels of profitability. In Chapters 7 and 8, we referred to the overall cost of long-term capital as a main criterion by which to judge the desirability of business investments. We established that only projects providing a time-adjusted cash flow return above the cost of capital will create value for the company's shareholders.

In this chapter, we'll discuss in greater detail the cost of various types of capital employed in a business, examine how this cost is measured, and in what form and for which purposes this economic reality should affect business decision making. We'll begin by sketching out the types of decisions for which cost of capital considerations are important. Then we'll discuss the cost of the different types of capital used, including operating funds, long-term debt, and shareholder equity (preferred stock and common equity).

Given the specific costs of each of these types of capital, we'll derive an approach to determining the overall corporate weighted cost of capital, and discuss the use of this cost concept in relation to the various return standards for business investments. We applied the cost of capital-based standards to the examples in Chapters 7 and 8, and we'll use them again in Chapters 11 and 12. As usual, the chapter will end with a list of key issues.

Decisional Context

The decisional context we've used all along stressed the interrelationship of investment, operations, and financing. We observed that, over time, most management decisions cause cash movements in one form or another. However, we didn't deal directly with the sources of the various types of funds employed in managing the system's cash flows, and did not dwell on their respective costs.

The dynamics of the business system require that funds be available at any time—temporarily or permanently—from a variety of sources, provided internally or externally. Key internal sources are cash flows from profitable operations or shifts in existing funds commitments. Key external sources are borrowing or raising new equity. Because the basic purpose of investing in, operating, and financing a business is to increase the economic value of the owners' stake over time, management decisions should create economic value for the shareholders by generating after-tax results that are higher than the cost of all the supporting capital inputs. This point was made repeatedly throughout the book, and we'll now take up in detail the main aspects of the cost aspect of this trade-off.

Investment Decisions

In Chapter 7 we discussed the various economic measures used to judge the desirability of an investment, and in Chapter 8 we demonstrated their use in a variety of investment decisions and trade-offs. All of these measures had in common the basic requirement that a project provide an economic return. This implies that the capital investment and all costs must be recovered, including an appropriate compensation to the providers of the various types of funds committed to the project. We also established that minimum standards for investments had to be set high enough to compensate both for the project's specific risk and for the opportunity loss of forgoing the returns from any alternative uses of the funds invested. Such alternative investments in the company's normal activities or in new initiatives were similarly assumed to adequately compensate both shareholders and lenders for providing their capital. We then suggested that the company's overall cost of capital, when used as a minimum standard for the economic desirability of investments, implicitly embodied all of these requirements, and value would be created if a project's cash flow performance exceeded the company's cost of capital.

The analytical methods discussed in Chapter 7 did not, however, directly include any financing costs; rather, the cash outflows and inflows as defined represented only investment outlays on the one hand, and incremental after-tax operating benefits and capital recoveries on the other. These cash flows were then discounted at a return standard that implicitly allowed for the recovery of all actual costs and opportunity costs combined. Importantly, we didn't take into account the cost of the specific funds to be used for financing the project, instead letting at all times a broad overall standard represent the combined cost of all types of funding employed by the company.

Accordingly, the economic results from a business investment have to be sufficiently attractive to justify allocation of part of the various long-term funds available to the company, because business investments generally have a fairly long-term economic life span. Here we must recognize an important principle, derived from our discussion of the business system in Chapter 2: Normally, the funds for new investments come from a pool of different sources, none of which can or should be specifically identified with any particular project under review. Instead, any funds used for investment purposes represent the mix contained in the pool, and therefore should carry the overall cost of the company's long-term funding, as suggested by Figure 9–1. There we see the basic combination of debt and equity, in whatever proportions management deems an appropriate level, supporting working capital, fixed assets of all types, and any other assets employed by the company.

Given the long-term nature of commitments for working capital, facilities, technology, etc., these investments are normally backed by the long-term capital structure of a company. This structure may employ different degrees of leverage and a whole range of financial instruments, and it may change over time as the company's business patterns develop. The important point is that the long-term pool of funds is the relevant source of funding—not any particular increment of financing which the company may be using at a given point in time to augment its capital structure. Therefore, the weighted cost of capital measure, which we'll discuss shortly, is the most significant criterion of cost in the capital budgeting and investment analysis context.

Operating Decisions

The time horizon for operating decisions is generally shorter than that of the typical business investment. Nonetheless, operational funds movements, such as increases or decreases in trade credit—both used and extended—and swings in cash balances and accruals as described in Chapter 3 do involve costs, both in the form of out-of-pocket charges and opportunity costs. For example, a near-term decision to take purchase discounts might involve significant economic benefits when

---

F I G U R E   9–1

Long-Term Funds Commitments versus Long-Term Sources

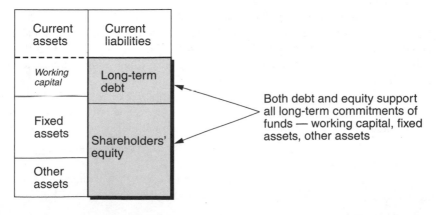

weighed against the cost of any incremental borrowing necessary to take advantage of the discount. Cash management decisions to minimize bank balances can eliminate the opportunity costs inherent in idle funds. In fact, there are myriad circumstances in which near-term decisions can cause or eliminate the cost of employing funds, as these decisions are often directly linked to incremental sources that entail specific costs. We'll discuss some of these shortly.

Financing Decisions

There are costs connected with obtaining financing and compensating providers of various sources of funds, both short-term and long-term, which must be considered by management in making any financing decision. Clearly, using any type of funds entails an economic cost to the company in one form or another. One of management's obligations is to develop a pattern of funding that both matches the risk/reward profile of the business and is sufficiently adapted to meeting the evolving needs of the company. At the same time, the use of long-term funds entails meeting the expectations of creditors, and meeting or preferably exceeding the expectations of the providers of equity funds, the company's shareholders. We'll discuss the major financing choices and the framework for analyzing them in the next chapter.

Cost of Operating Funds

In the course of operations, a business commonly carries many types of debt, including trade obligations (in the form of accounts and notes payable), short- and intermediate-term credit, notes payable to banks or individuals, tax accruals owed various government agencies, wages due employees, payments due on installment purchases, and lease obligations. For all types of debt, including long-term obligations in the company's capital structure, the specific cost of borrowing can be determined rather easily. Normally, debt arrangements carry stated interest provisions that call for interest payments during the debt period, at its end, or as an advance deduction from principal. The last of these provisions is called discounting. In all cases, the specific cost of debt is simply the direct cost of the interest commitment.

We also must remember that under current IRS taxation guidelines, interest payments of all kinds are tax deductible for corporations. Because of this feature, the net cost of interest to corporations (at least for those with sufficient profits to be liable for taxes or able to apply tax-averaging provisions) is the annual interest multiplied by a factor (f) of one minus the applicable tax rate.

For example, if a corporation pays 8 percent per year on the principal of a note and its effective tax rate (t) for any incremental revenue or cost is 34 percent, the net annual effective interest cost (i) of this note will be:

$$f = 1 - t$$
$$f = 1 - 0.34 = 0.66$$
$$i = 8\% \times 0.66 = 5.28\% \text{ (after taxes)}$$

Tax deductibility effectively reduces the cost of debt to a net amount after the prevailing tax rate is applied, if the company is in a position where changes in net income affect the amount of taxes due. This tax advantage might also be enjoyed by individuals in some circumstances, such as in the case of home mortgage interest deductions. However, the specific cost of other forms of capital (such as dividends on preferred stock) is not tax deductible for corporations at this time, as we'll see later.

We can define operating debt as short- or intermediate-term revolving obligations incurred in the ordinary daily operations of most businesses. Some of these debt funds are provided by creditors free of charge for short periods, under trade terms generally accepted in the industry or service sector in which the company operates.

Foremost in this category are accounts payable, which are the amounts owed vendors for goods or services purchased. Depending on the terms of the purchase agreement, the company being billed for goods and services can hold off payment for 10 or 15 days, or as long as 45 or even 60 days. In the interim, it can make use of the funds without incurring any specific cost. Recall from Chapter 3 that such trade credit is in fact a significant funds source that is rolled over continuously, and that grows or declines with the volume of operations.

In many cases, suppliers offer their customers a discount for early payment. For example, the supplier's terms might provide for a 2 percent reduction in the invoice amount if payment is received within 10 days (2/10), or 3 percent within 15 days (3/15) of the date of the invoice. This practice, common in many business sectors, allows the customer effectively to reduce the original cost of the goods or service by the specified discount. The incentive is intended to speed up the vendor's collections and thus reduce the level of the vendor's funds tied up in customer credit.

If the buyer lets the discount period lapse, however, the invoice amount becomes due and payable in full at the end of the period specified (n/30, n/45, and so on), although in practice these terms are rarely observed with precision. Failure to take advantage of the trade discount, and thereby prolonging the time during which the buyer can make alternative use of the funds, results in a definite opportunity cost. While often ignored, this cost can be quite sizable.

For instance, if the credit terms are 2/10, n/30, the cost of using the funds for the extra 20 days amounts to a loss of 2 percent of the invoice amount, or an annual rate of 36 percent! The calculation is quite simple:

$$\frac{360 \text{ days}}{20 \text{ days}} \times 2\% = 36\% \text{ (before taxes)}$$

In effect, the company loses, as taxable income, the cash discount it would otherwise have earned. To arrive at the net cost, the cash discount must be reduced by the taxes that would have been paid on the lost income. If we assume taxes to be 34 percent, the net cost for using the creditor's funds for the extra 20 days amounts to

$$1 - 0.34 = 0.66$$
$$2\% \times 0.66 = 1.32\% \text{ (after taxes)}$$

The annualization is calculated as

$$\frac{360 \text{ days}}{20 \text{ days}} \times 1.32\% = 23.76\% \text{ (after taxes)}$$

This cost is very high, especially when compared to the after-tax cost of the prime interest rate, which is the rate normally charged large corporations of impeccable credit rating—or even relative to the after-tax cost of much higher interest rates smaller companies pay to borrow operating funds.

Some companies, especially small and rapidly growing enterprises, make it a practice to use accounts payable as a convenient source of credit, often unilaterally exceeding the outside limits of credit terms by significant periods. The longer the funds are kept, of course, the lower the specific cost of accounts payable becomes, as trade creditors normally do not charge interest unless the receivable has to be renegotiated. In extreme cases, trade creditors might force the customer to convert unpaid amounts into notes payable due on specific dates, with or without interest. This is usually done—albeit reluctantly—by vendors who wish to establish a somewhat stronger claim against the customer's resources.

It's clearly a poor practice for any borrower to violate stipulated trade credit terms, both from the standpoint of business reputation and continuing creditworthiness. Prospective creditors will take such tardy performance into account when evaluating the customer's credit history, as such information is readily available from the databases of credit rating agencies. This is an implicit economic cost which must be considered in addition to the specific monetary cost incurred with trade credit.

Another form of operating debt includes short-term notes and installment contracts, where interest is either charged ahead of time or added to the amount of principal stated in the contract. For example, a one-year, $1,000 note which carries an interest rate of 9 percent will provide the debtor with only $910 in ready cash if the note is "discounted" by deducting the interest in advance. The effective cost before taxes is higher than the stated interest, because the company is in effect paying $90 for the privilege of borrowing $910 for one year:

$$\frac{\$90}{\$910} = 9.89\% \text{ (before taxes)}$$

The adjustment for income taxes is handled exactly as shown in the last example.

In the case of an installment contract for, say, $1,000 payable in four equal quarterly installments, with annual interest of 10 percent on the original balance, the effective cost of interest is far higher than stated, because decreasing amounts of principal will be outstanding over the term of the contract as the quarterly payments amortize the principal, while providing interest on the rapidly declining balance. The precise cost of 15.7 percent can be easily determined with a calculator or a spreadsheet, using the present value approach discussed in Chapters 7 and 8.

We can use an averaging process as a quick method of determining the approximate effective cost. Over the term of the contract, the amount of principal will decline from $1000 to zero, with the average outstanding balance of roughly one-half of this range, or $500. The contractual interest was 10 percent on $1,000, or $100, one-quarter of which was added to each of the four payments. When we relate the total interest paid to the average amount of funds used by the borrowing company during the term of the contract, the approximate cost doubles, as follows:

$$\frac{\$100}{\$500} = 20\% \text{ (before taxes)}$$

The actual result of 15.7 percent is lower because in our example interest in effect is also paid on the installment basis. (The adjustment for income taxes is the same as before.) If the contract ran for more than one year, the interest cost must be annualized, that is, the amount of interest must be allocated to the specific time period involved to derive the true cost per year, which is the normal period of comparison. More complex financial arrangements are normally handled with present value techniques. The computerized systems used by banks and other lending institutions routinely calculate the payments and charges precisely, and they are legally bound to disclose the effective cost of the arrangement on an annualized basis. The simple averaging technique shown earlier is useful as a quick check in many circumstances, including personal finance, to approximate the effective cost of credit for rough initial comparisons.

The discussion so far has focused on the specific cost of operational debt, which can range from zero to substantial annual rates of interest. This specific cost is not the only aspect of debt, however. As already mentioned in earlier chapters, repayment of the loan is required, which commits part of the company's future cash flows to that purpose. The obligation to repay the loan principal in a timely fashion forces the financial manager to forecast and plan cash receipts and disbursements with care. The projections could indicate that refinancing might be desirable when the amount becomes due. The basic techniques of making cash flow projections as discussed in Chapter 5 are applicable here.

Another element of the burden of debt, as already mentioned, is the impact various forms of debt obligations have on a company's creditworthiness in relation to current and future funding requirements. In other words, the balance between owners' equity and other people's money might become precarious and forestall borrowing of any kind for some time until the company has worked itself out from under its debt obligations. Highly debt-leveraged operations can be costly, both in terms of the risk of not meeting obligations as they fall due, and in having to turn to much more expensive sources of credit or equity funds as additional needs arise.

Cost of Long-Term Debt

Most companies employ at least some form of long-term debt obligation to support part of their permanent financing needs arising from major capital outlays, growth of operations, or replacement of other types of capital. This type of debt becomes integral to the long-term capital structure of the company. Examples are bonds of various types issued by a company and traded in the financial markets and long-term borrowing arrangements with banks and other financial institutions.

As we'll discuss in Chapter 10, management must make well-planned decisions when determining an appropriate level of debt in the capital structure, weighing the cost, risk, and debt service involved relative to the prospective uses of the funds. Long-term debt commitments by their very nature have a much more lasting impact on a company's situation than do short-term, working capital, financing, or intermediate-term loans.

The specific cost of long-term debt is expressed in the stated annual interest rate of the financial instrument involved. For example, a 9 percent debenture bond, which is an unsecured (no specific assets are pledged) general debt obligation of the company, has a specific after-tax cost of

$$9\% \times (1 - .34) = 5.94\%$$

if we assume that the company is able to take advantage of the interest deduction. An incremental tax rate of 34 percent was used. In addition, we'll assume that the bond had been sold at a price that nets the company its par value (face value). The stated annual interest rate (coupon rate) of a bond is based on the par value, that is, 100 percent of the principal due at a specified future date—regardless of the actual proceeds received by the issuing company. These proceeds often vary because marketable debt securities are generally sold at the best possible price obtainable in the market through underwriters who take some or all of the risk of marketing the issue for a small percentage of the gross receipts. Legal and registration expenses also are borne by the company. Therefore, depending on the issue price, which is related to prevailing interest yields and the quality of the company's credit rating, the company might actually receive net proceeds at a discount (below par value), or it might receive a small premium over par.

In either case, the specific cost has to be adjusted to take the actual proceeds into account. The effect is similar to the short-term loan discussed earlier, on which the interest was due in advance and which therefore entailed a specific cost somewhat higher than the stated rate. If we assume that instead of 100 percent of par value, the company received 95 percent for its debentures after all expenses and commissions, the effective after-tax cost with a 9 percent coupon rate is as follows:

$$0.09 \,(1 - .34) \times \frac{1}{.95} = 6.25\%$$

Apart from the specific cost of interest, long-term debt also again involves repayment of the principal. There are many types of repayment provisions, generally structured to fit the nature of the company and the type of risks the debt holder visualizes. Periodic repayment requirements can be met through a sinking fund set aside for that purpose and held in trust by a depository institution. Partial or full principal payments due at the end of the lending period are called balloon payments.

The basic point to remember is that debt instruments, even if long-term, must in some form and at some time be repaid, or at least rolled over into new debt. The cost of this repayment is implicit in the need to carefully plan future cash flows, and also to consider the ability to achieve future refinancing if the funds needs are likely to continue or even grow. Recall the discussion in Chapter 5 of funds projections.

Another implicit cost of long-term debt involves the nature and degree of restrictions normally embodied in the debt agreement (indenture). Such provisions can limit management's ability to use other forms of credit (e.g., leasing), they might specify minimum levels of some financial ratios (e.g., working capital proportions or debt burden coverage), or they might limit the amount of dividends that can be paid to shareholders. At times, specific assets might have to be pledged as security. Any set of such provisions carries an implicit cost in that it limits management's freedom of choice in making decisions. The greater the perceived risk of the indebtedness, the greater the restrictions are likely to be. One of the effects can be a reduction in the ability to grow through new investment, which can lead to lost opportunities from a market and strategic standpoint. Profitable growth depends, of course, on appropriate funding policies and options, as we discussed in the sustainable growth discussion of Chapter 6.

The rationale for debt restrictions was presented in the discussion of financial ratios from the point of view of lenders (Chapter 4). Not to be overlooked is the introduction of financial leverage into the capital structure, as discussed in Chapter 6. The implicit cost of this condition again depends on the degree of risk exposure caused by specific company and industry conditions.

Cost of Shareholders' Equity

Preferred Stock

This form of equity ownership is conceptually at the midway point between debt and common stock. Although subordinated to the various creditors of the corporation, the preferred shareholder has a claim on corporate earnings that ranks ahead of the common shareholders' position up to the amount of the stated preferred dividend. In liquidation, the preferred shareholders' claims are satisfied prior to the residual claims of the holders of common stock.

The specific cost of preferred stock is normally higher than that of debt with a similar quality rating. Because of the near-equity status of preferred stock, preferred dividends as of this writing are not tax deductible for the issuing corporation and are therefore an outflow of after-tax funds. For instance, an 11 percent preferred stock, issued at par (net of expenses), costs the corporation 11 percent after taxes. For each dollar of dividends to be paid on this preferred stock, the corporation must therefore earn, before taxes:

$$\$1.00 \times \frac{1}{1 - .34} = \$1.52$$

as compared to $1 for every dollar of interest paid on a long-term debt obligation. Where the 9 percent bond in the previous section had an after-tax cost of 5.94 percent, the 11 percent preferred stock has an after-tax cost of 11 percent. The stated dividend rate of a preferred stock therefore is directly comparable to the tax-adjusted interest rate of a bond.

We can easily compare the cost to the company of long-term debt and preferred stock if we assume that they were issued at prices that result in proceeds exactly equal to the par (face) value. When proceeds do not equal par value, as often happens because of market conditions, the cost must be based on the proceeds to obtain the effective cost as discussed above.

The additional implicit cost of preferred stock lies in the fact that it is a security senior to common stock, and the dividend claims of its holders rank ahead of common dividends. In addition, the essentially fixed nature of preferred dividends (they can be omitted only under serious circumstances) introduces a degree of financial leverage with varying earnings levels. Preferred stock being closer in concept to owners' equity than to debt, however, makes the implicit costs of its encumbrances far less serious than those of debt.

Common Equity

The holder of common shares is the residual owner of the corporation, with a claim extending to all assets and earnings not subject to prior claims. Common shareholders provide long-term funds with the expectation of being rewarded with both dividends and an increase in the economic value of their shares. This value accretion consists of the combined impact of (it is hoped) growing earnings and growing dividends on the market value of the shares. In turn, the market value is impacted by general economic conditions and by risks specific to the industry and to the individual company. We have already referred to the concept of total shareholder return (TSR) as an expression of this dual expectation of dividends and share price appreciation. In other words, in the case of common stock, we are dealing with more variables, while contractual provisions for compensation, such as coupon interest or the stated preferred dividend rate, are absent. As a result, the specific cost of common equity requires a more complex evaluation than we encountered with either debt or preferred stock.

The cost of common equity has to be viewed in an opportunity framework. The investor has provided funds to the corporation expecting to receive the combined economic return of dividends declared by the board of directors and future appreciation in market value. The investment was made—presumably on a logical basis—because the level and nature of the risk embodied in the company and its business reasonably matched the investor's own risk preference. In addition, the investor's expectations about earnings, dividends, and market appreciation were considered satisfactory.

The investor made this choice, however, by forgoing other investment opportunities. Moreover, the commitment was made under a condition of uncertainty about future results, because the only hard data available to any investor are past performance statistics. Therefore, measuring the cost of the shareholders' funds to the corporation is a challenge that must address investor expectations about the risk/reward trade-off executed by investing in this opportunity. In other words, the company must strive to compensate the shareholder with an economic return implicit in its past performance but most importantly in its future outlook, and relative to the potential returns from peer companies and from the stock market as a whole.

Several approaches to measuring the cost of common equity are used in practice; all involve many assumptions and quite a bit of judgment. The greatest difficulty lies in finding a specific linkage with the collective risk/reward judgments continuously made in the security markets, judgments that drive the market value of the common shares. We'll discuss two major methods:

1. The dividend approach.

2. The risk assessment approach based on the capital asset pricing model (CAPM).

The dividend approach is fairly straightforward; in effect it directly values expected future streams of dividends. But it is limited by highly simplifying assumptions. The risk assessment method, in contrast, approximates shareholder return expectations by adding to a "normalized" rate of return on securities in general a calculated numerical risk premium that is company-specific. As we'll see, it's the only approach that arrives at an economic return for the specific security relative to average yields experienced in the securities markets.

Dividend Approach to Cost of Common Equity
A way of dealing with at least one of the measurable benefits obtained by the shareholder is to use annual dividends to estimate the cost of common equity. This

is a cash flow method that parallels the measures for the other forms of capital. Yet the approach suffers from serious oversimplification, because companies vary greatly in their rate of dividend payout, and the method does not specifically address the effect of reinvestment of retained earnings. Remember, common shareholders are the residual owners of all earnings not reserved for other obligations, and dividends paid are usually only a portion of the earnings accruing to common shares.

In its simplest form, the dividend approach is the same as the dividend yield, which we discussed as one of the market indicators in Chapter 2:

$$\text{Cost of common equity} = \frac{\text{Projected dividend per share}}{\text{Current market price per share}}$$

$$k_e = \frac{dps}{P}$$

Introducing estimated growth in dividends into the formula is an improvement that implicitly recognizes the effect of reinvestment on the value received by shareholders. The assumption here is that over time, successful reinvestment of retained earnings will lead to growing earnings and thus growing dividends. The mathematics of the formula allow us simply to add the assumed rate of growth in dividends to the equation shown above. We begin with the dividend yield and add a stable percentage rate of dividend growth (g) to simulate the overall expectations of the shareholders:

$$k_e = \frac{dps}{P} + g$$

The difficulty, however, lies in determining the specific dividend growth rate, which must be based on our best assumptions about future performance, tempered by past experience. Many estimating processes can be used. In Chapter 6, we discussed the concept of sustainable growth, which assumed stable investment, payout, and financing policies. This might yield clues to the growth rate that would be appropriate for the dividend approach, but the process really requires projecting expected future dividend policies as set by the company's directors. If significant changes in dividend policy can be expected, the analyst might want to modify the approach, making a series of year-by-year assumptions and in effect, calculating a composite of future dividend growth patterns from these yearly forecasts.

A word about taxes is necessary here. In the dividend approach, we're dealing with after-tax cash flows from the company's viewpoint. Common dividends, like preferred dividends, are not tax deductible and must be paid out of after-tax earnings. No adjustment is therefore necessary in the result to make it comparable with the after-tax cost of debt and preferred stock.

The shareholder is judging the opportunity to earn an economic return on the same basis. However, interest and dividends are taxable income to the recipient. Because personal tax conditions vary greatly, one more adjustment is necessary from the investor's point of view to assess investment options objectively.

Yet the business analyst cannot perform the calculation for the shareholder without knowledge of the individual's tax status. Consequently, the only working assumption we can make in this context is that most investors are subject to some taxation; we can arrive at financial results that are consistent up to the point at which the individual investor must calculate the personal tax impact.

Risk Assessment Approach to Cost of Common Equity

As we said earlier, the risk assessment method doesn't rely on specific estimates of present and future earnings or dividends. Instead, a normal market return is developed from published data on financial returns and yields, which is adjusted by a company-specific risk premium or discount. The rationale is based on the assumption that a company's cost of equity in terms of shareholder return expectations is related to the relative risk of its common stock. The greater this relative risk, the greater the premium—in the form of an additional economic return over and above a normalized return—that should be expected by an investor. This approach makes intuitive sense and also can be demonstrated statistically.

At any time, the securities markets yield a spread of rates of return ranging from those on essentially risk-free government securities at the low end of the scale (5 to 7 percent), to the sizable returns from highly speculative securities, including high-yield but risky junk bonds (15 to 18 percent or more). The risk/return trade-off inherent in the many classes of security investments is reflected in this spread. Risk is defined as the variability of returns inherent in the type of security, while return is defined as the total economic return obtained from the security, including both interest or dividends and changes in market value.

A number of specific methods have been developed over the years to express the risk premium concept of return on common equity—which reflects the cost of common equity to the corporation—as a methodology both theoretically acceptable and practically usable. While no individual method is totally satisfactory in these terms, the most widely accepted is the capital asset pricing model (CAPM). We'll discuss some of its salient features here, but the conceptual and theoretical underpinnings are extensive and far beyond the scope of this book. The reader is encouraged to explore the references at the end of the chapter for more extensive treatments of the evolution, theory, and validation of the CAPM.

Three elements are required in applying the capital asset pricing model approach, and each must be estimated carefully:

- Level of return from a risk-free investment.
- Level of return from securities of average risk.
- Expression of relative risk of the company's securities.

The first element is a judgment about the basic return of a security from which all risk has been excluded. The purpose is to find the lowest part of the range of yields currently experienced in the securities markets as the starting point from which to build up the higher, risk-adjusted return specific to the particular common stock. Long-term U.S. government obligations are commonly used as a surrogate for such a risk-free return. The yields on U.S. government obligations are widely quoted and accessible, both for the present and for historical periods. For our purposes, current yields can be used, possibly adjusted for expected changes, such as the inflation outlook during the next several years. Precision is not possible here, and reasonable approximations supported by the analyst's judgment are quite workable.

The second element is an estimate of the return from a comparable type of security of average risk. This is needed because the CAPM approach develops a specific adjustment for the relative riskiness of the particular security as compared to an average or baseline. For our purposes, we can use an estimate of the total expected return for the Standard & Poor's 500 Index, a broad-based measure of the price levels of the common stocks of 500 widely traded companies. Such projections of the total return—a combination of dividends and market appreciation—that is expected from the companies represented in the index are frequently made by security analysts and published in financial services and newsletters (see Appendix II). While the S&P 500 Index provides a broad-based estimate of return, more specific indexes could be chosen. Again, the analyst must exercise judgment in using projections of future economic returns. The main point is to obtain a reasonable approximation of the average return from average investments of the type being evaluated.

The third element required is an expression of relative risk, which is based on the variability of returns of the particular security being analyzed. The definition of risk is very specific in the CAPM approach, and this has caused some controversy. Risk is not defined as total variability of returns, but rather, as the covariance of the particular stock's returns with those of assets of average risk. The assumption here is that an investor does not focus on the total variability of return experienced with each individual security, but rather on how each security affects the variability of the total return from the portfolio held by the investor. Note, however, that significant changes in a company's capital structure will tend to affect the company's relative risk as well as its covariance with the portfolio.

Risk, therefore, is a very relative concept in the CAPM, and its specific definition might not be acceptable to everyone. We'll ignore the arguments for and against this risk definition in our discussion, and concentrate instead on how risk is recognized in the CAPM approach to arrive at a company-specific return. This risk measure, in the form of the covariance of an individual stock's returns with that of the portfolio of stocks of average risk, is called beta (β). It is found by linear regression of past monthly total returns of the particular security against a baseline such as the S&P 500 Index. Services like Value Line list the current β for publicly traded securities as a matter of course.

How are these three elements combined to arrive at an expected return and the company's cost for a particular equity security? As we stated earlier, the CAPM method defines the cost of common equity as the combination of the risk-free return and a risk premium that has been adjusted for the specific company risk.

The CAPM formula is

$$k_e = R_f + \beta(R_m - R_f)$$

where

k_e is the cost of equity capital.
R_f is the risk-free return.
β is the company's covariance of returns against the portfolio
R_m is the average return on common stocks.

The company's β is expressed as a simple factor that is used to multiply the difference between the expected return on the average portfolio and the expected risk-free return. This difference, of course, equals the risk premium inherent in the portfolio. The β factor adjusts this average risk premium to reflect the individual stock's higher or lower relative riskiness. β goes above 1.0 as the relative risk of the stock exceeds the average, and drops below 1.0 when the relative risk is less than average.

The calculation itself is quite simple, while deriving the inputs is not, as we've already observed. To illustrate, let's arbitrarily choose a risk-free rate of return of 6.5 percent, an S&P 500 return estimate of 11.5 percent, and a company with a fairly "risky" β of 1.4. The cost of equity in this hypothetical example would be

$$k_e = 6.5 + 1.4(11.5 - 6.5) = 13.5\%$$

composed of the risk-free return of 6.5 percent plus the calculated company-specific risk premium of 7.0 percent, for a total of 13.5 percent.

A large number of issues surface when the CAPM or related measures are used to derive the cost of securities. One of these, already mentioned, is the quality of the estimate of both the risk-free return and the average return on a portfolio of common stocks. While the return on long-term U.S. government securities is a reasonable surrogate for the former, estimating an average portfolio return is fraught with conceptual problems. If β is the sole indicator of relative risk, the nature of the portfolio against which covariance is measured is clearly important. Broad averages such as the S&P 500 might or might not be appropriate under the circumstances. Also, there is the problem of using past data, particularly for variability of returns, in estimating the future relationships that indicate shareholder expectations. Finally, there is the issue of the effect of changes in a company's financial leverage.

Consequently, the results of these calculations, as with most types of financial analysis, should be used with caution and a great deal of commonsense judgment.

Inflation

So far we've been talking about the cost of capital without specific reference to the impact of inflation. We could do this because no adjustment is in fact needed. The risk-free return on a government bond does implicitly allow for the expected level of inflation, inasmuch as expectations about future inflationary conditions affect the yield from such securities. When inflation abates, the yields decline—as occurred dramatically in the mid-1980s and early 1990s. When inflation expectations rise, so do bond yields. The same is true of the yields from other financial instruments.

If no inflation existed, risk-free returns would probably be in the range of 3 to 4 percent, the basic interest rate. In fact, not just the CAPM, but all of the measures of cost of capital we've been discussing include expected inflationary effects in that estimates of future returns take these expectations into account. The spectrum of returns ranging from risk-free bonds to those on speculative securities also is consistent in reflecting the effects of inflation.

To summarize, it should be obvious by now that the cost of common equity, apart from the specific method of calculation, is generally higher than the cost of interest-bearing securities or preferred stocks. As we said at the beginning of this section, the residual claim represented by common shares involves the highest risk/reward trade-off. Thus, returns expected of common shares are higher, which in turn, must translate into the highest cost of capital from the corporation's standpoint. This fact will become even more important when we examine the alternative choices of financing new funds requirements, the subject of the next chapter.

Weighted Cost of Capital

Having determined the specific costs of the various types of capital individually, we now have all the specific cost inputs needed to make some of the funding decisions listed earlier. But because most companies use more than one form of long-term capital in funding investments and operations, and because the mix of sources used for long-term financing can change over time, it's necessary to examine the cost of the company's capital structure as a whole. The result we're looking for is a cost of capital figure that is weighted to reflect the mix of the various capital sources used as a matter of policy. It encompasses the cost of compensating long-term creditors and preferred shareholders in terms of the specific provisions applicable to them, and of rewarding the holders of common stock in terms of the risk-adjusted return they expect.

Several issues have to be resolved in determining an overall corporate cost of capital. The first is generating appropriate costs for the different types of long-term capital employed, which we have already done conceptually. The second is a decision about the weights, or proportions, of each type of capital in the structure to be analyzed. The third is the question of whether to apply market values versus book values of the various categories of capital in arriving at the weighting. It's only then that we can calculate a weighted cost of capital that is meaningful for the intended purpose.

Cost Choices

First to be resolved is the question of whether it is relevant to consider the past costs of existing securities in a company's capital structure, or alternatively, the incremental costs involved in adding newly issued securities. Quite often the debt and preferred stock section of the balance sheet lists a whole array of past issues, many of which carry interest or dividend rates that differ significantly from current experience. Obligations that are 5, 10, or 15 years old likely carry stated costs that are no longer relevant today. Moreover, the various methods of arriving at the cost of common equity were based on future expectations, which are not necessarily consistent with past debt or preferred costs. To solve this dilemma, we must again apply the principle established early in this book: The purpose of the analysis always determines the choice of data and methodology.

Normally, the key purpose of calculating a weighted cost of capital is for use in decisions about new business investments, serving as a standard of return that will adequately compensate all providers of capital. Unless a company undergoes significant restructuring, the funds for new capital commitments are likely to come from current internal cash flow, augmented by new debt, new equity, or both. This is an incremental condition, because the choices for adding new investments are still being made. Consequently, the cost of capital measure most appropriate here is based on the expected incremental costs of the various forms of capital employed by the company. As we already know, past decisions on investments and financing are sunk costs, and not relevant here.

Weighting the Proportions

As already mentioned, we're deriving a weighted cost that reflects the normal proportions of the different types of capital in a company's capital structure. Again, significant issues arise. The current capital structure as reflected on the balance sheet is the result of past management decisions on funding both investments and operations. The question to be asked here is whether the types and proportions of capital in this structure are likely to hold in the future, that is, whether they match the strategic plans of management. The intended capital budget supporting the company's future strategy, particularly when calling for sizable outlays, might indeed cause significant shifts in the long-term financing pattern. Also, management might choose to make gradual modifications to its financial policies which, over time, can cause sizable adjustments in the capital structure. (Recall the discussion in Chapter 6 of the impact of policy changes.)

In other cases, management might well be satisfied with the current proportions of the company's capital structure as a long-term objective. Yet the incremental capital required from time to time is normally raised in blocks limited to one form of security, that is, debt, preferred stock, or common equity. Therefore, in the near term, any one type of capital might be emphasized more than the long-term proportions desired would suggest. Capital must be raised in response to market conditions, and the choice of which type is appropriate at any given point is based on a series of considerations that we'll explore in the next chapter.

The analyst has to resolve the dilemma caused by such divergences with judgment. Given the fact that a company's conditions never remain static in the long run, the choice of capital structure proportions has to be a compromise intended to approximate the conditions relevant for purposes of analysis. Precision becomes secondary to common sense. Current proportions are a good starting point, but should normally be modified by specific assumptions about the future direction of the company's long-term financing. It also might be useful to generate a range of assumptions to bracket the findings, which as we know is a form of sensitivity analysis.

One common way of dealing with the issue of weights is to identify a "target" level of debt versus equity, which management identifies as a longer-term objective, even though near-term fluctuation might occur. This is done to relate the cost of capital to the strategic direction of the company, and also to avoid introducing fluctuations in the cost of capital measure which, after all, is to serve as a long-term gauge for value creation. But even this approach of necessity rests on assumptions and judgments.

Market versus Book Values

The weights to be assigned to different types of capital are going to be clearly different if we choose to apply current market values as contrasted with the stated values on the right-hand side of the balance sheet. Again, we must be guided by the purpose of the analysis to decide which value is relevant. If we're interested in a criterion against which to judge expected returns from future investments, the most common use of the cost of capital, we should use the current market values of the various types of capital of the company, because these values reflect the expectations of both creditors and shareholders. The latter certainly didn't invest in the book value of common equity, which usually differs significantly from the current share value as traded in the market. Further, it is management's obligation to meet the expectations of the shareholders in terms of the future economic value to be created by investments and operations, and to compensate creditors out of future earnings. Stated book values, as we observed before, are static and not responsive to changing performance or values.

The choice of market values also complements the use of incremental funding in that both are expressed in current market terms. The market value of common equity automatically (and implicitly) includes retained earnings as reported on the balance sheet. Although some believe that retained earnings bear no cost, this is a misconception. In fact, retained earnings represent part of the residual claim of the shareholders, even if they are imperfectly valued on the balance sheet because of required accounting conventions.

In this area, there are again conceptual issues and arguments that can be raised for and against market value weights. One of these has to do with a company that is experiencing financing requirements rather different from the historical pattern reflected in its capital structure. There it can be argued that a book value approach might be more suitable. Again, we must leave the in-depth exploration of these concepts to the reader, because they go beyond the scope of this book.

Calculating the Weighted Cost of Capital

Let's now turn to a simplified example of calculating a weighted cost of capital for a hypothetical company. This will allow us to demonstrate the basic mechanics of what we now understand to be a process that involves a great deal of judgment. We'll use the condensed balance sheet of ABC Corporation in Figure 9–2, augmented by some additional data and assumptions.

The company has three types of long-term capital, that is, long-term debt, preferred stock, and common equity. We assume that it could issue new bonds at an effective cost of 8.5 percent, and new preferred stock at an effective cost of 10 percent, based on proceeds from expected pricing in the market and after applicable underwriting and legal expenses. Note that these current costs are below the rates the company has been paying on its long-term capital as stated in the balance sheet, and it would most likely be prudent for management to consider refinancing at currently prevailing lower rates. ABC's common stock is currently trading between $63 and $67, and the most recent earnings per share were $4.72. Dividends per share last year were $2.50. The company's β, as calculated by security analysts, is 1.1, a fairly average risk. We further assume that the estimated risk-free return is 6.5 percent, and the best available forecast for the total return from the S&P 500 is 13 percent.

Overall company prospects are assumed to be satisfactory, and security analysts are forecasting normal growth in earnings at about 8 percent. Given this background, it's possible to calculate a weighted cost of capital. As we proceed, the choices to be made will be highlighted.

The respective costs of the three types of capital employed can be derived as shown on the next page. Note that we are employing the incremental cost of funds in each case, rather than the past costs as reflected in the balance sheet, where outstanding bonds carry a rate of 10 percent and preferred stock a dividend rate of 12 percent. The calculations for each type of capital appear as follows, using the methods discussed earlier:

FIGURE 9–2

ABC CORPORATION
Condensed Balance Sheet
($ thousands)

Assets		Liabilities and Net Worth	
Current assets	$27,500	Current liabilities	$ 9,500
Fixed assets (net)	35,000	Bonds (10%)	12,000
Other assets	1,500	Preferred stock (12%)	6,000
Total assets	$64,000	Common stock (1.0 million shares)	10,000
		Retained earnings	26,500
		Total liabilities and net worth	$64,000

Long-term debt: $k_d = 8.5 \times (1 - .34) = 5.61\%$ after taxes

Preferred stock: $k_p = 10.0\%$ after taxes

Common equity: $k_e = 6.5 + 1.1\,(13.0 - 6.5) = 13.65\%$ after taxes

The cost of debt was based on the effective cost of 8.5 percent and adjusted for taxes, while the effective cost of preferred stock required no tax adjustment. The CAPM was used for the common equity calculation. The CAPM figure of 13.65 percent can be compared to the less satisfactory answer obtained using the dividend approach, which provides an alternative lower result. This is a function of the current dividend rate and the expected dividend growth rate:

$$\text{Common equity: } k_e = \frac{\$2.50}{\$65} + 8.0\% = 11.85\% \text{ after taxes}$$

It's not uncommon to find that the two approaches to determining the cost of equity provide rather different results, as the data and assumptions going into the calculations are not comparable. We already highlighted the most significant issues when we discussed each measure earlier.

The weights to be used in calculating the corporate cost of capital depend both on the relative stability of the current capital structure and the relevance of market values to the results. Let's assume that management is satisfied with the current capital structure as its target level and is likely to raise funds in the same proportions over time. Let's further assume that the existing bonds of the company are currently trading at 117⅝ (a $1,000 bond with a coupon rate of 10 percent is worth a premium price of about $1,176.50, in view of the decline in bond yields), while the existing preferred stock with a $12 dividend rate is trading at 120 because of the decline in preferred yields (each share with a nominal value of $100 is currently worth about $120.00).

As Figure 9–3 shows, the following proportions result when we list both book value and market value for each type of capital. Depending on the way management assesses its future needs, the proportions could remain as shown in the table, or they could be altogether different.

Assuming that no significant change is foreseen, we can calculate the weighted cost of capital for both the market and book value (Figure 9–4). The

---

FIGURE 9–3

Capital Structure of ABC Corporation

	Book Value	Proportion	Market Value	Proportion
Bonds	$12,000	22.0%	$14,118	16.5%
Preferred stock	6,000	11.0	7,200	8.3
Common equity	36,500	67.0	65,000	75.3
Totals	$54,500	100.0%	$86,318	100.0%

FIGURE 9–4

Weighted Cost of Capital for ABC Corporation

	Book Value Weighting			Market Value Weighting		
	Cost	Weight	Composite	Cost	Weight	Composite
Bonds	5.61%	.22	1.23%	5.61%	.164	0.92%
Preferred stock	10.00	.11	1.10	10.00	.083	0.83
Common equity	13.65	.67	9.14	13.65	.753	10.28
Totals		1.00	11.47%		1.000	12.03%

results don't differ materially in this case. Differences would become significant only after more than one percentage point.

Given that all the assumptions and choices needed to make the calculations involved some margin of error, the results should be liberally rounded off in all cases before the measure is used as a decision criterion. We can say that under the stipulated conditions for ABC Corporation, the weighted cost of incremental capital is approximately 11.5 to 12 percent.

If the measure is used to judge the expected return from new investments, it should be viewed as a minimum standard of return from investments with comparable risk characteristics. The weighted cost of capital becomes the discount rate to determine net present values as discussed in Chapter 7. Remember, it represents the boundary between projects that create value and those that destroy value for the shareholders.

Cost of Capital and Return Standards

We've stated all along that the basic purpose of deriving a weighted cost of capital was to find a reasonable criterion for measuring new investments. This amounts to establishing a level of return high enough to compensate all providers of funds according to their expectations. By definition, projects with a positive net present value when their cash flows are discounted at this return standard would create economic value for the shareholders in the form of growing dividends and market appreciation.

However, using the weighted cost of capital for this purpose warrants further discussion. In this section, we'll examine more closely the notion of using the measure as a *cutoff rate,* and then discuss the question of projects in different *risk categories.* We'll also review the problem of the *multibusiness* firm, in which a variety of business risks are combined. Finally, we'll touch on the issue of modified standards using *multiple discount rates.* In all of these areas, a balance has to be found between the theoretically desirable and the practically doable.

Cost of Capital as a Cutoff Rate

In a *single-business company* with fairly definable risk characteristics, the weighted cost of capital as calculated here can serve as a cutoff rate in assessing capital investment projects ranked in declining order of economic desirability. If consistent analytical methods and judgments are applied to projecting the project cash flows, and if the risks inherent in the projects are similar and have been consistently estimated and tested through sensitivity analysis, then acceptance or rejection can be decided with this minimum return standard built into the net present value calculations. We're assuming that the company can finance all of the projects being considered at the same incremental cost of capital and without significantly changing the capital structure.

The weighted cost of capital works well in this idealized condition because the risk premium built into the measure, the proportions of the sources of new funds, and the range of risks embodied in the projects are all consistent with each other as well as the business risk inherent in the company. When some of these conditions change, however, managerial judgment must be exercised to modify the cost of capital and its application.

One common problem, even in the single-business firm, is the real possibility that the amount of potential capital spending will exceed readily available financing to some degree. If the list of projects contains many investments that more than meet the standard, they might be attractive enough for management to modify the company's capital structure to accommodate them—if the management team has the capacity to implement all of them. Then the weighted cost of capital will likely change.

Increasing leverage might introduce additional risk, thus exerting upward pressure on the cost of both debt and equity. A significant increase in the equity base will result in near-term dilution of earnings per share, thus affecting the market value of the stock and possibly the β of the company's common stock as judged by security analysts. While the changes might be manageable, the point is that the process of business investment and the selection of appropriate standards is never a static exercise.

Another practical issue is management's attitude toward taking business risks. Knowing that the analyses underlying business investment projects contain many uncertainties, management might wish to set the cutoff rate arbitrarily higher than the weighted cost of capital. This is done to allow for estimating errors—and even for deliberate bias in the preparation of the estimates, which is not at all uncommon in most organizations where managers compete for funds. There also might be a desire to play it safer in view of the limited reliability of the return standard itself. This adjustment, however, shouldn't be considered a substitute for using the best possible analytical effort and decision analysis tools to sharpen and test the cash flow patterns underlying the investment proposals. As we observed in Chapters 7 and 8, risk and uncertainty are a function of the many variables of an investment, which must be understood, quantified, and subjected to sensitivity analysis before appropriate return standards are applied to expected outcome.

From a conceptual standpoint, using cutoff rates significantly higher than the cost of capital might cause opportunity losses, because potentially worthwhile projects are likely to be rejected. From a practical standpoint, however, it might be prudent to leave a margin for error by adding some points to the cost of capital before using it as a cutoff rate. Of course, it's still possible at any time to reach below such a higher standard if a project has many other strategic or operational advantages that mitigate the effects of its marginal economic performance. But care must be taken to judge the impact of cutoff rates on the behavior of managers both in sponsoring risky projects and in potentially biasing their analyses to fit the higher standard expected. It's possible that over time the risk profile of the company's portfolio could be altered.

Finally, we must reiterate that capital budgeting and project selection are not merely numerical processes. Even in the most tightly focused single-product company, where all levels of management have firsthand knowledge about the intricacies of the business and its competitive setting, the decision process is always a combination of judgments affected by personal preferences, group dynamics, and the pressures of organizational realities.

Risk Categories

By definition, the weighted cost of capital represents a company's unique relative risk and particular capital structure. Yet, in a sense, this is misleading because even in the single-business company, different investment projects do involve different degrees of risk. Normally, a company encounters a variety of classes of investments ranging from replacement of equipment and facilities to expansion in existing markets, and beyond that to ventures into new products or services, or into entirely new markets, as well as into new technology.

The degree of risk inherent in these classes of investments will differ, sometimes materially, even though the products and services involved are within the scope of a single industry with a definable overall risk. Replacement of physical assets to continue serving a proven market where the company holds a strong position is far less risky and permits more reliable estimates of cash flow benefits than entering a new domestic or even international market.

A common way of handling such divergences is to set a higher discount standard for projects that are perceived to be riskier. A hierarchy of minimum rates of return can be established, somewhat arbitrarily, that ranges upward from the weighted cost of capital cutoff point. For example, if the weighted cost of capital is, say, 12 percent, that standard can be applied to ordinary replacements and expansion in markets where the company has a position. A standard of 14 or 15 percent can be applied to entering related markets, while a risky new venture might be measured at a premium standard of even 20 percent or higher.

As we demonstrated earlier in discussing the power of discounting, particularly at the higher rates, the chances of riskier projects being acceptable will be severely tested under such conditions. Yet such a demanding risk/reward trade-off standard might be appropriate if management's risk preferences are quite conservative.

On the other hand, it's often argued—particularly in a single-business company—that the weighted cost of capital implicitly embodies the whole range of risks normally encountered while participating and growing in that business. Consequently, one can even stipulate that the range of discount standards should be grouped around the weighted cost of capital. In effect, this allows the less risky projects to be discounted at a return standard below the weighted cost of capital, while riskier ones would be tested at or above that level. When all projects are combined, the result should be an average return at or above the weighted cost of capital.

This approach would require, however, that the proportions of projects being approved in the various risk classes be carefully monitored to ensure that the overall average will achieve the desired result over time. Otherwise, the company could encounter significant deviations from expected performance. Moreover, we must remember that shareholder value can grow only if investment returns exceed the cost of capital in the long run.

An additional practical issue tends to support raising the return standards for the different classes of capital projects. Every company faces a certain percentage of capital expenditures that yield no definable cash flow benefits. Among these are mandated outlays for environmental protection, investments for improved infrastructure of facilities, and expenditures for office space and equipment.

A strong argument can be made that funds required for these purposes must in fact be economically carried along by the expected cash flow benefits obtained from all other productive investments. By definition, therefore, the total amount of capital invested should provide a return sufficient to meet or exceed the weighted cost of capital. If some part of the capital budget is economically neutral, the returns from the economically positive projects will have to be higher to make up for such "nonproductive" investments. If management chooses to adjust its return standards for this condition, the modification will likely involve a fair degree of judgment about the mix and characteristics of the expected project portfolio.

Our discussion has gone beyond the purely analytical aspects of the subject and we've pointed out many practical issues involved in choosing and using economic measures for business decisions, of which discount standards are only one form. It's important to remember that the actual procedures employed by a company are likely to allow for a fair degree of judgmental override of the quantitative results of any financial analysis. This includes the specific return standards for capital investments, which are likely to be modified from time to time, to assist not only in project-specific economic assessment, but also in shifting the strategic emphasis between classes of investments. Senior management must, of course, continuously monitor and guide the pattern of investments they wish to undertake so that shareholder expectations are met. The pattern of investments suggested by the economic analyses and the return standards can and should be modified to fit the changing strategic direction of a company.

Cost of Capital in Multibusiness Companies

The issues involved in setting appropriate return standards become even more complex when a company has several divisions or subsidiaries engaged in rather different businesses and markets that vary greatly in their risk characteristics. While it's possible to calculate an overall cost of capital for the company with the help of a β that reflects the company's covariance of consolidated returns with the market return, it's far more difficult to derive equivalent cost of capital standards for the individual operating divisions. Most commonly, a multibusiness company has a single capital structure that supplies funds for the various businesses. Therefore, capital cannot be apportioned to the different risk categories on the basis of individual cost of capital standards that employ specific betas and debt ratings. These would be available only if the divisions were autonomous companies whose shares are traded in the securities markets.

The approach often used under such conditions is to estimate a series of surrogate costs of capital based on costs for independent companies that are comparable to the various businesses, if that's at all possible. From this background, a group of individual standards can be developed for the multibusiness company— modified with a great deal of judgment—that are similar to the array of risk categories in a single-business company.

Obviously, the apportionment of capital in a multibusiness setting also is complicated by the practical issue of divisional managements competing for limited funds while having to meet different standards. Corporate management must be very careful first to establish broad allocations of funds to the various operating divisions that match the desired corporate strategic emphasis, after having valued the respective business strategies in an overall portfolio sense. Then projects can be ranked within those individual blocks of allocated funds according to the different discount rates, and decisions can be made to accept or reject specific investments.

A predictable consequence of such an approach, however, is the dilemma of having to refuse specific higher-return (and perhaps higher-risk) opportunities in one division, whose overall allocation is exhausted, in favor of lower-return (and perhaps lower-risk) opportunities in another division. This dilemma has to be resolved by corporate management, who is responsible for developing and monitoring the strategic direction of the total company, including the desired business risk profile of the company's portfolio. The main point to remember is that top management needs to shape the company's overall capital investment portfolio in line with shareholder expectations, so that the sum of the parts can be expected to meet or exceed the corporate weighted cost of capital standard.

As we'll discuss in Chapter 12, the cost of capital also is used to determine whether individual lines of business in a diversified company are contributing to or detracting from shareholder value creation. Here the point is to test past and prospective overall cash flows from each business unit as a whole in relation to a minimum cash flow return standard based on the cost of capital.

Multiple Rate Analysis

One additional technical observation should be made here. Some practitioners argue for applying different discount rates to different portions of the cash flow pattern of a single project when calculating the measures of economic desirability, in order to reflect the relative riskiness of the various elements of the project. In effect, this is one more risk adjustment beyond the risk premium already inherent in a particular discount standard. For example, an investment can be separated into elements that carry a business risk, such as products or services, and elements that carry an investment risk, like land or other resources underlying the former. There are many variations of this approach, although it's not widely used in practice.

It should be apparent that because of the uncertainties inherent in project analysis and the complexities of establishing several standards, multiple rate analysis might not be warranted in most normal business investment situations. At the same time, different standards might indeed be necessary in assessing specialized projects, such as real estate investments, complex leasing proposals, natural resources investments, and other uniquely structured cash flow proposals. Such special conditions can involve financial contracts integral to the projects themselves, or require economic judgments about rather different stages in a given project.

In those cases, it is appropriate to discount portions of project cash flows at rates that reflect their contractual nature, as compared with other portions of the cash flow pattern that are subject to the uncertainties of operating in the business environment. These analytical refinements are too specific to be covered here, but are dealt with in the reference materials listed at the end of the chapter.

Key Issues

The following is a recap of the key issues raised directly or indirectly in this chapter. They are enumerated here to help the reader keep the techniques discussed within the perspective of financial theory and business practice.

1. The specific costs to a company of various types of indebtedness and preferred securities are readily apparent in the tax-adjusted cash obligations incurred, but it's difficult to measure the secondary costs implicit in debt service, credit rating, and market assessment.
2. Determining the cost of equity capital is intricately linked to the risk/reward expectations of the financial markets, because the cost of equity must be expressed in terms of an expected economic return for the shareholders of the company.
3. Simple surrogates for the cost of equity capital, such as earnings and dividend models, suffer both from variability of underlying conditions, which can distort their results, and from conceptual shortcomings.
4. The conceptual link established by modern financial theory between general financial market expectations and the value of an individual

company's equity securities remains an approximation based on a series of simplifying assumptions.

5. The use of a company-specific risk factor (β) to adjust average return expectations is a valid theoretical concept, but both definition and measurement of this factor remain open to disagreement and continue to pose practical problems.

6. The development of a weighted cost of capital raises significant questions regarding not only the elements composing the various costs, but also regarding the weights to be used and the concept of measuring incremental funding.

7. The use of a weighted cost of capital in setting business investment return standards is conceptually useful for projects within a company's normal range of risk, but the measure might need modification for business investments of dissimilar risk.

8. The theory of finance continues to evolve, but as new concepts generated are introduced and refined in the decision-making process, careful linkages to both data sources and the organization have to be established in order to make practical application both understandable and feasible.

9. Objective analytical approaches to business investment assessment are only one important input in the choices management must make. Individual and group attitudes, preferences, and judgments exert significant influences over interpretation and decision processes in the areas of investment, operations, and financing.

10. The precision implied in the calculations of economic measures like cost of capital or net present value must be tempered by the knowledge that the data and assumptions underlying them are potentially subject to a wide range of error.

Summary

In this chapter, we sketched out the rationale for determining the costs of various forms of financing as an input in making different types of financial decisions. We found that the specific cost of debt, both short-term and long-term, was relatively easy to calculate, given the nature of the contracts underlying it in most cases. The same was true for preferred stock. We also found that the fixed nature of the obligations incurred with debt and preferred stock raised a host of secondary considerations that exact an economic cost from the company in terms of debt service and restrictive covenants. Establishing the cost of common equity was particularly challenging because of the residual claim common shareholders have on the company, and because of their risk/reward expectations, which are reflected in the market's valuation of the shares.

After discussing techniques for calculating the respective costs of the three basic types of financing, and pointing out the theoretical and practical caveats, we developed the weighted cost of capital as an input to investment analysis. It was characterized as the dividing line between projects that added value and those that destroyed value for the shareholders. We found that use of the weighted cost of capital as a minimum standard for discounting investment cash flows is affected by the way project and business risks are interpreted within the corporate portfolio, and by the attitudes of corporate decision makers. At the same time, we found the approximate weighted cost of capital to be a conceptually appropriate target around which to build a series of return standards befitting a particular company's range of businesses and the investments and risks connected with them.

Analytical Support

Financial Genome, the commercially available financial analysis and planning software described in Appendix I, has the capability to develop and display the cost of capital of a company in various forms, calculated automatically from appropriate input data as well as databases. (see "Downloads Available" on p. 431)

Selected References

Brealey, Richard, and Stewart Myers. *Principles of Corporate Finance.* 5th ed. Burr Ridge, IL: Irwin/McGraw-Hill, 1996.

Ross, Stephen A.; Randolph W. Westerfield; and Jeffrey Jaffe. *Corporate Finance.* 5th ed. Burr Ridge, IL: Irwin/McGraw-Hill, 1999.

Weston, J. Fred; Scott Besley; and Eugene Brigham. *Essentials of Managerial Finance.* 11th ed. Chicago: Dryden Press, 1997.

CHAPTER 10

ANALYSIS OF FINANCING CHOICES

Let's now turn to analyzing the third aspect of the three-part decisional systems context introduced in Chapter 2: investment, operations, and financing. We'll concentrate on the choices available in arranging a company's long-term financing, while setting aside the incremental operational funds sources used routinely by companies in line with practices in a particular industry or service, and broadly discussed in Chapter 3. We choose this focus because, as we observed earlier, the nature and pattern of long-term funding sources is intricately connected with the types of business investments made and is critical to the growth, stability, or decline of operations. Indeed, management must fund its strategic business design with an appropriate mix of capital sources that will assist in bringing about the desired increase in shareholder value.

This chapter will deal with the key considerations in assessing the basic financing options open to management. While the choice among long-term debt, preferred, and common equity is blurred by a bewildering array of modifications and specialized instruments in each category, we'll discuss only the main characteristics of the three basic types of securities. Because our emphasis is on quantitative analysis, we must keep in mind that many other considerations enter into these choices. For example, the specific type of business and the industry in which it operates will affect the long-term capital structure chosen at various stages of a company's development, as will the preferences and experiences of senior management and the board of directors. These aspects cannot be adequately covered within the scope of this book.

We'll begin with a broad framework for analysis that defines the key areas to be analyzed and weighed in choosing sources of long-term financing. Next, we'll look at the techniques of calculating the impact on a company's financial performance resulting from the introduction of new capital supplied by each of the three basic sources. Then we'll turn to a graphic representation of these results, the range of earnings (EBIT) break-even chart, in order to demonstrate the dynamic impact that funds choices have on changing company conditions. After touching on leasing as a special source, we'll briefly discuss capital structure proportions and list the key issues involved in the area of funds choices.

Framework for Analysis

Several key elements must be considered and weighed when a company is faced with raising additional (incremental) long-term funds. We'll take up the five most important ones in some detail:

- Cost.
- Risk exposure.
- Flexibility.
- Timing.
- Control.

This discussion is intended to serve as a conceptual checklist to ensure that the most important considerations have been covered in the choice of long-term financing.

Cost of Incremental Funds

One of the main criteria for choosing from among alternative sources of additional long-term capital is the cost involved in obtaining and servicing the funds. In Chapter 9, we discussed in detail the specific and implicit costs a company incurs in using debt, preferred stock, or common equity.

As a general rule, we found that funds raised with various forms of debt are least costly in specific terms, in part because the interest paid by the borrowing company is tax deductible under current U.S. laws. The actual rate of interest charged on incremental debt will depend, of course, on the credit rating of the company and on the degree of leverage introduced into the capital structure by the new debt, as discussed in Chapter 6. In other words, the specific cost will be affected not only by current market conditions for all long-term debt instruments, but also as a function of the company-specific risk as perceived by lenders, underwriters, and investors. As we mentioned at the time, other costs are also implicit in raising long-term debt, including legal and underwriting expenses connected with the issue, and the nature and severity of any restrictions imposed by the creditors.

The stated cost of preferred stock is generally higher than debt, partly because preferred dividends are not tax deductible, and partly because preferred stock has a somewhat weaker position on the risk/reward hierarchy. Holders of these shares expect a higher return to compensate for their ownership risk. The comparative specific cost of preferred stock is relatively easy to calculate. The dividend level is clearly defined, and legal and underwriting costs incurred at the time of the issue are reflected in the net proceeds to the company. However, at times a variety of specific provisions can involve implicit costs to the company.

In Chapter 9 we found that determining the cost of common equity turned out to be a fairly complex task. It involved constructing a theoretical framework within which to assess the risk/reward expectations of the shareholder. Direct approaches (shortcuts) to measuring the specific cost of common equity were found wanting because they didn't address the company's relative risk as reflected in common share values. We had to use a more integrated framework involving some surrogates and approximations to arrive at a practical result based on the theoretical model.

The cost of common equity based on the CAPM approach could be directly compared to the specific costs of debt and preferred stock, and it also could be used to arrive at a weighted overall cost of the company's capital structure. As we'll see shortly, however, increasing common equity in the capital structure by issuing new shares involves additional considerations. The incremental shares dilute earnings per share, require additional and even growing dividends where these are paid, and also change the capital structure proportions. These effects introduce implicit economic costs or advantages into the funding picture.

Risk Exposure

If we use variability of earnings as a working definition of risk, we find that a company's risk is affected by the specific cost commitments, such as interest on debt or dividends on preferred shares, that each funding source entails. These commitments introduce financial leverage effects in the company's earnings performance, or will heighten any financial leverage already existing. As we discussed in Chapter 6, the use of instruments involving fixed financial charges will widen the swings in earnings as economic and operating conditions change.

Given the responsibility for providing holders of common shares with growing economic value, management must therefore expend much thought and care in determining the appropriate mix of debt and equity in the company's capital structure. This balance involves providing enough lower-cost debt to boost the shareholders' returns, but not so much debt as to endanger shareholder value creation during periods of low earnings, to arrive at a mix of capital sources carefully tailored to industry and company conditions.

The ultimate risk, of course, is that a company will not be able to fulfill its debt service obligations. The proportion of debt in the capital structure, and similarly, the proportion of preferred stock, affects the degree of risk of partial or total default. Analyzing risk exposure is based on establishing a historical pattern of earnings variability and cash flows from which future conditions are projected. These must take into account the extent to which a company's strategy is changing, any shifts in exposure to the business cycle, shifting competitive pressures, and potential operating inefficiencies.

Clearly, company-specific risk (earnings variability) and the company's ability to service its debt burden are intimately related to the particular characteristics of the business or businesses in which the company operates. Moreover, they're affected by general economic conditions—apart from management's ability to generate satisfactory operating performance.

The degree of financial leverage advisable and prudent will therefore vary greatly among different industries and services, and also will depend on the firm's relative competitive position and maturity stage. A new business entails a far different risk exposure for the creditor than does the established industry leader, apart from specific industry conditions.

Flexibility

The third area we must consider is the question of flexibility, defined here as the range of future funding options that remain open once a specific alternative has been chosen. As each increment of financing is completed, the choice among future alternatives might be more limited during the next round of raising capital. For example, if long-term debt obligations are chosen as a major funding source, the level of total debt in the capital structure, restrictive covenants, encumbered assets, and other constraints that impose minimum financial ratios might mean that the company can use only common equity as a future source of capital for some time ahead.

Flexibility essentially requires forward planning. Careful consideration must be given to matching strategic plans and corporate financial policies. Potential acquisitions, expansion, and diversification all are affected by the degree of flexibility management has in choosing appropriate funding, and by the funds drain resulting from servicing debt commitments or preferred dividends. To the extent possible, management must coordinate its planned future cash flows and investment patterns with the pattern of successive rounds of financing that will support them. Being in a situation where future funds sources are limited to only one option because of present commitments can pose a significant problem. Changing conditions in the financial markets for different types of securities might make this single option unappealing or even unavailable when funds needs become critical.

Timing

The fourth element in choosing long-term funding is the timing of the transaction. Timing is important in relation to the movement of prices and yields in the securities markets. Shifting conditions in these markets affect the specific cost a company incurs with each option, in the form of the stated interest rate on new debt or the preferred dividend rate carried by new preferred stock, as well as in terms of the net proceeds to be received from each of the alternatives. Therefore, the timing of the issue will affect the cost spread between the several funding alternatives available. Also, specific market conditions might in fact either preclude or distinctly favor particular choices.

For instance, in times of depressed stock prices, bonds might prove to be the most suitable alternative from the standpoint of both cost and market demand. Inasmuch as the proceeds from any issue depend on the success of the placement—public or private—of the securities, the conditions encountered in the stock or bond markets can seriously affect the choice. Potential uncertainty in financial markets is therefore a strong argument for always maintaining some degree of flexibility in the capital structure.

Control

Finally, the degree of ownership control of the company held by existing shareholders is an important factor as funding choices are considered. Obviously, when new shares of common stock are issued to new shareholders, the effect is a dilution of both earnings per share and the proportion of ownership of the existing shareholders. Such dilution becomes a significant issue for the owners of companies that could be subject to potential takeovers. In the past decade, the issue of control has been raised to new heights in the many battles over control during the corporate merger and acquisition boom.

Even if debt or preferred stock is used as the source of long-term funding, existing shareholders can be affected indirectly because restrictive provisions and covenants might be necessary to obtain bond financing, or because concessions must be made to protect the rights of the more senior preferred shareholders.

Dilution of ownership is a very important issue in closely held corporations, particularly new ventures. In such situations, founders of the company or the major shareholders might exercise full effective control over the company. Issuing new shares will dilute both control over the direction of the company and the key shareholders' ability to enjoy the major share of economic value growth from successful performance. Dilution of earnings and possible retardation of growth in earnings per share brought about by diluting common equity ownership is, of course, not limited to closely held companies. Rather, it's a general phenomenon that we'll discuss shortly.

Finally, dilution of control and earnings is a major consideration in convertibility, a feature found in certain bonds and preferred stocks. This provision allows conversion of the security into common stock under specified conditions of timing and price. In effect, such instruments are hybrid securities, as they represent delayed issues of common stock at a price higher than the market value of the common stock at the time the convertible bond or preferred stock is issued. We mentioned this feature in earlier chapters in terms of its effect on financial ratios, particularly when discussing the concept of diluted earnings per share, and we'll return to it later in this chapter.

Control becomes an issue in convertible financing options because the eventual conversion of the bond or preferred stock will add new common shares to the capital structure and thus cause dilution. The ultimate effect is just like a direct issue of new common stock.

The Choice

It should be clear from this brief résumé of the considerations involved that any decision about alternative sources of long-term funding can't be based on cost alone, even though cost is a very important factor and must be analyzed early in the decision-making process. Unfortunately, there are no hard-and-fast rules spelling out precisely how the final decision should be made, because the choice depends so much on the conditions prevailing in the company and in the securities markets at the time, and on the preferences of the board and senior management. The best approach is to consider carefully the five areas we've presented above and to examine the pros and cons of each as an input to the decision. Needless to say, one very significant consideration is the effect of each funding source on a company's future earnings performance. In the section that follows, we'll examine methods of calculating this effect.

Techniques of Calculation

For purposes of illustration, we'll employ the basic statements of a hypothetical company, ABC Corporation. The company is weighing alternative ways of raising $10 million to support the introduction of a new product. After analyzing the corporation's current performance, we'll successively discuss the impact on that performance level caused by introducing long-term debt, preferred stock, and common equity, in equal amounts of $10 million each. We'll focus on the implications of financing alternatives on the company's reported earnings, but will also test the cash flow implications of the choices to be made.

ABC's abbreviated balance sheet is shown in Figure 10–1. The company currently has 1 million shares of common stock outstanding, with a par value of $10 per share. From the company's income statement (not shown), we learn that

---

FIGURE 10–1

ABC CORPORATION
Balance Sheet
($ millions)

Assets		Liabilities and Net Worth	
Current assets	$15	Current liabilities	$ 7
Fixed assets (net)	29	Common stock.	10
Other assets	1	Retained earning	28
Total assets	$45	Total liabilities and net worth	$45

ABC Corporation has earned $9 million before taxes on sales of $115 million in the most recent year. Income taxes paid amounted to $3.06 million, an effective rate of 34 percent.

Current Performance

We begin our appraisal of the current performance of ABC Corporation by calculating the earnings per share (EPS) of common stock. Throughout the chapter, this format of calculating EPS and related measures will be used. It's a step-by-step analysis of the earnings impact of each type of long-term capital.

   First, we'll establish the earnings before interest and taxes (EBIT), a measure we discussed in Chapter 4. From that figure we must subtract a variety of charges applicable to different long-term funds. The first of these is interest charges on long-term debt. Normally short-term interest can be ignored unless it's a significant amount, because we assume—given the temporary nature of short-term obligations that arise from ongoing operations—that the related interest charges have been properly deducted from income before arriving at the EBIT figure.

   The calculations of earnings per share are shown in Figure 10–2. A provision is made in the table for both long-term interest and preferred dividends. No amounts are shown for these, however, because our hypothetical company at this point has neither long-term debt nor preferred stock outstanding. The calculations result in earnings available to common stock of $5.94 per share. From that figure we must subtract $2.50, which represents a cash dividend voted by the board of directors. We find that this fairly high level of dividend payout (between 40 and 50 percent of earnings) has been maintained for many years, impacting ABC's

FIGURE 10–2	
ABC CORPORATION	
Earnings per Share Calculation	
($000, except per share figures)	
Earnings before interest and taxes (EBIT)........................	$9,000
Less: interest charges on long-term debt........................	-0-
Earnings before income taxes...................................	9,000
Less: Income taxes at 34%....................................	3,060
Earnings after income taxes...................................	5,940
Less: Preferred dividends	-0-
Earnings available for common stock	$5,940
Common shares outstanding (number)...........................	1 million
Earnings per share (EPS)	$5.94
Less: Common dividends per share.............................	2.50
Retained earnings per share	$3.44
Retained earnings in total	$3,440

financing flexibility somewhat. The company's earnings have steadily grown by about 4 percent on average over the past decade. The stock is widely held and traded, and currently commands a market price ranging from about $38 to $47, which means it's trading at roughly seven to eight times earnings. The latest security analyst's report suggests a β of 0.9, while the risk-free rate of return is judged to be 6.5 percent, and the expected stock market return from the S&P 500 is forecast at 14.0 percent.

Long-Term Debt in the Capital Structure

As debt is introduced into this structure, both the financial condition and the earnings performance of ABC Corporation are significantly affected. To raise the $10 million needed to fund the new product, management has found that it's possible, as one alternative, to issue debenture bonds. Debentures are not secured by any specific assets of the company; instead they're issued against the company's general credit standing. These bonds, under assumed market conditions, will carry an interest (coupon) rate of 11.5 percent, will become due 20 years from date of issue, and will entail a sinking fund provision of $400,000 per year beginning with the fifth year. The balance outstanding at the end of 20 years will be repaid as a balloon payment of $4 million. The company expects to raise the full $10 million from the bond issue after all underwriting expenses, in effect receiving the par value.

Once the new product financed with the proceeds has been successfully introduced, the company projects incremental earnings of at least $2.0 million before taxes. Little risk of product obsolescence or major competitive inroads is expected by management for the next 5 to 10 years, because the company has developed a unique process protected by careful patent coverage.

We can now trace the impact of long-term debt on the company's performance, observing both the change in earnings and dividends, and the specific cost of the newly created debt itself. (A fairly high interest rate and preferred dividend were chosen for this illustration to make the impact of the choices more visible in the graphic analysis shown later.) We'll analyze two contrasting conditions:

- The immediate impact of the $10 million debt without any offsetting benefits from the new product.
- The improved conditions expected once the investment has become operative and the new product has begun to generate earnings, probably after one year.

The results of the two calculations are shown in Figure 10–3. The instantaneous effect of adding debt is a reduction of the earnings available for common stock. This is caused by the stated interest cost of 11.5 percent on $10 million of bonds, or $1,150,000 before taxes. Earnings after interest and taxes drop by $759,000 as compared to the initial conditions in Figure 10–2. This earnings

FIGURE   10–3

ABC CORPORATION
Earnings per Share with New Bond Issue
($ thousands, except per share figures)

	Before New Product	With New Product
Earnings before interest and taxes (EBIT)	$ 9,000	$ 11,000
Less: Interest charges on long-term debt	1,150	1,150
Earnings before income taxes	7,850	9,850
Less: Income taxes at 34%	2,669	3,349
Earnings after income taxes	5,181	6,501
Less: Preferred dividends	-0-	-0-
Earnings available for common stock	$ 5,181	$ 6,501
Common shares outstanding (number)	1 million	1 million
Earnings per share (EPS)	$ 5.18	$ 6.50
Less: Common dividends per share	2.50	2.50
Retained earnings per share	$ 2.68	$ 4.00
Retained earnings in total	$ 2,681	$ 4,001
Original EPS (Figure 9–2)	$ 5.94	$ 5.94
Change in EPS	−0.76	+0.56
Percent change in EPS	−12.8%	+9.4%

reduction represents, of course, the after-tax cost of the bond interest, or $1,150,000 times $(1 - .34)$.

As a consequence, earnings per share decline to $5.18, a drop of 76 cents, or an immediate dilution of 12.8 percent from the prior level. This change is purely due to the incremental interest cost, which on a per share basis amounts to the same 76 cents, that is, the after-tax interest of $759,000 divided by one million shares. In Chapter 8 we discussed the stated annual cost of debt funds, defined as the tax-adjusted rate of interest carried by the debt instrument. Assuming an effective tax rate of 34 percent in our example, the stated cost of debt for ABC Corporation is therefore 7.59 percent. We also explained in Chapter 9 that the specific annual cost of debt is found by relating the stated annual cost to the actual proceeds received. If these proceeds differ from the par value of the debt instrument, the specific annual cost of the debt will, of course, be higher or lower than the stated rate.

In the case of ABC Corporation, we assumed that net proceeds were effectively at par, and therefore the specific cost of ABC's new debt is also 7.59 percent, a figure which we'll compare with the specific cost of the other alternatives for raising capital.

When we turn to the second column of Figure 10–3, we find that the assumed successful introduction of the new product will more than compensate ABC Company for the earnings impact of the interest paid on the bonds. In other words, the investment project is earning more than the specific cost of the debt employed to fund it. After-tax earnings have risen to $6,501,000, a net increase of $561,000 over the original $5,940,000 in Figure 10–2. As a consequence, earnings per share rose 56 cents above the original $5.94, an increase of almost 10 percent.

By more than offsetting the total after-tax interest cost of the debentures of $759,000, the successfully implemented new investment is projected to boost the common shares' earnings. Incremental earnings of $1,320,000 ($2 million pretax earnings less tax at 34 percent) significantly exceed the incremental cost of $759,000. Therefore, the investment—if ABC's earnings assumptions prove realistic—has made possible an increment of economic value. In effect, the financial leverage introduced with the debt alternative is positive.

Yet, several questions might be asked. For example, suppose the investment earned just $759,000 after taxes, exactly covering the cost of the debt supporting it and maintaining the shareholders' position just as before in terms of earnings per share. Would the investment still be justified? Would this mean that the investment was made at no cost to the shareholders?

At first glance, one might believe this, but a number of issues must be considered here. First of all, no mention has been made of the sinking fund obligations which will begin five years hence and which represent a cash outlay of $400,000 per year. Such principal payments are not tax deductible and must be paid out of the after-tax cash flow generated by the company. Thus, debt service (burden coverage) will require 40 cents per share over and above the interest cost of 76 cents per share, for a total of $1.16 per share. The $400,000 will no longer be available for dividends or other corporate purposes, because it is committed to the repayment of debt principal. If we suppose that earnings from the investment exactly equaled the interest cost of the debt, how would the company repay the principal? At what point are the shareholders better off than they were before?

There's an obvious fallacy in this line of discussion. It stems from the use of accounting earnings to represent the benefits of the project and comparing these to the after-tax cost of the debt capital used to finance it. This isn't a proper economic comparison, as we pointed out in Chapters 8 and 9. Only a discounted cash flow analysis can determine the true economic cost/benefit trade-off. We could say that the project was exactly yielding the specific cost of the debt capital associated with it only if the net present value of the project was exactly zero when we discount the incremental annual cash flows at 7.59 percent.

This result would then represent an internal rate of return of 7.59 percent, a level of economic performance that would scarcely be acceptable to management. Yet even under that limited condition, the project's cash flows (as contrasted to the accounting profit recorded in the operating statement) would have to be higher than the $759,000 after-tax earnings required to pay only the interest on the bonds. This must be so because under the present value framework of investment analysis, the incremental cash flows associated with a project must not only provide the specified return but also amortize the investment itself, as we saw in Chapters 7 and 8.

Let's now return to the real purpose of this analytical framework. Our analysis isn't designed to judge the desirability of the investment; we must assume that this has been adequately done by management. Instead, we're interested only in which alternative form for financing the approved investment is most advantageous for the company under the specific circumstances presented. In this context, the impact of each alternative on the company's earnings is one of several aspects considered when deciding on new funding.

In the case of debt, which under normal conditions is the lowest-cost alternative, we would indeed expect a financial leverage effect in favor of the shareholder. When the project was chosen, it must have met a return standard based approximately on the weighted cost of capital—a return which is far higher than the cost of debt capital alone. In summary, the introduction of debt immediately dilutes earnings per share, but this impact is followed by a boost in earnings per share when the project's reported accounting earnings exceed the interest cost as reflected in the company's income statement. Also, the company must allow for the future sinking fund payments from a cash flow planning standpoint, because beginning with the fifth year, 40 cents per share of the company's cash flow will be committed annually to repayment of principal.

It's generally useful to examine the implications of these facts under a variety of conditions, that is, the risk posed by earnings fluctuations in both the basic business and in the new products' incremental profit contribution, which all along we've assumed to be successful. We'll take such variations into account later.

Preferred Stock in the Capital Structure

ABC Corporation could also meet its long-term financing needs with an alternative issue of $10 million of preferred stock, at $100 per share, which carries a stated dividend rate of 12.5 percent. For simplicity, we'll again assume that the net proceeds to the company will be equivalent to the nominal price of $100, after legal and underwriting expenses. Figure 10–4 analyzes the conditions before and after implementation of the new product investment.

This time we find a more severe drop in the earnings available for common stock, due to the impact of the preferred dividends of $1.25 million per year. Not only is the stated cost (as well as the specific cost, given that the net proceeds were again at par) of the new preferred stock higher by one full percentage point than the stated cost of the bonds, but also the dividends paid on the preferred stock are not tax deductible under current laws. In fact, we're dealing with an alternative which costs, in comparable terms, 12.5 percent after taxes versus 7.59 percent after taxes for the bonds.

Therefore, the immediate dilution in earnings with the preferred issue is $1.25 per share, or 21 percent, when compared to the initial situation. Over time, as the earnings from the new product are realized, the eventual increase in earnings per share amounts to only 7 cents, or a slight improvement of 1.2 percent.

FIGURE 10–4

ABC CORPORATION
Earnings per Share with New Preferred Stock Issue
($000, except per share figures)

	Before New Product	With New Product
Earnings before interest and taxes (EBIT)..........	$9,000	$11,000
Less: Interest charges on long-term debt	-0-	-0-
Earnings before income taxes...................	9,000	11,000
Less: Income taxes at 34%	3,060	3,740
Earnings after income taxes	5,940	7,260
Less: Preferred dividends	1,250	1,250
Earnings available for common stock	$4,690	$ 6,010
Common shares outstanding (number)............	1 million	1 million
Earnings per share (EPS)	$4.69	$ 6.01
Less: Common dividends per share	2.50	2.50
Retained earnings per share....................	$ 2.19	$ 3.51
Retained earnings in total	$2,190	$ 3,510
Original EPS (Figure 9–2)	$ 5.94	$ 5.94
Change in EPS	−1.25	+0.07
Percent change in EPS	−21.0%	+1.2%

The $1.25 million annual commitment of after-tax funds for dividends leaves very little room for any net gain in reported profit from the earnings generated by the investment—which we know are estimated as $2.0 million before taxes and $1,320,000 after taxes.

In this situation, the assumed conditions allow for very limited financial leverage. Only little more than a 1 percent rise in earnings per share is achieved over the starting level, whereas the fixed after-tax financing costs have nearly doubled when compared to the bond alternative. Earnings per share would be unchanged if the product were to achieve minimum earnings in the amount of the pretax cost of preferred dividends:

$$\frac{\$1,250,000}{(1-.34)} = \$1,894,000$$

At that level, the incremental earnings from the new product would just offset the incremental financing cost—a break-even situation. Note that the sizable earnings requirement of almost $1.9 million is two-thirds larger than the $1,150,000 pretax interest cost with the bond alternative.

Common Stock in the Capital Structure

A new issue of common stock as the third alternative for raising $10 million has an even more severe impact on earnings. Let's assume that ABC Corporation will issue 275,000 new shares at a net price to the company of $36.36 after underwrit-

FIGURE   10–5

ABC CORPORATION
Earnings per Share with New Common Stock Issue
($000, except per share figures)

	Before New Product	With New Product
Earnings before interest and taxes (EBIT)	$9,000	$11,000
Less: Interest charges on long-term debt	-0-	-0-
Earnings before income taxes	9,000	11,000
Less: Federal income taxes at 34%	3,060	3,740
Earnings after income taxes	5,940	7,260
Less: Preferred dividends	-0-	-0-
Earnings available for common stock	$5,940	$7,260
Common shares outstanding (number)	1.275 million	1.275 million
Earnings per share (EPS)	$ 4.66	$ 5.69
Less: Common dividends per share	2.50	2.50
Retained earnings per share	$ 2.16	$ 3.19
Retained earnings in total	$2,752	$4,072
Original EPS (Figure 9–2)	$5.94	$ 5.94
Change in EPS	−1.28	−0.25
Percent change in EPS	−21.5%	−4.2%

ers' fees and legal expenses are met. Such a discount from the current market price of $40 should help ensure successful placement of the issue. The number of shares outstanding thus increases by 27.5 percent over the current 1.0 million shares. Figure 10–5 shows the impact on earnings in the same way as was done for the other two alternatives.

We observe that immediate dilution is a full $1.28 per share, a drop of 21.5 percent, which is the highest impact of the three choices analyzed. Common stock, in terms of this comparison, is the costliest form of capital—if only because it results in the greatest immediate dilution in the earnings of current shareholders.

Moreover, there also will be an annual cash drain of at least $687,500 in after-tax earnings from the 275,000 new shares, if the current $2.50 annual dividend on common stock is maintained. Further, we can project that this cash drain could grow at the historical earnings growth rate of 4 percent per year. This assumption will hold if the directors continue their policy of declaring regular cash dividends at a fairly constant payout rate from future earnings that continue growing. For the present, the pretax earnings required to cover the $2.50 per share dividend amount to:

$$\$2.50 \times 275,000 \text{ shares} = \$687,500 \text{ (after taxes)}$$

$$\frac{\$687,500}{(1 - .34)} = \$1,042,000 \text{ (before taxes)}$$

We can directly compare this earnings requirement of about $1.05 million to the alternative bond requirement of $1.15 million and the preferred stock requirement of $1.90 million. From both an earnings and a cash-planning standpoint, these amounts and the differences between them are clearly significant.

The effect of immediate dilution of earnings is only part of the consideration. There will be the second-stage effect of continuing dilution, because in contrast to the other two types of capital, the new common shares created represent an ongoing residual claim on corporate earnings on a par with that of the existing shares. Thus, the rate of growth in earnings per share experienced to date will be slowed in the future, merely because more shares will be outstanding—unless, of course, the earnings provided by the investment of the proceeds are superior in level and potential growth to the existing earnings performance.

When we turn to the second column of Figure 10–5, it's apparent that despite the incremental earnings from the new product, a net dilution of earnings per share in the amount of 25 cents, or 4.2 percent, will in fact continue. The contribution of the new product to reported earnings wasn't sufficient to meet the earnings claims of the new shareholders and maintain the old per share earnings level. The negative impact on earnings of the common stock alternative thus is greater than the earnings generated by the new capital raised.

Up to this point, we've dealt with the earnings impact of common stock financing. To find a first rough approximation of the specific cost of this alternative, we can establish as a minimum condition the maintenance of the old earnings per share level, and relate this to the proceeds from each new share of common stock. The current EPS of $5.94 (Figure 10–2) and the proceeds of $36.36 result in a cost of about 16 percent.

$$\frac{\$5.94}{\$36.36} = 16.34\% \text{ (after taxes)}$$

Recall from the discussion in Chapter 9, however, that using accounting earnings in measuring the cost of common equity is not appropriate. If we employ the dividend approach to find the specific cost of the incremental common stock, as discussed in Chapter 8, we must relate the current dividend per share to the net price received, and add prospective dividend growth. We know that the company has experienced fairly consistent growth in earnings of 4 percent per year, and we'll assume that, given a constant rate of dividend payout, common dividends will continue to grow at the same rate. The result is a cost of about 11 percent:

$$\frac{\$2.50}{\$36.36} + 4.0\% = 10.9\%$$

As we stated in Chapter 8, however, the dividend approach is limited in concept and usefulness. Therefore, let's now use the background data provided to test the specific cost of capital for ABC's common equity with the CAPM approach explained in Chapter 9.

The resulting cost of common equity, k_e, is approximately 13.25 percent when we put into the CAPM formula the risk-free return R_f of 6.5 percent, the β of 0.9, and the expected average return R_m represented by the S&P 500 estimate of 14 percent:

$$k_e = R_f + \beta \, (R_m - R_f)$$
$$k_e = 6.5 + 0.9 \, (14.0 - 6.5)$$
$$= 13.25\%$$

This result is the most credible one for judging the specific cost of the common stock. It can be compared to the specific cost of the bonds of 7.59 percent, and that of the preferred stock of 12.5 percent.

Clearly, the common equity alternative is the most expensive source of financing, and we have already established that the dilution effect is also serious. In addition, the cash flow requirements for paying the current dividend of $2.50 per share plus any future increases in the common dividend have to be planned for. Because it's difficult to keep all of these quantitative aspects visible in our deliberations, let's turn to a graphic representation of the various earnings and dilution effects to compare the relative position of the three alternatives.

Range of Earnings Chart

We've referred several times to changes in the earnings performance of the company and the different impact the three basic financing alternatives have under varying conditions. The static format of analysis we've used so far doesn't readily allow us to explore the range of possibilities as earnings change, or to visualize the sensitivity of the alternative funding sources to these changes. It would be quite laborious to calculate earnings per share and other data for a great number of earnings levels and assumptions. Instead, we can exploit the direct linear relationships that exist between the quantitative factors analyzed.

A graphic break-even approach can be used to compare the earnings impact of alternative sources of financing. In this section, we'll show how such a model, keyed to fluctuations in EBIT and resulting EPS levels, can be employed to display important quantitative aspects of the relative desirability of the choices available. As we'll see, the break-even model allows us to perform a variety of analytical tests with ease.

To begin with, we've summarized the data for ABC Corporation in Figure 10–6. Variations in these data can then be displayed graphically in a simple break-even chart which shows earnings per share (EPS) on the vertical axis and EBIT on the horizontal axis. This EBIT chart allows us to plot on straight lines the EPS for each alternative under varying conditions, and to find the break-even points between them.

Commonly, one of the reference points is the intersection of each line with the horizontal axis, that is, the exact spot where EPS is zero. These points can be found easily by working the EPS calculations backward, that is, starting with an

FIGURE 10-6

ABC CORPORATION
Recap of EPS Analyses with New Product
($ thousands, except per share figures)

	Original	Debt	Preferred	Common
EBIT	$9,000	$11,000	$11,000	$11,000
Less: Interest.	-0-	1,150	-0-	-0-
Earnings before taxes	9,000	9,850	11,000	11,000
Less: Taxes at 34%	3,060	3,349	3,740	3,740
Earnings after taxes	5,940	6,501	7,260	7,260
Less: Preferred dividends . . .	-0-	-0-	1,250	-0-
Earnings available for common stock	$5,940	$6,501	$6,010	$ 7,260
Common shares outstanding (number)	1 million	1 million	1 million	1.275 million
Earnings per share (EPS)	$5.94	$6.50	$6.01	$ 5.69
Less: Common dividends per share	2.50	2.50	2.50	2.50
Retained earnings per share . . .	$3.44	$4.00	$3.51	$3.19
Retained earnings in total	$3,440	$4,001	$3,510	$ 4,072
Change from original EPS		−12.8%	−21.0%	−21.5%
Final change in EPS		+9.4%	+1.2%	−4.2%
Specific cost		7.59%	12.5%	13.25%

assumed EPS of zero and deriving an EBIT that just provides for this condition. The calculation is shown in Figure 10–7 for the original situation and for each of the three alternatives. The data in Figures 10–6 and 10–7 give us sufficient points with which to draw the linear functions of EPS and EBIT for the various alternatives, as shown in Figure 10–8.

FIGURE 10-7

ABC CORPORATION
Zero EPS Calculation
($ thousands, except per share figures)

	Original	Debt	Preferred	Common
EPS	-0-	-0-	-0-	-0-
Common shares	1 million	1 million	1 million	1.275 million
Earnings to common	-0-	-0-	-0-	-0-
Preferred dividends	-0-	-0-	$1,250	-0-
Earnings after taxes	-0-	-0-	1,250	-0-
Taxes at 34%	-0-	-0-	644	-0-
Earnings before taxes	-0-	-0-	1,894	-0-
Interest	-0-	$1,150	-0-	-0-
EBIT for zero EPS	-0-	$1,150	$1,894	-0-

FIGURE   10–8

ABC CORPORATION*
Range of EBIT and EPS Chart

*This diagram is available in an interactive format (TFA Template)—see "Analytical Support" on p. 354.

We can quickly observe that the conclusions about the earnings impact of the alternatives we drew from the two EBIT levels previously analyzed, $9 million and $11 million, hold true over the fairly wide range of earnings presented. That is, every alternative considered causes a significant reduction in earnings per share relative to the original condition.

There's a major new observation, however. Under the common stock alternative, the slope of the EPS line is different. In fact, the line for common stock intersects both the debt and the preferred stock lines at different points in the graph. The latter two lines are parallel with each other and also with the line representing the original situation, both appearing to the right of the original line. The lesser slope of the common stock line is easily explained. Introducing new shares of common stock results in a proportional dilution of earnings per share at all EBIT levels. As a consequence, the incremental shares cause earnings per share to rise less rapidly with growth in EBIT. In contrast, the parallel shift by the debt and preferred stock lines to the right of the original line is caused by the introduction of fixed interest or dividend charges, while at the same time the number of common shares outstanding remains constant over the EBIT range studied.

The significance of the two intersections should now become apparent. They are break-even points at which, for a given EBIT level, the EPS for the common stock alternative and one of the other two alternatives are the same. Note that the break-even point of common stock line with the bond alternative occurs at about $5.3 million EBIT, while the break-even point of common stock with preferred stock occurs at about $8.8 million EBIT.

Below about $5.0 million EBIT, therefore, the common stock alternative causes the least EPS dilution, while above $9 million EBIT, it causes the worst relative dilution in EPS. Recall that ABC's current EBIT level is $9.0 million, and is expected to be at least $11 million once the new product is fully contributing its projected earnings. Both break-even points thus lie below the likely future EBIT performance, which makes the common stock alternative the costliest in terms of earnings dilution.

Therefore, it's not possible to assess the three alternatives without first defining a "normal" range of EBIT for the company's expected performance, given that relative earnings effects of the three alternatives are different over the wide range of EBIT shown. If future EBIT levels could in fact be expected to occur fairly well within the two break-even points, common stock looks more attractive than preferred stock from the standpoint of EPS dilution, but worse than debt. If EBIT can be expected to grow and move fairly well to the right of the second break-even point, as is almost certain in the case of ABC Corporation, new common stock is not only least attractive from the standpoint of EPS dilution, but will remain so.

All of these considerations depend, of course, on unchanging assumptions about the terms under which the three forms of incremental capital could be issued. If we can expect any of these terms to change significantly, such as the offering price of the common stock, or the terms of the bond, an entirely new chart must be drawn up, or we must at least reflect any possible discontinuities in cost or proportions of the alternatives as EBIT levels change.

The intersections between the EPS lines that represent the EBIT break-even points for the common stock alternative with the other two choices can be calculated easily. For this purpose, we formulate simple equations for the conditions underlying any intersecting pair of lines. EPS are then set as equal for the two alternatives, and the equations are solved for the specific EBIT level at which this condition holds.

To illustrate, let's first establish the following definitions:

E = EBIT level for any break-even point with the common stock
   alternative.
i = Annual interest on bonds in dollars (before taxes).
t = Tax rate applicable to the company.
d = Annual preferred dividends in dollars.
s = Number of common shares outstanding.

The equation for any of the EPS lines can be found by substituting known facts for the symbols in the following generalized equation:

$$\text{EPS} = \frac{(E - i)(1 - t) - d}{s}$$

We can now find the EBIT break-even levels for bonds and common stock at the point of EPS equality. For this purpose, we fill in the data for the two expressions and set them as equal:

$$\begin{array}{cc} \textit{Bonds} & \textit{Common} \\ \dfrac{(E - \$1,150,000).66 - 0}{1,000,000} & = \dfrac{(E - 0).66 - 0}{1,275,000} \end{array}$$

When we solve for E we obtain the following result:

$$0.66E - \$759,000 = \frac{0.66E}{1.275}$$

$$0.842E - \$967,725 = 0.66E$$

$$E = \$5,317,000$$

This break-even level of $5.32 million can easily be verified graphically in Figure 10–8. When the same approach is applied to the preferred and common stock alternatives, the following result emerges:

$$\begin{array}{cc} \textit{Preferred} & \textit{Common} \\ \dfrac{(E - 0).66 - \$1,250,000}{1,000,000} & = \dfrac{(E - 0).66 - 0}{1,275,000} \end{array}$$

$$0.66E - \$1,250,000 = \frac{0.66E}{1.275}$$

$$0.842E - \$1,593,750 = 0.66E$$

$$E = \$8,757,000$$

Again, the chart can be used to verify the break-even level of $8.76 million.

We also can use the EBIT chart to show the impact of different assumptions about common dividends on the three alternatives. For example, the horizontal line at $2.50 in the chart represents the current annual common dividend. Where this line intersects any alternative EPS line we can read off the minimum level of EBIT required to supply this dividend. Similarly, it's possible to reflect in the chart the earnings requirements for sinking funds or other regular repayment provisions. In effect, such annual provisions commit a portion of future earnings for this purpose.

We can develop the effect of these requirements by carrying the calculations one step further and arriving at the so-called uncommitted earnings per share (UEPS) for each alternative after provision for any repayments. We simply subtract the per share cost of such repayments (that require after-tax dollars) from the respective EPS of the alternative thus affected, and redraw the lines in the chart. The result will be a parallel shift of the affected line to the right of its prior position.

For example, the sinking fund requirement of $400,000 per year in the bond alternative would represent 40 cents per share, and the new line for bonds would move to the right by this amount over its whole range. Similarly, the intersection at the zero EPS point, currently $1,150,000 EBIT, would move right to a zero UEPS point of $1,756,000. This shift reflects the sinking fund requirement of $400,000 per year, which translates into an incremental pretax earnings requirement of $400,000 ÷ (1 − 0.34), or $606,000. In this case, the UEPS line for bonds would move very close to the EPS line for preferred stock in Figure 10–8.

By now the usefulness of this framework for a dynamic analysis of the earnings impact of various financing alternatives should be clear. The reader is invited to think through the implications of the variety of tests that can be applied. It's possible, for example, to determine the minimum EBIT level under each alternative that would cover the current common dividend of $2.50 per share, while assuming a variety of different payout ratios, such as 50 percent or 40 percent. For example, with an assumed 50 percent payout, EPS would have to be $5. A horizontal line would be drawn at the $5 EPS level, and its intersection with the lines of the various alternatives would represent the minimum EBIT levels for the $2.50 dividend. The analyst would have to assess the likelihood of EBIT declining to this level, and judge whether this endangers the current dividend payout. Other tests can be applied, of course, depending on the particular circumstances of the company.

While we've concentrated on the implications for recorded accounting earnings involved in the choice, it should be clear that the framework also can be used to work through the cash flow implications of each of the results, by translating the respective EBIT levels into equivalent cash flow from operations, as discussed in Chapters 3 and 4. This would bring the analysis closer to the valuation concepts we'll take up in the final chapter—recognizing that cash flows are the ultimate drivers of company performance and value. Among the extra steps required are calculating the tax shield effect of depreciation and depletion write-offs, elimination of other accounting adjustments, and recognition of new investment requirements. A spreadsheet analysis can of course be used to make the multiple calculations required.

Again we must emphasize, however, that any one specific EBIT chart works only under fixed assumptions about proceeds and stable rates of interest and preferred dividends. If there's reason to believe that any of the key assumptions might change, the EPS lines on the graph must be adjusted. Obviously, any changes in the relative costs of the various alternatives will also have an effect. As the spread between the alternatives increases, for example, the differences in earnings impact will widen, and thus the distance between the parallel lines will increase. This simply reflects that imposing higher-cost fixed obligations depresses EPS.

Enlarging the amount of capital issued also has an effect, because the slope of the line is determined by the amount of leverage already present in the existing capital structure. In other words, if there's already some debt and preferred stock in the capital structure, the basic EPS would rise and fall much more sharply with changes in EBIT. Any increases in the fixed-cost alternatives would simply magnify this leverage. At the same time, the slope of the EPS line for common equity is governed by the relative number of shares issued, which in turn is related to the degree of earnings dilution, as demonstrated in the example.

Financial planning models or spreadsheet analyses can be used to enhance the basic framework demonstrated here. The point to remember, however, is that the process in essence quantifies the relative impact of the alternatives on reported accounting earnings. This effect is but one of the many factors that have to be weighed in making funding choices. As we mentioned in the beginning of this chapter, the conceptual and practical setting for the eventual decision is far more inclusive than this graphic expression of respective break-even conditions suggests. Strategic plans for the future, risk expectations, market factors, the specific criteria we listed, and current company conditions all have to enter the final judgment.

The Optimal Capital Structure

A great deal of theoretical and practical effort continues to be expended on determining the optimal mix of different long-term capital sources in a company's capital structure. This book is not the place to explore the many intricate conceptual issues involved, but some discussion is in order. We've referred many times to the fact that financial decision making involves a series of economic trade-offs as well as the personal judgments and risk preferences of the key managers and directors. Such is the case with the design and modification of capital structure proportions, which ultimately must be judged in terms of their support of value creation over time.

One of the key trade-offs is risk versus reward. Introducing leverage into a capital structure will, as we've observed before, tend to lower the overall cost of capital because of the least-cost aspect of debt (due to the tax deductibility of interest, as discussed in Chapter 9). This is not a static condition, however, because as we've mentioned, increasing amounts of debt expose the company to greater risk of earnings (and cash flow) variability, as well as potential default on the principal. Theoretical models of finding the optimal cost of capital take into account the dynamics of changing proportions of debt, preferred stock, and equity. Many studies have shown that, as a general rule, the cost of capital will tend to be lowest at debt proportions of around one-third versus two-thirds of equity in various forms. The specific risk characteristics of the company and its industry clearly will affect this general result. The evidence also shows that the overall cost of capital generally moves in a relatively narrow band between the extremes of leverage conditions, usually no more than two percentage points. But as we said before, the specific cost involved in financing is but one of many other considerations entering the complex trade-offs in capital structure planning.

One of the key considerations in shaping the capital structure is the relative growth performance and outlook of the company. Empirical studies have shown that fast-growing companies tend to create superior value through a capital structure with a conservative debt level, allowing them to maintain flexibility in accessing financial markets. This is generally accompanied by low dividend payout and emphasis on internal funds sources in financing growth. Additional equity is raised only when absolutely necessary to maintain profitable growth, while new debt is limited by relatively modest leverage targets. Overall, the focus must be on funding successful investments to sustain the growth pattern without excesses in funding choices, and exceeding the expectations of the market in implementing them.

In contrast, slow-growing companies that generate sizable cash flows can create superior value by disposing of the excess cash through share repurchases, reducing the equity base. Here the trade-off is simply between the quality and risk of perceived reinvestment opportunities on the one hand, and the impact of returning excess cash to the shareholders on the other. Given that attractive internal investment opportunities tend to be limited in slow growth situations, it might be economically advantageous to increase financial leverage even further and borrow funds for more share repurchases. The effect will generally be a rise in the value of the stock as fewer shares are left outstanding, and because of the proportional lessening of the dividend payments. Such a policy will not be sustainable in the long run, of course, because at some point the equity base will shrink to insignificance and expectations about future cash flows will diminish.

It should be added here that the effect of restructuring and the more successful performance achieved by many companies in the first half of this decade have led to a definite shift toward more conservative capital structures. Strong cash flows obtained from disposals of underperforming businesses and leaner ongoing operations have often been applied to reducing the temporarily inflated debt proportions of many companies. This was in part a reaction to the heavy—at times extreme—use of leverage during the 80s, which apart from greater risk exposure had not been justified by the results of the investments made with these funds.

The drive to create shareholder value in the past decade has included a rethinking of sustainable capital structure proportions in relation to business performance and outlook and not just from the standpoint of minimizing the cost of capital. Ultimately, of course, we must view the optimal capital structure in the broad context of our business system model as discussed in Chapter 2. It cannot be separated from the investment, operational, and financing variables we identified in all parts of the system.

Some Special Forms of Financing

Our earlier discussion focused on the very basic choice between debt, preferred stock, and common stock, setting aside the many variations often found in these instruments as well as in other specialized forms of financing. We'll now briefly cover several more specialized areas of financing choices, namely leasing, convertible bonds and preferred stocks, rights offerings, and warrants.

Leasing

We've referred to leasing at several points in this book. Leasing is a special form of financing that gives a business access to a whole range of assets, from buildings to aircraft and rail cars, and from automobiles to computers, without having to acquire these items outright. The lessee pays an agreed-upon periodic fee for use of the asset, set at a level that covers the lessor's ownership costs, financing and tax expenses, and also provides an economic return to the lessor. Lease contracts and provisions can vary widely, but they fall into two basic categories:

- Operating leases.
- Capital (financial) leases.

An *operating lease* essentially reflects the pure choice of leasing rather than owning. The lessee can use the asset for a specified period, usually less than the physical life, assumes none of the risks of ownership or technical obsolescence, and can replace or upgrade the asset while the lessor assumes the task of disposing of the used items. The latter provision is particularly appealing in the case of computers or technical equipment. The lessee, in effect, incurs only a tax-deductible periodic expense, while the lessor receives a stream of taxable payments against which are offset the ownership costs as well as any services provided the lessee. The lessor enjoys the tax shield effect of depreciation, and must decide what to do with the used asset at the end of the lease term.

A *capital lease* essentially represents a form of long-term financing, because title to the asset will be transferred to the lessee at the end of the lease term, directly or via a nominal purchase option. The specific choice to be made lies in the nature of the financing arrangement, viewed as a trade-off between a long-term debt issue supporting immediate ownership versus a leasing contract providing eventual ownership. The lease obligation, just like debt, is fixed, and the lease payment is based on recovering the value of the asset for the lessor and the cost of any other services provided. Long-term lease contracts, particularly for buildings, can extend over many years and thus become, in fact, part of a company's financial structure.

The impact of a lease on a company's financial statements differs between the two major types. Operating leases enter the income statement via tax-deductible lease costs, but do not affect the balance sheet directly, even though the lease contract usually extends over several periods. Instead, if operating leases are material in the cost structure of the company, a footnote disclosing the current and future annual lease totals is required to accompany the financial statements, disclosing the size of this "off-balance sheet" obligation. Because ownership remains with the lessor, the assets involved are not reflected on the balance sheet of the lessee.

In contrast, capital leases are reflected in a company's financial statements both on the balance sheet, where the asset involved is recorded, and offset on the liability side by the capitalized value of the lease payments. In effect, a capital lease has a recorded impact quite similar to a secured loan arrangement, and the total lease obligation is viewed as debt along with conventional long-term debt arrangements. The periodic lease payments are included as an operating expense in the income statement. Under current accounting rules, any lease which has just one of the following four attributes must be considered a capital lease and recorded on the balance sheet:

- Ownership is transferred to the lessee before expiration of the lease.
- The lessee can purchase the asset for a low price upon expiration of the lease.
- The lease term is for at least 75 percent of the asset's economic life.
- The present value of the lease payments is at least 90% of the asset's value.

From a tax standpoint, the periodic lease payments made by the lessee are tax deductible, while the tax shield effect of depreciation remains with the lessor, offset against taxable lease payments collected. The IRS is very specific about distinguishing between genuine leases and installment purchases or secured loans in order to allow a tax deduction of the lease payment by the lessee.

As we might expect, any company that leases a significant portion of its assets has less flexibility in its financing choices. The effect is the same as that of a large outstanding long-term debt. Also, fixed leasing charges introduce a degree of leverage into the company's operations that is quite comparable to leverage resulting from other sources, as discussed in Chapter 6.

Because leasing involves a choice of owning versus leasing, or leasing versus borrowing, the basic analytical process should be based on a comparison of the respective tax-adjusted cash flows. Using the present value techniques of Chapters 7 and 8, the analyst can develop comparative cash flow patterns for the alternatives involved. One of the basic patterns is the analysis of the cost of ownership, from which a break-even lease payment can be calculated, as shown in Figure 10–9. A seven-year life has been assumed for an equipment investment, with recovery of the residual book value at the end of Year 7. Maintenance and support costs are growing slightly as the equipment ages, and accelerated depreciation has been used to calculate the tax shield effect.

The net present value cost at 12 percent of owning the equipment is about $107,000, which can be converted into an annualized equivalent cost of $23,360,

Present Value Analysis of Cost of Ownership ($ thousands)

	Year 0	Year 1	Year 2	Year 3	Year 4	Year 5	Year 6	Year 7
Cost of equipment and recovery.	$−100,000	0	0	0	0	0	0	$ 4,450
Maintenance, insurance, support costs	0	$−15,000	$−15,000	$−16,000	$−16,000	$−17,000	$−17,000	−18,000
Tax rate		36%	36%	36%	36%	36%	36%	36%
After-tax cash cost.	0	−9,600	−9,600	−10,240	−10,240	−10,880	−10,880	−11,520
Depreciation tax shield*		9,146	15,674	11,194	7,994	5,715	5,715	−3,430
Operating cash outflows	0	−454	6,074	954	−2,246	−5,165	−5,165	−14,950
Present value factors @ 12%	1.000	0.893	0.797	0.712	0.636	0.567	0.507	0.452
Present values of equipment cash flows.	−100,000	0	0	0	0	0	0	2,011
Present values of operating cash flows.	0	−406	4,841	679	−1,429	−2,928	−2,619	−6,758
Present values of total cash flows.	$−100,000	$ −406	$ 4,841	$ 679	$ −1,429	$ −2,928	$ −2,619	$ −4,746
Net present value @ 12% . . . .$−106,608								
Annualized net present value @ 12% . . . . −23,360								
Pretax equivalent lease payment @ 36% tax rate 36,500								

*Based on 7-year accelerated depreciation percentages (14.29%; 24.49%; 17.49%, 12.49%; 8.93%; 8.93%; 8.93%; 4.45% residual).

as was discussed in Chapter 7 (on a spreadsheet, use the *pmt* function, specifying the discount rate, the number of periods, and the present value). Assuming that the lessor has similar ownership costs, the minimum lease payment required to earn the lessor a 12 percent cash flow return would be the pretax equivalent of $36,500 per year. From the lessee's standpoint, this lease payment represents a break-even level between leasing and owning, from which any significant deviation would have to be evaluated. Similar analyses can be developed for other potential alternatives, always being careful to lay out cash flows and tax implications properly.

There are many considerations involved in the choice of leasing versus ownership beyond the purely financial trade-offs. Very importantly, the analysis of leasing as a financing choice can come only after the cash flow economics of the investment project itself have indicated that it will indeed add value to the company. Thereafter, leasing can properly be considered as merely one form of financing. We'll not deal with the specific cash flow implications of the many types of leasing arrangements available, because they are too specialized and complex to be covered here. But we must recognize that leasing often involves an economic cost, because especially in operating lease arrangements the lessor must be compensated for providing, financing, servicing, and replacing the asset. By definition, leasing charges must be high enough to make leasing attractive for the lessor as the investor in the asset. At the same time, the lessor is often able to use economies of scale in acquiring and servicing the assets that might favorably affect the cost of leasing, as is the case with major equipment leasing companies, for example.

In the comparative analysis of the final choice between leasing and owner-ship we have to weigh such elements as the periodic expense to the lessee, any technological advantages from being able to use the latest in facilities and equip-ment, services received as part of the contract, the flexibility of not being tied down by ownership, and the impact on the company's financial position. As in all financial analyses, the choice is based on both quantifiable data and management judgment. In some industries, leasing is part of the normal way of doing business. For example, in wholesaling, warehouses are commonly leased, and in the trans-portation industry, leasing of rolling stock, trucks, and aircraft prevails. In other areas, the choice of leasing is wide open and depends on what financing alterna-tive is considered advantageous at the time.

Convertible Securities

As we stated earlier, convertibility into common shares is a feature sometimes added to issues of bonds or preferred stocks for reasons of marketability and tim-ing. The essence of convertibility is simply that the issuing company is in effect able to sell common shares at prices higher than those prevailing at the time the bond or preferred stock is issued. This is due to the fact that the conversion price for the common stock it represents is set at an expected future level, based on the company's value growth experience and expectation.

The conversion price is the basis for the conversion ratio set for the bond or preferred issue. For example, a new $100 convertible preferred might have a con-version ratio of 3, that is, each share of preferred stock is convertible into three shares of common stock. This represents a conversion price of $33.33 per com-mon share, while the company's shares might currently be trading in the $25 to $27 range. The difference between current price and the conversion price is called the conversion premium. The same approach applies to bonds, which are usually denominated in thousand-dollar units.

Given the expectation that the company's common stock will in time exceed the conversion price, the bond or preferred stock will trade at values that reflect both the underlying interest or dividend yield, and the conversion value itself. Initially the stated yield will predominate, but when common share prices begin to exceed the conversion price, the price of the bond or preferred stock will be boosted to reflect the current market value of the underlying common shares. This is the point at which conversion becomes increasingly attractive to the investor. If share prices remain below the conversion price, however, the conversion value will always be the floor value for the bond or preferred—while the actual price will depend on the yield provided by the stated interest rate or the preferred dividend.

Given the potential attraction of conversion to the investor, the issuing company usually pays a somewhat lower rate of interest or preferred dividend on these instruments. To limit the time period over which these securities are out-standing, the company can usually force conversion—once the market price of common stock has reached the conversion price—by exercising the call provision (the right of the company to redeem all or part of the issue) included in most convertible issues. This provision is usually based on a predetermined price close to the conversion price.

Convertibility adds a number of considerations to the three basic choices discussed earlier. Because successful convertible issues eventually result in an increase in common shares, the delayed impact on control, earnings per share, and the amount of future common dividends must be taken into account in the analysis. The graphic display used earlier can be applied by showing this alternative in two forms:

- The convertible bond or preferred as a straight bond or preferred.
- The additional common shares from eventual conversion.

As long as significant convertible issues remain outstanding, companies are required to calculate diluted earnings per share, as discussed in Chapter 4.

Stock Rights

A so-called rights offering is a form of common stock financing that minimizes the dilution of existing shareholders' proportional holdings. Also referred to as a privileged subscription, such an offering provides to each existing shareholder a proportional number of rights to purchase a specified number of new common shares from the company at an advantageous subscription price during a limited time period, after which the rights expire. The number of rights issued matches the number of shares of common stock outstanding, and a defined number of rights are necessary to purchase each share of new stock. Rights are issued as special certificates and are often traded on securities exchanges or in the over-the-counter market.

To illustrate, if the XYZ Company has 1 million common shares outstanding and wishes to sell 250,000 new shares, 1 million rights will be issued to existing shareholders with the provision that 4 rights are required to purchase a new share of stock at the subscription price. If the subscription price is $30, while the current market price is $40, a shareholder has to surrender 4 rights and $30 to the company to receive another share currently worth $40.

A company is attracted to this course of action because, apart from limiting the potential for dilution of control, it is a direct appeal for funds to a group of investors already familiar with its history and outlook. If so inclined, a shareholder will exercise the rights by purchasing directly from the company the number of shares specified at the set subscription price. If the shareholder isn't interested, the rights can be sold as such, because they'll reflect the value differential between the subscription price and the market price of the stock. We'll return to determining the value of rights to the investor in Chapter 11.

The analytical implications of this alternative are quite similar to those of a public offering, which we assumed to be the case earlier in the chapter. The subscription price might differ somewhat from the price the underwriters provide in a public offering, but otherwise the analysis will parallel the common stock alternative we explored.

Warrants

Warrants are a form of corporate security that entitles the holder to purchase a specified number of common shares at a fixed exercise price over a stated period of time. Some warrants have no expiration date. They are issued as an added incentive for investors to purchase a new public issue of bonds, or a private placement of loans or bonds. Sometimes warrants are issued as part of an offering of common stock. The proportion of warrants issued with the new offering will vary depending on the exercise price and the degree of incentive desired to move the new debt issue into the hands of investors. Warrants are attached to these new securities as part of the offering, but in most cases, they can be detached by the holder and sold separately if desired. Numerous warrants are traded at any time in the securities markets.

In effect, a warrant gives the holder the option to buy common stock if it's advantageous to do so, for example, if the exercise price is below the market price. Just as in the case of rights, when a warrant is exercised, the funds go directly to the company. Since warrants, in contrast to rights, are valid for relatively long time periods, there is the potential for earnings dilution from unexpired warrants. Companies with significant numbers of warrants outstanding must calculate diluted earnings per share, just as in the case of convertible issues outstanding (Chapter 4).

The main implication for analysis of a new debt offering with attached warrants is the need to recognize the potential funds inflow from new shares as warrants are exercised, and the earnings dilution from these shares. Our graphic analysis has to be modified to allow for the combination of these effects. We'll return to the value of warrants in Chapter 11.

Key Issues

The following is a recap of the key issues raised directly or indirectly in this chapter. They are enumerated here to help the reader keep the analysis techniques discussed within the perspective of financial theory and business practice.

1. The choice among different types of long-term financing is inextricably connected with the business strategy of a company. The final choice must match the risk/reward characteristics inherent in both strategy and financing, and should support value creation over the long term.

2. The cost of different types of capital is only one element on which
    a decision about new funding is based. While debt is generally the
    lowest-cost alternative (due to tax deductibility of interest) and
    common equity the highest-cost alternative, the need to build
    and maintain an appropriate balance in the capital structure often
    overrides the cost criterion.

3. Several non-cost elements, such as risk, flexibility, timing, and
    shareholder control as well as management preferences, have to be
    weighed in relation to both changing market conditions and the
    company's future policies.

4. New financing at times might represent a significant proportion of the
    existing capital structure. How these funds are raised can cause shifts
    away from a firm's ideal target capital structure. Because a block of one
    form of long-term capital was chosen at one point in time, management
    might be limited in the choices for the next round of financing. To
    compensate for this imbalance, a compromise mix of funds might
    have to be used.

5. The specific provisions of a new issue of securities are generally
    tailor-made for the situation. Investment bankers, underwriters, and
    management collaborate to negotiate the design and price of a financial
    instrument that reflects market conditions, the company's credit rating
    and reputation, risk assessment, the company's strategic plans, and
    current financial practices.

6. As a company's capital structure changes, so does its weighted cost of
    capital. However, temporary shifts resulting from adding blocks of new
    capital should not affect the return standards based on cost of capital,
    unless there is a deliberate and permanent change in the company's
    policies.

7. New common equity has the long-term effect of diluting both
    ownership and earnings per share. This is true whether the new shares
    are directly issued or brought about by conversion of other securities,
    or by exercise of warrants. The decision as to whether to issue new
    common shares, therefore, must be closely tied to the expected
    results from the strategic plans in place. It also involves weighing the
    advantages of introducing new permanent equity capital into the capital
    structure.

8. Leasing as a form of financing is based on a series of cash flow and
    operational trade-offs that must be weighed in relation to both the
    company's capital structure and its business direction. It cannot serve as
    a means of justification for obtaining the asset involved; only economic
    analysis is the appropriate foundation for adding investments.

Summary

In this chapter we've reviewed both the decisional framework and some of the techniques used to analyze the different types of long-term funds. We focused on the three basic alternatives open to management: long-term debt, preferred stock, and common equity, leaving the discussion of the many specialized aspects of funding instruments to be pursued in the reference materials at the end of the chapter.

We found that the choice of financing alternatives is a complex mixture of analysis and judgment. Several areas of consideration were highlighted. We reviewed the cost to the company, the relative risks, and the issues of flexibility, timing, and control with respect to the various funding sources. We found that many of the aspects involved in choosing types of capital went beyond quantifiable data.

We also focused on the impact of each financing alternative on the reported earnings of a company, and then developed a break-even graph relating EPS and EBIT. This simple model allowed us to test visually the earnings impact of the alternatives over the whole dynamic range of potential earnings levels. The graph suggested the potential use of broader financial models or computer spreadsheets with which to simulate more fully the impact of alternative financing packages or changing conditions. Very importantly, we pointed out that the optimal capital structure is not a function of earnings impact alone, but the result of weighing the key characteristics of the business and its performance and longer-term outlook to arrive at a mix that will sustain value creation.

We briefly examined the key aspects of other specialized forms of financing, convertible securities, rights, warrants, and leasing and suggested the kind of analytical considerations applicable to these modified conditions.

Analytical Support

Financial Genome, the commercially available financial analysis and planning software described in Appendix I, has the capability to develop and display full-fledged financial analyses under different financing assumptions from input data and built-in databases. The software is also accompanied by an interactive template (TFA Template under "extras"), which allows the user to study the impact on EBIT and EPS of different financing alternatives, based on the analysis and diagram in Figure 10–8 on page 341. It displays the results on the range of EBIT and EPS graph and on an abbreviated balance sheet. The historical database on TRW Inc. contained in the software also can be used to develop inputs to this financing template. (see "Downloads Available" on p. 431)

Selected References

Brealey, Richard, and Stewart Myers. *Principles of Corporate Finance.* 5th ed. New York: McGraw-Hill, 1996.

Hull, John. *Options, Futures and Other Derivative Securities.* New York: Prentice-Hall, 1993.

Ross, Stephen; Randolph Westerfield; and Jeffrey Jaffe. *Corporate Finance.* 5th ed. Burr Ridge, IL: Irwin/McGraw-Hill, 1999.

Weston, J. Fred; Scott Besley; and Eugene Brigham. *Essentials of Managerial Finance.* 11th ed. Chicago, IL: Dryden Press, 1997.

CHAPTER 11

VALUATION AND BUSINESS PERFORMANCE

Throughout this book, we've stressed that managers must primarily focus their decision making about investments, operations, and financing on the creation of economic value for the company's shareholders. Now let's put shareholder value into a broader context by examining the key concepts of value and relating them to successful business performance. Earlier we discussed such categories as the recorded values reflected in a company's financial statements, the economic values represented by the cash flows generated through capital investments, and the market value of shares or debt instruments. In each case, value was viewed in a specific context of analysis and assessment, but not necessarily against the full dynamics of management strategies and decisions that underlie the performance of any business.

We'll discuss the meaning of value in a variety of common situations where valuation is required. We'll not only define several concepts of value in more precise terms, but also once again use some of the now familiar analytical approaches that can be applied to the process of valuation. Foremost among these, of course, is the present value analysis of future cash flows (the main subject of Chapters 7 and 8), which is the common underpinning of modern valuation principles and shareholder value creation. In the final chapter we'll integrate the various concepts into an overview of value-based management, returning to the systems approach first discussed in Chapter 2 and using it to provide a consistent perspective of successful value creation.

We'll begin here with some basic definitions of value as found in business practice. Next, we'll take the point of view of the investor assessing the value of the main forms of securities issued by a company, and the point of view of the creditor judging the value of the company's obligations. Finally, we'll discuss the key issues involved in valuing an ongoing business as the basis for determining whether shareholder value is being created—the principal objective of modern management. As we've emphasized throughout this book, the linkage between cash flows and the creation of economic value is the ultimate expression of success or failure of business decisions on investment, operating, and financing. Recognition of this linkage spurred the wave of takeovers and restructuring activities of the 1980s—essentially a reassessment of the effectiveness with which resources were employed by target companies—leading to redeployment of those resources in alternative ways expected to generate higher cash flows and returns to the shareholders. But the failure to recognize these linkages at the turn of the century led to the bubble and deflation in the dot.com business valuations as we discussed in Chapter 1.

Definitions of Value

It'll be useful to refresh our memory briefly about the different types of value we've encountered so far, and to state as clearly as possible what they represent and for what purposes they might be appropriate. In this enumeration we'll demonstrate that only some of these concepts are really useful for what we now understand to be the economic task of value creation in a business setting.

Economic Value

This concept, used throughout the book as the relevant term for shareholder value creation, relates to the basic ability of an asset—or a claim—to provide a stream of after-tax cash flows to the holder. Such cash flows can be generated through earnings, or contractual payments, and/or partial or total liquidation at a future point. As earlier chapters said, economic value is essentially a cash flow trade-off concept. The value of any asset is defined as the amount of cash a buyer is willing to give up now—its present value—in exchange for a pattern of future expected cash flows. Therefore, economic value is very much a future-oriented concept. It's determined by estimating and assessing prospective future cash flows, including proceeds from the ultimate disposal of the asset itself. Remember that past costs and expenditures caused by prior decisions are sunk costs and thus irrelevant from an economic standpoint.

As we'll see, economic value underlies some of the other common concepts of value because it's based on a trade-off logic that is quite natural to the process of investing. Calculating economic value is not without practical difficulties, however. Recall that a representative discount rate (cost of capital or return standard) has to be selected and applied to the expected positive and negative cash flows over a defined period of time. The cash flows themselves are often difficult to estimate, and they might also include specific assumptions about any recoverable cash from liquidation, or about any ongoing value remaining at the termination point of the analysis. The process in effect determines today's equivalents of the cash flow amounts expected to occur in different parts of the time spectrum, based on a great deal of judgment.

Recall also the need for risk assessment, both in determining the cash flow pattern itself and in setting the appropriate return standard. In other words, economic value isn't absolute; it's the result of the relative risk assessment of future expectations. In fact, economic value is closely tied to individual risk preferences, because different individuals will arrive at different valuation results due to their varying perceptions of risk. Yet, whether or not these aspects are made explicit in a given situation, the principle of economic value is at the core of all business decisions on investment, operating, and financing.

Market Value

Also referred to as fair market value, this is the value of any asset, or collection of assets, when traded in an organized market—or negotiated between private parties—in an unencumbered transaction without duress. The various securities and commodities exchanges are examples of organized markets, as are literally thousands of regional and local markets and exchanges that enable buyers and sellers to find mutually acceptable values for all kinds of tangible and intangible assets. Market value is, of course, also established through transactions between individuals when no organized market is conveniently available.

Again, there's nothing absolute in market value. Instead, it represents a momentary consensus of two or more parties. In a sense, the parties to a transaction adjust their respective individual assessments of the asset's economic value sufficiently to arrive at the consensus. The market value at any one time can therefore be subject to the preferences and even whims of the individuals involved, the psychological climate prevalent in an organized stock exchange, the heat of a takeover battle, significant industry developments, shifts in economic and political conditions, and so forth. Moreover, the volume of trading in the asset or security will influence the value placed on it by buyers and sellers.

Despite its potential variability, market value is generally regarded as a reasonable criterion in estimating the current value of individual balance sheet assets and liabilities, as contrasted with their recorded value. It's frequently used in inventory valuation and in capital investment analysis where future recovery values have to be estimated. On a larger scale, mergers and purchases of going concerns are also based on market values negotiated by the parties involved. As was the case with economic value, there are practical problems associated with establishing market value. A true market value can be found only by actually engaging in a transaction. Thus, unless the item is in fact traded, any market value assigned to it remains merely an estimate, which will tend to shift as conditions change and the perceptions of the parties are altered.

But even if market quotations are readily available, certain judgments apply. For example, popular common stocks traded on the major exchanges have widely quoted market prices, yet frequently there are significant price fluctuations even within a day's trading, and the volume of shares changing hands on a given day might vary greatly—affecting the relevance of the quotations for all other shares being held. Also, overall market movements will affect individual stocks. Thus, market value based on many similar transactions can be fixed only within a given range, which in turn, is tied to the trading conditions of the day, week, or month. For items that are traded infrequently or in relatively small numbers, estimating a realistic transaction value can become even more difficult. Yet the fact remains that market value is one of the most significant value concepts used in financial/economic analysis. It is closely related to economic value, because it ultimately is based on the parties' expectations about future cash flows to be derived from the asset or business involved.

Book Value

Recall from Chapter 2 that the book value of an asset or liability is the stated value as reflected on the balance sheet, which has been recorded and at times modified according to generally accepted accounting principles. While book value is handled consistently for accounting purposes, it usually bears little relationship to current economic value. It's a historical value that, at one time, might have represented market value, but the passage of time and changes in economic conditions increasingly distort it. Assets of a long-term nature are particularly subject to changes in economic value over time. The frequently quoted book value of common shares, which represents the shareholder's proportional claim on the composite net result of all past transactions in assets, liabilities, and operations, is especially subject to distortion. As a residual amount it is affected by all past and present accounting adjustments as well as value changes. Its usefulness for economic analysis is therefore questionable under most circumstances.

Liquidation Value

This value relates to the special condition when a company needs to liquidate part or all of its assets and claims. In essence, it's an abnormal situation where time pressures and even duress distort the value assessments made by buyers and sellers. Under the cloud of impending business failure or intense pressure from creditors, management will find that liquidation values generally are considerably below potential market values. The setting for the negotiations is adversely affected by the known disadvantage under which the selling party must act in the transaction. As a consequence, liquidation value is really applicable only for the limited purpose intended. Nevertheless, it's sometimes used to value assets of unproved businesses as a more realistic basis for analysis than by estimating highly uncertain cash flow patterns when testing such aspects as creditworthiness.

Breakup Value

A variation of liquidation value, breakup value is related to corporate takeover and restructuring activities, as discussed later. On the assumption that the combined economic values of the individual segments of a multibusiness company exceed the company's value as an entity—because of inadequate past management or current opportunities that were not recognized earlier—the company is broken up into salable components for disposal to other buyers. Any redundant assets, such as excess real estate, are also sold for their current values.

Note that breakup value is usually realized on business segments with on-going operations, and less frequently through forced liquidation of individual assets supporting these business segments, as would be the case in a bankruptcy sale, for example. Any redundant assets not required for ongoing operations might, of course, be liquidated as such. Estimates of breakup value are a critical element in the analysis preceding takeover bids.

Reproduction Value

This is the amount that would be required to replace an existing fixed asset in kind. In other words, it's the like-for-like replacement cost of a machine, facility, or other similar asset. Reproduction value is, in fact, one of several yardsticks used in judging the worth of the assets of an ongoing business. Determining reproduction value of specific assets is an estimate largely based on engineering judgments.

There are several practical problems involved. The most important is whether the fixed asset in question could, or would, in fact be reproduced exactly as it was constructed originally. Most physical assets are subject to some pattern of technological obsolescence with the passage of time, in addition to physical wear and tear. There's also the problem of estimating the currently applicable cost of actually reproducing the item in kind. For purposes of analysis, reproduction value often becomes just one checkpoint in assessing the market value of the assets of a going business.

Collateral Value

This is the value of an asset that is used as security for a loan or other type of credit. The collateral value is generally considered the maximum amount of credit that can be extended against a pledge of the asset. With their own security in mind, creditors usually set the collateral value lower than the market value of an asset. This provides a cushion of safety in case of default, and the risk preference of the individual creditor will determine the magnitude of the often arbitrary downward adjustment. Where no market value can be readily estimated, the collateral value is set on a purely judgmental basis, the creditor being in a position to allow for as much of a margin of safety as is deemed advisable in the particular circumstances.

Assessed Value

This value concept is established in local governmental statutes as the basis for property taxation. The rules governing assessment practices vary widely, and might or might not take market values into account. Use of assessed values is limited to raising tax revenues, and therefore such values bear little relationship to the other value concepts.

Appraised Value

Appraised value is subjectively determined and used when the asset involved has no clearly definable market value. An effort is usually made to find evidence of transactions that are reasonably comparable to the asset being appraised. Often used in transactions of considerable size—especially in the case of commercial or residential real estate—appraised value is determined by an impartial expert accepted by both parties to the transaction, whose knowledge of the type of asset involved can narrow the gap that might exist between buyer and seller, or at least establish a bargaining range. The quality of the estimate depends on the expertise of the appraiser and on the availability of comparable situations. Again, individual ability and preference enter into the value equation. Only rarely will different appraisals yield exactly the same results, and ranges of value are used at times.

Going Concern Value

This concept applies economic valuation to a business in operation. A company viewed as a going concern is expected to produce a series of future cash flows that the potential buyer must value to arrive at a price for the business as a whole. Note that the same concept applies to valuing whole business segments of a company when its breakup value is established, as discussed earlier. Apart from the specific valuation techniques used, which we'll discuss later, the concept requires that the business be viewed as a "living system" of investments, operations, and financing rather than a mere collection of assets and liabilities.

Recall our earlier strong emphasis on the fact that economic value is created by a positive trade-off of future cash flows for present commitments and outlays. As we'll see in Chapter 12, the going concern value is useful when comparative cash flow analyses, singly and in combination, are developed for setting value-based management goals and for acquisitions and mergers. Going concern value also enters the cash flow analysis as the final estimate at the end of the analysis period, where it represents the ongoing value of the business in relation to future performance. The continuing challenge to the analyst is to properly weigh this future value as well as the overall pattern of estimated cash flows.

Shareholder Value

As we've stated repeatedly, shareholder value is created when the returns generated from existing and new investments consistently exceed the cost of capital of the company. It represents the total increase in the economic value of the business over time. This value in turn is reflected in the form of a growing periodic total return to shareholders as measured by the combination of dividends and capital gains or losses achieved, which can be compared to overall market returns or the returns achieved by selected peer companies or industry groupings. Shareholder value, the ultimate expression of corporate success, is closely tied to cash flow trade-offs and return expectations that are the basis of economic value. We'll discuss the concept in more detail in Chapter 12.

In summary, we've discussed a number of value definitions. Some were specialized yardsticks designed for specific situations. Many are directly or indirectly related to economic value. We've again defined economic value as the present value of future cash flows, discounted at the investor's risk-adjusted standard. As we know, this value concept is broadly applicable as the underpinning of shareholder value creation, and we'll use it extensively as we examine various decision areas where value measures are needed.

Value to the Investor

As in Chapters 6, 9, and 10, we'll concentrate only on the three main types of corporate securities—bonds, preferred stock, and common stock—in discussing the techniques involved to assess value and yield. For our purposes here, value is defined as the current attractiveness of the investment to the investor in present value terms, while yield represents the internal rate of return (IRR) earned by the investor on the price paid for the investment. We'll briefly discuss major provisions in the basic securities types insofar as they might affect their value and yield. The techniques covered should appear quite familiar to the reader because they closely relate to the various analytical approaches presented in earlier chapters.

Bond Values

Valuing a bond is normally fairly straightforward. A typical bond issued by a corporation is a simple debt instrument. Its basic provisions generally entail a series of contractual semiannual interest payments, defined as a fixed rate based on the bond's stated par (face) value (usually $1,000). The legal contract, or indenture, promises repayment of the principal (nominal value) at a specified maturity date a number of years in the future. The two basic characteristics, defined interest payments and repayment stipulations, are encountered in most normal debt arrangements. Complicating aspects are sometimes found in provisions such as conversion into common stock at a predetermined exchange value, or payment of interest only when earned by the issuing company. We'll review some of these specialized features later.

A bond's basic value rests on the investor's assessment of the relative attractiveness of the expected stream of future interest receipts and the prospect for eventual recovery of the principal at maturity. Of course, there's normally no obligation for the investor to hold the bond until maturity because most bonds can be traded readily in the securities markets. Still, the risk underlying the bond contract must be considered here in terms of the issuing company's future ability to generate sufficient cash with which to pay both interest and principal. The collective judgment of security analysts and investors about the issuing company's prospects influences the price level at which the bond is publicly traded, which is further affected by prevailing interest rates in the economy. Also, the bond is likely to be rated by financial services like Moody's and Standard & Poor's and placed in a particular risk category relative to other bonds.

To determine a bond's value, we must first calculate the present value of the interest payments received up to the maturity date and add to this the present value of the ultimate principal repayment. You'll recognize this method as comparable with the process of calculating the present value of business investment expenditures shown in Chapter 7. The discount rate applied is the risk-adjusted interest rate that represents the investor's own standard of measuring debt investment opportunities within a range of acceptable risk. For example, an investor with an 8 percent annual interest return standard would value a bond with a coupon interest rate of 6 percent annually significantly lower than its par value. The calculation is shown in Figure 11–1. The investor's annual standard of 8 percent is equivalent to a semiannual standard of 4 percent, a restatement for

FIGURE 11–1

Bond Valuation

Date of analysis:	July 1, 2000
Face value (par) of bond:	$1,000
Maturity date:	July 1, 2014
Bond interest (coupon rate):	6% per year
Interest receipts:	$30 semiannually

	Total Cash Flow	Present Value Factors, 4 Percent*	Present Value
28 receipts of $30 over 14 years (28 periods)	$ 840	16.663 (× $30)	$499.89
Receipt of principal 14 years hence (28 periods)	1,000	0.333	333.00
Totals	$1,840		$832.89

*From Table 7–II and 7–I (end of Chapter 7), respectively.

purposes of calculation that's necessary to match the semiannual interest payments paid by most bonds.

The resulting value, $832.89, represents the maximum price our investor should be willing to pay—or the minimum price at which the investor should be willing to sell—if the investor normally expects a return (yield) of 8 percent from this type of investment. This particular bond should therefore be acquired only at a price considerably below (at a discount from) par. Note that the stated interest rate on the bond is relevant only for determining the semiannual cash receipts in absolute dollar terms.

The actual valuation of the bond and the cash flows it represents therefore depends on the investor's opportunity rate (return standard). In other words, the desired yield determines the appropriate price, and vice versa. This relationship also applies, of course, to the market quotations for publicly traded bonds. The quoted price, or value, is a function of the current yield collectively desired by the many buyers and sellers of these debt instruments, which in turn is based on general interest rate conditions.

If our investor were for some unrealistic reason satisfied with the very low annual yield of only 4 percent from holding the same bond (equivalent to 2 percent per six-month period), the value to the investor would rise considerably above par, as shown in Figure 11–2. Under these assumed conditions, the investor should be willing to pay a premium of up to $212.43 for the $1,000 bond, because the personal return standard is lower than the stated interest rate. If the investor's own standard and the coupon interest rate were to coincide precisely, the value of the bond would, of course, exactly match the par value of $1,000.

In fact, the quoted market price of any bond will tend to approach the par value as it reaches maturity, because at that point, the only representative value will be the imminent repayment of the principal—assuming, of course, that the company is financially able to pay as the amount becomes due.

FIGURE 11–2

Bond Valuation with Lower Return Standard (4 percent per year)

	Total Cash Flow	Present Value Factors, 2 Percent*	Present Value
28 receipts of $30 over 14 years (28 periods)......................	$ 840	21.281 (× $30)	$ 638.43
Receipt of principal 14 years hence (28 periods)......................	1,000	0.574	574.00
Totals...........................	$1,840		$1,212.43

*From Tables 7–II and 7–I (end of Chapter 7), respectively.

Bond Yields

A related but common task for the analyst or investor is the calculation of the yield produced by various bonds, when quoted prices differ from par value. The key to this analysis again is the relationship of value and yield as discussed above, and the technique used is a present value calculation that in effect determines the internal rate of return (IRR) of the cash flow patterns generated by the bond over its remaining life.

The method is identical to that used for assessing the cash flows of any business investment proposal. The key difference in the data is that the individual investor's calculations are based on pretax cash flows that must be adjusted in each case by the investor for his or her personal tax situation. Other minor differences are the cash incidence in a semiannual pattern, and the form in which bond prices (the net investment) are quoted. Published prices are normally stated as a percentage of par. For example, a bond quoted at 103⅜ has a price of $1,033.75. The change to decimal trading in process in early 2001 will make these quotations easier to handle.

Bond yield tables have long been employed to determine a bond's internal rate of return, or yield. While today's computers and calculators have financial routines that make direct calculation routine, we'll nevertheless take a quick look at a yield table, mainly to help the reader understand the examples by visual inspection of the relationships. Bond yield tables are finely graduated present value tables that list the whole potential range of stated interest rates, subdivided into fractional progressions of as little as $\frac{1}{32}$ of a point. They're far more detailed than the present value tables used in Chapters 7 and 8.

For example, Figure 11–3 is a small segment of such a yield table, in this case for a bond with a coupon interest rate of precisely 6 percent. The columns

FIGURE 11–3

Bond Yield Table (sample section for a 6 percent rate)

			Price Given Years or Periods to Maturity			
Yield to Maturity	13 Years (26 periods)	13½ Years (27 periods)	14 Years (28 periods)	14½ Years (29 periods)	15 Years (30 periods)	15½ Years (31 periods)
3.80%	1.224 043	1.230 661	1.237 155	1.243 528	1.249 782	1.255 919
3.85	1.218 284	1.224 709	1.231 012	1.237 196	1.243 263	1.249 215
3.90	1.212 559	1.218 793	1.224 907	1.230 904	1.236 787	1.242 557
3.95	1.206 868	1.212 913	1.218 841	1.224 654	1.230 354	1.235 944
4.00	1.201 210	1.207 068	1.212 812*	1.218 443	1.223 964	1.229 377
4.05	1.195 585	1.201 260	1.206 821	1.212 273	1.217 616	1.222 853
4.10	1.189 993	1.195 486	1.200 868	1.206 142	1.211 310	1.216 375
4.15	1.184 434	1.189 747	1.194 952	1.200 051	1.205 046	1.209 940
4.20	1.178 908	1.184 043	1.189 073	1.193 999	1.198 823	1.203 549
4.25	1.173 414	1.178 374	1.183 230	1.187 985	1.192 642	1.197 201

*This example was used in Figure 11–2 (slight difference due to rounding of present value factors). Note that prices are given in the form of a 7-digit multiplier, which is applied against a $1,000 par value.

show the number of 6-month periods remaining in the life of the bond, while the rows display the yield to maturity. The yield to maturity simply refers to the yield obtained by the investor if the bond were actually held until its par value is repaid at the maturity date. If the investor were to sell at an earlier date, the market price of the bond received at that time would be substituted for par value in calculating the return. As a result, the yield achieved for the period up to the date of sale might differ from the yield to maturity if the bond is trading above or below par. We can quickly find the bond's yield to maturity at any given purchase price in the bond yield tables. Conversely, it's also possible to find the exact price (value) that corresponds to any particular desired yield to maturity. Our example of the 6 percent bond used in the previous section (Figure 11–1) is represented on the 4 percent yield line and in the 28-period column of the bond yield table segment reproduced in Figure 11–3. Bond yield tables provide a visual impression of the progression or regression of prices and yields which is, of course, purely based on their mathematical relationship, as discussed in Chapter 7. A calculator or spreadsheet program goes through the same steps and formulas as were used to generate the tables.

Yield to maturity can be approximated by using a shortcut method, if neither a computer nor a bond table is handy. If we assume that our 6 percent bond was quoted at a price of $832.89 on July 1, 2000 (which was the result of our earlier calculation), the discount from the par value of $1,000 is $167.11. The investor will thus not only receive the coupon interest of $30 each for 28 periods, but will also earn the discount of $167.11, if the bond is held to maturity and if the principal payment of $1,000 is received.

The shortcut method approximates the true yield by adjusting the periodic interest payment with a proportional amortization of this discount. The first step reflects the common accounting practice of amortizing discounts or premiums over the life of the bond. In our example, the discount of $167.11 is therefore divided by the remaining 28 periods, and the resulting periodic value increment of $5.97 is added to the periodic interest receipt of $30. The adjusted six-month earnings pattern is now $35.97 per period.

The next step relates the adjusted periodic earnings of $35.97 to the average investment outstanding during the remaining life of the bond. The price paid by the investor is $832.89, while the investment's value will rise to $1,000 at maturity. The average of the two values is one-half of the sum, or $916.45. We can then calculate the periodic yield to maturity (based on the six-month interest period) by relating the periodic earnings of $35.97 to the average investment outstanding, or we can find the annual yield to maturity by relating two six-months earnings amounts of $35.97 each to the average investment:

$$\text{Yield} = \frac{2 \times \$35.97}{\$916.45} = 7.85\% \text{ per year}$$

This result is slightly below the precise yield of 8 percent per year on which our original calculation was built. The averaging shortcut will always introduce some error, because it imperfectly simulates what is in fact a progressive present value structure. As yield rates and the number of time periods increase, larger errors will result. Yet the rough calculation provides a satisfactory result for use as an initial analytical check.

Had a premium been involved (that is, had the purchase price been above the par value of the bond), the shortcut calculation would, in contrast, reduce the periodic interest earnings by the proportional amortization of the premium. The second example discussed in the previous section (Figure 11–2) posed such a condition.

The result would appear as follows, again representing a close approximation of the true 4 percent solution:

$$\text{Yield} = \frac{2 \times (\$30.00 - \$7.59)}{(\$1,212.43 + \$1,000) \div 2} = 4.05\% \text{ per year}$$

In summary, bond yield calculations involve a fairly straightforward determination of the internal rate of return of future cash flows generated by the bond investment at a known present price. As in the case of a business capital investment, a trade-off of current outlays for future cash flows under conditions of uncertainty is involved. Yield and value are mathematically related and this relationship can be utilized to locate either result in preset bond yield tables, or to solve the analysis directly with a programmed calculator or spreadsheet.

Bond Provisions and Value

The simple value and yield relationships discussed so far are, of course, affected by the specific conditions surrounding the company and its industry, and also by additional provisions in the specific bond indenture itself. The issuer's ability to pay must be assessed through careful analysis of the company's earnings pattern and projections of expected performance. The techniques discussed in the early chapters of this book are helpful in this process. Ability to pay is a function of the projected cash flows and how well these flows cover debt service of both interest and principal. Sensitivity analysis based on high and low estimates of performance can be useful here, as can more sophisticated analytical modeling.

Variations in the bond indenture also will affect the value and the yield earned. To illustrate, we'll refer only to the major types of bond variations here. Mortgage bonds are secured by specific assets of the issuing firm. Because of this relationship, the bondholders have a cushion against default on the principal. This reduces the risk for the investor, and accordingly the coupon interest rate offered with mortgage bonds might be somewhat lower than that of unsecured debenture bonds, resulting in a reduced yield to the investor. Income bonds are at the other extreme on the risk spectrum because not only are they unsecured, but they also pay interest only if the earnings of the company reach a specified minimum level. Their coupon interest rate and yield level will be correspondingly high.

Convertible bonds, as we already observed, add the attraction of the holders' eventual participation in the potential market appreciation of common stock for which the bond can be exchanged at a set price. Therefore, the coupon rate of interest can be set at a somewhat lower level than that of a straight bond. In Chapter 10 we noted that the value of convertible bonds is affected by

- The market's assessment of the likely performance of the common stock.
- The gap between the stipulated conversion price and the current price of the common stock.
- The coupon interest it pays semiannually.

Normally, the conversion price is set higher than the prevailing market value of the common stock at the time of issue, to allow for expected value growth of the common stock over time. Conversion is essentially at the investor's discretion when found advantageous, although the indenture usually stipulates a time limit. Moreover, the issuing company usually has the right to call the bonds for redemption at a slight premium price after a certain date, thus forcing the investor to act. As common share prices approach and surpass the conversion price, the bond's value will rise above par because of the growing value of the equivalent common shares it represents.

A more recent phenomenon in the bond markets is the use of so-called junk bonds, extensively promoted by some investment bankers to support company takeovers that use very high levels of debt, or for leveraged buyouts by groups of managers or investors that similarly rely on extremely high financial leverage to finance the purchase of the company involved. These securities are in effect subordinated to (ranking below) the claims of other creditors in case of default and are sold under often highly risky circumstances, because the amount of indebtedness involved in some of these transactions exceeds what are normally considered prudent levels. The yields provided by these unsecured instruments are usually commensurate with the high risk perceived by investors, and defaults are not uncommon.

Many other modifications and provisions are possible to tailor bonds of various types to the needs of the issuing company and to the prevailing conditions in the securities markets. The many variations in bond provisions and their impact on value and yield call for careful judgments that go beyond the direct analytical techniques we discussed. We repeat that the calculations described are but the starting point, and no hard-and-fast rules exist for mechanically weighing all aspects of bond valuation. In the final analysis, value and yield must be adjusted with due regard to the investor's economic and risk preferences, in line with the specific objectives in owning debt instruments. The references at the end of the chapter cover these aspects in greater detail.

Preferred Stock Values

By its very nature, preferred stock represents a middle ground between debt and common equity ownership. The security provides a series of cash dividend payments, but normally has no specific provision (or expectation) for repayment of the par value of the stock. However, at times preferred stock carries a call provision, which allows the issuing company to retire part or all of the stock during a specific time period by paying a small premium over the stated value of the stock.

While the investor enjoys a preferential position over common stock with regard to current dividends and also to recovery of principal in the case of liquidation of the enterprise, preferred dividends might in fact not be paid if the company's performance is poor, a decision made by the board of directors. Such an event will, of course, adversely affect the value of the stock.

Preferred dividends, like common dividends, are declared at the discretion of the board of directors and, if missed currently, might not be made up in future periods, unless the preferred issue carries specific legal requirements to the contrary. Such provisions, for example, might call for cumulating past unpaid dividends until the company is in a position to afford declaring dividends of any kind. At other times, particularly in new companies, preferred stocks might carry a participation feature, which requires the board of directors to declare preferred dividends higher than the stated rate if earnings exceed a stipulated minimum level. But these two special situations are infrequent.

The task of valuing preferred stock, therefore, has to be based on less-definite conditions than was the case with bonds, because the only reasonably certain element is the stated annual dividend, which was originally set as a percentage of stated value. For example, an 8 percent preferred stock usually refers to a $100 share of stock which is expected to pay a dividend of $8 per year, most likely in quarterly installments, a pattern normally matching that for common stocks. The investor is faced with valuing this stream of prospective cash dividends. If the price paid for a share of preferred stock was $100, and the stock is held indefinitely, the yield under these circumstances would be 8 percent, assuming that the company is likely to be able to pay the dividend regularly.

If the price paid was more or less than the stated value, the yield could be found by relating the amount of the dividend to the actual price per share:

$$\text{Yield} = \frac{\text{Annual dividend per share}}{\text{Price paid per share}}$$

If the investor could expect to sell the stock at $110 five years hence, the exact yield of this combination of expected cash flows can be determined by using either present value techniques or the shortcut methods discussed earlier in the section on bonds.

However, estimating a future recovery value involves a good deal of conjecture. In contrast to bonds, preferred shares have no specific maturity date or par value to be paid at maturity. The actual price of a preferred stock traded in the securities markets depends both on company performance and on the collective value the securities markets place on the given preferred issue. In turn, this price level reflects the risk/reward trade-off demanded for the whole spectrum of investments at the time. The value range will depend not only on the respective risk premiums assigned to individual securities, but also on the inflationary expectations underlying the economy that are reflected in the risk-free rate to which risk premiums are added. Value might be a little easier to estimate if the stock carries a mandatory call provision applicable at a specific future date and price, especially if the date of analysis is close to that time.

When we look at preferred stock values from the viewpoint of investing, we should use the investor's own return standard to arrive at the maximum price the investor should be willing to pay for the stock, or the minimum price at which the investor should be willing to sell. We simply relate the stipulated dividend rate to our investor's required return—relevant for the level of risk implicit in the preferred issue—to arrive at the answer. If the return standard were 9 percent against which to test the 8 percent preferred, we would determine the investor-specific value as follows:

$$\text{Value per share} = \frac{\text{Stated dividend rate}}{\text{Required return}} = \frac{0.08}{0.09} = \$88.89$$

If the investor were satisfied with only a 7 percent return, the value would be:

$$\text{Value per share} = \frac{0.08}{0.07} = \$114.28$$

The judgments that remain to be made, of course, relate to any uncertainty in the future dividend pattern, and any likely material change in the future value of the stock, either due to changing market conditions, or because of a scheduled call for redemption at a premium price.

Preferred Stock Provisions and Value

As in the case of bonds, there are many modifications in the provisions of preferred stocks that can affect their value in the market. We mentioned earlier that some preferred stocks, particularly in newly established companies, contain a participation feature, which entitles the preferred holder to higher dividends, if corporate earnings exceed a set level. This feature can favorably affect the potential yield, and thus the valuation of the stock, depending on the prospects that the company will in fact reach this higher earnings level.

A much more common feature, similar to some bonds, is convertibility, the possibility of changing the preferred ownership position into that of common stock, as discussed in Chapter 10. As in the case of convertible bonds, however, the value of this feature can't be calculated precisely. Yet, as the price of common stock reaches and exceeds the stated conversion price, the price of the convertible preferred stock will tend to reflect the market value of the equivalent number of common shares. Before this point is reached, the convertible preferred stock's value will largely be considered the same as a regular preferred, and based essentially on the stated dividend. Convertibility is generally accompanied by a call provision, at a premium price, which enables the company to force conversion when conditions are advantageous.

In summary, the challenge of preferred stock valuation also goes beyond the simple techniques we have shown. In the end, decisions should be made only after careful assessment of the relative attractiveness of the specific features and conditions surrounding a particular company's preferred stock, and its place in the desired range of the risk/reward spectrum of the individual or institutional investor.

Common Stock Values

The most complex valuation problem is encountered when we turn to common stock, because by definition common stock represents the residual claim of owners on the total performance and outlook of the issuing corporation. We found this to be true when we examined the cost of capital from the point of view of the corporation in Chapter 9.

Common stock valuation is especially difficult because shareholders carry full ownership risks, yet have residual claims on both assets and earnings only after all other claims have been satisfied. Thus, an investment in common stock involves sharing both risks and rewards. This heightens the uncertainty about potential dividend receipts and any future gain or loss in recovering the price paid for the shares. As a consequence, measurement techniques have to deal with variables subject to a high degree of judgment.

The rewards of successful common stock ownership are several: cash dividends (and sometimes additional stock distributions in lieu of cash), and growth in recorded equity from growing earnings, whose underlying cash flows are reinvested by management in total or in part. Most important, however, is the past and prospective cash flow performance of the company, which is the basis for potential appreciation (or decline) of the stock's market price and resulting capital gains or losses. We've stated many times that shareholder value creation depends on the combination of dividends and capital gains or losses achieved over time, expressed in the form of total shareholder return, or TSR. As we observed in Chapter 9, there are many practical and theoretical issues surrounding the interpretation and measurement of these elements. Here we'll focus on ways of developing reasonable approximations of common share values, and similarly, show approximations of the yield an investor derives from a common stock investment.

Earnings and Common Stock Value

The quickest—if simplistic—way to approach the valuation of a share of common stock is to estimate the likely future level of earnings per share, and to capitalize these earnings at an appropriate earnings multiple (price/earnings ratio) that reflects expectations about the company and its industry:

$$\text{Value per share} = \text{Earnings per share} \times \text{Price/earnings ratio}$$

There are, of course, serious shortcomings in using projected accounting earnings as a measure of shareholder expectations. Since ultimately all economic value derives from cash flows, using the surrogate of earnings per share can't capture the full impact on value. Moreover, the approach is static unless any potential growth or decline in earnings is built in. Finally, there remains the basic problem of forecasting the earnings pattern itself, both for the company and its industry.

A more specific, cash-based approach to estimating common share value is to capitalize expected dividends. The size, regularity, and trend in dividend payout to shareholders has an important effect on the value of a share of common stock, being one of the elements of shareholder value creation. Yet there's also a degree of uncertainty about the receipt of any series of future dividends. Not only will such dividends depend on the ability of the company to perform successfully, but also any dividends paid are declared at the discretion of the corporate board of directors.

No general rule applies in this area—dividend policies can range from no cash payment at all to regular payments of 75 percent or more of current earnings. At times, dividends paid might even exceed current earnings, because the company is unwilling to cut the current dividend per share during a temporary earnings slump. Most boards of directors see some value in a consistent pattern of dividend payments, and major adjustments in the size of the dividend, up or down, are made very reluctantly.

The approach to valuation via dividends involves projecting the expected dividends per share and discounting them by the return standard appropriate for the investor. Several major issues arise here.

First, the current level of dividends paid is likely to change over time. For example, in a successful, growing company dividends, as well as earnings, are likely to grow. The problem is to make the projection of future dividends realistic, even though past performance is the only available guide. If a company has been paying a steadily growing dividend over many years, an extrapolation of this past trend might be reasonable. But this pattern must be tempered by subjective judgments about the outlook for the company and its industry. Companies with more erratic patterns of earnings and dividends, however, pose a greater challenge, as do young growth companies which pay no dividends in the early stages of their life cycle.

The second issue is the method of calculation. The most common format is the so-called dividend discount model, or dividend growth model, which appears below in its simplest form. The formula is a restatement of the dividend approach we used as one way of calculating the cost of equity in Chapter 9. In that approach, we defined the cost of common equity as the ratio of the current dividend to the current market price plus the expected rate of growth of future dividends. Here, instead of solving for the cost of equity, which is the investor's expectation of return, we solve for the value, or price, of the stock:

$$\text{Value per share} = \frac{\text{Current dividend}}{\text{Discount rate (Investor's expectation of return)} - \text{Dividend growth rate}}$$

This particular formula is based on the idea that the value of a share of stock is the sum of the present values of a series of growing annual dividend payments, discounted at the investor's return expectation for this class of risk. The formula also permits using the less realistic assumption of a constantly declining dividend. But either way it implies an ongoing series of payments in perpetuity, and it also implies a constant annual rate of growth or decline in the dividend payment.

Note, however, that this model would give an invalid answer for a company paying dividends expected to grow as fast or faster than the discount rate, because then the denominator would become zero or even negative. Clearly, under such a happy condition, the investor's return expectation should be reexamined and raised, or the stock should be considered as being outside the investor's risk/ reward spectrum.

The dividend discount model is related mathematically to an annuity formula (see Chapter 7) which assumes a constant growth rate and constant discount rate. The valuation it provides implicitly includes any appreciation in the stock's future market value as management reinvests the retained portion of the growing earnings. This condition holds because in the model, the market value of the stock at any future time is defined as the present value at that point of the ensuing stream of growing dividends.

The simplifying assumption of a constant rate of growth in dividends can be modified if a more erratic pattern of future dividends is expected. The calculation then becomes a present value analysis of uneven annual cash flows up to a selected point in the future. If the analyst wishes to assume that the dividend growth rate will stabilize at some future time, the basic formula can then be inserted and its result discounted to the present. Remember, however, that forecasting a precise pattern of dividends is problematic under most circumstances, and the analyst should look for reasonable approximations.

The dividend discount model (and earnings multiples) does not take into account the general trends and specific fluctuations in the securities markets. Obviously, the market value of specific shares can't be independent of movements in the securities markets as a whole, which are caused by economic factors like inflation, industry conditions, taxation, political events, and myriad other factors. Therefore, the economic returns a company achieves on the assets invested tend to be recognized in the relative market value of its shares, that is, relative to share values of its peers and within the context of overall market movements. Moreover, the value of a company's shares reflects the collective performance assessments by security analysts, institutional and individual investors, and the resulting demand for, or lack of interest in, those shares. While very important, these considerations are beyond the scope of this book.

Common Stock Yield and Investor Expectations

In Chapter 4, we presented two simple yardsticks for measuring the owners' return on investment in common stock. One of these was the earnings yield, a simple ratio of current or projected earnings per share to the current market price. The other was the inverse relationship, the so-called price/earnings ratio. As we pointed out, these simple ratios are static expressions based on readily available data and should only serve as temporary rough indicators of the real investor's yield created by a company's economic performance, that is, the cash flow pattern generated and projected.

The two yardsticks are useful mainly for a comparative analysis of companies or industry groupings, but must be supplemented by more insights if the analyst wishes to approximate the actual economic yield of a stock. Any serious examination of value or yield relative to the expectations of the shareholder should use more sophisticated techniques, such as the capital asset pricing model (CAPM, discussed in Chapter 9), which take into account market risk, specific company risk, portfolio considerations, and investors' risk preferences.

A third measure, most important for measuring shareholder value creation, is total shareholder return, or TSR, as we discussed in Chapter 4. This is an expression of the actual yield achieved over a period of time when a share of stock is acquired at the beginning of the period and sold at the end. The combination of dividends received during the period and the gain or loss achieved from the change in the share price is then related to the initial investment, as reflected in Figure 11–4. This calculation, which is published widely for publicly held companies in statistical compilations such as the Fortune 500 represents a direct approach to measuring the yield for the investor.

Yield, of course, is a function of the risk exposure chosen by an investor. A great deal of research has improved our understanding of the relative performance of common stocks within the broad movements of the security markets. This has resulted in refined definitions of the systematic risk underlying a diversified portfolio of stocks traded and the unsystematic (avoidable) risk of a

F I G U R E   11–4

Total Shareholder Return—the Components

particular security. As we discussed in Chapter 9, the CAPM relates the relative risk of a security to the risk of the market portfolio through a calculated factor, β, which indicates the difference in the risk characteristics of the stock versus the risk characteristics of the portfolio. The β factor is applied to the market portfolio's overall risk premium, defined in terms of the historical trend in returns earned over and above the risk-free return from the safest type of investment, such as long-term U.S. government bonds.

Thus, the expected yield of a particular common stock is the sum of the risk-free return and a risk premium, which is the risk premium earned in the total portfolio of stocks, adjusted by the inherent riskiness β of the particular security. We described the formula in Chapter 9:

$$\text{Yield} = R_f + \beta \ (R_m - R_f)$$

where

R_f is the risk-free return
β is the particular stock's covariance of variability in returns (the specific measure of riskiness)
R_m is the average return expected on common stocks

Fortunately, as we've mentioned, the β for publicly traded companies is published routinely in financial services such as *Value Line*. Current indications of the risk-free rate prevalent at the time and estimates of the return from groups of common stocks are also available in published sources.

We've only touched on some of the techniques used to determine value and yield for common stocks. Much more practical and theoretical insight is needed to deal confidently with the complex issues involved. The references listed at the end of this chapter provide more information.

Other Considerations in Valuing Common Stock

The book value per share of common stock is often quoted in financial references and company reviews. As we observed before, this figure represents the recorded residual claim of the shareholder as stated on the balance sheet. Book value is an accumulation of past transactions and values and does not reflect current economic value, which is based on potential earnings or dividends. It's only under unusual circumstances that book value per share will be reasonably representative of anything approximating the economic value of a share of common stock. This might be true, for example, if a company has either just been started, or is about to be liquidated. Under normal conditions, however, book value per share will tend to become increasingly remote from current values, because under current accounting rules, positive changes in the values of existing assets are rarely, if ever, reflected on the books. The book-to-market ratio discussed in Chapter 4 is used as a rough indicator of this divergence, and a book value that is close to or even exceeding market value might suggest the issuing company is under-performing, a situation that could invite takeover attempts by aggressive investors or corporations.

Market values of common stocks have been treated very lightly in our discussion, because a book on financial analysis techniques is not the place in which to explore the complex workings of the securities markets. Earlier we established the principle that in the broadest sense the stock market bases value on expected future cash flows, which are implicitly discounted by a rate of return reflecting the current outlook for the economy and the market as a whole. Key factors driving this rate of return are inflation expectations and projected tax rates. A rise in either of these will tend to lower the stock market valuation, while lower inflation and tax rates will boost it.

Within the general market trends the share prices of individual companies are similarly driven by cash flow expectations. The relative performance of a company's shares depends largely on these cash flows, but also to a significant extent on the trading pattern and volume of the particular stock. Suffice it to say here that if the following several basic conditions are met, quotations of a stock in the securities markets can reasonably be assumed to represent the underlying economic value based on the current and prospective performance of a company.

- The stock should be traded frequently and in fairly sizable volume. Small transactions between a few individuals cannot be a fair indication of the overall market value of a large company, even though the transaction prices are properly quoted on a given day.

- Share ownership should ideally be widespread so that trading does not involve moving large blocks of shares between a small number of concerned parties.

- The stock should be publicly traded on one or more stock exchanges, or be part of the increasingly important NASDAQ market.

Even if all of these conditions are met, the market value of a stock at any point might not necessarily reflect the true potential of the company. External factors, such as changes in the economy, publicity about the company and its industry, or takeover attempts, can affect the price at which the stock is traded. To help them understand this context, analysts will study the range within which market values have moved. Preferably this is done over at least one year and usually longer. Analysts will chart the behavior of specific share prices relative to market averages and composite averages for the industry peer group, using current databases for the process. Historical data and charting of key variables of publicly held companies are available online from a large variety of service providers. (See Appendix III)

As we'll see later when we'll discuss the valuation of a total company, there's also a difference between (1) valuing individual shares, (2) valuing the fraction of a company's shares traded normally in the stock market on a daily basis, and (3) the value of all shares at a given point of time. In most cases, partial trading can be viewed as establishing the value of minority holdings, that is, the value of partial positions in the company's equity—which is what current quotations represent. When it comes to valuing the total equity of a company, however, for example in the case of an acquisition, experience has shown again and again that the market price of recent partial trading and the value of the total enterprise in play for acquisition can differ widely, usually leading to a premium for the total company. The basic reason is that an acquisition transaction dramatically narrows the number of parties involved in trading, significantly increases the volume of shares traded, and introduces competitive bidding to realize synergistic and other advantages envisioned by the acquirers.

Specialized Valuation Issues

Rights and Warrants

In Chapter 10 we discussed the main aspects of rights and warrants from the perspective of the issuing company. We'll now turn briefly to illustrating the value of these specialized forms of financing to the investor.

Rights values arise from the fact that these securities entitle the holder to purchase additional common shares of the company at a price often significantly below the prevailing market price. For example, an investor holding five common shares has received five rights that represent the opportunity to purchase one new share of common stock at $30. The current market value of the existing common stock is $40.

Our investor's initial position is as follows:

Number of shares.	5
Number of rights.	5
Value of 5 shares @ $40	$200
Subscription price.	$30

After exercising the rights and paying $30 to the company, the shareholder's position will be:

Number of shares.	6
Value of investment	$230.00
Investment per share	$ 38.33
Value of a right	$ 1.67 (Old value − new value)

The market value of the company's shares after all rights have been exercised will in fact tend to approximate $38.33, because the new shares were offered at a significant discount, in the ratio of one new share for each five old shares held. When a rights offering is announced, the shares of the company will trade *cum rights* from the effective date (holder-of-record date) until the specified date at which the stock becomes *ex rights*. At that time, the decline in price reflecting the value of the now separate rights will take place.

The value to the investor of each right is therefore the proportional discount provided by the rights offering, as related to the ratio of old and new shares. Rights are often traded in the market at the approximate level of the calculated value. Both the value of common stock ex rights, and the value of rights themselves will, of course, be influenced by general movements in the securities markets that are independent of the particular company's circumstances.

Warrants have value directly related to the market price of the common shares of the company. Unlike rights, warrants are not issued proportionally to all common shareholders, but are most frequently attached to issues of new debt and occasionally to new issues of common. Moreover, warrants tend to have expiration dates far longer than rights, and in some cases have no expiration at all. In effect, warrants are options entitling the holder to purchase a new share of common at a fixed exercise price for an extended period of time.

The value of the warrant therefore will be directly related to the difference between the exercise price and the expected market value of the common during the usually lengthy exercise period. If the common stock continually trades at or below the exercise price, the value of the warrant will approach zero as the expiration date draws near and no change is foreseen. If the market value of the common rises above the exercise price, and especially if it's expected to grow in the future during the remainder of the exercise period, the value of the warrant will rise in concert.

Options

Given the rapid increase in the importance of options trading in the money and securities markets, at least some brief reference should be made to this highly specialized form of investing and the basic valuation aspects involved. Rights and warrants as discussed above are in effect options extended by the issuing company to purchase additional shares at a set price, and we saw how the interplay of the trend in the company's market price, the exercise price, and the exercise period affected the value of these instruments. The broader concept of options refers to a form of security which permits the holder to buy or sell an asset at a specified price for a specified period of time. Options to buy are named *call options,* while options to sell are named *put options.* The underlying asset's specified price is called the exercise or strike price, while the date at the end of the exercise period is its maturity. Options can be purchased in the option markets for a price, called the premium. It reflects, at the time of purchase, the value of the privilege to buy or sell the asset involved under the conditions specified, in light of the current expectations about future movements in the value of the asset.

Options are a way to guarantee the amount of a purchase or sale under uncertain future conditions for a relatively small current investment, but the value of this opportunity rises and falls with the movements in the market price of the asset. A put option to sell stock at a given price will become worthless if the market price matches or falls below the strike price as the maturity date arrives, while it can become quite valuable when the reverse is true. Similarly, a call option to purchase a foreign currency at a certain value to the dollar will grow in value as the market quotations exceed the strike price, and lose value as they drop lower, expiring worthless. Options can be useful in taking a position in a stock or other asset for a partial investment, with the opportunity to leverage a significant return on this investment if the option speculation is successful, while limiting a potential loss to the premium paid. Options are also ideal hedging devices, used by investors and corporate managers to offset exposure in currency or securities with matching options that "bet the other way."

The specific valuation techniques dealing with options and the many risk/reward patterns and trade-offs are too specialized to cover in this space. They are based in large part on the Black Scholes valuation formulas that established the analytical foundation. Apart from detailed texts on the subject, there are software models available to assist in the analysis of options. and the interested reader should turn to the references at the end of the chapter.

Business Valuation

Managers, investors, and investment bankers need to know how to measure the total value of a business as an ongoing entity. Whether it's a multibusiness global corporation, any of its individual operations, or a small single-business company, there are many occasions when obtaining a current valuation is necessary. The most obvious use for such a valuation arises when purchase or sale of a company or a line of business is being considered. The wave of acquisitions, mergers, and hostile takeovers in the past decade involved thousands upon thousands of valuations.

A similar type of valuation is useful when a company, for purposes of internal restructuring, disposes of certain product lines or operating divisions. The buyers might be other companies, groups of investors, or even the existing management, who might want to acquire the division financed through a leveraged buyout (a purchase based on using a high proportion of debt in excess of normal capital structure proportions). Regardless of the form of the purchase, sale, or restructuring, both the buyer and the seller need to arrive at a reasonable approximation of the economic value of the company or line of business as a going concern.

Another important use of business valuation—related to the ones mentioned—stems from the growing recognition of value-based management as the critical focus for successful performance. Managing for shareholder value has become a key strategic objective for corporate managers. Many successful companies measure economic value creation for the company as a whole and for its major businesses and reward the management team accordingly. In this context, the business is periodically valued with various techniques to determine progress against planned performance, and to set the appropriate incentive compensation awards. We'll discuss value-based management in more detail in Chapter 12, where we'll review the broad implications of shareholder value creation—the concept with which we began the book.

At this point we'll first discuss the basic concepts of valuing the equity of a company, then valuing the company as a whole. In each case, we'll use cash flow techniques which apply to most valuation situations.

Valuing the Equity

The value of a company's equity can be calculated by estimating the future cash flows accruing to the shareholders. The process is quite comparable to the business investment techniques we developed in Chapter 7. In essence, the stake of the shareholders in the company is (1) the present value of the total pattern of expected common dividends paid, carefully choosing an analysis period that is reasonable for the type of industry—3 to 5 years for fast-changing industries like computers, and 10 to 20 years for resource-based industries like forest products or oil—plus (2) the present value of the expected worth of the equity at the end of the analysis period.

We can express this definition in a formula:

VE = PV (of expected cash dividends) + PV (of value of equity at end of period)

Note that these cash flows are expectations, just as they are encountered in all types of business investments. Note also that this approach differs from the dividend discount model in that it establishes a definite time period and substitutes a direct estimate of the future value of the equity at the end of the period versus the simple assumption about a perpetually growing dividend.

The process is carried out by discounting the pattern of annual dividends and the ending equity value at the company's cost of equity capital, which reflects the risk to the owners of the equity. This cost is not the weighted average cost of capital, which is based on a combination of debt and equity in the company's capital structure, but rather the higher cost of the equity alone.

The pattern of estimated dividend cash flows can rise or decline, depending on the analytical assumptions underlying the expectations of the analyst. Similarly, the estimate of the ending value of the total equity might be based on a variety of assumptions, ranging from a simple dividend or earnings multiple to a detailed assessment of the company's competitive viability.

In the attempt to focus specifically on the value of the company's equity, however, this approach blurs the contribution from the successful use of leverage. Remember, the dividend cash flow to shareholders is made possible not only through successful investment of equity funds, but also from earnings exceeding the cost of long-term financing used in the capital structure. In fact, the common theme established early in the book was that the economic success of any company had to come from exceeding the weighted overall cost of capital in all of its present and future investments. As we'll see in a moment, it's far more useful to approach valuing shareholder equity by first valuing the total company and then subtracting the value of the debt.

Valuing the Total Company

As we've said before, any ongoing business represents a series of expected future cash flows. To arrive at the total value of the company, we must therefore transform past and projected earnings performance into a net cash flow framework, just as if we were calculating the desirability of a capital investment project as discussed in Chapters 7 and 8. The particular cash flow employed for this purpose is free cash flow, which is defined as the after-tax cash flow from operations before interest, reduced by any funds required for additional working capital and net new business investments. This cash flow represents the cash available for investors and creditors after the ongoing investment needs of the business have been met. Note that this definition matches the principles we employed in Chapters 7 and 8, where the cash flow pattern of an investment was developed independent of any compensation to the providers of the funds (interest and dividends), because the cost of capital used for discounting embodied the weighted average of shareholder and creditor expectations.

Several steps are normally used to arrive at the free cash flow pattern. The first is to forecast the operating earnings of the business for a reasonable number of years into the future. The starting point for deriving operating earnings relevant for this purpose is EBIAT, that is, earnings before interest, but after taxes, or EBIT $(1 - \text{tax rate})$, as was discussed in Chapter 4. The reason for using tax-adjusted EBIT is that we are looking for the cash flows remaining after all operating costs and expenses—of which income taxes are one element—but before any financing considerations, just as we did in the case of analyzing business investments in Chapters 7 and 8. Any significant nonoperating earnings or expenses after applicable taxes, such as investment income, or restructuring costs, should be recognized and eliminated in the period they occur, that is, by subtracting nonoperating income and adding nonoperating expenses to EBIAT.

Developing the expected earnings pattern calls for a variety of assumptions and judgments. The simplest way to project, of course, would be to keep the current level of earnings constant. Under most circumstances, however, such a simplification would not be realistic. If operating earnings can be expected to grow or decline, or follow a pronounced cyclical pattern, it's necessary to make a year-by-year projection for as far into the future as possible under the circumstances.

The second step is to convert the operating earnings pattern into cash flows, by adjusting the after-tax earnings for noncash elements such as depreciation and amortization, and for deferred taxes, as we discussed in Chapters 4 and 7.

The third step is to estimate the future investment outlays deemed necessary to support both the present level of earnings and any anticipated changes in operations in line with the company's overall strategy. These include spending on new property, plant, and equipment, major programs such as research and development projects, and all incremental working capital requirements, including planned acquisitions. The outlays will be reduced by any planned disposals of existing assets, or divestment of lines of business.

While such estimates can be quite speculative, it's normally unrealistic to assume that earnings of an ongoing business will continue at current levels. Unquestionably, there will have to be periodic infusions of capital for replacement and upgrading of existing equipment, not to mention the funding requirements to support growing volume (or capital releases from volume declines), as discussed in Chapter 3. There we observed that a rule of thumb commonly used to project these capital expenditures is that in order to maintain the present level of earnings, an amount close or equal to annual depreciation must be reinvested each year. Additional investments for expansion or new products and services and their effect on earnings are estimated as separate, distinct outlays with ensuing periodic cash inflows.

The fourth step is to determine whether there are any nonoperating assets that are separate from the ongoing operations, such as cash, marketable securities, unused land, and so on, some of which might create nonoperating income or expenses, or simply be redundant values. Such assets should be separated out in the analysis and in the end added to the operational firm valuation.

The final step in setting up the pattern for valuing an ongoing business involves truncating the analysis after an appropriate number of years and deriving an estimate for the ongoing value (market value) of the business at the termination point. It corresponds to the terminal value concept we discussed in Chapters 7 and 8 for doing project analysis. By definition, this ongoing value should be the sum of the present values of all future cash flows from that point on. Some analysts assume level cash flows (an annuity) for the indefinite future (perpetuity assumption), using the expected free cash flow of the first year beyond the termination point for the purpose. This no-growth expectation is calculated simply by dividing the expected future annual free cash flow by the weighted average cost of capital or similar standard to arrive at the ongoing value of the business (recall the discussion of annuities in Chapter 7). Where continuous growth is expected, one can use the so-called perpetual growth formula, which divides the expected annual free cash flow in the first year beyond the cutoff by the cost of capital less the growth rate:

$$\text{Ongoing value} = \frac{\text{Free cash flow}_{t+1}}{k_w - g}$$

Note that this formulation is limited to growth rates lower than the cost of capital because the result becomes meaningless when growth is equal to or in excess of the cost of capital. At times it might be necessary to assume a declining cash flow pattern that reflects competitive and technological uncertainty, which would alter the formula above into adding the rate of decline to the cost of capital in the denominator, instead of subtracting the growth rate.

The added difficulty of forecasting operations beyond the end of the chosen analysis period suggests that we also find an acceptable shortcut answer for the ongoing value. A common way of dealing with the problem is to use a price to earnings multiple that might be warranted at that point, i.e., to set the value of the business at the termination point based on 10, 15, or 20 times the after-tax earnings in that year. The multiple chosen will depend on the nature of the business and the trends in the industry it represents. Because of the power of discounting, such an approximation of the ongoing value will generally suffice at least for an initial valuation result. At times the ongoing value is simply represented by the estimated book value of the business, although this is probably a less satisfactory shortcut than the earnings multiple for the reasons we discussed in earlier chapters.

Once all the cash flow elements have been estimated, they can be assembled in the form of a spreadsheet as shown in the generalized format of Figure 11–5, which parallels the various examples we gave in Chapter 8. The resulting annual net cash flows (free cash flow) represent the cash available to the company to support its obligations to all providers of the long-term funds, i.e., the payment of

FIGURE 11–5

Total Company Valuation—A Numerical Example*

	Present	Year 1	Year 2	Year 3	Year 4	Year 5	Year 6
EBIT $(1 - t)$		$10,000	$12,000	$13,000	$12,000	$13,500	$ 12,500
Add: write-offs and noncash items.		6,500	7,000	8,600	9,300	9,900	11,900
Less: net new working capital		−1,200	−1,400	−1,800	500	−1,600	−2,000
Less: net new capital investments.		−8,000	−15,000	−10,200	−11,000	−22,000	−10,000
Add/less: significant nonoperating items		500	−300	400	1,200	−800	0
Free cash flow		7,800	2,300	10,000	12,000	−1,000	12,400
Ongoing value @ 15 times earnings		—	—	—	—	—	187,500
Present value factors @ 12%		0.893	0.797	0.712	0.636	0.567	0.507
Present values @ cost of capital		6,965	1,833	7,120	7,632	−567	101,349
Cumulative present values.		$ 6,965	$ 8,799	$15,919	$23,551	$22,984	$124,333
Firm value	$124.3 million						
Nonoperating assets (cash, marketable securities, etc.). . .	5.7 million						
Total value	$130.0 million						
Value of outstanding long-term debt.	40.0 million						
Value of shareholders' equity . . .	$ 90.0 million						

*This exhibit is available in an interactive format (TFA Template)—see "Analytical Support" on p. 389.

interest, dividends, and potential repayment of debt or even repurchase of its own shares.

After discounting the pattern of annual cash flows over the chosen time frame at the appropriate return standard, normally the weighted average cost of capital, the resulting net present value should be a reasonable approximation of the value of the total business. Note that the nonoperating assets were added to the operational firm value to arrive at the total value. In our example we've shown an assumed value of $5.7 million, which raises the total value to $130.0 million. The quality of the result depends, of course, on the quality of the estimates that were used in deriving it. The analyst should employ extensive sensitivity analysis to test the likely range of outcomes, testing different discount rates and especially different estimates of the ongoing value. In this example the ongoing value based on the no-growth assumption would be $100 million, when we use a free cash flow estimate of $12 million, divided by the cost of capital of 12 percent. With a five percent perpetual growth assumption, the ongoing value would be $12 million divided by a net factor of 7 percent, or $171 million. While the impact of discounting moderates the significance of the ongoing value somewhat (the discount factor in Year 6 at 12 percent is 0.507), the discounted difference between the earnings multiple assumption of $187.5 million we used, and the no-growth free cash flow result of $100 million is still a highly significant $44 million ($87.5 × 0.507), or about one-third of the final result. It's not unusual to find such sizable ranges of outcomes in what amounts to a quantification of future expectations, not historical data.

It'll be useful to demonstrate visually how the firm value developed by this present value analysis relates to the company's capital structure. What we've developed by discounting the net cash flow stream and the assumed ongoing value, plus nonoperating assets, is the approximate fair market value of the company's overall capitalization. Figure 11–6 demonstrates that the total recorded value of a business is the sum of its working capital, fixed assets, and other assets, which are financed by the combination of long-term debt and equity. The present value approach has enabled us to express this accounting value in current economic terms—a present value which might be higher or lower than the recorded values on the balance sheet, and which also depends, of course, on all the assumptions implicit in the cash flow forecasts including the ongoing value. Only by coincidence will the two values be precisely equal, because as we discussed in Chapter 2, recorded values on the balance sheet reflect historical transaction values which tend to become obsolete with the passage of time.

It should be evident that to arrive at the market value of the shareholders' equity, we must subtract the value of the long-term debt from the adjusted present value result—which is the market value of the total business, also called value of the firm or enterprise value. In our example, therefore, the value of the shareholders' equity is $90.0 million. It might be necessary to restate the value of long-term debt based on the current yields prevailing for debt of similar risk, as we discussed earlier in this chapter, rather than the recorded values on the balance sheet. For example, if current interest rates are higher than the stated rates for the company's debt, the value of the debt will be lower than recorded, and vice versa.

FIGURE 11–6

Present Value of Business Cash Flows and the Capital Structure

By observing this principle, we remain consistent with the weighted average cost of capital yardstick that was applied in discounting the cash flow pattern, a measure which contains the cost of incremental debt, as we recall from Chapter 9. A similar deduction must be made for any preferred stock contained in the capital structure.

We've now achieved a direct valuation of the company's common equity by means of an economic (cash flow) approach which is conceptually superior to the simpler devices discussed in the common stock section of this chapter, although subject to the range of assumptions underlying it. This approach is the basis for much of the analytical work underlying modern security analysis, where the use of cash flow analysis has begun to overshadow most other methodologies.

In a multibusiness company, the approach can be refined by developing operating cash flow patterns for each of the business units, and discounting these individual patterns at the corporate cost of capital. If the businesses differ widely in their risk/reward conditions, one can apply different discount standards that reflect these differences, as discussed in Chapter 8. In recent years, testing the present value of individual business units' cash flow patterns to determine the relative contribution to the total value of the corporation has become widely accepted.

Yet, given the nature of the estimates underlying the analysis, there's nothing automatic about the use of such values in an actual transaction involving the sale of a company or any of its parts. Different analysts and certainly buyers and sellers will use their own sets of assumptions in developing their respective

results. There should also be efforts to test the analytical results against comparable transactions, to the extent these are available and relevant.

The actual value finally agreed upon in any transaction between a buyer and
a seller will depend on many more factors, not the least of which are the differences in assessing business risk and in the return expectations of the parties involved, as well as the in the negotiating stance and skills used by them. We'll
return to the subject of valuation of a company or combination of companies
within the context of shareholder value creation in Chapter 12.

Using Shortcuts in Valuing an Ongoing Business

In the previous example, an earnings multiple based on EBIT was used to derive
the ongoing value of the business. This multiple simply indicated what a particular level of current or projected earnings was "worth" at the termination point
of the analysis. After-tax earnings or after-tax operating profit are often used as
well. Closely related to the price/earnings ratio, this rule of thumb is often applied
to quickly value a company, and the result can be an "opener" in initial negotiations. Never precise, the earnings multiple is derived from rough statistical
comparisons of similar transactions, and from a comparative evaluation of the
performance of the price/earnings ratios of companies in the industry. Other multiples encountered at times, especially with smaller companies or new businesses,
include multiples of sales, or even derived sales volumes based on an estimated
customer group.

When an actual earnings multiple is turned into a ratio of estimated earnings
to value, it provides a rough estimate of the rate of return on the purchase or selling price—assuming that the earnings chosen are representative of what the future
will bring. When taken as only one of the indicators of value within a whole array
of negotiating data, the earnings multiple and the related crude rate of return have
some merit.

Other shortcuts in valuing an ongoing business involve determining the
total market value of common and preferred equity from market quotations—in
itself somewhat of a challenge in view of stock market fluctuations—and adjusting this total for any long-term debt to be assumed in the transaction. One issue
involved in this approach is the question of how representative the market quotations are depending on the trading pattern and volume of the particular stock.
At times, when no publicly traded securities are involved, the book value of the
business is examined as an indicator of value. Needless to say, the fact that
recorded values don't necessarily reflect economic values can be a significant
problem.

All of these results can at one time or another enter into the deliberations,
but considerable judgment must be exercised to determine their relevance in the
particular case. In most situations, the discounted cash flow approach will be the
conceptually most convincing measure, despite the difficulties of estimating
the cash flow pattern in specific terms.

Key Issues

The following is a recap of the key issues raised directly or indirectly in this chapter. They are enumerated here to help the reader keep the techniques discussed within the perspective of financial theory and business practice.

1. The concept of value is not independent of the purpose for which it is used, and its definition and meaning can vary widely with respect to the conditions and circumstances to which it is applied.

2. The value of a security is a function of the expectations about future performance placed upon it, which can be individual judgments as well as collective judgments representing a market.

3. Investors approach the valuation of an investment proposition in terms of their individual risk preferences and thus will differ widely in assessing the attractiveness of an investment.

4. While the securities markets provide momentary indications, the relative value of a share of common stock in the market at any time is a combination of future expectations, residual claims, and assessments of general and specific risk, subject to economic and business conditions and the decisions of management and the board of directors. It's also affected by the breadth of trading in the security.

5. Valuation techniques are essentially assessment tools that attempt to quantify available objective data and estimates. Yet such quantification will always remain in part subjective, and in part impacted by forces beyond the individual parties' control.

6. Valuation of a security or a business is distorted by the same elements that distort other types of financial analysis: price-level changes, accounting conventions, economic conditions, market fluctuations, and many subjective intangible factors.

7. Validation of results achieved from valuation projects ultimately has to await actual performance in the future; this is why the importance of sound judgments at the time of the analysis cannot be overstated.

Summary

In this chapter, we've brought together a whole range of concepts and basic techniques to provide the reader with an overview of how to value assets, securities, and business operations. To set the stage, we discussed key definitions of value, and then took the viewpoint of the investor assessing the value of the three main forms of securities issued by a company. After covering both value and yield in these situations, we expanded our view to encompass the valuation of an ongoing business. Our purpose was to find basic ways of setting the value in transactions such as sale of a business, restructuring, or the combination of companies in the form of a merger or acquisition.

We found that methods were available for deriving such values, but that the specific assumptions and the background of the transaction added many, often complex, dimensions to the basic calculations. We demonstrated the valuation of a business specifically in cash flow terms, and showed how a company's equity can be valued based on cash flow expectations, quite similar to the business investment analysis we discussed in Chapter 8. Ultimately, value will always remain partially subjective and will be settled in an exchange between interested parties—but managing effectively for economic performance and value will always remain the basic obligation of management.

Analytical Support

Financial Genome, the commercially available financial analysis and planning software described in Appendix I, has the capability to develop and display integrated financial projections directly from input data and built-in data bases, using the application's forecasting capabilities. It can automatically derive accounting measures as well as common cash flow inputs to valuation analysis. The software is also accompanied by an interactive template (TFA Template under "extras") for the cash flow valuation of a business, based on Figure 11–5 on page 384, which can be used to calculate present values and the equity valuation for any pattern of inputs and discount rates. The historical database on TRW Inc. contained in the software can be used to develop projected statements and free cash flow as an input to the valuation template. (see "Downloads Available" on p. 431)

Selected References

Brealey, Richard, and Stewart Myers. *Principles of Corporate Finance.* 5th ed. Burr Ridge, IL: Irwin/McGraw-Hill, 1996.

Copeland, Tom; Tim Koller; and Jack Murrin. *Measuring and Managing the Value of Companies.* 2nd ed. New York: John Wiley & Sons, 1995.

Cornell, Bradford. *Corporate Valuation: Tools for Effective Appraisal and Decision Making.* Burr Ridge, IL: Business One Irwin, 1993.

Jones, Gary E., and Dirk Van Dyke, *The Business of Business Valuation.* Burr Ridge, IL: McGraw-Hill, 1998.

Pratt, Shannon P. *Valuing a Business: The Analysis and Appraisal of Closely Held Companies.* 3rd ed. Burr Ridge, IL: Irwin/McGraw-Hill, 1995.

Rappaport, Alfred. *Creating Shareholder Value.* Revised ed. New York: Free Press, 1998.

Ross, Stephen; Randolph Westerfield; and Jeffrey Jaffe. *Corporate Finance.* 5th ed. Burr Ridge, IL: Irwin/McGraw-Hill, 1999.

Weston, Fred; Scott Besley; and Eugene Brigham. *Essentials of Managerial Finance.* 11th ed. Hinsdale, IL: Dryden Press, 1996.

CHAPTER 12

MANAGING FOR
SHAREHOLDER VALUE

We now return to the primary concept we established at the beginning of this book, namely, that the basic obligation of the management of any company is to make investment, operating, and financing decisions that will enhance shareholder value over the long term. Our discussion of valuing business cash flows in Chapter 11 strongly suggested that management should periodically reexamine the company's policies and strategies to test whether its basic obligation of creating shareholder value is in fact being met. We recall that increasing shareholder value depends on making new investments that exceed the cost of capital—an expression of investor expectations—as well as managing all existing investments for cash flow results that similarly exceed investor expectations.

The most beneficial aspect of the growing emphasis on shareholder value creation over the past decade has been the widespread rediscovery of management fundamentals—even if at times under threat of dismissal by hostile raiders. Despite the periodic lapses of economic discipline exemplified in the recent dot.com bubble, which we discussed in Chapter 1, there has been real progress made with the prospect of more to come. Growing numbers of corporate managers, in the U.S. and in other parts of the world, are tackling the critical task of creating value for their shareholders. They are doing this by reexamining the structure and functioning of their company as a whole and by placing greater emphasis on making their decisions, large and small, on the basis of sound economic trade-offs. The basic imperative of requiring all investments to earn above the cost of capital has been rediscovered as a practical—even if difficult to achieve—goal. Vast efforts at restructuring, increasing cost-effectiveness, making disinvestments and acquisitions, and developing value-based processes, data flows, measures, and incentives are being carried out in the name of shareholder value creation. In fact, testing the efficiency with which all resources are employed and defining the relative contribution from various business segments with an objective "outside" orientation has become commonplace in many companies. One could argue that this approach should really have been commonplace all along, because of the long-established fact that all business decisions have an economic basis—whether this is recognized or not. A number of specialized measures and valuation methodologies have emerged in support of value-based management principles, which we'll discuss later in this chapter.

Shareholder Value Creation in Perspective

Before we turn to a detailed discussion of value-based measurement techniques, it'll be useful to revisit the business system as shown in Figure 12–1 to provide an overall perspective for the various analytical processes presented in this book, and to review their relationship to shareholder value creation. Two additional

FIGURE 12–1

Shareholder Value Creation in a Business System Context

overview perspectives in Figures 12–2 and 12–3 also will help set the stage for this chapter.

As the upper part of the diagram shows, companies focusing on shareholder value will tailor their analytical processes and physical implementation to achieve economic (cash flow) returns above the cost of capital on new investments as well as on existing investments, making sure that return goals are set at appropriate levels and in the proper economic context. We recall the discussion of Chapters 7, 8, and 9 in which the principles and the measures supporting this approach were presented. One of the key issues to be faced in this area, however, is the dichotomy between the economic analysis of new investments, where expected cash flow patterns can be judged in an incremental fashion, and the analysis of the existing investment base, where normal accounting data and recorded values are the main source of information. It is here where much of the development of value-based methodologies has taken place, in an effort to close the conceptual gap between cash flow economics and ratio-based conventional analysis.

The midsection of the diagram reflects our familiar set of operational trade-offs, which in a value creation context, should be made with long-term cash flow generation in mind. Excellent product and service offerings, competitive advantage, and cost-effectiveness are the underlying driving forces, but the many decisions supporting daily activities require not only an analytical understanding of their cash flow impact, but also measures and incentives that reinforce economic decision making. Again, the increasing emphasis on value-based management is fueling a shift away from accounting-based methodology toward cash flow frameworks. We encountered some of this trend in our discussion of the analytical approaches of earlier chapters, and we'll expand on the measures and their implications later in this chapter.

The bottom part of the diagram deals with the financing aspects of value creation, where we recognize the many trade-offs we've encountered in Chapters 6, 9, and 10. Companies with a value orientation consciously manage these trade-offs for long-term cash flow generation, and view the disposition of profits and the target dimensions of the capital structure as critical supportive elements in their strategic planning. Choices that affect dividend payout, changes in leverage, repurchase of shares, and funding of future opportunities are made against the criterion of value creation. The trade-offs chosen here can at times significantly affect the direction of the company's strategy.

Another overview of the integration of financial, strategic, and operational activities supporting shareholder value creation is provided in Figure 12–2. Here we see the core concept of earning in excess of the cost of capital surrounded by the key management activities, starting at the top with the evaluation and selection of sound strategies, leading to broad resource allocation and the analysis of specific business investments. In this area the analytical tools of Chapters 7 and 8 come into play. This is followed by the identification of those elements and variables that drive value creation, which form the basis for operational targets and the

FIGURE   12-2

Shareholder Value Creation in a Management Context

measures by which performance is gauged. Here the materials of Chapters 3, 4, and 5 have relevance. Next is the critical area of designing incentives for managers to act in an economic fashion, and to support a long-term view of decision making. We've not focused on such incentive programs because they are beyond the scope of this book. However, financial and other measures selected for the purpose must reinforce the economic (cash flow) orientation we have stressed throughout.

Finally, there's the broad strategic issue of the portfolio of activities carried on by the company, which is intimately connected with the capital structure proportions and trade-offs. Here the materials in Chapters 6, 9, 10, and 11 are the appropriate background.

Let's now turn to a final summary overview of the major elements of shareholder value creation and their relationship to the three areas of management decisions: investments, operations, and financing. The diagram in Figure 12–3 will be useful in tying together the various concepts we've discussed. It's designed to assist the reader in visualizing the linkage between management decisions and shareholder value. The diagram shows the three basic types of decisions on the left and identifies their key impacts on the cash flows that are the drivers for creating value. The combination of investment and operating decisions generates cash flow from operations after taxes, or free cash flow, while the financing decisions influence the capital structure and the level of the weighted cost of capital of the company. Applying the cost of capital—which of course reflects expected investor returns—as a discount rate to the free cash flow and ongoing value determines the total shareholder value, as discussed in Chapter 11. At the same time, product life cycles, competition, and many other influences affect the

Shareholder Value Creation in a Cash Flow Context

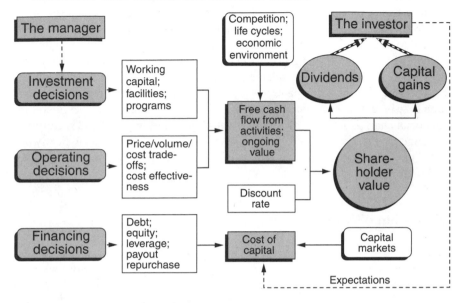

size and variability of these projected cash flows. In turn, the capital markets influence the investor's return expectation.

Alternatively, the right side of the diagram shows that shareholder value
also can be viewed in the form of total shareholder return (TSR), which we know
to be the combination of cash dividends and realized capital gains, when seen
through the eyes of the shareholder. This investor viewpoint is inseparable from
the basic driving force of the business—cash flow patterns—for it is positive free
cash flow that will permit the company to pay dividends in the first place, and also
will boost the market value of the shares, enabling the investor to realize capital
gains. Naturally, it's possible to create value by minimizing dividends and reinvesting all funds in soundly based opportunities. The value increase would then
come from capital appreciation, assuming successful implementation and expected growth in cash flow performance. Conversely, under conditions where
sound new opportunities are not available, it might be best for the shareholders
that the company repurchase shares rather than invest in mediocre business projects to avoid destroying value.

What are the implications of the three overviews we've just presented? Note
that we've once more returned to a systems view of the corporation, driven by the
same three basic management decisions, but stressing even more the cash flow patterns that are the economic underpinning of performance and value. All financial
analysis techniques and methodologies discussed in this book are ultimately related
to the business system and its strategic context as viewed here and in Chapter 2,

and it's important that the analytical use of any measure, or a combination of measures, be judged in this sense.

The basic message of managing for shareholder value is nothing more than management's obligation to base all of its investment, operating, and financing decisions on an economic—cash flow—rationale, and to manage all resources entrusted to its care for superior economic returns. Over time, consistency in this approach will generate growing shareholder value, and relative growth in share price performance. If this sounds fundamental, it's intended to be, since the challenge for the 21st century is competitive survival through managing better in a world arena—where economic fundamentals are gaining dominance over ideology. Financial analysis in its many forms, as introduced in Chapter 2 and specifically explained in the remainder of this book, is an essential toolkit for analytically oriented persons of any viewpoint, as they judge the financial/economic performance and outlook of any business.

Evolution of Value-Based Methodologies

Over the last two decades, a number of value-based methodologies have evolved and are gaining increasing acceptance. Their basic aim is to link performance expressed in past and expected cash flow patterns or their surrogates to the market value of a company as a whole and to the relative price level of its common shares. They have become popular within the context of value-based management processes, and various consulting firms use these approaches to establish a firm connection between management actions and shareholder value results. Moreover, such programs relate cash flow thinking and results to management incentive pay. They are designed to provide a coherent set of economic principles that should guide a company's planning processes, investment policies, financing choices, operational decisions, and management incentives toward increasing shareholder value, as displayed earlier in our overviews.

The change in thinking underlying these processes is exemplified in the simple diagram of Figure 12–4, which displays the significant shift in emphasis as reflected in the way corporate performance is being measured.

Prior to the 1980s, management emphasis in the majority of situations tended to be on achieving consistently high profit margins. The asset base necessary to support operations was of secondary importance, almost an afterthought, as indicated by the separation border. The idea was that if margins were high enough, asset recovery and returns would take care of themselves, as would funding of new investment needs for rapid growth. Needless to say, companies applying this way of thinking did not make the best use of invested funds, and asset effectiveness was problematic. In the '80s the emphasis shifted toward growth of profits in absolute terms, again with a focus on the operating statement and less attention paid to asset effectiveness. With some luck, sufficient profit growth would support existing and new investments, but this mindset still left asset effectiveness open to real questions.

F I G U R E   12–4

The Changing Emphasis in Corporate Performance Measures

*EVA is a registered trademark of Stern Stewart & Co.

It wasn't until the '90s that formal closure began between the asset base and operating profits, usually in the form of a percent return of profits on assets, expressed in a variety of ways. While recorded values and accounting-based profit could introduce distortions, and while using short-term returns as a goal could lead to less than optimal new investment actions, combining assets and profitability was a significant step toward a more integrated way of judging results and making new decisions. As more economic and integrated measures began to be used in practice, growing efforts were made to deal with the shortcomings of accounting-based thinking, and to provide more meaningful signals to managers at all levels. Shareholder value creation was introduced and was based on a variety of adjusted data representing the asset base and operating results.

One key element was the rediscovery of the cost of capital (which first appeared in economic literature around 1890!) as a key criterion for judging performance. The concept of economic profit was defined as the excess of adjusted earnings over the cost of the adjusted resources supporting them. Another key element was the rediscovery of cash flow as the driver of value, whether in the form of free cash flow for judging a whole company, or net cash flows for investment proposals. Various cash flow measures gained importance, among them cash flow return on investment (CFROI) in a variety of forms. The common theme during this evolution was the belated recognition that any business entity is in fact an economic system which has to be judged over a reasonable time horizon with performance and value criteria that reflect and encourage the cash flow trade-offs underlying management decisions, incentives, execution, and results.

A Review of Key Measures

At this point we should review in broad terms the key performance and value measures encountered in current business practice, and to comment in more detail on several of the emerging tools that support shareholder value creation. We've grouped the measures into earnings, cash flow, and value categories, and will take up each area in sequence.

Earnings Measures

The five measures in this area are the traditional ways of stating earnings or relating earnings to different expressions of invested capital, which we discussed in Chapter 4. They are being supplanted increasingly by cash flow and value-based measures, especially for internal planning, analysis, and evaluation purposes. We list them here more for completeness than for their current relevance.

- Earnings per share (EPS) is accounting net income after taxes divided by the number of shares outstanding.
- Return on investment (ROI) is accounting profit divided by the book value of the investment supporting the operations, both defined in a variety of ways.
- Return on net assets (RONA), or return on capitalization, is after-tax accounting operating profit (NOPAT) divided by the book value of total assets less current liabilities.
- Return on capital employed (ROCE) is accounting operating profit (NOPAT) over the book value of assets supporting the operations.
- Return on equity (ROE) is accounting net income after taxes divided by the book value of shareholders' equity.

EPS, one of the most commonly quoted indices of performance, which we discussed in several places in this book, has declined from its former pre-eminence. While still tracked by security analysts as an indicator of near-term performance, and used in simple valuation situations via the earnings multiple, EPS expresses only the income side of the accounting spectrum. Moreover, it is subject to the many rules of accounting that have moved performance data further and further away from cash flow. In addition, the number of shares outstanding will fluctuate even more in these days of share buybacks, and will affect the level and trend of this measure.

ROI is the simplest way of expressing the profitability of asset use, and in its unadjusted form remains a basic accounting measure, not an expression of economic performance. The accounting earnings reflect many noncash charges and additions, while the book value of the investment is a recorded value, not a current economic value. It might be useful as an approximation, but can often be unreliable because of the nature of accounting data, as we mentioned in Chapter 4.

RONA has become fairly popular, using a more focused operating profit related to the net assets, or capitalization, as recorded on the balance sheet. It still suffers from some of the same accounting issues as ROI, especially in the valuation of the asset base.

ROCE is a further modification, focusing on operating profit and operating assets, but with similar accounting issues remaining. Mostly applied to internal goal setting, it helps to make asset utilization a performance issue, at least near-term. It does not, however, relate well to economic measures used in judging new investments, nor does it assist in making day-to-day decisions on an economic basis.

ROE is the relationship of accounting net profit to the recorded residual ownership claim of the common shareholders, a recorded value buffeted by a whole host of set-asides, reserves, and reclassifications. Still widely quoted and at times used in goal setting, the measure by its very nature cannot reflect the economic performance of a company. Apart from the usual accounting issues it's also affected by the financial leverage employed by a company. Beside the measure's shortcomings for internal use, the leverage distortion makes peer comparisons more difficult, when capital structures vary.

Cash Flow Measures

The more recent approaches to performance and value measurement are invariably based on cash flow analysis, with much emphasis placed on removing accounting allocations and noncash adjustments to arrive at cash provided by operations and cash invested to support the operations. They relate closely to commonly used economic criteria like net present value and internal rate of return, thus linking the economic approach to new investments with the assessment of ongoing operations. We've discussed many of these already in earlier chapters, and will take up the most current ones later in this section.

- Free cash flow is operating cash flow (net income after taxes plus depreciation and amortization, but often adjusted to remove interest expense), less new business investments (including changes in working capital) plus dispositions of assets.

- Cash flow return on gross investment (ROGI) is operating cash flow (net income after taxes plus depreciation and amortization) divided by gross assets (before accumulated depreciation).

- Cash flow return on investment (CFROI) is the internal rate of return over the life of the investment, based on operating cash inflows, cash investment outflows, and cash recoveries. It involves a variety of adjustments to arrive at operating cash flows and the cash value of the asset base involved, as we'll demonstrate.

- Total shareholder return (TSR) is the yield to the investor from shares held over one or several periods, calculated from the combination of dividends and change in share value.

- Total business return (TBR) is the internal rate of return from a business unit or unlisted company over one or several periods, from the combination of cash flows and change in capital value. It involves a variety of adjustments to develop beginning and ending values of the business.

Free cash flow has become a commonly accepted concept, useful as an economic criterion for periodic results, but, even more importantly, representing a key element in the valuation of companies and their parts, as well as in strategic planning analyses.

ROGI at times serves as a simple substitute for a periodic economic return, relating operating cash flows to recorded operating assets—which have been "grossed up" by adding back accumulated depreciation to provide a surrogate for current values of the asset base. It can be a useful approximation to a more rigorous cash flow analysis in many situations, but could introduce some distortions because in effect it relies on the original cost of assets of different ages as a broad surrogate for current value.

CFROI, in its most sophisticated form, is an economic return developed for the company or its parts, representing an internal rate of return over the average life of the operating assets involved. It's directly comparable to the cost of capital, and to the results from cash-flow-based new investment analyses. The methodology requires a series of adjustments and several conceptual constructs, as we'll discuss later.

TSR has become a popular concept, used and published widely, because it expresses the annual return achieved by an investor from holding a company's shares over a specified period of time, based on dividends and change in market value. It links to a company's cost of capital calculation as an expression of the shareholder expectations to be considered in establishing the cost of equity capital.

TBR is a parallel measure to CFROI, designed to measure the internal rate of return of business units or other entities, based on free cash flow and estimates of the beginning and ending values of the entity, much like the analysis of an investment project as presented in Chapter 8.

Value Measures

The seven value measures listed here similarly reflect the evolution from simple multiples to present value cash flow concepts. Again we've discussed several of the basic measures in earlier chapters, but later we'll go into more detail about the most important ones for current value-based management practice.

- Earnings multiples are based on total income after taxes or EPS multiplied by a judgmental factor. They are related to the price/earnings ratio, which is often employed as a guide for the factor used.

- Cash flow multiples are a modification of earnings multiples, using total income after taxes plus depreciation and amortization, or the same on a per share basis, multiplied by a judgmental factor.

- Economic profit, or economic value added (EVA),* is the difference between operating profit after taxes (NOPAT) and a capital charge, which is based on the cost of capital times the net operating assets employed. It's also expressed as the change in economic profit from period to period. The measure requires a variety of adjustments to operating profit and the asset base, as we'll see.

- Market value added (MVA) is the difference between the book value of the total invested capital and the market value of the various forms of capital. It requires a variety of adjustments to the recorded values and a careful judgment about how representative current share values are.

- Cash value added (CVA) is the difference between the required annual cash flow to amortize an investment (using the cost of capital as the discount factor), and the actual cash flows generated, expressed as a present value differential.

- Shareholder value (SHV), as we know, is the present value of the estimated future free cash flows over the planning period, discounted at the company's cost of capital, plus the present value of the ongoing value of the business, plus any nonoperating assets (such as marketable securities and other investments), less the amount of long-term debt outstanding. It represents the present value of shareholders' equity under the assumed conditions.

- Shareholder value added (SVA) is the change in total shareholder value, either from period to period or over a longer planning time span, using the process of calculating shareholder value (SHV) as described above for each data point.

Earnings multiples are still a popular way of establishing a "ball park" figure for the value of a business, even though accounting earnings are subject to many potential distortions from an economic standpoint.

Cash flow multiples represent an effort to reflect operating cash flows, even though in their simplest form only depreciation and amortization is added back. Again, they are useful mainly as a first estimate before applying more sophisticated techniques.

EVA, the concept popularized by Stern Stewart & Co., is a form of economic profit derived from the excess (or deficit) of operating earnings after subtracting the cost of capital of the assets employed. With a variety of adjustments to both operating profit and the asset base, this approach can be used to track changes in value creation from period to period, and to establish a valuation of the company. Economic profit is not a new principle, because in its basic form it

---

*EVA is a registered trademark of Stern Stewart & Co.

simply states that a company or a business unit is adding value when after-tax earnings before interest are higher than the weighted cost of capital of the resources employed in the creation of these earnings.

MVA is an expression of the value created by a business in excess of the amount of the invested capital as shown on the balance sheet, on a periodic basis as well as over a longer time span. Given that the base is recorded capital, a variety of adjustments are required to make the measure meaningful.

CVA establishes the economic value created, in cash flow terms, over and above the cash flows required to recover the capital employed in a business, using the cost of capital as a standard. It closely parallels the net present value criterion and it is consistent with internal investment analyses.

SHV is, of course, the familiar concept of letting expected cash flows represent the present value of shareholders' equity as a measure of value creation of the total company. Discussed in Chapter 11, this model of value representation underlies much of the value-based management activity extant in modern corporate America.

SVA has become a useful addition to the concept of total shareholder value, because of the importance of establishing trends in value creation when assessing corporate strategic plans and their impact over a period of time. It's also used in assessing the value creation potential from combinations and acquisitions, as we'll see later.

Economic Profit and CFROI

We'll now discuss, in a little more detail, two of the most popular measures currently in use in value-based management processes. As we've stated before, economic profit (EVA) represents a yardstick for measuring whether a business is earning above the cost of capital of the resources (capital base) it employs. The calculation is a straightforward subtraction of the cost of capital from net operating profit:

$$EVA = NOPAT - Ck$$

where

$NOPAT$ = Operating profit after taxes (adjusted)
C = Capital base employed (net of depreciation)
k = Weighted average cost of capital

Note that the formula as stated relies on reported earnings and the recorded capital base supporting these earnings, not on cash flows. In effect, EVA is determined by subtracting from operating earnings a capital charge for the book value of the money invested in the company by owners and creditors. For a business unit, the capital charge is usually based on the net assets employed. At first glance, EVA therefore appears to be more of an accounting-based than an economic measure. In practice, however, Stern Stewart & Co. makes a large series of adjustments when working with client companies. These adjustments are made to calibrate the measure more closely to an economic cash flow basis, in an effort to parallel the economic valuation concepts we discussed earlier (see the references at the end of the chapter). Moreover, the EVA approach is applied not only to measuring current performance but also to measuring new investments and to developing incentive compensation.

What are some of the key adjustments used in applying the EVA concept? Starting with the accounting statements of a company, the first step is to derive an adjusted NOPAT, while the second is the development of the relevant capital base. The major adjustments in the NOPAT and capital base calculations occur in the following areas:

- Operating lease expenses.
- Major research and development expenses.
- Major advertising and promotion expenses.
- Inventory value adjustment (LIFO).
- Deferred income taxes.
- Goodwill amortization.
- Separation of nonoperating assets.

In the case of operating leases, an adjustment becomes necessary because there's a preference for showing the unrecorded value of the leased assets as part of the capital base, and removing the imputed interest expense on these leased assets from the income statement. The lease payments are capitalized on the balance sheet, with an offsetting matching liability, and the capital value is amortized over the appropriate time period. This amortization expense is then subtracted from earnings in arriving at NOPAT.

The effects of research and development as well as advertising and promotion expenditures incurred in a given period often extend into future periods, although current accounting rules require the total expense to be charged to the period in which it was incurred. The adjustment to NOPAT involves removing these expenses from the income statement, capitalizing them as part of the capital base, and amortizing them over an appropriate time period. This periodic amortization, a smaller amount, is then subtracted from earnings in arriving at NOPAT.

Inventory values under LIFO can, over time, become understated because the recorded cost of the earlier items in inventory remains unchanged, while recent additions are charged into cost of goods sold. To adjust for this disparity, inventories on the balance sheet are restated to current higher values, with an offsetting increase to earnings. This adjustment also is referred to as adding back the change in the LIFO reserve.

Deferred income taxes, as we discussed in earlier chapters, arise from timing differences between taxes due on corporate tax returns and those reflected on the books. In an effort to represent the cash taxes actually paid during a period, the change in deferred taxes is added or subtracted in the revised NOPAT calculation.

Finally, where sizable goodwill amounts are carried on the balance sheet, the periodic amortization reflected on the income statement is reversed so that earnings are higher. Goodwill remains unchanged on the balance sheet, on the assumption that this asset is a permanent part of the capital base.

In most cases, the net effect of these adjustments will result in a somewhat higher NOPAT and an expanded capital base, but not necessarily in proportion to their impact on the EVA calculation.

How is the result of the EVA calculation to be interpreted? There are two ways of looking at the outcome. The first is an absolute determination of whether periodic earnings have exceeded or fallen short of earning the cost of capital. The second interpretation tracks the change from period to period, to reflect the amount of value creation. For example, let's assume that in 1999 a company fell short of earning the cost of capital by $200 million, but in 2000 achieved a positive economic profit of $50 million. Under the first interpretation, economic profit was highly negative in 1999, and positive in 2000. Under the second interpretation, the company's management created $250 million of economic profit between 1999 and 2000, by having reversed the negative results of 1999 into positive territory in 2000. From a value-based management standpoint, both interpretations are used, the first usually for goal setting in operations, planning, and investment, and the second as an incentive to bring about change. As we'll see shortly, such economic profit analyses are best viewed over several periods, because being modified accounting results they are subject to some of the same period-to-period distortions as unadjusted accounting measures.

CFROI, the most sophisticated and empirically grounded methodology for value-based management, was developed over many years of statistical analysis by the former HOLT Value Associates, now functioning both as a part of The Boston Consulting Group and separately as Holt Value Associates LP. This cash-flow–based approach, originally intended as an analytical guide for portfolio managers, is based on translating a company's financial results through a variety of adjustments into a current-dollar cash flow return on investment (CFROI) measure, which expresses the company's economic performance. This concept, when applied to expected cash flows and combined with projected growth in the company's asset base, can then be used in a proprietary analytical model to calculate the company's market value. The HOLT model recognizes the adjusted cash flow contributions from existing assets and combines them with new investment cash flows, all on a comparable economic basis. This culminates in the concept of *cash value added (CVA)*, which amounts to finding the economic value created by successful business strategies and investments over and above earning the cost of capital on a discounted cash flow basis.

In effect, the HOLT model transforms a company's financial data into a consistent series of economic "project" cash flows that, when discounted at an empirically derived investor's return standard (generalized cost of capital for the market as a whole), permits calculation of the relative market value of the company's capitalization. In most cases, the calculated share values not only track very closely with historical price patterns but also become predictors for an expected market value based on a company's strategic plans—if the assumed plan cash flows are realized in the future, of course. The model is a highly integrated and sophisticated application of the economic cash flow principles we've discussed throughout this book (see the references at the end of the chapter for additional reading).

The CFROI performance measure itself can be illustrated by the diagram in Figure 12–5, where the data are taken from the financial statements of a company after a variety of adjustments, some similar to the ones we described for the EVA process. In contrast to EVA, however, the approach is strictly cash flow based, and the data are adjusted to a current-dollar basis. Note that the diagram is a present value analysis of the current value of the gross investment in the company, a level cash flow projection over 12 years, the average asset life assumed, and the value of nondepreciating assets recovered at the end of 12 years. In this example, the result is an internal rate of return of 20 percent, which represents the cash flow return earned by the company in the current year. The reason the cash flow pattern was extended over the assumed average life of the assets and a recovery was provided is simply that the CFROI concept is designed to parallel the familiar new project economics cash flow patterns we discussed in Chapters 7 and 8. There we emphasized that the economic life and any recoveries must be taken into account to be able to calculate an internal rate of return. The CFROI result expresses only the performance for the year under analysis. The CFROI for the next year would be based on that year's cash flows, extended over the assumed asset life, using asset values adjusted as necessary for the current investment as well as for the assumed capital recovery at the end, and the process is repeated for ensuing years.

FIGURE   12–5

A CFROI Perspective (thousands of dollars)

Annual aftertax adjusted cash flow before interest: $800
(Current-year cash flow assumed to continue)

Value of nondepreciating assets: $400

Current-dollar gross cash invested: $3,600

Average asset life assumed: 12 years

Result: CFROI is 20%
(the internal rate of return of this cash flow pattern)

The adjustments underlying the data in Figure 12–5 are made in three areas. The first involves transforming accounting net income into a gross cash annual flow. The following changes were made:

Accounting net income:	$425
Add back depreciation effect, other noncash charges	200
Add back tax-adjusted interest expense	75
Add back tax-adjusted operating lease expense (see below)	50
Adjust for inventory valuation (LIFO reserve)	40
Adjust for inflation	10
Current dollar gross cash flow:	$800

When appropriate, adjustments to add back unusual advance expenditures on research and promotion also are made. Note the inflation adjustment, which currently is not large in U.S. companies, but can be significant in other economies.

The second area involves transforming recorded assets into a current cash value investment base. The following changes were made:

Recorded total assets:	$3,125
Add back accumulated depreciation to arrive at original cost	950
Adjust gross fixed assets for current dollar value	575
Capitalize operating leases to show imputed asset value	350
Subtract non-interest-bearing liabilities	(1,100)
Subtract goodwill	(300)
Current dollar gross cash investment:	$3,600

Note that the adjustment to transform the original cost of fixed assets into a current-dollar equivalent is a significant amount, which is based on choosing appropriate inflation measures. Non-interest–bearing liabilities, such as accounts payable, accruals, taxes payable, and other noncontractual liabilities, are subtracted to arrive at a modified net asset figure. Importantly, goodwill is subtracted as irrelevant to the economics of this calculation, because the fixed asset adjustment to current values stands as a surrogate for goodwill arising from the premium paid for purchased assets.

The third area involves the development of a cost of capital standard in real (noninflationary) terms, which is based on a real risk-free interest rate, a real stock market premium, and a real interest cost of debt. The HOLT methodology uses a market-based cost of capital in those terms, rather than a company-specific cost of capital as discussed in Chapter 9, on the assumption that individual company risk (β) is expressed in the expected cash flow performance.

As we mentioned earlier, the CFROI calculation is one of the measures used in the HOLT methodology to judge whether a company is performing above the cost of capital in any given period. Because it's a strictly cash-based measure, CFROI is directly comparable to the cost of capital criterion. CFROI reappears in the HOLT methodology as part of an overall performance profile which links CFROI performance, past and projected investment growth, and competitive impact into a valuation framework that expresses past and prospective share price performance. The competitive impact is recognized in the form of a fade effect (reducing extraordinary results over time as unsustainable), and is incorporated into the judgment about the ongoing value of the business. We've given only a brief overview of this highly integrated methodology here; for more information the reader should turn to the references at the end of the chapter.

How can we compare economic profit and CFROI with some of the other measures? The table in Figure 12–6 is a highly simplified example of how the various approaches apply in the case of a company with an initial investment of $12 million, including $2 million of working capital, level net operating profit after taxes (NOPAT) of $825,000, and an economic life of eight years. We'll assume that no additional investments are required, that the working capital will be recovered in Year 8, and that all excess cash is paid out to the owners. In a real situation there would be more complex conditions, but for purposes of illustration this stripped-down example will provide acceptable indications.

First we show an economic profit analysis, in which a cost of capital charge of 10 percent is applied to the declining book value of the investment base. This charge is offset against the level annual NOPAT of $825,000. Note that during the first three years the economic profit is negative, with breakeven achieved in Year 4, and with growing positive amounts in the remaining years. Given that we've assumed a level annual NOPAT, this pattern is not surprising, because the capital charge is being applied every year to a declining investment base. When we use a 10 percent discount rate to the individual annual economic profit results, the net present value is 0, suggesting that in this simplified example the company is earning exactly its cost of capital.

The same result is achieved when we proceed with a basic CFROI analysis as shown in the middle of the table. First we move from accounting NOPAT to a periodic operating cash flow by adding back the noncash depreciation effect, arriving at a level $2.075 million. This parallels the approach we used with new investment projects, as described in Chapters 7 and 8. Moving on, we find that in this instance the investment base does not decline, because we are recovering the initial cash investment from future cash flows via a level capital charge plus a level capital amortization. The former is simply a 10 percent charge against the initial investment base. The second, in effect, represents an annuity that will build up to a future value of $12 million at 10 percent in Year 8, an amount sufficient to recover the initial investment. Note that the combined capital charge and capital amortization is exactly equal to the operating cash flow of $2,075 million, indicating that the internal rate of return of this business is exactly 10 percent.

The major difference between the economic profit and the cash flow return approaches is the respective periodic patterns and their interpretation. Note that the end results are the same, namely a net present value of zero and an internal rate of return of 10 percent. The meaning of the periodic elements as shown, however, is quite different, because in the case of economic profit we're observing an adjusted accounting profit as well as a declining capital base as reflected on the books of the company. In the case of CFROI we are dealing with after-tax cash flows in every instance that over time provide a recovery of the investment and a

FIGURE 12-6

An Illustration of Economic Profit, CFROI, and Earnings Measures (thousands of dollars)*

Economic Profit Analysis	Year 0	Year 1	Year 2	Year 3	Year 4	Year 5	Year 6	Year 7	Year 8
Book value of fixed investment (beginning)	—	$10,000	$8,750	$7,500	$6,250	$5,000	$3,750	$2,500	$1,250
Working capital	—	2,000	2,000	2,000	2,000	2,000	2,000	2,000	2,000
Total book value	—	12,000	10,750	9,500	8,250	7,000	5,750	4,500	3,250
Cost of capital	—	10%	10%	10%	10%	10%	10%	10%	10%
Capital charge @ 10%	—	$1,200	$1,075	$950	825	700	575	450	325
NOPAT	—	825	825	825	$825	$700	$575	$450	$325
Economic profit (EVA)	—	825	825	825	825	825	825	825	825
	—	−375	−250	−125	0	125	250	375	500
Net present value of economic profits @ 10%	—0—								
Cash Flow Return on Investment Analysis									
NOPAT	—	825	825	825	825	825	825	825	825
Add back depreciation effect	—	1,250	1,250	1,250	1,250	1,250	1,250	1,250	1,250
Operating cash flow generated	—	2,075	2,075	2,075	2,075	2,075	2,075	2,075	2,075
Initial investment	12,000	12,000	12,000	12,000	12,000	12,000	12,000	12,000	12,000
Cost of capital		10%	10%	10%	10%	10%	10%	10%	10%
Capital charge @ 10%	—	1,200	1,200	1,200	1,200	1,200	1,200	1,200	1,200
Capital amortization @ 10%	—	875	875	875	875	875	875	875	875
Terminal recovery of working capital	—	0	0	0	0	0	0	0	2,000
Total cash flow required	$−12,000	$ 2,075	$ 2,075	$ 2,075	$ 2,075	$ 2,075	$ 2,075	$ 2,075	$ 4,075
Present value of future cash flows	12,000								
Net present value @ 10%	—0—								
Other Measures									
ROE		6.9%	7.7%	8.7%	10.0%	11.8%	14.3%	18.3%	25.4%
ROCE/RONA		6.9	7.7	8.7	10.0	11.8	14.3	18.3	25.4
ROGI		17.3	17.3	17.3	17.3	17.3	17.3	17.3	17.3
CFROI		10.0	10.0	10.0	10.0	10.0	10.0	10.0	10.0

*This exhibit is available in an interactive format (TFA Template)—see "Analytical Support" on p. 423.

cash flow return of 10 percent. The economic profit pattern shares the distortion inherent in accounting return measures, which is caused by the depreciation effect. CFROI provides a level reading because the depreciation effect has been canceled out. Accordingly, in interpreting economic profit movements over time this effect must be taken into account when, for example, judging the impact of new investments that will temporarily depress the results of early years. Similarly, goal setting in profit plans has to be done with proper attention to the accounting implications.

At the bottom of Figure 12–6 we've listed the results for two common accounting measures, return on equity and return on capital employed. In this example they are equivalent, because we haven't used financial leverage, and they show the rapidly rising pattern that is also inherent in economic profit. The third measure, return on gross investment, shows a level result, because we know that this is a simple surrogate for cash flow return. Note, however, that ROGI here is significantly higher than the true cash flow return we've calculated, an illustration of how such shortcuts can give distorted results. Figure 12–7 shows in symbolic form the basic divergence of accounting and cash flow measures over time on a new business or investment project. Typically, the accounting return rises sharply as depreciation reduces the capital base, while the cash flow return over the period is positive and level, with a positive net present value over the life span of the analysis.

Another way of showing the separation of accounting measures and economic results is displayed in Figure 12-8, the left portion of which we encountered in Chapter 4 (page 136) during our discussion of the interrelationship of ratios. This time we're contrasting the family of accounting ratios that build up to the return on equity with a symbolic diagram of the shareholder value creation principles just discussed. Note the conceptual separation of the two approaches,

---

F I G U R E   12–7

The Divergence of Accounting and Cash Flow Measures

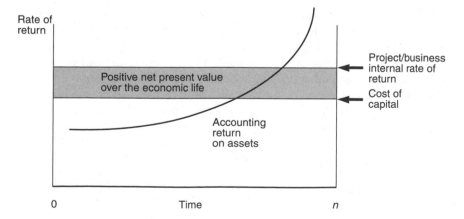

FIGURE 12–8

Another View of Accounting vs. Cash Flow Performance

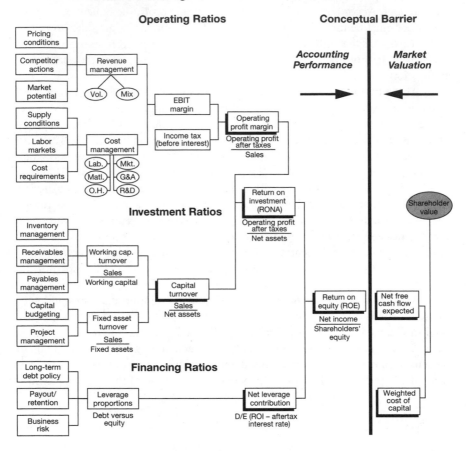

but also note that the basic performance drivers on the far left of the diagram are indeed the same for accounting results and for cash flow generation.

This is a critical insight, because the issue facing companies as they move toward shareholder value creation is how to reach across this barrier and link the basic performance drivers to near-term and long-term management decisions. This requires performance measures and incentives that will ensure long-term cash flow results. To a large extent, the accounting ratios and measures in the center of the diagram can be a distraction if they remain the main focus of management attention, for it can be shown that if cash flow results are indeed the foremost management goal, over time the accounting results will tend to fall in line. But the reverse is not necessarily true. A glance at the listings of the best-performing companies in the Fortune 500 ranked by shareholder return and by various accounting measures will tend to confirm that superior shareholder value creation over time is reflected in strong accounting results.

This brief overview of the value-based measures in current use was intended to provide enough of an insight for the reader to recognize the principles, and to encourage further study of the much more extensive and specialized references listed. Every one of the economic measures discussed has advantages and drawbacks. This is especially true in the complexities of implementation and in the process and attitudinal changes required to move from existing methodologies and thought patterns to an organizational culture that enhances shareholder value creation. For these reasons the results from value-based management efforts vary significantly from company to company, but in the aggregate the new concepts are making a significant contribution to better management decisions and corporate performance.

Creating Value in Restructuring and Combinations

One of the ways management attempts to create shareholder value is through changing the structure of the organization or combining the company with other entities to achieve greater efficiency, placing more emphasis on core activities, a broader business base, greater mass in a given line of business, and so on. The 1990s witnessed unprecedented activity in restructuring, reengineering, and streamlining, as well as record levels of mergers and acquisitions not only in the U.S. but worldwide. Records were set both in numbers and in the size of the combinations, such as the Daimler-Chrysler and Exxon-Mobil combinations, and the more recent AOL-TimesWarner merger. Despite the popularity of such efforts, a variety of retrospective studies have shown that mergers and acquisitions create shareholder value only in a surprisingly small proportion of the cases, because of the premium prices usually paid, and the difficulties both in melding disparate organizations and achieving expected synergies. Restructuring and reengineering have a better track record, as management or takeover teams focus on running existing businesses better, and eliminating activities not related to core capabilities. We'll discuss only some of the more common concepts of financial analysis relative to this topic, suggesting that the reader turn to the references for coverage of the highly specialized and voluminous techniques and methodologies involved.

Restructuring and Value

The opportunity to restructure arises from the perception—by management or by interested outside parties—that a *value gap* exists between the value actually being created by a company and the potential value achievable under changed circumstances. In simple terms, this value gap is the difference between the present value of the company's projected cash flows under existing conditions, and the present value of a different and usually higher cash flow pattern expected from the restructured company. The attraction for the acquirer in a corporate takeover is to realize the potential benefits implicit in the perceived value gap. Depending on the circumstances, the value gap can at times support sizable premiums in the price bidding usually encountered in takeover situations. However, the final result frequently creates a reverse value gap, since an excessive premium was paid in the heat of the contest. Moreover, unanticipated difficulties are often encountered in implementing changes in managing the combined entity and ultimately in adapting the corporate cultures, which are necessary steps in realizing the greater portion of the benefits envisioned.

It's beyond the scope of this book to develop all aspects of the rationale and the special considerations and techniques employed by corporate takeover specialists, leveraged buyout consultants, and investment bankers. We cannot cover the large variety of equity and debt instruments, including junk bonds with premium yields, which are used to achieve the restructuring of large and small companies. Instead, we'll briefly discuss the economic rationale and basic analytical approach to determining the value gap. For this purpose, the most common reasons that explain the value gap should be listed first.

Underperformance by parts or all of a company is likely to be the most important cause of lowered values. In thousands of situations, the historical record and projected performance by existing management using existing strategies and policies can be used to demonstrate that performance is inferior to that of appropriate peer companies. Such a record is usually directly reflected in relative share price levels. Whether restructuring is initiated by the board of directors from within, or through friendly or hostile initiatives by outsiders, the aim is to raise lagging performance and cash flow expectations. Revision of business strategies, improved cost-effectiveness and technology, reduction of unnecessary expenses, and more aggressive management of the company's resources are commonly used to achieve such results.

Disposal of selected lines of business is an extension of the improvement strategies mentioned above. Here the considerations might involve the sale of poorly performing segments and reinvestment of the proceeds in more promising parts of the company. An alternative use of such funds can be the distribution to owners in the form of special dividends—or the repurchase of the company's shares in the market, which in recent years has become an increasingly popular way of creating value with excess cash. Successful lines of business can also be sold with the idea of realizing the economic gains from such "stars," and using the proceeds to fund potential successes remaining in the company's portfolio. Another aspect of such a sale is to focus management attention more sharply on lines of activity it can competently manage for long-term success. Not to be overlooked is the fact that from an acquirer's point of view, proceeds from the sale of part of a company can help finance the acquisition transaction itself.

Eliminating redundant assets is often used as a means of freeing economic value that tends to remain hidden, involving such assets as unused real estate, financial investments, and even excessive amounts of cash bearing only minimal returns. Restructuring analysis in effect focuses on separating those economic values that are necessary to carry on the desired activities from those that can be "cashed in" as not relevant to the core purposes of the new company.

It should be clear that the point of view of restructuring—whether done externally or internally—is to develop, in essence, a break-up value of the company, carefully examining each business unit and all major operating and nonoperating assets held. The next step is to look for ways of not only improving operating cash flows but also realizing the economic values of resources that can be stripped away without affecting the chosen direction.

From an analytical standpoint, the approach is quite similar to the present value cash flow valuation discussed earlier. The main difference is that a set of estimates is used, which identifies specific enhancements in the cash flow pattern, as well as disposal values from businesses or from redundant resources.

If our earlier analysis can be stated as

$$\text{Value} = PV \, (\text{Free cash flow} + \text{Ongoing value})$$

the restructuring approach can be stated as

$$\text{Value} = PV \, (\text{Free cash flow} + \text{Ongoing value}) + PV \, (\text{Enhancements})$$
$$+ \, PV \, (\text{Disposal proceeds} - \text{Cash flow lost from disposals})$$

and the value gap will be the difference between the two results, the specifics of which are developed using the present value patterns discussed in Chapters 8 and 11. A key attraction to the external restructurer is, of course, obtaining control of the higher cash flows expected from the process.

It should be noted that two other aspects enter the picture. First, if a company changes hands in a restructuring, the depreciation basis for the assets involved is usually increased because of the higher values involved in the transaction, which under the purchase method of accounting are then recorded on the combined set of books at the new level. A portion of this recorded value increase translates directly into a stream of future cash flows because of the tax shield effect of depreciation. For example, if the acquired company's depreciable assets have a book value of $500 million, but are written up to $650 million because of the premium paid during the acquisition, the acquiring company will gain the cash value of the tax shield on the $150 million depreciation differential during the remaining life of the assets. If the company's effective tax rate is 40 percent, a total of $60 million in cash flow, spread over the remaining asset lives, will be created, assuming the company has sufficient earnings to take advantage of these write-offs. The present value of this cash flow pattern is a direct offset to the price premium the acquiring company is paying. In effect, the U.S. government is helping to finance the transaction in such cases.

Second, if the restructuring introduces higher financial leverage, as is often the case, the impact on the accounting return on shareholders' equity can be favorable, even though the cash flow pattern might be adversely affected in the near term due to significant interest charges. As the risk exposure increases, expectations about the company's likely performance can shift, affecting the valuation of the future cash flows downward as higher discount rates must be employed to value the expected cash flow pattern. The key to success in restructuring, as in any significant change introduced to a business organization, lies in the implementation—and it's here that the track record of existing management or that of the new group involved will be scrutinized by analysts to gauge the likelihood of realizing the expected benefits.

Combinations and Synergy

Another form of restructuring is found in the combination of two or more hitherto independent companies. The rationale often claimed for acquisitions and mergers is that synergy between the entities will bring real economic benefits. While empirical studies have cast serious doubt on whether business combinations are as mutually beneficial as hoped, it's tempting to assume that joining two separate businesses, particularly in the same industry, will tend to bring about some operating or market efficiencies. Examples might include the potential of fully engaging partially utilized manufacturing facilities or warehousing space; eliminating duplicate delivery systems or service networks; and consolidating certain activities, such as marketing and selling, support staff, and administration. Many of these benefits also are expected when complementary companies or even those in different businesses are combined. In recent years there's been increasing emphasis on combining already large businesses into huge entities, with the argument that success in industries such as automobiles, oil, banking, aerospace and defense, and communications depended in part on having critical mass and market strength, with attendant benefits in such areas as vendor relationships and global product/service patterns.

The impact of synergy can be felt in two major ways. The more specific benefits are identifiable cash flow improvements, for example, lower expenses that result from consolidation and reduction of facilities and staffs, and higher contribution from improved market position and coverage. The expected levels of these cash flow benefits must be estimated when an acquisition or merger is considered. Such estimates will, of course, vary in quality depending on how quantifiable the various opportunities for improvement are. There also are likely to be the kinds of tax shield and leverage effects we discussed in the previous section. All of these elements are then combined in the cash flow analysis pattern on a before-and-after basis to test for value creation.

A more general benefit is the expected impact on share price caused by the hoped-for cash flow improvements. This is ultimately where shareholder value improvement is recognized. The stock of the combined company might become more attractive to investors and thus achieve a higher market price, reflecting the benefits of the combination. Security analysts and the investment community generally expect combinations that are considered synergistic to result not only in a more profitable company, but possibly one poised for faster growth, with a stronger market position, or subject to lesser earnings fluctuations as the cycles of the individual businesses offset each other. The expectations implicit in this reassessment and successful implementation may in time improve the total share-holder return achieved.

Possible profit improvements resulting from a business combination can be analyzed to the extent they are quantifiable. To do this, the analyst uses two sets of pro forma statements. One set shows the projected net profits and cash flow patterns from each company separately, while the other reflects the combined company and includes the envisioned improvements. These statements then become the basis for comparative ratio analysis and for calculating the value of the individual companies and the combined entity with various methods. Once the cash flow patterns have been determined from this analysis, the various present value measures we've discussed can be applied.

At times it can be useful to determine separately the present value of all the synergistic cash flow benefits that were identified. This present value then can be used as a rough guide as the terms of the merger are being negotiated, because the value of realistic synergy expectations should be considered in setting the value premium the acquirer has to pay. In the end, however, the basis for valuation is likely to be a combination of present value analyses, rules of thumb, earnings and share price considerations, and a variety of tangible and intangible factors.

Combinations and Share Values

When an exchange of common stock is involved in an acquisition or merger agreement, as is true in many cases, the valuation challenge is extended. The eco-nomic valuation of the cash flow patterns, in which performance and synergistic expectations are expressed on an economic basis, should be the basis from which the parties proceed. The issue becomes one of translating those valuation results into the medium of currently traded shares as valued in the stock market. This process requires arriving at a mutually acceptable interpretation of the respective values of the two different securities, as well as finding an appropriate ratio of ex-change based on these shares. One aspect of this exchange is the usually signifi-cant premium (between 15 and 25 percent is the usual range) paid over what might be considered an initial fair economic value of the acquired company. While in the end a numerical solution is applied, the underlying values and the premium will be the result of extensive negotiation and a certain amount of "horse trading."

As the two stocks are valued, any differences in the quality and breadth of trading in the securities markets can be an important factor. If, for example, a large, well-established company acquires a new and fast-growing company, the market value assessment of the acquirer's stock is likely to be more reliable than that of the candidate, whose stock might be thinly traded and unproved, or it might reflect excessive speculation. But even if they had comparable market exposure, the inherent difference in the nature and performance of the two companies might exhibit itself in, among other indicators, a pronounced difference in price/earnings ratios. In effect, this means one company's performance is valued less highly in the market than the other's by this measure. This difference will tend to influence valuation of the stocks and the final price negotiated—apart from the specific cash flow expectations that have been developed for economic valuation.

We'll demonstrate just a few key calculations needed to arrive at the basis of exchange from this standpoint, using a simplified example. Let's assume that Acquirer Corporation and Candidate, Inc., have the following key dimensions and performance data at the time of their merger negotiations:

Key Data	Acquirer Corporation	Candidate, Inc.
Current earnings	$50 million	$10 million
Number of shares	10 million	10 million
Earnings per share	$ 5.00	$ 1.00
Current market price	$60.00	$15.00
Price/earnings ratio	12.0	15.0

Negotiations between the management teams have reached a point where, after Candidate has rejected several offers, Acquirer now considers a price premium of about 20 percent over the current market value of Candidate's stock necessary to close the deal. This calls for an exchange ratio of $18/$60, or about 0.3 shares of Acquirer stock for each share of Candidate stock. The impact on Acquirer's accounting records is as follows, at the combined current levels of earnings that include no synergistic benefits:

Acquirer Corporation

Combined earnings	$60 million
Number of shares (10.0 + 3.0 million)	13 million
New earnings per share	$4.62
Old earnings per share	$5.00
Immediate dilution	$0.38

Under these conditions, Acquirer suffers an immediate dilution of 38 cents per share from the combination. Yet the fact that the stock of Candidate has a higher price/earnings ratio suggests that the smaller company enjoys desirable attributes and expectations about them, which might include high growth in earnings, a technologically protected position, and so on.

Acquirer must therefore consider two points. First, are the earnings of Candidate likely to grow at a rate that will close the gap in earnings per share relatively quickly, aided by any synergistic benefits available now? Second, is the inclusion of Candidate likely to change the risk/reward characteristics of the combined company so as to improve the price/earnings ratio—and thus help overcome the dilution in the accounting results?

In our example, the earnings gap to be filled is 13 million shares times 38 cents, or almost $5 million in annual earnings—just to return to the current level of Acquirer's earnings per share. How much in synergistic benefits can be expected? Perhaps the ratio of exchange has to be reconsidered in this light. But will the smaller company even be interested in being acquired at less than a 20 percent premium over market, a not uncommon inducement?

Note that if we assume a reversal of the price/earnings ratios in the example, both the terms of the offer and the reported performance of the combined companies will change dramatically. At 15 times earnings, the price of Acquirer will be $75 per share, while at 12 times earnings, Candidate will trade at $12 per share. Given a 20 percent acquisition premium for Candidate's stock, the exchange ratio will be $14.40 ÷ $75, or 0.192 shares of Acquirer for each share of Candidate. This calls for 1.92 million new shares of Acquirer, and the new earnings per share will amount to $60,000,000 ÷ 11,920,000 shares, or $5.03 per share, a slight net improvement even before any synergistic benefits are considered. In this changed situation, both parties will be better off immediately in their recorded results, simply because we assume the price/earnings ratios to be reversed. It's possible, of course, that a company acquired at a premium—which has caused the combined earnings per share to drop initially—might more than offset the gap with higher growth and synergistic benefits later. This will depend on the relative sizes of the two companies as well as on the value and exchange considerations discussed.

We've given but one simplified example, and therefore only a quick glimpse of the nature of these earnings-based deliberations involved in exchanges of stock, which usually are superimposed on the detailed cash flow economics used in valuing the companies. Note that this viewpoint deals with but one of the many issues underlying the valuation process in mergers and acquisitions. However, it's this concept that receives the most public attention in the financial community, because it deals with the visible effect of the deal on the companies' current financial statements and share data. But to ensure that expectations about shareholder value creation are reasonable, merger transactions must always go beyond earnings dilution issues to careful projections of the separate and combined earnings and cash flow patterns, and an assessment of the likely market response into the foreseeable future. Again the reader is encouraged to turn to the specialized literature on mergers and acquisitions to expand on the simple indications we've provided here.

Integration of Value Analysis

We've covered a large variety of value concepts and valuation approaches in the prior chapter and in this current discussion, ranging all the way from simple rules of thumb to economic cash flow models. We've used some illustrative examples from time to time in applying the formulas, but also have recognized that valuation is one of the more difficult areas of financial analysis that must be practiced with complex integrative situations. Such detailed case examples go beyond the scope of this book, but they can be readily found in more extensive finance texts and case books, such as we've listed at the end of each chapter.

To round out our discussion, we'll touch on a series of key judgmental areas that are commonly encountered in the valuation process, and provide a broad framework within which to view the practice. Some of these elements have come up in earlier discussions, but we believe that the reader might find it useful to have an overview context summarized in this fashion as we complete the final chapter. We'll address the following points:

- Perspectives in valuation.
- Dealing with expectations.
- Choosing the time period.
- Developing the pattern.
- Estimating ongoing values.
- Using comparables for validation.
- Results and negotiation.

Perspectives

No value judgment can be derived without a proper perspective on the nature of the issue being addressed. In Chapter 11 we presented a variety of definitions of value, each of which was based on a particular perspective that made it relevant. But even within a particular category, such as deriving the economic value of a business, there are different perspectives that must be defined and understood before the methodology and analytical framework are chosen. For example, are we establishing the value of equity for purposes of an exchange of shares, or are we determining the total business value? Are we attempting to value a business unit in order to set incentive plan targets for its management? Is the purpose of the analysis to establish a negotiating basis for a contested acquisition, or are we contemplating the sale of a successful business unit? In every case there will not only be differences in the specific inputs and even the methodology chosen, but also differences in the interpretation of the results. It also matters greatly whether there are parties involved with widely differing views of value, such as groups negotiating a merger. There is simply no generalized analytical or negotiation pattern that can serve all purposes, although in every one of these situations, an effort at economic cash flow analysis in one form or another should be undertaken to establish a sound basis. Let's remember that valuations, while more complex than most other decisions, do involve economic trade-offs—a concept we established early on and applied throughout this book.

As we've observed before, solid preparatory thinking to frame an analytical task is much more important than the application of the tools themselves. This is particularly true in business valuation analysis, because most issues in this area usually have to be viewed within a very complex framework and against a strategic background. When a business entity is valued in part or as a whole, the judgments required extend directly or indirectly to the relevant success factors that drive the business—with a future-oriented mindset.

Expectations

These are the basis for most valuation approaches, because it's fair to say that the economic value of an object or a business entity reflects the future benefits to be obtained from owning it. These benefits, whether stated in the form of earnings, cash flows, or expected recoveries, always will be estimates of future, uncertain events that are subject to both specific and general risk exposure. We've encountered this principle in earlier chapters, and observed that depending on the importance of the analytical task, a degree of sensitivity analysis should be performed to scope the impact of changes in variables and in the expected risk patterns. Given the importance of valuing businesses as a whole or in major segments, the need for at least developing ranges of estimates should be obvious. This requires that the drivers behind earnings and cash flows be understood and the major variables be tested for changes in projected conditions. It's simply not sufficient just to project current earnings or cash flow levels and to hope that these are indicative of the future.

Time Period

The period chosen for a business valuation most often depends on the nature of the activity in which the company or unit being analyzed is engaged. There also might be a time horizon specific to a situation, such as a planned strategic change or a limited life cycle due to expiring patents. The changes occurring in many products and services in high technology industries are so frequent and extensive that time horizons of more than three years can be quite unrealistic. In cyclical industries, the time horizon should extend for at least one business cycle, while multibusiness companies with a portfolio mix of ascending, declining, and new venture business units can likely be valued over a five- to eight-year period. The main point is that the time horizon has to be a function of the economic circumstances, not the apparent neatness and convenience of a five- or ten-year pattern. One of the important judgments involved is what values to assign to assets or a going business at the end of the period, as we've observed before, and we'll summarize this area shortly.

Cash Flow Pattern

The economic valuation process depends greatly on establishing a realistic pattern of expected cash flows, just as we discussed in Chapters 7 and 8 for business investments. It's critical that the earnings stream expected during the time period under analysis not only reflect the ongoing operations of the company or business unit, but also be adjusted for planned strategic investments, divestments, potential synergies from combinations, major research outlays, and planned restructuring. In other words, the pattern of inflows and outflows should represent, as closely as possible, a strategic plan for the business under review.

Just as important is the need to be consistent in the adjustments for accounting processes, such as depreciation, amortization, and other elements that might or might not affect cash flows. This includes the tax shield benefits that can arise from revaluing assets in the case of a purchase, among others. In most analyses, the data will be expressed in a form closely related to free cash flow, while in simpler situations earnings-based approaches can be used.

It's good practice to base the analysis on cash flows early on in the process. This allows the analyst to deal consistently with the cash-in, cash-out trade-offs that underlie value, which can then be alternatively tested and expanded to consider the impact of accounting implications through earnings-based analyses, and against any shortcut approaches that appear reasonable in the context.

Ongoing Values

This aspect of value analysis is probably the least comfortable for analysts to deal with. The ongoing or terminal value at the point where the analysis is truncated on the time scale is in itself a business valuation of a continuing operation—but several years removed from the present. Obviously, the shorter the time period, the more this value can affect the result because of the time-value effect of discounting. But more important is the issue of how to set a realistic figure, when the pattern of expected cash flows leading up to this value was difficult enough to establish. In earlier chapters we discussed using price/earnings ratios, capitalizing the last year's cash flows (perpetuity assumption), using some operational rule of thumb, or employing growth formulas.

Any one of these processes doesn't substitute for the careful judgment required to assess, from a broad strategic standpoint, whether the company or business unit will indeed be viable at the end point of the analysis. Is it realistic to assume steady growth, continued competitive strength, and repeated technological success? For example, it's probably a sound assumption that a level of performance far above a company's peers cannot be sustained indefinitely, because competitive pressures will inevitably moderate results. The analyst must address these issues during the valuation process and not let the convenience of simple rules of thumb or multiples take over. Ending values also are an area where ranges of estimates and sensitivity analysis should be employed, to scope the possible variations and their impact on the results.

Comparables

Part of the analytical challenge is the calibration of the results obtained against available real-world experience. In other words, the value derived from a thorough analysis of a particular company or business unit should be tested against comparable companies or business units as a matter of course. In fact, it's sound practice to attempt to calibrate the major assumptions used during the process of developing the time pattern and ending values. At the same time, we must be realistic about the amount and quality of data available for this purpose, and about the differences that invariably affect the matching of the subject company or business unit with peers.

The very effort of developing comparable values and indicators, however, forces the analyst to be thoughtful about the realism of the assumptions used in the analysis. If profit margins, growth rates, investment patterns, and research outlays differ materially from comparable companies, the resulting cash flow pattern should be assessed critically. Furthermore, comparable companies or businesses are likely to be competitors, and trying to bring their dimensions into the analysis necessarily introduces a strategic perspective. Finally, if the valuation results are to be used in negotiation, there's every reason to believe that comparables will be brought up in one form or another.

Negotiations

Inevitably, negotiations affect the extent and direction of any valuation process. While objectivity for any analytical task is a worthwhile goal, the pressure of securing an advantageous negotiation position at the outset and during the deliberations will spur the parties to interpret the data and results from this perspective. Here the notion of using ranges as well as minimum and maximum acceptable results becomes commonplace. The practical implication for analysis is simply that the perspective of the analyst must change, in order to take into account the tactics and strategies employed by the parties involved. The analysis likely should be made from more than one viewpoint. Analytical tools used will usually be similar, but it's also to be expected that the parties will emphasize those approaches that favor their position. This shouldn't be surprising, for as we've said many times, financial/economic analysis is not a freestanding activity, but intricately related to the specific needs and issues surrounding it and affected by the vagaries of human judgment.

Key Issues

The following is a recap of the key issues raised directly or indirectly in this chapter. They are enumerated here to help the reader keep the techniques discussed within the perspective of financial theory and business practice.

1. Managing for shareholder value goes far beyond selection of appropriate measurements. It requires an integrated set of management processes tying together strategy, investment analysis, operational effectiveness, financial management, and evaluation and compensation—a systems approach to sound management.

2. The challenge of shareholder value creation can be stated simply: consistently exceeding the cost of capital in the performance of existing and new investments. However, bringing about value creation is the result of the very complex task of managing all aspects of the business system well.

3. Measures that gauge and reinforce shareholder value creation tend to reach beyond accounting results, because they should tie to the expectations of a cash-flow–driven market. Accounting results will usually follow in time when decisions on investments, operations, and financing are driven by cash flow considerations—not the other way around.

4. There's no one single measure or value-based approach that is or should be the obvious choice for every management team. Significant trade-offs are encountered in the areas of complexity, changing the organization's mindset, the degree of improvement likely, and precision of the process chosen. Measures must be judged within the framework of the capabilities of the total business system.

5. Valuation of businesses undergoing restructuring or combinations is only in part an economic cash flow exercise; there are many dimensions of expressing value and exchange parameters that fall back on accounting data and even purely judgmental aspects.

6. Proper framing of valuation tasks requires a critical set of judgments that are common to all economic investment deliberations. Effort spent early on this aspect will pay off in improved validity and relevance of the results.

7. Valuing a business for sale or purchase is one of the most complex tasks an analyst can undertake. It calls for skills in projection of earnings and cash flows, assessment of risk, strategic insight, and interpretation of the impact of combining management styles, operations, and resources.

8. While accounting analyses are typically a significant part of the valuation process, especially in public transactions like mergers and acquisitions, the economic base established by cash flow approaches is critical to successful decision making.

9. Shareholder value is the ultimate result of successful investments, operations, and financing carried out by management within an economic framework. However, the link between a company's current and prospective performance in these areas and the market value of its common stock at a particular time is not necessarily direct or directly measurable, because of the combination of forces acting on the stock market.

Summary

In this final chapter, we came full circle by again taking a systems approach to managing effectively, and we placed the relevant analytical techniques in proper perspective within this larger setting. We began with an overview of the value implications of managing the business system well, and provided further overviews of the many relationships of management processes and management decisions to the basic goal of shareholder value creation.

We then reviewed the evolution of selected financial measures in their movement toward cash-flow–based concepts, and placed them in the same perspective. We brought the more conventional measures covered in Chapter 4 together with the newer concepts applied in current value-based practice, and described the more common adjustments required for them as well as their meaning. A comparative example was used to show the different implications of the measures, and we pointed to the need for further study and analysis to deal with the refinements implied in value-based approaches.

Restructuring and combinations were covered in the broader context of cash flow analysis and the economic trade-offs involved, supplemented by the more important implications of earnings-based results as they affect exchanges of shares and reported financial data.

Finally we returned to the need for defining the judgmental dimensions of valuation analysis, a theme we had touched upon in earlier chapters, indicating that inasmuch as business valuation is a highly complex matter going beyond the analytical measures themselves, a clear understanding of these judgmental aspects is critical.

Ultimately, valuation will remain partly subjective, and where appropriate will be settled in an exchange between interested parties—but targeting and implementing the company's investments, operations, and financing for economic performance and shareholder value will always be the basic obligation of management.

Analytical Support

Financial Genome, the commercially available financial analysis and planning software described in Appendix I, has the capability to develop many of the business valuation measures and valuation terms directly from databases, spreadsheets and direct input data, using the application's forecasting capabilities. It can automatically derive accounting measures as well as common cash flow inputs to valuation analysis. The software is also accompanied by a general purpose interactive template (TFA Template under "extras") for the cash flow valuation of a business as described in Chapter 11, based on Figure 11–5 on 384, which can be used to calculate present values and the equity valuation for any pattern of inputs and discount rates. Another interactive template allows the user to view the impact of changes in key assumptions on various accounting and cash flow measures discussed in this Chapter, based on Figure 12–6 on page 408. (see "Downloads Available" on p. 431)

Selected References

Brealey, Richard, and Stewart Myers. *Principles of Corporate Finance*. 5th ed. Burr Ridge, IL: Irwin/McGraw-Hill, 1996.

The Boston Consulting Group. *Value Based Management: A Framework for Managing Value Creation*. Chicago: The Boston Consulting Group, 1993. (Holt Value Concepts.)

Copeland, Tom; Tim Koller; and Jack Murrin. *Measuring and Managing the Value of Companies*. 2nd ed. New York: John Wiley & Sons, 1995.

Knight, James A. *Value Based Management: Developing a Systematic Approach to Creating Shareholder Value*. Burr Ridge, IL: Irwin/McGraw-Hill, 1998.

Madden, Bartley J., *Cash Flow Return on Investment (CFROI) Valuation: A Total Systems Approach for Valuing the Firm*. Butterworth/Heinemann, 1999. (Holt Value Concepts.)

Martin, John D., and J. William Petty, *Value Based Management*. New York: The Financial Management Association Survey and Synthesis Series, 2000.

McTaggart, James M.; Peter W. Kontes; and Michael C. Mankins. *The Value Imperative*. New York: Free Press, 1994.

Pratt, Shannon P. *Valuing a Business: The Analysis and Appraisal of Closely Held Companies*. 3rd ed. New York: Irwin/McGraw-Hill, 1995.

Rappaport, Alfred. *Creating Shareholder Value*. Revised ed. New York: Free Press, 1998.

Ross, Stephen; Randolph Westerfield; and Jeffrey Jaffe. *Corporate Finance*. 5th ed. Burr Ridge, IL: Irwin/McGraw-Hill, 1999.

Stern, Joel M.; John S. Shiely; and Irwin Ross. *The EVA Challenge: Implementing Value Added Change in an Organization*. New York: John Wiley & Sons, 2001

Stewart, G. Bennett, III. *The Quest for Value*. New York: Harper Business, 1991. (Stern Stewart & Co. EVA concepts.)

Weston, Fred; Scott Besley; and Eugene Brigham. *Essentials of Managerial Finance*. 11th ed. Hinsdale, IL: Dryden Press, 1996.

Financial Analysis Using *Financial Genome*

An advanced financial analysis, statement generation and business planning software application called *Financial Genome* is available for purchase by interested users of this book. It's based on patented technology developed by Modernsoft, Inc., and can be downloaded from **www.modernsoft.com.** This unique add-in program for Excel 2000 (or later) running on Windows 95 (or later) is a professional application which empowers the spreadsheet user to do financial analysis and pro forma projections with ease, speed and accuracy. While adding a financial structure to spreadsheets, *Financial Genome* maintains their full flexibility, and it is far more intuitive to use than conventional spreadsheets.

Financial Genome easily accommodates widely different business analytical needs and projections. It links together a comprehensive, knowledge-based financial dictionary of terms and relationships, an analytical engine, and data base access. The built-in financial knowledge ensures internal consistency, avoidance of spreadsheet errors, convenient data access, ready project setup, and true analytical and formatting flexibility. The internal help system at any time allows the user to view the definitions of financial terms, and their relationships to formulas and statements. The software reflects the structure and definitions of financial analysis concepts and tools as discussed in this book.

The application contains an example data base to get started, and a data base for TRW which ties to the company's statements reproduced in the early chapters of this book. The software is accompanied by a series of interactive templates and graphic displays that relate directly to the various diagrams and analytical layouts covered in this book, designed to allow the user trace the effect of varying assumptions. *Financial Genome* and its accompanying templates also serve as learning tools, reinforcing the insights gained from reading this book and other financial literature. Learning is enhanced by the transparent structure and capabilities of the application, which allows the user to check understanding of terms and relationships on the fly, as well as through experimenting with the graphic displays in the accompanying templates.

Financial Genome as a Financial Analysis and Planning Tool

This professional software enables the user to:

- Input a typical set of financial data about a business from spreadsheets, data bases, or direct input.
- Manipulate selected data for free-form analysis.

- Create a wide range of financial reports and special statements.
- Do fully integrated financial forecasting and planning.

All of this can be done without the need to create formulas or relationships, or identifying spreadsheet cell locations. At the core of the application is the *Financial Dictionary*, which contains over 350 common financial terms, statements, and ratios, as well as the built-in knowledge of all the relationships between the terms and statements, and the formulas underlying them. Once a set of input data is entered into the program, or a database is accessed, the application ensures full consistency as the analysis proceeds, because statements, ratios and special analytical views are created automatically. All calculated terms are prepared by the application from the individual inputs, which ensures accuracy. Assumptions and data values can be changed at the user's option.

A full range of features allows customization of the analysis by changing term names and statement formats, expanding or collapsing details, creating new relationships, changing time frames and databases, etc. At any point the user can display the definitions and relationships underlying any term or statement used, and access the complete built-in help system for further background information.

The following capabilities are available for the *Financial Genome* user to perform financial analysis as described in this book or in other financial texts:

- Display selected financial data individually or in any combination, and perform financial analysis using the built-in relationships or by creating new ones:

    Use a familiar spreadsheet structure to display and manipulate data or groups of data.

    Keep track of the data necessary for the analysis on an automatic input statement.

    Choose annual, quarterly, or monthly time periods.

- Use *GenomeLink* to map data from spreadsheets or data bases to *Financial Genome:*

    After mapping, freely use the data as an internal data base for analysis

    Create internal data bases from ad hoc analyses

- Automatically create the following standard financial statements:

    Income statement.

    Balance sheet.

    Cash flow statement.

    Statement of changes in shareholders' equity.

- Automatically create a special statement listing the typical assumptions used for pro forma financial forecasts:

Forecast drivers for use in developing an integrated financial plan.

Display of matching historical data for these forecast drivers.

- Ability to create financial forecasts and integrated financial plans:

  Use the built-in forecast drivers for making key assumptions.

  Override with and/or add own assumptions.

  Test and modify data for full integration among statements.

- Automatically create the following special performance statements:

  Ratios statement (all major financial ratios grouped by the three decision areas).

  Performance analysis statement displaying key performance measures.

- Automatically create the following economic analysis statements:

  NOPAT analysis for deriving economic profit.

  Capital base analysis for deriving economic profit.

  Cost of capital analysis by category and various weighted proportions.

  Economic profit analysis combining all of the above.

- Ability to modify built-in terms, statements, sections of statements, and free-form analyses:

  Rename, itemize, and duplicate individual terms.

  Move terms and groups of terms on the sheet.

  Expand and collapse statement detail.

  Modify groupings, names, headings.

  Customize formatting for printing.

- Ability to override any data input or user assumptions:

  To modify conditions.

  To perform what-if analysis.

  Can return to original data base values at any time

- Ability to change databases and timing:

  Switch to new database.

  Manually override data.

  Change analysis time periods.

- Ability to access Excel's many features for data manipulation and formatting:

  Financial formulas and relationships.

  Cell formatting, outlining, colors, highlighting, etc.

- Ability to print out analyses and retain projects:

    Format print output as desired.

    Print statements as from any Excel spreadsheet.

    Save project files for future access and use.

These capabilities allow the user to do professional financial analysis on typical sets of data, with the assurance that there'll be accuracy and internal consistency as long as the input data themselves are correct. The analytical process can be applied to funds flow analysis as described in Chapter 3, the performance analysis of Chapter 4, the projections of Chapter 5, the growth conditions of Chapter 6, the present value analyses of Chapters 7, 8, 11 and 12 (templates), the cost of capital analyses of Chapter 9, and the financing options of Chapter 10. Because the interrelationships of the business system are embodied in *Financial Genome,* it has capability to develop a consistent and fully integrated set of financial statements, views, and performance analyses.

The process of analysis is based on the familiar look and feel of the Excel application, but it's driven by a sophisticated underlying knowledge structure and the patented *FinGen* technology. An intuitive control panel and a set of special tools are provided, which expand the standard Excel capabilities and tool bars.

Financial Genome as a Learning Device and Guide

The software contains a fully integrated help system that allows the user at any time to display not only the definitions of terms but also their relationships to other terms and their place in the analytical structure. Thus it's possible to check one's understanding of the underlying concepts step by step as the analysis proceeds. When automatic financial statements or collections of terms like ratios are called forth by the user, it's similarly possible to check and display the underlying structure for any term or group of terms, thus reinforcing the learning process. The user can learn by doing individual analytical tasks, checking the progress as desired, and also can learn by investigating the background and meaning of automatically calculated data, ratios, and statements. All definitions and terminology are closely aligned with the materials in this book, and the help system incorporates definitions selected from this book.

The special templates accompanying the software are designed as interactive and visual learning devices, allowing the user to trace the impact of changing assumptions on financial statements, analytical layouts, and key conceptual diagrams as discussed in this book. There are templates for all of the major diagrams and displays, designed both for learning and also for application in a professional setting when appropriate. A chapter-by-chapter description of the templates and use of *Financial Genome* follows:

Chapter 1:   As a stage-setting discussion it contains no analytical processes.

Chapter 2:   The business system in Figure 2–4 on page 28 is a key diagram that also reappears together with the growth model templates of Chapter 6. The interactive template for the business system contains live cells for every element, which display the changing conditions and allow the user to interact and modify at will. A list of key assumptions drives the template, and the results are also reflected on a linked balance sheet, income statement, and cash flow statement. In addition, a live bar graph displays the changes in funds uses and sources. The user's input assumptions cover key operating, investment and financing decisions and policies, and the template functions as a closed system that responds to any one or a combination of changes. By toggling between assumptions and results, the user can trace the impact of the changing cash flows implicit in all parts of the structure and enhance the understanding of the dynamics of the business system.

Chapter 3:   The funds flow analysis covered here does not require special templates, as *Financial Genome* has the built-in capability to create cash flow statements automatically from spreadsheet input data or databases.

Chapter 4:   The full ratio structure underlying the performance analysis in this chapter is automatically created by *Financial Genome,* and the user can request and display any single ratio, group of ratios, or a complete ratio statement from the underlying data. Definitions are available instantly. A special interactive template provides a visual representation of the impact on return on equity from changes in the underlying drivers. Based on the systems view of key ratios and their elements in Figure 4–4 on page 136, the template allows the user to trace simultaneous changes in all elements affected by a change in assumptions. A linked balance sheet, income statement, and cash flow statement accompany the diagram to give the user the corresponding impact on the financial statements.

Chapter 5:   The pro forma analysis discussed here is integral to *Financial Genome,* which in the forecasting mode can create a full set of integrated pro forma financial statements, ratios, and performance analyses based on the user's assumptions about forecast drivers and expected conditions. It provides financial closure by identifying the fund need or excess under any set of assumptions the user wishes to try. A special interactive template illustrates the interrelated conditions for developing a cash budget, requiring a variety of assumptions to be derived first. The template assists the user in building up a set of conditions over a six-month period, including sales forecasts and collection of receivables, inventory movements based on purchasing patterns, and changes in accruals. The template accepts key assumptions, displays staggered collection patterns, account receivable patterns, an inventory analysis, and accrued liability changes. All of these are linked to live displays of the cash budget, pro forma income statement, and balance sheet, and provide an internally consistent set of results that culminate in the cumulative cash flow for the period. Changing any or several of the assumptions allows the user to visualize the impact on cash requirements and on the financial statements.

Chapter 6:   The business dynamics of this chapter are supported by four templates, each of which allows interactive simulation of changes in policies and operational decisions. The first template illustrates operational break-even analysis, based on Figure 6–2 on page 198, where changes in price, variable costs, and fixed cost can be traced on a live graph. The second template displays the sustainable growth equation on page 215 with live cells, linked to the analytical format of the financial growth model in Figure 6–7 on page 208. Also linked to this model is a live representation of the business system of Figure 2–4 on page 28, together with a balance sheet, an income statement and cash flow statement, and a bar graph illustrating changes in uses and sources. This complete model allows the user to study growth conditions and to view them from all major viewpoints. The third template, a companion to the second template, allows the user to establish different sets of financial and investment policies in the growth model format of Figure 6–9 on page 213, and to view a series of different cases side by side. The fourth template is an interactive representation of the five-year projection of conditions and policies of Figure 6–10 on page 218, which the user can vary at will and study the impact of different assumptions on the results.

Chapters 7 and 8:   The present value analysis concepts and structures are supported by a general-purpose template which allows the user to input any desired return standard, cash flow pattern, depreciation tax shield, capital investments and recoveries, and to obtain the results of all present value measures, displayed in the spreadsheet format used in both chapters (see pages 237, 238, 273, and 274 to 281). The template is accompanied by a bar graph display showing the size of movements in investment and operational cash flows, and the depreciation tax shield.

Chapter 9:   The cost of capital calculations are directly supported by *Financial Genome's* built-in capability to develop the cost of capital for each element of the capital structure and to develop weighted average costs based on market values, book values, and target proportions. The user is required only to provide the necessary inputs requested by the software.

Chapter 10:   Financing choices are supported by a template that calculates and displays graphically the range of EBIT and earnings per share (EPS) conditions discussed in the chapter. The user can vary the conditions underlying different financing alternatives and observe the impact on the balance sheet and on the separate calculations of EPS and zero EPS. A live graph based on Figure 10–8 on page 341 displays the varying conditions. The impact of different financing choices is also implicit in the forecasting results obtained with *Financial Genome.*

Chapter 11: Business valuation as discussed here is directly supported by the forecasting capabilities of *Financial Genome,* which can derive both accounting measures and ratios as well as cash flow inputs such as EBIT, NOPAT, free cash flow, and others. An general purpose valuation template modeled on Figure 11–5 on page 384 allows the user to calculate the cash flow valuation of a company, based on projections of EBIT, depreciation, changes in working capital, investment changes, and an estimate of ongoing value. It's based on the same spreadsheet format as the general purpose present value template for Chapters 7 and 8.

Chapter 12:   Shareholder value management covers an overview of key measures, including proprietary approaches, which cannot be replicated as discussed here. A basic CFROI calculation can be developed using the present value template provided, while a comparison of measures can be viewed interactively in the special template based on Figure 12–6 on page 408. *Financial Genome* has the built-in capability to calculate economic profit, based on the user's inputs and assumptions.

While primarily designed as educational tools, the graphic templates can also serve the professional user, for example, to demonstrate the results of policy choices. The general purpose templates like the present value analysis and business valuation structures can be used for many practical applications. As a result, this professional software application, together with the interactive templates, assists both the student and the practitioner in performing financial analysis better, faster, and with greater insight.

How to Obtain *Financial Genome*

- *Financial Genome* can be downloaded for a free thirty-day trial from Modernsoft's web site: **http://www.modernsoft.com** and locating the download section on the site. The download requires a minimum of 5 megabytes of disk space.
- System requirements are Microsoft Excel 2000 and later and Windows 95/98/NT4/2000 (only US English versions in all cases)
- Downloads available are:
    1) The *Financial Genome* software, including the "TFA templates" for this book (contained in the "extras" folder of the software)
    2) Quickstart guide
    3) Graphic tutorial
    4) TFA templates for this book as a separate file
- The software can be purchased by credit card after download by registering and following the on-line instructions.

APPENDIX II

Glossary of Key Terms and Concepts*

Accelerated depreciation Patterns of *depreciation* write-offs that place larger proportions into the early years of an *asset*'s book life, rather than into the later years, either for accounting or for tax deduction purposes.

Accounting earnings The difference between recognized *revenues* and *expenses* during an accounting period, based on generally accepted accounting principles.

Accounts payable (payables) Obligations owed to trade creditors and suppliers as incurred in the normal course of business; also called *trade credit.*

Accounts payable days A translation of *accounts payable* into the days of average purchases outstanding at a point in time; used as an indicator of the effectiveness with which *trade credit* is employed.

Accounts receivable (receivables) Obligations owed by customers and other parties as incurred in the normal course of business.

Accounts receivable days A measure of the credit quality of *accounts receivable,* which expresses outstanding receivables as days' sales outstanding in terms of average daily sales; can be compared with the *credit terms* under which sales were made.

Accruals Recognition of *revenues* or *expenses* when earned or incurred, without regard to the actual timing of the cash transactions; used in the accrual method of accounting.

Accumulated depreciation The total of past periodic depreciation charges applicable to depreciable assets carried on a company's *balance sheet,* shown as a deduction from gross property, plant, and equipment.

Acid test A stringent measure of *liquidity* relating current cash *assets* (cash, cash equivalents, and receivables) to *current liabilities.*

Activity-based analysis A form of *economic analysis* that develops the specific *costs* and *benefits* generated by an activity, product line, or business segment, based on the physical processes and resource requirements underlying each subpart.

Aftertax cash flow Cash generated from *operations* or from an *investment* net of income taxes, derived by adding back non-cash charges like *depreciation* to aftertax earnings.

Aftertax value Net *revenue,* net *cost,* or net *investment* after adjusting for the effect of applicable income taxes.

Allocation An assignment or distribution of *costs* or *revenues* to products, activity centers, or other entities using a common basis.

Amortization A periodic charge reflecting the decline in the recorded value of an *intangible asset* over a specified number of years.

Annualized net present value The transformation of a *net present value* into an equivalent series of annual cash flows over the life of the project, used in judging the proposal's margin of *risk.*

Annuity A uniform series of payments or receipts over a specified number of periods.

Asset A physical or intangible item of value to a company or an individual.

Asset turnover An expression of the effectiveness with which *assets* generate sales, defined as the ratio of *net sales* to total assets.

---

* Items shown in italics are defined separately.

Balance sheet A *financial statement* reflecting the recorded values of all *assets, liabilities*, and *owners' equity* at a point in time.

Balloon payment A significant *principal* payment due at the end of the term of a financial obligation.

Bankruptcy A legal process of disposing of the *assets* of a business or individual to satisfy creditors' claims in total or in part, and protecting the debtor(s) from further legal action.

Benefit (cost/benefit) The positive element in an *economic trade-off* which relates *economic earnings* to *economic costs* in an *investment, operating*, or *financing* decision.

Beta (β) A calculated form of expressing the specific (systematic) risk of a company's *common stock* relative to the stock market as a whole. (Cf. *volatility*.)

Bond A financial instrument representing a form of corporate *long-term debt* issued to investors; a variety of different types of bonds exist.

Bond rating A published ranking of a *bond* developed by financial organizations to express its relative soundness on a defined scale.

Book value The recorded value of an *asset* or *liability* as reflected in the *financial statements* of a company or individual.

Book value of equity The recorded value of *owners' (shareholders') equity* on a company's *balance sheet*, representing the owners' residual claim on the *assets*.

Break-even analysis Determining the level of sales at which a company will just recover *fixed* and *variable costs*; a zero-profit condition.

Breakup value The value realized from separating the parts of a multibusiness company and disposing of them individually.

Burden The combination of *interest* charges and current *principal* payments required by a financial obligation.

Burden coverage The ratio of periodic *income* before taxes to the corresponding amount of *burden*, adjusted for income taxes; a test of the ability to service a *debt* obligation.

Business risk The risk inherent in the expected *cash flows* from *investments* and *operations*, apart from the risk inherent in the form of *financing* used.

Business system A dynamic representation of the key elements and relationships governing *investments, operations*, and *financing* of a business entity. (Cf. *financial model*.)

Call provision A provision permitting the issuing company to redeem in part or in total a *bond* or *preferred stock* issue at a date determined by the company.

Capital The total amount of long-term *funds* committed to an enterprise in the form of ownership *equity* and long-term *debt*.

Capital asset pricing model (CAPM) An analytical approach to calculating the cost of *shareholders' equity*, using a *risk-free interest rate*, a *risk premium* (market premium), and a company-specific risk assessment *beta (β)*.

Capital budget A selected group of *investment* projects approved in principle for implementation, pending individual approval, and related closely to a company's business strategies.

Capital expenditures Expenditures made during a stated period for investments in new *fixed assets*, for the purpose of replacement, expansion, or new business opportunities.

Capital investment A relatively long-term commitment of funds to a project expected to generate positive net *cash flows* over time.

Capitalization The sum of all long-term sources of *capital* of a company, also derived by subtracting *current liabilities* from total *assets*.

Capital rationing   The allocation of limited *investment* funds to a selection of investment projects smaller than all currently acceptable projects; a fairly common condition.

Capital structure   The relative proportions of different sources of *capital* used in the long-term funding of the *investments* and *operations* of a company.

Cash   The amount of readily available currency owned by a company at a stated period in time.

Cash accounting   A method of accounting in which *revenues* and *expenses* and all other transactions are recognized when cash changes hands, in contrast to the *accrual* method of accounting.

Cash budget   A periodic projection of cash receipts and cash disbursements over a specified length of time. (Cf. *cash flow forecast.*)

Cash flow   The positive (inflow) or negative (outflow) movements of cash caused by an activity over a specific period of time.

Cash flow analysis   An economic method of analysis that employs the positive (inflow) and negative (outflow) movements of cash caused by an activity to determine the relative desirability of the activity; usually involves *discounted cash flow* methodology.

Cash flow cycle   The periodic movement of cash through an enterprise, caused by *investment, operating*, and *financing* decisions.

Cash flow forecast   A periodic forecast of cash movements through an enterprise, recognizing sources and uses of funds.

Cash flow from operations   Cash generated or used by the operations of a business over a specified period of time; usually derived by adjusting aftertax *net profit* for *noncash* charges and *noncash* receipts.

Cash flow return on investment (CFROI)   The relationship of operational *cash flows* to the cash value of the assets employed in generating them. In its most sophisticated form, it employs present value techniques.

Cash flow statement   A *financial statement* listing the cash impact of the activities of a business over a specified period of time, separating the *cash flows* into the areas of *operations, investments*, and *financing*. (Cf. *funds flow statement.*)

Cash value added (CVA)   A form of *net present value* analysis expressing the increase in present value caused by a business investment, a strategic plan, or the operations of a business unit.

Collection period   The average number of days over which *accounts receivable* are outstanding, either in total or by defined categories; a measure of the effectiveness with which customer *credit* is managed.

Common dividends   The total amount of dividends paid to a company's *common* shareholders in the form of cash or stock.

Common shares (common stock)   Securities representing a direct ownership interest in a corporation and a residual claim on the *assets*.

Common shares outstanding—basic   The number of *common shares* of a company issued and actually outstanding at a point in time, used in calculating *earnings per share—basic*.

Common shares outstanding—diluted   The number of *common shares* of a company issued and actually outstanding at a point in time, plus the number of shares potentially outstanding from exercise of stock options, rights and warrants, and securities convertible into common shares, used in calculating *earnings per share—diluted*.

Common-size financial statements   A ratio analysis of *balance sheets* and *income statements* in which all elements are represented as a percentage of *assets* or *net sales,* respectively. Used in analyzing trends and in comparing statements from different companies.

Comparables   Selected *assets* or business entities chosen by analysts to establish comparability with an asset or business being valued; used in determining the *fair market value* in the absence of market transactions.

Compounding The process of calculating the growing value of a sum of money over time, caused by the periodic interest earned and by the reinvestment of such interest.

Constant-dollar analysis The adjustment of financial magnitudes for inflation to reflect a common dollar value basis (using dollar values of a specified point in time), and the use of these adjusted values in accounting or *economic analysis*.

Consumer price index (CPI) An index provided by the U.S. government that represents the periodic change in the cost of a selected group of items purchased by consumers; used as a measure of *inflation*.

Contribution analysis A method of analysis that determines the relative excess of revenue over variable costs of product lines, business segments, and activities, and judges the contribution made toward meeting *fixed costs*, overhead, and *profits*.

Contribution margin The excess (or deficit) of revenue over the variable costs of products or services, at times also the excess (or deficit) of revenue over the total cost of products or services *(cost of goods or services sold)*.

Conversion ratio The stated number of *common shares* or other securities into which a *convertible security* may be exchanged.

Conversion value The *market value* represented by the *common shares* or other *assets* into which a *convertible security* may be exchanged.

Convertible security A financial security that may be exchanged at the option of the holder into another security or *asset* with a prescribed *conversion ratio*.

Cost The transaction value at which an *asset* was acquired; also, any periodic *expense* recognized against matching periodic *revenue*.

Cost of capital (weighted average cost of capital, hurdle rate) The weighted average of the aftertax cost to a company of all forms of long-term financing used; employed as a minimum standard for the return to be earned on new *investments*.

Cost of debt The *cost* to a company of employing *debt*, developed from the aftertax interest charges of various forms of debt.

Cost of equity The *cost* to a company of employing *common shareholders'* funds, developed from the investors' expectations about the return from holding such shares, usually in the form of the combination of dividends and capital gains.

Cost of goods (services) sold (cost of sales) The total of all *costs* and *expenses* incurred in producing, or acquiring, goods or services for sale.

Cost of preferred stock The *cost* to a company of employing *preferred shareholders'* funds, developed from the pretax preferred dividend required by preferred holders.

Coupon rate The stated interest rate specified on the interest coupons attached to *bonds*, as contrasted with the *yield* obtained on a bond, which relates the coupon rate to the *market value* of the bond.

Covenant Provision in the *bond* agreement specifying restrictions or other requirements that the issuer has to observe to maintain the bond's *credit* rating.

Coverage Relationship of fixed requirements, such as interest or *burden* connected with *debt*, to operating income before or after taxes. (Cf. *times interest earned, times burden covered.*)

Credit (creditworthiness) The recognized ability of an individual or company to assume indebtedness with the prospect of properly servicing such *debt*.

Cumulative effect of accounting changes The aftertax effect of changes in accounting methods used by a company, shown as a line item in the *income statement* and used in arriving at *net income*.

Cumulative preferred stock A form of *preferred stock* that carries the provision that any unpaid dividends accumulate for later payment, and must be paid in full before common dividends may be declared.

Current asset   Any *asset* on the *balance sheet* with a short-term expectation of being turned into cash, such as *cash, receivables,* and inventories; usually considered as having a one-year time horizon or less.

Current-dollar accounting   The adjustment of historical financial magnitudes for inflation to reflect current-dollar values (adjusting for price changes) and the use of these adjusted values in accounting or economic analysis. (Cf. *constant-dollar analysis.*)

Current liability   Any *liability* on the *balance sheet* with a short-term maturity, usually payable within one year, such as *accounts payable* and accrued taxes.

Current portion of long-term debt   The proportion of a long-term *liability* that is due and payable within one year.

Current ratio   A common measure of *liquidity* that relates the sum of *current assets* to the sum of *current liabilities.*

Current-value basis   The restatement of the recorded values of selected *assets* in current-dollar terms to reflect price changes. (Cf. *current-dollar accounting.*)

Cutoff rate   The minimum *rate of return* (*hurdle rate*) that *capital investment* projects have to meet, usually based on the *cost of capital* or a judgmentally adjusted standard.

Cyclical variations   The impact on a company's *funds flows* from the operational changes caused by business cycles.

Days' sales   A measure of the credit quality of *accounts receivable,* which expresses outstanding receivables in terms of average daily *sales;* can be compared with the *credit* terms under which sales were made.

Debt (liability)   An obligation to pay amounts due (and interest if required) under specified terms, or to provide goods or services to others.

Debt to assets   A ratio relating outstanding *debt* obligations (usually *long-term debt* but at times all types of debt) to total *assets;* used as a measure of *financial leverage.* (Cf. *debt to equity.*)

Debt to capitalization   A ratio relating *long-term debt* to a company's *capitalization;* used as a measure of *financial leverage* as found in the *capital structure.* (Cf. *debt to equity.*)

Debt to equity   A ratio relating outstanding *debt* obligations (usually *long-term debt* but at times all types of debt) to *shareholders' equity;* used as a measure of *financial leverage.*

Default   Failure to make a payment on a *debt* obligation when due.

Deferred charges   A provision recorded on the *balance sheet* to reflect expenses incurred, but applicable to future accounting periods.

Deferred income taxes   A provision for income tax *liabilities* or income tax *assets* recorded on the *balance sheet,* arising from timing differences between recognized tax liabilities in a company's accounting system and tax liabilities reported to the tax authorities.

Deflation   A decline in general price levels. (Cf. *inflation.*)

Depreciation   The decline in an *asset*'s value, from use or obsolescence, that's recognized in the accounting system and for income tax purposes as a periodic allocation (*write-off*) against income of a portion of the original *cost* of the *asset.* (Cf. *accelerated depreciation; noncash charges.*)

Dilution   The proportional reduction of *earnings per share* or *book value* per share from an increase in the number of shares outstanding, either from a new issue or from conversion of *convertible securities* outstanding.

Discounted cash flow   The *discounting* methodology employed in determining the economic attractiveness of *capital investment* projects, which reduces the value of future cash receipts or payments.

Discounted cash flow rate of return (DCF) The rate of return (*yield*) that equates a project's cash inflows and outflows over its economic life; also called *internal rate of return*.

Discounting The process of calculating the reduced value of a future sum or series of sums of money in proportion to the opportunity of earning interest and the distance in time of payment or receipt. (Cf. *compounding, present value*.)

Discount rate The rate of return or standard used in calculating the *present value* of future *cash flows*, using the *discounting process*.

Disinvestment The act of disposing of assets or whole business segments, caused by a reassessment of the strategic fit of these assets; the opposite of *investment*.

Dispositions The net value received from the sale of operations, lines of business, or divisions of a company during a stated period.

Diversification The process of investing in a number of unrelated or partially interrelated *assets* or activities to achieve a more stable performance of the business *portfolio*.

Dividend coverage Relationship of the amount of common and/or preferred dividends to aftertax *earnings* of a company; a test of the ability of the company to pay current level of dividends.

Dividend discount model A valuation method for *common stock* that employs the *present value* of expected future dividends and any change in the expected level of dividends.

Dividend payout A ratio relating the amount of dividends distributed to the aftertax *earnings* of a corporation to derive the percentage of *earnings* paid to shareholders.

Dividend yield The current return to shareholders from dividends received over a specified period, derived by dividing dividends per share by the current average market price of the *stock*. (Cf. *yield*.)

Dynamic analysis A method of analyzing business decisions that incorporates the effect of likely changes in key variables, as contrasted with fixed assumptions. (Cf. *sensitivity analysis*.)

Earnings (income, net income, profit, net profit) The difference between all recorded *revenues* and all related *costs* and *expenses* for a specified period, using generally accepted accounting principles.

Earnings before interest and taxes (EBIT) An expression of a company's earning power before the effects of financing and taxation; used in a variety of *financial analyses*.

Earnings per share (EPS) The proportional share of a corporation's *earnings* that can be claimed by each share of *common stock* outstanding, derived by dividing aftertax earnings after payment of preferred dividends by the average number of common shares outstanding during the period. (Cf. *earnings per share—basic*.)

Earnings per share—basic A company's earnings per share calculated on the basis of the average of all common shares actually outstanding. (Cf. *common shares outstanding—basic*.)

Earnings per share—diluted A company's earnings per share calculated on the basis of the average of all common shares actually outstanding at a point in time, plus the number of shares potentially outstanding from exercise of stock options, rights and warrants, and securities convertible into common shares. (Cf. *common shares outstanding—diluted*.)

Earnings yield The current return to shareholders from *earnings* recorded for a specified period, derived by dividing periodic earnings by the *stock*'s current or average market price. (Cf. *yield*.)

Economic analysis The development of the economic impact of a business decision that determines the actual *trade-off* between *economic costs* and *benefits* in a cash flow framework independent of accounting conventions.

Economic benefit   The consequence of a decision that causes an ultimate increase in present and future *cash flows*.

Economic cost   The consequence of a decision that causes an ultimate reduction in present and future *cash flows*.

Economic earnings (loss)   The net result of a *trade-off* between *economic benefits* and *economic costs*.

Economic life   The time over which a current or future *investment* can be expected to provide *economic benefits*, which is independent of the physical life of any *assets* involved.

Economic profit   The amount of aftertax net operating profit (NOPAT) earned on the capital base supporting the activity relative to the company's *weighted average cost of capital* applied to the capital base.

Economic return   A measure of the earnings power of an *investment* in terms of net *cash flows* generated by the *capital* committed. (Cf. *discounted cash flow*.)

Economic trade-off   The comparison of the *economic benefits* and *economic costs* caused by a business decision using a cash flow framework.

Economic value   The *net present value* of all future *economic benefits* and *costs* expected from an existing or prospective *investment*.

Economic value added (EVA™)   A form of expressing the value created by investing in projects whose returns exceed the company's *cost of capital*. The simplest way is to show the difference between annual *profits* (or *cash flow*) and the cost of the assets employed. The concept is also applied to the companies and divisions as a whole.

Enterprise value (firm value)   The *net present value* of all estimated future *cash flows* to be generated by a business.

Equity (owners' equity, net worth, shareholders' equity)   The recorded ownership claim of common and preferred shareholders in a corporation as reflected on the *balance sheet*. Also defined as total *assets* less all *liabilities*.

Equivalence   A point of indifference at which the *present value* of future *cash flows* reflects the return expectations of a prospective investor.

Expected return (expectation)   A weighted average of alternative outcomes of an *investment*, using the respective probabilities as weights.

Expense   A periodic offset against *revenue* recognized under generally accepted accounting principles, representing either a direct cash outlay or an *allocation* or *accrual* of past and future outlays.

Extraordinary items   The aftertax impact of *costs* or *revenues* encountered on a nonrecurring basis outside the normal operations of a company during a stated period.

Fair market value (FMV)   The price for an *asset* on which two rational parties with sufficient information would agree in the absence of negotiating pressure.

Financial Accounting Standards Board (FASB)   The official rule-making institute of the accounting community, which is privately funded by the profession.

Financial analysis   The process of determining and weighing the financial impact of business decisions.

Financial flexibility   The ability to maintain alternative choices for raising additional *capital* while preserving a *capital structure* appropriate to the risks and conditions of a company's business.

Financial Genome   A professional software application by Modernsoft, Inc. designed for financial analysis, statement preparation, and financial planning.

Financial growth plan   A model of future financial flows that tracks the results of key *investment*, *operational*, and *financing* dimensions under a variety of assumptions about strategies, policies, and business conditions.

Financial leverage The magnifying (or diminishing) effect on *return on equity* from the use of *debt* in the *capital structure*, caused by introducing fixed interest charges against the returns obtained from the incremental funds invested. (Cf. *operating leverage*.)

Financial model The representation in a computer program of key financial dimensions of a business system for purposes of simulating the impact of management decisions. (Cf. *financial growth plan*.)

Financial statements Key periodic statements prepared under generally accepted accounting principles, which represent the financial condition of a company (*balance sheet*), the operating results (*income statement*), the changes in *funds flows* (*cash flow statement*), and the changes in *owners' equity* (*statement of changes in shareholders' equity*).

Financing The provision of *funds* from internal or external sources to support the *investments* and *operations* of a business.

First-in, first-out (FIFO) A method of accounting for inventory in which the oldest item is assumed to be used or sold first. (Cf. *last-in, first-out*.)

Fixed assets Any tangible *asset* on the *balance sheet* considered to have a life or usefulness for a business in excess of one year, such as land, buildings, and machinery. (Cf. *current assets*.)

Fixed costs Any *cost* that doesn't vary with changes in the volume of operations over time.

Fixed-income security Any security that provides an unchanging stream of interest or dividends to the holder over its life.

Foreign exchange exposure The potential loss from an unexpected change in currency exchange rates affecting *investments* or *operations*.

Free cash flow The net *cash flow* available to a company after providing for all acceptable new *investments* to support its strategy, before any dividend payments or changes in *financing*.

Fully diluted earnings per share *Earnings per share* which are calculated on the assumption that all outstanding *convertible securities* and *warrants* have been converted into the appropriate number of common shares, raising the denominator and reducing *earnings per share*.

Funds A general term denoting means of payment, often equated with cash.

Funds flow (cash flow) The movement of *funds* of all types through a business over time, ultimately resulting in changes in *cash*.

Funds flow statement A *financial statement* prepared to display the *funds* movements in a business over a specified period of time, separated into sections on *operations, investment, financing,* and cash balances. (Cf. *Cash flow statement*)

Going-concern value The *net present value* of the expected future *cash flows* generated by a business from its normal operations. (Cf. *economic value, enterprise value*.)

Goodwill A category of intangible asset representing the excess paid over recorded values for acquisitions. It is generally amortized over specific time periods.

Gross margin The difference between *net sales* and *cost of goods sold* (or *cost of services provided*), generally expressed as a ratio of this difference divided by net sales.

Growth/decline variations The impact on a company's *funds flows* from the operational changes caused by growth or decline in the volume of business.

Hedge A strategy to neutralize the risk of an *investment* by engaging in offsetting contracts whereby potential gains and losses will cancel each other.

Historical cost principle An accounting principle requiring the recording of transactions and the maintenance of recorded values at the actual level incurred, regardless of any subsequent changes in the value of the *assets* or *liabilities* involved.

Hurdle rate   A minimum standard for the return required of an *investment*, used in selecting from alternative investment choices.

Income   The difference between the *revenues* and the matching *costs* and *expenses* for a specified period. (Cf. *earnings*.)

Income statement (operating statement, profit and loss statement)   A *financial statement* reporting the periodic *revenues* and matching *costs* and *expenses* for a specified period, and deriving the *income* for the period.

Incremental analysis   A method of analysis that focuses on the impact of changes caused by a business decision.

Inflation   An increase in general price levels, the opposite of *deflation*.

Inflation premium   The increased *return on investment* required to compensate the holders for expected *inflation*.

Insolvency   The condition where an individual's or company's *liabilities* exceed the realizable value of the *assets* held.

Intangibles   A category of asset representing intangible values such as patents, software, and *goodwill* from acquisitions. These are generally amortized over specific time periods.

Interest coverage   Relationship of periodic interest expense to operating *income* before or after taxes, used to judge a company's ability to pay interest charges. (Cf. *times interest earned*.)

Internal rate of return (IRR)   The *discount rate* that equates the cash inflows and cash outflows of an *investment* project, resulting in a *net present value* of zero. (Cf. *rate of return, yield*.)

Inventory turnover   A ratio that relates ending inventory or average inventory to the *cost of goods sold* for a specified period of time; used in judging the effectiveness with which inventories are controlled.

Inventory valuation   Any adjustment to recorded inventory values to correct for differences between historical *costs* and current prices, also affecting *cost of goods sold*.

Investment(s)   The commitment of *funds* for purposes of obtaining an *economic return* over a period of time, usually in the form of periodic *cash flows* and/or a *terminal value*.

Investment value   The value of a *convertible security* based strictly on its characteristics as a *fixed-income security*, without regard to its conversion provision.

Junk bond   Any *bond* issued by corporations with risk characteristics higher than what's normally rated as investment-grade risk (normal risk exposure).

Last-in, first-out (LIFO)   A method of accounting for inventory in which the newest item is assumed to be used or sold first. (Cf. *first-in, first-out*.)

Leasing   The process of contracting for the use of *assets* owned by others over a specified period of time, in exchange for a stipulated pattern of periodic payments.

Leverage   The magnifying effect from volume changes on *profits* caused by fixed elements in a company's *cost* structure, or the magnifying effect from profit changes on *return on equity* caused by *fixed-cost debt* obligations in the *capital structure*. (Cf. *financial leverage, operating leverage*.)

Leveraged buyout (LBO)   The acquisition of a business by investors using a high percentage of *debt* carried by the business itself.

Liability   An obligation to pay a specified amount or to perform a service; at times also the recognized potential obligation to pay or perform a service (contingent liability).

Liquid asset   An *asset* that can be rapidly converted into cash without suffering a significant reduction in value, usually classified as a *current asset*.

Liquidation   The process of terminating a business entity by selling its *assets*, paying off its *liabilities*, and distributing any remaining cash to its owners.

Liquidation value   The estimated value of a business based on *liquidation* of its *assets*.

Liquidity   The degree to which a company is readily able to meet its current obligations from *liquid assets*. (Cf. *acid test, current ratio*.)

Long-term debt   Any *debt* obligation of a company with a maturity of more than one year.

Managerial economics   The methodology underlying the analysis and resolution of the *economic (cash flow) trade-offs* involved in making management decisions.

Marginal costs (revenues)   Increments of *costs* and *revenues* attributable to changes in a variable affecting an issue being decided.

Market to book value   The relationship between the current market price of *common stock* and its recorded *book value*, a ratio often used in judging the performance of a company's *stock*.

Market value   The value of an *asset* as determined in an unconstrained market of multiple buyers and sellers, such as a securities exchange.

Market value added (MVA)   The difference between the recorded value of a company's *capitalization* and the current market value of the securities representing it.

Market value of equity   The combined value of all *common shares* of a company at current market prices. (Cf. *book value of equity*.)

Market value of firm   The *market value* of a company's *equity* plus the market value of its *debt*.

Minority interest   A small portion of shareholders' equity held by outsiders in a corporate entity acquired by a company.

Monetary asset   Any *asset* defined in terms of units of currency, such as *cash* and *accounts receivable*.

Multiple hurdle rates   A set of minimum return standards in a company that are used to judge the desirability of *investments* in activities or lines of business with widely different risk characteristics.

Mutually exclusive alternatives   Alternative *investments* for achieving the same objective, of which only one can be undertaken.

Net assets   Total *assets* less *current liabilities*, as recorded on the *balance sheet*.

Net assets turnover   An expression of the effectiveness with which assets generate *sales,* defined as the ratio of sales to *net assets,* on an average or ending value basis.

Net income (loss)   The difference between periodic *revenues* and matching *costs* and *expenses*. (Cf. *earnings, net profit, profit*.)

Net income available for common dividends   *Net income* adjusted for any *preferred* dividends declared during the period, representing the residual claim of the *common* shareholders.

Net investment   The commitment of new *funds* to an *investment* project, net of any funds recovered due to the decision to make the investment, adjusted for tax implications.

Net operating profit after tax (NOPAT)   Net profit from operations before *interest* and nonoperating income or expenses, adjusted for applicable income taxes. Used in a variety of ratios and valuation concepts.

Net present value (NPV)   The difference between the *present values* of cash inflows and outflows from an *investment*, representing the net gain or loss in value expected from the investment relative to the earnings standard applied.

Net profit   The difference between periodic *revenues* and matching *costs* and *expenses,* after applicable income taxes. (Cf. *earnings, net income, profit.*)

Net property, plant and equipment   The residual recorded value of *property, plant and equipment,* after deducting the amount of applicable *accumulated depreciation* to date.

Net sales   Total *revenue* from sales for a specified period, less adjustments such as returns, allowances, and sales discounts.

Net worth   The recorded value of *shareholders' equity* on the *balance sheet.*

Nominal amount   Any quantity not adjusted for changes in the purchasing power of the currency in which it's recorded. (Cf. *real amount.*)

Noncash item   An *expense* or *revenue* recognized in the accounting process that doesn't represent a *cash flow* during the period, such as *depreciation* or unrealized income or gains.

Notes payable   Debt obligations representing trade or other credit extended to a company, generally interest-bearing commitments.

Ongoing value   The value of a business or activity that is assumed to be continuing at the termination point of a discounted cash flow analysis for valuation purposes, also referred to as *terminal value.*

Operating cash flow   The net *cash flow* generated by the operations of a business during a specified period, usually on an aftertax basis and adjusted for all noncash accounting elements such as depreciation and amortization.

Operating funds   *Funds* required to support current operations, such as the various *working capital* items.

Operating leverage   The magnifying (or diminishing) effect of volume changes on *profits* caused by the *fixed costs* in the company's operations.

Operating statement (income statement)   A *financial statement* reporting the *revenues* and matching *costs* and *expenses* for a specified period, and deriving the *net income.*

Operational analysis   The various methods of analyzing the specific and comparative aspects of a company's operating performance.

Operations   The activities in a company that support the basic purpose of the business, generating *revenues* and managing related *costs* and *expenses* for profitable results.

Opportunity cost   *Economic benefits* forgone by selecting one alternative course of action over another.

Opportunity rate of return   A rate of return standard reflecting the long-term level of returns expected in a business, often based on a company's *cost of capital.*

Option   A contractual opportunity to purchase or sell an *asset* or security at a predetermined price, without the obligation of doing so.

Over-the-counter market (OTC)   A market network among security dealers that permits electronic trading of securities not listed on a formal securities exchange.

Owners' equity   The recorded value of *preferred* and *common* shareholders' claims against the *assets* on a company's *balance sheet;* also, the proprietors' recorded claims in the case of an unincorporated business or partnership. (Cf. *equity, shareholders' equity.*)

Paid-in capital   The recorded amount of *capital* provided by shareholders on the *balance sheet,* as contrasted with *retained earnings.*

Par value   The *nominal* value established by the issuer of a security, as contrasted with the *market value* of the security. In the case of a *bond,* the issuing company contracts to pay the par value at maturity.

Payables   See *accounts payable.*

Payables period   A translation of *accounts payable* into the days of average purchases outstanding at a point in time; used as an indicator of the effectiveness with which *trade credit* is employed.

Payback period   The period of time over which the *cash flows* from an *investment* are expected to recover the initial outlay.

Perpetuity   A series of level periodic receipts or payments (*annuity*) expected to last forever.

Plug figure   A common term used to represent an unknown variable in a financial analysis, such as the amount of *financing* required in a pro forma projection. (Cf. *pro forma statement.*)

Portfolio   A set of diverse *investments* held by an individual or a company.

Preferred stock   A special class of capital stock, usually with a dividend provision, that receives a form of preference over *common stock* in its claims on *earnings* and *assets.*

Prepaid expenses   The portion of any expenses paid during a stated period but applicable to future periods, shown as a *current asset* on the *balance sheet.*

Present value   The value today of a future sum or series of sums of money, calculated by *discounting* the future sums with an appropriate discount rate.

Present value payback   The point in the *economic life* of an *investment* project at which the cumulative *present value* of *cash inflows* equals the present value of the cash outflows.

Price to earnings (P/E)   The relationship of the market price of a share of *stock* to the most recent *earnings per share* over 12 months; used as a rough indicator of what investors are willing to pay for $1 of a company's *earnings.*

Principal   The original amount of a loan or *bond*, also called face value, on which the rate of interest to be paid is based.

Private placement   The sale of securities to a selected group of investors rather than through a public offering.

Profit   The difference between periodic *revenues* and matching *costs* and *expenses.* (Cf. *earnings, net profit.*)

Profitability index (benefit/cost ratio, BCR)   A measure of *investment* desirability, defined as the *present value* of all cash inflows expected over the *economic life* of a project divided by the present value of the cash outflows.

Profit center   An organizational segment of a business in which *revenues, costs*, and *expenses* can be recognized separately, allowing the activity to be managed for *profit* performance.

Pro forma statement   A projected *financial statement* reflecting the financial impact of a set of assumed conditions for a specified future period.

Projection   A forecast of the quantitative implications of a set of assumed conditions.

Provision for income taxes   The amount of income taxes recognized as an expense for a stated period on the *income statement,* as distinguished from the amount of income taxes reported to the tax authorities. Any difference is due to differences in the timing and pattern of revenues and expenses reported for tax purposes, and this amount is recognized as *deferred income taxes* on the *balance sheet.*

Public issue (public offering)   The sale of newly issued securities to the public through underwriters. (Cf. *private placement.*)

Purchasing power parity   A condition in which commodities in different countries cost the same amount when prices are expressed in a given currency, due to expected adjustments in foreign exchange rates.

Quick ratio (acid test)   A stringent measure of *liquidity* relating current cash *assets* (cash, cash equivalents, and *receivables*) to *current liabilities.*

Quick sale value   The value of an asset or business when assumed to be sold under hurried conditions, resulting generally in a lower valuation than *market value.*

Range of earnings chart (EBIT chart)
A graphic representation of the related changes in *earnings before interest and taxes* (*EBIT*) and *earnings per share* under various financing alternatives.

Rate of return   The level of *earnings* attained or expected from an *investment* over a period of time. (Cf. *yield*.)

Ratio analysis   The use of a variety of ratios in analyzing the financial performance and condition of a business from various viewpoints, such as managers', owners', and creditors'.

Real amount   Any quantity that has been adjusted for changes in the purchasing power of the currency in which it's recorded. (Cf. *nominal amount*.)

Realized income   *Earnings* or gains that are recognized as the result of a transaction, as contrasted with earnings or gains that exist on paper only.

Receivables   See *accounts receivable*.

Recovery value (terminal value)   The value of any *assets* or future *profits* expected to be realized at the end of the *economic life* of an *investment*, net of taxes.

Redundant assets   Any *assets* held by a company that don't contribute returns appropriate for the lines of business principally engaged in; these are candidates for *disinvestment* (divestiture).

Relevant costs   Identifiable *cost* or *expense* elements that are expected to change in response to a decision being analyzed.

Relevant revenues   Identifiable *revenue* elements that are expected to change in response to a decision being analyzed.

Reserves   Portions of *shareholders' equity* set aside on the *balance sheet* in recognition of contingencies and potential *liabilities*.

Retained earnings (earned surplus)   The cumulative amount of past and current *earnings* retained and reinvested in a corporation, instead of being distributed to shareholders in the form of dividends.

Return on assets (ROA or ROAE)   The relationship of annual aftertax *earnings* to total *assets* (average or ending balance), used as a measure of the productivity of the assets a company employs to generate the earnings. At times aftertax earnings are adjusted for interest to eliminate the impact of *financing*.

Return on capitalization (invested capital) (ROC)   The relationship of annual *earnings* before interest, after taxes to the *capitalization* (average or ending balance); used as a measure of the productivity of a company's invested *capital* regardless of the amount of *financial leverage* employed. (Cf. *return on net assets*.)

Return on equity (net worth) (ROE)   The relationship of annual aftertax *earnings* to the recorded *shareholders' equity*. Used as a measure of the effectiveness with which shareholder funds have been invested.

Return on investment (ROI)   The relationship of annual aftertax *earnings* to the *book value* (average or ending balance) of the *asset*, business, or *profit center* generating these earnings. Used as a measure of the productivity of the *investment*. (Cf. *return on assets*.)

Return on net assets (RONA)   The relationship of annual *earnings* before interest, after taxes to total *assets* less *current liabilities* (*net assets*) (average or ending balance), used as a measure of the productivity of a company's invested *capital* regardless of the amount of *financial leverage* employed. (Cf. *return on capitalization*.)

Revenue (sales)   The recorded incidence of a sale of goods and/or services as recognized in the accounting system.

Risk-adjusted return standard (discount rate, hurdle rate, cost of capital)   A minimum *discount rate* that has been adjusted upward to include a specified risk premium.

Risk allowance   A provision for risk in an analysis, such as lowering a project's expected *cash flows* or using a *risk-adjusted return standard*.

Risk analysis A process of integrating risk dimensions into an analysis, such as using *sensitivity analysis* or modeling outcomes that have been adjusted by probabilistic methods.

Risk aversion A subjective unwillingness to accept a given level of risk unless a significant *economic trade-off* can be realized.

Risk-free interest rate The assumed *yield* obtainable on a guaranteed security in the absence of *inflation*, generally represented by U.S. Treasury bonds.

Risk premium (market premium) The increased return required from an *investment* to compensate the holder for the level of risk involved, generally represented by the difference between expected returns from a stock market portfolio and the risk-free interest rate. It is used as an input in determining the cost of *shareholders' equity* when calculating the cost of capital.

Sales (revenue) The recorded incidence of a sale of goods and/or services as recognized in the accounting system.

Sales per employee The ratio of annual sales to the number of employees (average or ending) as an expression of the effectiveness with which human capital is employed.

Seasonal variations The impact on a company's *funds flows* from the operational changes caused by seasonal business conditions.

Secured creditor A creditor whose claim is backed by the pledge of a specified *asset*, the proceeds of which will go to the creditor in case of *liquidation*.

Securities and Exchange Commission (SEC) The regulatory body established by the federal government to oversee securities markets.

Senior creditor Any creditor with specific claims on *income* or *assets* that rank ahead of that of general (unsecured) creditors.

Sensitivity analysis The process of testing the impact on the results of an analysis from changes in one or more of the input variables.

Sequential outlays One or more future *investment* outlays expected during the *economic life* of an investment project, which should be taken into account in judging the project's overall desirability.

Shareholders' equity The recorded value of the residual claims of all shareholders as reflected on the *balance sheet*.

Shareholder value The economic value created by successfully investing in activities whose returns exceed the company's *cost of capital,* which will cause growth in *total shareholder return.*

Share price appreciation The change in the *market value* of preferred and common shares over time.

Share repurchases (stock buyback) The purchase by a company of its own shares in the market, using available funds to reduce the number of shares outstanding versus investing those funds internally or paying an increased dividend.

Shelf registration The filing, under *SEC* rules, of a general-purpose prospectus outlining possible financing plans for up to two years, to speed up the actual issue when the timing is considered appropriate.

Short-term liabilities *Debt* obligations due within 12 months of the date of a *balance sheet*. Generally listed under *current liabilities*.

Simulation The process of modeling the potential outcomes of a financial plan or *investment* proposal, taking into account alternative assumptions about key variables and policies, and calculating the results using computer programs. (Cf. *sensitivity analysis*)

Sinking fund A separate pool of cash, often held in trust, into which periodic payments are made for the future redemption of an obligation.

Solvency The condition of an individual or company in which obligations can be paid when due.

Sources and uses statement A *financial statement* that separates all *funds* inflows and outflows for a given period of time, derived from changes in *balance sheet* accounts and supplemented with *operating statement* data. (Cf. *cash flow statement*)

Spot market A market in which prices of securities or commodities are determined for immediate transactions.

Spread The difference between the issue price of a new security and the net amount received by the issuing company, caused by underwriting commissions and *expenses*. Also, the difference between the *cost of capital* and the returns achieved on an *investment*.

Stock General term used in referring to *common stock*; also applied to *preferred stock*.

Stock market risk premium The premium in return to the investor governed by the risk of investing in the stock market versus risk-free long-term government bonds. Used in calculating the cost of capital. (Cf. *risk premium*)

Stock option A contractual arrangement allowing selected corporate employees to purchase a specified number of shares at a set price within a specified period of time; used as an incentive for key personnel.

Straight-line depreciation A pattern of *depreciation* write-offs that charges level amounts during the *asset*'s book life, for either accounting or tax deduction purposes.

Subordinated creditor A creditor whose claim is specifically designated as ranking below the claims of other creditors of a company.

Sunk cost A past outlay of *funds* that can't be recovered or changed by a current or future decision, and which is therefore irrelevant in the analysis of future actions.

Sustainable growth rate The rate of growth in *equity* or sales volume that a company can maintain without changing its *return on assets, asset turnover, debt to equity*, and *dividend payout*, and while keeping its *capital structure* proportions at their current levels.

Synergy The assumed *economic benefits* to be obtained from a successful combination of two businesses due to increased efficiency, economies of scale, and mutual reinforcement of business effectiveness.

Tax shield The impact on a company's income tax obligations from a change in a tax-deductible expense, such as *depreciation* or interest, defined as the amount of change times the applicable tax rate. It assumes that the company has sufficient taxable income to offset the change in the *expense*.

Terminal value (recovery value) The value of any *assets* or future *cash flows* expected to be realized at the end of the *economic life* of an *investment*, net of taxes.

Time lags The elapsed time between the recorded incidence of a transaction and its actual cash impact.

Times burden covered The relationship of the amount of debt *burden* during a period to *earnings* before interest and taxes. Used as a measure of a company's ability to service its *debt*.

Times interest earned The relationship of the amount of periodic interest expense to *earnings* before interest and taxes. Used as a measure of a company's ability to make regular interest payments.

Time value of money The *discounted* or *compounded* value of a sum of money over a specified period of time, using a specified discount or compound rate. (Cf. *present value*.)

Total shareholder return (TSR) The *economic return* to shareholders in the form of dividends and capital gains or losses from *share price appreciation* or decline realized during a specified period.

Trade credit Credit extended to a company in the course of normal business operations by its suppliers. (Cf. *accounts payable*.)

Trade-off The process of judging the relative advantage or disadvantage from making a decision that involves identified *economic benefits* and *costs*, generally in a cash flow framework.

Trade payables Amounts owed to a company's suppliers of goods and services. (Cf. *accounts payable*.)

Transfer price An internally established price level at which units of a company trade goods or services with each other.

Treasury stock The value stated at acquisition cost of a company's own common shares which were purchased in the stock market and are held in safekeeping for future use. Shown as a subtraction from *shareholders' equity* on the *balance sheet*.

Trend analysis A method of analysis that applies judgmental or statistical methods to historical series of data for the purpose of judging performance or making informed projections of future conditions.

Uncommitted earnings per share (UEPS) *Earnings per share* adjusted for the effect of future *sinking fund* payments and other repayment provisions, used in judging alternative financing possibilities.

Underwriter Investment banker or a group (syndicate) of investment bankers used by a corporation in marketing new securities issues to the public, guaranteeing a specific price to the issuing company. (Cf. *public offering*.)

Unrealized income (gain) *Earnings* or gains that are recognized on paper without the benefit of a transaction, as contrasted with earnings or gains that are realized through actual transactions. (Cf. *realized income*.)

Variable cost Any *cost* or *expense* that varies with operating volume over a specified period. (Cf. *fixed cost*.)

Volatility The risk introduced by past and expected fluctuations in a company's *earnings*, often expressed as β (*beta*).

Warrant A financial instrument issued to investors giving them the option to purchase additional shares at a specified price. Usually issued in connection with a new security issue.

Weighted average cost of capital Overall *cost of capital* derived by weighting the respective *costs* of different parts of a company's *capital structure* by their proportions.

Working capital (net working capital) The difference between *current assets* and *current liabilities* as recorded on the *balance sheet*, representing the amount of *operating funds* that is financed by the company's *capital structure*.

Working capital cycle The periodic transformation of *working capital* components into cash inflows and outflows.

Working capital turnover The relationship of sales to average *working capital* expressed as the number of times *working capital* is turned over during the period. It is an indicator of the effectiveness with which *working capital* is managed.

Write-offs Accounting entries that allocate portions of past outlays into appropriate operating periods, such as *depreciation* and *amortization*.

Yield The *rate of return* earned by an *investment*'s cash inflows and outflows during a specified period. (Cf. *internal rate of return*.)

Yield to maturity The *internal rate of return* earned by a *bond* when held to maturity.

APPENDIX III

Financial Information and On-Line Sources

While this book's orientation is techniques of financial analysis, many uses of the tools we've discussed suggest the need for information beyond that stipulated or available directly. Successful application of financial analysis requires that you be familiar with at least the main sources of financial information, and how to obtain the necessary inputs for your analysis. For this reason, we've devoted this appendix to a brief review of common data sources; where required we've also given some guidance for interpreting the financial data presented. Information sources listed here will give you the background to make more sophisticated decisions about company performance, new financing, temporary borrowing, investments, credit, capital budgeting, and so on.

The rise of the internet has literally opened a world of data sources and up-to-the-minute information to anyone willing to browse among the exploding number of web sites being made available. These sources complement, continuously update, and expand what used to be limited to the printed page in newspapers, magazines, and reference books. Accordingly, we'll address both on-line and printed sources where appropriate within the major topics covered in this appendix, while realizing that the fast-changing environment of data access will render this presentation partially obsolete in a relatively short time. The on-line sources are listed first, with brief explanations of the contents that can be accessed, while more detailed descriptions are provided with the print sources.

Several of the major search engines currently available offer access to a broad range of financial information. Foremost among these at the time of this writing is *Yahoo Finance*, which provides up-to-the-minute summary information on U.S. and international financial market data, stock and other securities quotations, individual company stock data and charts, financial news, and much more. Infoseek, Lycos, and Excite each offer a selection of financial data, news, and a variety of information for individuals and businesses, as well as links to a large number of information sites on financial offerings by colleges and universities. It's generally useful to browse these extensive sites, searching for "finance" to see firsthand the type of information available.

Yahoo: **http://finance.yahoo.com**
Infoseek: **http://infoseek.com**
Lycos: **http://www.lycos.com**
Excite: **http://www.excite.com**

In keeping with the nature of this book, this overview is meant only as an introduction to sources of current financial, periodic financial, and background company and business information. The reader is encouraged to search both the internet as well as depository libraries for information relevant to specific inquiries, using the special catalog and information links of the latter.

Current Financial Information

The common way to keep abreast of financial developments has long been to scan the daily financial pages of national, metropolitan, and regional newspapers. The most complete and widely read financial coverage is found in *The Wall Street Journal* (**http://www.dowjones.com**) and *The New York Times* (**http://www. nytimes.com**) which contain detailed information on securities and commodity markets; news, feature articles, and statistics on economic and business conditions; news and earnings reports for individual companies; dividend announcements; currency, commodity, and trading data; and a great deal of coverage of international business and economic conditions. Major U.S. and Canadian dailies also carry key financial and economic data, but their coverage and emphasis vary greatly. Smaller and regional papers often provide only selected highlights tailored to the area and the readership. As we'll show, most of this information can be found on the internet through the various service sites now available on line.

The bulk of the materials shown in the financial pages involve securities transactions and current financial data. This information isn't entirely self-explanatory. We'll describe the meaning of some of the abbreviations and symbols used in *The Wall Street Journal* listings for stock transactions, bond transactions, and other key financial data. Other newspapers generally present data in a fairly comparable fashion, but in less detail.

Stock Quotations

On-Line Stock Market Data
Major on-line sources for current information about individual securities prices, trading volumes, and averages include the following exchange sites:

NYSE: **http://www.nyse.com**

NASDAQ: **http://www.nasdaq.com** and **http://www.nasdaq-online.com**

These sites provide current market averages, indexes and trading data, as well as securities quotations, paralleling many of the listings found in the financial pages, but offering easy and immediate access.

On-Line Company Data
A growing number of web sites make available up-to-date company information in a variety of formats, including charts of share price movements and other data. Many of these require subscriptions to obtain highly detailed company analyses,

but most offer brief profiles and highlights for free. Again we suggest that the interested reader browse these sites to gain a sense of what information is available:

Bloomberg.com: **http://www.bloomberg.com**

Corporate Information Research Site:
http:/www.corporateinformation.com

Fortune 500 Companies: **http://pathfinder.com/fortune**

Hoover's Online: **http://www.hoovers.com**

Security APL Quote: **http://www.secapl.com**

Stockmaster: **http://www.stockmaster.com**

Stock Selector: **http://www.stockselector.com**

Stock Smart: **http://www.stocksmart.com**

Wall Street Research Network: **http://www.wsrn.com**

Wright's Investor Service: **http://www.wisi.com**

Zack's Investment Research: **http://www.zacks.com**

Printed Stock Market Data

Transactions executed on organized exchanges—New York Stock Exchange (NYSE), American Stock Exchange (AMEX) (which is now part of NASDAQ), and several regional exchanges—and the rapidly growing electronic network of the National Association of Securities Dealers (NASDAQ) are listed the following day in the financial pages of most newspapers. The format is generally comparable, although the detail provided and the number of companies covered will vary.

Daily trading statistics for the NYSE, AMEX, and NASDAQ are summarized under two overall headings, *Stock Market Data Bank* and *The Dow Jones Averages,* while composite transactions of individual securities are listed alphabetically by company. The Stock Market Data Bank shows the movement of the major indexes, that is, the Dow Jones Averages, The New York Stock Exchange index, Standard & Poor's Indexes, the NASDAQ Stock Market index, and a selection of other indexes. These are reflected in terms of the daily high, low and close, the net change, the change over the past twelve months, and the change from last year end. Next is a listing, by major exchange, of the most active issues, the price percentage gainers and losers, volume percentage leaders, and a summary of issues traded, advances, declines, new highs, new lows, etc., as well as hourly volumes of trading on the NYSE. The Dow Jones Averages are graphed over six months with daily ranges, covering the 30 industrials, the 20 transportation stock, and 15 utility stocks. These summaries provide an overview of the market's mood and direction.

The various stock price averages and indexes are popular and important clues to the stock market's behavior in general. They're calculated daily and in most cases continuously from on-line databases. The averages are followed by analysts, investors, and financial managers who interpret market movements to decide on purchase or sale of securities, or to assess various types of new securities. Because the various averages involve a selected and relatively small number of stocks, their upward or downward movement over time isn't necessarily a predictor of the likely movement of any particular stock or of the overall market.

As we've discussed in Chapters 10 and 11, there are many factors underlying the value and market position of a particular security, the most important being the current and prospective operating circumstances of the company and the cash flows generated in response to these. The market's atmosphere and general economic conditions will certainly influence the particular stock's behavior, but we must caution against the adage that a "rising tide lifts all ships in the harbor" (a gross oversimplification of stock market behavior). The limitations of stock indexes are those of averages in general, which can only be broad indicators of a likely trend against which all particulars of a security have to be compared.

The most commonly quoted and publicized stock price averages are the Dow Jones averages of 30 industrial, 20 transportation, and 15 utility stocks, and the composite average of all those 65 securities. The Dow Jones Industrial Average contains the most well-known companies in the United States, such as IBM, General Motors, General Electric, 3M, Coca-Cola, and Procter & Gamble. Because it's heavily weighted toward these "blue-chip" securities—many of which have performed less strongly than newer and more fashionable companies—the Dow Jones average isn't particularly applicable for analysis of securities of lesser-known companies, specialized "growth situations," internet companies, and conglomerates.

The New York Times average of 50 stocks includes 25 transportation issues and 25 industrial stocks. This average is also somewhat weighted in favor of blue chips. The Standard & Poor's averages—composite indexes of 425 industrial stocks, 50 utilities, and 25 transportation companies, and a combination of all these averages in the S&P 500—are more broadly based and more closely approximate the average price level of all stocks listed on the New York Stock Exchange, because the S&P 500 includes about one-quarter of the issues actively traded there.

The NASDAQ composite average is a broad sampling of the many issues traded electronically through a wide network of security dealers. These quotations have achieved growing recognition over the past decade and represent a vast grouping of new, emerging, and fast-growing securities as well as securities of large numbers of smaller, well-established companies.

Because stock transactions are electronically tracked, the current level of the various averages is always available almost instantaneously during the trading day. Continuous adjustments are made for stock splits, stock dividends, and many changes in the corporate structure of the companies in the index. Some references at the end of this appendix detail how the indexes are calculated.

Individual stock quotations from the NYSE are generally presented in a tabular, common format. The various columns show the high and low achieved during the past 52 weeks, the name of the company, the stock exchange symbol, the annual dividend, the current dividend yield, the price/earnings ratio, the day's volume of trading in hundreds of shares, and the high, low and closing price for the day. The quotations are accompanied by a large number of symbols and footnotes to provide further insight for the reader. For example, the notation "e" next to a company's dividend indicates that a dividend was declared but that there is no regular dividend rate. The letter "g" next to a company's name indicates that dividends are paid in Canadian dollars, while the stock is traded in U.S. dollars and no dividend yield is shown. If a preferred stock is traded, the symbol "pf" is added right after the name. The symbol "s" next to the high for a stock indicates a stock dividend or split, while the "n" with a company's name indicates a stock newly issued in the past 52 weeks. An upright black arrow at the beginning of the line indicates that a new 52-week high has been reached, while an inverse arrow indicates a new low.

The symbol "vj" ahead of the name indicates a state of bankruptcy and that no dividend is paid, and the letter "m" signals that the dividend was omitted during the past 52 weeks. Finally, "wt" with a company's name designates the issue as a warrant (trading separately from its related stock), while a new stock "wi" is trading on a "when issued" basis. Many other symbols refer mostly to dividend exceptions, and all are explained in the footnotes to the listing, as are the definitions of the listing categories themselves.

Individual listings of stock transactions in the *Wall Street Journal* are supplemented by various summaries of overall trading figures in the *Stock Market Data Bank,* which shows such statistics as the day's most active stocks. The *Diary* for the past two trading days covering the NYSE and NASDAQ/AMEX shows the number of issues traded, advancing and declining issues, volume leaders, leaders in price gains and declines, etc.

Quotations of transactions on the AMEX are printed in a similar format. Transactions on regional exchanges, such as the Pacific Stock Exchange in San Francisco and the Midwest Stock Exchange in Chicago, are often listed together with the most important quotations on the major Canadian stock exchanges in Toronto and Montreal. These transactions are usually quoted in less detail. Normally, only the number of shares traded, the high and low prices, and the closing prices with changes from the previous close are listed. At times, the quotations are limited to volume and closing prices only.

Quotations of transactions in the fast-growing NASDAQ market follow the basic format of the NYSE, except that notations indicating special conditions are incorporated into the four- or five-letter listing symbol. If a fifth letter is used, its special meaning is keyed to a symbol explanation below the NASDAQ listing. For example, the letter "F" indicates a foreign stock, while an "A" indicates a Class A stock. A huge volume of securities is traded in the NASDAQ system outside the organized exchanges, in an auction market consisting of hundreds of security dealers and individuals in all parts of the country. They're electronically linked via extensive computer networks, in an amazingly flexible arrangement which allows trading between prospective buyers and sellers of such securities as government bonds, state and municipal bonds, stocks and bonds of smaller and newer companies, bank stocks, mutual funds, insurance companies, small issues, and infrequently traded issues. A special listing of NASDAQ Small-Cap Issues is devoted to mostly new companies with a relatively small capitalization. Because of the limited trading in these stocks, the listing is confined to the name, the annual dividend, the volume traded in hundreds of shares, the last transaction price, and the change from the prior level.

Foreign Exchanges

Some of the larger newspapers carry limited quotations from major foreign stock exchanges. Trading of internationally recognized securities on the Paris, London, Tokyo, or Frankfurt stock exchanges is reported in the currency of the country involved. At times, the financial pages may contain current stock averages for foreign countries, supplemented by accounts of major activities there. *The Wall Street Journal* presents the Dow Jones World Stock Indexes, which reflect market trends in major regions of the world. Closing prices and changes from the prior trading day are provided for many industrial groupings and for major regions such as the United States, the Americas, Europe, and Asia-Pacific.

Mutual Funds

Mutual funds are professionally managed investment pools. A share of a mutual fund represents an investment in a portfolio of different securities, which may be oriented toward a variety of investment objectives such as earnings or capital appreciation. These funds have gained in importance in recent years, and mutual fund trading is quoted in most major newspapers. Price ranges are provided by the National Association of Securities Dealers (NASDAQ) and can be found on the NASDAQ web site listed earlier.

The quotes normally show the investment objectives incorporated in the name of the specific fund under the heading to the management company, defined in many categories, including capital appreciation (CAP) and growth and income (G&I) for stock funds, short-term (BST) and high-yield taxable (BHI) for taxable bond funds, and intermediate-term (IDM) and high-yield municipal (HYM) for municipal bond funds. Next is given the net asset value per share (NAV), followed by the net change in NAV from the previous day. Finally, the total return is provided in percent for the year to date.

A variety of mutual fund indexes developed by Lipper are quoted to show daily trends in major categories, such as growth funds, small company growth funds, and gold funds, as well as bond indexes for different funds such as world income or general municipals.

Options

Options (which are essentially contracts to buy or sell a security on a future date and at a stipulated price) are traded on various exchanges and are listed in terms of closing prices for "puts" (sales prices) and "calls" (purchase prices) for several months in the future. This specialized market has grown rapidly in recent

years as has the market for commodity futures, which similarly represent contracts for future sales and purchases of certain commodities and are quoted in the
financial pages.

Option quotations provide the option and strike price, the expiration date,
volume of trades during a given day, and the last trade in dollars plus fractions.
The 40 most active contracts the exchange traded on are identified, as are the net
change from the prior trading day, the closing price, and the "open interest" (options outstanding) from the prior trading day.

Bond Quotations

The three major types of bonds—corporate, state and municipal, and federal government—represent a huge market involving both the organized exchanges and
the NASDAQ market. In fact, the overwhelming majority of government bonds
of both types are traded in the NASDAQ market, while the majority of corporate
bond issues are traded on the stock exchanges.

The first column lists the abbreviated name of the issuing company, accompanied by the coupon interest rate and the maturity date indicated by the last
two digits of the year. Next is shown the current yield, followed by the volume
traded in thousands of dollars (most bonds are denominated at $1,000 each), the
closing price, and the net change from the prior trading day's closing price. The
most important difference to remember vis-à-vis stock quotations is that bond
prices are quoted in percentages of par value, expressed in fractions no smaller
than one-eighth of a percent, although the switch to decimal quotations in early
2001 is beginning to change this practice. The symbols used with individual
bond quotations parallel those discussed earlier. For example, "cv" indicates that
the bond is convertible into common stock, and the price will reflect the share
values of the common represented by each bond. The symbol "cld" indicates that
the bond has just been called for redemption, while "dc" refers to a bond selling
at a deep discount. The symbol "na" indicates that there is no interest accrual,
usually associated with a bond from which investors expect little interest recovery beyond the principal due.

A slightly different method is used to list current quotations for government
agency bonds and miscellaneous securities traded over the counter. We find that
these securities are listed in terms of bid and asked quotations, which represent the
price desired for purchase or sale on the trading day but don't necessarily denote
specific transactions. Another important difference reflected in this example is the
custom of quoting prices in percentage of par value, this time stated in terms of
fractions of a percent in 32ds of a point. Thus, a quote of 141:07 means a price of
1,410 7/32 percent or $1,412.19 per $1,000 of par value. The final column shows
the yield to maturity, which reflects the return on investment earned at the current
price if the bond is held to its maturity date and redeemed at par.

U.S. government securities as well as other debt instruments will be affected by the general outlook for interest rates. U.S. government securities will
tend to yield a lower return than most corporate and other public bonds, because

the likelihood of default is extremely remote and the purchaser is normally looking for a safe investment with an assured long-term or short-term yield. Also, they
generally are exempt from state income taxes.

As we found in the case of the stock market quotations, bond market listings
are supplemented by a variety of reports on the volume of trading, bonds averages, summaries of advancing and declining conditions, highs and lows for the
year, and so on. Again, these provide the investor with a general feel for the daily
movements of the bond markets and interest rate conditions. The most commonly
used averages are the Dow Jones Bond Averages (20 bonds, including 10 public
utilities and 10 industrials), Merrill Lynch Corporate Debt Issues, and Lehman
Brothers U.S. Securities Indexes. Bond averages are calculated in percentages of
par, as were the quotations themselves.

Other Financial Data

Most papers list, in one form or another, so-called leading, coincident, and lagging
business and economic indicators—such as indexes of industrial production,
freight car loadings, prices, output in the automotive industry, and steel production—both in feature stories and in tabular form. When supplemented by reports
of earnings and dividend declarations of individual corporations, news about corporate management, analysis and announcement of new financing, and industry
analysis, this information can provide a broad background for financial analysis.

Among the more specialized data in the financial pages are listings of transactions in the commodities markets. Commodities include a great variety of basic
raw materials such as cotton, lumber, copper, and rubber as well as foods such as
coffee, corn, and wheat. The best-known exchange for commodity trading is the
Chicago Board of Trade. More specialized exchanges include the New York Cotton Exchange or international exchanges such as the London Metal Exchange.
Commodities may be traded on a spot basis; that is, the commodity is purchased
outright at the time. Commodities futures are also traded. These are contracts to
buy or sell a commodity at a specified price at some point in the future. The commodities market is far too varied to describe here, but we should take a quick look
at how commodities are quoted.

The information on commodities trading provided by most sources usually
involves opening and closing transactions as well as highs and lows for the trading day and the season. Changes from the previous trading day are also often
listed. A variety of indexes are available, such as the Dow Jones Spot Index, Dow
Jones Futures Index, and Reuters United Kingdom Index. A company whose operations depend to a large extent on raw materials traded in a spot or futures market can be severely influenced by fluctuations in spot or futures prices. Because
fluctuations in commodities markets can be severe, traders in these markets often
hedge. This involves arrangements to both buy and sell the same commodity,
which will "cover" the trader for shifts in prices. References at the end of this appendix provide detailed information on commodities trading.

Foreign Exchange

Most newspapers list the major currencies of the world in equivalents of U.S. dollars. Normally the quotations represent selling prices of bank transfers in the United States for payment abroad, and quotations are given for the current trading day as well as for the previous day. Also, prices for foreign bank notes are often quoted in equivalents of U.S. dollars on both buying and selling bases.

Financial and Economic Information

Apart from the current financial data contained in daily newspapers, a wealth of information is provided by various financial, economic, and business periodicals. Furthermore, readily available reference works contain periodic listings and analyses of financial information oriented toward the investor and financial analyst. The advent of the computer has made possible the rapid collection and analysis of company and economic data, and current information can now be obtained on-line through database access or in hard copy on a timely basis. The most important sources of periodic financial and business information are discussed next.

Business and Economic Magazines

Major Periodicals

For general business coverage, *Business Week* (**http://www.businessweek.com**) remains one of the most useful and widely read publications. The magazine covers current developments in business and economics, both national and international. It analyzes major events and reports on individual companies, stock markets, labor, business education, and so on with a selective listing of economic indicators as well as a special index of business activity.

For more detailed coverage of stock quotations, security offerings, banking developments, and financial, industrial, and commodity trends, the *Commercial and Financial Chronicle* is the most comprehensive print source available. *The Wall Street Transcript* (**http://twst.com**) analyzes securities from a great variety of individual companies, on both a financial and economic basis, and assesses the technical indications of stock market charts. It discusses major corporate presentations to security analysts about past performance and future plans, and features roundtable discussions on industry groups by security analysts.

Barron's (**http://www.barrons.com**) covers business trends in terms of individual companies as well as major industries, and provides much information about corporate securities. The section "Stock Market at a Glance" is a useful and detailed picture of the securities markets. *Fortune* magazine (**http://pathfinder.com/fortune**) offers biweekly comments on national economic trends. It profiles major U.S. and international executives in addition to giving detailed articles on industr.y, company, and socioeconomic trends. The magazine's annual listing and ranking of the Fortune 500 (the best-performing U.S. companies) and similar listings of banks and major foreign companies are useful references, also obtainable from the magazine's web site.

Semimonthly *Forbes* magazine (**http://www.forbes.com**) takes the investor's viewpoint, providing detailed and searching analyses of individual companies and their managements. The annual January issue, which reviews the performance of major U.S. industries, is an excellent source of information on industry trends and ranks companies by a series of criteria.

For an international outlook, the weekly British magazine *The Economist* (**http://www.economist.com**) surveys international and United Kingdom developments in politics, economics, and business, and also discusses U.S. developments and business conditions in depth, supplemented by special features. It can be considered an international *Business Week*, as can *World Business*.

Economic and business trends are covered in considerable detail in publications of major commercial banks such as the *National City Bank Monthly Letter* and *New England Letter* of the First National Bank of Boston. The various Federal Reserve banks' general bulletins and regional bulletins contain regional economic data, and the St. Louis Federal Reserve Bank has an especially useful web site (**http://stls-frb.org/fred**) which contains economic data series and a wide variety of statistics.

The bimonthly *Harvard Business Review* (**http://hbsp.harvard.edu**), a highly regarded forum for discussion of management concepts and tools, includes financial insights from practitioners and academicians for an extensive worldwide readership of business executives. Several other major business schools publish journals of similar orientation, and most of these can be found on web sites specific to the journal or to the university.

Dun's Review presents trade indexes, data on business failures, and key financial ratios in addition to articles about industry and commerce. *Nation's Business*, a publication of the U.S. Chamber of Commerce, presents general articles on business subjects. The *Federal Reserve Bulletin* contains much statistical data on business and government finances, both domestic and international. The *Survey of Current Business* also provides extensive business statistics.

Detailed stock exchange quotations and data about many unlisted securities (those not traded on a recognized exchange), foreign exchange, and money rates are contained in the *Bank and Quotation Record*. The quarterly *Journal of Finance* presents articles on finance, investments, economics, money, and credit, including international aspects of these topics.

Other Periodicals

Many specialized periodicals are published by trade associations and banking, commercial, and trading groups too numerous to mention. Also useful are the great variety of U.S. government surveys and publications, statistical papers provided by the United Nations and its major agencies, and the various analyses and reviews in academic journals. The end of this appendix lists several books that provide detailed guidelines on and descriptions of the type of information available from various sources.

Listed below are some major periodicals that deal directly with, or relate to, corporate finance. Many other relevant publications are also available. Some publications are specialized and oriented toward a specific community of interest; others deal with financial conditions in foreign countries. The titles are largely self-explanatory:

Banker's Magazine	*Journal of Banking and Finance*
CFO Magazine	*Journal of Commerce*
Corporate Financing	*Management Accounting*
Credit and Financial Management	*Mergers and Acquisitions*
Finance	(US and British editions)
Financial Analysts Journal	*National Tax Journal*
Financial Executive	*Managerial Finance*
Financial Management	*World Financial Markets*
Financial World	

Other Background Information

Annual Reports

The most commonly used reference source about the current affairs of publicly held corporations is the annual report furnished to shareholders, supplemented by briefer quarterly reports. The formats used by individual corporations vary widely from detailed coverage (that may even include current corporate, industry, and national issues) to a bare minimum disclosure of financial results. Nevertheless, the annual report is generally an important direct source of financial information. Because the disclosure requirements of the Securities and Exchange Commission (SEC), the recommendations of the accounting profession, and state laws have become more and more demanding over time, the analyst can usually count on annual reports presenting a fairly consistent set of data. Annual reports can be obtained directly from the companies by looking up their addresses in the web sites listed earlier, or from services provided by newspapers and periodicals, such as *The Wall Street Journal,* which indicates which company's reports are available in its stock quotation columns.

Financial Manuals and Services

Most current financial and economic information is now available through various on-line services and information subscription services. This includes information available in published manuals and services. The most popular and best-known set of these is provided by Moody's **(http://www.moodys.com),** with Standard & Poor's **(http://www.standardpoors.com)** a close second. Moody's publishes several volumes: *Industrials; Banks and Finance; Insurance; Public Utilities; Transportation; Municipals; Government; OTC* (over the counter); and *International.* These manuals are published each year and contain up-to-date key historical data, financial statements, securities price ranges, dividend records, and debt ratings for a large number of companies, including practically all publicly held corporations. Moody's manuals are updated through semiweekly supplements with detailed cross-references.

Moody's *Quarterly Handbook* gives one-page summaries of key financial and operating data for major publicly held corporations. Furthermore, Moody's weekly stock and bond surveys analyze market and industry conditions. Besides its semiweekly *Dividend Record*, a semimonthly *Bond Record* contains current prices, earnings, and ratings of most important bonds traded in this country.

Standard & Poor's publications include the *Standard Corporation Records*. This financial information about a large number of companies is published in loose-leaf format and is updated through daily supplements. A useful S&P publication, the *Analysts Handbook*, provides industry surveys with key financial data on individual companies and some industries. Standard & Poor's other services include several dealing with the bond market, weekly forecasts of the security markets, securities statistics, and a monthly earnings and stock rating guide. Standard and Poor's also provides the *Compustat* service, which makes available in electronic form highly detailed up-to-date company statistics for analysis purposes.

Financial services similar to Moody's and Standard & Poor's are provided by Fitch's *Corporation Manuals* and by more specialized manuals such as Walker's *Manual of Unlisted Stocks.* An almost overwhelming flow of information, judgments, and analyses of individual companies from an investor's standpoint is provided by the major brokerage houses. Furthermore, services available to individuals on a subscription basis provide up-to-date financial analyses and evaluations of individual companies and their securities. The most important among these services are *Value Line* **(http://www.valueline.com)** *United Business Service, Babson's,* and *Investor's Management Sciences.* The *Value Line* investment survey provides ratings and reports on companies, with selections and opinions for the investor, while *Investor's Management Services* concentrates on providing a great deal of standardized statistical information as the basis for making analytical judgments. *Dun & Bradstreet's* **(http://www.dnb.com)** credit information services help in evaluating small or unlisted companies.

Business to Government Reporting

More specific details about company operations can often be found in the annual statement that corporations must file with the SEC in Washington, DC. This information is filed on Form 10-K and supplemented by quarterly 10-Q reports. Furthermore, when a corporation wants to issue new securities in significant amounts or alter its capital structure in a major way, the detailed proposal that must be filed with the SEC, the *prospectus*, is generally a more complete source of company background data than is the normal annual report. It will cover the history of the company, ownership patterns, directors and top management, financial and operating data, products, facilities, and information regarding the intended use of the new funds. Most of these publicly filed reports are now available on-line via the SEC's "Edgar" service **(http://www.sec.gov/edgarhp.htm).**

If a company is closely held (most of the shares are held by founders, their families, and key employees) or too small to be listed by the key financial services, information about its financial operations can often be obtained from the corporation records departments of the states in which the company does business. Again, these reports are open to the public for inspection.

Trade Associations

Trade associations, which number in the hundreds, are a prime source of information about their respective industries. A great deal of statistical information is available annually or more often and covers products, services, finances, and performance criteria applicable to the industry or trade group. Often financial and performance data are grouped by types and sizes of firms to make overall statistics on the industry more applicable to a particular operation. Trade associations include the American Electronics Association, Automotive Parts and Accessories Association, and the American Paper Institute, to name but a few. Sources for listings and addresses of these associations and their publications can be found in the references at the end of the appendix or on-line through the Yahoo search engine.

Econometric Services

Many forecasts of U.S. and international economic conditions are available to the financial analyst. Based on econometric models developed by a variety of academic institutions and economic advisory services, these forecasts of the U.S. economy and more recently of other countries' economies as well can provide valuable clues regarding the likely movement of the economy within which financial conditions must be viewed. Among the widely quoted and used econometric models are those developed by the Wharton School at the University of Pennsylvania, Data Resources Inc., and Chase Econometric Associates. Many corporations subscribe to such forecasting services and use the projections in their operational and financial planning. Increasingly, corporate and academic economists are testing their own assumptions about economic trends with the help of econometric models. Another feature of these services is the growing variety of on-line databases containing a vast array of statistical and financial information for immediate access.

While we've merely touched on the major sources of specific or general information on financial business affairs, the reader is encouraged to make use of the sources discussed as well as the references at the end of this appendix. In addition, a great deal of information is available from various business libraries in corporations, colleges, and universities as well as from local institutions. The problem facing a financial analyst, whether student or professional, isn't a lack of data; rather, it's selecting what's truly relevant.

Selected References

Fabozzi, Frank J., and Franco Modigliani. *Capital Markets.* Upper Saddle River, NJ: Prentice Hall, Inc., 1996.

Ibbotson, Roger G., and Rex A. Sinquefield. *Stocks, Bonds, Bills and Inflation.* Chicago: Ibbotson Associates. (Annual yearbook.)

Lehmann, Michael B. *The Dow Jones-Irwin Guide to Using The Wall Street Journal.* Burr Ridge, IL: Dow Jones-Irwin, 1990.

Novallo, Annette. *Information Industry Directory.* 14th ed. Detroit: Gale Research, 1993.

Pierce, Phyllis S., ed. *The Dow Jones Averages 1885–1990.* Burr Ridge, IL: Business One-Irwin, 1991.

Virtual Finance Library, Ohio State University **(http://www.cob.ohio-state.edu/dept/fin/overview.htm).**

Way, James, ed. *Encyclopedia of Business Information Sources.* 9th ed. Detroit: Gale Research, 1992.

APPENDIX IV

Basic Inflation Concepts

Throughout this book we've referred to inflation's distorting effects on financial decisions and analysis. In this appendix, we'll offer a brief commentary on the basic nature of the often misunderstood phenomenon of inflation. Financial transactions are carried out and recorded with the help of a common medium of exchange, such as U.S. dollars. Variations in this medium will affect the numerical meaning of these transactions. But we know that underlying the transactions are economic trade-offs; that is, values are given and received. We must be careful not to confuse changes in economic values with changes in the medium used to effect and account for these transactions. We'll examine the ramifications of this important distinction in several contexts below.

Price Level Changes

The economic values of goods and services invariably change over time. The reason for this is as basic as human nature: The law of supply and demand operates, in an uncontrolled market environment, to increase the value of goods and services that are in short supply, and to decrease the value of those available in abundance. This shift in relative values takes place even in a primitive barter economy that doesn't utilize any currency at all. The ratio of exchange of coconuts for beans, for example, will move in favor of coconuts when they're scarce, and in favor of beans when these are out of season.

Many seasonal agricultural products go through a familiar price cycle, beginning with their temporary unavailability, on to the first arrivals in the marketplace, and eventually to an abundance before they become unavailable again. This phenomenon is not limited to seasonal goods, however. Natural resources go through cycles of availability, be it from the need to set up the expensive infrastructure to exploit new sources as old ones expire, or from extreme concerted actions such as OPEC's moves to limit production in the 1970s and 80s that caused world oil prices to surge because of the cartel's control of over half the world's production. As alternative sources of oil and other energy were stimulated by the high prices, the cartel's power began to wane, hastened by inevitable squabbles among the member countries trying to look out for their own interests—and oil prices settled on a much lower, more sustainable level.

We know that the economic value of manufactured goods is similarly subject to the law of supply and demand. For example, as new technology emerges in the market, such as the first digital watches or compact disk players, or successive waves of innovation in electronic chips and other components, the price commanded by the early units will be well above the prices charged later on, after many suppliers have entered the market and competed for a share of industrial or consumer demand. The same is true of all goods and services for which there are present or potential alternative suppliers, domestic or international.

Our point here is that the economic value underlying personal, commercial, and financial transactions is determined by forces that are largely independent of the monetary expression in which they're recorded. As we'll see, an analysis of price level changes ideally should separate the change in price levels caused by shifts in economic value from those caused by changes in the currency itself. Accurate separation of the two is difficult in practice, but necessary for understanding the meaning of financial projections.

Monetary Inflation

Another phenomenon affecting transaction values is any basic change in the purchasing power of the currency. There are many reasons underlying the decline or strengthening of a currency's value as a medium of exchange. One of the most important factors causing inflationary declines in purchasing power is the amount of currency in circulation relative to economic activity. If the government raises the money supply faster than required to accommodate the growth in economic activity, there will literally be more dollars chasing relatively fewer goods and services, and thus the stated dollar prices for all goods and services will rise—even though the basic demand for any specific item may be unchanged.

This description is oversimplified, of course. A great many more factors affect currency values. One of these is the impact of government deficits and the way they are financed. Another is the value of the dollar relative to other currencies and the impact of exchange rates on international trade. In addition, international money flows and investment in response to more attractive investment opportunities cause shifts in the values of national currencies over and above the effects of the individual countries' fiscal and economic conditions. Union negotiations, wage settlements, and cost of living adjustments in wages, pensions, and social security are also related to changing currency values. Every nation's central bank—the Federal Reserve bank in the case of the United States—is vital in the process because its policies affect both the size of the money supply and the level of interest rates. These in turn affect government fiscal policies, business activity, international trade and money flows, etc. And ultimately, serious declines in the value of a currency can also affect the basic supply and demand of goods and services, as, for example, when customers and businesses buy ahead to beat anticipated price increases.

The point here isn't to systematically analyze inflation and its causes, but rather to make the basic distinction between economic and monetary changes influencing price levels. Suffice it to say that price level changes due to monetary effects are largely the ones that distort economic values of personal and commercial transactions. If monetary conditions remained stable (that is, if the amount of currency in circulation always matched the level of economic activity), price level changes would reflect only changes in economic values—something we've agreed is at the core of management's efforts to improve the shareholders' economic condition. Because monetary stability is an unrealistic expectation, however, the challenge remains to make the analysis of the actual conditions affecting prices and economic values truly meaningful.

Nominal and Real Dollars

Business and personal transactions are expressed in terms of *nominal* dollars, also called current dollars, that reflect today's prices, unadjusted or altered in any way. For accounting purposes, nominal dollars are used every day to record transactions. However, when dollar prices change over time, the amounts recorded in the past no longer reflect current prices, either in terms of the underlying economic values or in terms of the value of the currency at the moment.

To deal with changes in the value of the currency, economists have devised *price indexes* intended to separate, at least in part, monetary distortions from fluctuations in economic value. Such an index is constructed by measuring the aggregate change in the prices of a representative group of products and services as a surrogate for the change in the value of the currency. Yet we already know that any goods and services chosen for this purpose are themselves also subject to changes in supply and demand, apart from mere currency fluctuations. But there's no direct way to measure changes in currency values as such. Inevitably, therefore, the price index approach involves mixing demand/supply conditions and currency values, and the only hope is that the selection of goods and services employed in a given index is broad enough to compensate somewhat for the underlying demand/supply conditions.

The *consumer price index*, a popular index of inflation, is calculated in this fashion. It's based on frequent sampling of the prices of a "market basket" of goods and services purchased by U.S. consumers, including food, housing, clothing, and transportation. The composition and weighting of this basket is changed gradually to reflect changing habits and tastes, although there is much room for argument about how representative and up-to-date the selection is. Another popular index applicable to business is the *producer price index*, based on a representative weighted sampling of the wholesale prices of goods produced. Other indexes deal with wholesale commodity prices and a variety of specialized groupings of products and services.

The broadest index in common use is applied to the gross national product as a whole, the so-called *GNP deflator*, which expresses the price changes experienced in the total range of goods and services produced in the U.S. economy. Based on broad statistical sampling, the current level of the GNP deflator is announced frequently throughout the year in connection with other economic statistics about business and government activity. All of these indexes are prepared by calculating the changes in prices from those of a selected base year, which is changed only infrequently to avoid having to adjust comparative statistical series whenever the base year is changed.

The price indexes are used to translate nominal dollar values in government statistics and business reports into *real dollar values*. This involves converting nominal dollar values to a chosen standard so that past and present dollar transactions can be compared in equivalent terms. For example, to compare this year's performance of the economy to that of last year, we may choose to express current economic statistics using last year's dollars as the standard. Last year's dollars are then called real, and today's data are expressed in these real terms. To do this, we simply adjust today's dollars by the amount of inflation experienced since last year. If inflation this year was 3.0 percent over last year as expressed in the GNP deflator, every nominal dollar figure for this year would be adjusted downward by 3.0 percent. The result would be an expression of this year's results in terms of real dollars, which are based on the prior year.

A real dollar is thus simply a nominal dollar that has been adjusted to the price level of a particular stated base year, using one of the applicable price indexes. The base chosen can be any year, as long as past or future years are consistently stated in terms of the currency value for the base year. In fact, real dollars are often called *constant dollars*, a name that simply recognizes that they're derived from a constant base. The process of adjustment has the following effect: During inflationary periods, the real dollars for the years preceding the base year will be adjusted upward, while the real dollars of future years will be adjusted downward. The reverse is true, of course, if the period involves deflation instead.

To illustrate, let's assume that the following price developments took place during a five-year period. We're using the producer price index (PPI). This index was constructed on the basis of Year 0. In the following table, we've set Year 3 as the base year for our analysis.

	Year 1	Year 2	Year 3	Year 4	Year 5
Producer price index (Year 0)..........	1.09	1.15	1.21	1.25	1.33
Producer price index (Year 3)..........	0.90	0.95	1.00	1.03	1.10
Real value of $100 (Base Year 3)........	$111	$105	$100	$97	$91

Note that two steps were involved. First, the producer price index had to be adjusted for our chosen base, Year 3. That is, the index had to be set at 1.00 for Year 3 and then all index numbers were divided by the value of the index for the base year, which is 1.21. (However, the index could have been constructed on any other year because an index measures price changes year by year from whatever starting point is chosen.) The next step was to divide the adjusted index values on the second line into the nominal dollars of each year. We chose to use the amount of $100 for all years, but the process applies, of course, to any amount of nominal dollars in any one of the years. Using a single round figure permitted us to illustrate the shifts in value with a same dollar amount.

The example clearly shows that a dollar's purchasing power in Year 4 versus Year 3 declined by 3 percent. The implication from a business point of view is that a company must increase its nominal earnings power by 3 percent in order to keep up with inflation in the prices it must pay for goods and services. Anything less than that will leave the owners worse off.

This simple process allows us to convert nominal dollars into inflation-adjusted real dollars. Problems arise in choosing the proper index for a business situation, and also from the fact that the index embodies changes in economic value as well as in currency value, as we discussed earlier. Much thought has been expended on refining the process of inflation adjustment, but in the end, the judgment about its usefulness depends on the purpose of the analysis and the degree of accuracy desired.

Applications of Inflation Adjustment in Financial Analysis

Restatement of company data or projections in real dollar terms is at times useful to assess whether the company's performance has kept up with shifts in currency values. Such restatement may be used to value a company's assets and liabilities, or to show the real growth or decline in sales and earnings. As we observed, publicly traded companies are obligated to include an annual inflation-adjusted restatement of key data in their published shareholder reports.

Much effort can be spent on adjusting financial projections for inflation, particularly in the area of capital investment analysis. There are no truly satisfactory general rules for this process, however. When an analyst must project cash flows from a major capital investment, the easiest approach continues to be projection in nominal dollars, taking into account expected cost and price increases of the key variables involved, tailored specifically to the conditions of the business. The discount standard applied against the projection must also be based on nominal return expectations that, of course, embody the inflationary outlook.

To refine the analysis, many companies prepare projections in real dollars, attempting to forecast the true economic increases or decreases in costs and prices. Then an appropriate inflation index is applied to the figures to convert them into nominal dollars. The problem is, however, that the margin between revenues and costs may widen unduly, simply because the same inflation index is applied to the larger revenue numbers and to the smaller cost numbers. Often arbitrary adjustments have to be made to keep the margin spread manageable.

Another approach involves developing projections expressed in real dollars and discounting these with a return standard that has also been converted into real returns. The result will be internally consistent as far as the project is concerned. However, the result is not readily comparable with the current overall performance of the business—recorded and expressed in nominal dollar terms—unless the company has also found a way to convert and measure ongoing performance in real dollar terms. Some companies are beginning to experiment with such restated reports and measures, but the approach involves a massive effort, both in terms of data preparation and education of personnel generating and using the projections and performance data. It's instinctively easier to think about business in nominal dollars than real dollars, and progress in this area is being made only gradually. The complexities are such that the financial and planning staffs of companies wishing to use this approach face a lengthy conceptual and practical conversion problem.

Impact of Inflation

To restate quickly, the basic impact of inflation—and the much less common opposite situation, deflation—is a growing distortion of recorded values on a company's financial statements, and an ongoing partial distortion of operating results. Accounting methods discussed in Chapters 1 and 2 are designed to make the effect of the inflationary distortion at least consistent. In terms of cash flows, inflation distorts a company's tax payments if the taxes due are based on low historical cost apportionment, and it results in a cash drain if dividends are higher than they would be if real-dollar earnings were considered, to name two examples. Inflation also affects financing conditions, particularly the repayment of principal on long-term debt obligations. As we observed before, however, the mediating influence of interest rates—which respond to inflation expectations—tends to prevent windfalls for the borrower looking to repay debt with "cheap" dollars. Normally, over the long run, distortions from inflation affect lenders and borrowers alike. Relative advantages gained by one over the other are only temporary.

    Overall, the subject of inflation adjustments continues to evolve in financial analysis. It's unlikely that totally consistent methods that are generally applicable will be found.

APPENDIX V

Some Issues in Multinational Financial Analysis

In Chapter 3 we developed the principles of performance analysis and stressed the need for management to derive an economic return from the resources entrusted to them. The analysis involved such measures as profit margins, return on assets, and return on net worth, seen from different points of view. We also related the various measures within a system of ratios to show the different levers management can use to improve the profitability of the business and to create shareholder value. We'll briefly discuss some of the challenges generally encountered in measuring multibusiness companies, and then turn to the particular issues arising from operating with different national currencies.

General Performance Analysis Challenges

Performance measures work best when applied to a total business entity, where investment, operations, and financing are collectively controlled and managed by a management team. It's possible to derive both return on investment (ROI) and return on equity (ROE)—the latter allowing for the effect of financial leverage. Recall the expanded formula for return on equity,

$$\text{ROE} = \frac{\text{Net profit}}{\text{Sales}} \times \frac{\text{Sales}}{\text{Assets}} \times \frac{\text{Assets}}{\text{Assets} - \text{Liabilities}}$$

where the first element represents operations, the second element investment, and the third financial leverage. Also, as we discussed in Chapters 10 and 11, various cash flow analysis approaches can be applied to judge the performance and the value of the company.

Complications arise when the measures are applied to segments of a multiunit company, where individual units are responsible for investment and operations only, and financing remains a corporate headquarters function. In this case, the units are normally measured on a return on investment basis only, employing concepts such as return on total assets (ROA), return on net assets (RONA), or return on average assets employed (ROAE), modified to suit the needs of the particular company. The management of financial leverage doesn't enter in here. Recall the formula for return on assets,

$$\text{ROA} = \frac{\text{Net profit}}{\text{Sales}} \times \frac{\text{Sales}}{\text{Assets}}$$

which, when applied to an operating unit, relates the unit's net profit (before or after taxes) to the unit's sales and its identifiable assets. Again, we can use cash flow measures to judge the performance and the value of business units, but these require a variety of adjustments to make sure that all relevant cash flow elements have been considered, and that the appropriate return standards are applied.

Further complications arise when units within a large corporation supply goods and services to each other. The most difficult aspect is the issue of setting appropriate transfer prices for the value of the goods and services moving between units of the corporation. At times, readily available, clearly established market prices can be used to value these transfers. More often than not, however, transfer prices have to be set through negotiation or even by corporate decree. There are no entirely satisfactory approaches to resolving this often vexing issue, which not only can cause serious distortions in the results of individual units, but—even more significantly—may distort the decisions of unit managers and cause them to over- or underinvest, or to suboptimize their operations.

International Performance Analysis Challenges

The issue of measuring the performance of a business becomes particularly challenging when operations extend into the international arena, either when divisions are operating entirely within a foreign country, or when organizational entities perform transactions in several currencies. In the former situation, the division usually can be viewed as a rather independent entity—albeit operating with a foreign currency—while in the latter case, the flow of goods and services across borders introduces significant measurement problems. All of the measurement issues we mentioned earlier usually apply to foreign operations as well, but in addition there's the problem of measuring the impact of absolute and relative changes in the different currencies involved.

Foreign Subsidiaries Operating in a Single Country

The simplest case involves a wholly owned subsidiary, which for all practical purposes acts as part of the host country, and which keeps its books and financial statements in the local currency. The key measurements in which the U.S. parent company will be interested are current earnings performance and the valuation of the subsidiary.

Given that all transactions and cost accounting steps are carried out in the local currency, the calculation of earnings performance through various ratios will be internally consistent and unaffected by currency fluctuations and exchange rates. Whether the subsidiary operates in German marks, English pounds, or Brazilian cruzeiros, performance measures will indicate the effectiveness with which the subsidiary's assets are employed, and various ratios used to measure performance will give appropriate readings.

Since the U.S. parent company will also be interested in viewing the level of earnings as expressed in U.S. dollars, particularly for purposes of consolidating the earnings, exchange rates must be brought into play. We can represent the situation in the form of some simple formulas, revisiting the discussions of Chapters 3 and 5. If we simulate the subsidiary's earnings in dollars $(E_\$)$ by denoting unit price (P), variable costs (C), fixed costs (F), unit volume (V), and exchange rate (R), and denote all relevant components in terms of the foreign currency (f), the simple equation is

$$\text{Subsidiary } E_\$ = R\,[(P_f - C_f)\,V - F_f]$$

Clearly the exchange rate R affects all financial terms in the formulation, and the dollar earnings reported will be a function of the level of exchange between the dollar and the foreign currency involved. There's nothing the subsidiary management can do about the exchange rate, which may fluctuate wildly or may be very stable. The subsidiary's earnings as such aren't affected—only their expression in dollar terms will be altered. The U.S. parent, on the other hand, may be quite affected by rising or falling exchange rates that will change the subsidiary's dollar earnings. We observed some of these effects in TRW's financial statements in Chapter 3.

When we wish to develop the dollar return on investment (return on assets) of the subsidiary $(ROI_\$)$, the only additional item needed to complete the formula is the amount of the subsidiary's assets denoted in the foreign currency (A_f):

$$ROI_\$ = \frac{R\,[(P_f - C_f)\,V - F_f]}{R \times A_f} = \frac{(P_f - C_f)\,V - F_f}{A_f} = ROI_f$$

Note that the exchange rate R drops out of the equation and the return on investment in dollar terms is equivalent to the return in foreign currency terms. As we stated earlier, ratio analysis performed on an entity with consistent accounting in a single currency will provide meaningful results independent of exchange rate concerns. Only the distortions inherent in the accounting system itself, as discussed in Chapters 2 and 3, will affect the stated amount of the division's assets.

The implications of this discussion are rather straightforward. The management of a subsidiary operating as a unit completely within a given country can be judged by using all standard ratios expressed in the local currency. But the inclusion of the subsidiary's foreign currency earnings in consolidated U.S. financial statements will be affected by any movement in the dollar exchange rates, as will the recording of foreign assets in U.S. dollar terms. The U.S. parent's financial statements may have to be adjusted frequently to account for exchange rate differences alone.

Distortions arising from significant inflationary trends will affect a foreign subsidiary in much the same way as businesses experienced inflation in the United States during the 1970s. In essence, recorded asset values will tend to be understated over time. To the extent that inflationary conditions in the foreign country exceed U.S. levels, it may be desirable to revalue the foreign subsidiary's balance sheet elements for analysis purposes to make sure that ratios derived from the statement are internally consistent.

Valuation of the subsidiary in cash flow terms can be done by expressing the expected cash inflows in the foreign currency and discounting these to arrive at the present value, as we did in Chapter 10. Note that the issues of price, volume, and cost as well as terminal value will remain consistent through the use of the foreign currency in which they occur. All of the issues surrounding the estimates of future conditions in markets, costs, economic developments, and so on will apply here as they would in the United States. The final result can then be translated into U.S. dollars at the prevailing exchange rate, if desired.

Subsidiaries Operating across Foreign Borders

A more common consequence of the continued expansion of international trade is the need for a corporate entity to do business in several countries and in their respective currencies. Now the issue of exchange rates begins to loom large, for both earnings calculations and performance measures will be affected by the mix of currencies on the company's books. Let's take the simplified example of a so-called *cross-border subsidiary* that imports goods from the U.S. parent company and sells these goods within the foreign country in which it operates. Let's further assume that the U.S. parent requires payment for the goods in dollars, while the subsidiary quotes and sells the goods in the local currency. Moreover, all other costs of the subsidiary will be incurred in the local currency as well.

We can again write the equation for the dollar earnings of the subsidiary ($E_\$$), taking into account the fact that its variable costs are incurred in dollars:

$$\text{Subsidiary } E_\$ = R\left[(P_f - \frac{C_\$}{R})\,V - F_f\right]$$

This equation simply describes the subsidiary's condition in which prices and fixed costs have to be converted into dollars, while variable costs are already incurred in dollars.

The complications that can arise from this situation are apparent. No longer does the exchange rate simply apply to earnings as it did in the case of the single-country subsidiary. Now the exchange rate additionally affects a highly significant cost element in the subsidiary's cost structure. Any movement in the exchange rate during a period of operations will directly affect the subsidiary's cost of goods sold. For example, if the foreign currency weakens from four units per U.S. dollar to six, the subsidiary has suffered a 50 percent increase in its cost of goods sold because it must obtain dollars for payment to its U.S. parent that have become 50 percent more expensive. This could severely affect the subsidiary's competitive position in the local market unless it can readily pass on this price increase. An opposite effect will, of course, occur if the exchange rate moves in favor of the local currency, such as from four units per U.S. dollar to three.

The impact on the subsidiary's performance measures of exchange rate movement depends on a number of factors. If significant price changes in the subsidiary's cost of goods sold due to the U.S. dollar exchange rate don't affect its market position because it can adjust the price of the goods based on the change in cost—a highly unrealistic assumption—the performance ratios are likely to be unaffected. In reality, changes in the cost of goods sold will normally impact the subsidiary's ability to compete locally, and attempts to price according to cost will not only affect the volume of units sold, but also change operational costs because of these volume changes.

It's not possible to develop a simple formula approach here, because the total operating system of the subsidiary will be affected in largely unpredictable ways. For example, any attempted price changes are likely to be less than proportional to the change in the cost of goods sold, in order to minimize the competitive impact. Market reactions to these price changes will largely depend on the subsidiary's market position, the quality and price of competitive goods, the availability of competitive substitutes from sources not subject to similar exchange rate fluctuations, and so on. It will usually be best to model the major dimensions of the subsidiary's business system and to simulate a variety of assumptions about price, volume, and cost changes.

The basic calculation in Figure V–1 shows the type of analysis that will help gauge the effect on the subsidiary's earnings and ROA under several assumed conditions. Clearly, more specific knowledge about local market conditions would have to be applied to refine the range of estimates, and more of the underlying variables would have to be modeled to obtain a clearer picture of the impact of currency exchange rates.

FIGURE V–1

Impact on Subsidiary Earnings and ROA Using Several Assumed Exchange Rate Conditions

		Current Period		
Variable	Prior Period	Constant Exchange Rate	Dollar Strengthens	Dollar Weakens
Exchange Rate (R)............	$0.25	$0.25	$0.17	$0.33
(U.S. dollars/foreign currency)				
Selling price per unit (P_t)	f50.00	f55.00	f75.00	f50.00
Purchased cost per unit (C_s)	$10.00	$10.00	$10.00	$10.00
Purchased cost per unit (C_t).....	f40.00	f40.00	f60.00	f30.00
Number of units sold (V)	1,000	1,000	750	1,100
Subsidiary assets (A_t)..........	f30,000	f30,000	f36,000	f27,000
Earnings, ROI in foreign currency:				
Revenues................	f50,000	f55,000	f56,250	f55,000
Cost of goods sold	40,000	40,000	45,000	33,000
Fixed costs...............	5,000	5,000	5,000	5,000
Earnings.................	5,000	10,000	6,250	17,000
ROI....................	17%	33%	17%	63%
Earnings in U.S. dollars	$1,250	$2,500	$1,063	$5,610

This set of assumptions reflects conditions in two time periods, with exchange rates allowed to move significantly in the current period away from the conditions of the prior period. The foreign selling price was assumed to increase slightly in the current period under stable exchange rates (second column). The impact of this 10 percent price increase is a doubling of foreign earnings from f5,000 to f10,000, and a parallel doubling of the dollar earnings. Note that the ROI reflects this doubling as well.

As the dollar strengthens in the third column, the foreign purchase cost per unit jumps 50 percent, and the subsidiary tries to increase the price to recover the extra cost. This is likely to depress the volume sold—here it's assumed to drop by 25 percent. Higher-cost inventories will also increase the subsidiary's asset base by an assumed f6,000. While earnings in the foreign currency decline by 37.5 percent, the ROI is cut in half because of the impact of higher-cost inventories on the asset base. The dollar earnings, however, suffer an even greater decline due to the strengthening of the dollar exchange rate.

The fourth column reflects a weakening of the dollar, which makes U.S. goods cheaper to import. In fact, the cost to the subsidiary drops to 50 percent of the stronger dollar condition in the third column. We assume that the subsidiary will pass on much of this in the form of a lower price, which raises the number of units sold by 10 percent, to 1,100. Revenues are now the same as in the case of the stable exchange rate in the second column. Note, however, the impact of the reduction in costs on the foreign earnings, which soar to f17,000 and are reflected in the ROI of 63 percent—which in turn is boosted by the drop in assets due to lower-cost inventories. In addition, the weaker dollar exchange rate escalates the dollar earnings to more than twice the level of the second column, an increase of 124 percent!

It should be clear from this highly simplified example that we must thoroughly analyze the dynamics of the foreign markets and conditions in addition to assessing the mere reflection of currency exchange rates as changes occur. You're invited to trace through a variety of assumptions in this simple model to gain further insight into the dynamics at play.

More complexity is introduced when differing inflation rates in various countries are taken into account. As was experienced in the United States during the 1970s, inflationary conditions don't necessarily increase operating earnings proportionally, as the prices of inputs like materials, labor, and fuel don't necessarily move in concert. Thus, a detailed analysis of the impact of foreign operations requires much more insight than this brief exposure could provide.

We should briefly mention another aspect of foreign currency transactions here. Companies engaged in buying, selling, and operating in various foreign currencies will use, whenever possible, the concept of *hedging* to protect themselves from even temporary exposure to currency fluctuations. In simple terms, hedging involves the simultaneous purchase or sale of foreign currency contracts that offset the amounts of the commercial transaction undertaken. For example, if a U.S. company sells goods into a foreign market and expects to be paid in the foreign currency some 30 or 60 days hence, the company's treasurer may execute a simultaneous contract to sell an equivalent amount of foreign currency at that time, but based on today's exchange rate. Such a currency contract, called a *forward trade*, exemplifies a common transaction in the worldwide market for currencies. The purpose of currency hedging is in effect to lock in the prevailing exchange rate and to avoid the risk of fluctuations. Again, there are many more aspects of foreign currency management than we can cover in a book of this scope. Readers should turn to specialized materials on these subjects for in-depth coverage.

INDEX